FIVE DECADES OF ECONOMIC DEVELOPMENT AND SOCIAL CHANGE IN VILLAGE INDIA

By the same author:

1. Administrative and Development Planning in India/V. Nath
2. Development: A Saga of Two Words/V. Nath
3. Economic Development and Planning in India/V. Nath
4. Regional Development and Planning in India/V. Nath (Edited by S.K. Aggarwal)
5. Rural Development and Planning in India/V. Nath
6. Urbanization, Urban Development & Metropolitan Cities in India/V. Nath (Edited by S.K. Aggarwal)

About the Editor

Kamla Nath is a development economist who has worked in studies on women's economic role in developing countries like India, West Africa and the Middle East. Her professional interests include project identification, implementation and evaluation of projects and programmes for integration of women in development of the developing countries.

She has undertaken consultancies on behalf of the World Bank, UNIFEM, UNIDO, UNDP and UNESCO in India and in West Africa. She worked briefly as a lecturer in Economics in Delhi University and conducted field studies on changes in women's economic role, and patterns of living, consumption and social practices as result of economic development in India, Middle East and West Africa.

She was attached to The African Studies Center of University of Boston, USA as a senior research fellow and with Center for Social Research, New Delhi India as a Consultant. She is heading an NGO SarvSaandesh and The Nath Foundation.

About the Author

Dr. Vishwambhar Nath spent his entire career as a development economist in India, the Middle East and Africa. Born in Lahore on July 14, 1923, Dr. Nath trained as a geographer and economist joined the Indian Planning Commission in 1950. He worked on the Census of India and led the Project Evaluation Organization (PEO) of the Planning Commission to evaluate the Community Development Programme. Later assignments in the Planning Commission included work in the Natural Resources and Urban Planning Divisions. In between in 1957, he joined the Indian Administrative Service (IAS) and was the District Collector in Sawai Madhopur and Pali districts in Rajasthan. This volume is based on his work in Sawai Madhopur and later in the Punjab. From 1966 to 1984 Dr. Nath worked with the United Nations as a development economist in the Middle East and West Africa and worked as a Senior Research Fellow at the Asian Development Studies Center of Boston University USA and at the Center for Policy Research in New Delhi.. His academic interests include work in Economic Development, Regional Planning , Urbanization, Rural Development and Administration and Planning.

Five Decades of Economic Development and Social Change in Village India

V. Nath

Editor
Kamla Nath

CONCEPT PUBLISHING COMPANY PVT. LTD.
NEW DELHI-110059

ISBN-13 : 978-81-8069-958-0

First Published 2013

Published and Printed by

Concept
Since 1974

Concept Publishing Company Pvt. Ltd.
A/15-16, Commercial Block, Mohan Garden
New Delhi-110059 (India)
T. 25351460, 25351794, *F*: 091-11-25357109
E: publishing@conceptpub.com, W: www.conceptpub.com

Editorial Office: H-13, Bali Nagar, New Delhi-110 015, India.

Cataloging in Publication Data--*Courtesy:* D.K. Agencies (P) Ltd. <docinfo@dkagencies.com>

Nath, V. (Vishwambhar), 1923-2002.
Five decades of economic development and social change in village India / V. Nath; editor, Kamla Nath.
p. cm.
Includes bibliographical references (p.) and index.
ISBN 9788180699580

1. Economic development--India—Sawai Madhopur (District) 2. Economic development—India—Ludhiana (District) 3. Social change—India—Sawai Madhopur (District) 4. Social change—India—Ludhiana (District) 5. Rural development India—Sawai Madhopur (District) 6. Rural development—India—Ludhiana (District) I. Nath, Kamia. II. Title.

DDC 338.09544 23

Prologue*

The studies the results of which are described in the following pages were conducted in three villages of Sawai Madhopur district in Eastern Rajasthan and one village in Punjab first in 1961 and 1963 respectively. The repeat studies have been done in 2001 and 1975 respectively. They show changes in the economic activities, the income and level of living on the one hand and on social changes relating particularly to inter-caste relations and the position of women. The studies show also the effects of land reforms, the various rural development programmes and the economic and political changes in the country during the five decades.

Sawai Madhopur district, located in south eastern Rajasthan**, is a backward district of the State which is among the most backward states in India. It formed part of the former Jaipur State before the accession of the princely states to the Indian Union, and now forms part of the Jaipur division of Rajasthan. Surrounded by Dausa district in the north, Tonk district in the east, Bundi district in the southeast, Karauli district (which in 1961 was part of Sawai Madhopur) in the northwest and west and the Chambal River and Kota district in the southwest. Sawai Madhopur is the administrative headquarters of Sawai Madhopur District. It is home to the Ranthambore National Park and the historic Ranthambore fortress, which lies within the national park.

This area was ruled by Raja Hammir Dev (a Meena king) of Chauhan lineage along with his Gujjar (Cattleherdes) relatives. The area was destroyed by Allaudin Khiljee. As of 2001 Census of India, the bifurcated district of Sawai Madhopur had a population of 1117057? Males constitute 53 per cent of the population and females 47 per cent. It has an average literacy rate of 64 per cent, higher than the national average of 59.5 per cent, male literacy is 75 per cent; and female is 52 per cent and 16 per cent of the population is under 6 years of age (Population Census 2001).

---

* The Prologue is based on several scattered writings of the author on the subject collected by the Editor.

** See map below. In 1961 the entire area of Karauli (which is now a separate district) formed part of Sawai Madhopur district.

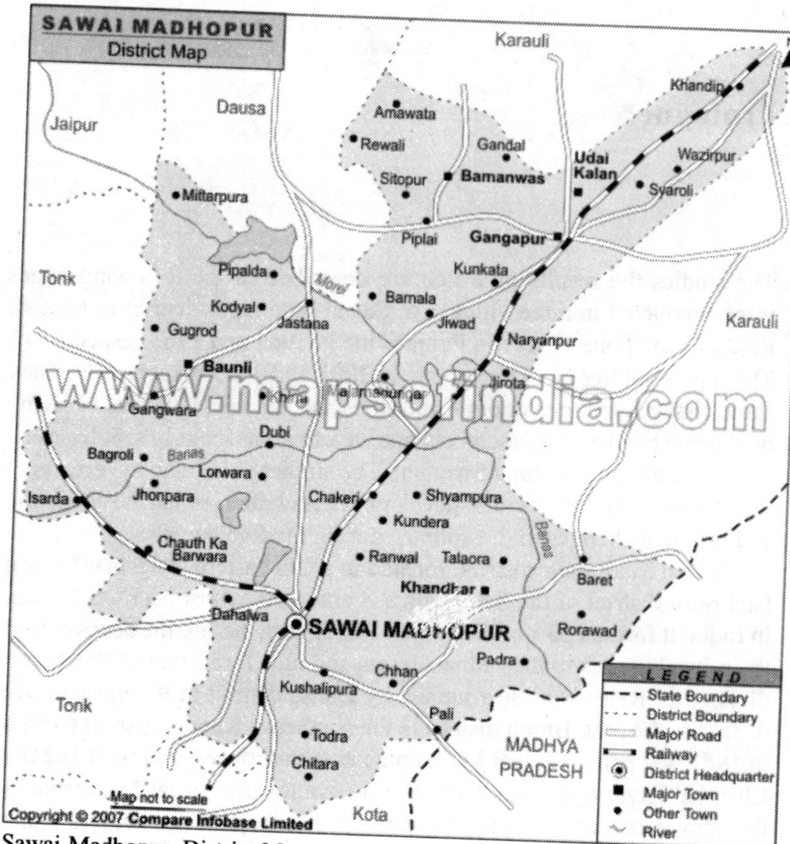

Sawai Madhopur, District Map

Sawai Madhopur, the district headquarter is located about 130 km. from Jaipur, the capital of Rajasthan. This town, which is now commonly known as the "Sawai Madhopur City", lies in a narrow valley between two parallel hills, at the South Western edge of the Ranthambhore National Park. It was built as a planned city by Maharaja Sawai Madho Singh of Jaipur (1750-1768), who named the township after himself. Sawai Madhopur is famous for its guavas, affectionately known as "Madhopur guavas" in Rajasthan.

The most famous Fort of Ranthambhor located in the National Park is reputed to have been built in 944 AD by brave Chauhan warrior after receiving the blessings of an ascetic. Further additions were made to it by subsequent rulers. The Ranthambhor Fort is one of the oldest in

Rajasthan. Located securely at a vantage point of 250 meters above the forested valley, it is built on an awesome scale. In order to check the growing influence of the Marathas, Sawai Madho Singh I, the ruler of Jaipur State, unsuccessfully, requested the Mughal emperor, in 1763, to hand over the Ranthambhore Fort to him. Soon after the ruler fortified the nearby village of Sherpur and renamed it Sawai Madhopur. The village now is known as Sherpur Khilchipur.

The Sawai Madhopur town is connected with Jaipur by a road, which was motorable only during the dry season (1961), and the railway. Sawai Madhopur or rather Maantown, the suburb in which the offices of the collector and other district officers are located, is the junction station where railway lines between Delhi and Mumbai and Maantown to Jaipur meet. Almost half of the district is hilly and is covered with thorn forest. The remaining area is plain. Annual rainfall, of about 80-100 cm., is quite dependable so that the plains produce large crops of cereals including wheat, corn, sorghum, millets and grams and oil seeds. The area is irrigated by wells and a large number of tanks. In recent years, a large proportion of the wells have been fitted with diesel operated pumps.

Maantown is located at the edge of the forest and the game sanctuary which is a major tourist attraction because of presence in it of tigers and other beasts and a wide variety of birds and is located about 10 km. from it. The villages selected for the study are all located in the plain, between 3-8 km. from the collector's office. Their population ranged between 500-2000 in 1961 and is estimated at 1000-8000 now (2001).

The Punjab Study

The village selected for the study in Punjab is located about two km. from the tehsil headquarter town Samrala of Ludhiana district. Punjab is about the most developed State in the country with the highest level of per capita income and level of living. Ludhiana which had a population of almost one million in 1961 is an industrial city in which a variety of machine tools and consumer durables are manufactured in a large number of medium sized industrial units. The Punjab Agricultural University is located in it. The district has led the State in increase in agricultural output after availability of dwarf high yield varieties of wheat in the late 1970s. The village selected for the study had a population of about 2000 in 1961; almost all its cropped area was irrigated by surface wells fitted with electric pumps for irrigation. Use of tractors and other machine driven farm implements such as maize shellers and thrashing machines for wheat was already well established by the early 1960s. The village is multi-caste with Jat Sikh cultivators and the scheduled castes, farmers, agricultural labourers, artisans constituting most of the population. Brahmin and Sikh traders who had migrated from West Punjab in 1947 formed about 10 per cent of the population. Except the Brahmins, the rest of the population is Sikh. Kamla Nath studied the work patterns of women and their attitudes and consumption patterns in an adjoining village which was similar to Otalan in every way. The reason for selecting a different village by Kamla Nath was the progressive attitude of the Pradhan of the village and his wife and their readiness to assist in everyway the study by her. She is thankful to the family of the Pradhan who not only encouraged and assisted Kamla Nath in conduct of the study but on several occasion served tea and delicious *sarso ka sag* and *makki ki roti,* which appeared to be the staple during the winter months of January-Februray, the timing of the study. Kamla Nath did not, however, take part in the repeat study in 1975.

The first study in the Rajasthan villages was done in 1961 when the author was the Collector of the district. He had a deep interest in study of changes in economic and social conditions of village people as a result of land reforms and the various rural development programmes that had been initiated in the early 1950s. Before coming to the district, he had been Deputy Director and Director of the Programme Evaluation Organization of the Planning Commission and Director of Research at the Central Institute of Community Development located in Mussorie: it is called National Institute of Rural Development now and is located in a suburb of Hyderabad in Andhra Pradesh. His wife, Kamla Nath joined him in the studies because she was distressed by the poverty, ignorance and low level of living of women in the villages selected for the study in Rajasthan. Trained as an economist, she had never seen such poverty and desperation. The Punjab village was studied by both Dr. and Mrs. Nath in 1963 when Dr. Nath was working in the Planning Commission. They spent five weeks in the villages and about four months in analyzing the data and preparing the report. The latter was published in five successive issues of the *Economic and Political Weekly*, Mumbai in April-May, 1965. It was re-published by the Weekly as a monograph entitled the "New Village". The findings of the repeat study of the Punjab village, '*The New Village: Twelve Years After*' was also published (Noble and Dutt)***.

*** Nobble, Allen and Dutt, Ashok K: "*Indian Urbanization and Planning—Vehicles of Modernization*" McGraw Hill Publishers 1977.

The report on the study of Rajasthan villages has remained unpublished. However, article based on the study was published under the title 'Village Caste and Community'in Economic Weekly in 1962. This is included in this volume.

The repeat study has been done in the Rajasthan villages in January 2001, by Kamla Nath and Dr. D.K. Giri, an economist trained in England and then a professor at Jawaharlal Nehru University in Delhi; two researchers assisted them. Dr. Nath could not participate in the field work but has provided valuable analytical insight based on his experience of the study in 1961.

A similar repeat study in the Punjab village was proposed to be done by Dr. Giri and the two researchers who were suppose to spend one week in studying the present economic and social condition of the village. However the repeat study could not be undertaken.

Dr. Nath had visited the Rajasthan villages for a day in 1976 and had found that there was not much change in the villages except for rural electrification which had resulted in use of electricity for lighting in the houses of the better off residents of the villages. It had resulted also in fitting of electricity operated irrigation pumps but there was no real noticeable change. The Punjab village was visited by Dr. Nath for a week in 1976. He found major changes in its population and economy. A large number of small farmers had left the village, by selling or leasing their land to large farmers and had gone themselves to the terrai sub-mountain area of Uttar Pradesh or Haryana where they could get land at low prices and develop large farms in which they could produce large crops of wheat, rice and oil seeds (and cotton in Haryana). The scheduled caste labourers were not working on farms but in the Samrala market, loading and unloading cereals (wheat, maize, and sorghum and oil seeds). They had joined the army in increasing number. There was large import of labourers from Bihar and eastern Uttar Pradesh from October-May i.e. in the busy agriculture season when the crops grown in the summer (kharif) of sorghum and millets had to be harvested and winter (rabi) season crops wheat, gram and oil seeds had to be planted (during October-December) and harvested (during March to May).

Some small farmers had sold their lands and had gone to U.K. to work there as unskilled labourers in factories. The elders of the village talked ruefully of *increase in drinking* among the large farmers who had become quite rich because of high yields of their crops for which high minimum prices had been fixed by the Government of India.

The repeat study showed further socio-economic changes in both the Rajasthan villages and the Punjab village since the early 1960s. For the convenience of the readers, the study is divided into two parts so that the changes in each set of villages can be described in a way that can be readily understood. Self-sustaining nature of the changes have been analyzed to ascertain that they have not put undue stress on the natural resources or that progress of one section of the population has not been at the expense of others.

Section A of this volume give details of the Rajasthan Study as analyzed by the author and contained in Chapters 1-7 and the two Appendices. Chapter 8 gives description of the changes in socio-economic conditions of the villages since 1961 and projects the changes into foreseeable future. It also analyses the self-sustaining nature of the changes and recommends additional initiatives to connect the changes in the macro economy with the development of the area. The author could not go to the villages in 2000 but sent a team of researchers to resurvey the villages. Based on the findings of the research team and additional material collected by the author through correspondence with the main informers, he analyzed the changes in the forty years since the initial study..

Section B covers the study of the Punjab villages conducted in 1963 and recording the impact of technological change in irrigated lands of east Punjab (Chapter 10). The study of impact of technological change and economic development on women in the Punjab village, studied by Kamla Nath is given in Chapter 11. The contents of Chapter 10 and 11 were published in *Economic and Political Weekly* in the 1960s. The findings of the repeat study in the East Punjab village which also captures the effect of Green revolution done in 1975 were presented at an international seminar and published in 1976 (Chapter 12).

Chapter 13 captures the change in rural areas and in agriculture development at the macro level and similarities and/or differences in the findings of the micro studies and development in rural India based on the macro data.

What next!

Based on the development in agriculture and rural farmers over a period of more than half a century it is still difficult to project which way the farming sector and rural communities will go in the next couple of decades.

The author's imagination was tickled by seeing what was happening in India and what he had observed had happened in some other farming communities like USA, France, and Japan etc.

According to the author, the farmers of Sawai Madhopur are likely to follow the same pattern as the Punjab farmers. There is a tendency to over-invest, once the returns of initial investment become apparent. Eventually too many people make too many investments in the same thing and there is a winnowing out of the marginal producers. The remaining producers consolidate the farms into larger tracts and can make use of the efficiencies of large scale mechanization. If the experience of Punjab is repeated in Sawai Madhopur, there will be fewer farm families, larger farms and greater mechanization. The farmers, who succeed, will be more prosperous.

But it need not be this way.

It is instructive at this point to review the way farming has been organized in the United States, France and Japan. The different structures supply us an alternative way to look at the future.

American farming is characterized by mega farms and a high level of automation. The food industry in the United States is homogenous and national. Farm produce, whether it is wheat, fowl or dairy are collected at central points, processed and distributed nationally. The chicken breasts purchased in Maine are exactly the same as the chicken breasts purchased in Honolulu, and they are both packaged in a factory in Arkansas; same with cheese, milk, bread, etc. Scale brings efficiencies to the production of food and also allows national standards of cleanliness to be enforced. The food is cheap and good. But the food is the same everywhere and is neither as tasty nor as healthy as small batch food processing would allow it to be. As a result, there is now the emergence of local bakeries and food processors who service a local, more affluent clientele and fine dining restaurants. Locally grown tomatoes and herbs and lettuce are finding a preferred position in many restaurants; local (sometimes neighbourhood) bakeries are finding unexpected success because they can vary their offerings and experiment with different ingredients.

French farming has always maintained its local traditions. The local markets with fruits, vegetables and other farm products (jams, jellies, mustards, herbs, etc.) complement the local bakery and the local boulangerie (meat shop). Farm employment remains relatively high and vibrantly innovative. Recently, high priced French jams have been finding success in specialty food stores in the United States. While the food is more varied and innovative, healthier and tastier, the cost of the food is significantly higher. The French consumer is more than willing to pay the higher prices; after all he is French!

The farm sector in Japan has an interesting twist. Japanese farmers form a strong political block and have been able to have many protectionist laws passed. Japan is dotted with small inefficient rice farms and the farmers are protected by competition from other countries ("Japanese rice is just better than Chinese rice"). Due to the regulation of the market, the Japanese food market is neither as vibrant as the French market, nor as efficient and inexpensive as the American market. It is a politically driven market.

We would recommend that the farmers of Sawai Madhopur or Punjab do not ask the politician for help in safeguarding their farms.

It is clear that the Indian food market is beginning to be dominated by large scale national and international food processors. The American model of food production and distribution will eventually be the way the Indian market is organized. We do not have the cultural snobbery or affinity to local produce that the French have; our industrialists have also shown an unseemly adeptness to manipulate the political system to their own uses, so the Japanese model is unlikely here.

However, India is a much more varied society than America and there will be a better possibility of regional producers of particular products to flourish. In the case of Sawai Madhopur, the area has been found to be exceptionally suitable for the growing of guavas. Additionally, there is a local sweet called *rabri* (a milk dish)—for which the area is famous. Proper branding of these products would lead to the movement of farming from commodity products to higher margin products. A guava canning factory, a Tiger brand of guava juice with extra protein, Sawai Madhopur *rabri* are all possibilities.

There will continue to be a viable farming community in Sawai Madhopur—many people will continue to produce commodity items for sale to large food processors, and there will be some local products which may find regional or national fame.

It is clear, however, that many farmers will not be able to survive. The children of the farmers will move to cities, many will enter service industries like trucking and retailing. In order for the children to continue to progress and become wealthier, it is crucial that they are educated and trained. Higher education results in greater individual productivity, which means increasing wealth.

There is one unique thing about Sawai Madhopur which separates it from many other villages in India. It is the location of one of three forest reserves for the endangered Bengal tiger. The Bengal tiger is a magnificent species and has caught the fancy of conservation groups around the world; it is one of three "glamour endangered species", the other two being whales and the bald eagle.

It would be to the benefit of Sawai Madhopur to establish itself as a centre for tiger research. This will bring in good service jobs to the area, as well as increase the level of education for the local population. As tiger research increases and the number of tigers increase, there will be a larger number of tourists visiting the Ranthambore forest reserve which will lead to more jobs in the tourist industry.

If the local or state government establishes a plan to purchase the farms of bankrupt farmers to expand the Ranthambore forest reserve, the economic development of the area will be assured. We will then have come full circle—from 1961 when the Chamars wanted to cut the forest so that they could have cultivable land, to 2010, when farms will be given back to the forest and to the tiger, so that people from around the world can visit and see it. Sawai Madhopur has a rare resource in the tiger and the forest; the development of the area and the wealth of its people will be most benefited by the conservation of the forest and its expansion. Who could have imagined that in 1961?

2nd October 2010 **Kamla Nath**

Preface

I was working as the Collector of Sawai Madhopur District. On my visits to some of the villages in the district I was fascinated by the speed of social change within the feudal atmosphere of the villages. The villagers were adapting themselves to new ideas and adjusting themselves to increasingly rapid change. There were also the young village leaders who found the change stimulating—even exciting. Most of them enjoyed their new role as representatives of the people in village institutions like the *panchayat* and cooperatives; others had already begun to see the problems ahead and were beginning to be dissatisfied.

Then there were the middle aged and old people who had seen their entire way of life change. They were trying to make adjustment in their personal and group relations, in their ways of thinking and doing things, with only a limited comprehension of significance of all that was happening. Among them were small ex-*jagirdars* or kinsmen or the former servants of the *Jagirdars* who looked back upon *jagir* time with nostalgia. They knew that the 'old days' would not return. Many of them were frankly critical of several aspects of the *jagirdari* system or of individual *jagirdars*. But they were always ready to talk about the past. In my discussions in villages, references to social and economic change came up frequently. The phrase "all has changed" was a recurring theme. I was encouraged to take up work in this field by the favourable response of people of Raipur village, which I had selected for a more intimate knowledge of village life. These people were enthusiastic in explaining the history of social tradition of their village, the conditions in the time of Jaipur State, and the changes which had occurred in the social and economic relations of different castes and groups.

An official like the Collector of a district has many disadvantages in undertaking a study of this kind. He can obviously not live in the village that he studies. He has to go behind the first answer to his questions rather more frequently than other investigators need to as people have a tendency to answer to please; caste and group leaders want to report things which all show them in a favourable light. Leaders of lower castes always want to talk about their difficulties. I am conscious of these limitations and knew that try as I might I cannot get over them completely. On the other hand the job has some advantages. The collector's multi faced work brings him in contact with village people at many points and gives him opportunity to deal with such varied problems that he gets a complete view of rural life. Thus he sees a village leader as a spokesman of his caste or his village and again as a party in a land dispute; he sees him inter-acting with other leaders in the *Panchayt Samiti* and as a member of one of the political groups in the district. When he sees a village divided on a land dispute, he knows the rights involved and why particular leaders take particular sides. Finally, as he is acquainted with developments in a whole region, he can see the trends and problems of the village, which he studies in the regional perspective.

A large number of people have assisted me in various stages of this work. First among these are the leaders and the people of the selected villages. With many of them, particularly the *Srapanchas* of Manpur and Raipur, I spent hours in discussions. After they understood the objective nature of these studies, they did all they could to make them a success. Among village level officials, the *Patwaris* were particularly helpful. They made available valuable back ground data on agriculture and other aspects of economic life of the villages. They were also helpful in explaining many facts about local customs and usage. Rukam Chand Sharma the *Patwari* of Manpur gave me valuable assistance in the household surveys. Among the other colleagues and staff of the district I should like to mention Vas Dev Chopra, a young trainee of the Rajasthan Administrative service who spent many hours assisting me with the household surveys. Dr. Robert, D. Campbell (then in India with the Ford Foundation) edited the entire manuscript and made invaluable suggestions. Assistant in typing and preparation of the manuscript has been given by K.L.C. and S.K.P. I take this opportunity also to express my gratitude to Shri B. Mehta, Chief Secretary, Government of Rajasthan. There are many others in Sawai Madhapur and Delhi who have regarded this as a labour of love and I can only express my appreciation for their assistance. It was their encouragement and abiding interest in this work which has enabled me to complete it. Finally I am grateful to my wife for participation in this work, constant encouragement and many helpful suggestions. She did the field work and the first draft of the study on women.

The views expressed here are entirely my own and neither the Rajasthan government nor the Planning Commission with which I am associated have any responsibility for them.

New Delhi
February 9, 1965.

V. Nath

Contents

Introduction

India's villagers like peasant communities in all developing countries, are experiencing rapid change. The agents of change are reforms in land tenure and economic influence—new production techniques new consumption goods, modern services such as transport and telecommunications and preventive medicine; and new concepts such as social equality and political democracy. They affect villages through increasing contact of the rural people with the outside and through operation of development programmes and other measure undertaken by governments. The latter are most important change influences at the present time when governments of most developing countries are carrying out programmes of economic development and social change. In India, the post-independence years have seen introduction of a number of development programmes and measures of institutional reforms. The Community development and other programmes introduced as part of the Five Year Plans have resulted in rapid extension of social services in the villages: they also represent a concerted effort to modernize agriculture, village industries and other aspects of the rural economy. The institutional reform measures range from land reforms (abolition of *Zamindari* and *Jagirdari*) and establishment of democratic institutions like the village *panchayts*, to such social reforms as abolition of untouchability, and a code of personal law for the Hindus.

Indian rural society shares with peasant societies the world over, such attributes as preponderance of agriculture in economic activity, age old techniques and very low levels of living. It shares with peasant societies in many countries of Asia the situation of large numbers of people subsisting on limited area of agricultural land. Consequently, most cultivators in India have very small holdings and there are considerable numbers of landless people, who subsist on agricultural and non agricultural labour. They may practice their ancestral crafts part-time. Most of them belong to the scheduled castes some of whom were untouchable, until untouchability was abolished by law after the country became independent. They have the lowest income and social status in rural society.

But the social system of Indian village has certain distinctive features, which have been described in village studies conducted by sociologists and cultural anthropologist in recent years. The principal features of the social system are:

Division of society into castes, each associated traditionally with a particular occupation and each having a well defined social status;

Organization of economic relations with the individual village as the unit. Traditionally these relations were regulated through the *Jajmani*[1] *system*, which is payment made by the cultivators in kind (grain or other produce) for the goods and services, furnished to them by the artisans and services castes.

A social status system under which the status of each caste is precisely stated. The high castes (Brahmins, Rajputs and Mahajans) have the highest social status, while the artisan or service castes, practicing dirty occupations such as scavenging, tanning and leather work, have the lowest status. Differences in social status are expressed in innumerable ways, of which practices relating to touch, acceptance of food and drink are the most obvious. Untouchability of the scheduled castes is the best known among these practices.

The disparity between these features of the traditional social system and the new change influences needs to be noted. The caste system, with its accent on differential social status is the antithesis of social equality. Association of caste with occupation and the *Jajmani* system, and an economy and society in which techniques, productivity and level of living do not change appreciably over long periods and in which use of cash is limited are incompatible with rapidly changing techniques of productivity and the level of income and rapid movement of people from one occupation (or group of occupations) to another.

The principal object of a study of social change is to describe the process through which a traditional society adapts itself to new change influences; how it modifies its structure and how individuals and groups in it change their patterns of work and living, their mutual inter-relations and their attitudes and values. The process which consists of constant action and reaction between the new change influence and the exciting social structure is the dominant and most fascinating aspect of change in village India. It is occurring in a situation which is essentially evolutionary, that is, in which the existing structure of society has not been disrupted. It is being accomplished by people who were brought up in the old social structure, but who are changing it to use new resources and meet new situations. At the same time they seek to moderate the impact of new change influences or to alter them to adapt them to their existing social situation. This is illustrated very well by the working of developmental institutions like statutory Village *Panchayats* and cooperative societies. These institutions have been established with certain ideas and objectives, and they are changing the social, political and economic structure of the villages. But institutions themselves undergo changes. The *Panchayat* or the cooperative of any village after the village people have worked with it for some time does not remain merely the product of the ideas and objectives with which it was established. It becomes what the people are able to make it in their attempt to adapt it to their existing social structure and economic and political conditions.

These studies show the processes of economic and social changes at work in a group of villages in Eastern Rajasthan, West Central India. Its working is all the more interesting here because the area is comparatively backward; it formed part of the princely State of Jaipur and held the feudal institution of *Jagirdari* as the principal system of land tenure until it was abolished in the 1950s. The social and economic changes experienced in most parts of British India in the period before Independence had been retarded here and the traditional social and economic structure and values were better preserved. But in the years after Independence, social, economic and political changes in the area have been more rapid than in most parts of British India, because the area had to make up for the handicap of the past while participating in contemporary changes. This situation has many advantages as well as some disadvantages for analysis of social changes. As the change process is faster its outlines are sharper and more clearly observable. On the other hand as a number of change influences are working simultaneously, the contribution of an individual influence in the change process cannot be easily determined. Moreover, since the observer is so close in time to rapid change, the significance and long term durability of individual change is more difficult to assess.

Description of Studies

The studies are based on fieldwork in a group of four villages of Sawai Madhapur district of Rajasthan where the author was posted as collector and District Development Officer during 1960-1962.[2] They are grouped into four parts. The first two studies are relating to caste and describe its role in current occupational and social change. Chapter 1 analyses changes in occupation in a large multi-cast village (Raipur), which is conveniently located for availing of the new opportunities of employment in industry and services and in which a considerable number of people have availed of these opportunities. It describes the response of village people to the new employment opportunities, and the influence of the caste in conditioning the response. Chapter 2—From Untouchables to Peasant Proprietors—The Study of the Berwa Chamars—describes what is perhaps the most important recent event in the breakdown of the *Jajmani* system in this area—abandonment by the chamars of their traditional occupation of flaying of hides and skins of dead animals and leather work and repudiation of other obligations to the village community to become cultivators on small areas of land allotted to them by the Government. This change besides transforming the social and economic status of the chammars, a large cast in this area, has had a far-reaching influence on the economic, social and political life of the area.

The two studies in Part II are concerned with the experience of the village people with democratic institution of local government and development, the *Panchayats*, *Panchayat* Samiti[3] and the cooperative societies. Chapter 3 describes the working of institutions, the *panchayat* and the cooperative, in Raipur. It is concerned especially with the conflict, which is posing as a major problem in the working of these institutions. It shows how several of the disputes are related to interpersonal and inter-groups conflicts within the villages and how these in turn are related to the process of rapid social and economic change in the village, with its resultant disturbance to the traditional power structure and prestige and influence of different families and groups.

Chapter 4 describes the new leadership which is emerging in these villages with the establishment of democratic institutions. It consists of profiles of 15 selected members of *Panchayat Samitis* and shows the kind of persons these new leaders are, how they view their new roles as representative of the people in democratic institutions and what expectations they and the people who have selected them, have from them and from these institutions.

Chapter 5 describes the changes in attitudes, social customs and practices which affect women more than men with a focus on customs relating to marriage, and the joint family, participation of women in work on the farms, education of women, treatment of disease, maternity and child care, etc. It describes the changes in these customs and shows how they are related to the other social and economic changes described in these studies. For example, it shows that in certain areas of social custom (e.g. marriage) different segments of rural society are coming closer together, because the traditional differences between the high castes the cultivating castes and the scheduled castes are being reduced; but at the same time new differences (patterns of food consumption, dress) are being introduced as a result of occupational changes.

The last two chapters are really analytical essays. They seek to review the findings of different studies as part of single process of social and economic change. Chapter 6 analyses these findings in relation to caste; Chapter 7 analyses the effects of social changes on the character of the village community and the feeling of belonging to the village.

Chapter 9 includes findings of a revisit to the three of the four villages in 2001, almost forty years after the initial study, by author's wife Kamla Nath, Dr. D.K. Giri Director Schumacher Centre and a team of researchers.

The two Appendices (i) on *Panchayats* and *Panchayat Samitis* and (ii) on District Revenue Administration describe the structures of these important institutions in the development and social change process in village India.

The Villages

Field work for the studies was done in four villages, Raipur, Manpur, Bijaipur and Chainpur,[4] all located within an 8 km of Sawai Madhapur. It extended over a period of 16 month, from February 1961 to June 1962. This was a period of considerable political activity in the area. When the studies began the *Panchayat* Elections, which were held all over Rajasthan in December 1960, had just been completed. They ended, four months after the country wide General Election of 1962. As mentioned in the preface the inspiration for the studies was provided by the fascinating spectacle of an area coming out of its feudal past and trying to adjust itself to new social and economic influences, new political ideas and institutions. By the time the author decided to take up detailed studies of social change, he had been in the area for four month and had become generally acquainted with its social and economic conditions. This acquaintance and the opportunities of visit to large number of villages, discussions with village leaders and settling disputes about ownership of land and their development problems have provided the back-drop of these studies.

Among the villages studied, Raipur is by far the most important because Chapter 1 and 3, and a portion of Chapter 5 deal with it. It is a large, multi-caste village (population 2850 in 1961) situated 5 miles from Sawai Madhapur railway station and Maan Town in which the offices of the Collector, the Superintendent of Police and other offices of the district are located, with which it is connected by an all weather motorable road. Among the other villages Manpur (which forms the subject of the case description of the chamar in Chapter 2) is also a rather large, multi-caste village with a population of about 2200 (in 1961). Bijaipur and Chainpur (described in Chapter 5) are small, essentially single caste, hamlet—like villages. Bijaipur is village of the Meenas, the principle cultivating caste in the area while Chainpur is a village of chamars.

Taken together these studies present a detailed picture of the economic and social life of Raipur and less detailed picture of the other three villages. Chapter 1 describes the economic activities of the people of Raipur; chapter 3 besides describing the working of the *panchayats* and the other institutions in it, gives a detailed account of the socio-political situation in the village. Chapter 5 describes the pattern of living and social customs of the Bramhins, an important caste of the village. Chapter 7 also uses Raipur as a case example to describe the changes in the character of the village community and the feeling for the villager over a period of years. The author has not attempted to present detailed account of life in only one village, a method which has been followed by many sociologists and anthropologists in their recent village studies. The value of this method for a study of social process is recognized. The method makes possible a degree of analysis in depth, especially of inter-personal and inter-group relations, which is not possible in studies painted on a wider canvas. It is recognized also that the Indian village—with its different castes bound together in an intricate system of socio-economic relationships embodied in the traditional *Jajmani* system—has been considered to be almost ideal subject for such a study. But the author had to modify the approach of studying only one village, when after several months of work in Raipur he came to the conclusion that study of one village alone would not be adequate for describing the social changes in progress in this area and that a more fruitful approach would be to select certain aspects of social change for detailed description in more than one village. Secondly, he felt convinced that for certain purposes it would be helpful to give a regional picture. Thus the study of change in occupation and social position of the Chamars is essentially a regional study which has affected a large area in eastern Rajasthan and adjoining areas of Utter Pradesh in which the Berwa chamars live and the case description of the village Manpur, has been given primarily to illustrate the kind of changes that have occurred in the area. This village was selected for this description, in preference to Raipur, because it illustrates both the significant aspects of change: (i) the chamars of the villages giving up their occupation and continuing to live there to change their economic and social status, and (ii) immigration into the village of the group of chamars who had settled as cultivators-cum-labourers on newly reclaimed land. Raipur has experienced only the former. Chapter 4 similarly is regional in scope and attempts to give a cross-section of the new leadership which has come up in the area with the formation of the *Panchaayts* and the *Panchayat Samitis*.

The approach of selecting certain topics for detailed study has led the author to write each chapter as a more or less self-contained one. Each chapter began with an introduction which explains the ideas which led to the selection of the subject, the method of collecting the date for it and concludes with an analytical section which sets out its principal findings. An exception has been made in case of Chapter 4: the introduction and the analytical section have been combined.

Method of Data Collection

In each of the selected villages' data on composition of the households, land ownership and cultivation, and economic activities were obtained through a household census. Other data and their methods of collection varied with the scope and the purpose of the different studies. Thus Chapter 3, data on the working of the *Panchayats* and the cooperative society and on village disputes were collected through discussions with village people and examination of the records of these institutions and of the Revenue Department. For Chapter 5 it was necessary to conduct a sample survey of 25 per cent of the households in the three selected groups—this was in addition to the census of all households—besides interviews with key respondents like the Gram Sevika (woman extension worker). Chapter 4 is based entirely on the author's personal acquaintance with villages' leaders whom he had occasion to meet and observe at work in their villages and or in *Panchayats* and *Panchayat Samitis.*

In most studies of this kind, the formal collection of data through household surveys, examination of records of institutions, attending meetings of the institutions is only a part of the work, and some of the more important observations are based on personal contacts with the people for a long period. The author knew the people of Raipur for about 16 months and of Manpur for about a year. He visited these villages frequently and participated in many of their social activities like festivals, marriages and *keertans* (devotional music sessions). His wife similarly visited the women of Raipur and the other villages selected for Chapter 5.

It is assumed that the reader is familiar with the main development programmes which have been undertaken in the Indian villages in post Independence years. Accordingly, no attempt has been made to explain these. Readers who are not familiar with the programmes will find the Bibliography at the end useful. However, two notes one on *Panchayat* and *Panchaayt Samitis* and the other on the district revenue administration have been given in the appendices. The first note explains the main features of *Panchayat* and *Panchayat Samities* as constituted in Rajsthan, and has been given to facilitate understanding of Chapter 3 and 4. The second note explains the main features of the districts revenue administration, references to which have been made at various places in these studies. Some readers may find it more convenient to go through these notes before beginning the studies.

Repeat Studies

The villages were revisited for two weeks by Mrs Kamla Nath and Dr. Giri, a social scientist in January 2000. The changes that had occurred over a period of 40 years have been described in Chapter 8 along with the initial conditions relating to Chapter 1, 2 and 5. This has not been possible for Chapter 3 and 4 because a detailed study of village leaders or working of *Panchayats* and cooperatives was not feasible. The remarks on these by the selected village leaders have been taken from interviews with the village leaders of Raipur, Manpur and Bijaipur. The Chapter 8 analyses also the self-sustainability of the changes and developments in the area based on findings of this longitudinal study over four decades of development.

The Setting

Sawai Madhapur is a small district headquarter town with a population of about 20,000 (1961). Its position as a railway junction with Mumbai and Delhi,[5] and the fact that it contained in 1961 a large cement factory, gave it some importance as a transport and industrial Centre. The area[6] formed part of the former Jaipur State, and its capital, Jaipur city, which is easily approachable (130 km away, three hours by train), has been its city for a long time. The people of the area have had a strong feeling of 'belonging to Jaipur' which has coninued after the formation of Rajasthan. Jaipur is the capital of the new state and has the best schools, colleges, hospitals and various other institutions. Accordingly, the people of the area continue to look to it for political and administrative directions and for obtaining various services, as they used to do in the past.

This is a historical area which was an important theatre of political activity in medieval India. The Ranthambhore Fort located about 10 km to the north of Sawai Madhopur towns was one of the most famous Forts and seat of power in north India. It was the scene of a famous battle between a *Pathan* ruler of Delhi and a local Rajput prince, early in the fourteenth century. The Rajput lost the battle and with it control over the Fort and the area; but their chivalry in battle and the sacrifice of their women, who immolated themselves before the final capture of the Fort by the *Pathans*, are still remembered in innumerable folk songs. In subsequent centuries control over the Fort passed through various hands; it was one of the major Forts of North India and every ruler of Delhi tried to capture it. The Fort stands deserted and dilapidated now; but a temple located within it is among the foremost places of pilgrims in Rajastan. A fair is held at the temple annually in August-September.

Most of the larger villages in the area are old and claim to have been in existence for several centuries. Thus the residents of Raipur claim that a village of the name has existed within a radius of one mile of its present site since the time of this historic battle. The present *abadi* (habitation area) of the village is stated to be less than one hundred years old; but the ruins of an earlier *abadi* located about a mile to the east can be seen in a fair state of preservation. The villagers can distinguish the *mohallas* (quarters) of different caste within it and have recently renovated two temples which are used for worship on certain festivals. The Brahmins and the Mahajans of Raipur are particularly proud of the historic past of their village. Some of them have in their possession old books, papers and other objects to remind them of it. The people of Mannpur similarly claim that their village is several hundred years old and relate the history of various rulers who have held sway over it. An old largely dilapidated fort stands at the southern end of the village, a mute reminder of its historical past.

Most of the smaller villages, on the other hand, are recent in origin. These villages located on the open plain, lacked the natural protection essential for preservation of settlement through periods of warfare, and their location has been shifting. Thus Bijaipur is less than a century old. Chainpur, the Chammar village, is in a separate category altogether. It is one of the settlements founded as a result of the recent migration of Chammars and is less than 20 years old.

Jagirdari

Jagirdari was a very important institution in Jaipur state, as in most other princely states of Rajasthan: more than 80 per cent of the villages of Jaipur State were under *Jagirdars*. In this area also, most villages were under *jagirdars*, and they were very powerful locally. But most of the *Jagirdars* of the area had limited jurisdiction as their *Jagir* extended to very few villages. The biggest, having 30 to 40 villages, could only be considered medium sized. Their power was due not so much to their wealth or size of their *Jagirs* as to the fact that they belonged to the same branch of the *kachwaha* Rajput[7] clan to which the ruling family of the state belonged. Several were related to the ruling family[8] and were very influential at the Court. Secondly, the power of the Rajput *jagirdars* rested purely on their position as *Jagirdars*: it was not buttressed by the presence of a large number of Rajputs in the villages, for their number was quite small. The villages which were headquarters of *Jagirdars* had a few Rajputs families living in them; most others had no Rajputs at all. After the abolition of *Jagirdari* a number of *Jagirdars* who earlier lived in their villages moved to Jaipur and other towns; as a result the social influence of the Rajput has almost disappeared. This situation is quite different from that in many districts of Western Rajasthan in which large numbers of Rajputs live in the villages and continue to be a social and political force in the area even after the abolition of *Jagirdari*.

Although *jagirdari* is often considered to be a system of land tenure like *Zamindari* in Utter Pradesh and other states, it was much more. It would be more correct to regard it as the apex of a whole complex of institutions—political, social and economic. Therefore, its abolition in the early 1950s did not merely mean termination of a system of land tenure. It meant bringing to formal end the feudal social and political order which had disappeared in British India much earlier but which had been preserved in the princely states as a result of an extraordinary combination of circumstances. An idea of the changes which have occurred with the abolition of *jagirdari* may be had from the following brief description of the role and functions of *jagirdars* and conditions of *jagir* villages.

The *jagirdars* considered themselves virtual masters of their villages. The largest *jagirdars* of Jaipur state, who had wide administrative and judicial powers, were in fact regarded as sub-rulers by the state. But even the medium sized and small *jagirdars*, like those of this area, who did not have any judicial powers and whose administrative powers are also limited, considered themselves to be the 'rulers' of their villages and the cultivators and the other people living in them, as their subjects. The use of the word *Thakur* (i.e. master) for all *jagirdars* and of *Darbar* (i.e. court of the state) which was used also for the ruler of Jaipur, for some of the larger *jagirdars*, gives an indication of the local power and prestige of the *Jagirdars*.

All land in *jagir* villages is the property of *jagirdar*, and the cultivators were considered to be the tenants. The tax on land collected was regarded as his share of produce. It was called rent, not land revenue, and it was in most villages collected through physical divisions of the produce on the threshing floor. The *jagirdar* had full control over all uncultivated land in his villages and gave permission for its use for cultivation, grazing and removal of forest produce, building houses, etc.; he charged fees for granting such permission. He maintained his own administrative agency for collection of land revenue, maintenance of land records, exercising control over the cultivated lands and other purposes. In case of most large and medium sized *jagirs* the organization of this agency was with *Patwaris*[9] (village accountants) and *patels* at the village levels and its methods of working (e.g. preparation of the record for every plot of land, conducting inspection of crops at every cropping season) were similar to those followed by the revenue Department of Jaipur state.

The *Jagirdars* were also considered to be responsible for welfare of their people. They were expected to undertake construction of such public works as roads, tanks and wells, to provide facilities for education and medical care; and to take interest in all aspects of economic, social and cultural welfare of their people. But the performance of different *Jagirdars* in this field varied very greatly, depending upon the interest of the individual *Jagirdars*, and the size and income of his *jagir*. Some of the more progressive and enthusiastic *Jagirdars* took a keen interest in these activities so much so that the people of their villages still remember their work with gratitude. But the majority did little. As a result, the standard of development of these services was rather low in most *jagir* villages and these were considered to be more backward than the *Khalsa* villages—i.e. villages administered directly by the State. But even the state did much less than what has been done in the years after the formation of Rajasthan. An idea of the difference between conditions in the time of the Jaipur state and after Independence may be had by comparison of school facilities in 1948 and 1962. In 1948 there was no high school and just one middle school (in Sawai Madhopur town) in the whole of Sawai Madhopur *tehsil*, and even large villages like Manpur did not have a primary school. But in 1962 the *tehsil* had 3 higher secondary schools and nearly a hundred primary schools. Communications, health and other services were similarly undeveloped earlier and have expanded greatly in recent years.

But the *Jagirdars* (and Jaipur state) took keen interest in several aspects of the welfare of their people to which the new secular state pays little or no attention. They took interest in socio-religious activities like the celebration of religious festivals and the support of temples, Brahmins and holy men. The most common method of such support was making grants of rent-free land.[10] The *jagirdars* were also active in enforcement of the *jajmani* systems and other traditional obligations of particular caste to the village community and themselves. Their support of the *jajmani* system was due partly to the fact that they had a vested interest in its preservation. They saw clearly that the village artisans and service castes would continue to serve them only as long as they serve the village community. But there was another reason also. The *jagirdars* entire outlook was oriented towards preservation of traditional practices and was against change. They considered themselves to be the upholder of tradition—traditional values, religious practice, and social customs and as 'defenders of the faith'. Their neglect of formal school education was also due partly to the attitude against change and partly to the fear that if their people got educated they would be less willing to submit to their local authority. The whole atmosphere was one of a feudal paternalistic autocracy.

It is true that the areas was not isolated from British India and could not but feel the impact of the social, political and economic forces that were gathering momentum there. The effects of the movement for Independence of the country and of ideas like representative governments, social equality, abolition of untouchability, uplift of the scheduled castes, abolition of *Jagirdars* and *Zamindars* and giving lands to the tillers of the soil had begun to be felt in the area in the 1930s and especially in the 1940s. Migration to British India (e.g. of chammar labours to industrial centres and other towns) was one means of inflow of new ideas. Commerce and communication were others. The Frontier Mail train[11] passed through the area every day and a wide variety of consumer goods was imported from British India. But even the influence of these economic factors was considerably moderated by the various restrictions on commerce imposed by the Jaipur state. Jaipur, like most other princely states had its own customs under which heavy duties were placed on import and export of goods. Besides, import or export of certain goods was not permitted. Thus *dalda* (hydrogenated vegetable oil which is used as a substitute for *ghee*)[12] could not be imported into the area of the State and *ghee* and milch animals could not be exported. Export of fuel wood was similarly prohibited. As a result the price structure of the area was significantly different from that of neighbouring areas of British India. Manufactured goods like cloth were more expensive, milk and ghee were cheap; wood for fuel and most other uses was available to the cultivators at a nominal cost. The villagers often refer to the low prices of milk and *ghee* and virtual free availability of wood during the rule of Jaipur state; the high prices and scarcity of these commodities now is one of their main grievances against 'changed times'.

Accordingly, integration of Jaipur with Rajasthan and abolition of *jagirdari* did not merely mean a change of government or of a system of land tenure. These brought the feudal way of life to an end and made the area a full participant in the social political and economic evolution of the country.

The Castes

The Meenas are the principle caste of landowner cultivators in the area. They are also the most numerous caste; but their number is not overwhelming, being estimated at only about 25 per cent of the rural population (1931) census.[13] Other castes, notably Chammars among the scheduled castes, Malis and Jats among the cultivating castes, and Brahmins and Mahajans among the high castes are also present in large number. The Meenas are most numerous in small villages and hamlets; but in the medium sized or large villages which are multi-caste in character, their number is rather small. The Meenas of this district as also of several adjoining districts of eastern Rajasthan are a cultivating, landowning caste with social customs and practices very similar to those of other such castes. But they are classified as a scheduled tribe and receive the concessions and preferences given by the government to these tribes. This classification is due to the fact that the Meenas of several districts of southern and south western Rajasthan are a backward tribe of shifting cultivators with a tradition of thieving; they were classified as a criminal tribe until this classification was abolished after independence. They have been settling down as cultivators in recent years but are still quite backward and poor. The difference between the two groups is explained by the local Meenas by stating that they themselves are *ujala* (literally clean) or *Zamindars* (literally Land-owner) Meenas; while the backward group with tradition of thieving are *chowkidar* (literally watchman)[14] Meenas. They explain that the two groups are separate, and there is no inter-marriage between them. However, the political leaders of the Meenas of this area are quite keen to preserve their status as a scheduled tribe, because this status brings advantages like reservation of seats in government services and in the state legislature.[15]

Geography

The climate, soils and cropping pattern of the area are very similar to those of the central Indian plain and are quite different from those of the semi-desert or desert areas of western Rajasthan. The average rainfall of Sawai Madhopur is more than about 30 inches per year. Two crops *kharif* (monsoon) and *rabi* (post monsoon), are grown without irrigation. The principal crops *jowar* (sorghum) in the *kharif* and wheat, barley and gram in the *rabi* are also characteristic of a humid rather than a dry climate. The hills in the eastern part of the *tehsil* are covered with forests and contain considerable wild life (especially tigers and several varieties of antelopes). Malaria was the major disease which took a heavy toll of life every year until its eradication in the late 50s through the national malaria eradication programe. Prevalence of Malaria is considered to be one reason for the relative backwardness of the area.

Pressure of the population on the land is not high. Land holdings are fairly large by Indian standards, ranging between 10 and 20 acres per cultivating family. The number of landless is moderate, 20 per cent or less in most villages and fairly large areas of cultivable land were available for cultivation until recently. These have been brought under cultivation during the last three decades and especially in the years since Independence, and this expansion of cultivation had an important influence on social change in the area. On the other hand, agriculture is rather precarious, techniques are poor, and crop yields are low. Most of the cropped area is rain fed and suffers from the vagaries of the monsoon. The irrigated area is very small, only 7 per cent of the total cropped area of the *tahsil*. Cultivation on the unirrigated land is extensive and the farmers do not apply even farm-yard manure to the fields. Use of improved seed, chemical fertilizers, pesticides and other improved techniques is confined to the small area of irrigated land. Some what larger holdings should not, therefore, lead one to infer a high standard of agricultural prosperity. The incomes and levels of living are quite low, as will be seen from observation in studies undertaken in the area.

The Period

The most important events influencing social change in the area during the last 25 years have been the merger of Jaipur state with Rajasthan and the abolition of *Jagirdari*. But these have come among several others in a change packed period, which can be considered to have started in 1942, after Japan entered Second World War and occupied Burma.

Second World War had started nearly three year earlier, but its influence in Indian villages became marked only in 1942 when prices of foodgrains began to increase rapidly, following stoppage of imports of rice from Burma, and large numbers of people began to get employment in various war works and industries. The former brought substantial gains to the cultivators; the latter meant more work and higher earnings for the labourers. But both placed a severe strain on the *jajmani* system. When the price of the foodgrains started shooting up, the cultivators found it more attractive to sell their foodgrains and to pay for the goods and the services, which they used to obtain earlier under the *jajmani* system, in cash. Compulsory procurement of foodgrains by the state, rationing in the towns, and other control measures, further increased the tendency among the cultivators not to part with their food grains. It is true that no large War work or industry was located within this area; but increased employments in works and industries in other areas to which people from this area used to go for work had the same effect as would have been produced by increase in employment within the area. It led to an increase in emigration resulting in scarce labour and higher wages. Moreover, higher earnings and greater exposure to urban influences made performance of the traditional tasks under the *jajmani* system increasingly distasteful to the Chammars and other labouring castes. The younger men especially resented having to perform these traditional tasks. The role of these economic influences in the movement for change among the Chammar has been explained at some length in chapter 2.

Independence

Independence of the country in 1947 and integration of Jaipur and other princely States to form the new state of Rajasthan in 1949 were the next big events. The latter had more immediate significance for this area because it meant a complete change in its political administration. Moreover, this change meant that the local socio-political structure (in which *jagirdari* was the most important institution) would change soon. It was known that the new government of the Congress Party was committed to abolition of *jagirdari* and would take this step as soon as possible. The law abolishing *jagirdari* was passed by the legislature of Rajsthan in 1952; but several of the administrative steps which helped effect the change were initiated earlier. Two of these were 'settlement and survey', and the posting of revenue staff of the government of Rajasthan in place of the staffs of the *jagirdars*. It has been mentioned above that the *jagirdars* had their own agency for collection of land revenue and maintenance of land records. With abolition of *jagirdari* both these functions would be taken over by the state government. But before this could be done it was essential to determine for each plot of land the right of ownership and the land revenue payable by the cultivators in cash. Determination of the latter was necessary because in most *jagir* villages rent used to be paid in kind. This operation of determining rights in land and the tax payable by each cultivator is called 'settlement and survey'. It was begun in this area as early as 1949, and was completed in different villages between 1952-1955. After its completion the revenue staffs of the *Jagirdars* were replaced by the *Patwaris* of the state government. The actual abolition of *Jagirdari* (called resumption of *Jagirs* by the State of Rajasthan) came in different villages between 1955 and 1958. But since these other steps had been taken earlier and direct relations established between the cultivators and the state, the final step of 'resumption' was no more than the culmination of a process.

Another important land reform measure was the Rajasthan Tenancy Act of 1955, which gave security of tenure to all cultivators and completed the process of giving 'land to the tiller' begun by abolition of *jagirdari*. The act was of particular benefit to the small cultivators especially of the scheduled castes, who had cultivated small areas taken on lease and had not enjoyed security of tenure earlier.

Independence of the country and formation of Rajasthan also marked the beginning of a series of political changes. The first General Election in 1952 was the first experience of the people with elections and caused much excitement in the area. From the point of view of social change, the impact of adult suffrage was perhaps as great as that of the elective process, because it introduced the people to a new principle of political power, the power of numbers. As they began to grasp the significance of winning an election by polling the largest number of votes, they realized that the basis of political power had changed decisively—from the authority of the individual *jagirdar* or the influence of a small high caste group, to numbers. Large castes and villages acquired a new political importance, because it began to be seen that their support could be decisive in an election.

The establishment of *Panchayts* in 1954 brought the democratic process closer and also made it more significant. It is true that *panchayts* had been formed in some villages even during the time of Jaipur state. Raipur was one such village. But these villages are few, and as the *Panchayts* were nominated bodies, they consisted mainly of persons who had held some hereditary office like that of *patel* or were recognized as leaders of their caste on account of wealth, prestige or influence, of the families. But the experiences of having elected *Panchayts* was entirely new, and its significance became increasingly clear as these bodies began to function and to exercise the powers conferred on them. The latest step in the political process has been the establishment, in 1959 of *Panchayt Samitis* and *Zila Parishads*, popular institutions constituted at the block and district level respectively, for direction of community development and other rural development programmes.

Development

The decade of the 1950s also saw a rapid increase in the pace of development activities, in building of roads, wells and tanks for irrigation and drinking water supply, and opening of schools, dispensaries, veterinary centres and other institutions providing other services. Emphasise on development activities became more pronounced after the opening in 1954 of the Sawai Madhopur Community Development Block. Thus a new type of administrative agency was introduced which had no regulatory functions but had responsibility only for development. Programmes for construction of various works and improvement of agriculture began to receive more funds and attention of staff. Eradication of malaria through the national Malaria Eradication Programme was another noteworthy development. It meant the end of the major public health problem of the area.

Another development of considerable local importance was establishment in 1950 of the cement factory at Sawai Madhopur. It meant a large increase in availability of non agricultural employment in the area. At the time of these studies, the cement factory employed about 2000 workers and its limestone quarries (at Phalodi, 10 miles to the south of

Sawai Madhopur) about 3000. The various public works undertaken as part of the Five-Year-Plan also provided considerable employment. The Sawai Madhopur railway station was expanded from time to time in order to cope with the increase in volume of traffic. In 1962, the large work of doubling the railway line, which provided employment to a large number of unskilled labourers, was in progress. Construction and repair of roads, laying of the transmission line from a hydro-electric power station located at Kotah to Sawai Madhopur and building of an electric sub-station at Sawai Madhopur were other major works in progress during the period of these studies.

Establishment of the cement factory and expansion of various government activities has also led to establishment of two new townships. A sizable township of about 6000 people has come up within the factory area. The tiny colonies of employees in the district head quarter offices and the railway station have grown and merged to form another township of nearly 2000 people. These townships have brought urban influences nearer to the villages included in these studies. They provided opportunities of employment and urban facilities like shops and restaurants; and created much large demand for agricultural products such as milk, vegetables and fruit.

This generally favourable economic situation, kept the prices of agricultural produce stable in 1950s after a period of rapid increase in the 1940s; reclamation and cultivation of large areas of cultivable waste lands and steady increase in non-agricultural employment has been a significant influence in the process of social change described in these studies. It has created an atmosphere favourable to change and has enabled the community to absorb the tensions arising from it. Thus, availability of cultivable waste lands and increase in opportunities of non-agricultural employment has been major factors in the smooth accomplishment of change in occupation among the Chammars.

Footnotes

1. The *jajmani* system is the system of economic exchanges between the cultivators and the others of the village community under which goods and services are supplied by village artisan and service castes to the cultivators against customary payments in grains at its harvest. The system is a well-known feature of Indian village life, though it is known by different names in different parts of the country. The term *jajmani* system has been used

here because it is the most widely used and readily understood. The system had been described in a number of studies on Indian villages. For a detailed recent description of the system in a north Indian village see Lewis; "*Village Life in Northern India*, 1958." chapter 2.

2. For a description of the work of the collector and district development officer, see Appendix II, 3 (p. 154-155).
3. For a note on these institutions see Appendix I, 3 pp. 148-153.
4. The names of the villages and the individual villagers mentioned in various studies are fictitious.
5. Sawai Madhopur is 224 miles from Delhi on the Delhi Bombay line of the Western railway.
6. Unless indicated otherwise the phrase 'this area' has been used for Sawai Madhopur *tehsil*, an administrative unit consisting of 204 villages with a population of about 140,000, according to the 1961 census.
7. The area is called *Rajwati* literally the home of *Rajwati* or kingly branch of the Kachwaha Rajput clan.
8. The present Maharaja of Jaipur is the son of *jagirdar* of this area. He was adopted as heir to the throne of Jaipur because the earlier ruler did not have any son. His predecessor had similarly gone in adoption from the same family.
9. *Patwari* is the village level official of the revenue department who maintains land records and assists the *patel* in collection of land revenue. The latter, men of prominent land owning families of the village are responsible for collection of land revenue for the state. For more detailed explanation see Appendix II.
10. Thus the *jagirdar* of Manpur had made grants of land to all the temples in the village, to individual Brahmins and also to the Rajput and other servants.
11. A well known train on the Delhi Bombay railway line.
12. Dalda is the trade name of the product of the particular manufacturer. But the term is widely used by the people of this area (as of most other parts of North India) for hydrogenated vegetable oil.
13. Figures on the population of individual castes have not been published after 1931 but the number of Meenas may be estimated approximately from the population of scheduled tribes given in 1961 census. This was 30,032 and formed 25.2 per cent of the rural population of the *tehsil*. As the Meenas are about the only scheduled tribe in the area—the number of other tribes is negligible—this number may be taken as giving a fair approximation of their numbers.
14. Besides being thieves, they were also excellent watchmen and were employed by the villagers in this capacity.
15. The propriety of classifying a cultivating owner group like the *Zamindar* Meenas as a scheduled tribe has been questioned on several occasion.

SECTION A
Economic Development and Social Change in Rajasthan

Social Change and the Village Community

Introduction

That the Indian village is a distinct socio-economic unit, whose inhabitants have strong community feelings, has been a dominant theme in writings on rural India during the last 100 years and more. Beginning with early British administrators[1], successive writers on rural India have emphasized this point. In recent years, sociologists studying villages have acknowledged the existence of the feeling of "belonging to the village" and have attempted to analyze the bonds that tie the villagers to his village and his caste, as contrasted with the nature of his contacts outside the village and the role of caste (which extends beyond the village). They have also dwelt at length on the questions whether the feelings for caste contributes to the feeling for the village or serve as alternative, competitive focus of community feeling. Perhaps, the most interesting discussion of the subject are in the studies of Srinivas, McKim Marriott, and Oscar Lewis, reported in 'village India'.[2]

In post-independence years, the idea that the people living in the village have a strong feelings of belonging together, has occupied an important place in thinking on the community development programme and on institutions like the *panchayat* and the cooperative. It is a central idea in the community development programme, in which village and community are considered to be almost synonymous. Many activities of the programme, such as public works, the expense of which is shared by government and the village people, are based on the recognition of the villagers' loyalty to their village. Moreover, it is thought that by affording such opportunities for collective endeavor, the community development programme itself strengthens the feeling for the village and helps build a stronger, healthier community life. Many of the institutions' activities included in the programme, such as organization of youth clubs, women's clubs and community Centres, attempt to foster community feelings as a primary objective.

In the village *Panchayat* similarly, the strong feelings of belonging, of members of one community, has been recognized as a major source of institutional strength. That such wide authority and comprehensive role in the economic and social advance of the rural people could be envisaged for an institutions are due, in the authors view, to implicit acceptance of the existence of this feeling. Moreover, the recent trend towards smaller *Panchayats* in several States has been motivated by the idea that the *Panchayat* will function better if the people of the Panchayat area regard it as an institution of the community, and that this can happen only if its area is co-terminus with the existing unit of community life, the village. "One village, one *Panchayat*"—this is the ideal. Bringing together two or more small villages into one *Panchayat* is recognized only as compromise which has to be adopted because it is not feasible, for economic and administrative reasons, to have a *Panchayat* for every small village.

In the case of cooperatives, there was for some time a controversy between the supporters of the comparatively large society, comprising a group of villages, and those who favoured the small society comprising a single village, or where necessary, a few small villages. The larger society was favoured on grounds of economic viability; the supporters of the small society should know each other personally and that the successful working of the society should rest on their strong sense of community.[3]

Yet, it is recognized by all who have anything to do with rural life that the feeling of belonging to the village is weakening and changing in character. No modern writer could follow Metcalfe or Munro, and call the village communities little republics. The changes of the last 100 years and more—political, economics and social—have produced enormous changes in the feeling for the village. With Raipur as the example, an attempt is made here to analyze the character of change in the feeling for the village as well as the influence contributing to it. The changes are brought out by contrasting the present position with that obtaining about 60 years ago, i.e., just before the railway line came into the area. This event greatly increased the contact of the village with the outside world and accelerated the process of economic and social change. Its first effect was migration of Brahmins to cities to work as cooks and priests. This throw back to a historic data helps clearer perception of the basic on which the feeling for the village rested in the past and the change influences working on it.

Raipur is an old village; the villagers believe it was founded at the time of the historic battle at the Ranthambhore Fort early in the 14th century. The feeling of continuous living in the same village for generations and centuries, typical of most Indian villages and a powerful factor in contributing to the sense of belonging to it, is particularly strong in Raipur, where there is the additional factor of pride in belonging to an historic village. This pride is shared by people of all castes, though the literate castes (Brahmin and Mahajan) feel it somewhat more strongly than others. It existed 60 years ago; the contacts of the village with the outside world were largely limited to some administrative and commercial relationships.

Administration was concerned primarily with maintenance of law and order and of collection of land revenue. Jaipur State had appointed *patels* and posted *patwari* within the village for collection of land revenue. The *tehsil* and the *thana* (police station), the two important administrative offices of the State, were located in Sawai Madhopur town, six miles from the village. The villagers understood very well the duties of the *patels* and the *patwari* and the functions of these two offices. They were also keenly aware that their village formed part of Jaipur State. There was a strong feeling of loyalty to the State and respect for the Ruler. But the administration had only limited functions: it did not enter into and affect the daily life of the villagers in innumerable ways as it does today.

The land of the village was the sole means of subsistence for the villagers. All castes depended upon it either directly as cultivators or indirectly as artisans, traders, priests etc., supplying goods or rendering services to the cultivators. Economic relations between different castes were regulated by the *jajmani* system under which the goods and services to be supplied by each caste and the payments to be made to it (mainly in grain) were specified in detail. All villagers, cultivators and non-cultivators, shared in the produce of the land; the non-cultivators had as much stake and interest in the agriculture prosperity of the village as the cultivators. A year of good crops meant plenty, one of poor crops meant hardship for all. The village was not merely a place to live: it was a sole theater of economic activity and its land was the sole means of subsistence.

Commerce with the outside world was limited. The principal exports from the village were some foodgrains and *ghee*. Imports were cloth, kerosene, salt and a few other consumer goods which had been introduced by this time. The village also served as a small commercial and service Centre for surrounding small villages. Its artisans sold leather goods, ornaments and *lac* bangles; its merchants distributed consumer goods, lend money and bought agricultural produce, and its Malis sold vegetables. Marriages of most castes were concentrated within a radius of 30 miles. Exception were Brahmins and Mahajans in case of whom marriage with families living at longer distances were more common. Marriages were a major source of contact with other villages because it was common to visit one's relatives.

Travel was limited. Most travel was confined to visiting relatives in nearby villages or going to Sawai Madhopur town. The only exception was pilgrimage to holy places. Pilgrimage to holy places was the principal form of travel to longer distances.

The village was by no means isolated although that might have been the case earlier. But its contact with the outside world was limited. What is more important, economic activity and day-to-day social life were concentrated in the village, and the outside world did not intrude into it and affect every aspect of life as it does today. As a result, the feeling of belonging to the village was all-pervading.

The feeling of belonging to one's caste was equally strong. Caste was the most important socio-economic institution in the life of village people. It was the basis of all marriages which were confined to caste. It determined occupation and social status; social and economic relations with people of other castes; marriage and other social customs; consumption especially preference for or avoidance of certain food; mode of dress; and values and outlook on life. Most villagers knew that their caste was found outside the village in neighboring villages and beyond. But consciousness of the distribution of caste beyond the marriage zone was vague, and what is more important, not meaningful; because the fact did not appear to be of any great significance to the average villager.

To sum up; the average villager felt that he belonged to a particular village and to a particular caste. Both loyalties were strong and keenly felt. The feeling for the village rested on contiguous living in the village *abadi*; concentration of economic activity and social relationship within the village, with the land of the village providing the sole means of substances and the *jajmani* system binding the different occupational and social groups (castes) in the case of economic and social relationship which gave all of them a stake in the prosperity of the village and very limited contacts with the outside world.

The feeling for the caste was based on the vital roles it had in all aspects of the social and economic life of individual. But one loyalty contributed to other: there were not many occasions when the villager found the two loyalties competitive or conflicting. There were occasional conflicts between castes, no doubt; but the role of caste as a basis of the *jajmani* system overrode these. Caste providing the social and economic stability and intra-group discipline essential for the functioning of the system. The socio-economic conception of the village uppermost in the mind of the villagers was of a unit composed of a number of castes, each of which performed an essential function and made possible its functioning as a unit. This was expressed in the locally popular saying, "the village is an entity composed of *saat jaat*."[4]

The position has changed radically during the past 60 years. The village is no longer the sole theater of economic activity; nor is its land the sole source of substances. Almost 40 per cent of the workers in Raipur (462 out of 1212) depend wholly or in large part upon income originating outside the village. The *jajamani* system has all but broken down. *Jajamani* relations are now confined only to a few castes—the Kumhars (potters), the Khatis (carpenters), the Lohars (blacksmiths) and the Nais (barbers). But even in these instances the traditional activities neither provide the main source of income for the caste nor form main basis of supply of goods and services furnished by the caste to village. Thus, only 4 out of 10 Kumhar families are engaged in their traditional occupation of making pots, and even these families supplement their earnings with other non-caste, sources of income. On the other hand only a minority of the village families use *jajamani* services. Non-cultivators and small part-time cultivators (e.g., Rehgars and Chamars 40% of all families in the village) do not participate in the *Jajamani* system at all. The main participant in the *jajamani* system are the cultivating owners—Meenas and Malis—and a few cultivating households among the high castes. But even the families who participate in the system obtain only a few specified goods and services obtained from the same artisans. Thus, only specified services like repairs to the plough are obtained from the Khatis under the *Jajmani* system, and all other goods, e.g., a *charpoy*, repairs to the house, are paid for in cash. Consequently, most of the transactions between the village artisans and other villagers are cash transactions, and the *Jajamani* system is of distinctly marginal significance in the economic life of the village.

Commerce with the outside world is extensive. A wide variety of manufactured goods is obtained from outside the village and earning money to pay for these, whether through sale of agricultural produce or through sale of one's labour, has become the most important objective of economic activity. Commercial contacts with the outside world are so active that a good deal of the buying and selling which would be done in the village is done in Sawai Madhopur town instead. A major part of the agricultural produce of the village is sold in the town, not to traders within the village, because prices are lower, or there is greater variety. Even goods of the type produced by local artisans are purchased outside the village, and village artisans on their part sell their good outside. The villagers buy country-type shoes, *charas*, and other leather goods produced by the village Rehgars from Sawai Madhopur town, from *haats* in other villages and form periodical fairs. The villages Rehgars similarly sell their products in fairs, *haats,* and Sawai Madhopur town. The Rehgars want a *haat* in the village so that they do not have to take their goods for sale outside. The village is part of a market area centreing on the town of Sawai Madhopur, which in turn is linked with the markets of the State and the nation, and economic influences originating outside the village are constantly impinging on it. Most villagers see this quite clearly. The average cultivator understands that variations in prices of agricultural produce are the result mainly of factors originating outside the village or local area. During the two years preceding these studies, the price of *gur*, an important source of cash for these cultivators, had been low. They knew that this was not due to any local factor—production in the area had been low in 1960-61 and prices should have been high—but to over production in the country. The white-collar workers in government service and the skilled and unskilled workers in the cement factory and the railway station all realize that their employment depends upon decisions taken by people at the State capital, Jaipur, or in distant places like Delhi, Bombay, and Calcutta.

Changes in contiguous living have not been as marked, because most of the people of the village continue to live in the village *abadi.* But there is a growing tendency to live outside. Nearly half the Meena households now live in the hamlet which has grown to its present size during the last sixty years. In addition, two hamlets, Chammar and *Rehgars*, have been established within the last twenty year; and a large proportion of families of these castes lived in them. The trend towards living outside the main *abadi* will grow. There is very little land available for expansion of housing within the *abadi,* and as population increase and rise in the standard of living leads to a desire for bigger, more spacious houses, there will be pressure to move out of the *abadi*. This may result in the establishment of one or more new hamlets at some distance from the *abadi* or in a tendency among cultivators owning land irrigated by wells to live, homestead fashions, near their wells.

Accordingly, all of the past reasons for the feeling of "belonging to the village" has been weakened and will weaken further as contacts with the outside world increase and economic activity outside the village becomes progressively more important. There is no influence in the development programme or development institutions which can counter this trend effectively. During eight years of community development programme, the only development activity in which the whole village participated as a unit was construction of middle school building. Participation was by no means equal: Brahmins and Mahajans made the largest contributions in money and were also the principal decision makers, and participation of the scheduled castes was nominal. Still, this was the only activity in which all castes participated; there has been no other. All other aspects of the community development programme, e.g., construction of drinking water wells and paving streets, have been done on a caste or *mohalla* (quarter of the village) basis, and if there has been a village contribution it has been only from members of the caste or residents of the *mohalla* concerned. The development institutions associated with the community development programme—the *Panchayat*, the cooperative society, the youth club, the women's club and the community Centre—do require association on a village wide basis. But none of these institutions have been successful in countering the above trend and fostering village wide association. The *Panchayat* (Chapter 3) serves more as an area of struggle for power than as a medium for village-wide cooperative action. The cooperative society is not functioning well. If it had been more active, it would have been the means of village wide association for certain economic purposes. On the other hand, it could also, like the *panchayat*, be an arena for caste or group competition. The youth club is dominated by educated young men, mostly of the high castes, and has never able to attract the youth of the cultivating or scheduled castes in large numbers. The women's club was also a high caste affair when it functioned. The community Centre is inactive.

The three later institutions are intended to serve as media of informal association and recreation on a village wide, supra-caste basis. But because they do not function, this objective is not being achieved, and informal association and recreation remain confined largely within castes. Probably this was always the case; but the changes of the last two decades and those which are occurring now tend to confine them more and not less within caste. This needs some explanation. The main forms of informal association and recreation within the village at present are: meetings of men at *hatais* (place of informal group meetings) in the evening and in shops in the village *bazaar* during the day; meetings of women at the wells, and *keertans* (singing of devotional songs) by the young men in the temples at night. Feasts, fairs, and religious festivals are other important occasions when villagers get together. Meetings at *hatais* are generally within caste, confined to neighbours. Meetings in the village *bazaar* are super-caste and are perhaps the most important means of day-to-day meetings between men of different castes. Meetings of women also have tended to become more caste base because the number of wells has increased in recent years and each caste, including the scheduled castes, has now got its own well. Feasts at weddings and funerals are also caste affairs because most of the invitees are relatives of the host and belong to his caste. *Keertans* are an increasingly popular source of recreation for the villagers, especially the young men. But these are organized in temples, most of which are caste temples, and *keertan* parties are unusually composed of members of the caste which patronizes and supports the temple. Most religious festivals are celebrated either in temples or in individual homes and do not afford opportunities for different castes to come together. There is only one festival in the year, the *Jaljhoolni Gyaras*, in which all, the Hindus of the village come together. But when the scheduled caste claimed the right to participate in this festival and the high castes opposed it, the disagreement became a cause of tension and actual violence. Therefore, participation in this festival at present serves more to emphasize caste feelings than to foster the feelings of belonging to a supra-caste entity—the village. In the days of Jaipur State and the *Jagirdar* there were rather more occasions for people of different castes to come together. The *Dussehra* and *Gangore*[5] festivals were celebrated by the State in the State capital and other large towns by the *Jagirdars* in their village at their own expense, and all people were expected to participate in these. Weddings and other ceremonies in the *jagirdars* homes were other occasions for people of different castes to come together, because they were all invited (or required) to attend. Integration of Jaipur State with Rajsthan has led to the disappearance of many opportunities for informal associations. The change is particularly marked in former *jaigir* villages like Manpur, and it is often mentioned by the villagers.

The school is at present the only institution in which there is effective, daily association on a village-wide, supra-caste basis. Moreover, this association is on the basis of equality, without regard either for the traditional ideas of caste status or of the new force of caste competition. It is of great significance for the future, because it will have a fundamental influence on the attitudes and behaviour of the generation now going to school. But its present influence is rather limited, because the school going youth form only a small part of population; as yet they have little influence on decision-making in the village.

The village is often thought of as a face-to-face society whose inhabitants see each other daily and do various activities together. This is undoubtedly true of small villages of agriculturists like Bijaipur or the hamlet of Manpur. But as the above description brings out, this is not true of multi-caste village like Raipur.

The traditional feelings of belonging to the multi-caste village was dependent to a large extent on isolation or limited contacts with the outside world and the very restricted, essentially static economic and social life institutionalized in the *jajmani* system. Moreover, the socio-economic system of the village was hierarchical in character and assigned a stated occupation, share in the economic product of the village, and most important, a particular social status, to each caste. It was inevitable, therefore, that with break-down of isolation, increasing participation in the nation's economic and political life, and spread of ideas of social and political equality, this structure of socio-economic relations should suffer violent convulsions. The feeling of belonging to the village should weaken.

But this feeling was essentially secular and integrative in character. It symbolized the contribution of different castes in the functioning of a secular, supra-caste social unit. The feeling for the caste on the other hand is essentially sectarian and divisive. Therefore, decline of the feelings for the village and strengthening of the feeling for the caste, together with the change in the role of caste feeling from contributor to the feeling for the village competitor, are matters for concern. This is especially so because the village, as stated above, will remain a principal unit of community life. In rural India and most activities of rural economic development and social advance will continue to be organized around it. Moreover, even though economic activity out side the village will become increasingly important in the life of the village people, they will continue to live in villages because of the very material advantages offered. Most of the people of Raipur who depend upon non-agricultural employment outside the village continue to live in the village, and even those who live outside for varying periods continue to maintain active links with the village (Chapter 1).

That small units of settlement and community life have an important place even in modern industrially advanced societies is demonstrated by the recent movement towards living in suburbs and small towns in western countries. The entire community development movement in the west is based on the belief that life in the small community offers a unique opportunity for expression of deep seated human urges—the feelings of belonging to a significant group, the desire to know and to be know in it and to work with other members of the group in meaningful activities. Western writing on community development constantly emphasized that life in a small community is richer and happier because of the opportunities of informal associations and collective effort for organizing recreation, social welfare and other activities that it offers.[6] In an old country like India the role of community development is much larger, because most economic development and social welfare programmes have to be organized around communities like the village.

But in order that the village may play the role envisaged for it, its social system must be organized on different principles. Unequal status of different castes and the *jajamani* system must go, replaced by social relations based on the principals of social and political equality, freedom of association and an opportunity for every individual to accept new patterns of economic activities. This involves changes in attitudes, ways of doing things, institutions and leadership: social strain and conflicts, such as those described in Chapter 3, are inevitable in the process. But it is in the degree that this transformation takes place, that administration of local affairs and organization of social and economic activities with the village as the unit will become successful and satisfying to the people, and they will have a new sense of belonging together and a new loyalty to the village community.

The new integration must be achieved primarily at the village level and with the village as the unit. The village has traditionally been the unit of settlement and of organization of social and economic relationship within rural society. And, it will remain so in future because the bulk of the rural population will continue to live in villages—in the present villages, in fact. It is, therefore, imperative that the village has a new social system through which the village people establish new patterns of social, political and economic inter-action, which are satisfying to them and enable them to live as members of one community without conflict. The traditional social system of the village had, in spite of all its other defects and draw-backs this cardinal virtue; it enabled different castes and groups to live together without serious conflict. Otherwise, it could not have survived the political convulsions and periods of anarchy and unrest which India experienced from time to time.

Footnotes

1. The following oft-quoted statement of Sir Charles Metcalf contained in his minute of 1830 expresses this view most forcefully:

   "The village communities are little republics, having nearly everything that they want within themselves, and almost independent of any foreign relations. They seem to last where nothing else lasts. Dynasty after dynasty tumbles down; revolution successes to revolution Hindu, Pathan, Moghal, Maratta, Sikh, English, are masters in turn; but the Village Communities remain the same. In time of trouble they arm and fortify themselves as hostile army passes through the country; the Village Community collect their cattle within their walls, and let the enemy pass unprovoked."

   As quoted in Dutt, R; *Economic History of India*, under early British rule, London, 1956, pp. 386-7.

   Metcalf had written about village communities in Northern India. Other British administrators of the time working in other parts of the country have expressed similar views. Thus, Munro in 1813 wrote about village communities in Madras as follows:

   "Every village with its twelve agendas, as they are dominated, is a petty commonwealth, with its Mokuddum, Potail, Rapod, Reddy of chief inhabitant at the head of it, and India is a great assemblage of such commonwealths. The inhabitants, during war, look chiefly to their own head-inhabitants; they give themselves no trouble about the breaking up and division of kingdoms while the village remains entire: they care not to what power it is transferred, on whomsoever it devolves, the internal management remains unaltered; the head-inhabitant is still the collector, magistrate, and head-farmer."—*ibid* page 141.

   And Elphinstone in 1819 wrote thus about village communities in the Deccan

   "In whatever point of view we examine the Native Government in the Deccan, the first and most important feature is the division into villages or township. These communities contain in miniature all the materials of a state within themselves, and are almost sufficient to protect their members, if all other governments are withdrawn. Though probably not compatible with a very good form of government, they are an excellent prevent the bad effects of its negligence and weakness, and even present some barrier against its tyranny and rapacity. "—*ibid* page 346.
2. Marriott, McKim (Ed) *Village India*, University of Chicago Press, Chicago 1955. Chapter I, VI, VII.
3. The two points of view have been summarized in the Report of the Committee on Cooperative Credit, Government of India, Ministry of Community Development and Cooperation, May 1960, Chapter V and VI.
4. *Saat jaat*, literally Seven castes. The word 'saat' here means multiple.
5. *Dussehra* or *Vijaya Dashami* is the festival which marks Ram's triumph

over the demon king Ravana. Celebration of Dussehra was very popular with Hindu princes.

Gangor is a popular festival in Rajasthan. On this occasion, women worship Gauri (wife of Shiva) and pray for marital happiness and fertility. In the larger villages and towns celebrations of the festival culminates in a colourful procession through the main streets of the images of Gouri and other Goddesses. During the time of Jaipur State, this festival was celebrated by the State Government in all towns with much pomp and ceremony. The people of Sawai Madhpur still remember the past grandeur of this festival.

6. See for instance, Morgan, Arthur E., *The Small Community*, New York, 1942; and other writings.

1

Caste and Occupational Mobility

Introduction

The traditional role of caste in determining occupation in rural India is well known. Each caste has a defined occupation: names of most castes were derived from the occupations followed by them. Thus, the word *kumhar* stands both for a potter and the caste of potters. Similarly, *sonar* stands for a goldsmith and the caste goldsmiths and *teli* for an oil presser and the caste of oil pressers.

The major change in this position came in the nineteenth century, when as a result of increasing competition from factory-made goods, many village crafts declined. Weaving is a notable example. The artisans affected by this decline joined agriculture in large numbers as small cultivating owners or more frequently as landless tenants or agricultural labourers. This process is well known and has been written about extensively.[1] In recent years however, as a result of increase in opportunities for employment in industries and services, an increasing number of villagers, especially those living in villages near industrial centres and other towns have found employment in these. The numbers in such employment will increase progressively as economic development proceeds and industries and service occupations expand. This study is concerned with the effects of this new situation. It describes the response of different castes in one village, Raipur, to new employment opportunities. The village is conveniently located for availing of these opportunities, as it is at a distance of about 8 kms from the cement factory and Sawai Madhpur railway station, both large employees of labour. Moreover, the Brahmins and other high castes of the village have been active in taking advantage of the opportunities of white-collar service in government, which have become available in recent years.

Raipur is a large multi-caste village with 535 households and a population of 2850 (in 1961)[2]. The village has a total of 26 castes. The Meenas with 110 households are the most numerous. The malis with 89 households, the Brahmins with 69 households and the Rehgars with 61 households are other important castes of the village. As many as 12 castes have 10 households or more; but no single caste has numerical dominance, because even the Meenas form no more than 20 per cent of the population of the village. (Table 1.1)

The main *abadi* (habitation, cluster of houses), of the village is located just off the road to Sawai Madhopur railway station. In addition there are three hamlets, one each of Meenas, the Rehgars and the Chammars. These are situated at distance of one quarter to one mile to the west to the maln *abadi*. The hamlet of the Meenas is quite old, but those of the Chanmars and the Rehgars have come up only during the last 20 years. The two *Bhangi* families live in shacks just outside the main *abadi.* About a mile to the east of the village, are the hill ranges which occupy a large area in the eastern part of Sawai Madhopur *tehsil* (map). This location of the village in the foot-hills influences the economic life of the village in several ways. First, it ensures a good supply of underground water for drinking and for irrigation. The village has 60 irrigation wells which irrigate nearly 300 acres of land, one-seventh of its total cropped area. The proportion is quite high for villages of this *tehsil*, being found only in a few other villages having similar favourable locations. But the productivity of the agricultural lands of the village is very uneven. The irrigated lands are very productive. They can be adequately irrigated because the wells have abundant water; they also receive soil and manure washed down form the hills during the monsoon. These intensively cultivated lands, which produce the highly remunerative crops of potatoes, sugarcane, chillies, onions and other vegetables, besides wheat and other grains, are about the most productive lands to be seen anywhere in this area. Some of the unirrigated lands of the village are also quite fertile. On the other hand, there are large areas of poor land, covered with the sand and coarse silt brought down by the hiil torrents. In recent years, these lands have been producing good crops of groundnut; but earlier when only *jowar* (sorghum) and *bajra* (millets) were grown in them, they gave low yields and were considered to be very poor. Secondly, the foot-hill location of the village enables a large number of people to find employment in occupations connected with exploitation of the resources of hills and forests e.g. grazing and cutting wood in the forests, or quarrying. This is one of the reasons that agriculture is comparatively less important in the economic life of the village.

Table 1.1: Land-holding and Cultivation by Principal Castes

Caste	Total number of households	No. of households owning land	Area owned (acres)	Net area given out(-) or taken in (+) for cultivation (acres)	No. of cultivating households	Area cultivated (acres)	Total No. of workers	No. engaged in cultivation.
I. High Caste Hindus	101*	90	463	–220	17	243	155	21
Brahmin	69	64	294	–121	12	173	98	15
Mahajan	24	22	114	–73	3	41	43	4
II. Cultivating Castes	219	192	1255	+450	184	1705	604	494
Meena	110	101	838	+245	96	1083	301	270
Mali	89	77	313	+183	75	496	251	195
Gujar	20	14	104	+22	13	126	52	29
III. Artisan Castes	38*	25	78	–50	9	28	91	5
Khati	13	11	45	–35		10	21	1
Kumhar	10	4	8		4	8	37	
IV. Scheduled Castes	115*	88	307	+94	84	401	250	108
Rehgar	61	52	145	+31	52	176	133	47
Chammar	35	33	143	+67	30	210	83	56
Koli	10						16	
V. Miscellaneous Hindu Castes	19	8	16	+11	5	27	45	9
VI. Moslems	43	30	119	–87	10	32	67	2
Faqir	20	14	19	–10	6	9	30	5
Moslim, other castes	18	13	76	–68	1	8	26	1
Total	535	433	2238**	+198**	309	2436**	1212	639

* Individual castes under the main caste groups, having less than ten households have not been listed. However, these have been given in the text wherever necessary.

** Difference between area cultivated and area owned of 198 acres is due to land taken from owners in other villages.

Method

Methods used for data collection for different aspects of the studies is given in the Introduction. The castes have been grouped together into the following six groups:

- the high caste Hindus;
- the cultivating castes;
- the artisans and clean service castes;
- the scheduled castes;
- the miscellaneous Hindu castes; and
- the Moslems.

The grouping of castes is based on economic and/or social similarity. Thus the cultivating caste group includes Meenas, Malis and Gujjars. The distinction between the artisans and clean service castes and the scheduled castes needs to be explained. The traditional occupation of all these castes is practice of a craft or rendering some service to the village people. But the scheduled castes have been separated from the others, because they have a markedly lower status; they are untouchables.

Ownership and Cultivation of Land

Some 433 out of 535 households or more than 80 per cent of the total are land owners; but about half of them have very small holdings of less than five acres. Those small land owners most of whom belong to the high castes, the artisan castes and the scheduled castes, depend primarily on non-agricultural occupations for their livelihood. They either give their small areas of land to others for cultivation on *batai*[3] —this is the practice followed by most small owners of the high castes—who cultivate the land by hiring bullocks for ploughing, sowing, etc. Their holdings are too small to enable them to take an adequate interest in the cultivation. Consequently, the number of cultivating households (309) is considerably smaller than the number of land owning households. Secondly, even among the households classified as cultivating, about a quarter (76) does not keep any bullocks. In the latter households the primary source of livelihood is practice of a traditional craft, agricultural and non-agricultural labour and cultivation of the small holdings only brings in a little extra cash or helps meet the foodgrains requirements of the household. The most common practice in these households is for the young men to do non-agricultural work and for the women and old folks to look after cultivation. Less than half the total number of household (233) in the village keep their own bullocks. A similar picture is revealed by figures on distribution of workers among different types of work given in Table 1.2. Out of a total of 1202 workers in the village, 639 are engaged in cultivation and 99 in labour—making a total of 738 workers in agricultural operations. But since many workers have more than one job—many of those who engage in cultivation take up other employment also—a better picture is obtained by analyzing the distribution of the total number of jobs. The latter total 1436 and the 738 agricultural jobs are just over half of these.

Table 1.2: Distribution of Workers in Raipur

	Total number of workers	1202
	Total number of jobs	1436
	Number engaged in	
(i)	**Cultivation**	639
(ii)	**Agricultural labour as**:	
	(a) unattached workers	83
	(b) *Halis* or attached workers	16
	Total	99
(iii)	**Casual or non-agricultural labour**	215
(iv)	**Service**	
	(a) white collar	56
	(b) class IV	17
	(c) as skilled workers	15
	(d) as unskilled workers	46
	Total	134
(v)	**Commerce: shop keeping and trade** (excluding money-lending and shops of artisans and skilled workers like goldsmiths and tailors	23
(vi)	**Skilled work**:	
	traditional crafts	59
	Other occupations:	
	(a) specified non-agricultural labour type occupations like stone quarrying, hauling wood, carrying milk etc	79
	(b) miscellaneous, including begging	21

There are several reasons why agriculture is less important in the economy of the village than one might expect. Firstly, Raipur like most other large villages in this area has a concentration of castes with an essentially non-cultivating tradition—the high castes, the artisan castes and the non-cultivating Moslems.[4] Secondly, the cultivated area of the village is small in comparison with its population. Including about 200 acres of land taken on lease from owners in other villages, the cultivators of Raipur cultivate a total of 2,436 acres. This gives an average of less than 8 acres per cultivating household, and if the 76 households of part-time cultivators are excluded, about 10 acres per households.

The latter figure is considerably lower than the average holdings in most villages in this area (17.3 acres in Manpur). Thirdly, the foot-hills location of Raipur enables a large number of its people to get their living from occupations based on the resources of hill and of forests. Finally, its location close to the two major sources of non-agricultural employment, the cement factory and the railway station, had enabled a large number of persons to avail of the employment opportunities in these. One of these sources of employment has been completely wiped out during the last forty years, the cement factory closed down; the opportunities of employment on the railways has increased manifolds instead with increase in the number of trains and rail tracks.

The castewise distribution of occupation is shown in detail in Table 1.3 and is discussed in the next section. The overall position for the village is summarized below:

Caste and Occupation

The High Caste Hindus

The high caste group includes besides the Brahmins and the Mahajans two small castes, the Kayastha and the Babaji with four households each. The Kayastha are the traditional white-collar workers of North India whose principal occupation was government service, mainly as clerks. Babaji (*Bairagi*) are the descendants of Sadhus (lit. mendicants) who served as priests in temples. Most Sadhus remained unmarried; but others took wives, and their descendants are grouped into these castes. These two castes because of their occupational and social affiliation with the high castes are conveniently considered in this group. The four Kayastha households of Raipur, descendents of a single ancestor have a total of 4 earners. Two of them are in white-collar service, while other two, in as many households, manage cultivation of their land with the help of *halis* (employed agricultural labourers). The Kayasthas are all well off and are also quite influential in village affairs. One of the old and respected leaders of the village is a Kayastha. The Babajis on the other hand, are landless and quite poor. Their interest is purely priestly: each of the four households manages a temple. Making Kanthis (rosaries of sacred thread) is a side activity which brings in a little extra income.

Table 1.3: Caste and Occupation: Principal Castes, Raipur

Caste	*Total no of households*	*Total number of workers*	*Number of workers engaged in:*											*Total number of jobs*
			Cultivators	*Agricultural labour (including halis)*	*Casual non-agricultural labour*	*Service***				*Commerce*	*Skilled Work*		*Other occupations (mainly unskilled labour type)*	
						White collar	*Class IV*	*Skilled work*	*Un-skilled labour*		*Traditional craft or occupation*	*Other*		
1	2	3	4	5	6	7	8	9	10	11	12	13	14	15
I. **High Caste Hindus**	**101**	**145**	**21**	–	**6**	**2**	**10**	–	**2**	**23**	**21**	**11**	**10**	**156**
Brahmin	69	98	15	–	5	46	9	–	–	2	11	9	9	107
Mahajan	24	33	4	–	1	4	1	–	1	21	–	2	1	35
II. **Cultivating Castes**	**219**	**604**	**494**	**60**	**67**	**2**	**2**	**4**	**20**	–	**5**	–	**5**	**659**
Meena	110	301	270	19	14	1	1	1	7	–	–	–	1	314
Mali	89	251	195	35	45	1	–	1	13	–	–	–	1	291
Gujar	20	52	29	6	8	–	1	2	–	–	5	–	3	54
III. **Artisan Castes**	**38**	**91**	**5**	–	**7**	**1**	**1**	**2**	**1**	–	**53**	**17**	**37**	**124**
Khati	13	21	1	–	2	–	–	2	–	–	17	17	–	39
Kumhar	10	37	–	–	–	–	–	–	22	–	12	–	37	49
IV. **Scheduled Castes**	**115**	**250**	**108**	**33**	**98**	–	–	**1**	–	–	**77**	**1**	**23**	**363**
Rehgar	61	133	47	29	59	–	–	–	17	–	65	–	–	217
Chammars	35	83	56	4	22	–	–	–	4	–	–	–	19	105
Koli	10	16		–	13	–	–	–	1	–	–	–	3	17
V **Miscellaneous Hindu Castes**	**19**	**45**	**9**	**6**	**16**	–	**3**	–	**1**	–	**6**	–	**6**	**47**

(*Contd.*)

Table 1.3 (*Contd.*)

1	2	3	4	5	6	7	8	9	10	11	12	13	14	15
VI. **Moslems**	**43**	**67**	**2**	–	**21**	**1**	**1**	**8**	**1**	–	**5**	**30**	**19**	**87**
Faqir	20	30	–	–	12	1	1	1	–	–	–	19	13	47
Moslem, other castes	18	26	1	–	8	–	–	4	–	–	–	10	4	27
Total	535	1202	639	99	215	56	17	15	146	46	167	59	100	1436

* The castes having ten or less than ten household, are not included in this table. But references have been made to them in the text wherever necessary.

** Total white collar workers in 2000 were 250.

The Brahmins

The Brahmins, with 69 households and 395 persons are the third largest caste in Raipur. Nearly all Brahmin households (64 out of 69) own some land; but the holdings of most households are very small—less than five acres. Holdings of this size are quite insufficient for making a living as non-cultivating owners. The result is that excepting nine households who manage cultivation with the help of *halis* and another three who do cultivation themselves, all others have given their lands for cultivation on *batai*. The total area cultivated by these 12 cultivators among the Brahmin is 173 acres; the remaining 121 acres, or nearly 40 per cent of the total area owned by the Brahmin land owners is cultivated by the people of other castes.

The high caste Hindus, the artisans and the Moslems[4] are the principal caste groups giving land for cultivation on *batai*. The Meenas and the *Malies*, both traditional cultivators, and the Chammars, who are making a bid to become cultivators, are the principal castes taking land on *betai* (Table 1.2).

Halis are men from landless or small land owner families of the cultivating castes or other clean castes who take up employment as agricultural labourers, usually on a one year contract. Their employers are generally land-owners of the high castes, whose land holding are large enough to enable them to employ *halis*. Out of 16 *halis* in the village as many as 14 are employed by owners of the high castes—9 Brahmins, 3 Mahajans and 2 Kayasthas. The remuneration of a *hali* ranges between Rs. 450 and 500 per year. In addition the *hali* is given perquisites, like a suit of cotton cloth, at each harvest. But no food is given by the employer.

Service, white-collar and other, is the most important means of livelihood of the Brahmins. Out of a total of 98 earners among them, as many as 56 are in service. Forty-six of these are in various white-collar jobs, 9 are in class IV services[5], and one is employed as an unskilled labourer in the public works department of the State. Most of the white-collar workers are employed as village level government servants—school teachers, *patwaris*, *vaidyas*[6], compounders, village level workers[7] of the *Panchayt* Samiti, secretaries of *Panchayt*s or cooperative societies, etc. The Brahmins have an overwhelming majority (46 out of 56) among the white-collar workers of the village. Among the remainder, 4 are Mahajans, 2 are Kayasthas and only 4 are from the non-high castes. Details of the types of job held by the white-collar workers of the village are shown in Table 1.4.

Table 1.4: Distribution of White-collar Workers of Raipur by Caste

	Bramins	*Other High Castes*	*Other Castes*	*total*
Patwaris	11	–	–	11
School teachers	11	3	1	15
Vaidyas	5	–	–	5
Compounders, Health Attendants etc	5	–	1	6
Village level workers, fieldsmen, Agricultural Extension Officers.	7	–	–	7
Others: secretaries of panchayts or cooperative societies, clerks etc.	7	3	2	12
Total	46	6	4	56

The nine Brahmins in class IV service work as peons, watchmen, guards, etc.—all jobs which do not require any education or skill. They are uneducated persons, who have taken up these jobs because they could not get anything better (Table 1.3).

The nine persons listed under other occupations are Brahmin widows who carry milk daily to the railway station-district headquarter colony. They receive between 50 and 70 paisa for carrying a vessel full of milk over a distance of 5 miles. This is hard work which one would imagine would be shunned by a literary, white-collar group. It is certainly not looked upon with favour; but the fact that poor widows resort to this hardest form of manual labour and do not take up a handicraft like embroidery or tailoring or basket making is an eloquent commentary on the Brahmins' lack of either aptitude or attention to skilled work.

Working as priests and cooks are other sources of livelihood for the Brahimns. Eleven persons work as priests, five in the village and six out side. The latter go to Kotah, Indore and other towns of Madhya Pradesh. Seven Brahmins work as cooks with *Seths* (rich merchants) in Bombay, Calcutta and other cities. All these men go out for work for a few months at a time and return to the village for a few months' stay before going out again. They go alone, leaving their families behind. Eleven Brahmins engage in moneylending; but since moneylending is only a side activity with them—cultivation, shop keeping, white-collar service etc. are other principal occupation.

Brahmins are generally considered to be a priestly caste. But it will be seen that only 11 out of a total 98 Brahmin workers of Raipur are priests, and even among them only 5 work in temple within the villages. The secular interests of the Brahmins of Raipur are far more important. The priests among them have special names, which also show that even traditionally this work had not been done by the majority but had been reserved for a limited number. Moreover, the Brahmins are not the only priestly group in the village (or in this area). Sadhus or their Babaji descendents look after many temples. Their own priest looks after the temple of the scheduled castes. Therefore, the popular notion that the Brahmins are (or were) mostly priest was not correct in case of Brahmins of Raipur or of this area. Their traditional position is more correctly stated as that of priests-cum-literacy men-cum-professionals, living partly by earnings of their professions and partly on income from rent-free grants[8] of land given for their subsistence, by the states or in *jagir* villages by the *jagirdars*. The Brahmins of Raipur were essentially literary people, with a tradition of Sanskrit learning. Most of them lived as non-cultivating owners of land and remained engaged in literary activities. Some of them took up practice as *vaidyas*, astrologers etc. The majority must have been only moderately well off or poor.

The first major change in their economic activity took place about 60 years ago (beginning of the twentieth century), when men from poor families began to move out of the village. Many of them succeeded in getting well paid jobs as cooks with Rajasthani businessmen in Bombay, Calcutta, and other cities. These businessman—all strict vegetarians themselves—preferred them as cooks because they were from their home state and were well versed in the art of vegetarian cooking.[9] As a result, work as cooks with business men became an important source of livelihood for the Brahmins of Raipur, earnings from which have helped many a family to progress from poverty to moderate well-being.

About 20 years ago (1940s), Brahmin young men began to enter government services, mostly as school teachers and *Patwaries* for which a high standards of education was not then required. The minimum educational qualification for appointment as *Patwari* was middle standard (eight years of school) and for a school teacher, matriculation. But in those days, when competition for these jobs was much less, a lower level of education was considered adequate. Several of the *Patwaris* from the villages (as also from other villages in this area) have had only 4 or 5 years of school education; others have had only the traditional Sanskrit educations from *pandits* (Brahmin scholars of Sanskrit) in the village. The Brahmins along with the Mahajans and other high castes were among the first to take advantage of the opportunities for upward movement in services which were becoming available at that time. But as education spread and the advantages of such services became better known, there has been increasing competition from the increasing number of educated young men of all castes.

Competition for these jobs in this area is still not as fierce as it is in many other parts of the country; but it is becoming increasingly keen. The response of the Brahmins to this situation is to give higher education to their sons, so that they can compete for posts like that of the *vaidya*, the Village Level Worker, and the Agricultural Extension Officer, for which a higher level of education (matriculation or above) or a technical qualification is required. As many as twelve Brahmins of Raipur are working in these posts: they are the only people from the village who do. It appears moreover that the Brahmins will be able to maintain a dominant position in these jobs in the future because far more Brahmins boys are going for education up to the matriculation stage and above, than boys of the other castes. This is brought out by the figures in Table 1.5.

Table 1.5: Education Level by Caste in Raipur Village: Number of Boys Receiving Education

Caste	*Primary Classes (I-V)*	*Post Primary Classes (VI-VIII)*	*Schools Outside the villages: Classes (IX t-XI)*
Brahmin	40	10	8
Other high castes (Mahajan, Kayasthe, Bairagi)	17	6	0
Meena	37	4	0
Mali	34	6	2
Muslim	29	2	0
Chammar	6	1	1
Rehgar	14	3	2
Total all castes	215	36	13

The educated Brahmin holding a white-collar job has both greater inclination and capacity to give his son an education which will equip him for a good white-collar job than has the illiterate Meena or Mail. The Brahmin would send his son to school even at a sacrifice, because he sees that the future of his son lies only in such service.

The difference between the Brahmins' attitude towards white-collar service and towards work as cook or priest is considerable. Persons who went out to work as cooks or priests were generally from poor Brahmin families with small holdings who could not make ends meet while living in the village. The work involved living away from the village for long period, disturbing family life and membership in the community, and was never favoured or held in high esteem by the other villagers. It was always regarded as a product of necessity, to be resorted to by a person who could not live on income from the family holding, even though several persons made good money in it and helped raise the economic levels of their families. Work as a priest was considered somewhat better than that as a cook; but both were considered lower than staying at home and managing the family lands. Consequently, going out for both these types of work proved to be a temporary phase in the history of the group. In many families the older men had gone out but the younger men have entered white-collar services—their education being financed by the earnings of the older men; "going out" has either ceased entirely or will cease as soon as the old men are too old to go.

But the attitude towards white-collar service is entirely different. Such service is held in high esteem. A job like that of the *vaidya* or an agricultural extension officer, which carries a good scale of pay, is coveted. Even that of the *Patwari* or the school teacher is prized. Young men from all Brahmin families, including those which have the largest land holdings and have traditionally been the most respected in the village, have accepted white-collar jobs. The essential qualification for these jobs—education and the nature of work are quite in accord with Brahmins' literary tradition. Moreover, acceptance of these jobs doesn't involve serious disturbance to family or community life. Most of the government servants have managed to be posted in villages within 20 miles of Raipur. They keep their families in the village and visit them on weekends and during leave periods. In this way they can look after their lands and participate in community affairs. The income of the government servant makes a major contribution to the income of his family, and since it is fairly good, being equal to or higher than what the family used to get from non-cultivating ownership of the land, the income level of the family goes up considerably. Secondly, the official position and contacts with other official are valuable assets for the family and for the faction to which it belongs.

With the growing importance of white-collar service as a source of livelihood, certain social and economic changes have been experienced by the group. The first and most obvious among these is increasing emphasis on education of both boys and girls. Almost all Brahmin boys are going to school, and as noticed above an increasing number are going out of the village for high school and higher education. The girls are being sent to the primary school in the village, because educated young men prefer educated girls for wives. Secondly, there is a marked change in the criterion of what constitute a good 'match' for marriage. It used to be the case that size of land holding and traditional prestige of the family were considered most important; now the pay and status of the job held by the young man are given first consideration. There is a growing competition for marrying daughters to young men with good jobs, and this had led in turn to increasingly elaborate marriages and larger dowries (see chapter 5).

Another set of changes is in level of living. This is a major contribution of white-collar service, which arises partly from higher incomes but even more from the new ideas and higher aspirations acquired through urban and service contacts. White-collar service has helped these Brahmins (many of whom were quite poor in the past) to attain lower middle class income and living standards. It has not made them rich; in fact no Brahmin family could be considered rich. They are a middle class group.

The Mahajans

Most Mahajans households are following their traditional occupation of petty shop keeping—distribution of commercial goods and buying of agricultural produce. All but three Mahajans reported this as their principal occupation. Three households of shopkeepers lend money as an additional sources of income. It may be noted that this petty commerce is almost entirely in the hands of Mahajans. They own 21 of the 23 general shops in the village, the remaining two being owned by Brahmins. Besides these shops, there are nine other shops in the village, which are owned by traditional craftsmen like *Sonars* (goldsmith), *Lakhare* (maker of *lac* bangles) or skilled workers like tailors and bicycle repairemen. But the owners of these shops have been classified under skilled work and not under commerce in Table 1.3.

Like the Brahmins, most Mahajan households also own small areas of land which they give out for cultivation on *batai*. Only three households with somewhat larger holdings, manage cultivation of these with the help of *halis*. None engages in cultivation itself. The number of Mahajans in white-collar services is small, a total of four. The Mahajans of this area are prominent in such service, but those of this village are obviously an exception. Two Mahajans are *halwais* who prepare food and sweetmeats on the occasion of marriages and other feasts. On account of caste considerations, this work can be done only by people of this caste, although both Brahmins and Mahajans of the village are expert at it. No other skilled work is done by Mahajans. But four persons including one in class IV service work on jobs of the unskilled labour type. One Mahajan widow carries milk to the colony. The absence of skilled workers among the Mahajans is as pronounced as among the Brahmins.

The Mahajans of Raipur are doing only moderately well. There are no rich men among them, and some whose business is not running well, are quite poor. One reason for this is that Raipur, unlike other large villages in the area, is not the commercial centre of a group of small villages in its vicinity, collecting their agricultural produce and distributing consumer goods. The area immediately behind Raipur is hilly and forested, with no village. Secondly, Raipur is so close to Sawai Madhopur town that its cultivators and those of the few villages in its vicinity find it more convenient to sell their produce and to do their marketing in the town itself.

The Cultivating Castes

The Meenas, the *Mails* and the Gujjars have been grouped together as cultivating castes. Among them, the Meenas devote themselves exclusively to cultivation of field crops. The *Malis* (market gardeners) take cultivation of vegetables and associated crops like chilies, onions and garlic, in addition to cultivation of field crops. They are the only people in the area who engage in production of vegetables. The Gujjars similarly have an active pastoral interest. Several families among them graze buffaloes in the hills and forests behind Raipur and sell their milk and ghee.

The Meenas

Out of 110 Meena households in the village as many as 101 are of land owners and 96 are of cultivators. The Meena land-owners own a total of 838 acres; but the area cultivated by the Meena cultivators is considerable larger—1083 acres, because a number of small owner cultivators take on additional area for cultivation on *batai*. Ninety per cent of the Meena earners (270 out of 301) are engaged in cultivation. Other work—agricultural labour, causal non-agricultural labour and service—is reported by only 44 workers. Most of the men in service have jobs involving unskilled labour; only two young men have better jobs. One of them is a skilled worker, while the other is a white-collar worker. The first endeavour of every Meena family is to subsist by cultivation of its own land. But, if the holding is too small, additional land is taken for cultivation on *batai*. Agricultural or non-agricultural labour or service are taken up only when the family is not successful in obtaining sufficient land for cultivation, attention is devoted exclusively to production of field crops. No Meena is engaged in commercial production or vegetable or milk or fruit, for all of which there is now a large and growing demand. Therefore, it would not be an exaggeration to say that the Meenas have remained singularly unresponsive to the new opportunities, both of non-agricultural employment and/or more remunerative types of farm production, which have arisen with the coming of the cement factory and expansion of the railway station district headquarter colony. This tendency had been noted again among the Meenas of Bijaipur (Chapter 5).

The Malis

Like the Meenas, the Malis are also concentrating on cultivation. Families having adequate holdings devote themselves exclusively to cultivation; others try to obtain additional land for cultivation on *batai*, and only those who do not own land and can not get sufficient land for cultivation have one and more members engaged in agricultural and non-agricultural labour. These latter are the main activities besides cultivations. 77 out of the 89 Mali households in the village are land-owners; 75 of them are cultivators. The latter include seven households which do not keep their own bullocks but cultivate their small holdings with the help of hired bullocks. The total area owned by the Malis is 313 acres; but the area cultivated by them is considerably larger, 496 acres.

Out of a total of 251 workers among the Malis 195 are engaged in cultivation, 35 take up agricultural labour and 45 do casual non-agricultural labour. The agricultural labourers include eight *halis*, half the total number of *halis* in the village. The Malis are preferred as *halis*, because they are a clean caste and because of their attitude for intensive cultivation on irrigated lands. Fifteen Mali young men are in service. But as many as 13 among these work as unskilled labourers—at the railway station, in P.W.D., and elsewhere. Only two young men, one a white-collar worker and the other a skilled worker in the cement factory, are in better type of service.

Even though the *Malis* are traditional producers of vegetables, production of vegetables for sale was reported by only 20 households. Production is mainly for meeting the demand of the village; no attempt is made to produce for urban markets. But even the demand of the village is not met fully and there is considerable import of vegetables and fruit from outside. Vendors from the town and the colony come to the village to sell vegetables and people who go out of the village for work, often bring vegetables and fruit for their home use while returning to the village. Earlier, Mali women of the village used to take vegetables for sale to nearby villages. But this practice was stopped by the caste *Panchayat* some years ago, when they decided against hawking of vegetables by the women both within and outside the village. Vegetable may now be sold only by sitting at the appointed place in the village bazaar. The economic advantage of growing vegetables for sale is well understood by the Malis and was discussed with the author at length. The households growing vegetables for sale had reported income raging from Rs. 150 to Rs. 500 per year from this source. The heads of many of them mentioned that they could get larger incomes if they gave more attention to production for the urban market. Some explained that growing of vegetables was remunerative, that a household could make a comfortable living with it on only one or two acres of land. They cited the example of Malis of a large village situated next to Sawai Madhopur town who were concentrating on productions of vegetables for the urban market and had become quite prosperous. They agreed that the irrigated land of the village, with its loose sandy soil and good fertility was very suitable for growing vegetables. Many stated that commercial production of vegetables was the best solution for the economic problem of a number of Mali household having very small holdings. But these economic considerations are not sufficient to alter the current pattern of discouraging cultivation of vegetables and concentrating on production of field crops, because the social motive of raising the status of the caste is far stronger. The social ambition of the Malis is to be recognized as the equal of the Meenas and they are trying to achieve this by adding to their land holdings, concentrating on cultivation of field crops, and discouraging or completely stopping practices, because of which they had been considered inferior to the Meenas in the past. Growing of vegetables is not encouraged in spite of its economic advantages, and drawing of water from wells for the families of the high castes, which was a traditional obligation of the Malis, has been stopped altogether.

But it is interesting to note that the above attitude towards production of vegetables does not extent to production of potatoes or chillies; both of these are important commercial crops of the village and the Malis are prominent in their production. The similarity of both crops with vegetables is recognized. Potatoes are eaten as a vegetable, and even though chillies are used as a condiment they are also considered to be a vegetable. But cultivation of potatoes has been taken up in recent years by all castes, including the Brahmins. The area under the crop has increased so much during the last 15 years (it was 28 acres in 1961) that it now competes with sugarcane as the most important commercial crop of the village. The Malis are the largest producers of the crop; but since others are also growing it, they feel that their social status does not suffer by growing it. Chillies similarly are grown by cultivators of all castes. Moreover, since they are marketed as a field crop and not as a vegetable, their cultivation is also not considered derogatory by the *Malis*.

The Gujjars

The Gujjars are partly cultivators and partly graziers. Among the 20 households in the village, 13 are included among cultivators; but only nine have enough interest in cultivation to keep their own bullocks, the rest cultivate their small holdings with the help of hired bullocks. Grazing buffaloes in the hill forests and selling their milk and ghee is the principal source of livelihood of the seven non-cultivating households. These households keep large herds of buffaloes, 10 to 50 in number. Men of these households spend most of their time with their animals in the forests, and in the rainy season, when travel to and fro is difficult, they remain in the forests for weeks together. Most of the milk which goes from the village for sale to the officer's colony comes from these herds; the village itself had no surplus for sale. In fact, most of the commercial milk supply in the area comes from Gujjars grazing buffaloes in the forests. The town of Sawai Madhopur, for instance, obtains its supply from Gujjars in the forests to the south and east of it.

This pastoral occupation of grazing buffaloes in the forests is followed only by the Gujjars of Raipur. Even sale of milk of a few buffaloes kept within the village is confined to the Gujjars and three households of the associated caste of Jansodis. However, sale of small quantities of goats' milk is reported by five families—three Moslems *Faqir*, one *Jogi* and one *Khangar*. It is possible that sale of milk has been under-reported. Thus, some cultivators may have been selling small quantities of milk, especially in the rainy season when they have a small surplus, but may not have reported it. Sale of goat's milk is also somewhat more widespread than reported. But there is no question about the main facts: (i) most of the milk for sale comes from herd of buffaloes grazing in the forests, (ii) these herds are kept by the Gujjars, and (iii) the sale of milk is also mainly in the hands of Gujjars.

As in case of vegetables, the demand for milk has increased greatly in recent years. But the supply position is even worse than that of vegetables. In the case of the latter, a part of the demand is met by import of milk. The local milk supply is inadequate to meet the larger demand and is also subject to large seasonal fluctuations. It is maximum in the rainy season when there is abundant grass in the forests, falls steeply in the winter, and is lowest in the hot dry months of April, May and June.

The Gujjars keep large herds of buffaloes in order to utilize all the grass available in the rainy season, but they do not practice any stall-feeding to maintain production during the winter or the dry summer months. The practice of obtaining milk from herds in the forests was quite well adapted to the conditions of an earlier day, when commercial demand for milk was limited and most of the milk was converted into *ghee* or *khoya* (milk solid used to preparing sweetmeats) for sales in Sawai Madhopur town and large villages like Raipur, or even for export to Jaipur. But it cannot meet present day needs. The people of the area are well aware of this. One hears frequent references in Raipur, in other villages, and in Sawai Madhopur town to the fact that milk and *ghee*, which were abundant and very cheap in this area until about 20 years ago, had become very expensive, and pure milk and ghee were not available even at the prevailing high prices. The Brahmins of Raipur were especially vociferous in complaining about the shortage of milk and *ghee*. Some of them remarked that "milk and ghee have now disappeared"

Social factors are partly responsible for milk supply not keeping pace with increase in demand. The cultivators have not started commercial milk production, because in this area as in most others in north India, there is a strong prejudice against sale of milk by cultivators.[10] The Gujjars have not shown interest in increasing production through stall feeding of buffaloes, again partly because of social considerations. Like the Malis, the Gujjars also regard their traditional work of keeping buffaloes and selling milk and *ghee* as inferior to cultivation and there is a tendency among them also to prefer cultivation of field crops and to get rid of some of the features of their traditional occupation which they consider derogatory. Thus, carrying of milk by Gujjar women for sale outside Raipur was stopped by the caste *Panchayat* some years ago. The women who now carry milk to the colony are all non-Gujjar, mostly Brahmin and Mahajan widows. It is an interesting commentary on the social changes of recent year that a job which has been abandoned by the caste which did it traditionally on the ground that it lowers its social status has been taken up by the poor and destitute of the highest castes.

It is true that the large demand for vegetables and milk is a recent phenomenon, resulting from establishment of the cement factory and expansion of the railway station district headquarter colony, and that the people of these villages have not had adequate time to change their production practices to meet it. It is most likely that in course of time the economic advantages of commercial production of vegetables and milk will assert itself and more attention will be given to their production. But the attitude mentioned above retards the adjustment of the supply to demand. They keep the Mails and the Gujjars from availing adequately of their new economic opportunities and make it difficult for people of other castes to engage in these types of production.

The Artisan and Clean Service Castes

This group includes the Khatis (carpenters), the Kumhars (potters), the Sonars (goldsmith), the Nais (barbers), the Telis (oil pressers) and the Lakhare (maker of *lac* bangles). The Sonars (five households) and the Lakharas (one household) are engaged exclusively in their traditional crafts. The Nais (four households) are also concerned primarily with their traditional occupation; the one notable exception is an educated young man who is working as a school teacher. The traditional occupation of oil pressing is followed in all the five Telis households; but in two of these, income from it is supplemented by causal non-agricultural labour.

The Khatis and the Kumhars are present in somewhat larger number, 13 and 10 households respectively, and their branching off into other occupations is more interesting. The traditional craft of carpentry is practiced in al! the Khati householders; 17 out of 21 members among them are engaged in it. These constitute the entire body of practicing carpenters in the village. But all of them are carpenters-cum-masons who have found the addition of mason's work to their traditional occupation an easy and profitable change. Mason's work has been paying well in recent years, because *pucca* houses are becoming increasingly popular. Raipur has become a minor centre of masons who are much in demand within the village and in neighbouring villages for building pucca houses. Besides the Khatis there are several Moslems masons in the village. But the latter do not do the carpenter's work. It is interesting to note that while the traditional craft of carpentry remains entirely in the hands of the Khatis, the new addition, mason's work, is not their exclusive preserve. In fact, the expanding occupation of the mason is a relatively "open" one, which has been taken up by number of castes in this area. In Sawai Madhopur town, and in some large villages of this area, the *Kolis* have become masons. In Chainpur several Chammars are working as masons. Two *Khatis* are employed as skilled workers in the cement factory; one of them is a carpenter, while the other is a fitter. The close affinity of these jobs to the traditional occupation of the *Khatis* is obvious.

The most important source of livelihood for the Kumhars is hauling of earth and wood with the help of their donkeys. All the 10 Kumhar households are engaged in this work. In six households it is the main source of livelihood; but in the other four, it supplements income from the traditional job of Kumhars in this area, which they continue to practice in most villages. They might have taken it up originally, because they have to keep donkeys to haul earth for making pots and found hauling of earth and other materials for house construction and other such activities a useful additional source of income. Bringing wood from the forests was added by the Kumhars of Raipur because the village is so close to the hills. In time, it grew to be their most important source of livelihood. But a few years ago the forest department of Rajasthan discontinued the practice of issuing permits for donkey loads of wood. This was done on the ground that the practice of issuing such permits was leading to over-exploitation and depletion of forests. The Kumhars, deprived of their source of livelihood at home, now go to forests in the southern part of the district and the adjoining districts of Morena in Madhya Pradesh. They stay in the forests from six to eight months in the year, coming back to the village only during the rainy season when it is not possible to work in the forests. Life is hard and the work does not pay too well. But it is interesting to note that the Kumhars have gone so far (30 to 50 miles from the village) in search of it.

The Kumhars have been agitating for restoration of the permit system so that they can resume the work in the forests near the village. About three year ago they formed a cooperative society with the object of getting a contract for felling a small block of forests. But they were not successful in getting the contract and the society failed. Another attempt to form a society was being made at the time of this study.

The Scheduled Castes

This group includes, besides the Chammars and the Rehgars, who are present in considerable numbers, the *Kolis* (weavers), the *Khatiks* (Hindu butchers) and the *Bhangis* (scavengers). The Kolis have given up these traditional craft of weaving altogether. They are all landless, are dependent entirely on non-agricultural labour and are poor. The Kolis in several other villages of the *tehsil* are quite well off. They are owners and cultivators of land and have also taken up stone quarrying and meson's work. A large proportion of the masons in Sawai Madhopur town and another town of this *tehsil* are Kolis. But the Kolis of Raipur have not taken advantage of these new cpportunities and remain poor.

The *Khatiks* (seven households) are still engaged mainly in their traditional occupation of keeping sheep and goats for sale of meat, wool, etc. All of them keep sheep and goats and sell wool. *Ghoghies* (coarse felt blankets used by villagers for protection against rain) are made in four households. There is no sale of meat within the village. But live animals are sold for meat in the weekly market held near the cement factory. Three Khatiks are engaged in cultivation of their small holdings, one is a skilled worker in the factory, and another has a bicycle repair-shop in the village. The local demand for meat has increased considerably after establishment of the cement factory and expansion of the colony. There is also a brisk and expanding trade in export of meat animals—sheep and goats—to Bombay and other cities served by the railway line which passes through Sawai Madhopur. The Khatiks of this village, as of many other villages in the area, have benefited from both these developments, and many of them have become quite prosperous. The only other people in this area who raise meat animals and trade in them are the Moslem *Beoparis* (traders) or *Kasais* (butchers). The export trade in meat animals is mainly in their hands. It may be noted that except for these two castes of traditional butchers, no other caste, Hindu or Muslim, has been attracted by the expanding demand and high prices of meat to take up either raising meat animals or selling them.

The two Bhangi families were brought to the village a few years ago, especially for doing the work of lifting of dead animals and flaying their carcasses, which had been stopped by the chamamrs. They are doing this work in addition to scavenging the village streets.

The Chammars

As this village had a large number of Rehger households, its Chammars never did any leather work. They would lift the dead animals, flay the carcass and hand over the raw hide to the Rehgars for tanning and making leather goods. They left this work, about 10 years ago, as part of the movement described in a later section, and are now dependent entirely upon cultivation and/or labour. Cultivation is a source of livelihood for as many as 30 among the 35 Chammar households but only 20 households keep bullocks; the rest cultivate their small parcels of land with the help of hired bullocks. The total area cultivated by the Chammars is 120 acres; the figure includes 67 acres taken for cultivation on *betai*. Casual non-agricultural labour and stone quarrying are other important activities of the Chammars; 22 persons live on non-agricultural labour and 15 on stone quarrying as source of income. Three men, who are more enterprising, have become stone quarry contractors. The Chammars and a few Muslims of Raipur are the only people who worked in the stone quarries. Here, as in case of the Ḳumbhars hauling wood in the forests, is an instance of a caste entering an occupation as a group and of other castes avoiding it. It is perfectly possible for other labouring castes of the village (e.g. the Rehgars and the Kolis) to take up stone quarrying and they will probably do so if this activity expands. But, in the present state of demand for labour in stone quarrying, the village is content to leave it largely to the Chammars.

The Rehgars

For the Rehgars, the ancestral occupation of tanning and making of leather goods continues to be an important source of livelihood. It is practiced in 36 out of 62 households and by 65 out of 135 workers. But most households practicing it have other sources of income also, mainly cultivation and/or labour. Cultivation is a source of income in as many as 52 households; but only 17 have sufficiently large holdings to keep bullocks. Non-agricultural labour, which is reported by 59 persons, is another important activity of the Rehgars. Seventeen persons, all young men, work in the cement factory, loading cement and unloading coal. They are the only people from the village who do this work. This in another striking instance of a caste entering a new economic activity as a group.

The standard of leather work of the Rehagars of Raipur is fair. They make *charas* (leather buckets used for drawing water from irrigation wells) and country type shoes of fairly good quality. Some of them are interested in expanding their business and improving techniques. Their leaders mentioned that they had made a request to the village *Panchayat* for starting a *haat* (weekly market) in the village, where they could sell their goods instead of having to take them to *haats* in Sawai Madhopur town or a neighbouring large village. They also complained that ever since the Chammars quit flaying carcasses and the work was taken up by the *Bhangis*, who did not know the job of flaying and were not interested in doing it well. They explained that an unblemished hide of full grown bullock was needed for making a *charass*; that such hides were available in the village in plenty when the Chammars used to do the flaying, but were not available any longer because the *Bhangis* did not take care to avoid bruising the hide while lifting the carcass or while flaying it. As a result the Rehgaras have to go to distant markets to obtain good hide or leather. "We have to go as far as Agra to buy leather", one of them remarked.

It is true that the Rehgars have not yet adopted any improved techniques in their work, nor learnt making western style shoes, which are much in demand in the village and which are already being produced by Rehgars of Sawai Madhopur and some large villages of the area. Similarly, no Rehgar has been enterprising enough to start a shoes making or shoe repairs shop in the factory township or the colony. But these developments will come in course of time, because the Reghars are taking an adequate interest in their traditional craft.

Miscellaneous Hindu Castes

This group includes castes like jansodi, Rana, Rao, Jogi or Nath, and Khengar. The Jansodis and the Raos are the *Charans*[11] of the Gujjars and the Meenas respectively. The Ranas, also called *Dholis*, are drum-beaters. The Jogi, worshippers of Shankar (Shiva the God of destruction in the Hindu Trinity) are traditional practitioners of magic cures, who also have the responsibility of protecting the village from calamities like Locust invasions.[12] The five castes have a total of 19 households, with 45 workers. Most of them are landless; labour, agricultural and non-agricultural is their principal economic activity. Ancestral occupations serve as subsidiary sources of incomes for some households. A few households have some other sources of income also. Thus, three Jansodi households are engaged in selling milk. Among the Ranas, three young men from as many households are employed in class IV service and among the Khangars one young man works as a Hali.

The Moslems:

There are 43 households of Muslims in the village, distributed by caste as follows:

(i)	Faqir	20
(ii)	Other castes: *sayid* pathan, Shaikh (julahas etc.)	18
(iii)	Lohar	5

The *Faqirs* are quite poor. Most of them are landless, or have very small holdings which they give out for cultivation on *batai*. Only six families cultivate a total of 9 acres, all with the help of hired bullocks. In the past, begging was their main source of livelihood. It is important even now because as many as seven households report begging, in the village or outside, as a source of livelihood. The fact that Raipur is a predominately Hindu village does not prevent the *faqirs*, who are Muslims, from practicing this occupation. Begging, like other traditional crafts or occupation is traditionally followed by particular castes, of which *faqir* is one; and the fact that they are Muslims does not make any difference to the villagers. Unskilled casual labour is another important source of livelihood for the *faqirs*; 12 persons are engaged in begging. Another four work on stone quarries in the hills. Three householders keep goats and sell some quantities of milk. Ten young men are members of the village band[13] which performs at marriages and other festive occasions. They are the only people in the band. Their income is not much at present; but the work has a good potential, because use of bands at marriages is becoming popular. Four men are working as tailors, two are masons and three are in service. Among the last, one is a white-collar worker, another is a skilled worker in the cement factory but the third is unskilled worker. Three *Faqir* women work as mid-wives. Traditionally this work is done by the chammars and *Faqir* women. One of the mid-wives is considered to be quite competent and is very popular among the Brahmin women of the village.

It will be seen from the above that the *Faqirs* follow a varicty of occupations, including tailoring and playing western-style musical instruments, which require acquisition of new skills. This tendency to take up any work that offers good remuneration, and especially to enter occupations requiring acquisition of new skills, is even more marked among the 'other Moslems', who do not suffer from the *Faqirs'* handicaps of poverty and illiteracy. Most of these 'other Muslims' were land owners and used to depend mainly upon income from land. The larger land owners lived as non cultivating owners as some Brahmins and other high caste land-owners still do; the smaller owners were cultivators-cum-labourers. The majority of the households (13 out of 18) still own land; but with the exception of one household, which cultivates a part of its holding with the help of hired labour, all others have given their land on *batai*. However, instead of going only after white-collar services, as most Hindu castes in similar position have done, they have taken on a variety of occupations including skilled and entrepreneurial occupation such as masonry, tailoring and contractors as shown in the Table 1.6.

Table 1.6: Skilled and entrepreneurial workers among other Moslem castes

	Total number of workers	26
	Number of engaged in:	
i)	Cultivation	1
ii)	Casual unskilled labour	8
iii)	Service as skilled workers	4
iv)	Skilled work in village (tailors, masons etc.)	10
v)	Entrepreneurial work (contractors)	2
vi)	Other work	2

There are five households of *Lohar* with a total of 11 workers. Five workers in three households are engaged in the traditional occupation of smithy (repair of agricultural implements and other work for the cultivators) under the *Jajmani* system; three work as skilled workers in the cement factory and one runs the flour mill in the village. The *Lohars* are the best qualified to avail of the new opportunities for skilled work offered by modern industry, and are availing of these fairly well.

Distribution of Skilled Workers

Skilled workers can be divided into three categories:

- those following their traditional craft or occupation; e.g. potters, barbers and leather workers;
- those in new occupations or in services as skilled workers e.g. tailors, repairmen, members of the village band, skilled workers in the cement factory; and
- others.

The Brahmins and the Mahajans who work as cook or *halwais*, have been placed in the last category because these occupations are the semi-traditional occupations of these castes.

The workers in these three categories classified according to caste are shown in Table 1.7.

The predominance of Moslems in occupations requiring acquisition of new skills is obvious. This proficiency is not confined to this village but it is found also in Sawai Madhopur town and in the area generally. The Moslims[14] are the one significant innovator group in the area; they are prominent in bringing new things and machines into the village and servicing, repairing and operating these. Driving and repair of motor vehicles; tailoring, operation of flour mills; repair and renting of bicycles,

Table 1.7: Castewise Distribution of Skilled Workers

Caste	*Craft/Occupation*	*number of workers*
I. Skilled Workers in Traditional Crafts/Occupations		
Rehgar	Leather worker	65
Lohar	Smith	5
Kumhar	Potter	12
Khati	Carpenter-cum-mason	17
Babaji	Maker of rosaries	10
Sonar	Goldsmith	8
Lakhara	maker of lac bangles	1
Teli	Oil presser	5
Khatik	maker of ghogis	6
Faqir	Mid-wife	3
II. Skilled Workers in New Occupations or Service		
Brahmin		2
Moslem-Faqir		19
Lohar		4
Other		14
Gujjar		2
Khatik		2
Mali		2
Meena		2
III. Others		
Brahmin	Cooks	7
Mahajan	Halwais	2

or sugar presses; formation of village bands and playing the gramophones at marriages—in every trade which requires introduction of new machines, the Moslems are prominent. A detailed investigation of the reasons for this phenomenon would be interesting. Two explanations come readily to mind: (1) Muslims are not tied by strong traditions to any particular remunerative occupation; and (2) as the caste-occupation association is not nearly as strong among Moslems as among Hindus; they have found themselves free to experiment with new technologies and occupations.

Analysis

This case study brings out the initial responses of a caste-based society to the new opportunities for urban/industrial employment and for production of new goods and services to meet new demands. The findings may now be summarized.

Different cartes avail of new opportunities in very different degrees. Thus the cultivating owner Meenas remain confined to cultivation and are very slow in availing of these opportunities, while Brahmins and Moslems have been quick in availing of these.

The decision to seek new occupation and the choice of a particular new occupation appears in most cases to be made more by caste then by individuals. Each caste appears to be selecting from among the new occupations those which it considers most suitable for itself. The phenomenon is somewhat like water seeking its level: each cast is seeking its level in the new urban/industrial society. The main criterion which makes a new occupation suitable for selection by a caste is: (a) that it should be allied to the traditional occupation of the caste, and (b) that it should maintain its relative social status among the castes. It should raise the social status of the caste, but it should not lower it. The economic returns from the occupation are of importance. An occupation allied to the traditional occupation of the caste is preferred because the caste already has the skills and the aptitude needed for that kind of work and finds it easy to adopt the new techniques and work patterns. The second criterion is of cultural importance in the current phase of social evolution, when the *Jajmani* system is breaking down and a number of castes are trying to raise their social status through leaving their traditional occupations, obligations to the village community, and other practices which they considered to be the symbols of their social inferiority.

Brahmins take to white-collar service or to occupations like cooking for which they are preferred, because of being the highest caste. Mahajans stay in commerce or like the Brahmins enter white-collar services. Both castes are conspicuous by their absence in the skilled occupations. Certain artisan castes have taken up the modern equivalent of their traditional occupations. Thus, *Lohars* have become fitters and smiths in the cement factory or machine-men running the flour mill in the village; a *Khatik* has got placement as a carpenter in the factory. Another response is branching off into occupations which are close to the traditional ones; *Khatiks* are becoming masons. But since the scope for both kinds of occupations is limited—these are possible only in case of castes whose skills are in ready demand in the new urban/industrial occupations, large numbers of traditional artisans have to resort only to cultivation and/or unskilled labour. The Chammars, the *Kumhars*, the *Kohlis*, and to an extent even the *Rehgars* furnish examples of this kind of change. These poor artisans are almost absent from the skills or white-collar occupations. But it is interesting to note that even within unskilled work different castes tend to specialize in different types of work. Thus *Kumhars* have taken up hauling of wood in the forests, Chammars quarrying of stones, and

Rehgars loading the coal in the cement factory. All these are different forms of the unskilled work, and other castes could have taken them up just as well. But they have not done so. This kind of 'specialization' arises mainly from the fact that when one individual makes a success of new type of work, others of the group who are known or related to him are attracted to it. The phenomenon is common to all groups. But the fact that the groups in this case are all caste based is only another indication that caste is still the primary social group in the village.

The one notable exception to the pattern of castes choosing new occupations and preferring those which are allied to their traditional ones is furnished by the Moslems, especially Moslems other than the *Faqirs*. This group has shown versatility—readiness and ability to go into different types of occupations, and a remarkable capacity to take up occupations requiring new skills. To an extent, the *Faqirs* and *Lohars* also follow this pattern

The increased demand for certain types of agricultural and life stock products—vegetables, milk, ghee, meat—has failed to evoke the response either of large numbers of new producers improving their methods. Production of vegetable remains entirely in the hands of the *Malis*, who have concentrated their attention to meeting the demands of the village and have not made any effort to produce for the new urban demands. Production of milk for sail similarly remains in the hands of the *Gujjars*, who have not given attention either to developing commercial dairying or even to systematic feeding of milch animals. The result is serious shortage of milk and ghee. One reason for this phenomenon is that production of theses items for consumption was not rated highly in the traditional value system. The main cultivators, the Meenas and the Jats, did not produce vegetables or milk, and the caste which did, was ranked lower than them. Keeping meat animals and selling meat were regarded as downright reprehensible jobs which only the *Khatiks*, whose social status was associated with the lowest, could take up. The economic opportunities in these forms of productions have come at a time when the traditional producers have an opportunity to raise their social status. The Mails and the *Gujjars* have now a chance to get more land, devote themselves entirely to cultivation of field crops and thus fulfil their social aspirations of being recognized as the equals of Meenas. The result is that the two forces, the economic and the social, operate in opposite directions and tend to cancel each other. There is no onrush of new producers; the traditional producers remain in production but do not pay adequate attention either to improving techniques or to expanding output rapidly.

Under these conditions the Marshallian concept of the "economic man"—each man choosing an occupation which is most ruminative for him—is of severely limited significance. The individual's choice of his occupations is limited to the restricted area which is defined for him by his caste. Thus, the educated Brahmin can become a *patwari* or school teacher or a Village Level Worker. With more education he could become a college lecturer or doctor or an engineer. But he is not free to become a skilled worker in the cement factory and cannot become a carpenter or a smith in the village. And in making its choice of occupation, the caste is influenced by several considerations of which the economic is only one and by no means the most important. Fairly remunerative new occupations are not taken up, and even existing ones are given up (e.g. giving up of flaying of carcasses and leather work by the chammars), because association with these runs against the social aspirations of the caste.

Curiously enough in this process, the "open" occupations, i.e. those which can be entered by any caste, are found at the two ends of the status scale. They are white-collar work and cultivation which are rated the highest and unskilled labour which is rated the lowest. Inclusion of white-collar services and cultivation in the 'open' group is easily understood. Both command high prestige; the former because of its association with high castes, reasonably good remuneration and other advantages, the latter because the land is the prime source of wealth and the power in an agricultural community. Unskilled work, which is the lowest and poorest paid of all occupations, comes in this category—of open occupations—because it is the refuge of all, from Brahmins to Chammars, who can not do better. It will be recalled that Brahmins take up services of the unskilled type and their widows carry milk; but they are almost absent from the skilled occupations. The main reason for this is that skilled work is to a large extent "closed". The traditional skills and crafts are completely "closed", because no caste would take up the traditional occupation of another. Even the new skilled occupations are largely closed, as we have seen, because these are entered mainly by the persons from castes having allied traditional occupations. The only examples of occupation requiring new skills which are partially 'open' are tailoring and cycle repairs, which have been taken up by Brahmins, Moslems, and *Khatiks*. What makes these particular occupations 'open' while most others remain "closed", is an interesting area of further study.

It will be argued that all these are initial responses, and that larger exposure to opportunities for employments and remunerative forms of production will evoke different responses in which the influence of economic factors will be more pronounced. There are some developments which point towards this possibility already. Thus, in the Chammar village Chainpur it is noticed that while the older Chammars are unskilled labourers, several of the young men have become skilled labourers in the factory, self-employed skilled workers (masons), and even entrepreneurs (contractors). Similar vertical mobility will occur in this village also: some of the sons and nephews or the neighbours of *Reghar* unskilled labourers in the factory will undoubtedly become skilled workers. Young men of the scheduled and cultivating castes will also join white-collar services in increasing numbers, as they get education and avail of facilities like reservation of seats for them in government service. The change is well advanced in many parts of the country and is also noticed here. But the basic question raised by the study is this: will these changes be rapid enough and what is more important extensive enough, to do anything more than modify the first responses described here? The latter are the natural responses to economic changes of a stratified society in which caste is the basic institution. These aim at preserving the structure of society and absorbing the shocks of urbanization and industrialization. The fact that the stratified structure of caste and the close association of the caste with occupation are well preserved even in a town like Sawai Madhopur and the recent growth of population, immigration of large numbers of people, and advance in techniques of new jobs, have not produced structural change in these, would lead one to the view that the caste structure may not be affected, except marginally, even with longer experiences with urban and industrial employment. Sawai Madhopur town differs little from Raipur in social organization or the social behaviour of its residents. Settlement of people of different castes in different quarters of the town, their following traditional occupations (Mahajans—commerce, *Julahas*—weaving, *Malis* –production of vegetables) are prominent features of its socio-economic life. Adoption of new forms of traditional occupations or addition of modern techniques to the latter are accomplished without disturbing caste-occupation association. Thus, Mahajans have taken up distribution of an innumerable variety of modern consumption goods; *Julahas* have installed power looms in place of handlooms; and *Rehgars* are making modern style shoes. The phenomena described in this study—caste remaining the primary group in choice of new occupations, and castes choosing occupations allied to their traditional ones and those which maintain their comparative social status—are just as noticeable in the Sawai Madhopur town as in Raipur. Again, as in the village, there is no occupational piracy; i.e. no caste takes up the traditional occupation of another. Even the recent repudiation of traditional practices and obligations by particular castes, e.g., of flaying of carcasses by the Chammars, of cleaning of utensils by the *Nais*, of carrying of water by the *Malis*, is as rigorous in the town as in any village. Socially, therefore, the town is as much an association of a number of castes as is the village. It is a large village!

However, experience in this area alone is not adequate to answer this question, which can only be answered on the basis of studies in villages and towns in different parts of the country which have had much longer experience with urban/industrial employment.

It is recognized that these social phenomena have considerable influence on economic growth. That demand for milk, vegetables and meat is not being met is a factor retarding growth. It means that opportunities for increasing production, income, and employment are not being availed of by individuals, and that the community is poorer—in money, income and in level of consumption—than it could be. Similarly, the shortage of persons who can handle machines (because there are few traditional Lohars who have the aptitude for handling machines and other castes are not willing to take up this work), is a serious impediment to technological change.

Technological change in agriculture and village industry would have been much more rapid in the area if larger numbers of village people could handle machines. On the other hand the aspiration of the Chammars to raise their social status has acted as a powerful stimulus to economic progress and has made them more responsive to new economic opportunities than are the other scheduled catses or even cultivating castes.

Aspirations and 'Open' and 'Closed' Occupation

The above findings can also be presented in terms of aspirations of different castes. This presentation is useful in that it provides a clear view of the future trends in social movement—changes in the composition of rural society and the social relationships within it. In order to facilitate understanding of the findings this presentation has been made only for the following castes:

- The high castes—Brahmin and Mahajans
- The cultivating castes—Meenas and Mali
- The clean artisan castes—Khati
- The scheduled castes—Chammars.

These castes can be taken as representative of their respective groups because even though the aspirations of the other castes in each group may be somewhat different, the differences would only be of degree, not of kind. Thus among the high castes, the aspirations of the Kayasthas are very similar to those of the Brahmins, and among the cultivating castes, the aspirations of *Gujjars* are similar to those of the *Malis*. Among the scheduled castes, while other castes like the *Rehgars* and the *Kolis* are not as keenly interested in becoming cultivating owners as the chammars are, the other aspects of the response are similar.

A distinction can be made between aspirations centreing on the village and those oriented outside. Aspirations, fulfilment of which brings higher economic and social status through work within the village, have been considered 'village centreed'; those which involve work outside the village for their fulfilment have been considered 'out oriented'. Thus ownership and cultivation of land is village-Centreed and white-collar service is outside-oriented, even though many Brahmin white-collar workers of Raipur keep their families within the village while working outside. The word "opportunity" has been used for occupations to which a caste does not aspire but which it accepts when it can not attain its aspiration. Unskilled labour is an opportunity for the high castes.

For the high castes the principal aspirations are outside the village. For the Brahmins white-collar service and profession constitute principal aspirations, while commerce is secondary. The Mahajans on the other hand, aspire equally to white-collar services and professions, and commerce. Unskilled service and labour (e.g. class IV services), is the opportunity for all members of the high caste who are not successful in their aspirations. Both Brahmins and Mahajans do not aspire to higher status within the village. The larger land owners among them would be content to maintain the non-cultivating owner status which they have enjoyed so far. Even cultivating ownership involves a reduction in social status for these casts. The principal aspirations of the cultivating castes are village-centreed. The major objective, social and economic, of the *Malis* is to attain the status of the Meenas. The Meenas have no desire for economic change within the village; their aspiration is mainly social and centre on improving the social status of the caste so that they can be recognized as the equals of cultivating owner castes of established social status like the Jats. Aspiration outside the village are weak for both these castes. White-collar service is the principal aspiration and unskilled labour the opportunity. The *Khatiks* similarly have no marked aspirations within the village. They are content to maintain their present social status and to make only marginal changes in their occupations. Outside the village their first preference is for practicing their traditional occupation of carpentry or its modern counter part, furniture making. But movement to skilled work outside the village does not mean any change in the status, and the aspiration to move out is not too strong. In case of Chammars, however, both village-centreed and out-oriented aspirations operate and both are strong. Within the village, the Chammars wish to become cultivating owners and the social equals of the Meenas. But they also want to go out to become unskilled workers and after acquiring skills or education they want to be skilled or white-collar workers. However, even unskilled work outside the village has been considered an aspiration in their case, because it meant an improvement in economic status and release from the position of inferiority within the village.

The concept of 'open' and 'closed' occupations; the ability of different castes to enter different occupations, traditional and new, and the facility of certain artisan castes to make the change from their traditional occupations to new skilled ones are another important aspect. The traditional crafts of *Khatiks*, *Lohar, Rehgar, Kumhar* and *Koli* are 'closed' because they would not be practiced by any other caste. The comparable new occupations are also practically closed, because other castes would not generally choose them. Analysis of different economic opportunity available to different castes in making a change from traditional to new occupations shows that *Lohars* and the *Khatiks* can make the change successfully because there is a large demand for their skills in the urban/ industrial economy. But the *Rehgars*, the *Kolis* and the *Kumhars* have much greater difficulty in making the change. In case of the latter two, especially, the urban demand for traditional skills is very limited and a substantial number must either learn new skills—even practicing the modern counterparts of their traditional occupations requires learning of entirely new skills because textile manufacture and pottery follow greatly advanced techniques, or as has been happening, join the ranks of unskilled labourers.

A few new skilled occupations are partially or mainly open. The occupations of motor driver, tailor and bicycle repairmen are the most 'open' among the new occupations, because all castes from the Brahmin to the Chammars can take these up. The occupation of mason is less open, because while a number of other castes join it, the high castes do not. The propensity of the 'other Moslems' in entering a variety of new skilled occupations is noteworthy.

Footnotes

1. Gadgil, D.R., *Industrial Evolution of India in Recent Times*. Bombay 1924, contains a good account.
2. According to the household survey, conducted as part of these studies.
3. *Batai*: crop sharing between the owner and the cultivator of land. Under the agreement most common in this area, the owner pays the land revenue and half share of the cost of seed and manure, the cultivator bears all other expenses of cultivation, and the produce is divided equally between them. But variations from this practice are made by agreement between the parties concerned.
4. There are in this area, Moslem castes like the *Gaddis* and the *Pathans* who are cultivators. But these are not found in this village. The Moslems of this village, all belong to castes with a non-cultivating tradition.
5. Class IV servants: persons employed by Government as peons, messengers, watch-men and primarily unskilled labourers are classified by it as 'Class IV servants'. This term has been retained because it refers to a category of persons, who while they do work which does not require any education or skill, get higher pay and have greater security of service than do other unskilled labourers.
6. *Vaidyas* are practitioners of the indigenous Ayurvedic system of medicine. All the *Vaidyas* of this village are in Government service and are posted in rural Ayurvedic dispensaries run by the state. One of them is posted in the dispensary of the village itself, the others work in dispensaries in neighbouring villages.
7. Village level workers are extension workers having responsibility for propagation of improved agricultural practices and other improvements sponsored under the community development programme. One V.L.W. is posted in a group of 5 to 10 villages.
8. Grant of rent-free lands was the most common method of supporting temples or individual Brahmins in this area.
9. Brahmins are generally preferred for the job of cooks especially in the more orthodox vegetarian Hindu homes, because they belong to the highest caste and are mostly vegetarian themselves.
10. In a popular saying which expresses this prejudice very well, selling milk is equated to selling one's son, which is the depth of degradation. But the prejudice does not extend to sale of *ghee* and many cultivators sell small quantities of *ghee*.
11. *Charans* were bards of Rajput princes who sang their praises and kept them company in battle and court. They also maintained family histories. This practice of having bards-cum-genealogists spread among other castes so that each caste began to have its own special caste of bards-cum-genealogists.
12. Only an occasional *Jogi* practices these now-a-days. The following two

experiences may be of interest in illustrating the present state of villagers' belief in the efficacy of the *Jogis'* methods in protecting the village from natural calamities. In the winter of 1961, there was a mild locust invasion in this area. A few swarms passed over some villages, but did not do much damage. Manpur was one such village. A swarm flew over it one afternoon but did not settle on its lands. When I visited the village in the evening, I found the villagers very happy that the swarm had passed over the village without doing any damage. They explained that the village *Jogi*—among 8 men of the caste, he was the only practicing *Jogi*—had performed the puja to ward off the locusts and had been successful. Some of them added that their *Jogi* had never failed them. But in the summer of 1962 when there was a very sever locust invasion in the district, intensive dusting operations had to be carried out in all these villages. Practically, the entire adult population of each village was mobilized and organized into parties for dusting the fields and other lands with B.H.C (a strong chemical pesticide). The villagers, men and women, came out in large numbers to do this work without any payment. They understood that this was the only way to protect their crops from total destruction. We seldom heard of *Jogis* in those days though it is possible that they may have also been asked to perform their *pujas*.

13. A small orchestra of western type musical instruments, mainly trumpets and flutes.
14. These remarks apply only to the traditionally non-cultivating groups among the Moslems. The traditional cultivating groups like the *Gaddis*, remain largely confined to cultivation and are not prominent as innovators or skilled workers.

2

From Untouchables to Peasant Proprietors

The Story of the Berwa Chammars

Introduction

One of the major social changes in this area has been that the Chammars have left their traditional obligation of flaying carcasses, doing leather work, and rendering certain services to the cultivators; and are devoting themselves entirely to cultivation and/or labour. This change began about 20 years ago (1940 or so) and had been completed in all villages of this area a few years before the study. It has brought a major change in economic activity and social status of the Chammars, transforming them from untouchables, at the bottom of the social scale, to cultivators-cum-labourers aspiring for social equality with other cultivating castes. It has also had far reaching repercussion on the social, economic, and political life of the area. The change is a product of the current process of social and political change; but it can also be considered a major event, a landmark, in that process[1].

The Berwa Chammars[2] are a large group in this area. The number is estimated at 10 per cent of the total[3] rural population and is next only to that of the Meenas. Until the early 1940s when this change began, they used to flay carcasses of dead cattle, tan the hides and make leather goods, and do various services (*beggars*)[4] for the cultivators and the villages. They also did agricultural and non-agricultural labour and cultivated small holdings which they owned and/or took on lease. Tanning of hides and making of leather goods is really the work for the *Rehgars* (lit. tanners and dyers of leather) and wherever the latter lived, they did this work while the Chammars did flaying. But since the *Rehgars* lived only in the large villages, in most small villages the Chammars did leather work as well. They were bound to the cultivators by contractual obligation embodied in the *Jajmani* system, and received fixed payment in grain at the time of harvest. The *beggars* for the cultivators consisted of various labour jobs in the field, in the home and on ceremonial occasion. The Chammars assisted the cultivators in thrashing grain and carrying the thrashed grain and chaff to stores in their homes. They cleaned the cattle shed, and did various jobs connected with cultivation. They were also available for hired labour whenever required: in fact, the Chammars formed the largest component of the agricultural labour force in the area. Their women similarly assisted the cultivators' women in making cow dung cakes and doing such arduous household tasks as grinding grain. Chammar men and women worked at the time of marriage and other ceremonies in the cultivator's home. The midwives were almost invariably Chammar or Muslim women. The Chammars had certain obligations towards the village also. They had the responsibility of looking after the visiting officials of the revenue department and other departments of the state government. They were required to carry their luggage, to bring *charpoys*, bedding, fuel and other supplies for them; to call the cultivators from their homes or field, when the official wanted to see them, and to remain in attendance for miscellaneous duties. They had also the responsibility of helping the *Patwaris* in tasks like measurement of fields. All in all, they were the general purpose servants of the cultivators and of the village, while their women had a similar role in the cultivators' homes.

Non-agricultural labour was another economic activity of the chammars, but as sufficient employment was not available within the area large numbers went for work outside it. This migration took two main forms: (i) seasonal migration to forests of Madhya Pradesh to make wood charcoal, and (ii) migration to towns, especially industrial centres like Indore and Ujjain in Madhya Pradesh and Ahmedabad in Gujurat, to work in industries, construction and other such work. Migration to the forests was seasonal. The migrants left home between November and January, and came back in June, just before the onset of the monsoon. But migration to the industrial centres tended to be more permanent, especially if the migrant was successful in finding permanent employment. It increased in volume in the 1930s and especially in the 1940s, with rapid expansion of employment in industries and public works as a result of Second World War.

Accordingly, the Chammars were not mere flayers of carcasses and workers in leather, as the name of the caste might suggest. Flaying and leather work were only two of their several economic activities, and in case of most families not the most important. But these were their traditional tasks, their obligations to the village community, and because of their association with these tasks they were untouchable, occupying almost the lowest position in rural society.

All this has changed during the last twenty years. The Chammars have stopped lifting dead cattle, flaying carcasses, making leather goods and doing various *beggars* for the cultivators. They have walked out of *Jajmani* system. Most of them are land owners and cultivators, though their holdings are small and they have either to take additional areas for cultivation on *betai* (share cropping), or to supplement their earnings from cultivation with agricultural or non-agricultural labour. The social transformation has been even greater. The Chammars feel that since they have given up their 'defiling' and 'servile' tasks, they should be treated as a clean caste of cultivating owners, the equal of the Meenas. The people of other castes are also very conscious of the change. They realize that the Chammars have become assertive and unwilling to tolerate social inequality, leave alone untouchability. The Meenas and other castes of traditional cultivating owners resent the changes the most, for reasons explained below.

Though these changes in occupation and social status of the Chammars are not confined to Sawai Madhopur *tehsil*; they are of regional occurrence. But in this *tehsil*, they have been accompanied by a large migration of Chammars, from villages in which they had been living for generations to other villages and to new settlements of their own. This migration, made possible by availability of unoccupied cultivable waste land in the foot hills, plains and valleys in the eastern part of the *tehsil*, has been a distinctive feature of the change in it. It has accelerated and facilitated the change in occupation and made possible attainment of the Chammars objective of becoming cultivating owners; and it has not brought acute social tension and conflict.

This study describes the change in occupation and social status of the Chammars and the migration which accompanied it.

The case description of Mainpur is based on the author's field work in the village over a period of more than a year. Data on economic activities of the Chammars were obtained through a household survey. Data on migration of Chammars were collected in all villages of the *tehsil* with the assistance of the *Patwaris*.[5] Most of the latter belong to the *tehsil* and have worked in it for a long period, and were quite familiar with the social and economic changes of recent years—including migration of the Chammars. This previous knowledge of migration was an advantage, because both the Chammars and other castes were reticent on the subject of migration. The Chammars were trying to forget their past—their earlier occupation, social position in the old villages, and migration. The Meenas and other cultivators, especially of villages from which Chammars had gone, were also not too keen to talk about these happenings[6].

The author met the *Patwaris* first in one of their monthly meetings in the *tehsil* office. The main facts about the migration of Chammars were discussed in this meeting, and the schedules to be used for collecting information for each village were explained. Two separate schedules were used, one for villages from which Chammars had left, and the other for villages of immigration. Both schedules were to be filled for villages which had experienced both emigration and immigration. The scheduled for villages of immigration sought information on the number of Chammar families that had left the village during the last 20 years, the year (s) of leaving, the motives and circumstances of leaving, especially whether it had been the result of quarrel with the cultivators or other castes in the village, and the village or villages to which they had gone (if known). The schedule for villages of immigration similarly sought information on the number of Chammar families that had arrived in the village during the last 20 years, the year(s) of arrival, the area occupied by them for cultivation, weather obtained through allotment, purchase or unauthorized occupation, and general information on their other economic activities with Chammar leaders and were to be checked and supplemented by discussion with other village leaders, by reference of revenue records, etc. But in village in which no Chammar family was living at the time of the survey, data had to be collected through discussions with the village leaders—the *Sarpanch* and other member of the *Panchayat*, and others. The *Patwaris* were requested to complete the schedules at their convenience during the course of a month and to bring them along at the next monthly meeting. At this meeting, the filled schedules for each village was scrutinized by the author and discussed with the *Patwari* concerned. In several cases, extremely useful comments and supplementary information were given by the *Patwari* or the land record inspector (a supervisory officer having jurisdiction over the area of about 10 *Patwaris*) who had been posted in that villages, when the migration of the Chammars actually took place.

Change in the Area

Before starting description of change in the *tehsil*, it would be appropriate to refer to the riots in 1939 between the Meenas and the Chammars in several villages of Lalsot *tehsil* of Jaipur district, located 30 miles to the north of Sawai Madhopur tehsil. Influences like spread of ideas of social and political equality and the feeling against untouchability and other disabilities suffered by the scheduled castes, had been working for quite some time, and the tension had been building up. These riots however, were the first violent expression of these. The riots were suppressed by the police of Jaipur state without much difficulty, but tension prevailed in the area for several months. During this time a number of villages were intensively patrolled and other necessary measures were taken by the police to prevent recurrence of violent outbreaks. But as subsequent events have shown, the riots were the signal for the start of a movement of far reaching significance which had continued to this day.

The main cause of the dispute between the two castes was the refusal of the Meenas to allow the Chammars to give elaborate feasts on marriage and other occasions, erect poles[7] before their houses and to allow Chammar women to wear *kari* (an ankle ornament) and other silver ornaments or walk through the village streets with their shoes on. Thus the stated points of the dispute were items of dress and social practices, which were popular among the Meenas (and other cultivating castes) and which the Chammars wanted to adopt. But this desire of the Chammars was regarded by the Meenas as an attempt to shake off their position of subservience and social inferiority. It is interesting to note that flaying of carcasses, leather work or beggar were not expressly mentioned in the dispute. But the inferiority of the Chammars was based upon these latter, and allowing them to adopt those of equality with the Meenas would have meant recognition of their claim to social equality. These implications were well understood by both the Meens and the Chammars. The item of dress and social practices served only as symbols of the social struggle.

The outcome of the riots could be considered to have been favourable to the Chammars. The riots were effectively suppressed, and large numbers of Meenas were punished for causing violence. What is more important, the Chammars were left with the clear impression that no attempt would be made by the state to enforce their customary obligations to the cultivators or to interface in any way with their struggle for social equality with the latter.

In Sawai Madhopur *tehsil*, trouble started in 1943-44 in village Surpur, 6 miles north of Sawai Madhopur town. This is a big village (present population about 3000) with a large population of Meenas; it has always been considered to be the leading Meena village of the *tehsil*. Moreover, it is surrounded by a number of small villages in which Meenas are predominant. Surpur and all the surrounding villages were *khalsa* villages, directly administrated by the Jaipur state. Predominance of

Meenas and absence of local *jagirdars* or even of large number of people of the high castes had made this group of villages a Meena stronghold. The points of dispute in this village included refusal of the Chammars to flay carcasses of dead cattle, besides the items of dress and social practices mentioned above. There was some violence, and the Chammars were turned out of the village by the cultivators. But they were assisted by the state in settling down three miles south of the village on cultivable waste land which was allotted to them, for settlement and cultivation. The state also helped them to establish a new, well planned village of their own. This clearly showed that the sympathies of the state and its local officers were with the Chammars.

Even before the quarrel in Surpur began, there had been some migration of Chammars, especially from small villages along the river Banas at the northern end of the tehsil. But the trouble in Surpur was the signal for quarrel between the Meenas and the Chammars and Chammars emigration from small villages in the entire Meena-dominated central and northern part of the *tehsil*. The quarrel and emmigration were confined however, from small villages in the Meena dominated zone: large villages in the Zone (e.g. Raipur), in which people of the high caste were present in large numbers, or villages located in the western part of the *tehsil* in which the *jagirdars* had a strong influence, were not thus affected. In the latter the occupational change was accomplished without emmigration: the Chammars continued to live in the villages with changed occupation and, gradually, social status. The rest of the community reconciled itself to the change, though as the experience of village Raipur brings out, strained relations and tensions arising from it continued to this day.

Migration of Chammars

The method of collection of data on migration has been explained above. The principal facts may now be summarized.

Out of a total 2122 Chammar families living in 199 villages of the *tehsil*[8], 712, or one-third of the total, are living in villages to which they moved during the last 20 years. In other words, one in every three rural Chammar families in the *tehsil* has been affected by the movement.

But the number of Chammar families reported to have left their villages during this period is only 495. This number is considerably smaller than the figure of immigrant families for the following reasons:

(a) Increase in the number of families, due to natural increase in population and subdivision of families after arrival in the new villages.

The influence of this factor was clearly seen in cases where inflow had been entirely from one village A to another village B. In all such cases the number of immigration families reported in village B was higher than the number of families reported to have left village A.

(b) Net immigration from outside the *tehsil*. While most of the migration has been within the *tehsil*, there has been some immigration from villages outside the *tehsil* also.

(c) Reporting on the number of families which had left the village cannot be as exact as on the number of families which have arrived; the latter are present in the village and the former are not! From experience in this survey it appears that there is tendency to underreport the out-migration.

Emigration of Chammar families has been reported from 55 villages, while immigration has been reported in 32 villages. The area of *tehsil* can be divided into three "movement zones. First from which there has been the heaviest emigration, which includes the villages of the central plain extending north from Sawai Madhopur town to the Banas River. The second zone, which has been the principal area of immigration, includes the villages to the east and south of Sawai Madhopur town and about 15 villages to the south-east of it (located south of the railway line to Jaipur). This zone contained most of the lands available for cultivation, which have been cleared and occupied by the immigrant Chammars. Most of the new Chammar settlements (including the hamlet of Manpur) are located in this zone. The villages in the western part of the *tehsil* forms the third zone, in which there has been practically no emigration or immigration Most of these villages were under *jagirdars* who had considerable local power, and who did not allow such a movement to develop. Figure on migration in the three zones are given in Table 2.1.

Table 2.1: Migration of Chammar Families

		Emmigration		*Immigration*		*Families in 1962*		
	Total No. of Villages	*No. of Villages Affected*	*No. of Families Living*	*No. of Villages*	*No of Families Arriving*	*No. of Villages*	*No. of Families*	*No. of Villages without Chammar Families*
ZONE I	93	48	451	8	115	37	504	56
ZONE II	58	1	4	18	523	34	972	24
ZONE III	48	6	40	6	74	35	646	13
Total No. of Village	199	55	495	32	712	106	2122	93

Movement from the old villages has been both by single families and by groups of families. Typically, a few families have left the village and settled down in a new location where they were able to get a sizable area of land for cultivation. In course of time, they have been joined by other families from their old or neighbouring villages, with the result that the hamlet grew in size. Thus the hamlet of Manpur which had 48 families at the time of this study, had started with only 20 families in 1994. Most Chammar hamlets have 10 to 30 households, though a few are larger.

Most families have moved only short distances.

Families moving	
Less than 5 miles	195
Between 5 to 10 miles	110
Between10 to 15 miles	34
Between 15 to 20 miles	89
Above 20 miles	284
Total	712

About 30 per cent of the families have moved less than 5 miles and as many as 60 per cent have moved less than 20 miles. Even among those which have moved 20 miles and over, the majority have moved less than 30 miles. The families moving less than 5 miles have left one village only to settle in the next or the next but one, where they could get land for cultivation. Movement under such distance can hardly be termed a migration—it would be recorded by statistics as inter-*tehsil* migration—and is more appropriately called a "drift"

It had been mentioned above, that the movement began before 1943 (samvat 2000[9]) and had continued to this days. The number of families moving in different five years periods is as follows:

1943 (s. 2000) and earlier	43 families
1944-48 (2001-05)	211 "
1949-53 (s. 2006-10)	184 "
1954-58 (s. 2011-15)	164 "
after1958 (s. 2015)	110 "
Total	712 "

The bulk of the movement took place within the 15 years period, 1944 to 1958, when nearly 80 per cent of the Chammar families moved. It began during Second World War, after the abrupt rise in prices in agricultural produce and was at its peak during the immediate post-war and post-independent years. It has decreased greatly after 1958, mainly because the culturable lands have been largely occupied and it is becoming increasingly difficult to get new lands for cultivation. The major political change in the area—integration of Jaipur state and formation of Rajasthan in 1949—has not had any marked influence on it, because the policies of both the Jaipur state and the present Rajasthan Government have been favourable to it. The attitude of Jaipur State was generally sympathetic towards the Chammars and its local officials helped them in settling on unoccupied culturable lands. The Rajasthan Government had given a preference in allotment of cultivable waste lands to the landless, especially of the scheduled castes. During the 1950s the movement was entirely to waste lands allotted by the Rajasthan Government or occupied by the Chammars in an unauthorized way and regularized later. There is still considerable pressure from Chammars for allotment of forest-covered lands in the foot-hills, plains and valleys in the southern part of the *tehsil*. Some small areas, which do not have a good forest cover, are allocated every year. But no large scale allotment is possible now, because further extension of cultivation into the hill slopes and valleys would lead to depletion of forests, accelerated soil erosion and other serious consequence for the agricultural economy of the area. Allotment of these small areas to the Chammars is now encountering increasing competition and resistance from the other cultivators and grazers. The owners of land of less than 10 acres are eligible for allotment of more land; Meenas, Malis, Gujjars and Jats, press their claims for allotment. They even claim preference on ground of being residents of the village in which the lands are located. In certain cases, there are residents from the village who are professional grazers, mostly Gujjars, whose cattle and buffaloes graze in those wooded areas, and who see in the allotment of these lands for cultivation the end of their grazing activity.

The Chammars gave two main reasons for their migration: increasing difficulty in obtaining land for cultivation on *batai* in the old villages; and attraction of obtaining land for cultivation in the new villages.

The conflicts arising from cessation of flaying and other *beggars* were scarcely mentioned. When asked about conflict in the old villages—the schedules contained a question on this—most of them replied that there was no such conflict and that they left entirely on their own accord. But the Meenas and other residents of the same village did not have much hesitation in referring to these conflicts and giving their details. Secondly, the Chammars were reluctant to discuss their former role of flayers of carcasses, leather workers and servants of the cultivators. They wanted this part of their story to be completely forgotten. They were anxious to emphasise, probably to bolster their claims for obtaining more land for cultivation, that they were cultivators earlier, are cultivators now, and had moved only because they could not get enough land for cultivation in the old villages and got it in the new. But almost invariable they added that they needed more land. This demand for additional lands always came up in the author's visits to the new Chammar settlements. One reason for this is that most of the settlements have a number of landless families. The success of the first settlers in getting land has attracted others but several of the latter have either not been able to get any land at all, or have got only small areas, which are not sufficient for their subsistence; they must rely rather heavily on labour. Seventy-four per cent of immigrant Chammar families (527 out of 712) have been successful in getting land for cultivation while 26 per cent are landless. The area owned by the land owing families totals 5300 acres, an average of a little more than 10 acres per family. The bulk of these areas have been obtained through allotment (including regularization of unauthorized possession); a small area totalling about 300 acres was reported to have been purchased. These 5300 acres are only 3 per cent of the cultivated area of the *tehsil*. That such a small area was sufficient to spark a movement of such magnitude and social significance is a fact of considerable importance for social policy.

Most of the land has been brought under cultivation after clearing the forests. The Chammars have done enormous labour and spent their meagre capital in cutting trees and bushes, preparing land for cultivation, building *kutcha* houses and cattle sheds, digging drinking water wells, and buying bullocks, seeds, implements and other essentials for cultivation. They have done all this and endured the hardship of living in new settlements, most of which were in the heart of the jungle when started, because of their determination to raise their social and economic status. This determination and the confidence which comes from successful achievement of an objective were noticeable in discussions in all the Chammar settlements visited by the author. These are also responsible for the spirit of going ahead, which appeared to be somewhat more pronounced among the Chammars than among most other castes in this area. Moreover, the Chammars regard their new settlements as their 'village' and are anxious to build their own wells, temples schools and other community facilities. A strong sense of community, of belonging to the new settlements, exists among them. Reference has been made to this feeling in both the Chammar settlements described in these studies—the hamlet of Manpur and the village Chainpur. It was visible in even small hamlets of 10 or 15 households. The existence of such a strong feeling of belonging together in settlements which are less than two decades old and to which many families have arrived during the last 5 or 10 years is due partly to the anxiety to avoid encountering the same kind of social disabilities which they suffered in the old villages, and partly in the fact that their relations with people of the surrounding villages are not good. The feelings of mutual indifference and dormant hostility between the Chammars of the hamlet and people of the main village described below in case of Manpur are found in a number of other Chammar settlements also. They originate partly in the opposition of the other castes to the Chammars leaving their traditional obligations, and partly in the fact that the cultivators and the grazers in the villages in which the new settlements are located were opposed to the coming of the Chammars. Their opposition was unsuccessful; but the hostility to the Chammars, who are still regarded as intruders, remains.

Most of the immigrant Chammar families have to supplement cultivation of their own lands, with one or more of the following:

- Taking in additional area for cultivation from neighbours;
- Agricultural or non-agricultural labour near their villages; and
- Seasonal migration for non-agricultural labour e.g. for charcoal-making in the forests of Madhya Pradesh.

Change in Village Manpur: A Caste Study

Manpur is a medium sized, multi-caste village with a population of about 2200, situated at a distance of 6 miles from Sawai Madhopur town. It has 88 households of Chammars of which 40 live in the main village and the remaining 48 are in a hamlet of their own about $1\frac{1}{2}$ miles to the east. The hamlet is a distinct entity by itself and could well be considered a separate village; but its inclusion within the administrative area of Manpur makes the Chammars the largest caste in the village. The other prominent castes of the village are Brahmin, Rajput and Mahajan among the High castes and the Meenas, Jats and Malis among the cultivating castes. The distribution of castes having more than 10 households each is given in Table 2.2.

The village had formed part of the *jagir* of a very powerful *jagirdar* of the area, who was moreover known for his ultra-conservative attitude. Secondly, because of its Rajput residents, many of whom were in the service of the *jagirdar*, enforcement of traditional *Jajmani* obligations to

Table 2.2: Number of Households and Population of Main Castes in Manpur 1961

Castes	*Households*	*Population*
Brahmin	32	137
Rajput	23	128
Mahajan	14	57
Jat	41	229
Meena	26	145
Mali	78	380
Gujjar	16	79
Kumhar	21	104
Chammar	88	544
Koli	10	60
Others	72	350
Total	421	2213

the community and of *beggars* for the *jagirdar* was as rigorous in this village, as perhaps in any other in this area. Moreover, as there were no families of Rehgars, the Chammars of this village did leather work in addition to flaying of carcasses; they supplied to the cultivators, as part of *jajmani* arrangement, shoes, *charas* and other requisites of cultivation like leather straps for hitching bullocks to the plough.

In the process of change in the position of the Chammars of Manpur, three events are noteworthy:

- Establishment of the hamlet in 1944 by 20 Chammar families coming from villages along the river Banas. These families came after leaving of flaying of carcasses and leather work in their old villages, and settled down here as cultivators-cum-labourers;
- Cessation in 1952 of traditional *beggars* for the *jagirdar* by the cultivators and other castes of the main village; and
- Cessation in 1956 of flaying of carcasses and leather work by the Chammars of the main villages.

Establishment of the hamlet was a significant event in the process of change in Manpur, because it gave the villagers their first experience with change among the Chammars. Cessation of *beggars* for the *jagirdar* was the first step in the process of repudiation of traditional obligations within the main village.

The original families from the Banas village were joined in course of time by others mostly from villages located within 5-10 miles of Manpur, as quarrel between the Meenas and the Chammars spread out to these. As a result of addition and division of the older families, the number of families in the hamlet had increased to 48 by 1961. The leaders of the hamlet stated that the first families moved out of the ancestral villages only because they were experiencing difficulty in obtaining land for cultivation and that there were no quarrels with the Meenas or other cultivators. They explained that they had petitioned the *jagirdar* of Manpur for allotment of 3,000 *bighas* (about 1900 acres) of culturable waste land in this area, and that their request was granted; but by the time they could move and occupy the land, only 500 *bighas* (312 acres) were left unoccupied, the remainder having been occupied through encroachments by the cultivators of Manpur and other neighbouring villages. The story is substantially correct and throws light on the attitude of the cultivators to settlement of the Chammars on unoccupied waste lands. The land allotted to the Chammars as well as most of land further south and east going up to the slopes of the hills, (about 2 miles further east from the hamlet) was uncultivated at that time. It was covered with trees and bushes, had abundant grass during the rains, and were used by the villagers for grazing of livestock and for obtaining fuel and timber. The land vested in the state (or in *jagir* villages like Manpur in the *jagirdars*) but the villagers were allowed the facilities of grazing and removal of forests produce on nominal payment. Moreover, the cultivators regarded the land as a reserve for future expansion of cultivation with increase in population; the right to land of their sons and grandsons when their existing holdings were no longer sufficient. Its occupation by the Chammars was, therefore, considered to be an encroachment by them which were additionally repugnant, because the Chammars were settling here after repudiating their customary obligations and in a bid to become the equals of the cultivators. These attitudes persist and are well brought out in the dispute relating to the cooperative farming society which occurred about two years before this study.

As part of a programme of encouraging cooperative farming in Rajasthan, a 'drive' to establish cooperative farming societies was launched in the district in 1959. The Chammars of small hamlet, three miles from Manpur, which had been established in the late forties, saw in this drive an opportunity to obtain land for cultivation. About 20 families, most of them landless, joined in farming in cooperative farming society. They were allotted 150 acres of land. The cooperative department of the state government gave a loan of Rs. 10,000 for land improvement, buying bullocks and agricultural implements. The allotment was opposed by the cultivators of 12 neighbouring villages (including Manpur) on the ground that the Chammars had no intension of practicing joint farming, that the society had been formed by them only to obtain land. They argued further that the land could not be allotted for cultivation under the law, because it was grazing land, in which their cattle had been grazing from 'time immemorial[10]. Besides making an application for cancellation of the allotment order, they physically prevented the Chammars from obtaining possession of the land, with the result that there was a scuffle between the two groups and a police case was registered. Finally, in the summer of 1960, the allotment question was decided in favour of the Chammars and they could thus take up clearance and cultivation of land in earnest only in 1961. At the time of the study, the Chammars had harvested one *kharif* crop, and were engaged in further clearance and improvement of land. They were also planning to build huts for permanent settlement.

The basic hostility of cultivators of Manpur (and other surrounding villages) to the new Chammar settlers, is a major factor to keeping the Chammars of the hamlet away from the people of Manpur. Their hamlet is included within the administrative area of Manpur; they are represented in its *panchayat* and cooperative society and have some economic relations with its people. But they consider themselves separate and are anxious to have their hamlets recognized as a separate village.

The trouble over *beggars* for the *Jagirdar* occurred in 1952. The *jagir* had not been resumed till then; it was formally resumed four years later. But *jagir* resumption was already in the air; the law abolishing *jagirs* had been passed by the legislature of Rajasthan and the process of taking over land records and revenue administration work from functionaries of the *Jagirdars* had started. Moreover, the first General Election (of 1952) had been held, elected *Panchayats* were going to be formed shortly, and new *ideas* of social and economic change—rights fort cultivators, political and social equality—were sweeping the area. The trouble started when some Mali and Meena cultivators of Manpur refused to give the customary *beggars* to the functionaries of the *Jagirdars*. The Malis used to draw water from wells for them and to supply vegetables, chillies, etc., free or at concessional rates: the Meenas would bring the bullock carts for their use. This refusal of the cultivators resulted in a quarrel between them and the local Rajputs, many of whom were in the service of the *Jagirdar*. A case was registered by the police and was sent for trial to the local magistrate. The latter found the servants of the *jagirdar* guilty of obtaining illegal *beggars* and awarded them small sentences of imprisonment. This decision was a complete defeat for them. The cultivators and most other villagers were happy with this decision, as it meant the end of their obligations to the *Jagirdar* and the power of the local Rajputs. One of their prominent supporters was Ram Singh, who had just then returned to the village after having lived 20 years outside. Even though a Rajput himself, he was much opposed to *Jagirdari* and all that it stood for (including accessories like *beggar*), because he had been deeply influenced by the idea of social and political equality and of giving land to the tiller during his stay outside the village. This action of his made him unpopular with has own caste men but very popular with people of the cultivating castes and the scheduled castes, and contributed to his rise to leadership in the village. He was nominated *Sarpanch* when the *Panchayat* was first formed in 1952; was elected unopposed when the first elected *Panchayat* was formed in 1954, and has continued to be *Sarpanch* ever since.

The Chammars of the main village decided to stop flaying of carcasses and leather work in 1956, soon after the formal resumption of the *jagir*. By this time, the movement of stopping this work had reached an advanced stage in the area—it had been completed in most villages and was going on in full swing in the rest. Resistance to this decision of the Chammars from the rest of the village was rather weak and was soon over. There was opposition from the cultivating owners, Jats, Malis and Meenas, who were the most affected by the decision, and also from the high caste Brahmins and Rajputs. There was some tension also and a quarrel was feared. The *Sarpanch*, Ram Singh, openly expressed himself in favour of the Chammars and encourage them in their stand. He also sent a report about tension in the village to the sub-divisional magistrate in Sawai Madhopur. This office visited the village and warned the villagers against any violence. There was no violence, however, the villagers accepted the decision of the Chammars and the tensions subsided after a few days. Ram Singh's attitude was welcomed by the Chammars and other scheduled castes; but was resented by the cultivators and the high castes. The cultivators had been happy with him because of his support to them on the issue of *beggars* for the *Jagirdar*, and had supported him in his election as *Sarpanch*. But after this incident they began to be suspicious of his motives and to oppose him in the *Panchayat* elections and in other village's affairs. This opposition of the cultivators and the Chammars support to him are important facts in the political life of the village.

Two other steps taken by the Chammars during the next two year completed the social part of the change process. A few months after they quit their traditional activities, they decided that their women would wear *karis* (silver ornaments for the ankles). Several of them got together and had these ornaments made from silversmiths in Sawai Madhopur town. They did this collectively, because they were apprehensive of opposition from the other villagers. But there was no opposition. Soon, after this the Chammars started making their temple *pucca*. The building was completed in 1958, and in the winter of that year they installed in it the idol of Dwarkadhish (lit. lord of Dwarka, another name of Shri Krishna)[11]. The installation ceremony was an elaborate one and included taking the idol in a procession through the village and a large community feast. The *Sarpanch* Ram Singh was with them at the head of the procession. This was an unprecedented event in the village and one not common in the area till then. The Chammars were very proud: they were installing their idol in the temple in the same way as the caste Hindus do. But the cultivators and the high castes were unhappy and angry; because they felt that the Chammars were going too far in their assertion of equality. The *Sarpanch* had sent a request to the police for making security arrangements partly because of these feelings and partly, it appears to the author, to impress upon the villagers his own support for the Chammars. The security arrangements were made and the whole incident passed off peacefully.

The Chammars have since organized a *keertan* (devotional music) partly in their temple on the model of similar parties in the caste Hindu temples. They follow Vaishnavite worship practices, even though the priest in that temple is a Chammar. On the occasion of *Jaljhoolni Gyares* (a festival coming in the month of September) they take out their idol in procession to the village tank, just as other castes do. However, it had been agreed between them and the other castes that their procession will start a few hours before the main procession of the village and will have returned to their temple before the latter starts.[12]

Effects of the Changes

Ever since the Chammars stopped flaying of carcasses, the village *Panchayat* gives a contract for this work. For several years, the contract was being taken by a Moslem contractor who employed the *Bhangis* of the village to do the work. But in 1961 the contract was taken by the village *Bhangis* themselves for a sum of Rs. 250. Addition of this work has meant a considerable addition to the income of the *Bhangis* (one extended family of 6 households). The cultivators allege that it has also made them arrogant because they feel that they are doing a 'dirty' and 'defiling' work which they alone are prepared to do. Some Mali cultivators having fertile, irrigated lands in the vicinity of the village *abadi* complained to the author about the damage done to their valuable crops of chillies, sugarcane, and vegetables, by the pigs who roam about everywhere; these pigs enter our fields and cause so much damage; but the *Panchayat* does not do anything to prevent this and we ourselves are afraid to tell the *Bhangis* lest they get annoyed and stop scavenging and lifting of dead animals."

The cultivators have suffered considerable economic loss as a result of this change, and have also been put to much inconvenience. They have lost all rights on the carcasses of the dead animals. Under the *Jajmani* arrangement, they used to get a fixed number of shoes, leather straps and other accessories of cultivation, and *charas* (if they had an irrigation well), in exchange for the hides of animals and the grain payment which they made to the Chammars who also undertook repairs of shoes and other leather goods. Now they receive nothing for the hide and have to buy all their requirements of leather goods in Sawai Madhopur town or in other villages where there are colonies of Rehgars. The nearest such village is three miles from Manpur. Moreover, they have to go to the town or to these villages for the smallest repairs. Apart from the unnecessary expenses of buying leather goods and paying for repairs, the inconvenience and waste of time involved in going a long distance from the village for the smallest repair job, causes much annoyance to the cultivators. Ram Singh said that in order to remove the repairs difficulty he was trying to get a Rehgar to come and settle down in this village. But no one had come till the end of this study. During the busy cultivation season (especially in October-November before *rabi* irrigation begins), itinerant Rehgar families come and camp in the village for a few days and undertake repairs of *charas* and other accessories of cultivation; but at other times no local service is available.[13] The community has suffered an economic loss also. The *Bhangis*, since they do not posses the traditional skill of flaying and are able to get the carcasses on a nominal payment, and know that they are doing a job which nobody else is prepared to do are not very careful in doing it. Several cultivators of Manpur mentioned that many hides were damaged by them through carelessness in dragging the dead animals or in flaying. The point was also brought up in Raipur, where the Rehgars were much more explicit in their complaint.

Some cultivators mentioned to me that many Chammars of the village regretted their decision of leaving flaying and leather work, because they had lost a good source of income and were not as well off as before. However, experience does not support this view. Evidence collected showed that the Chammars were better off than ever before, and that they were the one group whose economic level had shown the most marked improvement during the past ten years[14].

Social and Political Effects

One important result of these changes has been a marked reduction in untouchability. Untouchability has not disappeared altogether—it is still practiced by the orthodox; but there is a noticeable relaxation in the attitude and practice concerning it. Most educated young men and political leaders of the village express themselves against practice of untouchability and pay no attention to observe it themselves, especially when they are outside the village, one drinking water well—the best and most popular—is used by people of all castes (except the *Bhangis*), and Brahmin and Rajput women have no hesitation in drawing water from it at the same time when Chammar women are doing so. Chammar children go to the village school. Chammar members sit as equal on the *Panchyat* and the executive of the cooperative society. The villagers know that some *panchayts* in the *tehsil* already have Chammar *Sarpanchas* and that could happen in Manpur also, especially as the Chammars are the largest caste in the villages. They are particularly conscious of the fact that the Sarpanch Ram Singh could get re-elected in 1960 only on account of the solid support of the Chammars.

The Chammars themselves accept the change in their social position without any noticeable complex. In the meetings of the village *Panchayat* attend by the author. Chammar members participated as equal, did not show any tendency to sit on one side or to consider themselves inferior in any way. Whenever, he visited their hamlet, the Chammars would bring out the *charpoy* and the cotton blanket for him to sit on; and would offer to bring milk or water just like people in other villages.

Reduction in untouchability has been helped by certain changes in religious practices, personal hygiene and consumption among the Chammars. As mentioned earlier, the Chammars of the main village have rebuilt their temple and installed an idol of Sri Krishna in it with much ceremony, and are very enthusiastic about *keertans* (devotional music) and other aspects of Vaishnavite worship. The Chammars of the hamlet have shown similar enthusiasm for building their temple in the summer of 1962. This building—the only *pucca* building in the hamlet—which had cost them nearly Rs. 6000, was intended also to house the primary school and to serve as their community centre. The idol of the deity had not been installed till the end of this study. When asked about their plans for installation of the idol, their leaders stated that the installation ceremony would be accompanied by festivities culminating in a large feast in which Chammars from a number of surrounding villages would be fed. They explained that the ceremony and the feast would cost them at least Rs. 2000 and that they would do it during the winter of 1962-63, by which time they hoped to have enough money. They added "we are too poor to take up the whole burden at once."[15]

The temple building is a symbol both of their social aspiration and of their feeling of belonging to the new community, the hamlet. They want to worship in a temple of Sri Krishna, to have a proper installation ceremony for the idol, and to have a *keertan* (devotional music) party. They already have an active *keertan* party and are anxious to equip it properly with musical instruments.[16] In one discussion with the author they suggested that he might use his influence with the *Panchayat Samiti* to get a grant for musical instruments for their *keertan* party. The suggestion surprised the author at first; but on going into the matter further, he learnt that the *Panchayat Samiti* had given a grant to the *panchayat* of Manpur for buying musical instruments for the community centre, that the instruments had been bought, but were often used by the *keertan* party in one of the caste Hindus temples. This had given these people the impression that the *Panchayat Samiti* gave such grants and they wanted similar assistance for their own party.

Corresponding with this emphasis on Vaishnavite religious practice, there are certain changes in attitudes towards consumption of meat and alcoholic drinks, both of which are prohibited in Vaishnavite practice. The Chammars have always eaten meat and taken drink, and both these practices continue. In the sample survey on consumption, for instance, most Chammar households reported occasional consumption of meat. Drinking is also common among them. But the remarks of the two principal leaders of the hamlet are significant as they indicate an interesting change in attitude. They mentioned that they had given up eating of meat and drinking themselves and were advocating similar abstinence by other people of the hamlet. When asked the reasons for this they replied, "These things are not 'good', and are taking our people downwards".[17] It is most unlikely that this change in attitude among the leaders will lead to any significant reduction in eating meat or in drinking among the group; because increasing contacts with urban areas and participation in industrial and other non-agricultural jobs will be influence against it. It is relevant to mention here that consumption of meat and drink is quite high among the Chammars of Chainpur, who depend mainly upon industrial labour.

But the change in attitude of the leaders is of interest because it indicates an effort to follows the teachings of Vaishnavite religion.

There is also greater attention to personal cleanliness and to keeping their homes and surroundings clean. The hamlet is one of the cleanest villages in the area: the Chammar quarter in Manpur compare most favourably in cleanliness with the other parts of the village. As regards personal hygiene, the people of the other castes in Manpur freely admit that the Chammars are now much cleaner than they used to be.

The Chammars are beginning to show a keen interest in education also. There are 27 children from Chammar families of the main village in the village school. In addition, 15 boys from the hamlet go to a primary school in another village, a quarter mile away. The proportion of Chammar children of primary school age (6 to 11 years) going to school is lower than among the high castes, but it is considerably higher than among the Meenas, Malis, and Jats. This is brought out by the following figures in Table 2.3.

Table 2.3: Proportion of Children of primary school age in School by caste

Caste	*No. of children in primary school going age (6-11 yrs)*	*No. of children in primary (first five) classes in school*	*Per cent (3/2)*
High Castes			
Brahmin	13	13	100
Rajput	18	11	61.1
Mahajan	9	9	100
Cultivating Castes			
Meena	21	5	23.8
Mali	54	4	7.4
Jat	28	4	14.3
Chammar	84	26+15*	48.8

*In other schools

The Chammars of the hamlet want a new school to be opened in the hamlet.[18] When asked why they wanted another school when the existing school, was so conveniently located, they explained that their school would have a sufficient number of students, because the number of children going to school from their hamlet would double, and children from neighbouring Chammar hamlet would join it. The latter argument is interesting because it shows that they want the school to become an exclusive institute of the Chammars. It gives a significant insight into their desire to build a separate community life of their own. In support of their case for the school, they stated that the *pucca* building which they had constructed was eminently suitable for it. They argued that existence of the building was sufficient reason for their getting a school, because many villages had a school without satisfying this condition laid down by the government of providing a building. The school was desired partly for reasons of convenience, but even more for gaining recognition and prestige. Its establishment would mean, in effect, recognition by the government and the *Panchayat Samiti* of the hamlet as a separate entity and themselves as people of status.

The political influence of Chammars had grown steadily as the villagers have become more familiar with democratic process and especially since an opposition to *Sarpanch* Ram Singh has increased. As mentioned earlier, he was nominated *Sarpanch* in 1952 and was elected unopposed at first election of 1954 but in the election held in 1959 there was a contest, though the opposition was rather week and he was elected without much difficulty. In the latest election, however, the opposition was much stronger and he was elected by a margin of 68 votes (380 vote in favour, 312 against). In this election most people of cultivating owner castes voted against him; but the Chammars and other scheduled castes voted solidly in his favour, and his victory was due entirely to the latter's support. The high castes opposition to Ram Singh is due to various personal and fractional reasons. Many of them are dissatisfied with his conduct in various cases placed before the *Panchayat*. They are particularly unhappy about his role in the dispute between the Rajput families which have been growing for a number of years and as a result of which there is much bitterness among the Rajputs of the village. Many Mails, Meenas and Jats had similar reasons to be dissatisfied with him. But they (and to a lesser extent the high castes) are angry with him primarily because of his consistent support of the Chammars. Their opposition to him began when he supported the Chammars in their decision to stop flaying of carcasses, and it has grown as he has supported them on various other occasions. The Chammars and other scheduled castes, of course, support him for the same reasons.

The effect of this support pattern is reflected in the working of the *Panchayat*. The *Sarpanch* and the other members of the group are particular to ensure that the Chammars remain pleased with them, and get their due in all matters coming before the *Panchayat*. There are three representatives of the Chammars, two from the hamlet and one from the main village, in the 13-member *Panchayat*. But because of the support of the *Sarpanch* and his group, their influence is much greater then their numbers would suggest.

It will be seen that nearly three-quarters of the households own and cultivate land. But most of them have a second source of income also, usually agricultural and/or non-agricultural labour. This is reflected also in the figure on numbers of workers and jobs. 85 per cent of the workers (262 out of 311) are engaged in cultivation, but the total number of jobs (454) is nearly 50 per cent higher than the number of workers, which indicates that a large percentage of the workers do more than one job. The most common practise is for one or more persons in each cultivating households to take up work as a labourer at some time in the year. In most households the young men concentrate on labouring jobs while the women and the older folks devote themselves to cultivation. The latter may also take up agricultural or casual non-agricultural labour for short periods, but sustained non-agricultural work is done mostly by the young men.

The total area owned by the Chammars is 666.5 acres. But since a considerable acreage is taken on lease from other land-owners, of Manpur, and those of a small village adjoining a hamlet, the area cultivated by them is larger—911.5 acres. The Chammars of the main village are better off in land ownership and depend to a large extent on cultivation than do those of the hamlet. The number of landless households is smaller among them and the average area owned per land-owning household is higher. Moreover, since they are able to get a considerable area of land for cultivation on *batai*, from other land owners of Manpur, especially Brahmins, most cultivating households have fair-sized holdings. The average holding of 16.06 acres for Chammar cultivating household of the village is only slightly lower than the average for all cultivators of Manpur. The land is of fair productivity, though nearly all of it is unirrigated. There are several good cultivators among these Chammars. One family in particular, which constructed a small check dam on their land a few years ago with financial assistant from the community development block, is among the best cultivating families in the village. These Chammars can also get agricultural labour on the fields of other cultivators of Manpur quite easily. As a result, they depend much more on agricultural land and much less on nun-agricultural labour than do the Chammars of the hamlet. The principal forms of the non-agricultural labour in their case are casual labour and seasonal migration to the forests of Madhya Pradesh for making wood charcoal. They are conspicuous by their absence from work involving permanent or more or less continuous employment, such as permanent service in the cement factory and work on the railways, which are important source of livelihood for the Chammars of the hamlet.

In case of the latter, access to a smaller, poorer, agricultural resource on the one hand and nearness to principal sources of non-agricultural employment on the other, combine to produce a much greater dependence upon non-agricultural labour. It has been mentioned in the preceding section that in many of the new Chammar settlements the success of the first immigration in obtaining land attracted others to join them; but many among the latter were not able to get land. In this hamlet also, most of the landless householders are those who have come only during the last few years. Secondly, the holdings of even the land owners are smaller than those of the Chammars of the main village and since they are not able to get so much land for cultivation on *batai*—they are far from the main village and do not have established relations with its land-owners—their cultivated holdings are smaller still. Finally, the land is unirrigated and of low productivity. It is essentially marginal land which had not been brought under cultivation earlier by the cultivators of Manpur. Parts of it are subject to erosion or deposition of sand by small *nullahs* (rain torrents) coming down from the hills to the east. Nearly all of it is suitable only for growing a single crop (*jowar*) during the kharif season. A small holding of such land is quite inadequate for supporting a family. These people cannot get much agricultural labour also because of distance from the main village. They have, therefore, to depend mainly upon non-agricultural labour. But in obtaining the latter, they have an advantage over the Chammars of the main village because the hamlet is about one and a half miles to the principal sources of non-agricultural employment, the railway station and the cement factory. Moreover, the non-agricultural workers among them aim at finding permanent or semi-permanent employment; very few are casual labourers.

Patterns of Labour

Agricultural Labour

Agricultural labour is done mainly by the women; men prefer non-agricultural work. There are two reasons for this. Firstly, men do non-agricultural work because it pays better. The wages in non-agricultural work were higher by 25 to 50 paise per day than those in agricultural work because it was better. The wages in non-agricultural work were higher by 25 to paise per day than those in agricultural work during the period of the study. Secondly, agricultural labour is preferred for the women, because it does not involves going out of the village, and is the next best thing to working in the family holding, which is the social objective of these Chammars. They would like their women to work only on the family holding and not for wages, just as the women of the Meenas cultivators do. But since most households find it necessary to supplement income from cultivation with that from off-farm labour, they prefer that their women work as agricultural labourers. An interesting result of this attitude was reflected in this study. During the initial stages of the household survey the heads of most households stated that their women were busy only with work in the home or on their family holdings, and did not do any wage labour? Even heads of non-cultivating households reported that their women did not do any labour and spent their time in looking after the livestock; most kept a few animals. But after some months when better rapport had been established with these people and it became know that this statement was not correct, information on work by women was obtained through a re-canvass of the question for all the households.

Non-Agricultural Labour

The principal forms of non-agricultural labour are the followings:

- Seasonal migration to the forests of Madhya Pradesh to make wood charcoal;
- Migration to stone quarries in the Medak area of Kotah district, located about 25 miles to the south of the village;
- Labour on the railway;
- Permanent service in the cement factory, or its quarries; and
- Casual non-agricultural labour.

Seasonal migration to the forests of Madhya Pradesh has been a distinctive feature of the economic life of the Chammars (and other labouring castes) of this area for several decades. There are many old men both in the main village and the hamlet who can recall going to these forests for 30-40 years and of their parents' migration before them. The people going to the forests leave their homes in November, December or January after harvesting the kharif crop. They stay in the forests for 5 to 8 months and return home in June or early July, just in time for taking up kharif cultivation again. They have to come back in time even if they have no land, because no work can be done in the forests during the rainy season. Migration is by families. The presence of the women is essential for cooking food or looking after the huts when the family lives in the forests. Moreover, the women and the children work and make a sizable contribution to the family income. An average family, with both husband and wife working, usually has a net saving (after meeting expenses of living in the forests) of Rs. 300 to Rs. 400 during one working season.

This migration has played a very useful role in the economy of the Chammars, especially during the recent transitional period. It has helped them absorb the shock of loss of income from leaving their traditional occupation and meet the expenses (e.g. of buying bullocks, clearing land, building huts etc.) for starting cultivation in their new settlements. But in spite of these it is not looked upon with favour by the Chammars now, and as local employment opportunities increase, more and more of them are turning to these in preference to going to the forests. There are several reasons for the trend. Firstly, life in the forests is hard not altogether free from danger. Secondly, the work is exhausting and has a bad influence on health; long exposure to charcoal smoke has a tendency to cause lung diseases. Earnings are good; but since the money is paid in advance the worker is likely to fritters it away and remain chronically in debt. Finally, the work involves living away from home for long periods, with consequent disturbance to community life. But the migration still serves an insurance against poor times, and in a season in which the kharif crop is poor or local employment is scarce migration increases considerably. Thus, in the migration season of 1961-62, which followed a poor kharif crop, the number of persons going to the forests increased to 60 as compared to 36 in the previous season.

Migration to the stone quarries of Kotah district has started only during the last five years. But it is preferred to migration to the forests because wages are good, averaging about Rs. 2.50 per day, and as the quarries are only 25 miles away, it is not necessary for entire families to move. The men go alone leaving their families behind and visit them once or twice a week.

Work on the railway is the big source of local employment. But, all the persons engaged in it are young men from the hamlet. Wages are fairly good; a young man getting continuous employment makes about Rs. 50 per month. During the last few years, they have been also able to get employment for 6 to 8 months in the year and feel that they will become permanent employees in course of time.[19] Fairly good wages and the facility of commuting to work are the main advantages of this work. The worker does not have to leave his home and can even look after the family land and livestock in his spare time. Permanent service in the cement factory (or its quarries) is even better than the work on the railway. The minimum wage is Rs. 82 per month; those employed as skilled or semi skilled workers get much more. But the number of such workers is small, because it is difficult to get employment in the factory.

The casual labourers, most of them from the main village, find employment in odd jobs within the village and in various public works. The public works in progress during the period of this study were laying of transmission lines from a hydro electric station at Kotah to Sawai Madhopur and other places, construction of an electric substation at Sawai Madhopur, and construction of a road linking Manpur with a town 20 miles away.

The factory and railway workers and those going to the stone quarries—40 in all—are available for continuous non-agricultural employment. The factory workers are in permanent service already: the others work in their non-agricultural jobs for most of the year, and could work longer if work was available. The leaders of the hamlet indicated that about 50 men could take up full-time, non-agricultural work without detriment to cultivation. They said that they would welcome establishment of any industry which would provide such employment. They are an agricultural people, no doubt: every land-owning family cultivates its holdings and in our discussions they never failed to press their claim for being allotted more land. But they see clearly that their futures lies in non-agricultural work.

Analysis

The influences which have contributed to the changes described in this study and some of the effects of the change may now be recapitulated. Among the influences, perhaps the most important is the feeling against caste, social inequality and untouchability which began with the social and economic changes of the twentieth century and which was given such powerful impetus by Mahatma Gandhi during the Independence movement. It will be recalled that uplift of these scheduled castes and abolition of untouchability formed the central planks of the programme of social reform which Mahatma Gandhi placed before the nation during this movement. The Chammars of this area began to feel the influence of theses ideas during the late 1920s and especially during the 1930s when large number began to go out of the area for labour in industrial centres and other towns.

But while these influences were creating a certain restiveness among the Chammars—a symptom of which was the riot in Lalsot villages in

1939,—the immediate provocation for change in occupation, through repudiation of traditional obligations and large scale migration appears to have been provided by the economic changes occurring after the entry of Japan in Second World War. As mentioned in the introduction the sharp increase in prices of agricultural produce and scarcity of foodgrains on the one hand and greatly increased availability of employment at high wages in industries and other works in towns on the other combined to produce intolerable strains on the *Jajmani* system. It will be recalled that quarrels between the Chammars and the Meenas and the large scale migration of Chammars started in this area only after 1953, when these economic changes had began to have effect.

High prices and scarcity of foodgrains also brought to the landowners a sharp realization of the value of land as an instrument of production. Earlier, in the two decades of agricultural depression, when produce prices had been very low, and the cultivators frequently found it difficult even to pay the land revenue, ownership and especially cultivation of land were not so highly prized. The average Meena or Jat cultivating owner had therefore no hesitation in giving some of his land for cultivation to Chammars and others. In fact, the opposite situation of land owners, especially of the high castes, having difficulty in finding cultivators for their land was quite common. But with increase in prices of agricultural commodities, land acquired a new value, and land owners especially of the cultivating castes were less willing to give it for cultivation on the customary *batai* basis.

This tendency was aided by the growing realization of impending land reforms. The Indian National Congress had propagated its objective of land to the tiller for a long time, and was committed to its achievement through abolition of *Jagirdari* and *Zamindari* and other measures. The people of this area had known about these ideas. But these began to acquire a real significance for them only in the later War years, when people realized that the end of the War might bring major political and economic changes in the country and that the land reforms, including abolition of *jagirdari* and grant of right in land to any one who was cultivating it at the time, might be the most important among these. The steady rise in population also helped the process, because increasing number of cultivators found that their holdings were sufficient only for the growing numbers in their own families. It will be recalled that the Chammar leaders of the hamlet of Manpur, and of nearly all the villages covered by the survey of migration had mentioned that they had left their own village because they were having difficulties in obtaining land for cultivation.

Even after making allowance fir their unwillingness to talk about the quarrels with the cultivators arising from their refusal to do flaying and *beggars*, it has to be recognized that difficulty in obtaining land was a contributory factor in the migration of Chammars.

Another aspect of land policy of the new Rajasthan government has been to give preference to the landless, especially of the scheduled castes, in allotment of culturable wastelands for cultivation. The operation of the policy in this *tehsil*, where large areas of such lands were available, has greatly accelerated the process of occupational change among the Chammars. These lands have acted like a powerful magnet drawing the Chammars towards them. It must be made clear, however, that availability of such lands is not essential for the change in occupation of the Chammars, because change has taken place in other parts of this district, in other districts of Rajsthan, and in other States of northern India in which such lands were not available and no migration took place. But it has enabled the community to absorb the tensions created by the change. The majority of the Chammars have become cultivating owners and are better of than before. The Meenas and other traditional cultivators have also more land for themselves, and are happy with this result of the change however, keenly they might resent the other effects. On the other hand, in other parts of the district (e.g. the Hindon *tehsil*, 60 miles to the north of Sawai Madhopur) where the pressure of the population on land is high and Chammars have not been able to get much new land for cultivation there is keen competition between them and the other cultivators for the very small area of culturable waste lands that are available for the allotment, and there is also greater tension.

Abolition of *Jagirdari* itself assisted the change in several ways. First, it removed a powerful local influence which was for preservation of tradition and against change. It has been explained in the introduction that the *Jagirdars* were active in support of *Jajmani system*. Secondly, they did not allow any castes to become too assertive or powerful or social tensions to develop within their villages. The attitude of curbing "unhappiness" which was perhaps necessary for preserving their own position at the apex of the local power structure often worked against the Meenas, who were naturally the most powerful castes in the villages. But it also meant discouraging the aspirants of other castes which might disturb the traditional structure of social position and power. The influence of the *jagirdars* in curbing local tensions has been very clearly explained in this study; there were no quarrels between the Chammars and the cultivators and no emigration of the former in the *jagirdars'* villages in the western part of the *tehsil*.

During the 1950s the political and administrative change and special measures for uplift of scheduled castes proved to be noteworthy influences. These did not initiate the change in occupation of the Chammars or their migration, which were already under way. But they were major factors in acceptance by the rest of the community of the Chammars' right to give up their traditional occupation to seek a higher social status, and of the need for improvement in their economic and social condition. The political system is based on adult suffrage. Every politician understands the importance of the large vote bank of the scheduled castes in such a system and is anxious to win it. Among the Chammars themselves, realizations of the power of their number grows with every successive election. Moreover, reservation of seats for the scheduled castes in legislatures, *Panchayat* and other bodies has produced a crop of young leaders who understand the mechanism of the political system, are keenly aware of the numerical strength of their caste and are anxious to exploit it.

The establishment of *Panchayats* has made a major contribution in this process. In their absence, the influence of the political system would have been felt only at the time of the general election. But with them, it is felt all the time. The vary fact that Chammar members sit as equal with others in the *Panchayat*s makes the villages aware that social equality has come to stay. Moreover, every *Sarpanch* realises that the scheduled castes vote could be decisive in his election. The *Sarpanchas* of both Manpur and Raipur have been elected in the last election on the strength of the scheduled caste vote. There are many others in the area who are in a similar position.

Besides, the influence of the political process, the entire educational and propaganda machinery of the state has been directed towards spread of the ideas of social equality, abolition of untouchability and uplift of the scheduled castes. The intelligentsia which forms the bulk of the political leaders, official and the educators in rural areas also support this change. The other villagers under influence of the new ideas propagated by these educated people are less willing to assert their traditional superiority over the scheduled castes or to observe untouchability, which they are beginning to realize, is an offence under the law.

Finally, the fact that the Meenas, the principal cultivating owners in the area, do not have a very high social status has helped in the process of improvement of social status of the Chammars. This has worked somewhat as follows. The Chammars feel that the Meenas are not a high caste that

Meenas in other parts of Rajasthan are backward and depressed; but those of this area enjoy good social status and have risen to the position of the dominant caste only because they own and cultivate land. They have a applied the analogy to themselves and gone on to argue: "if we stop our 'defiling' work and get land for cultivation we can also become the equals of the Meenas: for, if Meenas can be cultivating owners, what is wrong with us?" But, if the bulk of the cultivators had belonged to a caste with recognized high status (e.g. the Rajputs or even the Jats); it is possible that the social change among the Chammars would have been less easy or less peaceful.

Effects of the Changes

The change had given the Chammars a powerful urge for economic and social advance. They are engaged in a constant endeavour to get more land for cultivation, though further progress in this is slow because of shortage of suitable unoccupied land and increasing competition from the traditional cultivators, especially the Meenas. They are also keen to get industrial employment and to climb up the occupation ladder through education and learning of new skills. Having a tradition of migration in search of labour, they were the first to go to work in the cement factory and its quarries and they form the largest constituent of the labour force in these. Most of them are still unskilled labourers; but the younger men are learning industrial skills, and getting better paid jobs as skilled or semi skilled workers. They are also quick at availing of the new employment opportunities in public works like the railway. Some enterprising young men are going into contract work, especially building and labour contracts in which they have an advantage because most of the labourers are men of their own caste. The Chammars living in larger villages or in villages nearer the town (e.g. Chainpur) are keen to send their boys to school (including high school) with the result that the number of young men with high school education is increasing slowly but steadily.[20] Many of these young men have availed of the scholarship given by the government for education of the scheduled castes. They are keenly aware that a proportion of the jobs in government service are reserved for the scheduled castes, and look forward to such service as their career in life.

Moreover, because of their association with non-agricultural and industrial labour, the Chammars have greater contact with towns than the pure cultivators like the Meenas and the Malis and are more affected by urban consumption partners and ways of thinking. This was noticed only in Manpur where the Chammars of the hamlet, were seen to be much ahead of the Meenas and the Malis in use of durable, urban type consumption goods such as bicycles and wrist-watches. Accordingly, the Chammars are not merely being lifted from being almost the lowest economic and social group within the village to equality with the cultivating owner castes; but in terms of many indicators of economic process, they are well ahead of the letter.

The change has also given the Chammars a powerful impetus for social advance. Beginning with change of name to Berwa, they have made a number of changes in individual or group behaviour—Vaishnavite religious worship, greater attention to personal cleanliness, discouraging women from labour outside the home or the family holding, adoption of customs of the Meenas or the high castes in marriage (Chapter 5), all of which are motivated by a powerful desire to be accepted as a clean caste by the rest of the community.

These changes in occupation and social conditions of the Chammars have had interesting results on the other sections of the community and the attitude of different castes to these are extremely significant and revealing. The Chammars repudiation of their traditional occupation and obligations has given the *jajmani* system a blow from which it can't recover. It has demonstrated that a determined group, could repudiate these obligations with success, and could even be better off in the process. The lesson has not been lost on the other castes, several of which have followed the Chammars to the extent of leaving their customary obligations to the community while they continue to practice their traditional occupations. Thus the *Nais* (barbers), while they continue to do the barber's work have stopped cleaning utensils. Similarly, the *Kumbhars* (potters), while continue to make pots have stopped drawing water from wells. The change is so widespread that it is extremely difficult to get any one to perform these services even in towns like Sawai Madhopur.

It has been explained earlier that the attitude of the traditional cultivating-owner castes like the Meenas has been hostile to the change. The phase of violent quarrels is over; but resentment against the Chammars persists. The reasons for these are both economic and social. Stoppage of flaying and leather work by the Chammars has caused serious economic loss to them. Moreover, they cannot obtain any longer the *beggar* services which the Chammars rendered. On the other hand, the Chammars are now competitors for allotment of culturable lands and claim preference on grounds of being landless and a scheduled caste. The Meenas also resent the fact that the Chammars, a large caste numerically, have become a major political force in the area. They have themselves realised this fact only recently: their domination of the *Panchayat Samiti* and a large number of *Panchayat*s in the area has become effective only after the elections in 1960. The Chammars on their part see the Meenas as their main opponents and obstacles to further progress. The memory of having to leave their villages is still fresh, and they encounter opposition from the Meenas in land allotment every day. The sentiments expressed by the Chammar leaders of the hamlet of Manpur (and also of Chainpur) that "the Meena dominated *Panchayat Samiti* will do nothing for us" is widely shared by the Chammars in this area.

In contrast, the high castes, though lacking in any great enthusiasm for the change, have not shown any active opposition to it. They understand the social implications of the change—decline in untouchability, the Chammars' aspiration to social equality with the cultivating owner castes and their adoption of Vaishnative worship and some of the customs of even the high castes. They see all these things happening and the orthodox among them are not happy. On the other hand, the educated young men, who have been influenced by the new ideas of social equality, and have a keen consciousness of the injustice of untouchability and other social disabilities suffered by the scheduled castes, are on the whole sympathetic to the Chammars. Indeed, it is most likely that as these trends continue and the Berwa Chammars, in course of time, make a claim for being recognized as a clean caste, the Brahmins and other high castes will not oppose them; opposition, if any, will come from the Meenas and other cultivating castes. The Brahmins will have no difficulty in making out of the Berwas, another caste of clean cultivators like the Meenas of this area and so many others in adjoining districts of Rajsthan.

Thus, opposition to the advance of the scheduled castes comes mainly from the traditional cultivating owner castes: the high castes are either indifferent or sympathetic. The attitude of the latter does not conform to the popularly held stereotype, that the high castes are opposed to abolition of untouchability or social inequality or that the impetus for continuance of these comes from them. This might have been the case in the past, it is not so in this area at present. Moreover, the opposition of the cultivating owner caste is not based on religious or ritualistic conditions: the main reasons for it are economic and social.

The changes in the occupation and social status of the Chammars have made a major contribution to social efficiency and in some ways also to social integration. Earlier a large caste, forming about one tenth of the entire rural population, was condemned to the lowest position in society because one of its several economics activities (flaying of carcasses) was considered defiling. The numbers belonging to it were much in excess of the numbers required for doing the work. An idea of the disparity between the numbers in the castes and the numbers required for the work may be had from the fact that while Manpur has 40 households of Chammars (in the main village), the entire work of flaying is now being looked after by 6 households of *Bhangis*—who do it in addition to scavenging! Similarly, while there are 35 houscholds of Chammars in Raipur, the flaying work is now being looked after by just two households of *Bhangis*. The situation in other villages from which Chammars have not moved is similar.

It has been mentioned that the *bhangis* do not do the work of flaying with care and that there is so much wastage of hides that villages like Raipur which were self-sufficient in leather earlier have to import leather now. If the movement against lifting of carcasses spreads further (it is already of regional occurrence), the problems of disposals of dead animals of on the one hand and supplies of leather and leather goods on the other may assume serious proportions. Secondly, it is possible that similar movements may develop among castes practicing other "dirty" occupations, e.g., *Bhangis* (scavenging), *Khatiks* (slaughter of sheep and goats). Therefore, for social progress to be ensured and no caste to remain condemned to a low social status because of association with a "dirty" occupation, technological change, which takes the 'dirty' aspect out of such occupation, is essential. The example of scavenging will make the point clear. It is considered to be the dirtiest of all occupations. But there is no stigma against its modern counterpart working as plumber or sanitary engineer and people from all castes, including the Brahmins, are doing this work in the cities.[21] This is true also of leather work to some extent. There is large number of high caste Hindus among technicians in modern tanneries and among the owners of shoe shops in cities though actual shoe making and tanning are still done by people of Chammars or equivalent castes. It is the author's belief that as the "dirty" aspects of these occupations are eliminated through technological advance, more and more members of high castes will be prepared to enter them and the prejudice against them will decline. Such technological change is undoubtedly expensive; but the social cost of not making it will be higher. The need of social integration and making all sections of society equal participants in economic and social progress make such technological change imperative.

Footnotes

1. For an account of changes experienced by Chammars in an eastern U.P. village, see Bernard S. Cohn: The Changing Status of a Depressed Caste, in Mackim Marriott; *Village India,* Chicago 1955.
2. The word *Berwa* is used only for Chammars of this and certain neighbouring districts. Apparently, it stands for a distinct ethnic group among the large number of such groups which practice these occupations in the different parts of northern India and are given the generic name of Chammars (from Sanskrit Charmakar, lit., worker in leather). The group, since it has stopped flaying and leather work, resents the use of the word 'Charmakar' preferring to be called *Berwa*. Use of the word '*berwa*' would have been quite appropriate and, in fact, better than 'Chammar'. But in this study the word 'Chammar' has been used in preference to *Berwa* or *Berwa* Chammars, only because the former brings out more clearly the social changes which forms the subject of this study and also aides in understanding the attitudes of the other castes towards the group
3. In 1931, they formed 11.5 per cent of the rural population; figures for later years are not available in the Census reports.
4. *Begar* (lit: forced work). The *Begar* system was part of the feudal way of life, under which different castes were required to perform specific tasks for the *jagirdar*, and the village community. Thus the *Nais* (barber) had the obligation to clean utensils, the *Kumhars* (potters) to draw water from wells, the Chammars to bring fuel, and do field labour and other miscellaneous work. These obligations were in addition to the occupational obligations of the castes.
5. The circle of a *Patwari* in this *tehsil* consisted of one to six villages, with a population of between 3000 and 5000.
6. In this connection the author's experience may be of some interest. He learnt about the change in occupation and social status of the Chammars soon after his arrival in the district. But the facts about the conflicts between the Chammars and the cultivators, and especially about the extent of the migration of Chammars and their settlements in new villages, came to his notice only slowly, over a period of months.
7. A raised platform along the front wall of the house used by the men as a place for sitting and gossiping.
8. The figures exclude Sawai Madhopur town, the cement factory township, and the 'villages' comprising the workers' colony of the quarries of the cement factory.
9. '*Samvat*', the year of the Bikrami Era. This era was used for most official purposes during the time of Jaipur state; is still used for revenue records by the Rajsthan Government, and is in common use in this area. The original figures had to be collected by the years of this era, because villagers invariably use this calendar.

10. Under the revenue laws of Rajasthan, land classified as grazing land cannot be allotted for cultivation.
11. All the temples in the village are Vaishnavite temples in which Vishnu (god of preservation in the Hindu trinity), is worshipped is one of his several incarnations. Sri Krishna, the hero of *Bhagawat Gita*, is the most popular incarnation of Vishnu in this area and is worshipped most.
12. This agreement was observed during 1961. The Chammars took out their procession early in the afternoon and had brought it back by about 5 p.m., when the main procession started. The desire of the scheduled castes to take out procession on this festival and the caste Hindus' opposition to it have led to several quarrels in villages of this area. Thus in 1960, there was a violent quarrel between the high castes and the *Rehgars* in a large village, located about 30 miles to the north of Sawai Madhopur.
13. During the winter of 1961, two *Rehgar* families from a neighbouring district of Madhya Pradesh had camped in the village.
14. Data of this survey have not been used in this study.
15. The installation of the idol was done in January 1963. On this occasion, about 6000 Chammars were fed in a giant caste feast, which cost about Rs. 3000.
16. The author was treated to a most delightful recital of *bhajans* (devotional songs) of Raidas and other poet-saints of the Bhakti Movement by the old Chammar who serves as their priest. Bhakti Movement, a movement for religious reform was at its height between the 15th and the 17th century. Many prominent religious teachers of North India were associated with it. They emphasized equality of man before God. advocated love of God and *Bhakti* (devotion to him) as the sole means of personal salvation: many expressed themselves against the caste system. One of these leaders was Raidas (or Ravidas), a Chammar from Varanasi. In large parts of North India he is regarded by the Chammars as their patron-saint and hero.
17. An instance of a caste giving up drinking in an effort to reform itself came to the author's notice during his visit to the area in July 1963. The *Rehgars* of the area are notorious for heavy drinking at marriages but in May 1963, a meeting of *Reghars* of 18 villages decided that they will not drink at marriages in future. The meetings were held in Raipur because *Rehgars* of the village have traditionally been *Chaudhries* (recognized leaders) of the caste in the area and because initiative for convening it was taken by two *Rehgar* leaders of the village. One of them has extensive political contacts including those with a member of parliament in New Delhi. When asked what had made them take this initiative they explained, "Our people waste much money on drinking at marriages. Some of them drink so much that they lie unconscious for a night or more. Others laugh at us. They also explained that the decision was being adhered to by the *Rehgars* of all the villages concerned and that the movement was spreading to other villages.
18. The school was opened in July 1963.

19. In 1962, they were expecting to get employment throughout the year, as work on doubling the railway line had started.
20. Several school teachers whom the author met during his visits to villages commented on the eagerness of Chammar and *Rehgar* boys to do well at school.
21. In post-Independence years, Indians have bought several reputed European firms of sanitary engineers. Besides, in cities like Delhi hundreds of people of high castes have set themselves up as sanitary engineers and contractors.

3

Conflict in Village Institutions

A Case Study

The problem of conflict in popular institutions, especially the *Panchayats* and the *Panchayat Samitis*, has been attracting increasing attention recently. Such conflicts, "group rivalry" or "party politics"[1] as it is loosely called, is a noticeable attribute of many of these institutions, and one which worries many policy makers and students of rural development programmes. Legislators, social workers, and officers (like the collectors and the *vikas adhekari*) who work with the village leaders and observe the working of village institutions come across numerous instances of such conflict. They may see rival groups in a *panchayat* taking their disputes to the *Panchayat Samiti*, marshalling support in the *samiti* for their respective contentions, or approaching different officials and non-officials for their support. Frequently, these disputes are brought to the collector or *vikas adhikari* for decision. The most common form of the conflict in the *panchayats* is that between the *Sarpanch* and his supporters and their opponents, who generally include the defeated candidates for the post of the *Sarpanch*. "Ineffectiveness" of the *panchayats* i.e., their poor performance in mobilizing participation for development works or in levying taxes is frequently attributed by the village leaders to these divisions and conflicts.

The subject of conflict in village institutions often comes up in meetings of the *Panchayat Samitis*, block and district level seminars, training camps for village leaders and various other places where rural problems are discussed. Here again the view that conflict leads to ineffectiveness of institutions is often repeated. The further view—that the formation and working of the *panchayats* have themselves contributed to conflicts and group rivalries within the villages and "destroyed" the unity of the villages—is also expressed frequently. The elective process is blamed as being the root cause and starting point of all these conflicts. These feelings against conflicts in village institutions and their contribution to ineffectiveness of institutions and increasing discord and conflict within the village, are not confined to the village, block or district levels. They are shared by many political leaders, officers and policy makers at the state and even national levels.

Concern with this problem arises partly from the fact that in a good deal of the thinking preceding the establishment of the *panchayats*, harmony and accord within the village and in the working of these institutions was held up not only as ideals but as attainable objectives. It was thought that these institutions would promote harmony within the village, partly because they would take power away from such interested and powerful persons as the village money-lenders, the land lords (*Jagirdars* in this area), the small town lawyers, and the village level revenue officials like the *Patwaris*, who had exploited the villagers, encouraged conflicts, and curbed growth of initiative and self-reliance among villagers. Unanimity in elections to *panchayats* was and is still held as a desirable objective, because it is considered to the starting point of harmonious working of the institutions[2]. Therefore, evidences of conflict in institutions and especially the view that working of the institutions itself contributes to increasing discord and conflict within the villages is very disturbing.

This study is concerned with conflict in the village and in village-level institutions—the *panchayat* and the cooperative society. It analysis the working of village institutions against the background of inter-personal and inter-group relations in the village. This approach has been adopted because of the belief that the working of village institutions is but one aspect of the functioning of the village as a social system. In Raipur, the village selected for the study, conflict was known to be pronounced. A village of this type was deliberately chosen to bring out more clearly the morphology and physiology of conflicts—the form which conflict takes, the various ways and issues through which it is expressed, and the factors which contribute to it. Raipur is not an average village or *panchayat*, and the pronounced conflicts found in it are not found in the majority of the *panchayats* in this area. Rather, it is a problem village. It could even be called a sick village. The considerations underlying its selection are not those of the statistician who selects a sample or the average to obtain a view of the larger whole: rather they are those of the pathologist who studies the sick to discover the causes of sickness.

The main facts about population, land use, cropping patterns, castes, and economic activity relating to the village had already been collected in the course of earlier studies, so it was possible to proceed directly to the study of village institutions. Informal discussions (without questionnaires) with key respondents were the principal method of the study. Such discussions were held with the *Sarpanch* and members of the present *panchayat*; the various ex-*Sarpanchs*; some of the defeated candidates for the offices of the *Sarpanch*; the chairman and the prominent members of the cooperative society; the secretary of the *panchayat* and the cooperative society; and persons who were reported to be leaders of particular castes or prominent in village affairs, weather or not they had ever held any office in village institutions. In addition several meetings of the cooperative society were attended. Discussions and meetings were held with various stakeholders. One of the *panchayat* meeting was styled as a meeting of the Gram Sabha[3] by the *Sarpanch*. But it was observed that the composition of this meeting was no different from that of the other meetings of the *panchayat*. It was also attended by same kind of people—members of the *panchayat*, other village leaders, and some onlookers—as the other meetings. There were no women present in any meeting of the *panchayat*, although there are two women co-opted members.

The records of the *panchayat* and the cooperative were examined in detail to obtain factual data on casework, taxes, annual budgets and expenditure on development works in case of *panchayat*; and on loans advanced, recoveries, over dues and distribution of agricultural supplies in case of the cooperative. Later, records were examined of cases in which appeals against the decisions of the *panchayat* had been filed with the *Panchayat Samiti*.

The 'revenue' disputes of the village—i.e., land disputes arising from encroachments on *rastas* (paths), from grazing in cultivated lands and pastures, etc.—were discussed with the village leaders, the *patels*, the *patwari* of the village, and the *tehsildar* of the area.[4] These disputes are a major source of conflict in the village. It may be recalled that among the Brahmins of this village there are 11 *patwaris*. Consequently, the issues in each revenue dispute and the legal rights of different parties are very well understood; the opposing factions are very well (often too well) briefed about their own "wrongs" done by their opponents, and there is great interest in these matters in the village.

The study begins with a historical review of the functioning of the *panchayat* since its formation in 1948. The working of the different *panchayats* formed since 1948 has been described in detail, because the *panchayat* was found to be the main institution in which group conflicts were expressed and the varying alignments of individuals and castes were reflected. The cooperative was much less important from this point of view: it was established much later and had had only a brief career as an effective institution. Its working has, therefore, been described more briefly. One section of the study is devoted to a description of the major disputes in the village. The concluding section contains some observations on the problem of conflict in village institutions.

Working of the Panchayats: A Review

The First Panchayat (1948-52)

The first *Panchayat* was set-up in the village in March 1948 under the Panchayat Act of the then Jaipur State. It was formed by nomination and could be considered "an assembly of village elders". It consisted mainly of people who because of their traditional position of prestige and authority in the village, deriving from large land holding or official positions, were recognized as leaders either of the village or of important castes. They were all men of middle or old age. Most of them have continued to play a prominent part in village affairs and are still recognized as leaders of the village or of their castes, weather they occupy any positions in the *panchayat* or not. The nomination to the *panchayat* was made by the *tehsildar*, who had visited the village for this purpose, based on a consensus of opinion of the assembled villagers. Several of the persons nominated to the *panchayat* were not very anxious for this position: but were persuaded by the other villagers to accept it. Their hesitation arose largely from their ignorance of the objects and functions of the new institutions. Moreover, as the village leaders explained, the attitude of the villagers towards the State at that time had an element of fear in it, and they were not over-anxious to be associated with state sponsored activities.

Under the Jaipur Panchayat Act, the *Sarpanch* was indirectly elected by the members of the *Panchayat*. In addition, the act provided for appointment of a *sabhapati* (chairman), who functioned as an elder statesman and adviser to the *panchayat*, especially in its case work. Hiralal, the first *Sarpanch*, was a Mahajan belonging to a prominent village family which had at one time functioned as keepers of village land records and collectors of the land revenue for Jaipur State. He continued as *Sarpanch* till 1952. In 1957, when the large sized cooperative society was established in the village, he was elected its first Vice Chairman. For some time now he has had no official role, but continues to be a leader of the high castes and an influential person in the village. The first *sabhapati* was an elderly Kayastha, a retired Mir Munshi (senior revenue officials) of a small princely State in Central India, who was greatly respected in the village for his sagacity, knowledge, and honesty. The old man is still living, still respected, and is consulted by villagers, especially the high caste Brahmins and Mahajans, in their personal affairs. But he has never contested an election nor been formally associated with any village institution since then.

The *panchayat* was given both judicial and administrative functions under the Act. But its powers were limited. Thus, it could not try criminal cases, and its civil jurisdiction was also limited to cases of the value of Rs. 20 only. Such powers as sanctioning mutations of land, recommending allotment of cultivable wastelands for cultivation, giving permission for construction of *pucca* houses in the village *abadi*—all of which are the chief sources of power of the present *panchayat*—were not vested in it. The *panchayat* had authority to give permission for construction of *kutcha* houses only.

The *panchayat* had been given powers of taxation under the Act and did make an attempt to levy the house tax as well as a tax on several professions. But its taxation effort was not very successful. The taxes were resented and there were protests against them from all sections of the village. The *Rehgars* took their protest to the state Government and were successful in getting the order of *panchayat* cancelled. Collection of taxes had been poor from the beginning; but after this decision of the government, no serious effort at collecting taxes was made by the *panchayat*. Consequently, its income remained meager—it was derived mainly from the operation of the cattle pound—and it could not do much in the way of undertaking development activities. But it must be said to its credit that it spent money on meeting two of the urgent needs of the village, conservancy and provision of watering place for the cattle.

The Second Panchayat (1952-54)

The first *panchayat* was succeeded by another nominated *panchayat* with a very similar composition. The old *sabhapati* and several of the members continued; but there was a new *Sarpanch*, Ramlal, an energetic, development-minded, forward looking Brahmin. He continued as *Sarpanch* in the third *panchayat* also and played an important part in the various development activities which were undertaken during the period of the *panchayat*.

The second *panchayat* continued the elementary civic activities of the first *panchayat* and also levied house and shop taxes. But collection of taxes continued to be poor, so that its income and activities also remained small. The period of this *panchayat* is best regarded as a 'period of waiting' for establishment of the new elected *panchayat*. A new Panchayat *Act* providing for elected *panchayats*, with greatly increased judicial and administrative powers and developmental functions, covering all villages of Rajsthan, was already under consideration in the state legislature in 1952, when the second *panchayat* was constituted. The act was passed by the legislature in 1953, and the new *panchayats* were established the following year.

The Third Panchayat (1954-58)

The establishment of the third *panchayat* marks a distinct break with the past, because it was an elected *panchayat*, represented a much larger geographic area, had greater power, and enjoyed a wider range of functions. The area of the new *panchayat* comprised 13 villagers—Raipur and 12 small villagers in the vicinity, with a total population of about 5,000. It was given jurisdiction in both civil and criminal cases; its civil jurisdiction was increased to include cases up to the value of Rs. 100. Moreover, very important revenue administrative functions—like sanction of uncontested mutation[5], checking of *Gasht Girdawari* (inspection of standing crops conducted by the *patwari*, once in every cropping season), sales of *abadi* lands with power of granting permissions for construction of both *kutcha* and *pucca* houses—were given to it. The Panchayat Act of 1953 drew its inspiration from the ideas about the role and functions of the *panchayats* embodied in the Constitution of India and in the First Five Year Plan. It constituted a major advance towards the objective of giving the villagers the maximum initiative in administering their own affairs and making the *panchayat* the principal agency for their economic development and social advance.

The Act had provided for elections on the basis of adult suffrage. But voting was to be by show of hands; voting by secret ballot was introduced much later (1960). The election of the *sarpanch* and other members of the new *panchayat* of Raipur were held in the school building, where a large number of people (mostly men) of Raipur and other villages of the *panchayat* had collected. The principal candidates for the office of *Sarpanch* were Ramlal, the incumbent *sarpanch*, and a young Meena, son of an influential Meena leader of Raipur, who had died a few months earlier. This young man had no claim to leadership himself, but was being proposed for the post of *Sarpanch* because of the position his father had occupied among the Meenas of Raipur and neighbouring villages. His supporters had carried on a campaign of "vote for the Meena" among the Meena of the *panchayat* area. They had also campaigned among the other cultivating castes like the *Malis* and the *Gujjars* in favour of support for a cultivator as against a non-cultivator. Accordingly, the large number of Meenas and other cultivators who had assembled in the school building had come with a decision to vote for the young Meena. They are clearly in the majority and were quite confident of their success. The fact of their majority was recognized by the returning officer, and Inspector of the *Panchayat* Department of the State and he was going to declare the Meena elected, when an objection against his eligibility for election was raised by a prominent lawyer-politician of the area, a supporter of Ramlal. It was contended by him that the Meena was too young to satisfy the age requirement of the office of *sarpanch*. This objection was accepted by the Returning Officer, the candidature of the Meena was rejected and Ramlal was declared elected unopposed. The decision was great disappointment for the Meenas. Most of them felt that the "objection" was a clever trick played by the lawyer and other supporters of Ramlal, and as subsequent events have proved, went away with a determination to mobilize their forces more effectively the next time. The caste feeling—"vote for the candidate of your own caste"—appeared at the first election and has become progressively stronger with each election since then.

The election of the *Sarpanch* has been described in some detail because in this *panchayat*, as in most others in this area, interest was centered on it. There were two reasons for this:

(i) The *sarpanch* was elected by the votes of the entire electorate of the *panchayat* area, while the other members were elected from individual villages or wards; and

(ii) The next Act had vested a large measure of executive authority in the *Sarpanch*, making him the key figure in the *panchayat*.

Elections to the post of *panchas* (members of the *panchayat* other than the *sarpanch*) did not evoke much interest. The *panchayat* had 13 *panchas*, of who six were from Raipur and seven from the other villages. Most of the latter were returned unopposed, the village sending their *patel* or other persons with land and an established position of prestige and authority.

The third *panchayat* stands midway between the first and the present *panchayat* not only in point of time, but also in its composition and in the experience of the people with democratic elective process. There was a keen contest for the election of *Sarpanch* but not for election of most of the other members. Moreover, while people with urban contacts and education had begun to come in—one Brahmin member and to an extent the *sarpanch* himself belonged to this class—the majority of the members belonged to the old established class of village leaders.

This *panchayat* was also not very successful in raising tax revenues, and its financial resources remained meager. But since large sums of money began to be available for works and other development activities through the community development block, instituted in October, 1954, and other developmental agencies as the Jal Board[6] and the District Board, the period of this *panchayat* was one of considerable developmental activity. The first major work undertaken in Raipur was construction of the middle school building. Construction of the school, the largest community effort made by the village in recent years, was described to the author in detail, because many village leaders still take considerable pride in this achievement and talk about it enthusiastically. The story is somewhat as follows.

In the summer of 1955, the collector of the district received a letter from the State Government sanctioning a grant of Rs. 10,000 for construction of a building for a middle school in any village, which could raise a contribution of Rs. 15,000 of its own and construction of the building within a month according to the building plan given by the State Education Department. On completion of the building, the State Government would open a middle school in the village. Several large villages of this area wanted to accept this offer—the first of its kind; but the time allowed to construct the building was so short that most of them found it difficult to fulfil this condition. The lawyer-politician mentioned above, who was a member of the State Legislature at that time and took a keen interest in the affairs of Raipur, played an important part in obtaining the grant for the village. He held preliminary discussions with the village leaders and was assured that the conditions laid down by the government would be fulfilled. He then conveyed this assurance to the collector and obtained from him the assurance that the government would do its part if the villagers did theirs. Work on construction of the building was then begun, and from the account given, it appears to have been carried out in an emotionally charged atmosphere in which everybody was expected to do his best to make this endeavor of the village a success. Cash contributions were raised from mahajans, Brahmins the majority of the cultivators, and others who could afford to pay in cash.[7] The cultivators who could not pay cash brought stones and other building materials in their bullock carts. Potters brought earth and other materials on their donkeys. The labouring castes like the Chammars and the *Rehgars* contributed their share in the form of unskilled labour.

There is no doubt that this was a genuine mobilization of local resources in which all sections of the village participated. The work went on day and night, and the village succeeded in completing the building by the prescribed date. It is a handsome building, which not only meets the specifications of the Education Department but also has a gate with two beautifully carved elephant-heads. Thus satisfying the aesthetic sense of the villagers and expressing their feeling for the collective enterprise. It remains the pride of the village, and an account of its construction was given with pride, mixed with regret that it would not be easy to repeat the performance in the present atmosphere of "division" in the village.

The government grant was received, the middle school was opened as promised, and with this a major felt need of the villagers, especially of the high caste Brahmins and Mahajans, was fulfilled. The Brahmins were very keen on the opening of the middle school in the village, because they felt that this would save them the expenditure, inconvenience, and risk involved in sending their boys outside the village. As for the risk—several parents explained that there was always a risk of the young boys getting spoiled while living in town away from their parents! The other castes also wanted the middle school—having a middle school or a high school in the village is a matter of pride for all villagers; but the gains to them were not so immediate. This is one reason why the Brahmins and other high castes were in the forefront of the movement for the school building and paid the major share of the cash contribution.

These different attitudes are repeated in the current discussion of a building for a girls' primary school. The school, now located in a Brahmin temple, must have a building of its own for two reasons: accommodation in the temple is insufficient, and the Brahmins object to Moslem girls and girls of the schedule castes entering their temple. Construction of a new building for a school was started three years ago, when a grant of Rs. 2500 was received from the community development block. But it has not been completed. Even the money given to the block has not been fully spent; a balance of Rs. 1000 is lying unspent with the *panchayat*. The building requires another Rs. 2,000 for its completion, so that Rs. 1000 must be raised from contribution within the village. The

Brahmins and the Mahajans are ready to give their contributions, because most of the girls going to school are their girls, but they want the other castes to contribute also, and the others are not willing.

Construction of the middle school building, though considered by all to be a successful endeavour of the community, has left behind a certain amount of dissatisfaction and ill-feeling. Two complaints are generally made by the villagers. First, it is alleged that many persons, including several Brahmins and Mahajans, did not pay the contributions. However, this did not affect the progress of work at the time, but it has left the feeling that many leading people of the village did not do their bit. Secondly, it is alleged that the accounts of expenditure on this building, as also of other works undertaken by this *panchayat*, were not properly maintained. And since *sarpanch* Ramlal, who was the principal figure in all these construction activities, was also the owner of a small stone quarry and a lime kiln, materials from which were used for these works, there is widespread suspicion that he profited from the effort. Allegations of misappropriation and management of *Panchayat* funds began to be made against him towards the end of his tenure as *Sarpanch*; they formed the main theme of the attack against him when he sought re-election in 1959. As explained below, similar allegations are being made against the two succeeding *Sarpanchas* also. The allegations were a prominent feature of two of the *panchayat* meetings attended by the author.

A number of other construction works were also taken up by this *panchayat* in Raipur and other villages of the *panchayat* area. Pavement of the village bazaar and of a street in the *Rehgar* quarter, repairs to two drinking water wells, construction of a residence for the village level worker and purchase and renovation of the building for the office of the *panchayat* were the other major public works in Raipur. The works in the other villages included repairs to two drinking water wells and construction of a building for the primary school. All these works were done with grants from the community development block or other development agencies, plus contributions raised from the villagers.

Besides construction of public works, a number of other development activities were taken up and development institutions established during the period of the *panchayat*. The large-sized cooperative society organized in 1957 was the most important institution; others were the *Yuvak Mandal* (youth club) and the *Mahila Mandal* (women's club). Among the development activities, organization of adult literacy classes and various recreation programmes were the most important.

Altogether, this was a period of considerable development activity in the village. The community development block had been started only recently, and there was no dearth of funds to give to any village which was responsive and willing to raise its share of contributions. The Block Development Officer of the time appears by all accounts to have been an enthusiastic worker who was genuinely interested in rural development work. Within the village a favourable combination of factors enabled it to take advantage of this situation. There was a concentration of educated people who appreciated the value of the various activities sponsored by the community development block. There was an enthusiastic *Sarpanch* who was interested in construction works and had sufficient confidence of the villagers to be able to raise the necessary contributions. As a result, the village received much more than its share of funds for works and development activities and of attention from the block staff. The staff visited it frequently and brought important visitors. It was considered a "most progressive" village, ranking second in this respect among the villages of the block. All in all, the period of this *panchayat* was one of enthusiasms, useful construction activities and progress. It is unfortunate that this progress has not been sustained.

But even this *panchayat* could not solve the problem of building up permanent sources of revenue. It could not levy any taxes nor create any other source of sizable permanent income. Its income was derived mainly from sale of *abudi* lands, fines of the cattle pound and other charges connected with case work, and grants from government. Together these totaled about Rs. 3,000 per year; most of the money was spent on meeting the establishment expenses and maintaining elementary services, such as sanitation and street lighting. The small surpluses that remained were spent in small grants for construction works and for purchase and repair of the *panchayat* building.

The Fourth Panchayat (March 1959 to December 1960)

The second *panchayat*, formed under the 1953 Act had the same jurisdiction and functions as its predecessor. But there was one major difference. Five years' experience with the previous *panchayat* had demonstrated to the villagers the extent of its power, especially in case work, its role in development activities and the importance given to it by government in various administrative matters. In addition, it was known that the *Panchayati Raj* scheme of constituting *Panchayat Samitis* and *Zilla Parishads* was going to be introduced in the state in October 1959 and that under it the *sarpanch* would be the controlling authority for community development and several other rural development programmes. Consequently, interest in election to the *panchayat* was much greater than it had been five years earlier, and the struggle to capture the power vested in this institution now began in earnest. There were six candidates for the post of *Sarpanch*: two Meenas, two Brahmins of which one was Ramlal, the sitting *Sarpanch*, and two Mahajans. Each of the six seats of *panchas* allotted to Raipur and most of those allotted to the other villages were keenly contested. Caste, which had already made its appearance in the 1954 election, now came to the fore. There was a keen contest for the office of the *Sarpanch*, the principal candidates being Ramlal and Manphool, the latter a Meena of Raipur. Manphool's election slogan was: "vote for the Meena and preserve Meena solidarity". The result of the election showed a marked polarization of voting between the Meenas and non-Meenas and between Raipur and other villages of then *Panchayat*. Manphool won by a margin of about 100 votes. Further, the small villages, in most of which Meenas are predominant, returned Meena representatives. Manphool's success was also due largely to their votes. But, within Raipur, where they are in a minority, the Meenas did not do well. Manphool received only a small percentage of the votes cast and only two Meenas were elected *panchas*, the remaining four being non-Meena. The election shows also that younger people were coming into the *panchayat*. The new *Sarpanch* was about 35, and three of the six members returned from Raipur were also young. But most of the members from the other villages were middle-aged people from respected families who were sent on the strength of the status and prestige of their families or for their own reputation for sagacity and tact, to a body of elected representatives who approached the people on the basis of caste and their individual capacity to do things and to get things done for them.

The period of this *panchayat* was rather brief, a total of 18 months, and was marked by a sharp decline in interest in development activities and works. Construction of works already in progress continued, and a few small new works were started also. But the earlier tempo could not be maintained. There were several reasons for this. First, obtaining grants for works had become more difficult. After the formation of the *Panchayat Samiti* in October 1959 there was keen competition for grants among the *Sarpanches* of different *panchayats* who composed the *samiti*, and villages like Raipur could not maintain the favoured position they had enjoyed earlier. Second, the process of sanction and disbursement of grants began to take much more time. The new *Vikas Adhikari* (the new name for the block development officer) was not as keen to disburse moneys and get construction works completed quickly as his predecessor had been. He was conscious of the curbs on his powers under the new Act and the need to comply with the procedures prescribed by it. Furthermore, the situation within the village was also not favourable to maintenance of the earlier tempo of construction works. Most of the urgent need of such works had been satisfied; the new *Sarpanch* lacked his predecessor's flair for these works, and since he faced much stiffer opposition within the village, he found it difficult to raise contributions. Finally, the limitations or defects of the development institutions which had been set up in quick succession in the period of the previous *panchayat* were beginning to be seen by the villagers, who were growing less enthusiastic about development activities. The cooperative society was having difficulties: its members were not repaying their loans. The women's club and the youth club had failed to arouse enthusiastic response. The women's club had ceased to function altogether after a short period of activity. The youth club continued to function but interest in its activities was not great. It had become another area for election contests and display of personal rivalry among the educated and urbanized young men of the village and the majority of villagers had lost interest in it.

The Present Panchayat (December 1960 to-date)

Election to the present *panchayat* was held in December 1960 under the amended Panchayat Act of 1960. The new Act had made major changes in the area, jurisdiction, and functions of village *panchayat* in the State (Appendix I.3). The area of the village *pancayat* was reduced in order to bring the institution closer to the village people. The judicial function was given to the newly found *Nyaya Panchayat* (judicial *panchayat*) to reduce conflicts in village *panchayats*, some of which were due to exercise of judicial powers.

The area of the new *Panchayat* of Raipur was limited to the village of Raipur, and two new *Panchayats* were formed for the other villages, comprised in the earlier *panchayat*. A separate *Nyaya Panchayat* was formed, with its headquarters in Raipur and with jurisdiction over about 30 villages. But this reduction in the area and functions of the village *panchayat* did not reduce the struggle for office; as will be seen from the following account, it was in fact keener than ever before.

The *Panchayat* had 13 members including the *Sarpanch*. Of these, 11 members were to be elected and two women co-opted by the elected members. There were contests for 10 of the 11 seats of elected members, and only one person, a representative from the *Rehgar* ward, was returned unopposed. The contest for the post of *Sarpanch* was the keenest of all and caused excitement not only in Raipur but also in the surrounding villages. The main contestants were Manphool, the sitting Meena *sarpanch*, and Prem Kumar, an educated young Brahmin. The latter won by the margin of only two votes. The system of voting by secret ballot was introduced in *panchayat* elections for the first time. Prem Kumar attributes his victory largely to his success in educating his supporters in the correct use of the secret ballot. He explained that he had polled fewer votes than his opponent but had won the election because a large number of the votes caste for his opponent were marked incorrectly and had to be rejected: the voters were not familiar with the technique of marking ballot papers. He added that he himself had taken great pains to understand the new method and explain it to his supporters, that he had even got specimen ballot papers printed and voting seals made in order to demonstrate their use. An educated young man and a white-collar worker—he is a clerk in the cement factory; he understood the importance of this work. His opponent however did not pay much attention to this part of the 'election effort'.

The result of the election was a surprise and caused considerable excitement in the village. The votes were counted three times to dispel any doubts about the result. Prem Kumar and his supporters allege that their opponents were so furious that they would have started a fight if the administrative arrangements for the election had been less adequate or the Returning Officer had lost his nerve. Prem Kumar alleges further that he was actually afraid of a violent attack on his person for several days after the contest. It is not possible to say whether his fears had any basis, because there was no violence in fact, and the excitement subsided after a few days. But even though there was no actual violence, then or later, the feeling of keen rivalry aroused by the election has remained and affects the working of the *panchayat* at every stop.

An election petition was filed by Manphool in the court of the Magistrate concerned, but it was rejected after a few months and the election of Prem Kumar was confirmed.

Caste, which had already appeared as a major factor in the two previous elections, was the dominant influence this time. The cry "*vote aur beti Meena ko*"[8] went round the whole area and became the most important election slogan. In most small *panchayats* in which the Meenas formed the majority, Meena candidates were elected *Sarpanchs*. In multi-caste villages like Raipur, canvassing for support was mainly along caste lines, with each candidate appealing to caste sentiments, trying to capture votes of particular caste groups, and assessing his chances of success in terms of ability to mobilize the votes of the most numerous castes. The following analysis of the voting pattern in this election was given by Prem Kumar and confirmed by his opponent:

(i) All the Chammars and the *Rehgars* voted solidly for Prem Kumar. Among the other scheduled castes and the poor artisan-cum-labourer castes like Kumhars, the majority voted for him.
(ii) All the Meenas voted solidly for their own caste man. Manphool, and the majority of the *Malis* and the *Gujjars* also voted in his favour;
(iii) The votes of the high caste Hindus and the Moslems were almost evenly divided.

It will be seen that the main supporters of Prem Kumar were the scheduled castes. He claims that they supported him because of their antipathy for the Meenas and the fact that he and his young associates had been 'bold enough to champion the cause of these underprivileged people'. The hostility between the Meenas and the Chammars is particularly strong in this village, where the cultivators have not yet reconciled themselves fully to the economic loss which the change in the occupation of the chammars has caused them. But Prem Kumar's opponents allege that the scheduled castes supported him because of various promises he had made to them. They said that he had promised support to the Chammars in allotment of the *charagah* (pasture) land and to the *Rehgars* in awarding the contract for lifting carcasses.

Among the Brahmins, Prem Kumar had the support of a number of young educated white-collar workers; but most others were opposed to him. The reasons for this opposition are interesting. The chief reason is that Prem Kumar belongs to a family which was rather poor until recently and was never included among the leading Brahmin families of the village. His family land holding is small, and his father had worked as a cook in Calcutta all his life. The economic position of the family had improved only in recent years after Prem Kumar got a well paid white-collar job. Most of the Brahmins are, therefore, jealous of his rise. Second, for some time before the election, Prem Kumar and his supporters had been making allegations against the older high caste leaders of the village, including Ramlal, the Brahmin *Sarpanch* of the 1954-59 *panchayat*, and Hiralal, the Mahajan, who ha been the first *Sarpanch*, alleging that both these men, (and their associates) had exploited their positions in village institutions for personal advantage. This propaganda had antagonized a large number of Brahmins and Mahajans. These high castes still do not regard Prem Kumar as their leader and in any matter of village wide or even caste-wide interest, prefer to speak through their older leaders.

The election gave Prem Kumar and his supporters an absolute majority within the *panchayat*. Besides Prem Kumar himself six of his supporters were elected while only four members of the rival group were elected. With the addition of two women co-opted members, the former now have nine votes in the *panchayat* as against the opponents' four. Therefore, they can carry the *panchayat*, and the opposition can express itself only by talking against the *panchayat* in the village.

The Working of the Panchayat

Prem Kumar is an enthusiastic young man with a genuine interest in development activities. Before becoming *Sarpanch*, he had been active in the cooperative society and the youth club, and his main slogan in the election campaign was that he would take greater interest in development activities, a duty neglected by his predecessor. However, the actual record of achievement of the new *panchayat* is little better than of the previous *panchayat*. As no new grant for works has been given by the *Panchayat Samiti,* the *panchayat* has only been able to complete the works in progress and to begin two new ones for which grants had been given earlier. Two drinking water wells have been repaired, a street in the *Rehgar* quarter has been paved, and construction of the girls' school building has begun. The difficulties in obtaining grants room the *Panchayat Samiti* which had begun to be experienced by the previous *panchayat* are now much greater. The *samiti* is now dominated by members from small villages which were somewhat neglected during the period of the community development block. They are anxious to make amends for this neglect and to get the maximum grants for their villages. The result is that bigger villages like Raipur which had got large grants during the block period are not receiving many grants now. Secondly, since Prem Kumar is a vocal opponent of the ruling group in the *Panchayat Samiti*, he has not been elected to any of the standing committees which control distribution of grants and loans.

The *panchayt* cannot find any money for construction works from its own resources also, because the changes made by the new Act have made its financial position even worse than that of its two predecessors.

As its area has been greatly reduced, its income is much less than before. The grant from the State Government, which is a proportion of the land revenue paid by the villages within the area of a *panchayat*, has also been reduced for the same reason. Transfer of case work to the *Nyaya Panchayat* has meant loss of income from this source. On the other hand, the establishment expenses continue almost on the old scale, because a full-time clerk and a peon are considered to be minimum needs of the *panchayat* of an 'important village' like Raipur. The panchayat's present income is somewhat over Rs. 2.000. It is derived mainly from sale of *abadi* lands, grants for permission either to build houses or to make repairs and additions to these, operation of the cattle pound, and grants from the government. Nearly 40 per cent of it goes for establishment expenses and most of the remainder is spent on maintenance of services—conservancy, lighting the village *bazaar*, and maintaining the water hut where people drink water during the summer. Nominal grants are given to the library; to the youth club for cultural activities; to the middle school for celebration of the Republic Day and other national festivals; and to maintain the radio set in the *panchayat* office. The *panchayat* has not levied any taxes, nor does it propose to do so. The *sarpanch* fully understands the need for taxation and has repeatedly expressed himself in favour of it. Indeed, one of the main points made against him in the election campaign was that he, an urbanized educated young man, would impose taxes. But after election he found that opposition to taxes is too strong and extends to all sections of the village—including his own supporters.

The *panchayat* has also not contributed to development activities in other ways. Thus, it has not used its influence to improve the working of the cooperative society, the Women's Club or the Youth Club. On the contrary the *Sarpanch* and his associates are opposed to the group now in power in the cooperative society, and this makes the task of revitalizing the society more difficult. The *panchayats* are also expected to take an active interest in agricultural improvement in their villages. But this *panchayat*, like its predecessors, has not made any noteworthy contribution in this direction. Raipur does have a number of progressive cultivators and both during the period of the community development block and later, it has received more than its share of funds for agricultural improvement, together with attention of the extension staff. During 1960-61, for instance, 20 cultivators of the village received a total of Rs. 22,500 in lands and grants from the *samiti* for various agricultural improvement activities. Raipur is one of the two selected villages of the *samiti* (called 'laboratory villages') in which an intensive agricultural improvement programme is being carried out. Moreover, because of its nearness to *samiti* and district offices, it is visited frequently by the extension officers of the *samiti* and district level officers of the State department of Agriculture. As a result, its agricultural improvement activities are quite carefully supervised and new activities, such as soil conservation, have been taken up. But the *panchayat* has taken no interest in agricultural improvement work either by way of popularizing acceptance of any improved agricultural practice or by mobilizing voluntary labour of cultivators for any land improvement work. The only interest shown by the present *sarpanch* is his complaint that the loans and grants recently given by the *Panchayat Samiti*—most of these have gone to his opponents—have not been utilized for the purposes for which they were given

Case Work

Even within the limited area of administrative case work now left to it, there is a growing tendency among the villagers not to accept the decisions of the *panchayat*. Appeals against these decisions have become almost routine. Out of 146 cases decided by the *panchayat* since its formation, 88 cases were contested. Most "cases" are applications from individuals relating to such small matters as repairing one's house and cutting a tree standing within one's own courtyard. The uncontested cases are those in which no objection against the request is raised by anybody and the *panchayat* passes an order, usually in favour of the applicant. The cases in which an objection is filed are called "contested", because the *panchayat* has to give a decision after hearing both parties. It is true that there are some cases in which the dispute between the parties is of long-standing, connected perhaps with inter-family or even inter-caste quarrels. Appeals against the decision of the *panchayat* are unavoidable in such cases. But the majority of even the contested cases relate to small matters; the objections are of a trivial or routine nature, and the case should end with the decision of the *panchayat*. Therefore, a situation like the one in this village in which a large number of the contested cases (17 out of 88) are taken in appeal, is an indication that factors other than the substance of the objection are at work.

The appeals go to the administration standing committee of the *Panchayat Samiti* where they remain pending for several months. Thus, out of the 17 appeals made to this body during a period of approximately

18 months from the inception of the *panchayat* in December 1960 till the end of the study in June 1962, only eight had been decided. And of these, only two had been disposed of within less than six months. This is not to suggest that the time taken by the *Panchayat Samiti* in deciding cases was too long. It is comparable to the time taken in other courts and is the result mainly of the procedures which have to be followed by it. But, as soon as an appeal is admitted by the *Panchayat Samiti* a 'stay order' is issued by it, and the decision of the *panchayat* becomes inoperative. Therefore, irrespective of whether the decision of the *panchayat* is finally upheld by the *samiti* or not, the very fact that an appeal is admitted reduces the authority and effectiveness of the *panchayat*.

The decisions of the *Panchayat Samiti* in the eight appeals have been as follows:

(i)	Decision of the *panchayat* upheld	2
(ii)	Appeal rejected for other reasons	2
(iii)	Case sent back to *panchayat* (for Reconsideration of its decision)	2
(iv)	Decision of the *panchayat* reversed	2

Thus the decisions of the *panchayat* were upheld in only two cases and not upheld in four. Further, in one of these cases in which the *panchayat's* decision was upheld, the *samiti* had not sent the file back to the *panchayat* till the end of this study that is more than nine months after making the decision.

Since the *Panchayat Samiti* has not accepted the decisions of the *panchayat* in several cases and has delayed sending the file of an important case, an impression has been created in the village that it is unfavourable to the *panchayat*. This impression is shared by both the supporters and the opponents of Prem Kumar. They would have been inclined to form such an impression even otherwise, on the following consideration:

(i) That the Meenas are the dominant group in the *Panchayat Samiti*, but are in the opposition in the *panchayat*;

(ii) That Prem Kumar is very vocal in his criticism of the dominant Meena group in the meetings of the *Panchayat Samiti*; and

(iii) That Manphool, the defeated Meena candidates for *sarpanch* is a near relation of an important functionary of the *Panchayat Samiti*.

These happenings have converted a pre-disposition into a belief. Whether the belief has any basis in fact or not is not as important as the fact that it exists and is held by both groups in the village.

Allegations and counter-allegations have become a prominent feature of the political life of the village. The main allegation against Prem Kumar is that he is partisan in his approach, that he has shown partiality in all the cases brought before the *panchayat*, and that he is creating trouble for his opponents, especially the Meenas, by digging up old issues which go against them. He is also charged with dishonesty. It is alleged that the accounts of the public works executed by the *panchayat* are not properly maintained, are never presented before the village, and are not available for inspection. It is also alleged that Prem Kumar and his close associate, the Mahajan *Upasarapanch* (Vice President), keep panchayat funds for long periods for personal or business uses. Finally, it is alleged by his opponents that ever since he lost control of the cooperative society, Prem Kumar has been encouraging members not to pay the dues of the society and that poor financial situation of the society is due partly to this propaganda and partly to the faulty policies regarding advance of credit followed by him and his predecessor, Hiralal Mahajan.

Prem Kumar's main counter-charge is that the prominent members of the opposite group are corrupt. The charge of financial corruption is made openly, and the charge of moral corruption is made in confidence. He explains that the accounts of the *panchayat* were in disorder when he took over because the previous *Sarpanchas*, especially Manphool, had kept *panchayat* funds for long periods for personal use and had not maintained proper accounts of public works. He alleges that work on the building for the girls school was not started by Manphool because he had spent the money received from the *Panchayat Samiti* and had said that he could not start the project because contributions were not forthcoming from the villagers. Prem Kumar alleges further that he experienced great difficulty in taking charge of the office of *sarpanch* and that the accounts were given to him only in April, 1961, four months after his election. He explains that Manphool had received a substantial *taccavi* loan for the *Panchayat Samiti* and that he utilized this money to pay back the *panchayat's* money which he had already spent.[9] To support these charges, Prem Kumar explains that Manphool has only a small holding which he does not attend to properly and that his expenses are much more than his income. Prem Kumar has also accused Ramlal, the Brahmin *Sarpanch* of the 1954-59 *panchayat*, who did not support him in his election, of not having maintained the accounts of the *panchayat* properly and having utilized the *panchayat's* money for his daughter's marriage. Another prominent member of the opposing group, Shankar, a *patel*, who holds an important office in the cooperative society, is charged with being a tout. It is alleged that he had established good relations with village level officials of the police, the Revenue and the Forests, departments of the State Government and used to take money from the villagers in police and Revenue cases on promise that he would get these officials to 'fix' the cases in their favour. It is also alleged that by making appropriate arrangements with the forest guards, he used to encourage the cultivators to steal wood and other forest produce from the forests. This man is also accused of being addicted to drinking and eating meat himself and of encouraging these practices among young men of the village, including those of the high castes. The gravity of this last charge can be appreciated only against the background of the attitude towards eating meat and drinking in the village. The Brahmins and the Mahajans of this village (and this area) have traditionally been strict vegetarians and teetotalers. As long as they lived only in the village, there was no difficulty in enforcing the prohibition against meat and drink on members of their castes. But in recent years, with large numbers of young men going into government service, enforcement of the prohibition has become more difficult, and the leaders of these castes admit that some young men have begun to eat meat and to drink, especially when they are in the company of their officers or colleagues. The action of a person who takes meat or drinks only outside the village, is regretted, but is not considered so very bad, because it is not seen by any other villagers. But indulgence in meat or drink within the village is considered reprehensible, because it is an open violation of the values of the castes. There is also the danger that the practice may spread among the young boys. Both, meat eating and drinking are not merely considered bad, they are sinful. And meat-eating is considered the worse of the two. Therefore, any person who encourages high caste young men to indulge in these things within the village is considered by the people of these castes to be a "Centre of vice". The charge reflects on the man in the eyes of the other castes as well: the *Malis* are vegetarian and practically teetotalers, the Meenas have also been giving up these practices in recent years; and even among the scheduled castes, especially the Chammars, the current trend is in favour of giving up meat eating and drinking.

The bad management of the cooperative society is also attributed by Prem Kumar and his supporters to the fact that key figures in it now are dishonest. They explain that loan receipts are poor because the cultivators have no faith in these dishonest people, who make no effort to collect the money.

Perm Kumar denies the charges of being anti-Meena or anti-cultivator; but he admits that he had taken up disputed matters (like cattle grazing in cultivated fields and encroachments by cultivators on the village *rastas* (paths), which hurt some cultivators. He explains that in all these matters, the 'illegal' and 'unjust' doings of a few offenders are causing losses to other cultivators and inconvenience to all the villagers; that his predecessors had not done anything about them because they were under the influence of the offenders, some of whom are prominent leaders of the village, but that he has shown courage and taken these matters up. The charge of financial irregularities is stoutly denied by him. In his defense, he explains that he has begun construction of the girl's school building, which had not been taken up by the earlier *panchayat*. He maintains that the accounts are open for inspection by the villagers or the officers at any time and that this charge is being made by his opponents only to cover up their own financial irregularities. Finally, he and his associates claim: "We young men are honest, educated and competent. We want to eradicate corruption in the *panchayat* and in the village, and since we have educated government servants among us, we know how to do it. The older leaders see us as a threat to their authority and their 'corrupt' ways, and this is the main reason why they are so opposed to us."

Whatever be the truth of these charges and counter charges, the important fact is that they are freely made and believed in the village and are taken to the *Panchayat Samiti*, to local politicians, and to the block and district level officers. The result is that an atmosphere of complaint and counter-complaint, in which the integrity and motives of every one are suspect, has been created.

The Cooperative Society

The Raipur Large-sized Multi-purpose Cooperative Society was established in November 1957 with 331 members from 12 villages, of which nearly half (158) were from Raipur. Organization of the society was part of the programme of organizing large-sized societies which was being undertaken all over Rajsthan at that time. The staff of the community development block and the Revenue Department took an active interest. In this village the village level worker of the block and the *patwari* were active in organization of the society as were some prominent Mahajans and Brahmins of the village, including Hiralal Mahajan. The latter was elected the first Vice-Chairman[10] of the society. The response from the cultivators of the village was quite good, and more than half of them joined the society.

The society has been concerned mainly with agricultural credit. During its first year it advanced short term loans totaling about Rs. 30,000. The loans advanced in subsequent years, their recoveries and over dues are given in Table 3.1.

Other activities of the society have included distribution of improved seed (mainly of wheat), and of chemical fertilizers and pesticides, according to the programmes of the community development block or the *Panchayat Samiti*. It also owns three *charkhis* (hand operated presses for making *gur* from sugarcane) which are rented to the cultivators.

Table 3.1: Short Term Loans (*Rupees*)

Year	*No of Loans*	*Loan Amount*	*Recovery*	*Overdue*
1957-58	158	29660	–	–
1958-59	106	17480	30973	6166
1959-60	167	32914	22854	4054
1960-61	42	6936	16099	3179
1961-62	66	13840	5186	25000 (approximate)
Medium Term Loans in Rs.				
1960-61	23	29000	1050	–
1961-62	–	–	6004	2239

The society began to run into difficulties on its second year, because recovery of loans was poor. The position improved slightly in the next two years but deteriorated further during 1961-62. As a result, large over dues have accumulated, the Central Cooperative Bank of the district refuses to give any further loans to the society, and the Cooperative Department is thinking of classifying it as a 'D' (poor) society.

Three reasons are given for poor recoveries of loans and accumulation of over dues.

(i) Over dues of small amounts are said to be due to a misunderstanding of the rules of the society. Members who took small loans paid the amounts back after deducting the share money contributed by them. Most of them joined the society under the impression that its loans were, like the *taccavi* loans of government, long-term loans. But when they were required to repay the loans the very next year they did not want to have anything further to do with the society. They paid up the amounts borrowed, minus their share money. It was not explained to them that this was not possible under the rules of the society and that they must deposit the full amount first and then wait for refunds.

(ii) Small amounts ranging between Rs. 50 and Rs. 200 are owned by a number of poor members of the village—mostly of the Moslem *Faqir*, artisan and scheduled castes. It is alleged that the Mahajans and other money-lenders of the village persuaded these people to become members, got them loans from the society, and utilized the amounts for payment of debts owing to themselves. Thus the bad debts of the money-lenders were cleared but the society was saddled with loans to a large number of poor people. These people would have had difficulty in repaying the loans in any case; but it is alleged that the money lenders are telling them not to worry about payments.

(iii) Larger amounts ranging between Rs. 250 and Rs. 750 are owed by some influential persons of the village.

At the time of this study, the society was in the hands of the group opposed to Prem Kumar. The Chairman was a Brahmin white-collar worker, but the chief men in it were Shankar Patel, and the Meena who had unsuccessfully contested election for *sarpanch* in 1954. This group had been in power for about six months. Earlier Prem Kumar's group was in control, with Prem Kumar himself as Vice Chairman of the society and Hiralal as its secretary. It is clear that, like the *panchayat*, the cooperative society has also become a medium for expression of the group conflicts in the villages; and the fact that it is now in the hands of the group opposed to that controlling the *panchayat* makes its position more difficult. A concerted village-wide effort is needed to improve the management of the society; but such an effort cannot be made in the present situation.

The Major Disputes

Charagah Land[11]

This dispute is over some 150 acres of land situated on the south eastern boundary of the village. Part of the area (about 25 acres) is *talab* (shallow tank), which has water standing on it during the rains. This area is cultivated after the monsoons, because the water dries up in time for sowing the *Rabi* crop. The soil is quite fertile due to the deposition of silt from the adjoining hills. The remaining area (about 125 acres) is undulating land or the sandy bed of the stream feeding into the *talab*; it is fit only for grazing. However, the entire area is recorded as *Sawai Chak Banjar* (government owned cultivable waste) in the records of the Revenue Department and is therefore available for allotment for cultivation. The dispute concerns the cultivable 25 acres. It began about 20 years ago (1943) when an attempt was first made to cultivate the land. At that time, the Grow More Food Campaign had been started by the Government of India, and efforts were being made all over the country to increase the area under cultivation. A lawyer-leader tried to take over this land for his personal cultivation; he got it ploughed and seeded. The villagers resented this intrusion by an outsider, because the area had all along been used for grazing, and the *talab* was particularly useful as a watering place for the cattle. They presented a united front against him under the leadership of Hiralal, the *sarpanch* of the first *panchayat*, and some *patels* of the village. The latter prevented the labourers employed by the lawyer from cultivating the land. There was a quarrel. The lawyer had a criminal case instituted against the village leaders, and some of them, including Hiralal, had to remain in judicial lock up for a brief period. But the case failed in appeal in the Sessions Court, and all were acquitted.

Therefore, no attempt was made to cultivate the land for a long time. But as population increased and all other cultivable lands were occupied, attention was again directed towards this land. In 1959, some Meenas of the hamlet tried to cultivate it but the villagers persuaded them against it. In the meantime, the Chammars had also been trying to get the land allotted to them. They had made several applications for allotment and had gone to Delhi to obtain support from certain members of the parliament belonging to the schedule castes. But since most of the villagers wanted the area to continue to be used as grazing ground, they filled applications opposing allotment. In 1960, the Tehsil Land Allotment Committee, after considering the various applications, for allotment and against it, decided that the land should not be allotted. The opponents of allotments had also requested that the land be reclassified as *charagah* in the records of the Revenue department, so that it could not be allotted in future. But the committee did not make any recommendation regarding reclassification.

In 1961, some applications for allotment were again submitted to the new Tehsil Allotment Committee. This time, the Committee accepted the applications of two Meenas and one Chammar of the village and allotted the land to them.

It will be recalled that Prem Kumar's opponents allege that he had promised the Chammars support in allotment of this land at the time of his election. But this allegation is denied by Prem Kumar. He says that he has always been with the rest of the village in its demand for retention of land in its present use. And, as proof of this, he produced an application which he had sent to the collector for retention of this land in its present use and for its reclassification *charagah.*[12]

Award of Contract for Flaying Carcasses of Dead Cattle

It has been explained earlier that after the Chammars stopped flaying carcasses, the *panchayats* of most villages began to award contracts for this work. But in this village although the Chammars had stopped doing such work about ten years ago, the contract arrangement by the *panchayat* had not been made until the issue was taken up by the present *panchayat* early in 1961.

It may help to explain the background of this situation. At the time when the Chammars stopped this work, there was no *Bhangi* family living in the village, and a *Bhangi* family living from a neighbouring village had to be brought in to do it. But after some time this family found employment in the cement factory and left. Thereafter, *Bhangis* from another village were tried; but their work was unsatisfactory. Finally the village leaders persuaded some *Bhangis* from another part of the district to come and settle down in the village. At the time of this study, two families of these *Bhangis* were doing the work. The village has about 60 families of *Rehgars* who continue their traditional work of tanning hides and making leather goods. The individual cultivators have made arrangements with the *Rehgars* under which the *Bhangi* delivers the raw hide to the *Rehgar* who works on it and makes some payment in kind or cash to the owner of the hide. There are conflicting reports on the subject of payment. Manphool and other leaders of the cultivators, who oppose the award of contract by the *panchayat*, say that this payment is substantial—that cultivators get *charas*, leather straps used for hitching bullocks to the plough and other requisites of cultivation practically as they used to get in the past when the chammars did the work. But Prem Kumar and his supporters refute this claim and say that while influential leaders like Manphool or some *patels* might get *charas*, nobody else gets it; that the majority of the cultivators get only the leather straps, and that Brahmins, artisans and others who keep only a few animals get little (e.g., a token payment of Rs. 2 to Rs. 5) or nothing. They argue that award of the contract by the *panchayat* would not cause a serious economic loss to the cultivators, but bring in a sizeable income to the *panchayat*, as evidenced by other *panchayats* in the area which do award contracts.

The attitude of different castes to the contract issue varies considerably. High castes and artisan, who keep only a few animals, generally favour it. For them the inconvenience of having to find somebody to lift the carcass of a dead animal is much greater than the small benefit they might get in exchange for the raw hide. The opposition to the contract comes mainly from the Meenas and other cultivators who have a good many animals and are more conscious of the economic loss.

The contract was awarded by the present *panchayat* immediately after it took over in January, 1961. It covered only the two remaining month, February and March, of the financial year 1960-61, and it was given to a young *Rehgar* of the village for Rs. 400. This young man is a member of the *panchayat* and is among the prominent supporters of the *Sarpanch.* The timing of the contract, immediately after the new *panchayat* assembled, and its award to a prominent supporter of the *Sarpanch*, aroused anger of the cultivators. Some of them are reported to have said that they would rather hitch the carcasses of their dead animals to their ploughs, take them outside the village themselves and bury them, than allow them to be removed under this contract. An appeal against the decision of the *panchayat* was immediately filed by their leaders before the *Panchayat Samiti*, and a stay order was obtained. The *samiti* took several months to consider the case and finally decided it in September 1961. As explained earlier, it has upheld the decision of the *panchayat* but has not sent back the case file so far, with the result that the practice obtaining before the award of the contract continues. Failure of the *samiti* to send the file back has confirmed the suspicions of Prem Kumar and his supporters that the *samiti* is pro-Meena and would favour Meenas, right or wrong. They say, and with some justification, that the *samiti* had no choice in its decision because most *panchayats* in the area already award these contracts, so that a different decision in this case would have upset the practice and created a furor in the *samiti*; but the effect of its decision has been nullified and made inoperative by its retention of the file.

Grazing of Cattle in the Kala Mal during the Rainy Season

The cultivated lands of the village are given different names by the villagers, depending upon the colour and texture of the soil and other factors which affect cultivation. *Kala Mal*[13] is a block of cultivated land situated to the west of the village near the hamlet; the soil is deep clay, dark brown in colour. The area is low-lying; water stands on it for several weeks during the rains and prevents cultivation. But it produces very good crops of wheat, barley and other grains during the *Rabi* season, because the soil is heavy and has plenty of sub-soil moisture. In fact, it is considered to be the best unirrigated land in the village. The land is owned by cultivators of the main village, mainly Brahmins and Meenas. But since it is located close to the houses of the Meenas of the hamlet they graze their cattle in the *mal* land, in small patches of uncultivated wasteland, and in their own fields with standing *kharif* crops instead of the grazing grounds of the village or to the hill forests where the cattle of the other villagers go, because the regular grazing lands are one-and half to two miles from the hamlet. Moreover, the route to them is blocked by water during the rains. Earlier when there were considerable areas of wasteland in the vicinity of the hamlet these were used for grazing. But with the allotment of most of these lands for cultivation, the problem has become more difficult because grazing is confined to the *mal* Land and the small patches of cultivable waste that remain. The situation leads to two difficulties which are the main reasons for the dispute:

(i) The cattle trample and compact the soil of the uncultivated land of the *mal*, with the result that plowing and preparation of the seed bed for the *rabi* crops becomes difficult; and
(ii) It is alleged that the owners allow their cattle, especially bullocks, to graze not only in their own field but also in those of their neighbors, thus spoiling their crops.

Prem Kumar and other opponents of the practice allege that as long as grazing is allowed in the *mal* land and in fields with standing crops these difficulties will continue. They say the practice must stop. The Meenas whose cattle graze in the area contended that the cattle graze only in the owners' fields or in wastelands; that they take good care to prevent cattle from going into the fields of others; but that they cannot stop the practice because they cannot send their cattle to the distant grazing grounds of the village. They also argue that the practice of grazing in these lands has been going on for generations, and nobody had raised any objection to it; but Prem Kumar has raised the issue only to harass the Meenas, who opposed him in his election.

There is no doubt that this became a major issue only after the present *panchayat* came to power and Prem Kumar started making a serious effort to stop the practice. It is true also that his attack has been motivated partly by partisan considerations. But there has been a feeling against this practice for a long time. Some Brahmins petitioned Hiralal, *Sarpanch* of the very first *panchayat* to stop it. He put the cattle of a few cultivators in the cattle ground and fined them. But since these aroused serious opposition from the cultivators, he went no further. The subsequent *Sarpanchas* took no action at all. But Prem Kumar started taking vigorous action in the very first year of his tenure. He put the cattle of a number of cultivators in the pond, fined the owners, spoke against the practice in the village, and wrote letters to the Collector and other officers concerned, asking their assistance in stopping it. These actions infuriated the Meenas, especially of the hamlet, who saw in them nothing but working of partisan politics. Those who had been fined filed an appeal to the *Panchayat Samiti*, which gave a stay order. This order is in force and the practice continues.

Encroachment of Rastas (Paths)

Several cultivators in this village, especially those owning land irrigated by wells, have encroached on the village *rastas* by extending the boundaries of their fields. Such encroachments are common in villages of this area, and are made by cultivators to add to their cultivated lands. The encroachments had made the *rastas* quite narrow at many points, making the passage of bullock carts difficult and at places impossible; there is a general feeling against them in the village. But since a number of influential cultivators were involved, the earlier *panchayats* took no effective action. The present *panchayat* took action in some cases and fined the offenders Rs. 11 each. The latter appealed to the *Panchayat Samiti*, which upheld the decision of the *panchayat*, but reduced the fines to the nominal figure of Rs. 1.25 each. The encroachments were not removed. The *Sarpanch* says that he is going to request the *Tehsildar* to take action to remove the encroachments and will also seek the assistance of the police if necessary. However, discussions with various village leaders left the impression that it will be difficult to get these encroachments removed, though the *Sarpanch* may be successful in getting the cultivators to take adjustment here and there to make movement of bullock carts possible.

The Dispute Over Land Used for Baking Pots of the Kumhars

This dispute is of recent origin and relates to a small piece of land within the *abadi* area of the village. It is alleged that a rich Meena cultivator who is influential and powerful within his caste because of his extensive money-lending had begun to extend his cattle shed. In doing this he encroached on the ovens in adjoining houses of the *Kumhars*. The latter submitted a petition to the village *panchayat*, which accepted it and ordered the Meena to remove the encroachment. He appealed to the *Panchayat Samiti,* which reversed the order of the *panchayat* and further directed the *Kumhars* to take their ovens outside the village. Against the decision of the *samiti*, the *Kumhars* moved a revision petition in the court of the Additional Collector; this is pending.

Prem Kumar and his supporters have made much political capital out of this decision of the *Panchayat Samiti*. They say that the encroachment by the Meena is unjust and that the decision of the *Panchayat Samiti* in supporting it has been motivated only by political and partisan considerations. Their argument is that these ovens are about a hundred years old; that the affected *Kumhars*, who are potters of the village, and their fore-fathers before them had been using them all these years, and that the ovens of the *Kumhars* in the village of this area are always located within their houses in the village *abadis*. But the *Panchayat Samiti* has chosen to disregard all these fact, and take a decision which penalizes these poor people and favours a rich and influential Meena—and it reverses the decision of the *panchayat*!

A Dispute among the Brahmins

With the exception of the potters' dispute, all the disputes described relate to matters of collective interest in which either the whole village or a considerable section of it is interested. In three of these disputes, one group or caste has one attitude while the others have the opposite attitude because of considerations such as economic interest, social prestige, and so on. The last dispute arose between individuals but was soon given a caste and factional colour. This dispute concerns members of only one caste, and it is described here in order to illustrate the type of situation which leads to bitter and long-standing disputes within a caste. About 20 years ago young widowed sister of three Brahmin brothers belonging to a prominent land-owning family of the village became pregnant as a result of illicit relations with a neighbour. The brothers, two of whom were educated white-collar workers, arranged for the delivery of the child in a hospital in Jaipur. The child died soon after birth and the brothers brought their sister back home to live with them as before. They were helped in the whole affair by a Brahmin young man, belonging to one of the leading landowning families of the village, who had been among the first to be educated and take a government job. He was much respected in the village because of his family background, his job, and his personal qualities. But the orthodox section of the Brahmins was vehemently opposed to this behaviour and decided to excommunicate them all.

The decision to ex-communicate, immediately led to a split in the caste, because the young Brahmin government servant and his family commanded considerable support. The division continued for almost 20 years, during which Brahmin families belonging to the opposing groups did not attend each others' marriages and other ceremonies. Finally, the rival groups were persuaded to come together, and on the occasion of the *Holi* of 1962, there was a formal reconciliation between them.

Analysis

The *panchayat* is an institution of power. Its developmental functions are undoubtedly important and will grow more so as economic development proceeds; but to the average villager the power role of the *panchayat* as an institution exercising local administrative authority—appears to be of much greater importance. Several powers of the *panchayat* are of vital importance to him, as for example permission to construct a new house or to extend an existing one, to attest a mutation of land; to recommend an application for allotment of land for cultivation or for grant of a *taccavi* loan or one for supply of scarce commodities like cement or corrugated iron sheets. Favourable action in cases involving exercise of any of these powers can be of considerable benefit to the villager involved while unfavourable action can cause him enormous loss and trouble. Thus the *panchayat's* refusal to grant a villager permission for constructing a *pucca* house could make things extremely difficult for him. The only remedy open to him in case of such a decision would be to make an appeal to the administration standing committee of the *Panchayat Samiti*. This will involve expense and delay, and if the *Sarpanch* is influential in the *samiti*, the chances of the decision of the *panchayat* being reversed are very small indeed. On the other hand the support of the *sarpanch*, who is a member of the land Allotment Committee, can make all the difference between acceptance or rejection of his application for allotment of land for cultivation.

Aside from the specific powers vested in the *Sarpanch* and members of the *panchayat*, these positions carry considerable prestige in official circles and afford opportunities for contact with officials of various departments of government—opportunities which can be utilized for getting the work of the supporters done and that of the opponents frustrated. Thus, a *Sarpanch* in an outlaying village, in which supervision by higher officers is not very intensive, can have things very much his own way by establishing good relations with the village level officials of the Revenue, Police, Forests and other Departments. He can encourage his supporters to occupy cultivable wastelands, encroach on *rastas* and unoccupied land within the village *abadi*, and see to it that either these encroachments are not noticed or that effective and timely action is not taken against them. In this way his supporters can enjoy the benefits for long periods. Even more important than what he really can or cannot do is the widespread belief among the villagers that he can get a great deal done. Acknowledgement of the power of the post depends upon this belief.

In case of the cooperative, the power role is not so pervasive, but it is still considerable. The power to grant or deny loans or to supply or deny essentials of good cultivation is not a small one. It does not appear so important at present, because cooperative credit and use of improved seeds are not widespread in this area. But the villager already understands the very considerable financial advantages which a cooperative society can confer on its members, and he realizes very well that it's Chairmanship or Treasure-ship gives considerable power of patronage.

But power attracts conflicts and it was almost inevitable that vesting of power in village institutions should be followed by conflicts among individuals and groups striving to capture it.

It was unavoidable also that the new institutions should take power away from the persons, groups and institutions who previously had power—and this of course creates conflicts. The cooperative takes away the power of the money lenders—not only the professional Mahajans or Brahmin money-lenders, but also the prosperous cultivator-cum-moneylenders among the Meenas and the *Malis*. It has been explained earlier how the moneylenders of Raipur captured the cooperative in the beginning and used its funds for their personal ends. In the *panchayat* conflict is more serous, because the *panchayat's* powers extend over a wider area and affect a much larger number of people in opposition of traditional power. One of the groups affected is the *patels*. Reference has been made earlier to the conflict between the present *Sarpanch* and one of the *patels*. This is a case of conflict between two individuals. But the two institutions are also in conflict, because most of the powers formerly enjoyed by the *patels* have now been conferred on the *panchayat*. The *Sarpanch* and other member of the *panchayat* are now consulted by the state government on every matter concerning the village, just as the *patels* were consulted in the past. The latter had (and still have) the function of supervising crop inspection and reporting an unauthorized encroachment on cultivable wastes, pastures or *rastas*; cultivation by other than owners, etc. But these powers have been conferred on the members of the *panchayat* also. Many of the *panchayat's* powers (sale of residential sites, permission to build or repair houses, advice in allotment of land) although not formally vested in the *patels* were in fact enjoyed by them, because the officials of the *tehsil* who had these powers generally relied upon their advice. The *patels* were the agents of the *raj* and nothing could be done in the village without their advice. The patel continues[15] and still has important functions; but most of their powers, and all of its prestige and recognition by the government have been given to the *panchayat*. Under these conditions, conflict between the two institutions is invertible, unless the *patels* capture the *panchayat*, as happens in many villages.

Another source of conflicts is rapid social and economic change in the village which leads to tensions and disputes between young and old, between castes and within castes and between families which enjoyed power and prestige in the past and those which are powerful now. The fore-going analysis reveals how several of the disputes in Raipur are connected with social and economic changes experienced by the village. The dispute about the award of contract for flaying carcasses has its origin in abandonment of this work by the Chammars. Similarly, the dispute about *charagah* land arises partly from the Chammars' desire to obtain more land for cultivation and thus to progress towards their goal of economic and social equality with the Meenas. The change which affects different families differently leads to tensions and conflicts within castes. The Brahmins furnish the best example of this. Earlier, when land was the main source of income, families which have large holdings were the richest and had all the prestige and power. But during the last 20 years a new source of income, prestige and power, has appeared in the shape of white-collar jobs. Several of the young men who have got good jobs belong to relatively poor families, while some rich families have suffered an eclipse because their sons have not been able to get good jobs. Prem Kumar's family was poor but he has a better education and a better job than most young men of families with large land holdings. Such disturbance of traditional position of prestige and power would create conflicts in any group, and the Brahmins of Raipur are no exception.

Finally, there is conflict between young and old. The present *panchayat* is composed predominantly of young men. The *Sarpanch*, the Upe-*Sarpanch* (Vice-President) and 8 out of 11 other members of the present *panchayat* are young persons. None of the "old leaders" of the village is included in it. But, even though the "old leaders" are not in the *panchayat*, they have not lost their "leadership" positions within the village. In fact, in most important matters concerning individual castes or even the whole village, "leadership" rests with them. The villagers consult them and entrust to them the responsibility of deciding a suitable course of action. During the course of this study, an attempt was made to collect names of prominent persons of this type. Certain names came up from different castes. There was general agreement about them; even Prem Kumar and other young members of the *panchayat* were agreed. Most of these people had been members of the first two *panchayats*. Some of them like Sankar Patel are involved in serious conflicts, with the *panchayat*. The attitude of most others, like Hiralal, is that of indifference or subdued hostility; it is not one of sympathy or support. They understand that sources of power have changed. Some of them might come back to the *panchayat*; others might not. But in either case, they will continue to hold their leadership positions, which only means that the village has a diarchy, with political power, deriving from an official institution, vested in one set of person and social power, deriving from the traditional ways of doing things, remaining with another.

The area of conflict would have been narrower, though the conflicts might have been less serious, if opportunities for entering and gaining control of the new institutions had been restricted. But since the village institutions are based on the principle of equal opportunity for all, as they must be in a democratic society, the area of competition and struggle extends to all sections of the village. Each caste and group feels that it has a voice in the election of the *Sarpanch* and that the *Sarpanch* could be one of its members. In any case, anyone who wishes to become *Sarpanch* must seek the support of every caste. As the most populous castes (Meenas, *Malis*, Chammars, and *Rehgars*) did not enjoy power in the past, they have a keen sense of 'newly found power'. Moreover, the current rivalry between them sharpens the struggle for political power. The election of the present *Sarpanch* with the support of the scheduled castes and in the teeth of opposition of the Meenas and other cultivating castes add to their rivalries, as do the actions of the *panchayat* in favouring the scheduled castes in some cases and in taking up issues in which the cultivating castes would be adversely affected. The Meenas suspect and fear that the *panchayat* is against them, and they are determined to capture power in the next election.

The study throws light also on the role of outside influences on conflicts in the village and in village institutions. Of course, no village institution could expect to function in isolation, unaffected by higher level political leaders. But in Raipur because of proximity to block and district head quarters, the interest and interference of outsiders has been rather more than in most other villages. It has been noted that each member of the State legislature has in his time tried to influence elections to the village *panchayat* and has taken sides in particular disputes in the village. Easy access to block and district officers also encourages individuals and groups within the village to go out and seek help from outsiders. The tendency has increased after the formation of the *Panchayat Samiti*. The *samiti* appears to the villagers of both the opposing groups to have become a party to disputes within the village, with the result that there is a growing tendency among them to fight their battles in the *samiti* and in other administrative offices and courts.

This tendency is not likely to diminish in future. On the contrary, it will increase as the contacts of the villagers with outside agencies, official and non-official, increase, and particularly as other political parties come into the field. So far, only the Congress Party has an organization in the area, and even its organization extends only to the block level, there being few persons who are identified with the Congress Party or with any political party at all in the villages. But this situation will change: the organization of the Congress Party will extend to the village level, and other parties will come into the field. Attempts will then be made by rival parties to attract different groups and individuals to their respective folds. Then a new political situation will develop. Prem Kumar and his supporters (or the scheduled castes as a group) will belong to political party-A and the ex-*Sarpanch* Manphool and his associates (or the Meenas as a caste) will join party-B; and the local inter-personal or inter-caste rivalries will be camouflaged in slogans of different political parties.

Before concluding, one point may be made, if only to counter an impression which may have been made, given the pre-occupation with conflict. It has been implied that conflicts affect the *panchayat's* capacity to raise resources or to undertake development activities. The resources of the Raipur *panchayat* are indeed meager, and it does not impose taxes. But the situation is not peculiar to this particular *panchayat*; nor is it due primarily to conflicts. The main reason is that all sections of the people of Raipur are opposed to taxation. The situation is not better in many *panchayats* in which there are no serious conflicts. It has been mentioned also that while the village did well in development works in the early years of the community development programme, progress has been slow in recent years. But again factors other than conflicts are largely responsible: fulfilment of most urgently felt needs and consequent absence of any major objective of collective endeavor, competition from other villages as a result of which grants are now not made by the *panchayt samiti* etc. When the villagers have before them a major work or activity which they consider essential for their village, the existence of conflicts in the *panchayat* or in the village will not prevent from mobilizing the necessary resources. This happened in two large villages in this area in the summer of 1961 and there is no reason to believe that it would not happen in Kaipur. Both these villages were (and continued to be later) torn by serious conflicts. But this did not prevent their constructing high school buildings costing between Rs. 20,000 and Rs. 30,000 each, all collected through contributions from the village people, and making successful efforts to influence officials and non-officials in agreeing to their demands that high schools be opened in their villages.

Conclusion

Conflict in village institutions is an inevitable consequence of their new roles of power and prestige. It arises because the institutions appear to be suitable forums for expression of rivalries between different castes, groups, and factions. It is a product of social, economic, and political change in the village, in which there is emergence of new aspirations, interests, and sources of power. It is a symptom of the process by which a traditionally hierarchical society is trying to adapt itself to democratic institutions. It has its undesirable features, of course: under certain conditions it could render village institutions ineffective and even vitiate the quality of village life. But only when its nature and significance in the present situation of change in the village is understood can appropriate measures be taken to check untoward developments.

Footnotes

1. The Hindi phrase *party bazzi* and the English phrase "party politics" are both frequently used by village leaders. The usage is not correct, because political parties are not involved in these conflicts described. But the phrase is significant, because it shows that the villagers consider the phenomenon of group rivalry within the village to be very similar to rivalry between political parties in the State legislature. The similarity is often expressly stated.

2. At the time of the 1960 *Panchayat* Elections, the Rajsthan Government had announced as an incentive to encourage unanimous elections and additional grant of 25 *naya paise* per head of population to all *panchayats* which held such elections.
3. Gram Sabha: the general body consisting of all adults in the village. Meetings of this body are supposed to be called by every *panchayat* twice a year.
4. This village has six *Patels* of which three are Meenas, two are Brahmins and one is a *Gujjar*. Earlier there were eight *patels* including two from among the *Malis*; but at the time of this study, no Mali was working as *patel*.
5. Mutation: transfer of land as a result of sale, succession, gift etc.
6. A special agency created for meeting the problem of rural water supply in Rajsthan. The Board has since been dissolved.
7. Such contributions are regarded as "voluntary donations", and are made by each head of household in accordance with his capacity to pay. However, considerable social pressure is exercised, especially on the heads of the more prosperous households, to ensure that their contribution is 'adequate'. The villagers think that once the more prosperous people come forward to pay adequately, the job of obtaining contributions from the others is relatively easy. Individual contributions are generally settled in informal meetings, e.g., of leaders of different castes in which the contribution of each family is announced, are often largely formal.
8. A Meena should give his vote only to a Meena, just as he gives his *beti* (daughter) in marriage only to a Meena.
9. This is one case cited by him in support of his contention, that the loans and grants given by the *Panchayat Samiti* during 1960-62 have been misused by the recipients.
10. At that time, the Block development Officer used to be the Chairman of all large sized societies of the block area, so that Vice Chairman of the society was the highest office open to a villager.
11. Grazing ground.
12. The application has since been accepted.
13. Black, unirrigated, cultivated land.
14. A festival which comes in February or March.
15. It was abolished in Rajsthan in 1963.

Appendix I.3
NOTES ON PANCHAYATS AND PANCHAYAT SAMITIS

The *panchayat* or village council is an elected institution having functions of local governments and development[1] at the village level. *Panchayats* were established in several of the former British Indian provinces (e.g. Madras, Bombay, U.P.) and some of the former princely States (e.g. Mysore) in 1920s and even earlier; but for the most part they have been created since Independence. Even where *panchayats* existed before independence they generally covered only a few villages and had very limited powers and functions. After Independence it became national and State policy to extend *panchayat* to all areas of the country, to form *panchayats* for all villages and to increase their functions and powers so as to give them an important role in local government and development programmes. The Constitution of India directs the States "to organize village panchayats and to endow them with such powers and authority as may be necessary to enable them to function as units of self-government".[2] Accordingly, States in which *panchayats* existed earlier extended them to all villages and gave them much larger powers and wider functions. In Rajasthan some of the more progressive princely States had established a few *panchayats* in the late 1940s. Jaipur was one of these States and Raipur was among the first villages of the States in which the *panchayats* were established. But in most villages in Rajasthan *panchayats* were constituted only in 1954 under the Rajasthan *Panchayat* Act of 1953.

The *panchayat* is intended to serve as the institution through which village people take initiative over a wide area of local administration, economic development, and social advance. Its functions include:

- *Municipal duties:* Maintenance of sanitation, providing street lighting.
- *Administrative duties:* Management of the village *abadi* (habitation area), pastures, woodlands and other common lands, tanks for irrigation and drinking water, roads, paths, etc.
- *Judicial duties:* Deciding petty disputes of a civil or criminal nature.
- A wide range of developmental activities.

In the latter field, the *panchayat* is expected to construct public works—drinking water wells, approach roads, school buildings—to encourage growth of other developmental institutions (cooperative societies, youth clubs, women's club), and to take steps to increase agricultural production, to improve cottage industries and crafts and to promote education, health, and social welfare. In other words, in addition to performing developmental functions specifically entrusted to it, the *panchayat* is expected to take an interest in all aspects of economic development and social advance of the village people. The range of functions of *panchayats* and their anticipated role in economic and social development are described in the following extract from the Second Five Year Plan[3]:

> "In the First Five Year Plan it was recommended that to enable *panchayats* to play their part in organizing village development programmes, legislation should confer on them certain functions related to village production programme and development of village land and resources. Recently, this proposal had been further examined. The functions of village *panchayats* may be distinguished broadly between two groups, administrative and judicial. Administrative functions may be divided conveniently between (1) civic, (2) development, (3) land Management and (4) land reforms. The civic functions of *panchayats* are embodied in legislation in different states in more or less similar terms. They include such tasks as village sanitation, registration of births, deaths, organization of village watch and ward, construction, maintenance and lighting of village streets,

The functions of village *panchayats* in relation to development may be set out as follows:

- farming programmes of production in the village; in association with cooperatives, farming budgets of requirements for supplies and finance for carrying out programmes; acting as a channel through which an increasing proportion of government assistance reaches the villages;
- developing common lands such as waste lands, forests, *abadi* sites, tanks, etc., including measures of soil conservation;
- construction, repair and maintenance of common village buildings, public wells, tanks, roads, etc;
- organization of mutual aid and joint effort in all activities;

- promotion of cooperative societies;
- organizing voluntary labour for community works;
- promoting small savings; and
- Improvement of livestock.

The functions of *panchayats* in respect of management of village lands and the implementation of land reforms are specially related to the lines along with it is proposed that the agrarian structure should be organized and are explained in Chapter IX. The main land management functions are:

- Regulation of the use of common lands such as waste lands, forests, *abadi* sites, tanks, etc.
- Cultivation of land set apart for the benefit of the village community, as in consolidation of holdings;
- Adaptation of standards of good management and cultivation to local conditions and their enforcement; and
- Association with the work of main tenancy of land records.

The functions of *panchayats* in relation to land reforms arising from legislation which may be enacted by each State. In the main, they entail the association of the village *panchayat* with activities such as:

(a) determination of land to be allotted to owners and tenants on the exercise of rights of resumption for personal cultivation;
(b) determination of surplus lands on the application of ceilings on agricultural holdings, and
(c) redistribution of surplus lands arising from the imposition of ceilings.

Village *panchayats* are already associated in several States in the work of consolidation of holdings.

The judicial functions of *panchayat* concern –

- the administration of civil and criminal justice,
- enforcement of minimum wages for agricultural workers, and
- simple disputes pertaining to land.

The common pattern in States for facilitating the exercise of these functions is to establish separate judicial *panchayts* whose territorial jurisdiction extends as a rule to a number of villages."

The specific functions of *panchayats* constituted under the Rajasthan *Panchayst* Act 1953[4] may be summarized as follows:

- civic functions like conservancy and street lighting;
- administrative functions, especially management of the village *abadi*, tanks, pastures, roads and paths and other lands belonging to the village community. Management includes the right to sell house/sites and to give permission for building houses in the *abadi* and the right to sell grass and other produce from the pastures and fish from the tanks; but it does not include the right to sell or take any action which might reduce the value of any of these community assets;
- judicial function viz. deciding civil and criminal disputes within certain stated limits;
- development functions similar to those enumerated in the above extract from the Second Five Year Plan.

In addition, the Act gave the *panchayat* and its president, the *Sarpanch*, very important advisory or executive functions in revenue matters. Thus the *Sarpanch* was to function as a member of the Land Allotment Advisory Committee when it considered cases of allotment of cultivable wastelands to landless persons in the area of the *panchayt*. He and other members of the *panchayat* were given powers of supervision of inspection of crops by the village *patwari*. The *panchayat* was also authorized to sanction certain kinds of mutations (transfer of rights in cultivated land). The institution was sought to be built up as the representative of State government in the village and provision was made for consultation with the *sarpanch* or with the *panchayat* as a body, in a variety of administrative matters.

Under this act, the area of a *panchayat* included one or more villages, with a total population of 5000 to 8000. Typically, it included a medium sized village with a population of between 1000 and 3000, which was the seat of the *panchayat*, and a number of small village located in the vicinity. In the Sawai Madhopur *Panchayat Samiti*, which has a rural population of about 80,000 in 1951, there were 16 *panchayats*.

The *Panchayat* Act of 1953 was amended in 1960 when major changes were made in the area and functions of the *panchayats*. The area of the *panchayats* was reduced to one village or a group of small villages with a total population of 1,500 to 2,000. This was done to bring the institution closer to village people. "One village, one *panchayat*" is the ideal, and *panchayats* are constituted for all large and medium sized villages; but the small village had to be grouped together because reducing the area of *panchaysts* too much was not considered feasible on administrative and economic grounds. As a result the total number of *panchayats* in the State increased from about 3,000 to nearly 74,000. In the Sawai Madhopur *Panchayat Samiti*, the increase was from 16 to 45.

The Amended Act also entrusted the judicial functions to separate body called the *Nayaya Panchayat* (judicial *panchayats*). As the above quotation from the Second Five Year Plan shows, many States already had *Nayaya Panchayat*. Their establishment had been recommended by the Study Team on Community Projects of the Committee on Plan Projects[5], in its report submitted to the Government of India in 1957. Entrusting the judicial functions to separate bodies is generally favoured on two grounds: (i) that it reduces conflicts in village *panchayats* many of which arise, it is argued, from the exercise of judicial powers, and (ii) that it enables the village *panchayats* to concentrate their attention on development activities. But even after the separation 'case work' arising from administrative functions—sale of *abadi* lands, giving permission to build or repair houses, clearing encroachment on pastures—continues to be a very important part of the work of village *panchyats* in this area. In most *panchayats* it took the major part of the time of the *panchayat* members. It was the main visible evidence of the functioning of *panchyats*, to which weekly meetings were almost entirely devoted.

The *Sarpanch* of the *panchayat* holds a very important position. He is its president as well as its executive head. In the latter capacity, he has charge of the *panchayat* office and is responsible for execution of all its decisions. Several important powers are vested in him personally. Moreover, as representative of the *panchayat* area in the *Panchayat Samiti*, the *sarpanch* is chiefly responsible for ensuring that the area gets adequate attention in all development programmes under the charge of the *samiti*. His election by a system of direct election (by all the voters of the *panchayat* area) gives him added importance. It makes him independent, to an extent, of the other members of the *panchayat*. He can continue in office even when the majority of the other members (called *panchas*) are opposed to him: he may be removed only by the votes of three-fourths of the *panchas*.

Each *panchayat* has a secretary to attune to clerical work. In many States, *panchayat* secretaries are appointed and paid for by the State Government. But in Rajasthan each *panchayat* appointments and pays for its own secretary.[6] Usually, an educated young man of the village is appointed, and he works on this job full or part-time depending upon the work load and the capacity of the *panchayat* to pay for his services.

The *Panchayat Samiti* is the block level institution responsible for policy making and execution of community development and other rural development programmes. The *Zila Parishad* is the district level institution responsible for coordination of development programmes within the districts. *Panchayats, Panchayat Samities* and *Zila Parishads* are collectively known as *Panchayati Raj* (governments by the *panchayats* and associated institutions of people) institutions. The establishment of *Panchayat Samiti* and *Zila Parishads* was recommended in 1957 by the Study Team of the Committee on Plan Projects mentioned above[7]. The recommendation was accepted and during the next few years most states took steps to establish these institutions. Rajasthan, which established them in October, 1959, was the first State to do so. Earlier, the community development programme had been executed by a team of officials under the leadership of the Block development officer and the general guidance of the District Development Officer (collector)

A *Panchayat Samiti* in Rajasthan is composed of the *sarapanches* of all the *panchayats* in its area and a certain number of co-opted members.[8] The latter are added to give representation to women and special groups like the scheduled castes and scheduled tribes, who may not be adequately represented otherwise; to special interests like the cooperative institutions; or to persons with experiences in administration, progressive farming, etc. The various *Panchayat Samitis* of Sawai Madhopur district have between 40 and 60 members, of which 8 to 10 members are co-opted and the rest are *Sarpanches*. The Chairman of the *Panchayat Samiti* is called the *Pradhan*. He has been given important executive functions, and his post has come to have considerable prestige and power. But the *Pradhan*, unlike the *Sarpanch* in the *Panchayat*, is indirectly elected by the members of the *Panchayat Samiti*, and can continue in office only as long s he enjoys their confidence. The Vikas Adhikari (the new name of the block development Officer) is the chief executive officer of the *Panchayat Samiti* and is responsible for implementation of the development programme and all decision of the *samiti*.

Panchayat Samities function through a number of standing committees. Among these, the standing committees on administration and finance is generally regarded as the most important, because it has powers of giving financial sanctions and the administrative control over the staff of the *samiti*. It is also the appellate body for cases decided by the village *panchayats*. The Rajasthan *Panchayat Smiti* and Zila Parishad Act provides for filing revisions against the decisions of this committee before the Collector under certain conditions, and also for appeals to higher courts.

Appendix II.3

NOTES ON DISTRICT REVENUE ADMINISTRATION[9]

The district is the principal administrative unit in India, below the State. The area and population of districts very greatly from State to State and within each State from district to district; but an idea of the size of the unit may be had from that fact that most districts contain one to two million people. Sawai Madhopur district, with a population of about 900,000 (1960 census), is smaller than an average Indian district, but is larger than the average district of Rajasthan.

The officer in charge of the district is called the Collector or Deputy Commissioner, different names being used in different States. He is responsible for collection of land revenue (tax on land) and maintenance of law and order. He also has important duties in the fields or development and general administration. During the British period revenue, law and order, and general administration functions of the Collector were most important; in post-Independence years, with the pronounced shift to development activities, the developmental function has become of primary importance. The collector is expected to take an active interest in progress of all development programmes and functioning of all developmental institutions in his district. For some programmes or institutions he may have direct responsibility; but even for those for which he has no direct responsibility, he is expected to keep himself informed about their progress and to give such guidance or assistance as may be needed from time to time. In Rajasthan, as in most other states, the Collector is also called the District Development Officer.

The districts are further divided into smaller units for development work and for revenue administration. The unit for development work is the community development block and that for revenue administration the *tehsil*.[10] As explained in Appendix I, development work in each community development block is carried out under the direction of its *Panchayat Samiti,* by a team of officials headed by the Vikas Adhikari. Revenue administration in the *tehsil* is under the charge of an officer called the *tehsildar*. The village level official of Revenue department is called the *Patwari*. He helps in collection of land revenue, maintains land records, including the record of right of each individual land holder, collects agricultural statistics, etc. An important function of the *Patwari* is to conduct *Gasht Girdawari* or field-to-field inspection of crops in every cropping season. The original objects of this inspection was to access the condition of the standing crops for purposes of tax collection, because tax relief like suspension or total remission of land revenue were granted on the basis of this assessment. But in recent years, when land reform legislation directed towards giving rights in land to the actual tillers of the soil has been introduced in all States, another purpose viz. recording the name of the actual cultivators of each field has become even more important.

Revenue administration in India is not concerned merely with collection of land revenue. This was undoubtedly the primary object of establishing it and might have been its most important function in the beginning. But since revenues administration was for a long time the only agency of government reaching down to the village level, a variety of functions were entrusted to it. Villagers often knew government only through the revenue (and police) administration, and they had a tendency to equate it with government. In post-Independence years, however, with the establishment of extension services and various developmental institutions at the village level, revenue administration had become less important. But even today its importance is much greater than collection of land revenue alone would warrant. One reason for this is that the allied functions of maintenance of land records and land management (e.g., allotment of cultivable waste lands for cultivation and checking unauthorized occupation of these and other uncultivated lands) are of vital importance to the villager. In Rajasthan, as in most States, popular institutions like the *panchayats*, and non-officials like the local M.L.As are associated with performance of the land management functions. Allotment of cultivable wastelands within the area of a *tehsil* is entrusted to a Tehsil Land Allotment Advisory Committee which is composed mainly of non-officials. The M.L.A. of the area is a member of this committee, and the *Sarpanch* of each *panchayat* is co-opted as a member when the committee considers cases of allotment of land in the area of the *panchayat*. But, since all the records relating to allotment of land and other land management functions are maintained by the revenue staff, and since revenue officers like the *Tehsildar* and the Collector have the ultimate responsibility for ensuring satisfactory performance of theses functions, the villagers continue to regard these functions as the responsibility of revenue administration.

Besides the *Patwari*, the other functionaries of the Revenue department at the village level are the *patels*. Most villages have several *patels*, whose specific function is to collect land revenue on behalf of the State. They receive a small commission for doing this work; the amount is quite small and is not an important source of income. But the *pateis*[11] are (and were more so in the past) important persons in their village. Their importance arises from the manner of their selection and from their treatment in the past as links between the administration and the village. *Patels* were selected from families of land-owner-cultivators who had large holdings and were known to be influential in the village. As the position was hereditary, going from father to son, selection of *patels* from a family meant official recognition of its influence within the village. It also meant a guarantee for its continuance for a long time, because the *patels* were considered to be the arms of the administration in the village and were consulted by local officials in all matters. The *patel* system was abolished in Rajasthan in 1963.

4

Emerging Leadership

Profiles of Village Leaders

Introduction

In the growth of new democratic institutions like the *Panchayati Raj* institutions, the people who come to these in the first few years have many important roles. The form and the structure of the institutions—composition, functions and powers relations with the state government and other bodies—are determined by the laws formed by the state government. But their actual working and the way in which they develop depend in large part on the thinking and action of their members. The *Panchayati Raj* institutions have been established with certain objectives and expectations. They are expected to function as agencies of self-government at various levels and to serve as major instruments of economic development and social advance of the rural people. But whether these expectations are fulfilled and the institutions assume the role advised for them, or they confine themselves to the more limited tasks of mentoring social service or executing certain development programmes or worse, become forms for expression of local group or personal rivalries. All this depends very largely upon the understanding of their members of the object and function of the institutions and of their own role in these and their ability to play this role successfully[1]. Accordingly, a study of members of the *Panchayati Raj* institutions is of great importance for understanding of their progress. It is important also for understanding the new trends for rural leadership. These institutions have brought new opportunities for exercise of power and leadership in the rural areas and are festering a new leadership, which is going to be increasingly important.

In recognition of the importance of the study of new leaders, fairly detailed data on some measurable attributes—age, education, caste, economic status etc.—has begun to be collected in Rajsthan (Government of Rajasthan 1960). This information is valuable in as much as it gives an idea of the social and economic background of these people. But it needs to be supplemented by more detailed studies of selected leaders, to show what kinds of persons they are, what influences bring them to the institutions, and what they seek to obtain from them; for themselves and for the people who have sent them there. Appendix 1.4 of this Chapter contains profiles of 15 selected members of *Panchayati Raj* institutions in Sawai Madhopur district of Eastern Rajasthan which throw light on these and related points.

The choice of persons for these profiles has been subjective. It has been influenced by the opportunity, which the author had of knowing members of these institutions and of seeing them at work. But within this limitation an attempt has been made to include the more important types of persons that one comes across in these institutions. Thus, included here are people from the dominant cultivating caste of the area, the Meenas, as also those from high castes like the Brahmins the Rajputs and the Mahajans; people with purely rural orientation and interests and those with their eyes focused on the town; people having no interest other than that of representing their village or castes, and those with political ambition, who see their present position in the Panchayati Raj institutions as a stepping stone to a more important political office, old and middle aged men as well as young men. Finally, to complete the picture, one woman and one representative of the scheduled caste have also been included. The woman is a co-opted member of a *Panchayat Samiti* but the scheduled caste representative is a *Sarpanch* and is a member of *Panchayat Samiti* in his own right as a village leader. Scheduled castes and women are not adequately represented in the *Panchayati Raj* institutions, and social provision has been made for their representation through cooption.

The collection is not representative in a purely statistical sense: i.e. different types of members of these institutions are not represented in it in the same proportions in which they would be found in an average institution like a *Panchayat Samiti*. The majority of members of a *Panchayat Samiti* are cultivators with some urban contacts and often also with some non-agricultural source of income. But these are represented in the study by no more than six profiles. On the other hand, other types like the small town leaders (Lal Chand) and smali town businessmen (Sagar Mal) have been included. The latter are not present in a *Panchayat Samiti* in large numbers. But when ever present they are influential, because of their education, wider knowledge and political and other contacts. This being a study of leaders, persons who occupy positions of influence and authority in *Panchayati Raj* institutions, it was considered more important to include in it different types of persons than to make a statistically valid representation of the membership of these institution.

The observations about each person are based on the author's personal acquaintance with him. He had an opportunity to know each one well, to see him function in various situations in his village and/or *Panchayati Raj* institution and to have informal discussions with him on various issues from time to time; these were not structured interviews.

Common Characteristics

When we think of village leaders, the type who readily comes to mind is an older middle-aged man, with little or no education, with a basically tradition-oriented outlook, and with his sphere of interest and knowledge limited to his own village or a few surrounding villages. Village leaders of this type (Raj mal and Harphool in this collection) are no doubt present in *Panchayati Raj* institutions, even in fair number in some but they are not in the majority, and what is more important, their influence is much less than their numbers. Most persons of this type are content to be back-benchers in the institutions, allowing to be guided by others. Further, even young, the literate or barely literate old world types, symbolized by Harphool are definitely on the way out. The average member of *Panchayati Raj* institutions is a young or middle aged man, educated and ressonably well-informed and standing midway in outlook, economic interest and social and personal contacts between the village and the town. He has his roots in the village people whom he represents, and he generally belongs to a family, which has been living in the village for generations. But he has also contacts with block and district level officials and political leaders. Moreover, he has a fair understanding of the economic system—prices, markets, scarcity of products like cement and steel, is well informed about land reform and other laws, which affect the village people, and has detailed knowledge of various development programmes, and of facilities like cooperative credit, *Taccavi* loans and grants which are available for their economic benefits.

Most of such leaders belong to the new middle class, which is emerging in rural India. Of the fifteen person figuring in these profiles, only one (Tara Chand) could be considered rich; all others are only moderately well off, with incomes ranging between Rupees 250-750 per month. None is poor! The cultivators among them are with comfortable holdings: several combine cultivation with other sources of income like money-lending, trade, or ownership of a small processing enterprise like a flour mill. This is true both of persons belonging to the purely cultivating Meena caste and of those who belong traditionally to non-cultivating castes; because none of them is an actual tiller of the soil. Some (like Amar Singh) manage their cultivation with the help of hired or attached labourers; others (like Sridher) have given their land on *betai*, still others (like Ram Pratap and Rajaram) who come from joint families of cultivators have other members of their families looking after cultivation. One would be justified in concluding that the time and the energy of the leader are more useful to his family or his village in the leadership role than in the role of the tiller of soil. There are several reasons why the leader does not cultivate his land himself, two among which are noteworthy. Firstly, it is not considered proper or dignified for a leader like a *Sarpanch* of the *Panchayat* or the *Pradhan* (chairman) of a *Panchayat Samiti* to do agricultural work himself. The entire value system of the village is against his doing such work. Secondly, the business of leadership takes considerable time and money and only those who can afford to spend these can enter it. Attending meetings of the *Panchayat Samiti* or of standing committees of the latter, and joining activities like seminars, training camps and study tours, participation in which is voluntary but expected, take time and require absence from home, sometimes for days together. Even more time is taken in looking after the problems, individual or collective, of the village people. These leaders participate in all activities, which bring their village or an individual villager in contact with the outside world. Leading a delegation of villagers before the Collector or a visiting Minister to represent for removal of a grievance or for obtaining an amenity for the village; helping an individual cultivator obtain a *taccavi* loan or grant from *Panchayat Samiti* or a permit for scarce material like cement; assisting a villager in a court case or in an appeal before the *Panchayat Samiti*—these are a few of the many things these leaders do. It was observed by the author that except the woman (Ram Devi) and the illiterate Meena lad (Harphool), all the persons figuring in these profiles spent a lot of time at a district or *Panchayat Samiti* headquarter towns. They were men about town in very real sense. The cultivator who has to earn his living with his own labour just cannot afford such expenditure of time or money.

Pre-occupation with work of this kind gives a revealing insight into what is perhaps the leader's most important role—that of link between the village and the outside world. The village people have always needed such links. Earlier, these were provided by better educated or urbanized villagers like the traders, richer cultivators, village level official like the *patwari* and in the *jagir* villages by the *jagirdars* and their servants. Now, this link is provided increasingly by members of *Panchayat Raj* institutions.

Most leaders have come to theses institutions because membership confirms prestige and gives opportunity for exercise of power. For some (like Ram Pratap and Raja Ram) membership of the institutions is merely a new expression or formal recognition of the traditional position of influence and prestige, which their family has enjoyed in the village or in the area—a modern symbol of a traditional position. For others (like Jai Singh and Raj Singh) who belong to families of former *Jagirdars*, it is an effort to retain some influence and prestige in their former *jagir* villages. But in case of some (like Ram Das) who belong to under-privileged castes, it is the symbol of the new, higher status of their caste and their own position as its leaders. In every case, it is the symbol also of personal success. Some of these leaders (like Ram Pratap and Jai Singh) are content to remain *Sarpanchas*, exercising power in their villages or small group of villages and being known as persons of consequence there; but others (like Raja Ram and Tara Chand) have ambitions of higher political offices. Several of them are disappointed that the powers and financial resources of these institutions do not measure up to their expectations, that the reality is much less than what they had been led to believe by the talk about these institutions in the months preceding the 1960 *Panhayat* election. This is particularly true of *Sarpanchas* of the new, small *panchayats* who are disappointed to find that the funds of the *panchayats* are very small and the *Sarpanchas* cannot increase it because of the strong opposition to taxes among the village people. They cannot expect to get large grants for works, etc., from the *Panchayat Samiti*, because the total amount available for such grants is limited and as a result all *panchayats* in the *samiti* area compete for them. They find that after being in office for more than a year they have not been able to take up any construction work in their villages, or show to the village people any other tangible evidence of the functioning of the *panchayat*. They understand the causes of this difficulty, but feel that the government should have seen it and provided against it while designing the institutions. Those (like Sager Lal and Amar Singh), who have experience of earlier *panchayats* which had larger area, more funds and also judicial powers, feel that 'nothing much is left in the *panchayats* now'.

Several of these leaders have good executive ability. In fact, both the quality and quantity of administrative calibre to be found in an average *Panchayat Samiti* in this area will give an outsider a pleasant surprise. But this ability is not finding adequate expression in organizing programmes of rapid economic development or social progress of the village people. Its main expression is in the enthusiasm for running the *panchayat* office but complete lack of interest in administrative matters, or in discussions of finer points in the Acts and rules. Some (like Suraj Mal and Tara Chand), who are *Pradhans* of *Panchayat Samiti*, tend to function more as executive heads of their institutions than as policy makers giving general directions to their Block Development Officers.

There are several reasons for these phenomenon, and they give a revealing insight into the capacity and limitations of these leaders for guiding programmes of economic development. One reason is that most of them have come to their present position in the *panchayat* or the *Panchayat Samiti* after keen contests and have to contend with strong opposition groups. Several of them have to concern themselves constantly with, maintaining or improving their position; even the others, whose positions are more secure, have to remain vigilant and see that they do things which keep their supporters pleased and their opponents in check. This political compulsion makes it necessary for them to concentrate attention on activities like case hearing in the *panchayats*, and distribution of grants and loans and for transfer of the staff in the *Panchayat Samitis*. These are the activities for which the supporters seek their intervention and by taking interest in which they can demonstrate to the supporters both their concern for them and their own effectiveness in the *panchayats* or in the *Panchayat Samitis*. Thus a *Sarpanch* who obtains a grant for construction of a drinking-water well or a community building in his village demonstrates to the village people that he is concerned with the development and is sufficiently influential in the *samiti* to get the grant sanctioned. If he gets a *Taccavi* loan sanctioned for a supporter or an appeal decided in his favour, he similarly demonstrates his willingness and capacity to help the supporter. The *pradhan* in the *Panchayat Samiti* has a similar compulsion in seeing that position of staff and distribution of grants and loans are favourable to the *Sarpanchas* supporting him. But the same political insight prevents them from taking unpopular actions like levying taxes and collecting contributions for community works and often leads them to give insufficient attention to agricultural extension.

As agricultural development is the most important function of *Panchayati Raj* institutions; the attitude of these leaders towards it needs some explanation. Here it will be useful to make a distinction between the operational aspects of agricultural work such as distribution of loans and supply of materials like chemical fertilizers and cement, and the purely educational and experimental aspects, which relate to propagation of new practices. These leaders are keenly interested in the operational aspects but lack interest in the educational and experimental aspects of agricultural extension. The reasons for it is not difficult to understand when we consider the position of a leader *viz a viz* a new practice, which is being advocated in his area by the agricultural extension workers. He finds that the benefits of the new practice are neither collective, nor immediate, nor even certain that they will accrue to individual cultivators. The benefits will accrue after a few months (when the crop is harvested) and only if the cultivators take adequate care of their crop and if the season is favourable. If the leader is a progressive farmer himself, he may take interest in the new practice, to the extent of having a demonstration conducted on his own field; and if it gives good results, of talking about it to friends. But, to the political being in him, which has to keep supporters pleased and opponents in check, interest in the improved practice starts only when it had already been proved successful and when the problems connected with it are not educational, but those of arranging supplies, credit, etc.

The Meena representatives are in some ways the most significant persons in these profiles. The whole complex of socio-political changes, described in these studies, has put the Meenas in a dominant position in local institutions in this area, and this dominance is likely to continue. Therefore, the working of the institutions and indeed the whole course of their development will be influenced very greatly by the personal qualities, the attitude and the behaviour of the Meena representatives. Here, as illustrative of the personality differences which will affect these institutions, let us consider Raja Ram and Ram Pratap on the one hand and Bal Ram and Tara Chand on the other. All four are Meenas and they must keep the interests of the Meenas in view and their Meena supporters pleased all the time. But the difference between the essentially reasonable attitude and action of the former, who will consider the claims of other groups in the village also in view and will try to meet them to the extent possible, and the aggressive casteist approach of the latter, is crucial, because the two approaches evoke very different reactions from the other members of the institutions. The former approach is essential, not merely for harmonious day-to-day working of the institutions but even more for their growth to position of key institutions of local government and development, which is envisaged for them.

Links in the Chain of Political Leadership

It has been mentioned above that these leaders function as links between the village and the outside world as well as in the chain of political leadership, which extends from the state level, through the district and the block, to the village. The various links in the chain are: the Minister, the member of the state legislative assembly (M.L.A), the *pradhan* of the *Panchayat Samiti*, the influential *Sarpancha* and members of *panchayats*. Before the establishment of the *Panchayati Raj* institutions, this leadership chain was incomplete because there was no effective, functional link between state level political leaders like the Ministers and the MLAs and village level leaders like the *Sarpanch* and members of the *panchayat*. These institutions have supplied the links by creating new area level leaders like the *Pradhans* and the influential *Sarpanchas*. These people, with active links 'downwards' with the village, function at the area level and they interact with the other area level leaders—the M.L.A., who has linkes 'upwards' at the State level. The interaction may be one of mutual support, especially at the time of his election, or the latter might themselves be dreaming of contesting election to the state legislature and be his potential rivals.[2] But the important fact is of interaction, which brings the two sets of area level leaders together, completes the political chain, and makes possible transmission of views, felt needs and problems of the villagers to the highest level of state administration far more affectivity, than was possible earlier.

Leaders and Representatives

The persons figuring in these profiles are representatives of their villages (or larger areas) in democratic institution. But are they "leaders" and if so, to what extent and in which areas of the social life of the village? It is necessary to raise these questions because there are different areas of social life of the village community, which have different leaders, and the fact that a person has been selected for a leadership role in one does not automatically make him a leader in all the others.

In the detailed study of Raipur village, it was found that the young *Sarpanch* of Raipur is not accepted as a leader of the village or even of his own caste for many purposes as do several other leaders figuring in these profiles. It is not possible to enter here into a detailed discussion of the nature of rural leadership or of the different kinds of leadership roles in a village community. But a brief reference to two different leadership roles will serve to illustrate the point. These are: exercise of political power in the village and maintenance of social norms. In the past the first role was played generally by the people having hereditary authority and prestige—the *patels*, the high caste Brahmins and Mahajans with wealth or large land holdings and the *Jagirdars* and their servants in the *jagir* villages. Frequently, village level government servants like the *Patwari* also shared this role. These people served also as the links of the village with the outside-world—for administrative, legal and most economic purposes. The role of maintaining social norms was also played sometimes by these holders of political power—the *Jagirdar*, who imposed his authority for maintenance of the *Jajmani* system. In his village he was an example of the person who combined the two roles; a better example was the wise *Jagirdar*, who was so respected by the village people that they took their inter-caste or inter-personal disputes to him voluntarily. The voluntary aspect was more clearly seen among the *patels*, who were often also the leaders of their caste and were prominent in maintaining social norms within it and in regulation of its relations with other castes. But, equally frequently the second role was played by the people who had no political power, e.g. old or middle-aged men of different castes. These persons were respected for their wisdom, cleverness or knowledge of traditional values; inter-personal and inter-caste disputes and cases involving transgression of traditional customs of the caste were refereed to them for decision and they are expected to speak for their caste or their village when any matter concerning these was under consideration. The role was played at intra-village meetings of caste leaders to settle a dispute in which. a woman married to a man has gone to live with another and the aggrieved party has moved the leaders for a settlement of *jhagra*[3].

The village people see their representatives in *Panchayati Raj* institutions pre-eminently in the role of holders of political power—as successors to *patels*, influential wealthy high caste men, and if one might say so, the *Jagirdars*. They understand that their position in these institutions gives them political power. But they are equally clear that the other role of maintenance of social norms does not flow to them by virtue of office. An individual member of a *Panchayati Raj* institution may perform this role (Raj Mal does it) in his village and/or (Raja Ram does it conspicuously) among the Meenas of the entire *Panchayat Samiti* area. But this is because of personal qualities and not due to official position; because other holders of similar positions (e.g., Sridhar and Ram Das) are specifically excluded from performance of this role.

It must be assumed that the second role is not important at present. Some aspects e.g., enforcing caste taboos in food and drink may be less important now. But, as we have seen in these studies, other aspects such as regulating changes in occupation and social custom among the scheduled castes and the cultivating castes, are more important, now than they were in the past. Consequently, the leaders who are entrusted with responsibility to maintain social norms have just as important a role in the social life of the village community as have members of *Panchayati Raj* institutions. Recognition of the existence of several leadership roles in a village community, and of the fact that members of *Panchayati Raj* institutions fill only one of these by virtue of their offices is essential for understanding the nature of these new leaders, and their positions in their villages.

Essentials for Leadership in PRIs

In 1961, as well as in 2001, there are two conditions that are essential for leadership in the village and in local institutions. These are brought out by examples of the leaders in the two villages, Manpur and Raipur, studied by the author in 1961; the villages were resurveyed in 2001. First, the leader should belong to a family with a large land holding or an established position of affluence or prestige in the village. In 1961, late Hari Singh, a Rajput with a large land holding in his family and who had been the principal functionary of the former *Jagirdar* of the village, was the *Sarpanch* of Maanpur *Panchayat*. He had been *sarpanch* since the *Panchayat* was established in 1952. His position was unquestioned for two reasons. First he had the qualities that kept the leaders of various communities (Rajputs, Mahajans, Meenas, *Mallies* and the scheduled castes) satisfied and had also established good relations with officials. In 2001, the *sarpanch* is a successful Mahajan businessman. But late Hari Singh's younger brother Mr. Suraj Bhan Singh, an ex-*sarpanch* of the village, is consulted by leaders of various castes in matters relating to the welfare of all the villages under the *Panchayat*. The leaders of the hamlets of the *Chammars* and the Meenas are also cultivators of more than average land holdings.

The second essential condition for leadership is that he should be convincingly vocal about the needs and problems of the village to the officials and at the same time convince the villagers that he can put forward the demands of all the villagers as well or better than any one else. Late Hari Singh had and Suraj Bhan Singh has these qualities.

In Raipur, the two most respected leaders in 1961 were (i) middle aged Meena with a large land holding. He had been a member of the first *Panchayat* established in 1952. The second leader was (ii) middle aged affluent Mahajan. The family owned a sizeable land holding and had besides, money-lending as a principal economic activity. He too had been a member and for many years *Sarpanch* of the *Panchayat* established in 1952. The two leaders had mobilized funds, labour and material contributions from the villagers for construction of the buildings of a middle school for boys and a primary school for girls, repair of the approach road to the village, pavement of streets in the habitation area of the village and construction of buildings for the *Panchayat* and the cooperative society cum-store for improved seed, fertilizers and other inputs. They had obtained grants or loans from the community development administration for construction of all these works and also for construction and repair of wells in the hamlets of the *Chammars* and *Gujjars*, located on the outskirts of the village.

Mr. Sham Lal Sharma, the *Sarpanch* of Raipur in 1961 was very critical of the regime of these leaders; he accused them of corruption, a charge that they reciprocated. But he recognized that he could not mobilize the funds for the works mentioned above that the traditional leaders had done. The maximum that he could do was to maintain these works and at the same time ensure that the *Panchayat* had enough funds for maintaining clean drains in the habitation area of the high castes. The villagers did not allow him to raise taxes to undertake any new development works. Although he was a well-paid clerk in the cement factory, he came from a poor family. Thus he lacked one essential condition for leadership.

In 1961, two essential conditions for position of leadership at the block and district level were also that the leader should be well off enough not to appear to utilize his leadership to enrich himself from the grants or loans that were available for development works in the villages and he should be convincingly vocal about the demands and the difficulties of the villagers to the officials.

The *Pradhan* (chairman) of the Sawai Madhopur *Panchayat Samiti* in 1961 was a middle-aged Meena from the central part of the *tehsil* which was the stronghold of the Meenas. His family had a large landholding and the Meena community had chosen him for being a convincingly vocal representative of the Meena caste. Furthermore, he had such personal qualities that the decisions of the *Panchayat Samiti* were seldom overturned by the District Development Officer or the Collector.

In 1961, the MLA of the Sawai Madhopur (unreserved) constituency was a reasonably successful Moslem lawyer. His brother was also a successful lawyer in the Collector's office. Furthermore, he had the backing of the mostly Moslem forest contractors who mobilized men and money for his campaign in return for his ability to get permission to cut forest and other favours from the Collector and the state government.

He was succeeded in the election of 1962 by a Rajput ex-*Jagirdar*, a traditional leader from a reasonably affluent family. Furthermore, he had the ability to approach the Meenas, *Malies* and the *Chammars* and to convince them that he would further their interests with the state government.

These conditions have remained unchanged in 2001, no matter who occupies the various positions in the *Panchayati Raj* institutions. The *Sarpanch* of Raipur in 2001 is a woman of washer men (Dhobi*)* caste, the lowest in an extremely caste conscious village. She is completely ineffective. She is accused also of corruption because her husband drinks. She was elected because the seat had been reserved for a member of the scheduled caste/scheduled tribe and also reserved for a woman. The scheduled castes and scheduled tribes community men could not decide on any one candidate and had put up several women. The *Dhobi* woman won the election primarily as a proxy candidate for whom all high caste voters voted. However, the real leader of the community remains a reasonably affluent Meena and two or more reasonably well off Mahajans and Brahmins.

In Maanpur while the *sarpanch* is a *Mahajan,* Suraj Bhan Singh, a Rajput and the ex-*sarpanch* is consulted in various matters for his traditional position in the village. The leaders of the hamlets of the *Chammars* and the Meenas are also farmers with relatively large land-holdings who are convincingly vocal about demands of their constituents.

Foot Notes

1. For one view of the influence of the attitude and the cultural orientation of the new leaders on the development of *Panchayati Raj* institutions see, Mathur P.C. (1964.)
2. Nine out of the ten *Pradhans* in Sawai Madhopur district took an active part in the general election of 1962. Three of them contested the election themselves; three were aspirants but could not get the backing of the Congress Party for their candidature, and three others were active campaigners for or against particular candidates.

3. *Jhagra*: payment received by husband whose wife has left him to live with another man.

References

Mathur P.C. (1964) : The Sociological Dimensions of *Panchayati Raj*, *Journal of the Indian Institute of Public Administration*, New Delhi, January-March.

Government of Rajsthan (1960), Evaluation Organization: *Panchayat Election in Rajasthan*, Jaipur.

Appendix 1.4
PROFILES OF VILLAGE LEADERS

Ram Pratap—Young Cultivator

Ram Pratap 40 is the *Sarpanch* of the newly created *panchayat*. He belongs to a prosperous, influential, and respected land-owning-cultivating Meena family. The family has the biggest landholding in the village and has enjoyed the position of being its most prosperous and influential family for a long time. It is also well known and respected, in its own caste, in the entire of the *Panchayat Samiti*. The family now consist of three brothers and own about 150 acres of good agricultural land in the village. One brother devotes himself entirely to cultivation while the other two spend time also in village's affairs and local politics. Ram Pratap is the middle brother. The oldest brother is the chairman of new *Nyaya (judicial) Panchayat* which has jurisdiction over seven *panchayat* circles and about 30 villages.

Ram Pratap is not new to local politics: he represented his village as member of the former *panchayat* for 3 years. But he has more authority and influence in his present position of *Sarpanch*. He is head of his own *panchayat*, and as a prominent member of the cultivating caste group, which dominates the *Panchayat Samiti* and is one of the most influential members of that body. An added source of power: he is related to and is a close associate of the *pradhan* of the *samiti*.

Like many other young or middle-aged leaders of his caste, Ram Pratap has rural and urban, agricultural and non-agricultural interests; in fact he stands between town and village in many ways. He has been educated, up to the primary standard.[1] While his principal economic interest is in cultivation and money-lending in the village, he also has a small retail shop in town. He goes to town often in connection with his business and political affairs. He is well acquainted with ways of commerce and of small town politics. His position in the *Panchayat Samiti* is making him increasingly acquainted with district and state level politics. However, he is by no means an urbanite: his primary interests are in the village and its affairs, and he comes to the town as a representative of his village and caste, not *vice-versa*.

1. Fifth class of school.

He is quiet and unassuming by temperament; but he had the confidence which comes from belonging to a substantial and respected family. He is not given to speech-making or throwing his weight about. Because of his position in his caste group and his relationship with the *pradhan*, he is influential in the *Panchayat Samiti*. His attitude towards officials is one of cooperation and tolerance. As he belongs to a family of hereditary *patels*, he knows official attitude and way of working quite well, and he is quite familiar with both the strength and weakness of the administration of the village, block and district levels. His relation with the *Vikas Adhikari* (Block Development Officer) and staff of the *Panchayat Samiti* are quite cordial.

Ram Pratap's position in the *panchayat* is an expression primarily of the position of influence and respect which his family has enjoyed in this village for a long time; his position in the *Panchayat Samiti* is an expression of the preponderance of his caste in the area. The family was respected and this man is judged to be a worthy member of the family and therefore considered quite suitable to lead the *panchayat* and to represent the village in the *samiti*.

Ram Pratap considers the *Panchayat Samiti* to be a continuation of the Community Development Block, which did good things for villages in the area; he feels that through his position in the *samiti* he can get things done for his villages and for members of his caste. However, he has been able to accomplish this objective only to the limited extent of getting loans for some cultivators. His village and *panchayat* circle have not got any funds for works programmes so far. He understands that this is due to shortage of funds with in the *samiti* and is not happy about the working of the *samiti* on this account. But he is very dissatisfied with the new small *panchayat* like the one he heads. He feels that these have neither power nor resources nor important functions. His *panchayat* consist of six small villages with a total population of about 2,500. Such sources of income as share of land revenue and sale of *abadi* lands-sources which brought substantial revenue to the former *panchayats*—bring in very little money now. The *panchayat* has not levied any taxes and had practically no money. The judicial function, which is the most important function of *panchayat* in the eyes of the villagers, has been transferred to the new *Nyaya Panchayats*. As an example of his *panchayat's* lack of power, Ram Pratap cited the instance of ill-treatment of the peon of the *panchayat* by the people of another village of the *panchayat* circle. The man was not allowed to enter the village when he went there on *panchayat's* work. Explaining the background of the incident, Ram Pratap mentioned that these people wanted the headquarters of the *panchayat* to be located in their own village and strongly represented anger at its location in Ram Pratap's village. They said that Ram Pratap's village is in one corner of the *panchayat* circle and is unapproachable during the rains while their own village was in the centre of *panchayat* circle and was accessible throughout the year. A more important reason was that the two villages had a long-standing feud, and these people did not want the *panchayat* headquarters to be located in a rival village. But, when their plea was rejected and Ram Pratap's village was finally selected because it was the largest village in the circle, they decided to boycott the *panchayat* election and the institution itself. In fact, people of this village and some sympathizers from other villages did not vote in the (1960) *panchayat* election. Their opposition continues, and their attitude towards the new *panchayat* is one of complete non-cooperation. Ram Pratap complained that the *panchayat* is powerless to do anything about it.

Ram Pratap is progressively taking more interest and spending more and more of his time in local "political work". He is very often at the district headquarter in connection with some work of *Panchayat Samiti* or the village. Currently he is spear-heading the demand of villagers for compensation for lands submerged and houses damaged by construction of an irrigation tank. The tank was constructed several years ago, but compensation has not been paid to the villagers so far. They also suffer great hardship during the rainy season when their village is almost surrounded by water. Ram Pratap feels that his village has a much better chance of getting a liberal settlement in this pre-election year (1961) than it would in other years. He had advocated the case before the local revenue officials; he has seen to it that they visit the spot and appreciate their difficulties; and he has sought the active support of the local M.L.A., and *pradhan* and had also been to the state capital and seen the ministers. His conduct in this case is an excellent illustration of the growing understanding among village leaders of the methods of obtaining action on their demands in a political democracy.

Bal Ram—Young Cultivator—Politician

Bal Ram is a self-made young man. He belongs to a poor cultivating family of *Chowkidar Meena* caste[2] and has attained his present position,

2. Certain castes and tribes were classified as criminal tribes during British times because of their tendency to commit crimes. The classification was abolished soon after Independence.

Sarpanch, of a large and important *panchayat* and an important executive of the *Panchayat Samiti* entirely through hard work, ability, and aggressive political campaigning. He is educated up to the eighth class and he has his service experience for several years. He started service with the *Jagirdar* of his village and was transferred to the subordinate service of the state when the *jagir* was resumed. He remained in state service for some years, and then resigned it to enter the Meena Reform Movement. His primary economic interest at present is a grain shop in the *panchayat* headquarter village, a trade of some local importance. His family lives in a nearby village, where they cultivate about 60 acres of land. Bal Ram has helped to acquire the land through allotment and purchase over the years. He is not rich and can barely manage to afford the standard of living and expense of travel, which his political activities require; but he is not poor either. However, his attitude is deeply collared by the poverty that he has known as a child.

Bal Ram gained his present position as a leader of his caste, via the Meena Reform Movement. This movement was aimed at modernization of the Meenas by encouraging modern education, and by abolishing a whole cluster of former caste-customs: group dancing at fairs, the use of heavy silver ornaments, distinctive peasant clothes, and a distinctive hair-do by the women, drinking and meat eating, child marriage, easy and frequent divorce, taking *Jhagra* money, etc. the movement was an organized articulation of the process of caste modernization; it began rapidly after the disappearance of the princely states. Bal Ram joined the movement in the early fifties after leaving state service. One of the things which prompted him to join this movement and which also accounts partly for his aggressiveness is the memory of the harsh treatment meted out to members of his caste during the time of the former Jaipur state, when they were classified as a criminal tribe. They were kept under surveillance and were often the victims of harsh treatment at the hands of petty police officials. He never suffered such treatment himself; but the sight of others suffering these inequities has left a deep impression on his young mind.

His attitude forms a fascinating study. He represents, at the local level, the militant and aggressive leadership, which has come up among the cultivating castes following disappearance of the *Jagirdari* and establishment of the democratic institutions. Leaders like Raja Ram represent the moderate section in the new leadership. He realizes that the basis of his leadership is caste and that he must retain the support of his caste to be elected to any political position. He appeals to caste loyalty in a frank and aggressive casteist fashion.

He is aggressive due partly to his feeling, perhaps unconscious, that as he belongs to the *Chowkidar Meena* group, his appeal must be more frankly casteist if he is to identify himself with the majority group and own their support. His aggression towards officials is due partly to his having been in a subordinate position in government earlier. He feels that he can now question and criticize the actions of official, whom he could only obey in the past and would have continued to obey if he had remained in service. However, he understands and respects government procedures and methods. He was in service too long not to have acquired the habit of respecting government orders!

Bal Ram is the leader of his faction in both his *panchayat* and the *Panchayat Samiti*. He became *Sarpanch* of his *panchayat* after a keen contest with a Mahajan rival who is much richer and whose family enjoys a position of respect in the village. His main supporters were the cultivating and lower castes, while his rival found support among the traders, Brahmins and other high castes. The election rivalry and prestige colour the attitudes and behaviour both by and towards him in the village. There are allegations of mismanagement of *panchayat* funds against him and he does not hesitate to deliver his counter punches whenever he has the opportunity. One result of the opposition has been his inability to impose any taxes. Even his very hard and successful work in getting the village a higher secondary school has not reduced the opposition. On the contrary, it has accentuated it because his rivals have interpreted the effort merely as a move to improving his own political prospects. Their judgment is not too unjust, because the effort did form part of his campaign to get political recognition and support for his claim to get the Congress Party ticket for election to the state legislature. In the *Panchayat Samiti*, he is a leading member of the dominant Meena group, and he has fully used the power, which this position gave him in getting *Taccavi* loans and other benefits for his supporters. This has created a certain feeling of dissatisfaction among the *samiti* members who do not belong to his group.

In spite of his partisanship and aggressiveness, Bal Ram could be a good development worker if he devoted his energies to this task. He demonstrated his capacities in the effort he made recently for establishment of the higher secondary school. He was active in mobilizing contributions for construction of the building and even more so in convincing the local officials, the MLA, and finally the ministers in Jaipur, that this was the most important demand of the village. He suggested that they must accept it if they were to win support in the election in this village and a large numbers of villages in the neighbourhood which would also derive benefit from the school. But his primary interest is in a political career. He is trying very hard to get the Congress Party ticket for election to the state legislature. He values his present position in the *Panchayat Samiti* and the power and the influence that it gives him in his village and the surrounding villages, even more so for the opportunity it offers for climbing to higher political positions. He feels that his caste needs "leaders" and he is one of them. Whether he succeeds in his political ambitions or not, will depend on his capacity to devote himself to the task and appeal aggressively to the caste consciousness of his people.

Jai Singh—Young Rajput

A young educated (up to the matriculation standard) Rajput, Jai Singh is the *Sarpanch* of a *Naya Panchayat*, which consists of five small villages with a population of about 2000. He is not an old resident of this village or even of this district. He makes a living by managing cultivation of his lands. Besides he operates a lime-kiln and lends money for additional income. He owes his political positions in the village partly due to his own personal qualities. He is a smart young politician who has successfully used the techniques of mobilizing local opinion behind a single issue to his own advantage. The issue is the location of headquarter of the new *Nyaya Panchayat*. He wants it shifted from a neighbouring village to his own village. His case is not strong: his village is smaller, much less important, and in many ways much less suitable for being the headquarters than the other villages. But he has been successful for his mobilizing, first people of his own *panchayat* circle, next of a majority of his members of the *Nyaya Panchayat* and finally of *Panchayat Samiti*. This is undoubtedly a major political accomplishment; it helped him in his candidature for *Sarpanch* and now makes him a prominent member of the *Panchayat Samiti*. Also, he wants to establish a grain market in his village. The prospectus for this are not bright, as the village is small, does not have good communications, and has no particular commercial potential. But his desire for development can be understood only as a typical reaction of a young man who has broken urban connections and is keen to re-create them in the village where he has come to settle down.

The small village is hardly sufficient to absorb his energies. He is a frequent visitor to the district town and to the state capital, and he maintains active contacts with district officials, local politicians, and member of the *Panchayat Samiti*. He is the young man about town. In an earlier age he would have been a member of the smart set, albeit of a small princely state (a role for which, alas, there is no scope today). His main motive in coming to the *panchayat* and the *Panchayat Samiti* is to establish his personal prestige and position in his own and surrounding villages and in the district headquarter town. He wants to be known and respected as a person of consequence in the area. His ambition is strictly local and is quite in accord with his *jagirdari* background. He has no great political ambition; though he may not rule out the prospect of becoming an M.L.A. or the *pradhan* of the *Panchayat Samiti* at some future date.

Sridhar—Educated Young Leader

Sridhar is the Brahmin *Sarpanch* of a large and prosperous village (population 5000), which has an important grain market. The village was the seat of an important *Jagirdar* of the former Jaipur state. Sridher's ancestors were tutors to the *Jagirdar's* sons and enjoyed a position of respect, influence, and authority in the village. Respect for the family has been an important factor in his election to the present position. The other factor has been the support of an old *vaidya*-cum-political worker who has lived in this village for about 25 years. Sridhar's family is not rich; but they are moderately well off. He himself manages the family lands (about 40 acres of good farm land) and has a share in a flour-mill in the village. The land has been given for cultivation on *batai* while the mill is being looked after by his partner. This economic interest guarantees him a comfortable, middle class living and also leaves him enough time for local politics.

Sridhar is well-educated (matriculation, Hindi *Sahitya Ratna*)[3] keen, and intelligent, with an interest in politics. He is the type who would have been an active fighter for freedom in the pre-Independence days and who joined the *Sarvodaya* movement[4] out of intellectual conviction. He has already worked for the *Bharat Sewak Samaj*[5] and for Harijan uplift; he still has considerable interest in constructive work. A fairly good speaker, he delights in public speaking and debate. He has considerable political ambition and would not mind making politics a career.

Before becoming *Sarpanch*, he was a member of the village *panchayat* for three years. He was elected *Sarpancha* after a very keen election contest in which there was some tension in the village. His principal rival was an influential Mahajan businessman who had been

---

3. A degree in Hindi
4. Bhoodan movement
5. An Association of voluntary service

Sarpanch for a number of years and who has the support of the businessmen, a numerous and powerful group in the commercial centre. Sridhar won with the support of the cultivators, artisans, *Chammars*, and people of the other low castes. The election campaign has left a deep rift in the village, which affects the working of the *panchayat*. The Mahajans are against him and his own attitudes and actions are quite partisan. He has made several complaints against the formal *Sarpanch* and his other political rivals. He has also talked about levying taxes on sales in the grain market, a move, which would affect the interest of the traders.

His village has made very good progress—economics and social-in the years following the formation of Rajsthan and abolition of *jagirdari*. A grain market has been established; business has increased enormously; a large number of *pucca* houses have been built, and a number of development works and social service institutions have been started. To some extent progress represented catching up with modern times and realizing the economic potentials of the village, both of which become possible after removal of the restriction on economic progress (e.g. on construction of *pucca* houses) which had prevailed in the *Jagirdar's* time. The village took an active interest in the Community Development work and a number of works and development activities concentrated in it. The higher secondary school and the dispensary are the most important institutions to be located in the village during recent years. The villagers have built a very good building for the school at the cost of about Rs. 40,000 and are particularly proud of this achievement. The *panchayat* has a substantial income because of the grain market and a fair, which is held annually at a local shrine; it has been an active institution.

Sridhar is anxious that this progress should continue. He takes an active interest in the work of *panchayat* and in development activity generally. He has proposed a number of taxes for increasing the income of *panchayat*. He is active in campaigning for improvement of existing development institutions and location of new ones. He is currently campaigning for the addition of science wing in the higher secondary school. He would like to see progress in his village and small industry attracted to it. He meets officials and non-officials frequently to overcome some local difficulty or to improve some institutions.

But he faces serious handicaps in working for the development of his village. In the *panchayat* and the village he has the stiff opposition of the traders and the others who opposed his election. As a result, it is likely that many of the taxes he is proposing will not be levied, and if levied, will not be collected. Contributions for development works cannot be obtained on any large scale for the same reasons. In the *Panchayat Samiti* he finds himself in a hopeless minority, because he does not belong to the cultivating caste group, which dominates its affairs. Moreover, the members of the *Panchayat Samiti* feel, not entirely without justification, that the village received its share of development funds during the time of the Community Development Block; that it is a rich semi-urban, commercial village which can afford to take up works on its own; and that no substantial development funds need be given to it now. Sridhar protests against this attitude of the *Panchayat Samiti* members but his protest has produced no affect so far. Finally, he is not a good executive. He is a thinker and a speaker, not a man of action. Many of his ideas will remain unimplemented because he neither has the personal qualities to implement them, nor the ability to mobilize the required support for them in the *panchayat* or the *Panchayat Samiti*.

His position as *Sarpanch* and member of the *Panchayat Samiti* gives him considerable authority and influence in the village. This is a great satisfaction for one whose family has enjoyed respect and authority in the village and who would like to see this position reaffirmed. Even more important, it gives him a chance to pursue his political career as he can meet people at the block, district, and even state level. He spends quite some time in these political contacts and is somewhat of a lieutenant of the local M.L.A. He realizes his handicaps in pursuing a political career; he does not belong to the dominant cultivating caste and is not rich. But he is more conscious of his assets—public speaking ability, intelligence, education and a personal charm, and feels that with these he can be a success. He has no immediate political objective, but in course of time he would not mind trying for positions like *pradhan* and M.L.A.

He is somewhat critical about the *Panchayat Samiti*. He feels keenly that this is a show for group and caste politics and *Sarpanchas* like himself who are in the minority cannot do much in it. He speaks openly and frequently against the partisan character of the *samiti* and is one of the most vocal critics in this area, of the whole system of *Panchayati Raj* institutions.

Ram-Das—Chammar Representative

Ram Das is the only *Sarpanch* of his caste in the *Panchayat Samiti* and one of the few in the district. He heads one of the newly created *panchayat* with jurisdiction over 5 small villages (population 3000). The villages are located near a town, and large numbers of people are engaged in them in non-agricultural occupations—industrial and casual labour, petty trade, and professions. The caste composition of the population is also very mixed, with no one caste predominant. Ram Das's own caste is in a small minority in these villages, and he has been elected with the support of the other castes, which makes his achievement even more creditable.

He represents the advanced group of the young men of his caste who depend upon non-agricultural labour and other non-agricultural occupations and who have been greatly affected by urban contacts. Educated up to the middle standard, he is a small contractor; he has the labour contracts for loading and unloading freight on the railway. His father was a railway employee, and his uncle had a similar labour contract in another part of the country. He was born and brought up in a non-agricultural environment and started life as small contractor-cum-businessman. After two failures, he settled down in his present business, which requires management of human beings; he successfully runs a business, which employs a labour force of about 600 men. This large labour force is an important resource for elections! Besides giving him his own voting strength, it provides him with the manpower so essential in fighting elections.

Although a non-agriculturist, he has some links with agriculture and rural life. Two of his brothers are engaged in cultivation. He wants to get them more land, and he would like to get some land for cultivation himself.

This is not his first entry into local politics. For several years, he was member of the former large *panchayat* of which his village then formed a part. Two years ago, he contested for the *Sarpanchship* of the *panchayat*. He was defeated, but he gave his opponent a very stiff fight. He says that he would have won but for the fraudulent practices of his opponent. He has won the present election by a comfortable margin.

Ram Das is very conscious of the fact that his caste, which forms a substantial section of the rural population, is seriously under-represented in the *Panchayat Samiti*. He would like to see this imbalance corrected at least in part, at the next *panchayat* election. He is aware of the special measure being taken for social and economic uplift of his caste and the social concessions being given to them; but he feels that what he has done is not enough, that much more should be done quickly. He feels particularly strongly about the *Panchayat Samiti's* reaction to the needs of his caste. He is himself a member of the standing committee which deals with programmes for the under-privileged groups; but he says that during his 10 months in the committee he has been able to get grant for only one drinking-water well for Harijans, and even in that he faced strong opposition from other members of the committee. He complained that the *Panchayat Samiti* was dominated by the Meenas and would not give a fair deal to his caste; but he emphasized that as long as he is there he would not let them have their own way entirely. "They are afraid of me", he added.

Besides looking after the interests of his caste in the *Panchayat Samiti*, Ram Das takes interest in the affairs of his village and is pressing for funds for development. However, in this also he is not very successful. He said that his village has several needs, of which a drinking water was most urgent. The villagers were prepared to contribute their share of the cost, but funds were not sanctioned by the *Panchayat Samiti*. "The *samiti* has not even given *panchayat* a grant for street lighting which it has given to most other *panchayats*". He said the discrimination has coloured his attitude towards the *Samiti* and he is quite critical of its working.

Like many other *Sarpanchas* of new small *panchayats*, he feels that the institutions have no resources, few functions, and very little powers. His *panchayat* has levied no taxes. Its meagre income comes mainly from the sale of *abadi* lands, which together with granting permits for construction of houses appears to him to be the only function of the *panchayat*. He is anxious to get more area converted into *abadi*, because sales of the house sites in the next *abadi* will, give the *panchayat* a good source of income. It will also help meet the need for more houses, the most urgently felt need in his village. He is also trying to get land allotted for a separate colony of Harijans. When asked about the power of *panchayats*, his first reply was that the judicial function had been taken away; the *panchayts* had "very little power left". As an example, he mentioned that a rival whom he had defeated in the election for *Sarpanch* has instigated some people of his village. The *panchayat* has served notices on these people, but was not in a position to do anything further, because it could not displease a fairly powerful section of the village.

As mentioned above, he is a competent and successful businessman; however, in spit of his economic and political success, he has not yet got over the self-consciousness and inferiority complex which one finds in many urbanized young and middle-aged persons of the *Chammar* caste. He is not aggressive; on the contrary he is shy and has a tendency to withdraw within himself.

He has given no indication yet of having any higher political ambition. His business absorbs most of his time and energy, and since he runs it by himself he has to give it his first attention. But he will probably not be opposed to seeking a political career somewhat later. He is young and has already made a bid for *Sarpanchship* of a large *panchayat*. He is quite aware of the fact that he has several advantages, some money, education, and contacts with officials and non-officials, executive ability—which is highly prized in political life and is so scarce among people of his caste.

Raja Ram—Prosperous Farmer-cum-Businessman

An important executive of *Panchayat Samiti*, Raja Ram comes from an old, respected and prosperous Meena family of a large village. Members of his extended family are influential and respected in the entire area of the *Panchayat Samiti.* They are also connected through marriage with many leading families of the caste in the area. His nephew is the *Sarpancha* of the village *panchayat*; other members of the extended family fill important positions in the cooperative society, the *panchayat* and the *Nyaya Panchayat*. Several *Sarpanchas, patels* and other leading persons of the *Panchayat Samiti* area are related to the family through marriage. They are solid rural people: not rich, but substantial and comfortable. Raja Ram and his two brothers owned a farm of about 100 acres. The land is cultivated by hired labour under the supervision of Raja Ram's brother. The farm is successful, sugarcane being especially remunerative. They attempted pump irrigation some years ago, but without conspicuous success. They are bold but rather conservative farmers and they have not made any major changes or technological improvements in their cultivation. Besides cultivation, they also lend money, and Raja Ram has an interest in a shop in the town.

Raja Ram is educated only up to the primary standard, and although he is quite familiar with urban ways, he is essentially a villager and a farmer. He is a quiet, unassuming, well-mannered person—intelligent, even shrewd, but completely honest. As a result, he commands respect and the complete confidences of *Sarpanchas* of his caste in the *Panchayat Samiti*. His present position in the *samiti* is due as much to his personal qualities as to the position of his family in the area. As he comes from a family of hereditary *patels*, he is familiar with local administration and has an attitude of cooperation and respect for officials. He is friendly with the officers of the *samiti* and sympathetic towards the lower staff. These attitudes and behaviour are in no small part responsible for the smooth functioning of the *samiti*.

Local politics is a hobby with him. He has been associated with the *Panchayat Samiti* ever since its formation in 1959. Earlier he had been a prominent member of the Block Development Committee of the Community Development Block. He has also interested himself in district and state level politics. He contested election (unsuccessfully) for the state legislature in 1957 and is counted among the probable local candidates for the next (1962) election.

The main source of his strength is of course the position of his family among the Meenas, who have emerged as the dominant social group in the area after abolition of *Jagirdari* and establishment of representative institutions. Members of the caste want their own representative in position of prestige and power. Raja Ram, worthy scion of an old and respectable family, fills this need admirably. Since his position rests in the support of people of his caste, he must do things to keep them pleased and must make an appeal to caste loyalties to retain his position. But he is not aggressive and does not encourage caste and community friction unnecessarily. He must favour members of his group and caste; but he would not do anything blatantly unjust. He is essentially a gentleman.

He sees his position in his *Panchayt Samiti* as a position of prestige and power, one which enables him to control financial and other benefits that flow from the state government for developing of rural areas. He and his supporters control the *Panchayat Samiti* fairly effectively and have no difficulty in directing the flow of benefits to villages and the people of their choice. He appreciates the advantages of *Panchayati Raj* institutions and feels that they give the rural people precisely the kind of say that they should have in development programmes. He is interested in their success. But he is quite conscious of their difficulties and weaknesses. His main complaint is that the *panchayats* and the *Panchayat Samitis* have such meagre resources. He thinks that many of the charges of discrimination levelled against him and his group by their rivals in the *Panchayat Samiti* would disappear if the *samiti* had more funds and could be more liberal in giving grants and loans.

Tara Chand—A Representative of the Cultivating Castes

Like Raja Ram, described above, Tara Chand is also an important executive of a *Panchayat Samiti*, belongs to one of the oldest, most influential and prosperous Meena families of a big village of his *Panchayat Samiti* area. The family owns a substantial acreage of rich farm land, a large portion of which is irrigated, and grows paddy; a highly remunerative crop. Tara Chand and other members of his family personally supervise the Cultivation of their land. They are known to be among the wealthiest cultivators in the *samiti* area. Tara Chand claims that he and other members of the family were instrumental in reviving cultivation of paddy in the village about 20 years ago, when they found that due to an increase in rainfall and sub-soil moisture (the village had been receiving canal irrigation for more than 50 years), their Jowar crop was not doing well. They experimented with paddy and found the result extremely satisfactory: paddy produce has increased considerably in this area during the last 15 years, and Tara Chand's family has made very good money.

After coming into the *Panchayat Samiti* two years ago, Tara Chand had taken an active interest in the agricultural improvement programme. His most important achievement has been repair and renovation of several small irrigation tanks. The *Panchayat Samiti* has a large number of such tanks built, and maintained by the cultivators themselves. Of late maintenance of these tanks has been in arrears and many of them have deteriorated. In 1961 a large sum of money was received for benefit of the schedule tribes, and six tanks located in Tara Chand's village were repaired with it. This work has benefited the land owning cultivators of his village, most of who belong to his caste. This shrewd peasant saw in the special fund, an opportunity to benefiting the cultivators of his village, including members of his own and extended families. The money was available without too much political pressure, and he quickly took it. Also, with the unerring eye of the shrewd peasant he used it for a work, which would yield benefits quickly and for a long time. This work has brought a solid benefit to cultivators of his village and greatly raised his stock.

Tara Chand is not well educated. He knows Hindi well, but not English. But he is a shrewd businessman and has plenty of commonsense. He is also tough: he has a strong will and is unquestionably the boss in whichever position he is. His supporters, as well as the staff of any institution in which he works, must obey him. He is a good friend but a bad enemy. However, his attitude towards officials is not without respect and understanding: it cannot but be influenced by the tradition of respect for and obedience to officials of the revenue department in his family of hereditary *patels.* The working of his *Panchayat Samiti* has not been marked by any serious feuds, but this is because he has been able to have his way in all matters of interest to him and his group.

He has taken an active interest in local and district politics for some time. He is an active party worker, has been an aspirant for legislative offices, and is planning to take an active part in the forthcoming elections. Politics to him is a means of asserting the position of his family in his caste, and of his caste in the block and the district. His family has been settled in this area for centuries and has enjoyed respect and influence in the village and the surrounding villages for decades. In recent years, they have made good money and have become known as wealthy people. They see political position as a means of asserting themselves. Tara Chand is the symbol of their influence and strength. Also behind him are his group in the villages. They are with him as against other leaders of his caste including the present member of the state legislature who also comes from the same village. He is frankly casteist, and his main political appeal is to caste solidarity. He is anxious to exploit fully the caste motive for enlisting support for himself in his political battle. He would also fight for continuation of the privileges enjoyed by members of his caste. But if he were trained to rise above narrow caste loyalty and take up a wider cause, he would prove to be a tough fighter. He is the material from which fighters for great causes are made by the leaders of political movements.

Raj Singh—A Representative of the Old Rural Elite

Raj Singh is a middle-aged Rajput and a former *Jagirdar*. He belongs to a family of small *Jagirdars* but is related to most of the leading *Jagirdar* families of this area. He is also an ex-soldier. He was an officer in the Jaipur state army for about 20 years; he was in the Indian army also and saw action during Second World War. He came back to settle down on his family land soon after Independence. *Jagirdari* abolition was in the air at the time, and his main object in coming back to his village was to prevent the family land from being lost to the tenants. Cultivation of this land is his main source of livelihood now. Part of the land has been given for cultivation on *batai*; the remainder is being cultivated by him with the help of *halis*. The standard of cultivation is only fair because Raj Singh is not a good manager. However, income from the land together with the Army pension give him enough to maintain a middle-class standard of living and especially to pay for the education of his sons, who are studying in schools and colleges in Jaipur. Like other educated Rajputs of the area, he sees education as the only salvation for members of his group, and to see his sons educated and well placed in service is his main objective in life now. He proposes to persuade one of his sons to stay on the land, and expects that the remaining three will be successful in getting good jobs in government and commercial firms.

Raj Singh is educated up to the matriculation standard. He is a quiet and undemanding person, who nevertheless impresses one with his dignity and self-confidence. He has a position of established respect among the

Rajputs of this area. Few of the former *Jagirdars* are living in the village now, and among those who are, there are few who are educated or have a modern outlook; so his position as a leader of the group in this area is undisputed.

He had taken an active interest in local affairs. He was the *Sarpanch* of the *panchayat* of his village for several years, and was re-elected in 1960. But he had to give up this position on election to his present post of *Pradhan* of the *Panchayat Samiti*. He is active also in the cooperative movement and holds important position in several cooperative institutions. He is also interested in the affairs of soldiers and former *Jagirdars*, and has served on local committees constituted from time to time for their welfare. All in all, he is an influential and respected member of his caste, people of his own and surrounding villages and the officers. Of course he has opposition. He was elected *Sarpanch* in 1960 only after a stiff fight and opposition to him in the *panchayat* circle and the *Panchayat Samiti*, continuous to be active. He sees that the membership in the *panchayat*, the *Panchayat Samiti* and the cooperative institutions confers prestige, power and influence. His family and the large Rajput ex-*jagirdar* group, to which he belongs, have always exercised power in the area, and his motive in seeking membership in these institutions is to maintain a position of power and respect. He explains that people of his caste and his village expected that he, as an intelligence, able and affluent member of a former *Jagirdar* family should take an active part in these institutions. But an element of gain is also mixed with this. "These are institution of power and if I and others (Rajput ex-*jagirdars*) like me do not take interest in them, their power might be used against us", he says. But he is satisfied with positions in local institutions and has no ambition with higher political office. He realizes that his caste and group affiliations and moderate personal income are serious handicaps in pursuing a political career. Besides by temperament and training, he is not a politician. He was brought up as a country gentleman and will be content to remain one.

Amar Singh—A Constructive Cultivator-Leader

Amar Singh, the Rajput *Sarpanch* of a medium sized village (population 2500), is in his middle fifties. He belongs to one of the Rajput families, which had rent-free grants from the *Jagirdar* of the village. The Rajputs, belonging to the same caste as the *Jagirdar*, were the most important people of the village at that time. But Amar Singh's family had little land, they were relatively poor, and had little influence in the village;

he has built the position which he enjoys in the village today, largely by himself.

He left the village as a young man about 35 years ago. He remained in the service of a *Jagirdar* in a neighbouring district for 20 years, and came back to settle down in the village about 15 years ago. Since his return he has improved his cultivation, increased his holding, and has gradually risen to the position of the leader of the village. He is *Sarpanch* of the *panchayat* and chairman of the large-sized cooperative society. What is more, he and his group (which includes his nephew and cousins, two leading Mahajans and some prominent cultivators) control almost all the important positions in village level institutions. The group controls all but two seats in the *panchayat*. Amar Singh's nephew is the representative of the village on the *Nyaya Panchayat*. A cousin is secretary of the cooperative society and a member of executive of the Land Mortgage Bank of the district. The group also represents the village on the district Cooperative Bank and the Cooperative Marketing Society.

Amar Singh has been *Sarpanch* of the *panchayat* ever since its formation in 1954. At first he was elected unopposed, but then in two elections he had contestants. The contest in 1960 was quite stiff, and he did not win by a comfortable margin. His support is either among the Rajputs and the Brahmins or among the *Chammars* and the other low castes. *Malis*, Jats, Meenas, *Gujjars*, etc. are not very happy with him; they did not vote for him at the last election. The support of the scheduled castes rests on the solid work, which he had done for them after coming back to the village. During his stay outside the village he was influenced by the ideology of the Congress Party and wanted to put it into practice on return. At that time the village was still under the *Jagirdar*. But he (Rajput) expressed himself in favour of abolition of *Jagirdari*, and lent active support to abolition of *begar* (forced labour). There were some incidents between the servants of *Jagirdar* and the villagers on the issue of *begar* in the early fifties, in which he expressed himself against the *Jagirdar*. This annoyed the *Jagirdar*, but it gave Amar Singh a standing in the village and especially among the low castes. He has also worked for abolition of untouchability, and on the two occasions when there were conflicts between the Chammars and the rest of the village, he supported the former. The first occasion was provided by the Chammars' decision to stop lifting carcasses and the second by their decision to build a temple and install an idol of Lord Krishna in it. The cultivators and the members of the high castes, including the Rajputs, have not appreciated his role in this case. They are jealous also of the monopoly in positions of the village level institutions, which Amar Singh and his supporter enjoy. Some of them complain that members of this group have used the positions for personal gain: spcifically, that they have themselves taken most of the *Taccavi* loans given by the Community Development Block. Others complain that the grants for construction of the school building and other works have not been properly utilized, and that money received from the government has been used personally for long periods before being spent for public works. The Meenas in particular, are so angry with him that they have completely boycotted the cooperative society.

These allegations are not without foundation. Amar Singh and members of his group have undoubtedly obtained *Taccavi* loans and other advantages from the Community Development Block. They have also been prominent in obtaining loans from the district Land Mortgage Bank. It is also true that some of the *taccavi* loans have not been properly utilized, and that construction of the works was delayed for long periods. On the other hand, one must give credit to Amar Singh for obtaining for the village almost every grant, loan and other facilities given by the Community Development Block. Almost every public work included in the programme of the Community Development Block—building for the village school, office of the *panchayat*, office-cum-godown of the cooperative society and residence of the V.L.W., two drinking water wells, and pavement of the village *Bazar*—was taken upon in the village. He obtained fund for theses works from the block and raised contributions from the village people. His village was judged to be one of the most responsive to development activities in the district in 1958 and was awarded a cash grant of Rs. 2000 for attaining this distinction. Amar Singh then saw the benefits available from the cooperative movement, especially from the new large-sized societies, which began to be established by the cooperative department after 1956. One such society was established in the village in 1957. He worked hard in building it up, and he is mainly responsible for bringing it to its present position: it has the highest loan operations of any society in the district, and is considered to be a 'model'. Even now he works constantly for the society; he particularly sees to it that recoveries are realized in full. He understands that good recovery of loans advanced, is the key to healthy functioning of the society and spares neither effort nor personal popularity to achieve it. Finally, he is the only village leader in this area who has grasped the value of the long-term loans offered by the newly opened Land mortgage Bank, and the village advances made by the bank to cultivators in this village—the only one in the district—are the result largely of his efforts.

Even his critics admit that he was a very competent and constructive worker that the various village institutions would not function well without his interest and effort.

All in all Amar Singh understands the essential nature of the new economic and political institutions very well, and he knows how to use them for the good of his village and himself. He keeps himself well informed about district and state level politics. But he has no political ambition, and is content to pass the rest of his life as a farmer and village leader. He has contacts in town: his daughter is married there, and one son is working there. But his own interest is in the village and in looking after his land.

Like so many others who have been associated with the Community Development Programme for a number of years and were *Sarpanchas* of former large multi-village *panchayats*, Amar Singh is very dissatisfied with the present *panchayats* and *Panchayat Samiti.* The *panchayat* which earlier had jurisdiction over ten villages and a substantial income, the jurisdiction of the present *panchayat* is limited to one village and its income is barely sufficient to meet the administrative expenses of keeping a clerk and a peon. The transfer of judicial function to the *Nyaya Panchayat* has robbed it much of its power. The new *Panchayat Samiti* is dominated by the Meenas with the result that non-Meenas like him are in a minority and have little say in its functioning. Amar Singh, in spite of his associations with the development institutions for a number of years, and his outstanding work for his village, has not been made a member of any standing committee of the *Panchayat Samiti*. Moreover, his village has not received any grant for a construction work or other development activity ever since the formation of the new *Panchayat Samiti*. All this cannot but make him unhappy.

Suraj Mal—Small Town Politician

An educated Mahajan about 35 years old, Suraj Mal is an important executive of a *Panchayat Samiti*. He comes from an old family of cultivators-cum-moneylenders in a village near the *Panchayat Samiti* headquarter town, and even though he is himself settled in a small business in the town, his links with the village remain active and close. His brothers are engaged in cultivation of the family holding, he himself has taken interest in its improvement. Recently, he helped his brothers obtain a large *Taccavi* loan for installation of a pump on the irrigation well. He has also been actively associated with the village *panchayat*. He was elected its *Sarpanch* in 1960, and gave up the position only on election to his present office in the *Panchayat Samiti*. But, his primary interest is in the town where he lives. He hopes that with the support of the town's people he can realize his ambition to achieve a position in state level politics.

He entered politics as a young man, fresh from college, 15 years ago. At that time, he came under the influence of a leading political figure of the state that aroused his interest in politics and gave him his first political lesson. He has been active in local politics ever since and has filled several important positions in local bodies. He came to politics not as a spokesman of any particular caste, community, or interest group; but only as an individual, with attractive personal qualities. He is a fairly effective street-corner speaker, a good debater and agitator, and a bit of a demagogue. He has administrative experience (of local bodies) and has good political contacts at the local and state levels. But he has his limitation also. His profession, even through it gives him time and inclination for political work, does not bring him much money; nor does it bring him into active contact with the people. He does not have the support of any powerful caste group or region. Finally, he is a faction leader, and lacks the qualities, which would win him support from all sides. His ambition is to enter state level politics by winning a seat in the state legislature, and it is towards this end that he is working all the time.

His position in the *Panchayat Samiti* gives him political influence and power, keeping busy with the game of small town and local area politics, and at the same time keeps himself in the limelight, for consideration for a position in state level politics. He takes active, continuous and detailed interest in the work of the *samiti*. He spends a lot of time in the *samiti* office; he tours extensively, takes an interest in the problems of the rural people and makes a sincere attempt to meet them in so far as this is possible within the limited resources and power of the *samiti*. He has acquired a thorough knowledge of the legislation relating to the *panchayat* and the *Panchayat Samiti* and various administrative procedures prescribed under it. He knows precisely what the member of the *Panchayat Samiti*, the block development officer and the other staff of the *samiti* can or cannot do. He is probably better informed about these things than the Block Development Officer himself. But his relations with the B.D.O. and other members of the *samiti* staff are not good. One reason for this is that his position in the *samiti* is not secure. His group does not have a comfortable majority in the *samiti*; the opposition is strong and active and has already made two attempts to unseat him. Therefore, he finds it necessary to keep members of his group and his supporters pleased and his opponents in check. He often interferes in appointment and transfer of *samiti* staff and violates prescribed procedures and rules in sanctioning loans, grants etc. This brings him in conflict with the Block Development Officer and other members of the *samiti* staff. A second reason is personal. He is capable of original and at times unorthodox ideas, and he is so carried away by them that he does not mind violating rules and procedures, and even risking administrative unfeasibility in their implementation. This quality, which could be an asset in a business executive—he would probably make a good one, is not without its handicaps in an executive of a *Panchayat Samiti*.

Lal Chand—Small Town Politician

A small town lawyer, Lal Chand, is one of the oldest, most active and prominent political workers in the district. He filled important positions in local political institutions and in the district organization of the Congress Party and was for some years a member of the state legislature. He is a clever, well-educated, extremely energetic and ambitious person with considerable political acumen and capacity for organization, who would have been successful in business or a profession anywhere.

His interest in local politics is purely professional; he does not represent any caste, economic interest group or village. It arose because his profession allowed him time and opportunity—for political activity. He was excited by the political support, saw that the rewards of success were good, and felt that with his ability, ambition and drive, he could make it. But he has not been successful so far. After some years of local political work he was elected a member of the state legislature in the early 1950s. But he could not advance to a position in the state cabinet—for which he had intense ambition—or even to retain his legislature seat. He now confines his activities to the local level and is at present a member of *Zila Parishad.* But he sees his present position in the institution primarily as a platform for continuing his political activity. It helps him to remain on the local political scene and keep trying for a position in state level politics. But he is little interested in rural development and welfare of the rural people, which are the primary object of the work of the *Zila Parishad.* His position in the institution is not too important; he lost the contest for an important position. But he is an influential member of the body because he is an eloquent speaker—often regarded as extremely effective behind the scene political worker. In one word, he is one of the many small town politicians who have gate-crashed into *Panchayati Raj* institutions and are using these merely as stepping stones to higher political office.

Sagar Mal—Small Town Businessman

Sagar Mal is an energetic, middle-aged businessman, who is *Sarpanch* of a large semi-urbanized village, located near the block headquarter town. He comes from one of the old and respected business families of his village. Educated up to the middle standard, he is established in a small construction contract business with work in and around the town.

Sagar Mal has taken an active interest in the affairs of the *panchayat* and in development activities in the village for almost a decade. He was a member of the *panchayat* for several years, was elected as *Sarpanch* in 1958, and was re-elected in 1960. This period has been one of rapid development and change for his village. With expansion of commerce and industry in the neighbouring town, the people of the village have been getting jobs in the town and nearby factory in increasing numbers, and outsiders with jobs in the town or the factory have been coming to live in the village. As a result, incomes have gone up, local business (retail distribution, etc.) has expanded; a large number of *pucca* houses have been built, and the village has been deeply affected by urban influences. It is fast becoming a suburb of the town and will before long form part of it. This period had also seen establishment of a number of institutions—a middle school, a primary school for girls, an *ayurvedic* dispensary and an animal husbandry centre—in the village. The village *Bazar* has been paved, and several new drinking water wells have been constructed with grants from the community development block. Agriculture has been improved, and is being gradually reorganized to supply for urban demand for milk, vegetables and fruit.

Sagar Mal has taken an active interest in development of the village. He has obtained grants for works from the Community Development Block and raised contributions within the village. His construction business brings him in close contact with block and district officers. He has also established good relations with officers, which also helps him in his business. Many of his critics in the village say that he has used his position as *Sarpanch* of the *panchayat* to build up these contacts and he has utilized them for furthering his business interests. But even they cannot deny that he has helped the village to get grants for works and to establish the new service institutions.

The *panchayat* of his village is quite wealthy. It has good sources of income—in cattle fair and in sale of *abadi* lands. Sagar mal has set up construction business in the town. But it is alleged by some of the block staff and by his critics in the village that the *panchayat* accounts are never in order and that Sagar Mal takes an inordinately long time in rendering accounts for grants given to his *panchayat*. However, there are no allegations against him either of appropriation of funds or of wasting money. Part of the account difficulty arose precisely from his over-enthusiastic interest in development work and anxiety for rapid development. He started several works in quick succession, diverting money granted for one work to another and *vice-versa* as need arose, with the result that the accounts got mixed up. It appears also that he did not always keep grants for these works strictly separate from investment in his town construction business.

He has a very active opposition in his village, especially among people of his own and other high castes, and he derives his support chiefly from the cultivators and scheduled castes. In the 1960 election, he was elected with the support of these castes; the high caste vote was largely against him. This opposition is due partly to old family rivalries: people of other old, wealthy, and respected high caste families are jealous of his position. Many others are annoyed with him because of his conduct as *Sarpanch*. They allege that many of his decision in cases brought before the *panchayat*, and other actions as *Sarpanch*, have been partisan or have been actuated more by expediency than by principles.

His influence in the affairs of the Community Development Block has also declined markedly after the constitution of the *Panchayat Samiti* in 1959, and especially after formation of the present *samiti* in 1961. Before the constitution of the *Panchayat Samiti*, he was among the most influential members of the Committee, which advised the Block Development Officers. He maintained good relations with officials and as his village is close to block headquarters, besides being rich and progressive, it received much more than its share of attention of the block staff and funds for development. After formation of the *Panchayat Samiti*, however, his influence decreased because the *samiti* began to be dominated by the Meenas. But he was still one of the fifteen *sarpanches* comprising the *samiti*. The present *Panchayat Samiti* however, has forty five *Sarpanchas*; the dominance of the Meenas has increased further, and non-Meenas like him have very little influences in it. Moreover, the Meena *Sarpanchas* coming from small villages feel,—not without justification—that Sagar Mal's village received more than its share of funds in the past and need not receive any large grant now. As a result, he is dissatisfied with the working of the *Panchayat Samiti*. He realizes that the *samiti* will continue to be dominated by the Meenas and that persons like him cannot have influence in it. He is, therefore, concentrating his energies in building up the *panchayat*. Fortunately for him, his *panchayat* is quite wealthy and its case-work and the other activities are enough to absorb his energies.

What does a person like Sagar Mal seeks in membership of the *panchayat* or the *Panchayat Samiti*? The answer lies in one word: recognition. He belongs to an old and respected family of the village. His position in the *panchayat* enables him to have an important say in village affairs and thus to re-assert and reinforce the family's position in the village. His membership in the *Panchayat Samiti* makes him as a person of some consequence in the local area. But like many others in this profile, Sagar Mal is quite satisfied with confining his political activity to the local level and has no keen ambition for higher political office. He is conscious of his limitations in pursuing a political career—small finances, business community background, limited education, etc.—and will probably not seek a political office like a seat in the state legislature for a long time.

Raj Mal—An Old Village Leader

An old man of about 60 years, Raj Mal, is *Sarpanch* of a large village. He comes from a high caste family of cultivators, which has been living in the village for centuries and is one of the oldest and most respected families in the entire area of the *Panchayat Samiti*. At one time, it was the largest joint family of cultivators in the area and the rulers of the Jaipur state had conferred a special honour on it. The family is now divided; but the members maintain good relations among themselves, and their support is an important source of strength for Raj Mal in his position in the *panchayat*.

He has fairly large agricultural holding: the land is highly productive, and the standard of cultivation is very high. Besides cultivation, Raj Mal lends money and has an interest in a flour-mill in the town. He is well off: indeed, he is one of the rich men of the village.

His village is about the most faction-ridden in the entire area of the *Panchayat Samiti*. It is a large village (population about 5000), with a concentration of Mahajans and Brahmins. Most of the people are educated. Many of them have left the village for government service or the business. Others remain behind and are engaged in some petty trade and money-lending, supplementing their earnings with income from non-cultivating ownership of small areas of ancestral lands. Most of those who have left live in the neighbouring towns and villages and continue to take interest in the affairs of "their own village". The businessmen continue to make contributions for projects of benefits to their caste or the village; they have recently made handsome contributions for construction of two major buildings—a higher secondary school and a primary health centre with a six-bed hospital. Both these institutions were located in this village because it satisfied the condition of local contribution laid down by the state government. But such outside interest and interference contributes to factional rivalries and quarrels within the village; though the main reason for these is that life in the village does not fully absorb the energies of these intelligent and educated people. The villagers frequently say that there are no large, well organized factions in their village, that there are no long standing disputes or deep seated reasons for quarrels, and that people quarrel simply because they must, or because every educated person feels that his opinion must be heard and accepted. "Every one is a 'leader' (*neta*) in this village", they explain.

Raj Mal has been the *Sarpanch* of the village *panchayat* for almost a decade. At the time of the latest (1960) *Panchayat* election, he was not too keen to enter the contest; but he was persuaded to do so at the last moment. He won by a comfortable margin. He is a soft-spoken, unassuming, rather shy, frail, old man. But he is neutral between the rival factions and has reputation for being sagacious and completely honest. His values and outlook are completely tradition-oriented, but he represents the best in tradition and faith in God and acting according to the *dharma* (righteousness). The villagers feel that they can trust him to take an impartial and intelligent view on any issue and to execute the decision with honesty. The traditional respect that his family has enjoyed reinforces the villagers' confidence in him. They know his limitations. They realize that he is not a dynamic personality, that he cannot speak eloquently and put the case of their village strongly in the *Panchayat Samiti*, and that he does not posses the energy to organize campaigns for particular causes within the village and to rush up to Sawai Madhopur or Jaipur to obtain support to them from officers, M.L.A.s, or Ministers. They understand very well that with a more vigorous *Sarpanch*, who could do all this and more, development of their village could have been faster and some of their present difficulties could have been removed. For example, they are very badly in need of an approach road: the village is eight miles from the metalled road and is completely isolated during the rains. More energetic *Sarpanch* could have got them a road. There are vigorous and forceful men in the village; but the villagers prefer Raj Mal because he is honest and wise. There is also the feeling that the record of development activity in his time, even though it has not been spectacular, has not been bad. Raj Mal has brought them together in spite of their quarrels and factions, and enabled them to mobilize contributions for major works like buildings for the higher secondary school and the primary health centre.

As *Sarpanch* of the *panchayat*, Raj Mal devotes his time mainly to resolving small disputes or attending to various administrative and municipal matters like granting permission for building a house or a shop; clearing encroachments; arranging street lighting, or cleaning the village *bazaar.* As this is a large village with a big *bazaar*, this work takes a lot of time. His *panchayat* has not suffered financial problem because the village is a commercial centre of some importance. In the *Panchayat Samiti*, his primary concern is to represent the interest of his village. He does not belong to the majority group in the *samiti* and is therefore, not an important member. But he is always heard with respect, because he represents the biggest village in the *samiti* area and because his personality inspires respect.

Even though he is a good cultivator himself, Raj Mal is not interested in such modern innovations as use of chemical fertilizers and pesticides. He believes in traditional methods of good farming. He cannot therefore be expected to act as an innovator or an unofficial extension worker. His main interest is in the works and programmes of the *Panchayat Samiti* and in obtaining *Taccavi* loans for cultivators of the village. Like many other experienced members of the *samiti*, he feels that funds for loans and grants are limited and committee discussions and procedural 'wrangles' are too many. He realizes that the *samiti* is dominated by the Meenas, who have their own way in everything and that he or others like him—high caste *sarpanchas* representing large villages—cannot influence its working much. But his attitude is one of quiet acceptance of this situation; there is no bitterness or rancour in it.

Harphool—A Representative of the Old World

Harphool is the sixty year old *Sarpanch* of a newly created *panchayat* having jurisdiction over six small villages (population about 1500). His own village, which is the head quarter of the *panchayat*, is a small single-caste village with only 65 households. He is the representative of the majority faction in the village and had won the *panchayat* election because of influence of the faction in this and other villages of the *panchayat* circle. His opponent, younger and wealthier, was the leader of the minority faction in the same village.

This is not Harphool's first experience with popular institutions. For nine years he was member of the large *panchayat* of which his village then formed part. He is also a prominent member of the successful cooperative society of his village. This is the first election contest however; earlier, he has always been returned unopposed. The contest has moreover badly split this small single caste village, which is known for its internal unity and enthusiasm for development works, and there is at present considerable bitterness among the rival factions. One cause of the bitterness is refusal of Harphool's faction to drawing of water by women of his opponents families from the well, located in their part of the village within the *abadi* and having abundant water throughout the year. The women of the families of opponents of Harphool's faction now draw water from another well, located at a distance of about one furlong (quarter of a mile). This causes them considerable hardship and these families are very angry with their opponents.

In the *Panchayat Samiti*, Harphool represents the old world, the traditional rural India; he is old, barely literate, steeped in tradition, and purely a cultivator whose interests are, confining to his fields, his village, and his relations and acquaintances in the surrounding villages. He is one of the few members of the *samiti* who cultivates his land. He has a holding of about forty acres, of which ten acres are irrigated. The income from this land is just sufficient to give him a comfortable living at the village standard. He is by no means rich, but he is comfortable and his satisfaction with life is enviable. Although a shrewd peasant, he is a back-bencher in the *Panchayat Samiti;* but as he forms part of the dominant Meena group, he is a member of an important standing committee of the *samiti*.

He has no knowledge of the *Panchayat Samiti Act* or of the prescribed rules and procedures, and he has to be guided in all these matters by officials or other members of the *samiti*. But he has plenty of common sense and knows what the interest of his village or his caste is. His primary interest in the *Panchayat Samiti* is to represent his village and his caste and he see that he can get for them grants and other benefits, which are obtainable through the *samiti*. In this he has been successful. He has been able to get a grant for repair to the village tank, the most keenly felt need of his village. But he feels that the formation of the *Panchayat Samiti* has not conferred any material benefits on the village people. He explained, "It is true, we make our own decisions now, in committee. But the money does not reach us in time because the new procedures are elaborate. Moreover, there is much less money now. Earlier, there was more money and the B.D.O. and extension officers of the Community Development

Block reached us and did their work quickly." This feeling is easily understandable, because his village did rather well during block times, being the recipient of a number of development works, including a school building, a drinking water well, and paved village streets.

Harphool is not enthusiastic about the new *panchayat* either. It has very little money, barely enough to pay the allowance of a school teacher who looks after its work part-time, has undertaken no development activity and has very limited power. About the only thing it has done so far, is to give permission for construction of a few *kucha* houses. "I did not want to start my career as *Sarpanch* with levying taxes on my own people", Harpool explained. He understands that with these limitations, the institutions cannot do more; but he is not too happy with its limited role.

Ram Devi—the Woman Member, an Extra Vote

Ram Devi, the wife of a young *Sarpanch*, is co-opted member of a *Panchayat Samiti* and had occupied this position for about two years. A young woman of about 30, she is educated up to about matriculation standard. She has four children, two of whom are quite young. She is entirely a housewife and her interests are all in the home: she does not do social or community welfare work among the women of her village. In the *Panchayat Samiti*, she is a member of an important standing committee; but her entire participation in the work of the *samiti* as confined to attending the meetings of the *samiti* and the standing committee. In spite of her education, her attitude and way of life remains tradition-oriented. She is not a woman of modern ideas, serving as an innovator or leader among the women of her village. Rather, she is an ordinary high caste village housewife confirming to the attitude and way of living of high caste rural women. In the home she represents traditions and orthodoxy and prevents her young husband from going too far from traditional practices. She is by no means an incompetent person. Quite the contrary, she is a competent housewife and mother. But she is just not up to the role of innovator, informal educator, and community leader that one might expect from educated women in her position. Her function in his *Panchayat Samiti* is merely that of an extra vote for her husband's group: she has no independent opinion on any issue. She is there because two women members have to be co-opted, and as there are very few literate woman in their own caste the Meenas who dominate the *Panchayat Samiti*, did not mind putting a high caste woman in the position.

5

Women in the Changing Society

Introduction

The different changes experienced by a society are part of a single social change process: changes in one part of social life have their repercussions on others, which in turn influence the first. The first four studies have been concerned with certain social changes, especially those relating to occupation and social status of particular castes and those resulting from the new political experiences of rural people. These and other changes currently in progress are bound to have their influence on the women. They affect the position of women in the home and in the community, their participation in economic activity and in decision-making; they affect customs of marriage, divorce, and re-marriage etc. This study is concerned with these and other aspects of social change. It is true that this is a very large field of enquiry and that the present small study is quite inadequate to cover it. But any study of social change which does not show how women participate in the change process and how change affects them is incomplete. Perhaps this study, inadequate though it is, will help build up a fuller picture of social change in this area.

The study is divided into four major areas:

- Certain aspects of consumption—notably food, dress and ornaments, and housing;
- Attitudes towards education of girls and towards treatment of disease;
- Experience with development programmes designed especially for women; and
- Marriage and the family—customs relating to marriage, e.g., age at marriage, selection of spouse, dowry and bride price, divorce and widow re-marriage; the position of women in the family and the joint family.

Method

The study was undertaken among women of three caste groups living in three different villages; the three groups were Meenas of Bijaipur, a small village about three miles from Sawai Madhopur railway station; the Chammars of Chainpur, a small Chammar village about a mile from the station, and the Brahmins of Raipur. The three groups represent the three major segments of rural society—peasant, scheduled caste and high caste. They also represent different degrees of dependence upon agriculture. The Meenas are pure agriculturalists; the Chammars depend primarily upon industrial and non-agricultural labour, while the Brahmins are non-cultivating land-owners-cum-white collar workers. The number of households in the three groups was Meena 55, Chammar 61, and Brahmin 69. A 25 per cent sample was taken in each case, so that a total of 47 households were included in the sample survey. But as one Meena family could not be covered the survey data relate to 46 families.

This method of the study, about adoption of three castes from three different villages rather than of selecting a sample of three castes from a multi-caste village like Raipur was preferred in spite of the advantage of the latter method, e.g. data on economic activity of different castes and their social inter-relations were already available for example for village Raipur. But the method of selecting two single caste villages and studying only Brahmins of Raipur, even though it involved more work, was selected because it depicted more clearly the effects of change influence on living patterns, attitudes, and social custom of the different segments of rural society in this area. The Meenas of Bijaipur are as unresponsive to non-agricultural employment as the Meenas of Raipur (or of the area generally). But the Brahmin and the Chammar groups selected for the study are ahead of their counter parts—the high castes and the scheduled castes—in most villages of this area, both in acceptance of new economic opportunities and adoption of urban patterns of living. As a result, the difference in occupation, patterns of living, and social attitudes among the three groups selected for the study are sharper than differences among difference castes in a single village. This sharper differentiation makes possible a clearer perception of the different ways in which change influences are affecting different segments of rural society.

The study collected demographic and detailed household data as well as data on size of holding, cultivation, and economic activities of each member of the household for the two single caste villages while similar data for Raipur had already been collected for the four studies described earlier. Data on the major areas of the study were collected in the second phase, based on interviews with women of the sample households and group discussions with them and other women of the caste.

The first two or three visits in each village were devoted to group discussions. In these the objects of the study were explained to the women, and ground prepared for individual interviews. In two of the villages Bijaipur and Chainpur, it was found useful to have as a companion a woman of the village who was literate, had a good knowledge of the customs of the group, and could understand the purpose of the study somewhat better. Her presence was found useful also in interpreting and explaining some of the words of the local dialect. In Bijaipur the *Gram Kaki*[2] functioned as the companion, while in Chainpur the wife of one of the Chammar leaders performed this function. In Raipur it was not necessary to have a companion because the Brahmin women were familiar with the studies. Moreover, they were more literate and better informed than women of the other two groups. Finally, they spoke Hindi, and there was no language difficulty in their case.

The purpose of the study was not too well understood in the Meena and Chammar villages in the beginning, and the women were suspicious that the wife of the District Collector should visit them and ask so many questions. But as the study progressed suspicion gave way to confidence and, especially in the Meena village, to affection and warmth. The affectionate and cheerful meetings with the Meena men and women in visits to their village during the latter part of the survey, and afterwards, was one of the most rewarding aspects of this study.

The Meenas of Bijaipur

Bijaipur is small village of 63 households (population 321) located 3 miles from the district headquarters railway station colony and 4 miles from Sawai Madhopur town. It is easily reached from the colony and Sawai Madhopur town, with which it is connected by a tarred road and a regular bus service. Of the 63 households, 55 are Meenas, 3 Lohars, 2 Ranas and one each of Kumhar, Khatik and Brahmin. For all practical purpose, it is a Meena village.

Economic Activities

Nearly all the Meena households (53 out of 55) are cultivators. Cultivation is the sole means of livelihood in most households; but in a few households, one or two young men have taken up casual wage labour, mostly at the railway station. There were two such households in the sample. Women work on the family holdings and do not normally work for wages. But women of poor and landless families accept work, agricultural or otherwise, within the village. One woman in the sample households was working as a casual labourer within the village at the time of this study. Altogether, labour, agricultural or non-agricultural, is of minor importance in the economy of the group.

The total area cultivated by the 53 cultivating households is 1014 acres, an average of 19.1 acres per households. Most households (41 out of 53) cultivate between 15 and 30 acres. The landholding position is not unsatisfactory. But since most of the land is unirrigated and grows only food grains, the income of most households is low.

The irrigated area—123 acres—gets its water from the village tank across the road from the main entrance to the village. In years of good rainfall the tank fills up and irrigates 100 to 150 acres of land; in dry years the area irrigated is much less. Irrigation water is for the *Rabi* crops, principally wheat and barley; the *Kharif* crops are not irrigated. The tank is used also for bathing laundering and watering animals. But its water is not used for drinking. There is a strong prejudice against drinking water from tanks in this area, and only water of wells and *bawris* (step wells) is considered fit for drinking. *Jowar* (sorghum) in the *kharif* and wheat, barley and gram in the *Rabi* are the principal crops grown. The best lands are reserved for cultivation of wheat which is the prized crop. The other *Rabi* grains or mixtures of grains (wheat-barley, gram-barley) are sown in lands which do not have enough moisture or fertility for wheat. The unirrigated *Rabi* crops depend entirely on the conserved sub-soil moisture of the preceding monsoon. In years of low rainfall, the area under wheat is reduced and that under the other *Rabi* grains increases, because most fields have sufficient moisture only for the latter.

Besides foodgrains, oil seeds, sesame in the *kharif* and linseed in the *Rabi*, are grown in small areas. No figures for area under vegetables were reported in the records of the Revenue Department, although each cultivator puts a few gourds along with his Jowar crop in a field which is most fertile or is nearest to his house. The area under fodder crops is also negligible—a total of 5 acres. Jowar fed green or as dry stalks, is the principal fodder given to the livestock.

In other words, the agricultural economy of the village is almost entirely dependent upon production of foodgrains, principally Jowar and wheat, barley and gram. These meet the people's needs for food grains and their sale is the only source of cash. This situation is not unusual in small villages of this area in which most of the land is unirrigated. The land of Bijaipur is considered to be quite fertile by the local staffs of the Revenue Department who give the following norms of yields for years of average rainfall:

Jowar	5 maunds* per acre.
Rabi grain	3-5 maunds per acre of unirrigated land and 6-10 maunds per acre of irrigated land

As a detailed economic survey was not conducted in the village, it is not possible to vouch for the accuracy of these figures or to give estimates of the income of the sample households. These figures have been mentioned to give an idea of the relative magnitudes involved. They explain, for instance, that an average Meena household, depending solely upon cultivation of about 20 acres of single cropped land to produce grains for both home consumption and sale, can have only a limited cash income.[3] Moreover, since the income comes in lump sums twice a year, a large part of it is spent in clearing past debits, making ornaments and clothes, and meeting expenses of marriages and other ceremonies. As a result, the households have very little disposable cash for the greater part of the year.

The chronic shortage of cash is an important fact in the life of the Meenas and one which sets them off from both the Chammar and the Brahmin groups included in this study. The latter depend mainly on wages or salaries and are paid regularly once a month, or oftener. Many of the differences between the Meenas and the other two groups in food and various other aspects of consumption can be adequately understood only if this major economic difference is kept in mind. Of course, the Meenas could have higher income by supplementing their earnings from agriculture and wage labour. Their village has an excellent location with reference to the major centres of non-agricultural-employment—the railway station, the cement factory and the Sawai Madhopur town, and one or more young men from each household could work as the earners for a part of the year at least, without undue interference with cultivation. Their failure to avail themselves of this opportunity is due entirely to a basic social attitude. They feel that they are cultivators, and cultivation

---

* a maund is a weight measurement equivalent of 39 kg. approximately.

is the only proper work for them. Non-agricultural labour would be considered by a Meena household only if it had no land or if it's holding were too small to support it. But even in such cases the first preference is to rent or share-crop additional land. Non-agricultural labour is accepted only if no land is available. Women are not allowed to engage in non-agricultural labour; it is below the dignity of a Meena woman. Even agricultural labour for wages on another's land is not considered quite proper, although it is accepted in case of need. The only proper thing for the Meena is to cultivate the land, and it is his woman's job to assist him.

Bijaipur, along with the other two villages included in this study, from part of the Sawai Madhopur Community Development Block, which had been in operation for about six years at the time of this study. Because it was near the block and district headquarters, and because it was a small village in which there were no serious dissensions, and people cooperated readily with the development workers, it did rather well in the community development programme. It was visited frequently by officials and other visitors and received more than its share of grants for public works. The major construction works undertaken with financial assistance from the block were construction of a primary school, a drinking water well (incomplete), and pavement of a large part of the village street. This was perhaps the only village in the block in which the expensive work of paving the village street was undertaken. The primary school was opened during the time of the Community Development Block and is attended by about 25 boys from the village. The paved street gives the village a neat look. It is unfortunate that the attempt to construct the drinking water well was not successful—the well caved in during digging—an additional well located close to the village *abadi* is the most keenly felt need of the village. There is only one other well in the village, which is located near the *abadi* and has water throughout the year.

The village formerly sent a representative to the *panchayat* located in a large village three miles away. Since December 1960, however, it has been the headquarters of a *panchayat* comprising four small villages besides Bijaipur. The election in December 1960 of the *Sarpanch* of the new *panchayat* was keenly contested between two Meenas of this village. Its only effect has been to create strong factional rivalries in a village which had been practically free from them earlier. But the *panchayat* has not been able to take up any community work or give any other evidence of its being active in the welfare of the village people.

Houses and Household Goods

The houses line both sides of a winding street which extends from one end of the village to the other. Excepting the house of one rich Meena, which is *pucca*, all houses are kutcha. They have mud walls and floors and roofs of crude baked tiles resting on a frame-work of light beams made from branches of trees. The people make the mud bricks, bake the tiles, and build the houses themselves. A house usually consists of three or four rooms built on three sides of a central courtyard. It has also a raised platform (called *pole*) in front, on either side of the entrance door. This platform serves as a sitting place for the men in the evening; the platform of a popular householder being used as a *hatai*.[4] Cattle are also kept within the house, usually at the back end of the courtyard some distance from the living rooms. A separate *nauhra* (cattle shed) is the preferred thing; but most families cannot afford it and have to be content with keeping the cattle at the end of the yard or in an enclosure attached to the house. There is another reason also for keeping cattle within the houses. They want to guard against theft or damage to their animals by a hostile neighbour. The rooms are all-purpose; every one serves as living room, bed-room and store room. Actually, life is not lived in the rooms to any extent. The men, and most women and children, work out in the fields most of the day. In the summer they sleep outdoors, in the yard or outside the house in the village street. The rooms are essentially places for keeping things—grains, *charpoys* and other crude furniture, bedding and clothing. Only in the winters or on rainy nights during the monsoons, are they used as bedrooms. Food is also cooked in the open for most of the year; a corner of one of the room is used as a kitchen only during the winter or on rainy days.

Many houses have two or more households living in them; they are of course congested. The 55 Meena house-holds (and two non-Meena households who share houses with them) used a total of 31 occupied dwellings. Only 9 of these were occupied by one household each; all the others had two or more households living in them:

One	hh	per dwelling	19	dwelling	19	households
Two	"	"	4	"	8	"
Three	"	"	6	"	18	"
Six	"	"	2	"	12	"
Total			31	"	57	"

One would not expect such congestion in a small village of cultivators. It arises partly from poverty and partly from the fact that village has no place to expand its *abadi*. The lands on all sides of the village *abadi* are irrigated, the best in the village, and their owners will not give them up. Another contributing factor is the prevailing practice of giving a room or two within the family house to each married son and daughter-in-law when they want to live separately. Additional rooms within the house will be constructed whenever the family can afford to do this, but the immediate need is met simply by crowding the rest of the family.

The interiors of the rooms are poor; the most conspicuous articles are a few *charpoys (*a reed woven bed), earthen pots and brass or aluminium utensils, one or more iron suit-cases, and the little clothing the family owns. Most of the men and women have only three or four ensembles at any one time. Furniture and objects of interior decoration are conspicuous by their absence. The prevailing drabness is relieved only by cheap pictures or calendars with pictures of Hindu gods and goddesses, film stars or national leaders like Gandhi and Nehru. Stores of grains are also kept within the rooms, usually in one or more big earthen cylinders (*kothis*). *Kothis* are usually decorated with crude designs painted in white lime or red clay; some of the designs were quite attractive, and a few even had small pieces of mirror fixed to them. The *Kothis* are used for storing milk, curd, cooked food, and money. Several households have large iron cylinders (also called *kothis*) about twice the size of a barrel. These are used for bringing drinking water at the time of feasts on marriages and other occasions. In recent years, they have become popular as wedding gifts.

The walls and floors of the houses are neatly plastered with mud by the women. The front walls on either side of the entrance are generally decorated with crude paintings in white lime by the women. Some of the houses have elaborate multi-coloured paintings drawn by an artist. Paintings on walls and mud *khothis* are the only evidence of artistic expression in the village. But these and the cleanliness of their rooms speak well of the love of beauty and neatness of the Meena women.

The houses, though extremely modest and bare looking, are quite comfortable. The mud walls and tile roofs keep them cool in summer and warm in winter. The *pucca* houses of the Brahmins of Raipur are much less comfortable, especially in the summer when they get quite hot. The houses in the Chammar village, with their small, congested rooms and roofs of corrugated iron sheets which get unbearably hot in the summer, are the most uncomfortable of all.[5]

The women do quite a lot of work in building and maintaining the houses. Like women in most Indian villages, they plaster the floors with cow-dung and mud once or twice a week. In addition, they help their men make mud bricks, bake tiles and repair and build houses. The building work is done generally in the summer months of May and June, after the *Rabi* harvest, a period when there is practically no works in the fields. It is necessary at this time to prepare the houses for the coming monsoon. The portions which have suffered damage during the rains are repaired, the whole house is plastered, and designs are painted on the walls. The tradition of plastering and beautifying houses at the time of Diwali[6] arises from this practical need.

Dress and Ornaments

The dress of the Meena women consists of a *ghagra* (wide, billowy long skirt reaching down to the ankles), a *lugari* (big scarf usually about three yards long) and a *kanchil*—a brief, tight, blouse—like garment which leaves the back and midriff of the wearer open, and covers only the breasts and upper arms. Nothing is worn above this garment while the women work in the field or in the house. But on more formal occasions, a long, loose fitting blouse, *kabza* is worn on top of the *choli*. The cloth for these garments used to be woven by local weavers and dyed and printed by dyers and calico printers in Sawai Madhopur town or large villages of this area. The locally-woven coarse cloth has been completely replaced by mill-made cloth; but the local dyeing and printing continue. The cloth is dyed almost invariably in dark colours—maroon, deep red, navy blue, or black (dark colours are preferred so that the garments will not show dirt), and printed in simple traditional designs. Traditionally, small variations in design and colour schemes identified different castes, so that it was possible to know the caste of the wearer simply by looking at her clothes. This is no longer the case, mainly because the traditional dress materials have been replaced by mill-made fabrics of great variety in design and colour. Chammars and Brahmins have completely replaced locally dyed and printed dress materials with nice fabrics. Among Brahmins the *ghagra* and *lugari* have themselves been replaced by the *saree* and the blouse. Departures from the traditional garments have been the minimum in case of the Meenas.

All women wear silver or silver-coated ornaments. Three pieces, the *khagali* (heavy necklace weighing two pounds or more), *kari* (anklet) and a bangle worn above the elbow, are made of silver. Besides these, they wear a number of silver-coated iron bangles which cover large portion of both arms. Each woman wears ornaments weighing 6 to 8 pounds. The weight and number of ornaments has increased during the last 20 years, as these people have become relatively prosperous. Earlier, most families could not afford to buy the full complement of ornaments.

There was striking similarity in the dress and ornaments of all Meena women, including those of the one rich Meena household. As dress and ornaments are the most common indicators of economic differences, greater variation was anticipated: it was expected that the women of the rich households would have more ornaments, or gold ornaments. It was also expected that they would not be working in the fields. But in all these respects the women of the rich household were no different from the other Meena women. The rich household has demonstrated its wealth by building a *pucca* house. But the interior of the house was very similar to that of all others in the village, and the absence of furniture and urban consumptions goods was equally noticeable in it.[7]

The men wear a white *kurta* (loose-fitting long shirt) a *dhoti*, and a turban. Stout country-made shoes of similar designs are worn by both men and women. Several men were seen wearing silver anklets or gold ear-rings. The girls wear the same dress as the women, and most boys wear the same dress as the men. But the few boys who go to the primary school wore a white or *khaki* shirt and *khaki* half-pants—the prescribed uniform.

Food

Meena food is a very simple. In fact, lack of variety, inadequate attention to cooking, and deficiency in essential nutrients (fats, animal proteins and the vitamins and minerals supplied by fruit and vegetables) is its chief characteristic. All the households eat *bejer* (barley and gram mixed), jowar and wheat. Even the most prosperous household has not switched over to exclusive use of superior food grain, wheat. The *Rabi* grains are eaten mainly in the summer and in the rainy period—i.e., after the *Rabi* harvest, while jowar is eaten during the first half of the year. The flour for *chapattis* (flat pancakes made with unleavened flour) is ground by the women at home, in spite of the fact that there are floor mills in several adjoining villages to which they could easily take their grain. *Chapattis*, eaten with a vegetable or pulse or with crushed raw onions; chillies or raw mangoes (in season), constitute the entire meal. The woman of the house tries to finish most of the cooking for the day in the morning before she goes for work in the field. Food is cooked and eaten to fill the stomach. There is no leisure to devote to elaborate cooking; nor is there time to look after the special food needs of the children. In the summer, the *chapattis* for the entire day are made in the morning, but the *curry* for the evening meal is prepared only in the evening because curry made in the morning would spoil by the evening. In winter the cooked food will last until the next meal or even until the next day without spoiling; but as people want to eat hot food, *chapattis* are made fresh at every meal and only the *curry* from the previous meal is used after re-heating. The children have to adapt themselves to this regimen. No food is prepared for them when they get hungry in the afternoon; they have to be content with munching *chapattis* prepared in the morning until something is cooked in the evening. This creates a serious nutrition problem.

Most households plant some vegetable vines with the *kharif* crops during the monsoon; but no particular attention is given to them. Moreover, the vegetables they produce last only a few weeks. There is no other local production of vegetables, because there are no Mali households in the village.[8] Some vegetables are bought in exchange for wheat when a vendor comes to the village. Otherwise pulses—mostly the home produced *moong* and gram—are the mainstay for *curries*. Onions, raw mangoes, green leaves of gram and *methi* (a leafy fodder crop) are also used in *curries*. Onions are the staple seasoning: they are used throughout the year. Raw mangoes are a principal ingredient in *curries* in the early summer, when they are in season. Consumption of other fruits is negligible. A little fruit is bought occasionally in the town.

Consumption of milk is low and highly variable and depends entirely upon whether the household has any milk animals and whether they are giving milk. Most households have one or more milch animals (cows or buffaloes) and have some milk during the monsoon months and two post-monsoon months, when there is grass in the fields and the animals give milk. But during the rest of the years, they are without milk. Of the 13 households in the sample, 8 had no milk at the time of the survey (conducted during the summer). The other 5 had small quantities (2 pounds a day or less) from a cow or a buffalo. Milk is not sold in the market. Few households have a surplus for sale, but even if they did, they would not sell it because of the strong prejudice against sale of milk by cultivators. When a Meena household has a small surplus of milk the women make *ghee* (clarified butter) out of it, which they might sell. More frequently however, the *ghee* is stored for use during winter or for special occasion like the periods after child birth. Eating of *ghee* after child birth is considered extremely beneficial for the health of the mother, and most women try to eat two to ten pounds of *ghee* at this time.

The shortage of milk is of course reflected on the health of the children; there are many cases of debility, and even death, from malnutrition. Figures on infant mortality are given at the end of the chapter. A number of cases of *sukha* (marasmus, a disease caused by acute protein deficiency in which the child becomes very thin) were seen in the village. A child is supposed to subsist on mother's milk until he is old enough to swallow solids (*chapattis*). He is given cow's or buffalo's milk only when an animal kept by the household is giving milk. No Meena would think of keeping another cow or even a goat to provide milk for a child. On contrast, Brahmins buy milk or keep a cow or a goat especially for their children.

Consumption of fats is very small. *Ghee* and oils are the only fats used in daily cooking. Nine out of the 13 sample families reported consumption of about 2 pounds of *ghee* per month. The other four used only oil, generally sesame or mustard oil. Use of *dalda* is avoided, because it is more expensive than oil and is also considered injurious to health. However, *dalda* is used extensively in feasts, when large numbers are to be fed. It is accepted as a substitute for *ghee* particularly for feasts.

Sweet dishes like *halwa* (a pudding) are eaten, mostly at feasts and rarely otherwise. *Gur* (unrefined brown sugar), eaten raw, is the only sweetening in the daily diet. Large feasts are the principle occasions which break the drabness and monotony of the daily diet of the Meena.

No consumption of meat, fish or poultry was reported by women of any household: they all claimed to be vegetarians. The Meenas were not vegetarians in the past, and there was considerable meat-eating among them, especially on festive occasions. But the recent Meena Reform Movement, aiming at raising their social status has emphasized abstinence from meat and drink, and now no one would admit these practices. Smoking the *hukkah* (hubble-bubble) and *beedies*[9] is common among the men, but women do not smoke.

In summary, cereals, supplemented by pulses and a few vegetables, constitute almost the entire diet. Consumption of animal proteins is minimal, being confined to a little milk or buttermilk when the household has these. Even consumption of fats and sugar is very small. Poverty, social attitudes (e.g., those against growing vegetables and producing milk for sale), and food taboos (e.g., not eating flesh) combine to produce a cereal-dominated diet. The monotony of food and lack of attention to cooking are better understood if two further facts are also kept in view.

(i) The desire to keep cash expenditure for food at a minimum. This stems partly from a serious lack of money, of course. But it also reflects the traditional agricultural way of life: farmers produce their own food and seldom buy food.

(ii) The time spent in cooking has been reduced to a minimum because women work in the fields.

Personal Hygiene and Medical Care

Women bathe about once a week in the winter and twice a week in the summer. They go to the village tank when the men are not around. During the rainy season, they bathe in a small *nullaha.* Men and children bathe oftener, especially in the summer, because they can bathe in the tank or wells when ever they feel like it. Women wash their hair with black mud taken from the tank once every two or three weeks and apply *ghee* to their hair afterwards. Clothes are changed every week or two and are washed with or without soap. Women do not generally use soap for bathing, but in recent years some of the men and especially the boys who go to the school have started using soap. The soap used is generally a washing soap, not toilet soap. There is no use of any cosmetics.

The village is not too far from Sawai Madhopur town and these people could use medical facilities of the hospital and the Ayurvedic dispensary without much difficulty. They could go to the medical dispensary in the district headquarters colony even more easily. But they use these facilities only rarely. Any small ailment is ignored at first, in the hope that it will be cured by itself. But if this does not happen, then, in case of aliments of women and children, the old Brahmin woman who is the *Gram Kaki* is consulted. She prescribes traditional home remedies. Alternatively, a barber's wife from an adjoining village is consulted. If the aliment does not disappear with such treatment, one of the two private practitioners in the town is consulted. One of this is a trained *vaidya* but other is only a *pansari,*[10] with no formal medical training. The medicines prescribed by these practitioners are taken only half-heartedly; the general belief is that the patient will get well if he is going to. The doctors in the hospital are consulted last of all. Only in cases of serious sickness, and often when it is too late. One reason they hesitate to go to the hospital is that it is very crowded and they have to wait a long time before they can see the doctors. Among the sample households, there were two cases of serious illness in which medical treatment had been obtained not only at the hospital in Sawai Madhopur, but also at bigger hospitals (Kotah in one case and

Jaipur in the other). In both cases, medical assistance was sought too late, and the patients, both middle aged men, died. We had an opportunity to discuss these cases with one of the doctors in the hospital at Sawai Madhopur. He said that if they had been brought for medical attention earlier both could have been saved.

There is no *dai* (midwife) in the village. The work of a midwife was done by the Chammar woman when the Chammars lived in the village. But since they left a few years ago the village has no midwife within it and relies on the services of a midwife from a neighbouring village. She is untrained and has no conception of sanitation or modern midwifery practices. If there is any delay in her arrival, the other women of the family or the neighbourhood help the mother. But they will not cut the umbilical cord, because this is considered to be midwife's work, which a Meena woman should not do. Sometimes, in case of trouble during labour, the man may, on the advice of the midwife, take his wife to the hospital. Such cases were rare.

Very high infant mortality results from such practices in nutrition and medical care. The women in the 13 sample households reported that of the 64 children ever born to them, only 34 were living. Most of the deaths had occurred when the children were very young. The main causes of deaths were reported to be "*sukha*" (marasmus, a disease arising from acute protein deficiency, as a result of which the child becomes very thin and is unable to digest any solids), "diareia", "the evil eye", and "not known". These attitudes are typically fatalistic and ignorant and are in marked contrast with those of the Brahmin and the Chammar groups studied. Even the latter showed a greater readiness to do something about sickness.

Education

The village primary school is attended by about 25 boys. A few of the older boys go to the middle school in a large village, four miles away. No girl goes to school. The reasons given for this were:

- "Education of girls is of no use. The work that a girl has to do when she grows up, in the home and in the fields, can be done very well without education. Education will only make her sophisticated; she will start behaving like a high caste woman and will not be prepared to work in the fields".

- "The presence of girls is necessary in the home, because they have to look after their younger brothers and sisters when the mother is working in the fields, and they help the mother in small household tasks when she comes back from the field."
- "Sending girls to a boy's school is not good".

The Development Programme for Women

The development programme for women (under the community development programme) included organization of cultural and recreational activities through *Mahila Mandals* (women's club); organization of classes to teach useful skills like stitching, embroidery and knitting; extension work in nutrition, personal hygiene, sanitation and child care; and home improvement, especially adoption of such improvements as the smokeless *chulha* (hearth) for cooking and *jaali* (cupboard with wire gauze doors and sides) for storing food. The activities were organized by the *Gram Sevika* (woman village-level worker) and the lady Social Education organizer with local assistance of the *Gram Kakis*. The *Gram Sevika* and the L.S.E.O. are trained extension workers, forming part of the staff of the community development block (now *Panchayt* Samiti). The *Gram Kaki* (lit. aunt of the village) is generally a middle aged woman who has a little education, some competence in crafts, and a progressive outlook. She is an honourary worker who is paid an honourarium of Rs. 15 per month and is expected to do extension work among the women while staying in her own home. The institution of *Gram Kaki* is peculiar to Rajasthan, though many other states have, or have had in the past, similar workers under other names.

At the time of this survey the *Panchayt Samiti* took no interest in these activities. Payment of honourarium to the *Gram Kaki* had been discontinued for some time, and their work was not being effectively supervised. As a result, many of the *Gram Kakis* felt rather neglected and were not taking much interest in their work. The observation about the development programme among women in this and other villages relate to activities taken up before the formation of the *Panchayat Samiti*, during the time of the community development block.

The *Gram Kaki* of this village is the old woman of the Brahmin household. She is a competent woman who is respected by other women and is consulted for small ailments and on various domestic matters. She is the best informed and most intelligent woman in the village and is without doubt the most suitable person for this job. She has been doing this work for some years. But the development activities have not made much progress. The *Gram Kaki* explained that she had been told by the extension workers to concentrate on two improvements, the *Magan chulah* and the *jaali*.[1 2] She had done this, but neither of the improvements had been accepted.

The *Magan Chulah* is designed to save time and fuel in cooking: it has three openings on which as many dishes can be cooked at the same time. But the village women did not consider *Magan Chullah* useful, because they rarely cook more than one dish at a time, and for this the traditional *chullah* is more economical of fuel. The *Gram Kaki* had been quite enthusiastic about propagation of the *Jaali* also. She had got half a dozen *Jalis* made at her own expense for demonstration and sale to the village women. But all of these were lying unused in her home. The village women did not use *Jaali* also because of its cost, and the fact that it occupied space in an already congested house. Some of them explained that they did not need the jaali because they did not keep much cooked food for any length of time. "Food Cooked in the morning was taken to the fields, and cooking for the evening was done only after they returned home", they said. This explanation is not correct however, because *chapattis* and other food cooked in the morning are generally kept until evening, or even until the next day. But such food can be kept in the mud cylinders which are used for grain storage, or in a *Chikka* (rope-basket) which can be made by the women themselves at little cost, so the *Jaali* is considered to be an unnecessary expense.

A sewing class had been organized in the village during the time of the community development block, and a sewing machine had been provided. But the machine had been out-of-order for several months and the *Gram Kaki* had not got it repaired at her own expense. Actually, she is not well trained in sewing, and the women continue to stitch some garments by hand while getting the others prepared by tailors in town.

Marriage Customs

Pre-puberty marriage for the girls is the rule. All the women interviewed had been married before puberty, usually between the ages of seven and twelve. The boys are also married young, generally between the ages of ten and fifteen. Boys who are not married at this age find it difficult to marry later. They or their parents have to pay a heavy bride price or have to be satisfied with a widow or a girl who has been left by her earlier husband or one who suffers from some physical defect. Some of them may never marry. There was one such case in the sample, a 55 year old man who could not get married for a long time because he was poor. His parents had died in childhood and there was nobody to help him. Finally, when he was 50, he succeeded in marrying a middle-aged woman and spent Rs. 500 on the marriage. But the woman ran away within a year of marriage, and he was left alone with his debt.

Gauna or *Saiya*, a ceremony to mark the commencement of conjugal living, takes place three, five or seven 7 years after marriage, when the girl is 14 to 16 years old. Most marriages are between residents of villages located within 20 miles[13] of each other. There is no marriage within the village, because these people consider children who lived in the same village to be brothers and sisters. Three *gotras* (lineages) are avoided in fixing marriages: those of the father, the mother and the father's mother. The initiative in making the match is generally taken by the boy's parents, because they are anxious to find a wife for their son. The girl's parents have no such anxiety. When a boy is 8 to 12 years old his parents start looking for a suitable girl for him. They begin to make informal preliminary enquiries on occasions like marriages and deaths when people of the caste gather. After these have been satisfactorily completed in a particular case, the girl's parents send the Brahmin of their village to see the boy and his home. Their main considerations are:

- That the family has enough land and a number of cows and bullocks; and
- That the boy is healthy.

The boy's parents similarly want the girl's family to have plenty of land. But an even more important consideration with them is that the girls be healthy and free from physical defects (like blindness or lameness). As the girl has to work in the home and the fields, they want to be sure that she will make a good worker. The boy's education or the girl's beauty is not really considered.

After the match is decided, a ceremonial gift of one rupees and a coconut are sent as *lagan* (token of engagement) from the girl's family. This is reciprocated by a gift, usually of a dress for the girl by the boy's family. A day before the marriage both the boy's and girl's families give a feast (*manda)* to their respective relatives and other people of their villages, with whom they have "relations"—i.e., are on terms of participating in feasts. This is the big marriage feast and the popular expression used for it is "that the whole village is invited". But in actual practice, the number of persons invited to the feast varies greatly, depending upon the economic status of the family and their "relations" with their fellow villagers and relatives. Relatives and other people of the caste from neighbouring villages with whom the family has "relations" join the feast; but those of the same village with whom the family does not have relations do not join. The prosperity of a person and the "quality" of the marriage are judged very largely by the numbers of people fed and the quality of food given at this *manda* feast. Serving five dishes, using *ghee* (or *dalda* which is accepted as a substitute) as the cooking medium, and using crystal sugar for the sweet dishes, are considered 'good'. Feeding 200 to 500 people at the *manda* feast is common among the Meenas and feeding one thousand people or more is not unusual. At two marriages in the sample households, 800 to 1000 people had been fed. Even larger numbers are fed at marriages in prosperous Mahajan or ex-*jagirdar* Rajput families.

Most marriages are celebrated on the Akha Teej day,[14] the popular saying being that one does not have to consult a Brahmin for fixing a marriage on this day. As there are so many marriages on the same day, the invitees get distributed so that each family has to feed, only a few people and to take only a small number with the marriage party. The concentration of marriages on one day appears to have arisen mainly because of the need to cut expenditure on marriage feasts. The choice of a day at this time of the year is in perfect accord with the prosperity level and work cycle of the cultivators. The *Rabi* crop has been harvested, and there is no work to be done in the fields till the onset of the monsoon, some two months away. The prosperity curve is at its peak, because the *Rabi* harvest has been gathered and the kharif was only four months earlier. But precisely because a marriage on this day saves expense, its avoidance has become a status symbol. The more prosperous Meena house holds avoid marriages on this day: their main motive is to give a large feast and prove their financial status.

Dowry and Bride Prices

The boy's parents have to incur considerable expenditure at the time of marriage. They must make heavy silver ornaments for the girl and take gifts like a *jajam* (a large, coarse cloth of printed cotton which serves as a carpet), and a *kothi* to her parents. The silver ornaments weigh 4 to 10 pounds and cost Rs. 400 to 1000. Ornaments weighing between 6 and 8 pounds are considered 'adequate' for an average cultivating family, so most families attempt to attain or exceed this level. The financial status of the boy's parents is judged by the kind of *manda* (feast) they give and the weight of the silver ornaments. One result of recent prosperity has been a progressive increase in the number and weight of silver ornaments. For example, in the marriage of most of the women of the sample households, which had taken place 15 year ago or earlier, silver ornaments weighing 1 to 4 pounds had been made by their husbands' parents. At that time, ornaments of one-and half lbs to two lbs were considered adequate. But when their sons and daughters married, the new standard was ornaments weighing 4 to 10 pounds! The weight of ornaments considered 'adequate' has increased by a factor of 3 or 4 during the course of one generation. Gold ornaments are a rarity: even a very prosperous Meena would give only one or two small ornaments of gold, weighing not more than one or two *tolas*[15] along with silver ornaments.

The ornaments remain with the girl's family until she takes them with her when she goes to live with her husband several years latter. The cost of the *jajam* and the *kothi* is paid by the girl's parents in many cases. It is customary for the boy's parents to make a donation to the temple of the girl's household. In many cases, the whole or large parts of the expenses of the girl's parents are paid by the boy's parents. The expenses of the girl's parents are limited. There is no dowry; the only gifts they give are two dresses (silk or cotton), one for the boy and the other for the girl. In most cases they bear the cost of feeding the marriage party and other expenses of marriage; but not in others. All this, as well as the practice of paying *jhagra* (the compensation) to the husband when a woman leaves him to live with another man, indicates the prevalence of bride price in the past. Payment of bride price is not very common now, and *roti-beti* (i.e., giving *the beti* (daughter) in marriage without any monetary consideration and also bearing the expenses of *roti* (feeding the marriage party) is the more common practice. Moreover, it is regarded as the only proper practice, and those who accept payment for expenses on their daughter's marriage will not admit it, because they feel they have failed to live by the caste norms. Only one women in the sample admitted that her parents had been repaid for expenses of the feast; all the others said that their marriages were on the basis of *roti-beti*. The marriages of sons and daughters celebrated by these women were also all reported to have been on the same basis.

An idea of the expenses currently incurred in marriages can be got from the data on ten marriages itemized below:

	Number of marriages	*The girls' parents*	*The boys' parents*
Daughter's marriages (sample households)	7	*Rs. 150 to ** Rs. 1000	@ Rs. 500 to Rs. 2000
Son's marriages (sample households)	3	Rs. 200 to 500	* Rs. 800 to Rs. 2000

* Incurred by the sample households.

@ Incurred by the other party, as reported by the sample households.

** The very high expenditure of Rs. 1000 in one case of a daughter's marriage included the cost of feast (in which about 1000 persons were fed) given by the father of the girl. This man was not rich; but he felt that he had to give a big feast because he was a leader of the village he was representative of the village in the multi-village *panchayat* at the time of this marriage and later (in 1960) was elected the *Sarpanch* of the *panchayat* of Bijaipur.

It is true that some of the money spent by the boy's parents (e.g., that on ornament) comes back to them after the girl comes to live with them. Until then the ornaments remain with the girl's parents. So the boy's parents are very anxious to keep the girl's parents pleased and especially to avoid offending or annoying them. Their fears of what might happen if the girl's parents are annoyed are very real, because there are cases, infrequent but not rare, in which the girl does not go to live with her husband after marriage but goes to another man, either because of a love affair with the latter or because her father is tempted to send her to a man from who he has received money. All such cases involve *jhagra*.

Dissolution of Marriage and Widow-Remarriage

There is no formal dissolution of marriage or re-marriage of a widow; but sitting in *nata*, a term which applies both to a widow going to live with another man and a woman leaving her husband to live with another man, is common. Similarly, the man is free to leave one woman and take another as wife. A widower, like Hindu widowers of all castes, can remarry.

There is no formal ceremony or celebration at *nata*; but the social attitude towards it is not altogether unfavourable. The *nata* of a widow or a woman who has been left by her husband is accepted as necessary; that of a young widow is considered desirable. But a woman who leaves one man and goes to live with another is not looked upon with favour, although even in this case the disapproval is due more to complication of *Jhagra*, possible litigation, and violence than to any strong feeling of wrong doing.

Leaving a spouse to take another is not considered very wrong, and the caste would not think of sanctions against either the man or the woman concerned. The prevailing attitude is that in certain circumstance this becomes necessary. The reasons considered adequate for dissolution of marriage are extremely interesting, because they are very matter of fact: a high value is not attached to preserving the marital link at all costs! A man may leave his wife if she is barren, or if she suffers from a physical defect, or is unable to work in the fields. For the woman cruelty of the husband or an inconsiderate attitude on the part of the mother-in-law are adequate reasons for leaving her husband.

The sample revealed two cases in which both husband and wife were living with their second spouses. In one case, the husband had left his first wife because she was lame and had married the present wife (ten years ago), who in turn had left her first husband. He had paid Rs. 5000 as *jhagra* to the first husband. In the other case, the husband was a widower and had re-married after paying *jhagra* of Rs. 625 to the first husband. In a third case, in which a daughter had been widowed and had remarried. The second husband had returned the ornaments given to her by the parents of the first husband, paid *jhagra* to them, made new ornaments for the woman and gave a marriage feast. The man had to sell all his land to do this! The woman's father died a few months after the marriage, so this son-in-law came to Bijaipur and started working on his father-in-law's land.

In all such cases, the right of the husband to the custody of his children, if any, and of sons to the property of their father is recognized. The actual arrangements vary in individual cases. For example, if the children are three years old or older, the woman may leave them in her husband's home; but if they are very young she will take them with her. Girls have no share in property. Boys can claim their father's land when they are of age.

The woman who is widowed or is left by her husband goes to live with her parents until another husband is found for her. There is no stigma or shame attached to this, nor do her parents feel that she is a burden to them. She works for her keep while she stays with them. In fact, the economic relation of women to farm work is the key to the entire structure of social relations and customs.

Jhagra

In all cases where a woman is married to one man but goes to live with another weather this happens before *gauna* or after, the first husband is entitled to receive from the new husband compensation, which is given the extremely significant name *jhagra* (dispute). The amount is decided by *panchas* (prominent persons of the caste, or the village) on an *ad hoc* basis. Usually the amount they fix has some relation to the marriage expenditure of the first husband, especially on ornaments and other gifts for the wife and money payment, if any, to her family. But as the word *Jhagra* indicates, settlement of compensation money is frequently the cause of dispute, and husbands and their families are anxious to avoid a situation in which they have to claim *jhagra* for a woman who has gone away.

Disputes, litigation and even violence are common in cases where a woman married to one man goes to live with another before *gauna*. The disputes and violence do not remain confined to the parties concerned i.e. families of the girl, the husband and the second man, but are taken up by caste men of their respective villages and even by those of surrounding villages. Very often, the people of the aggrieved party make an attempt to kidnap the woman or any other woman from the second man's village. This practice based on the principle of "blood for our blood: we shall take a woman from the village which has taken away a woman belonging to us", has greatly declined in recent decades; but it appears to have been the accepted practice of settling such cases in the past when enforcement of law and order by the State was not so effective. Even today many cases coming to the law courts involving "kidnapping of women" are seen on closer scrutiny to involve disputes of this kind.

The Joint Family[17]

The joint family is not as common as might be expected. Of the 55 Meena households in the village, only 11 could be considered joint families. In 10 of these, one married son and daughter-in-law were living with his parents. In the eleventh household however, two married brothers were living together along with their widowed mother. In the 13 sample households there were only two joint families.

Since child marriage is the rule and married boys and girls continue to live single for several years before they are joined by their spouses, the occasion of *gauna,* is more important in the evolution in the joint family than the marriage. At the time of *gauna*, the young wife invariable comes to live in the home of her husband's parents. She generally lives with them for a few years. Thereafter, quarrels begin between the mother-in-law and the daughter-in-law and the son and daughter-in-law start a separate kitchen, usually in a separate room in the same house. Separation of cooking may or may not be accompanied by separation of cultivation. It is not uncommon for land to be cultivated jointly for several years afterwards. Generally, one son and wife do not find it too difficult to live with his parents; the eldest son and his wife may continue to live with his parents for many years and an only son and wife may live with his parents as long as the latter live. The crisis point in the history of the family comes after the *gauna* of the second son, when two daughters-in-law begin to live together in the same house. It is not possible to sustain joint living long after this event, and in most cases the family breaks up into two or more units within a year or two or the second *gauna.* The only one case of two married brothers living together in the village mentioned above, is an exception and is recognized as such by all the villagers.

Several reasons were quoted for separate living by the women covered in the sample. For example, (i) the mothers-in-law make them do too much work in the house; (ii) they did not get enough food to eat; and (iii) they had no control over the produce or the income from land. In some cases the father divides the land when he finds that the son is lazy and irresponsible.

Joint family and joint living are undoubtedly held as ideals. But there is no strong feeling against separate living, which is viewed in an unemotional, matter-of-fact way. Separate living is not considered a misdemeanour on the part of the young couple or a calamity for the family, a view more likely to be taken among the high castes. It should also be noted that separation does not mean a clean and final break between the households concerned. Cultivation may continue to be joint for several years after separate living has commenced, and even after cultivation has been separated the bullocks may continue to be jointly owned.

As a result of this unemotional attitude towards separation, there are few cases of embittered relations between the parents and sons and daughters-in-law or between brothers and their wives. Lack of tension and bitterness among the women who had separated in recent years was quite evident. It is this which makes it possible for "separated" households to continue to live in the same house after separation.

The Chammars of Chainpur

Chainpur consists of 61 Chammar households with a total population of 324. It is located opposite the cement factory, about a mile from the district headquarters-railway station colony.

Chainpur was founded in 1945 by the Chammars of village Surpur after their quarrel with the Meenas described earlier. As a result they had to leave the old village. The state Government assisted their re-settlement by allotting them a block of cultivable wasteland. The present plan of their village, with its wide, straight central street and well-planed house sites, was given them by the then *Tehsildar* of the State. Without the sympathetic and generous attitude of the state these people could not have been resettled so easily.

During the last 20 years the original families from Surpur have been joined by a number of Chammar families—some from other villages of this area and others from Surpur who had been settled in industrial centres like Indore, Ujjain and Surajpur (Punjab). Several of the latter have come after establishment of the cement factory, which brought industrial labour similar to that which they were doing. Chainpur is regarded as the village of the Chammars of Surpur; others are considered outsiders, and if anyone is not liked (e.g. the contractor with whom they have been having a quarrel for almost two years), he is considered an intruder.

The village looks fairly clean and attractive at first sight because it is well designed. But a closer look will reveal that many of the house sites are congested. Congestion has resulted from continual additions to the original houses to accommodate the rapid increase in numbers. Houses which once had one or two families now have three four or even more families. Even people who took house sites two to four times in excess of their then requirements when the village was settled are experiencing shortage of space.

Economic Activity

Work in the cement factory is the principal economic activity: most of the men and about half of the working women are engaged in it (Table 5.1).

Most of the self-employed persons are also dependent, directly or indirectly, upon work in the factory. Ten of them are masons working mainly for contractors who undertakes various construction jobs in the factory and in the colony; three have shops in the factory, and one is a building contractor. Thus, nearly all the men are working either in the factory itself, or on jobs which derive substance from it. Twenty-six women workers, more than half of the total, get work in the factory. The remainder take up casual labour from time to time in addition to working on their small plots of land. But they also work either for the contractors working for the cement factory or on small building works in the colony.

Table 5.1: Occupational Distribution of Adults in Chainpur

	Male	*Female*
Total adults	86	86
Total workers	74	50
Permanent workers in factory	46	2
Skilled	18	
Unskilled	28	2
Workers with factory contractors	10	24
Self-employed persons	14	
Other occupation (mainly cultivation supplemented by causal labour)	4	24

While the majority of the men are permanent factory workers, only two women are permanent workers; all others work as casual labourers for a factory contractor. The difference is due partly to the management's preference for male workers and partly to the fact that the man is considered the principal earner (and gets the better paid job); the women's earning role is essentially subsidiary. There is also a tendency for women to stop working when the economic level of the household rises. Wives of permanent skilled workers who are paid well, or of self employed men, who have good incomes, do not go out for work. In some families where the father is an unskilled worker, but the son is a skilled worker, the mother may work, but the son's wife does not. Labour by the women has begun to be regarded as the product of economic want and even though women of large number of households still work, the ambition of every household is counter to this.

The minimum pay of a permanent worker in the factory is Rs. 82 per month. Many get more; some skilled workers make as much as Rs. 150 per month. Factory workers have complete security of job and are also entitled to such benefits as a bonus, earned leave, medical attendance under the employees' State Insurance Scheme and free education for children in the factory school. On the other hand, the wages of the contractors' workers range between Rs. 1.50 and 2.50 per day for men and between 1.00 and Rs. 1.75 per day for women. There is no security or even certainty of getting work everyday. There are periods, in the rainy season, when many workers are without employment for days together. A man working with a contractor, and getting work through the month, usually makes about Rs. 50 per month and a woman about Rs. 40 per month. Moreover, they do not enjoy the benefits mentioned above. Permanent factory workers are considered as a privileged group: there is constant endeavour, especially among the men, to get a permanent job in the factory.

The skilled or semi-skilled workers in the factory are mostly young men who work as fitters, helpers, wiremen, drivers, packers, etc. They constitute the first group of much larger numbers which will come from the younger generation now in a school. This generation, raised in an industrial labour environment, will find it easier to progress to skilled jobs than did their fathers or elder brothers who came from an agricultural-rural environment and for whom acceptance of industrial employment was it self a major change. Another happy sign is that many men work as masons, shopkeepers, and contractors and have income ranging between Rs. 1000 and 2000 per year. The entry of the Chammars into these skilled and entrepreneurial occupations is evidence of their willingness and capacity to take advantage of the varied opportunities for profitable work that an industrial environment offers.

Agriculture is not an important source of lively-hood for these people. Of the 61 households in the village 14 are landless and depend entirely upon non-agricultural income; the others have very small holdings (one-third of an acre to 5 acres). Cultivation of such a small plot of unirrigated land can do no more than meet a part of the foodgrain needs of a household, besides providing fodder for one or two milch animals. Still almost all the households cultivate small plots of land, and a few even take land on *batai* from others. Most do not keep bullocks—it is uneconomical to keep bullocks for such small plots—but get the land ploughed by cultivators in neighbouring villages. Cultivation is looked after by women and the old folks; the young men help on holidays, and if they are casual labourers they help when they are out of work.

More important than material benefits is the psychological satisfaction that cultivation brings the feelings of being land owner cultivators, firmly rooted to the soil and not shifters. This is especially important for the older people, who remember their migration from the old village. They want to be recognized as cultivators and to vindicate their stands against the Meenas. During the course of this study, several of the older people made a demand for allotment of additional land for cultivation. They argued that out of the land originally allotted to them by Jaipur State, a large area had been occupied by the cement factory. They felt entitled to allotment of land in lieu of it. They also made several complaints about the damage done to their crops by pigs and cattle kept by scavengers and other labourers living within the factory area. All these are typical peasant attitudes showing that even though industrial labour is their main source of income, the aspiration to posses and cultivate land continues to be strong among the older people. The younger people, while they do not oppose the demands of their elders, do not show similar interests in agriculture or keenness to posses land.

Income

The income of the 16 samples households ranges between Rs. 400 to Rs. 2,000 a year;[18] the average is a little over Rs. 1,400. Variations in income depend upon the number of earners in the households and the kind of work done. Where a man has a permanent unskilled labour job in the factory and his wife also works, the annual earnings of the household range between Rs. 1200 and Rs. 1500. Earnings are higher only in households in which the man is a skilled worker, shopkeeper, or contractor, or where there is more than one male earner in the household. The income level of the Chammars is somewhat higher than that of the Meenas. In spite of this, Chammar women complained about financial insecurity in the group discussions. In some cases, the husband spent money on drinking and gambling and did not give his wife enough money for the home. In others, the household had gone in debt because of an expensive marriage or chronic sickness. Some households, in which men were only casual labourers with contractors, were spending more than they made. The attraction of acquiring urban-type consumption goods and spending money on more expensive foods has proved too much for them. To some extent the feeling of insecurity was connected with being landless. Several women explained that they were not as well of as they used to be when they were "on the land". While this is not true—their incomes and levels of living are much higher than they ever were in the old village—the feeling of financial insecurity persists.

Houses and Households Goods

Continuous additions to the original houses meant that the majority of families now live in one or two room units side by side, as in a congested industrial colony; they have little privacy. A few families whose house sites are not so congested have independent, small two-or three room houses, with a small courtyard in front and another in the back; the latter is used for cattle or to grow vegetables. All houses are *kucha*, but most of them have straight, smooth walls made of well-shaped mud bricks and plastered with lime or mud. Some houses have cement floors, and others have mud floors. The smooth, straight walls and well built look of the houses are in sharp contrasts with the crude, unfinished look of the Meena houses of Bijaipur. Of course, this village contains a number of masons and one building contractor.

Many houses have roofs of corrugated iron sheet on one or two rooms. The number of houses with such roofs is increasing every year and would increase more rapidly if the sheets were easily available. The iron roofs plus congestion make these houses quite uncomfortable during the summer. Many women complained that their houses were as hot as ovens during the summer days. The Meena houses with their tile roofs and open courtyards are infinitely more comfortable, but in spite of these advantages, there is a marked preference for corrugated iron sheets and for the same reason as explained above in case of Bijaipur.

A higher income level than that of Meenas, together with the urban influence of the factory had made Chammar homes quite different from Meena homes. They contain much more furniture—charpoys, tables, chairs, and many urban-type consumption items. Crockery, brass and aluminium utensils, hurricane lanterns, kerosene cooking stoves, bicycles, and iron clothes boxes were found in most homes. An occasional home had a radio or phonograph, and in one there was a perambulator. Most homes also had calendars with picture of national heroes, Hindu gods and goddess, or film stars. The rooms looked crowded and less neat than rooms in Meena homes, and the distinctive Meena paintings on the *kothis* and the walls were conspicuously absent.

Dress and Ornament

Women's dress is basically like that of the Meena women—*ghagra, lugari*, and a garment above the waist. But the tight *kanchli*, which is still popular with the Meenas, has been replaced by a long loose-fitting blouse, *kabza*. The coarse, locally-printed materials still used extensively by the Meenas are not popular among Chammar women. There is increasing use of mile-made cloth. Older men still wear *dhoti, kurta* and turban; their dress is indistinguishable from that of the Meena men. But the dress of the young men, who worked as semi skilled or skilled workers in the factory, has undergone a marked change. They have started wearing bush-shirts, pants, pyjamas, *chappals* and western style shoes (instead of the old style *jootis*). They go about bare-headed and have their hair cut in western style. Several of them have cheap wrist watches and fountain pens which they are very fond of displaying. Similar changes have occurred among the Brahmin young men, of course. The stimulus in both cases is the same—non-agricultural employment outside the village.

Chammar women were traditionally not allowed to wear silver ornaments and the Chammars asserting the rights of their women to wear these ornaments was a major issue in the quarrel between them and the Meenas. These Chammars started making silver ornaments for their women only after settling down in this new village where they were free from restrictions. Now they have gone much farther then the Meenas in spending on ornaments. Most Meena women of Bijaipur (and this is true of Meena women in most villages in this area) have only three silver ornaments, the anklet, the elbow ornaments and the *khagali* (the heavy piece worn round the neck); they wore silver coated iron bangles. But practically all the Chammar women have all their ornaments made of solid silver. Some of the young Chammar women have even bought small gold ornaments like *tagri* and necklace. Gold ornaments are worn only by the high caste women in this area: the average Meena woman would not think of wearing them. In matters of dress and ornaments the Chammars have not only attained equality with the Meenas but have surpassed them and have begun to adopt some of the practices of the high castes.

Food

The traditional food consumption pattern of the Chammars in this area was similar to that of the Meenas but with two differences: all Chammars took meat, and many of them drank. These differences have remained; and larger differences caused by urban contact, higher income, and the necessity for buying most of their food, have been added. Food purchase is a factor of considerable importance in affecting choice of foods and introducing new foods, because a family which buys food is not restricted to traditional or locally produced foods but has a wider choice with the overall limitation of its budget. For example, the Meena do not buy milk or *ghee* and spend very little on oil, vegetables, or other food articles. The Chammars have more cash and have to buy most of their food. Limitation in choice of food is set by cash with the family and prevailing prices of the various consumption items. They buy what little milk they can afford. For cooking fat, they buy *dalda* or oil. They can afford either oil or *dalda* (which is a little more expensive than oil), but not pure *ghee*. They are not prejudiced against the use of *dalda* to the same degree as the Meenas or the Brahmins are. Since they have to buy both vegetables and pulses, and their only consideration is price, they are more ready to buy vegetables, especially when they are available and cheap. Finally, as a result of the urban contact, they consume more manufactured foods like white sugar and tea.

In more than half of the sample households (9 out of 16) full meals consisting of *chapattis* and one curry of vegetable or pulse were cooked twice a day. The ones who do not cook two meals reasoned lack of money and time with the women for this practice. In these households, women cooked curry only once a day and used curry from the earlier meal or *chutney* for the other meal.

Groceries are bought from shops in the factory area or in a market in the colony. Vegetables are bought from vendors. Tea drinking is much more widespread than in the other two groups. In the majority of households tea is made regularly in the winter and all members of the household take it. In a few households tea is drunk in the summer also. The tea habit is carried to the home from the factory, because many of the men who work in the factory take tea there. Sweets like *halwa* and *dalia* (two types of porridge) are also made frequently and Chammars consume more sugar than do the Meenas. Both white crystal sugar and *gur* are used. Several women said they used *gur* to wash down the cement which got into their throats when they worked in the factory. Fruit and sweetmeats are bought occasionally. Consumption of milk is small. Most families use just enough milk for tea. Children go without milk and suffer from malnutrition or sheer starvation until they are old enough to swallow solids. Cases of '*sukha*' (marasmus) are frequent. *Sukha* and diarrhoea were mentioned as the most frequent causes of death among children. The Chammars of this area eat meat and drink alcoholic beverages. The change to industrial occupation and higher income has increased consumption of both meat and drink. Most sample families eat meat twice a month. Drinking is common among men, and many of the women also drink. Expenditure on smoking is also more than among the Brahmins or the Meenas, one reason being that most of the Chammar women smoke while the Brahmin and the Meena women do not.

To sum up, there is greater variety in food than among the Meenas. Food is richer and there is greater use of manufactured foodstuffs, stimulants, and intoxicants.

Sanitation, Personal Hygiene and Medical care

The village is better off than most others in matters of sanitation. Its planned structure, with a wide, straight central street, is itself an enormous advantage, but an advantage progressively reduced now by increasing congestion in the house sites. The drinking water supply is much more abundant than in most villages of this area. The drinking water well of the village has abundant sweet water; some years ago the villagers built a well designed parapet wall and platform for drawing water, bathing, and washing clothes. These were built with financial assistance from the community development block. Paving for the main street of the village had also been promised by the block staff, but the promise has not been fulfilled. However, lack of pavement in the street causes no great hardship, except that the street is muddy for a few hours after a shower.

Women bathe more frequently than the Meena women of Bijaipur. Those who work in the factory take a bath daily, after work because they are covered with cement or coal dust, when they work. Soap is more commonly used than among the Meenas: its use was reported by all the sample households. Soap is used for washing clothes and for bathing but many of the older women continue to use mud to wash their hair. Several young women use cheep cosmetics like talcum powder, vaseline, and face cream. All these practices constitute a considerable advance over the practices of Meena women of Bijaipur.

This group is better served with medical facilities than either of the other two. The factory labourers are members of the Employees State Insurance Scheme (ESI) which covers both workers and families. Medical assistance is given at a well equipped and adequately staffed (two male doctors and one female doctor) hospital in the factory area. Doctors visit the village about twice a week. The value of these services is recognized by the people, who use them freely.

Other medical facilities within easy reach of the village (doctors of the two hospitals, the dispensary in the colony, and the two *vaidyas* and the *pansari* in the town) are also used, especially by those not covered by the E.S.I Scheme. In 8 out of the 16 sample households women referred to treatment obtained from the doctors of the E.S.I Scheme or in the town. There is greater consciousness of the need for proper treatment of disease, greater readiness to use the facilities available, and what is most important, greater willingness to spend time and money to be treated, than was the case with the Meenas. But it appears that sickness is also somewhat more prevalent in this group than in the other two. There were several cases of serious sickness (particularly tuberculosis) among the sample households, and there were many complaints of minor ailments. The general appearance of the women, in spite of their more varied and richer diet, was not as robust as that of the Meena women; and the survival rate of children was not much better than that among the Meenas. Of the 84 children born to women in the sample households, only 47 had survived. Most of the women who had lost children said that many of their children had died without treatment. Several of them mentioned that they would consult the doctor only in case of an emergency; for common aliments home remedies and magical cures would be resorted to. These facts and attitudes towards medical treatments are better understood if the following facts are kept in view.

Most heads of households, because of their industrial employment experience here and elsewhere, have known about and used medical facilities. This and the greater health hazards of industrial employment account for readiness to use medical facilities.

Adequate and convenient medical facilities have begun to be available only during the last five years, after the introduction of the E.S.I Scheme; even now only about half of the households in the village are benefited by these. For the others the cost and other difficulties of obtaining proper medical treatment encourage the tendency to avoid treatment as long as possible and to resort to traditional remedies.

The decision-makers in most households (middle-aged men and women) are illiterate; they did without medical facilities during their childhood or adult years, so that even though most of them could obtain medical treatment later, the attitude and habits of mind oriented towards resorting to magical cures or home remedies persist.

The higher incidence of serious sickness and the less robust physiques may be due to the fact that most of the men and many women have to do work which is arduous and involves exposure to coal and cement dust.

Education

Chammars are more conscious of the value of education than the Meenas. Most of the boys of school age (6 to 15 years) go to school, either to the primary school in the village or to the higher secondary school across the road; the latter is run by the cement factory for children of its labourers and other staff.

The villagers are proud of the school in their own village; they want it raised to the middle standard immediately and to the higher secondary standard eventually. When asked why they wanted another middle school in the village when there was a higher secondary school maintained by the factory for their benefit. The leaders replied that the standard of teaching was not good in the factory and was much better in their own school.[19] The present two-roomed school building was constructed some years ago, with financial assistance from the community development block. They were now adding seven rooms so that their school will be considered eligible for upgrading to the middle standard. They know that before raising a school, to the middle or the higher secondary standard the Rajasthan Government insists on a suitable building and they are prepared to fulfil this condition. Some of the young men are more concession-conscious, and they feel that as Chammars they are entitled to preferential treatment in this respect. They want the Government either to provide financial assistance for the new building, or better still, build the building for them.

Making a seven room addition is an enormous undertaking for a small Chammar village. The fact that they are prepared to do it is eloquent proof of their consciousness of the value of education. Education has begun to be regarded as the gateway to wider opportunities—better jobs, higher income and a better life. They know that educated young men of their caste can get jobs in government as clerks and other functionaries (they know about the special concession for the scheduled castes in government service), are accepted more easily for jobs in the factory, and have also much greater facilities in seeking work on their own.

But these attitudes relate only to education of boys: they do not extend to girls. Girls in most families do not go to school. The few girls who go to the village primary school are all from families of skilled workers or self-employed men whose wives do not work. The reasons given for not sending the girls to school were the same as those given by the Meena women: girls are needed in the home to look after younger brothers and sisters when mother is away at work, besides, girls' education is of no use. However, as urban contacts increase, education spreads among young men and more of them get skilled or white collared jobs, education among the girls will increase. As among the Brahmins, the competition for such young men as grooms for their daughters will lead an increasing number of parents to provide more education for their girls.

The Development Programme for Women

As Chainpur is located on a main road near block headquarters, it was much visited during the period of the community development block. A number of construction works were undertaken, and a programme of work among women was organized. The Lady Social Education Organizer and the *Gram Sevika* of the block visited frequently; they organized programmes of instruction in crafts and home improvement similar to those mentioned for Bijaipur. The block staff also distributed medicines. But all this activity had ceased. At the time of this study, there was no *Gram Kaki* in the village and no work was being done among the women. The earlier activities, while they must have been beneficial at the time, had also not left any appreciable impact; when questioned about them, women showed no particular interest.

Marriage Customs

The marriage customs of the Chammars are very similar to those of the Meenas, and changes in them have also been similar. Child marriage is still common; the most frequent age of marriage is 7 to 12 years for girls and 7 to 15 years for boys. *Ganua* takes place several years after marriage, when the girl is 14 to 16 years age. As among the Meenas, three *gotras*, those of the father, the mother and the father's mother are avoided. Most marriages are with Chammar families in neighbouring villages; but there are no marriages within the village because children drinking water from the same well are brothers and sisters. Some families have relations with Chammar families belonging to this area who are now settled in Indore and Ujjain in Madhya Pradesh and Surajpur in Punjab. They know these families from their ancestral villages or because they have themselves lived with them in these centres.

Until about 20 years ago marriage was a simple affair which involved little expense. A few people would go with the marriage party and would be given food only a little better than ordinary daily food. Little was spent on ornaments because Chammar women were not allowed to wear silver ornaments. But in recent years marriage expenses have increased considerably, and the trend is towards increasingly elaborate and expensive marriages. The boy's father is now expected to give the bride silver ornaments weighing 4 to 8 pounds. These ornaments remain with the girl's parents, until she comes to live with her husband after *gauna*, so the boy's parents in the pre-gauna period are in a subservient position. Again, as among the Meenas, the "whole village" is invited to the *manda* feast now-a-days and 3 to 5 dishes are served. Marriage parties have become much larger than before; the expense of feeding them has increased alarmingly. Urban contacts and the desire to raise social status have led to several other incidental expenses. A Chainpur boy was married while this study was in progress. The marriage party went to the bride's village in a chartered bus! And had a band, which was hired at a cost of more than Rs. 100. The boy belongs to a family which had been doing rather well—one of his brothers is a skilled worker in the factory. He himself is studying in the seventh class. The marriage party was well treated by the girl's parents; the food served was elaborate, and each member of the party was given a brass tumbler and a handkerchief. The girl's parents also gave a dowry consisting of clothes and other gifts. These practices, it will be noticed, are quite similar to those among the Brahmins, and the motives are also similar. The boy's family spent much on his marriage, to proclaim their new prosperity. For the girl's parent marrying their daughter to an educated young man of a prosperous family, who will most probably take up a white-collar job, is an incentive to spend more on the marriage. (Details of the expenditure on this marriage are shown in Table 5.2).

As among the Meenas, *roti-beti* marriage is the ideal, and taking bride price, or even the expenses of marriage, is not considered good. But payment of marriage expenses is more common among this group then among the Meenas. There is some hesitation in admitting acceptance of money on the marriage of a girl but not its payment on the marriage of a boy. In 7 of 16 sample households, wives of heads of household reported that at the time of their own marriages their husbands (or their parents) had paid marriage expenses to their parents. Two of them mentioned that *jhagra* money had been paid by their husbands as well. But in marriages which had taken place more recently, payment of expenses of marriage was reported in four out of six cases of sons' marriages, and its acceptance in four out of ten cases of daughters' marriages. Women in two households reported that they had given dowry and received bride price at different times, depending upon their circumstances at the time. One woman said that earlier, when they are well-off, they had spent nearly Rs. 1000 on the marriage of their first daughter; but more recently they had accepted Rs. 200 each on the occasion of marriages of two daughters. In an other case, the circumstances of the family had improved in recent years, and while for the marriages of two elder daughters they had received Rs. 40 each, on the marriage of the third, they had spent Rs. 400. More recently, this family had spent Rs. 150 on celebrating the betrothal of a grand-daughter. It is clear that the practices of paying bride price and giving dowry are in a transitional stage. The trend is towards replacement of bride price by dowry. But, bride price is still the norm, commonly restored to when the family is poor.

Table 5.2: Expenditure on Educated Chammars's Marriage

	Boy	*Girl*
Age	18 years	15 years
Education	Studying in seventh class	nil
Item of expenditure	Boy's side	Girl's side
(i) Manda feast to their respective village people		
No. of persons fed	200	200
No. of dishes	3	3
(ii) Marriage party		
No. of persons		40
No. of meals and dishes served at each meal		3 meals with 4 dishes at each meal
Gifts to each member of marriage party.		1 brass tumbler and 1 handkerchief
(iii) Ornaments and clothes		
Gold ornaments	Nil	Earning for the boy made of one gold sovereign (approx. value Rs. 125)
Silver ornaments	Rs. 400 worth	Rs. 200 worth
Clothes	Nil	1 ensemble for the girl
(iv) Other gifts		3 kitchen utensils for the couple's home
Total estimated expenditure	Rs. 900	Rs. 1500

* Incurred by the respondents

** Incurred by the other party, as reported by the respondents

Widow Re-marriage and Dissolution of Marriage

Chammar customs relating to widow-remarriage, dissolution of marriage, and *nata* are similar to those of the Meenas. Widow re-marriage is freely allowed. Dissolution of marriage is similarly allowed although not favoured, and the women exercise equal initiative with the men. The aggrieved husband of the woman who has gone away with another man is entitled to receive *jhagra*, fixed by an assembly of caste leaders. Women are sought after for marriage and respected after marriage: they are earning members of the household.

Polygamy

Monogamy is the rule with all the castes in the area. However, in the Chammar village there were two cases of bigamy (the only ones in all the three groups). In one case, the man had paid Rs. 500 as *jhagra* for his second wife because his first wife was barren. In the other case, the widow of an elder brother had begun to live with his married younger brother. As might be expected in both cases relations between the wives were not good.

The Joint Family

Joint families are less common than among the Meenas. The usual practice is for the son to start living separately from his parents immediately after, or shortly after *gauna*. Among the 16 sample households, there were only two cases of a married son and daughter-in-law living with his parents. In both cases the son had permanent skilled job in the factory, the family owned some land, and the daughter-in-law was not working. One reason for weakness of the joint family is absence of an economic bond. The bond of dependence upon the family land which is an important factor in keeping Meena families together does not operate in this group. Young men have separate incomes and are not dependent on their fathers. The young women want to live separately, because by doing so they can reduce their household work and take up a job which will increase their income. Furthermore, the young men are more urbanized and less under the influence of their parents. Finally there is much less fear that the caste or village will blame them for selfishness because even traditionally the joint family was not as strong among the Chammars as among the cultivators and the high castes.

The Attitude of the Enlightened Chammars Youth

The young men who have skilled or semi-skilled jobs in the factory are in some ways the most significant persons in this group. They are better off and better informed than their elders. The latter respect them and are proud of them; they know that the young men know more and have done much better than they themselves could. The attitudes and opinions of these young men have considerable influence on the thinking of the entire group. The young men are keenly aware of the low social status of their caste and of the social disabilities from which it suffers. They see the depressed condition of their brethren living in other villages. Many of them participated in the migration from Surpur as children, and others have heard about it from their parents. All are aware of it. At the same time, they are conscious of their superiority to the Meena agriculturists—in economic status, in level of living, and in knowledge of the outside world. They see wider opportunities opening before them and feel that they need not be inferior. They are also very conscious of the fact that the government wishes to raise their economic and social status and is taking a number of steps with this end in view. They know that untouchability has been abolished by law, that other practices like not allowing Chammars to draw water from wells used by caste Hindus are not looked upon with favour by the government, and that social concession (scholarship for education, reservation of seats in government service and legislature) are being given for their benefit.

These conflicting influences seem to produce an acute aggressiveness among the young men. In interviews they complained constantly—against the factory, against the Meenas, against individual officials, and against the government in general. "The factory has taken away our land; the cattle and pigs of workers living in the factory colony spoil our crops; the factory is not giving us electricity, the management is not giving us bonus"[20]. These were some of their grievances against the factory. There was not a word of acknowledgment of the high wages or other benefits which they got from the factory or of appreciation for the excellent health work done by doctors of the E.S.I Scheme. The main grievance against the Meena was that the 'Meena-dominated' *Panchayat Samiti* had not sanctioned any grants for works in their village; that promises to pave the village street and construct a model housing colony made earlier by the Block Development Officer but were not being fulfilled; and that scholarships for education of scheduled caste children which are provided by government, were not being given in the village by the *Samiti*. The officials were blamed because they 'did not listen to them'. The reasoning which leads them to adopt this kind of attitude may be summed up as follows:

> "We are entitled to social consideration. The government is giving a variety of concessions to us. People of our caste in other States and in other parts of Rajasthan are benefiting from these concessions. We are not getting enough, because of local factors like the unhelpful attitudes of the *Panchayat Samiti*.
>
> "But the nation is not doing us any favour by giving these special concessions and privileges. The scheduled castes have been

oppressed for long and these concessions are only small recompense for these oppressions.

"However as these concessions are being given, let us raise our demand as much as we can; because the more we demand the more we shall get, and the more we get, the better of we shall be".

The Brahmins of Raipur

Economic Activity

Traditionally the Brahmins of Raipur depend upon rent income from land for their living. Being a literacy and priestly caste, they did not cultivate the land themselves but gave it on *batai* and subsisted on the rent share. Some families which had fair-sized irrigated holdings were comfortable; but others with small holdings were quite poor. About sixty years ago men from families with small holdings started to migrate to cities to work as cooks or as priests, the next major change was when educated younger men became white-collar workers, and this brought to the caste considerable increases in income and in urban contacts, with concomitant changes in ways of living. The changes in food, dress, housing and marital custom described below are closely related to this change in occupation.*

Of the 18 households included in the sample, 17 owned land, a total of 85 acres. Only three households, owning a total of 31 acres, managed the farming themselves by employing *halis* (wage labourers) to do all the manual work; all the others had given the land on *batai.*

The sample households had a total of 53 adults, 25 earners. This is a smaller proportion of earners to total adults than in the other two castes, reflecting the fact that Brahmin women do not work outside the home, while Meena and Chammar women do. The earners included 13 white-collar workers from 12 households, 3 "farm managers" and 12 persons in other occupation. The latter include cooks for city merchants (5), priests in the village and outside (5), and two persons working as unskilled workers in the cement factory. In a number of households there was more than one earner, and in practically all there was more than one source of income. The annual income of the households ranged between Rs. 750 and Rs. 4000.[21]

* A detailed analysis of Economic Activity of Brahmins of Raipur and change in it were analysed by the author and are given in (Chapter I)

Houses and Household Goods

The central and south-eastern part of the village is the Brahmin quarter. Most of their houses are *pucca,* built entirely of stone and lime mortar; some of these are double storey. The remaining houses are in various stages of transition from the *kutcha* to the *pucca* state. In the latter, a portion consisting of one or two rooms may be entirely pucca while the rest of the house is *kutcha.* The living rooms are generally *pucca* or semi-*pucca* (stone walls, with roofs of corrugated iron sheet), and the entirely *kutcha* potions are generally those used as a cattle shed or for grain and fodder storage. Some of the *pucca* houses are quite old; but the majority of *pucca* houses and *pucca* additions and improvement have been built during the last 20 years. They are the product of the increasing prosperity of this period. Improving the family house, extending it, and making it *pucca* is the aspiration of every villager, especially those who find employment outside the village. The Brahmins are no exception. Investment in the family houses has taken a good part of savings first of those who went out of the cities as cooks and priests, and more recently of the larger numbers who have entered white-collar services.

The Brahmins quarter of Raipur is quite congested, in marked contrast to the open look of the Meena and the Chammar villages. One reason for this is the pattern of settlement of the Brahmin and other high castes in this area. They live in large numbers only in large or middle sized villages, and their houses are clustered in the central portions of these villages possibly as a security measure. The Brahmin quarter of Raipur has always been more densely inhabited than the Meena and Chammar quarters of Raipur. New houses and additions to older houses in recent years added to the congestion. Many families have renovated the space formerly occupied by the cattle shed, reducing the space available for animals and increasing the congestion.

Most Brahmin homes have the look of middle class urban homes. There are many more things—clothing, bed lines, furniture, iron boxes for keeping clothes, brass utensil, and various consumption goods—in them than in the homes of the Meenas of Bijaipur and even of the Chammars of Chainpur. Various urban-type consumption goods—crockery, bicycles, harmoniums, radios, clocks, calendars, and photographs, books, toys for children, cheap cosmetics—are to be seen in almost all homes. But the link with agriculture is also clearly observable. Each house has space for storage of foodgrains, a room or a portion of a room being reserved for this purpose. If the family has only one cow it will probably be tied in the courtyard in which case fodder is also stored within the house. But if the household has bullocks and a number of other animals they are housed in separate cattle shed (*nauhra*), along with the fodder. The interiors of the houses are neat and well scrubbed. Most house-wives pride themselves on the neatness of their houses. But the exteriors are not attractive partly because of the presence of stagnant water explained below.

As among the Meena and the Chammars, most Brahmin houses contain more than one family.

Dress and Ornaments

The traditional dress of Brahmin women was not very different from that of Meena women. They wore *ghagra, lugari* and *kanchi or kabza,* made of coarse *khaddar* (hand-spun, hand-woven cloth) and dyed and printed locally. The major difference was in colours: the Brahmin women generally wore lighter and brighter colours e.g. orange. The more prosperous Brahmin families used silk. Mil-made fabrics began to replace local hand-spun and hand-woven cloth earlier and spread more quickly among the Brahmins than among the other two groups. During the last 20 years women's dress has changed altogether, and the change has been from basic similarity with the dress of the peasant to that with the dress of the urban middle class, a change which is in accord with the group's change in occupation and mode of life. Young Brahmin women have discarded the *ghagra* and *lugari* altogether and have taken to wearing either the *sarees* and blouse in typical urban fashion, or a modified and urbanized version of the traditional dress which consists of a long skirt topped by a long muslin scarf (*chunnri*) and a blouse. Only a few of the older Brahmin women in the village wear the traditional dress. Use of the locally dyed and printed coarse cloth has disappeared altogether. The heavy silver ornaments worn by the Meena and Chammars women have also been discarded. Perhaps use of theses ornaments was less among Brahmin women than among the women of the other two castes even earlier. But it has almost disappeared during the last twenty years. The only silver ornaments now worn by the Brahmin women are light anklets; all other ornaments worn by them are of gold.

Similarly changes are to be seen in the dress of the men. The older men wear *dhoti* and the turban in the traditional style. But among the young men and boys the basic dress consists of an urban-style shirt, a *dhoti*, urban-styled shoes and chappals (sandals). Many of them wear pants, bush-shirts and jackets in winter. *Pyjamas*,[22] which were worn only by the Moslems in the past, are also worn by the young men. The boys usually wear shorts and shorts.

Food

The food of the Brahmins always contained more of the superior foodgrain, wheat and less of the coarse grain, jowar, bajra and gram, more milk, *ghee*, sugar and spices than did the food of the Meenas and the lower castes. Its cooking is also more sophisticated and elaborate. Because of their higher social and economic status and the fact that their women did not work outside the home, they had more money and time for household work. Moreover, being a literary people and bearers of the Hindu cultural tradition, they have a greater consciousness of the value of good food, especially of milk and *ghee*, whose nutritional qualities have been praised in all the Sanskrit texts. They also knew how to prepare good food. The fact that so many Brahmins from this village get jobs as cooks with rich merchants in Calcutta and Bombay shows clearly that the traditional standard of cooking among them was quite high and they were well versed in all the refinements of vegetarian cooking. This is a far cry from the crude cooking of the Meenas!

The changes of the last two decades have introduced more variety in food and further increased the tendency towards elaborate cooking. Most of the women interviewed said that the young educated white-collar workers are much fussier about food than men of the older generation. Some even complained that their entire time was taken up in cooking, especially on weekends and vacations when the men were at home. Hot food at every meal has become the rule, and the meal generally consists of *chapattis*, one or two curries prepared with vegetables or pulses, curd if available, and savouries (e.g. pickles). This is the typical menu for meals in an urban middle-class high caste family.

The cooking fats used are pure *ghee* (to the extent that it is available and is within the means of the family) and oil. *Dalda* is not used in ordinary cooking. But the quantity of *ghee* used is very small—2 to 4 pounds per month. *Dalda* is used for feasts as a substitute for *ghee*, which is expensive and difficult to obtain in large quantities required for such occasions. There is a marked preference for pure *ghee*, and all households try to buy as much of it for their daily cooking as they can afford. This preference arises from the importance given to pure *ghee* in the Sanskrit texts with which the Brahmins are familiar.

The price of *ghee* in the village was very high at the time of this survey, ranging between Rs. 3 and Rs. 3.50 per pound, and good *ghee* was not easily available even at this price. Village leaders claimed that their village had, because of its foot hill location, the advantage that they could buy *ghee* from Gujjars grazing buffaloes in the hill forests. But they admitted that adulteration was widespread and it was difficult to be sure about the quality of *ghee*. Many of the Brahmin elders were saddened at the "disappearance" of pure *ghee*, saying that it had become very expensive and was not available even at the prevailing high prices. Some of them attributed this change to the merger of Jaipur State with Rajasthan, explaining that during the time of the former State the import of *dalda* and export of *ghee* were not permitted. However, more revealing of the changes experienced by the group was following remark made by one man: "earlier, milk and *ghee* were very cheap, but we had no money to buy them; now we have the money, but milk and ghee are not available".

Brahmins consume more milk than do the other two groups. Two-thirds of the sample households, 12 out of 18, used milk, but the quantities were small, ranging from 1 pound to 4 pounds per day. Four households obtained milk from a goat or a cow kept especially for the young children; the remaining eight reported buying milk. They obviously realize the value of milk, especially for the young children, and most households are prepared to spend money for it. The village sends out substantial quantities of milk for sale to the railway station districts headquarters colony. Even so, milk is not freely available in the village and those who want to buy it have to make a long term arrangements with *Gujjars* or other suppliers.

Brahmins are strict vegetarians and teetotallers. Smoking is confined to men, but it is not favoured by the young men, among whom there are a number of non-smokers. The younger people use tea during the winter and in case of an ailment. But among the older generation there are still people who never take tea. Four old women in the sample households so stated. Moreover, few families drink tea during the summer; there were only two such families in the sample. In the summer, cooling drinks like buttermilk, *thandai* and *sharbat* are popular. As the sample survey was conducted during May and June, many women reported that they were taking *thandai* daily. It may be added that *thandai* with the intoxicant *bhang* (Indian hemp, *cannabis indicia*) added to it is the traditional favoured drink of Brahmin men.

Vegetables and fruits are much more commonly used by the Brahmins than by the Meenas. They are bought from the *Malis* in the village or the men bring them from the town when they return from work. Papaya and mango are available in the village in their seasons. The village has its own sweetmeat shops as well as vendors from the town. An ice cream vendor from the town was doing brisk business at the time of the survey.

Altogether, food has much more variety and its preparation is more elaborate and sophisticated than among the other two groups. It is the typical food of urban high caste families of the middle income group. But there is a pronounced deficiency of proteins. No meat, fish or poultry are eaten because of religious beliefs and milk consumption, in spite of full realization of its value, is also low. The physique of the Brahmins, both men and women, is noticeably weaker than that of the Meenas. This may be due partly to their sedentary mode of life, but the protein deficiency in the diet is also perhaps a contributing factor.

Personal Hygiene and Medical Care

Urban patterns have also been adopted in personal hygiene and adornment. Toilet and washing soap and hair oil are commonly used. Cheap cosmetics—face cream, Vaseline and talcum powder—are seen in many homes, although their use is not yet general. There is a great deal of variation in this respect between individuals and between families. Most of the younger women use soap and oil and also cosmetics. But several of the older women still retain the old habit of using mud to wash their hair and apply *ghee* thereafter. A daily bath is the rule, and clothes are washed as frequently as is considered necessary. The traditional Brahmin preference for a daily bath is a powerful factor in this. Men and boys generally bathe at the wells; women bathe in the houses with water brought from the wells. As there is no drainage system in the village, many houses have water standing in front of them. This is one reason why, in spite of greater prosperity, the general appearance of the Brahmin quarter of the village is not as neat as that of the Meena village. A proposal to built a set of bathroom for the use of the women has been pending with the village *panchayat* for several years.

Brahmins are aware of the importance of clean water for health. Most housewives screen the drinking water by placing a piece of muslin cloth on the mouth of the jar while drawing the water from the well. The practice is probably of no value as a preventive against spread of water borne diseases. But it shows a certain concern for sanitation.

Sickness receives relatively prompt and adequate attention by the Brahmins. This is due partly to the tradition of this literary group, which has always had some *vaidyas*, well versed in the traditional Ayurvedic system of medicine; but urban contacts, education, and white-collar service have also contributed to it. There are five *vaidyas* and six qualified compounders among the Brahmin white-collar workers in this village. The village has an Ayurvedic dispensary with a qualified *vaidya* and compounder. Medical assistance is more readily available than in the Meena village and is also more adequately utilized. The services of the doctors in the hospital in Sawai Madhopur are also frequently utilized. Complicated cases are taken to hospitals in Jaipur and Kotah. A woman in one of the sample households related an interesting case history of a number of operations for a uterine defect which she had had to undergo at various hospitals in Jaipur and Kotah.

But it must not be assumed that sickness receives adequate attention in the modern sense, or that the attitude towards medical treatment is basically science oriented instead of tradition-oriented. It is still the latter. For example, nearly all the women interviewed, including those in the families of the *vaidyas* and the compounders, reported that their deliveries were attended to by the village *dais* (midwives). The most popular among them is an old Muslim woman who is considered very competent. The *dai* follows traditional methods and has no training in modern midwifery practices. The only 'modern' innovation adopted by her is use of a razor blade, instead of knife, to cut the umbilical cord. But, two young women in the sample households who had returned for their confinement to their parental village, which had a medical dispensary, said that they had been attended by a trained midwife attached to the dispensary. These were the only exception to the rule. But their experience shows that younger women are prepared to use the services of trained midwives if they are available.

There are many cases of children who have suffered from malnutrition and of infant mortality resulting from neglect on the part of the mother and non-treatment of children's diseases. But these are not as common as among the Meenas and the Chammars. The young women particularly are conscious of the need for better nutrition and medical care of the children. The fact of this consciousness is clearly seen in the following figures on survival rate of children.

	Number of women	*Children born*	*Children surviving*
Married for 20 years and more	12	87	47
Married for less than 20 years	6	14	11

The survival rate of children born to older women is not very different from that of children of women of the other two groups; but among the children of young Brahmin mothers there is a marked change. This survey did not include study of fertility rates, attitudes towards family planning, etc., but the above data point significantly to the kind of changes which are coming in the group as a result of education.

Education

These Brahmins have an active literacy tradition, and the village is known in the area for the good scholars of Sanskrit it has produced from time to time. Sanskrit learning at home or from some *pundit* (Brahimn scholar of Sanskrit) in the village was quite common until recently. Many of the young men who later were educated and entered government service began their education in Sanskrit in the traditional way. But in recent years as there has been a complete change to school education the tradition of learning Sanskrit at home is dying out.

Nearly all the Brahmin boys of school-going age are in school. They constitute one-fifth of the boys in the village school. In addition, eight boys are studying outside the village. Education of girls is comparatively recent development. In the sample, most of the women below the age of 30 had had some education, primary school or less; but most of the older women were illiterate. Most Brahmin girls of the primary school going age are now being sent to the girls' primary school in the village. The prevailing attitude is that the girls must be educated through the primary stage. The principal reason for educating girls is that the educated young white collar workers, who receive first preference as bride grooms, want wives who have had enough education to be able to write a letter. Education up to the primary stage is meeting this requirement. Higher education is neither considered necessary nor practical in the absence of a middle school for girls in the village; the prevailing attitude is against sending girls to the boys' middle school. In another ten years or so, when there are even more men in government services and some men have become college lecturers or gazetted officers, there will probably be a demand for girls with higher education. The village may then want a middle school for girls, as many large villages in this area, with concentrations of Brahmins and Mahajans, have got already one or more middle/high schools for girls. But in the present stage of social advance of the group, a primary school for girls is deemed adequate.

The Development Programme for Women

The development programme for women, with its emphasis on teaching crafts (stitching and embroidery) and hygiene, nutrition, child health, etc., would be expected to have better chances of success in this urbanized, middle class group than in the other two. An adequate and well conceived programme, conducted through well trained personnel, would probably elicit a good response. The actual experience is different however. The village has a *Gram Kaki*, a young widow of the goldsmith caste. She has a sewing machine and conducts the prescribed programme of extension work among 20 families. But her work too had no impact among Brahmin women so far. She is a woman of a lower caste who has no more education or knowledge of crafts than many of the Brahmin house-wives. The latter can (and do) learn much more about modern fashions in clothes and stitching methods and other ways of doing new things from each other, from visiting relatives and friends, or from their men-folk, than they can from the *Gram-Kaki*. Moreover, it is well-known that this girl has been appointed a *Gram Kaki* only in order to provide her some financial assistance in her young widowhood.

Marriage Customs

The marriage customs of the Brahmin have always been different from those of the cultivating and the scheduled castes. The major differences are in matters of widow-remarriage and marriage dissolution. Both are permitted among the cultivating and the scheduled castes; but they are not permitted among the Brahmins. The man has the right to marry a second time while his first wife is living; he even has the right to forsake his wife without formal dissolution of the marriage. The woman has no such rights. These customs, generally associated with the entire Hindu society, are found in this area only among the Brahmin and other high castes, the Rajput and the Mahajan.

Until recently the age of marriage among Brahmins was not very different from that among the cultivating and the scheduled castes. Early marriages, with the girl 7 to 12 years old and the boy 7 to 15 years old with *gauna* several years after the marriage were the rule. Now this is changing. All the middle aged and older women (35 years older) in the sample households had been married at the age of 10 or 12 years. Several of the younger were also married at this age but the others were married when they were older, generally between 14 and 16 years. At present, the most frequent age of marriage is 14 to 16 years for girls and 18 to 22 years for boys.

Most marriages are arranged with Brahmin families in Sawai Madhopur town or in villages around Sawai Madhopur or neighbouring *tehsils*, generally within 30 miles of the village. In this respect, however, Brahmins practice differs somewhat from the practices of the Meenas and the Chammars. Marriage within the village is allowed, provided it is not within the prohibited *gotras*. However, such marriages (within the village) occur frequently; there were three cases among 18 sample households. Brahmins obviously do not share the prohibition against intra-village marriage which both the Meenas and the Chammars have. On the other hand, Brahmin marriages often link families who live considerable distances apart. Concentration of Brahmin families are found only in large or middle sized villages of this area, with the result that marriage among families located at distance of 50 or even 100 miles were not uncommon in the past. The recent emigration of Brahmins to cities had made this more common. For example, the girl whose marriage gifts are described below had married into a family, which lives in Ratlam, in Madhya Pradesh some 300 miles away. But the most important changes relating to marriage are that it has become more elaborate and expensive, and the burden of the expense has begun to fall increasingly on the girl's parents. A marriage 40 years ago was a comparatively simple and inexpensive affair. The marriage parties even at that time were large; parties of 100 to 200 persons were not uncommon for families with average land holdings. But the food served at the feasts was comparatively simple and the cost of ornaments, clothes and various ceremonies connected with marriage was nominal. At the time of engagement the girl's parent would send only one rupee and a coconut. The boy's parents made ornaments and clothes for the girl for the wedding ceremony; but they were fewer in number and less expensive than they are today. A few light silver ornaments, a gold *rakhri* weighing between one and two *tolas* and one dress were considered adequate. The girl's parents would give Rs. 5 at each of the three principal ceremonies connected with marriage—*agawani, hethlai* and *bidai*. In addition, they would give the mother-in-law a dress or a *lugari*. At the time of *gauna*, which took place after several years, the girl's father would again give the girl a dress and some ornaments.

Until recently, the overall expense was largely borne by the boy's parents, as is the case among the Meenas and the Chammars even today. The boy's parents were expected to make ornaments which remained with the girl and came back to them only when she came to live in their house. Frequently, they shared or paid for entirely the cost of the marriage feast at the girl's house. Bride price was looked down upon; but it was prevalent among the poor families, especially in the form of paying the expenses of marriage of the girl's parents. Finally, as in the case of the other two castes even today, the anxiety for marriage was all on the side of the boy's parents.

Fifteen to 20 years ago (in 1940s) marriages were becoming more expensive among the Brahmins. The boy's father made silver ornaments weighing four to ten lbs., a gold *rakhri,* and two ensembles for the girl. The food at the manda feast had become more elaborate. The girl's father was also supposed to serve more elaborate food to the marriage party. In addition, it had become the practice to give a small gift (of money about 4 annas—one-forth of a Rupee) to each member of the marriage party. All this meant a considerable increase in marriage expense for the girl's parents. But there was still some sharing of expenditure between the parents of the boy and the girl. If the marriage party stayed for more than three meals at the girl's house, the expenses of the fourth meal were met by the boy's parents. Similarly, while dowry had become common, it was small. Some silver ornaments, a few ensembles for the girl and a suit of clothes for the boy were considered adequate.

The last ten years or so (1950s) have witnessed a very real increase in marriage cost. Now the boy's father must make gold ornaments weighing five to ten or even fifteen *tolas* and two ensembles of clothes for the girl. Three gold ornaments, *rakhari, tagari* and a few thin gold bangles are considered the minimum. The *manda* feast is expected to be large and elaborate; between 200 and 500 guests must be served at least 5 dishes! The expenses of the girl's parents have increased even more. The marriage parties (200 or more persons are still common) must be fed during the entire time that they stay at the girl's home, and with 5 dishes at each meal. No part of these expenses is now borne by the boy's parents. The gifts given to the members of the marriage party have also increased in value. A gift of one rupee or a brass tumbler to each member of the marriage party is most common now and in one marriage celebrated in the village some months before this study, each member of the marriage party was given five brass utensils! The amounts given at the three marriage ceremonies observed ranged between Rs. 51 and 201; those for *hathlai* going up to Rs. 501 or more. Dowry consists of ornaments ranging from 2 to 10 *tolas* of gold, 5 ensembles for the girl, a suit of clothes and a gold ring for the boy, bedding kitchen utensils and other goods for the new couple's home; besides clothes for the father, the mother, sisters, and brothers and other near relatives of the boy. Durable and expensive consumption goods like a radio, a sewing machine, a bicycle, and a wrist watch have also begun to be given in the dowry, as is the practice among the urban high castes. Now-a-days the interval between marriages and *gauna* is much shorter, and the girl starts living with her husband soon, within a year or so after marriage. There is some small exchange of gifts at the time of the *gauna* ceremony too. The details of expenditure on two marriages in one sample households, 30 years apart, (Table 5.3) show how marriage expenses have gone up over the years. The household is a little more prosperous than average because it has more than average land holding (10 irrigated acres) and the head of the households is working as an agricultural extension agent.

Increasing elaboration of marriage is to be expected, with rise in income, because marriage is the occasion on which a newly rich family announces its new prosperity and an established family confirms its continued affluence. But higher standards of education and salaried jobs have also contributed to this. At one time the main criteria in fixing a match for a girl was the economic status, land holding, and reputation of the boy's family, and the boy's health. Families had small holdings and limited incomes and expenditure on marriages remained within reasonable limits. Now however, the principal criteria for selection of a good match are the boy's education and his job prospects. Boys with good education and good jobs are still not numerous, so there is a spirited competition among girl' parents. Larger dowries and elaborate expensive marriages are one result.

The Joint Family

The distribution of sample households by single and joint families is as follows:

- Single families—12—In five of these, the widowed father or mother of the husband lives with the married couple.

Table 5.3: Change in Expenditure on Brahmin Marriages

	Marriage of head of households, 35 years ago expenditure by Boy's side Girl's side		*Marriage of daughter of head 2 years ago expenditure by Boy's side Girls side*	
(i) Manda feast to their respective village people				
No. of persons fed	Boy's side 200	Girl's side 300	Boy's side 500	Girl's side 800
No. of dishes served	3	3	3	5 dishes, cooked in pure ghee
(ii) Marriage party				
No. of persons		100		125
No. of meals and dishes served at each meal.		4 meals with 4 dishes at each meal		4 meals with 4 dishes at each meal
Gift to each member of marriage party		nil		nil
(iii) Ornaments and clothes				
Gold ornaments	1 tola	Nil	10 tolas	2 tolas
Silver ornaments	200 tolas	Nominal, Rs. 25 worth	240 tolas	nil
Clothes	2 ensembles for the girl, 1 cotton, 1 silk	nil	2 silk ensembles for the girl	1 silk ensemble for the girl, 2 suits for the boy and clothes for the father mother and relations of the boy, of the value of about Rs. 200
(iv) Cash gifts on ceremonies				
Agwani		Nil		Rs. 101
Hathleva		Rs. 100		Rs. 1001
Bidai		Rs. 101		Rs. 201
(v) Other gifts		nil		Kitchen utensils for the couples home

- Joint families—6 —Married sons are living with their parents in their families, and two married brothers are living together in the other three.

These figures show that joint families are some what more common among the Brahmins than among the Meenas and the Chammars. The tradition of the joint family is stronger among the Brahmins than among the other two groups. And the present economic situation is also a factor contributing to the greater prevalence of joint families among them. In most households, one or more persons are engaged in white-collar service or other non-agricultural employment. Those who work in the town or in the factory can commute to work easily. They live in the family home in the village. Even those who have to live outside the village but can visit it on weekends and leave periods, prefer to keep their wives and children in the family home. This arrangement has several material advantages. It precludes thc inconvience of finding a rented house and the expense of maintaining a separate establishment. Houses are difficult to rent in the small villages in which most of these people are posted. Moreover, their salaries are not very high. If they kept their families with them, they would barely manage to live within their income and would go into debt when there was a sickness or other mishap in the family. On the other hand, the cost of keeping ones family in Raipur is much less. There is no house rent to bc paid and other household expenditure are also less, because food grains and milk are produced at home. Besides, if a man's wife and children live in the village and he visits frequently, it is easier to keep an eye on the land given on *batai*, especially to ensure that he gets his due share of the produce at harvest. There is the added security of living among one's own people, a real advantage when there is sickness in the family or when marriages are arranged. So most of the white collar workers keep their families in the village and make one of the following three living arrangements:

(i) The family of the white-collar worker lives with his parents or parent;

(ii) In case where the joint family has not broken up, the families of other married brothers also live with them; but where the joint family had broken up, the wife and children live separately in a portion of the ancestral house, weather formally divided among brothers or not.

One married son and daughter-in-law generally continue to live with his parents. The questions of break-up of the joint family arises only when two or more brothers are married. But it is not uncommon to find two married brothers living together.

Widow Remarraige and Status in the Family

The family status of a Brahmin woman was never equal to that of Meena or a scheduled caste woman. She did not work in the fields, nor did she work for wages; she was never considered an economic asset. Moreover, since a widow re-marriage was not allowed among the Brahmins and the woman was not permitted to leave her husband although her husband could leave her, her position was distinctly inferior. But so long as the people were poor, obtaining a wife was itself an achievement because of the overall shortage of women. The anxiety to obtain a wife was, with the boy's parents. Marriages were early and the boys who could not get married early, had to face much greater difficulty and to spend large amounts in getting married later. Some had to remain unmarried altogether. Bride price was not looked upon with favour, but it was frequently paid by those marrying late. The burden of the marriage expenses was mainly on the boy's parents, and marrying a girl was not a problem for her parents. The socio-economic changes of recent years have not affected the ban on widow re-marriage or the husband's right to leave his wife. On the contrary by adding the problem of finding suitable matches for girls and heavy expenses on girls marriage, they have made the position of women somewhat worse.

Analysis

This study reveals striking differences (in marriage customs and the position of women in the home) between the high castes on the one hand and the cultivating and the scheduled castes on the other. Ban on widow re-marriage and on divorce, dowry, and women's subservient position in the home, generally regarded as distinctive customs of Hindu society, are typical only of the Brahmins. The practices among the Chammars and Meenas are entirely different. The widow is allowed to sit in *nata*; dissolution of marriage is not considered good and is not frequent but it is allowed and the woman exercises the some initiative in this as the man. Dowry is absent, and the prevailing marriage practices point towards the prevalence of bride price in the recent past. The latter has almost disappeared among the Meenas; but it is still prevalent among the Chammars. The position of women in the home is also very different from that among the high castes. The woman is not a helpless creature fit only for home, a burden on her parents so long as she is not married and even thereafter, occupying a subordinate position in the home during her married life and condemned to a life of despised dependency should she be widowed. Instead, she is respected and feared; she has almost a dominant position in the home. The anxiety for marriage is all on the side of the boy's parents, because they know that if their son passes a certain age without getting married it will be difficult to find a wife for him. Accordingly the boy's parents take the initiative in fixing a marriage; they spend much more on it than the girl's parents do, and they take all possible care to please the girl's parents both before marriage and after marriage until she comes to live with her husband. The husband himself, after the wife comes to live with him, realises that she is his partner in the home and in work, that her contribution could make the difference between prosperity and want, and that if anything happens to her, or if she leaves him, he will find it extremely difficult to get another wife.

In our view, the most important reason for these difference is the economic fact that the women of the cultivating and the scheduled castes work outside the home and are economic assets to the family, while high caste women remain in the home and make no contribution to the family income. The entire superstructure of strikingly different social customs and attitudes seem to be built mainly on this single economic fact.

But it is significant that their own custom are regarded by the cultivating and the scheduled castes as the product of ignorance and want; the customs of the high castes are considered the mark of propriety and respectability; with growing prosperity, the trend is towards adopting high caste customs. Bride price is looked down upon, and *roti-beti* is considered proper. The prosperous Meena and the well-to-do Chammar wishes to give a dowry as well. Dissolution of marriage is becoming less free and the practice of *jhagra* and the Meena habit of kidnapping of women are looked upon with increasing disfavour. There is change even in the attitude towards work by women. The Chammars of Chainpur, copying the Meenas, want their women to work only on their own fields. The Chammar industrial workers of Chainpur are beginning to look down upon wage labour by women and the more prosperous among them, like the well paid skilled workers and the self-employed men, want their wives to stay at home, devoting themselves entirely to household work, just as the high caste women do. Boys with some education and a white-collar or skilled job, whose wives will not have to work, have begun to be sought after. The Chammars, giving dowry and sending girls to school, have already started to cater to them. These things hve not started among the Meenas, mainly because they continue to be predominately agricultural. The trend towards seeking boys with well-paid jobs and catering to their demands is most pronounced among the Brahmins. Among them the criteria of a good match have undergone a complete change in course of little more than a generation. Dowry, always present but quite nominal in the past, has become large and burdensome—the inevitable result of competition for boys with good jobs—and marriage has become a very expensive affairs.

But the trend towards adoption of high caste customs does not extend to widow re-marriage, and there is no evidence that the cultivating and scheduled castes will adopt high caste practices of prohibiting widow remarriage. Nor would such a movement be very easy. The practice regarding widow re-marriage is a vital matter for a caste. It has been a major determinant of social status in the past—the fundamental difference between high castes on the one side and cultivating and lower castes on the other, and it will not be possible to change it so easily. It is not certain that the change will be entirely in the direction of adoption of high caste practice by cultivating and scheduled castes. The high castes themselves are finding their customs increasingly difficult to maintain; there is growing opposition to it from urbanized and educated youth. It is quite possible that while the cultivating and scheduled castes move towards making widow re-marriage less easy (e.g., by prohibiting older widows or those with sons and land from remarrying), the change among the high castes may be in the direction of partial relaxation of the ban, especially in the case of young widows.

The social compulsion towards conspicuous and large expenditure on such ceremonial occasions as marriage and death almost forces each family to scrape the bottom of its financial barrel or to go beyond and borrow. This tendency has been commented upon by most writers on social or economic life in rural India, and there is no sign of its diminution. On the contrary, the effect of the economic and social changes of the last twenty years in this area, which have brought prosperity, or at least freedom from indigence, to an increasing number of rural people, has been to spread this tendency wider and to render ineffective the social restraints which had been imposed either from above (e.g., by the *Jagirdars*) or by the castes themselves. Expensive marriages and large feasts, which in the past were the prerogative of the wealthy, mostly the *Jagirdars* and the rich Mahajans, are now being indulged in by an ever-increasing number. Feasts for 400 to 500 guests are common among the Meenas, and even those for 800 to 1000 guests are not at all unusual. The more prosperous families in each caste want to imitate the ex-*jagirdar*, the rich Mahajan and the large cultivator; the poorer families imitate the more prosperous ones. In fact, expensive marriages and large feasts have become the accepted method of proclamation of prosperity by individual families and of freedom from traditional restraints by castes. The Chammars now invest heavily in silver ornaments. They have already outdone the Meenas in this respect and are trying to imitate the Brahmins by making gold ornaments.

Concentration of marriages on the Akha Teej day was another restraint exercised by the village community. But marriage on this day is beginning to be disfavoured precisely because it is not possible to give a large feast! Similarly, the small amount fixed by castes for particular marriage ceremonies, followed by all expect the very wealthy, 20 or 25 years ago, are no longer adhered to.

Among the Brahmins, among whom this process is best seen, no new norm have been fixed and giving the maximum on each occasion has become the criterion of a good marriage. It constitutes the single most important cause of indebtedness among all castes, from the highest to the lowest. It is a truism that the villager will starve his children but will not stint on ceremonial expenditure and will on the contrary go to any length in order not to loss face on such occasions.

In most Meena and Chammars households, if the children had no milk, the Meena women explained that the cow was dry and they could not afford to stall-feed her and get more milk, or the Chammar women explained that they could not afford to buy milk. But the same households were found to be going out of their way in incurring debts to meet expenditure on marriages and death feasts.

The social significance of these ceremonies is great, unquestionably. Marriages and other occasions when relatives and other people of the caste come together have an important social function. They serve as club, caste gathering, and fashion show for the women, matrimonial exchange, all in one. They could well be considered vital to the functioning of the caste as an institution and even to the entire social life of rural India today. The feasts on these occasions constitute the only break from the drabness and poverty of the villagers' daily food. Marriage ornaments are a kind of insurance for the woman—insurance as much against adversity as against disregard of her interests by her husband. But even when all this is taken into account, the wastefulness of a feast in which several hundred people are fed at one time, and its crushing burden on the poor family which spends an amount equal to its year's earnings and several years' savings, cannot but be deplored.

So far, neither social education nor legislation has had any effect on this expenditure. (No effective social education programme directed at reducing such expenditure has been undertaken. Legislation against death feasts was brought on the statute book in Rajsthan some years ago. Its only effect has been to change the name of this feast from *nukta* (death feast) to *gangoj* (feast given after a person has been to a holy place on the Ganga, usually Hardwar), and to add the cost of the trip to that of the feast. The feasts continue as before, only now more people go to Hardwar so that they can justify before the authorities the claim that the feast was a *gangoj* and not a *nukta*.

The Joint Family

The joint family is some what more common among the Brahmins of Raipur than among the other two groups. Among, the former the very practical advantages which joint living confers on the service men who are posted away from their homes but cannot afford to keep their families with them is a major factor favouring joint living. Among the Meenas, land acts as an influence in keeping families together; but separate living starts even when cultivation is joint and is in any case accepted as normal and inevitable. Among the Chammars the joint family was never as strong as among the other two groups; now it has almost disintegrated. The overall impression conveyed by the findings of this study is that the joint family is a much weaker institution than it is often represented to be in writings on village India. It is by no means comparable in social significance to caste.

Attitude Towards Education of Girls

It is interesting to note the effect of occupation on attitudes towards girls' education, and especially the social process through which the need for girls' education begins to be felt. The need for education begins to be felt when the change from an agricultural to a non-agricultural way of life takes place in the caste and more specially when a number of young men enter white collar, skilled or entrepreneurial work, after education and begin to demand that their wives have some education. This change is most pronounced among the Brahmins and is the main reason for sending girls to school. But it has also begun to be noticeable among the Chammars.

Consumption Patterns: The Influence of Occupation

The differences in consumption patterns of the three groups are striking. The Meenas have changed least from their traditional patterns in food, dress and ornaments, housing personal hygiene, etc.; the changes among the other two groups have been much greater. Distance from the town is not a factor in this: the Meena village is no farther from Sawai Madhopur town than the other two villages, and it is just as conveniently situated for obtaining consumption goods and services. Income and ready availability of cash are factors of some importance. The Brahmins have higher incomes; both the Brahmins and the Chammars have more cash than the Meenas, and for longer periods. But the Chammars are not much richer than the Meenas; on the contrary some of them are poor, and a large number, though better off than the Meenas, face greater financial insecurity.

Occupation is the main factor responsible for these differences. The Meenas remain the least affected by urban consumption patterns because they remain an agricultural group with non-agricultural sources of income contributing very little to their economy. Even with rise in income they do not incline so much towards acceptance of urban consumer goods, as toward peasant ways of conspicuous consumption—large feasts, for example. Brahmin consumption pattern tends to be similar to that of the literate, urban middle class, while Chammars have already begun to take on the colour of industrial labourers in this respect.

The marked, almost aggressive dissatisfaction of Chammars young men have been commented upon. Many of these are associated with an industrial way of life, and Chammars have begun to experience them even though they are living in a village and the older people among them are anxious to preserve their agricultural links. On the other hand, this group has achieved the maximum economic and social advance during the last two decades; it is making good use of the economic opportunities opening up for it and will probably do even better in future. Altogether, it appears to be the most interesting groups among the three, and we feel that a more detailed study of its problems and attitudes will be most rewarding.

Footnotes

1. It had been intended to include also study of attitudes of women towards political process like elections and towards institutions like the *panchayat* and the *Panchayat Samiti*. Women had been seen to participate in polling for the two elections, the *Panchayat* Election of December 1960 and the General Election of February 1962, in large numbers. The legislation relating to *Panchayti Raj* institutions provides for cooption of women as members of *Panchayats*, *Panchayat Samitis* and *Zila Prishads,* and in two of the three villages studied Raipur and Bijaipur, women had been co-opted as member of the village *panchayats*. But preliminary enquiries during the course of this study revealed a marked lack of interest in and awareness of political process and institutions among women in all the three villages. They knew about the existence of *panchayats* and *Panchayat Samitis* and that these bodies had women members; they had voted in the *panchayat* election. But they knew little else and showed no interest in the functioning of these bodies. Even the women members either did not attend meetings of these bodies or were silent spectators in the meetings, which they did attend. After the preliminary enquiries revealed this situation, a detailed study was not considered necessary.
2. *Gram Kaki*: (lit. aunt of the village). A woman of the village selected for assisting the extension workers of the community development programme in extension work among village women.
3. On basis of the above figures of per acre yields and the prices prevailing in 1961, the gross annual income of such cultivator comes to Rs. 1200.
4. *Hatai*: A place where men of a few neighbouring houses gather together for gossip.
5. But, in spite of this disadvantage of corrugated iron sheets, these are very much desired for roofing. Sheet roofs are preferred because they do not need to be repaired after each monsoon and replaced after two to four years, which tile roofs do. Besides, the labour of making tiles is saved. The number of houses with sheet roofs is small so far; but this is mainly because of non-availability of sheets. There is a keen demand for sheets and if they were available freely, a large number of houses will have sheet roofs.
6. *Dewali:* The festival of lights which comes a few weeks after the end of the monsoon.
7. This is true also of Meena women in other villages of the area. The author noticed during his visits to homes of prosperous Meena leaders (e.g. Ram Pratap, Raja Ram and Tara Chand described in study of Village Leaders) that their women dressed like other Meena women of the villages and also worked in the fields. Building *pucca* houses and giving large feasts on marriages, deaths and other occasions are the principal ways in which the prosperous Meena shows his wealth.

8. As explained in study on Caste and Occupations, only the *Malis* grow vegetables for sale.
9. *Beedi*: small cigarettes made by wrapping tobacco in *beedi* leaves.
10. *Pansari*: A merchant of traditional herbs and drugs.
11. An improved type of hearth originally designed by a Gandhian institute of rural development.
12. *Jaali*: A small cabinet for storing food. It has wire-gauze doors and sides in order to provide adequate aeration.
13. Since marriage parties used to go (and still do) to the bride's village by bullock-carts, the distance which a bullock-cart could cover during the course of a day was perhaps a factor in setting the limit on the distance within which marriages were fixed.
14. *Akha Teej*: Third day of the waxing moon in the lunar month of Baisakh. It usually comes in the first fortnight of May.
15. 1 *tola* = approx. 2/5 of an oz.
16. "He beats me. The mother-in-law makes me do all the work but would not give me food to eat", were some of the remarks made by the women of Bijaipur who had left their earlier husbands to live with the present ones.
17. The term 'Joint family' has been used here for all families in which two or more related couples are living together. A family in which one or more married sons are living with their parents, or two married brothers are living together, has been considered a joint family; but one in which one widowed parent is living with his/her married son and daughter-in-law has not been considered as a joint family.
18. Figures on incomes of permanent workers in the factory are fairly accurate; those on incomes of self-employed persons and workers with contractors are rough estimates.
19. This impression had been created because students of the factory school had not done well in the matriculation examination of 1960.
20. There was a dispute at the time about payment of bonus to workers between the management of the factory and the workers union.
21. One household consisting of an old widow, who subsist on food received in charity from other Brahmin households and a small income from two acres of unirrigated land has been excluded.
22. Pajamas were worn in the past only by the Moslems and the Rajputs. All other Hindu men wore the *dhoti* and the women wore the skirt.

6

Social Change and the Role of Caste

The changes described in these studies include:

- Change in occupation and work status of individuals and groups with consequent changes in production relationships within the village community;
- Change in consumption practices, especially use of new consumer goods and of modern services—education, health, transport, etc.,
- Change in certain social practices such as those relating to marriage, living in the joint family and religious worship; and
- Change in political relationships within the village community and in patterns of political institutions and leaders.

These changes have been accompanied by changes in attitudes, values, aspirations and goals of individuals and groups. They have changed the patterns of inter-action within groups and between groups in the village community, and have set in motion social movements of considerable magnitude.

The social matrix of rural life has consisted of the village and the caste, and the role of any individual in it could be very well identified with reference to these. In the words of Srinivas, "the village may then be described as a vertical entity made up of several horizontal layers each of which is caste", and again, "Rampura is a well defined structural unit which commands the loyalty of all who live there irrespective of their affiliation to different caste." (in Mackim Marriot)[1] This concern with caste and village arises from the fact that these are the two primary foci of community feeling in rural India.

Major Social Changes: A Recapitulation

Among the changes in occupation perhaps the most interesting is repudiation of their traditional occupations and obligations to the village community by castes like the Chammars. This change has had interesting social and political effects described earlier. Similar, though less important, changes have been experienced by other castes. A number of castes while continuing their traditional occupations have stopped rendering the supplementary services which they used to render to the village community. Thus the *Nais* (barbers) have stopped cleaning of utensils and the *Kumhars* (potters) no longer carry water from the wells. All these changes form part of the accelerated breakdown of the *Jajmani* system which began with rapid economic changes brought about by Second World War and has been helped by the social and political changes of the post-Independence years. However, in the motives for change, both the economic and the social are inextricably mixed. For the Chammars, the new opportunities for wage employment and for occupying cultivable wastelands were undoubtedly major factors motivating repudiation of the traditional occupation. But the strength of the social motive—raising the status of the caste—can scarcely be under-estimated. Its influence is clearly seen in the tendency to discourage women from doing wage labour. The rural Chammars of Manpur want their women to work, like the Meena women, only in the fields; the Chammar industrial labourers of Chainpur want their women to remain in the home. In both groups, a number of women continue to do wage labour; but the endeavour of the groups is to stop this practice as soon as possible.

Again the attitude of castes like the *Mali* and *Gujjar* towards their traditional occupations—producing vegetables and milk respectively—shows the strength of the desire to raise caste status. Both castes continue to follow their traditional occupations, but they prefer cultivation of field crops to these, even though production of vegetables and milk is very profitable and cultivation of field crops is not. They were not considered as 'proper cultivators' in the past, and were given a lower status then the Meenas. They now want to become 'proper cultivators' in an effort to achieve social equality with the cultivator-owner castes—Meena and Jat—which is the objective of all lower castes. The Meena or Jat cultivating owner, who has enough land to work with a good pair of bullocks, which he owns, and whose wife and other members of the family work only on the family holding (and do not seek wage labour outside) is their ideal. This explains the desire of all these castes to obtain land and become cultivating owners.

The Meenas have also been affected by this process; but in a different way. They have no incentive to occupational change, because they are cultivating owners already. But they are strongly disinclined towards 'accepting regressive change' such as combining wage labour with cultivation. The conspicuous failure of the Meenas of both Raipur and Bijaipur to take advantage of the opportunities of wage labour, even though this failure means lower income and level of living, can be explained only in this way.

The other aspects of occupational change relates to response to new employment opportunities. Here, the findings show caste in a new role—that of influencing choice of new occupations by individuals. The tendency of different castes to select different occupations (high castes—white-collar service and profession, scheduled castes—unskilled labour, artisans and Moslems—skilled work) is the main theme of this study. It brings out that each caste selects from among the new occupations those which will not interfere with its effort at social advance and which are allied to its traditional occupations. The result is that the individual's choice of occupation is limited, and the association of caste with occupation found in the village tends to be reproduced in urban and industrial communities.

Many of the changes in patterns of living and social customs are complementary to the changes in occupation. They are all directed towards adoption of higher caste practices and are motivated by the desire to raise the social status of the caste adopting them. Acceptance of vegetarianism and discouraging drinking among the rural Chammars, their adoption of Vaishnavite worship practices and the wearing of silver ornaments by their women are evidences of the change.

But the most striking change is in marriage customs. Changes already in evidence include discouragement of bride price; acceptance of *roti-beti* as the proper practice and the attempt of the well to do to give a dowry; discouraging dissolution of marriage; and frowning upon the practice of *Jhagra*. Even the increasing elaboration of marriage ceremonies—larger, more elaborate feasts; heavier silver ornaments; more elaborate Sanskrit ceremonies and introduction of innovations like band, fire-works and giving a gift to each member of the marriage party—is an aspect of the same process. The only area in which there is no marked change—and one in which the gap between the practices of the high castes and the others is continuing—is that of widow re-marriage. A difference in widow re-marriage practices has always been a basic social difference between the high castes and the others. This difference remains, probably because the cultivating and lower castes realise that the high caste practice is unsuitable for their needs and ways of life.

The Meenas too have a strong motivation for making these changes in social customs. Their traditional social status has not been very high—they are still considered a backward group—and they wish to attain social equality with cultivating castes of recognized status like the Jats. Their principal response to change influence was embodied in the Meena reform movement which was strong in this area in 1940s. This movement, besides advocating the changes in social customs noted above, also discouraged such distinctive Meena practices as group dancing by men and women at fairs and other festive occasions, easy divorce and kidnapping of women.

The attitude of the Meenas to their classification as a scheduled tribe gives a revealing insight into the different motives and aspirations within the caste. Most Meena leaders are anxious to retain the scheduled tribe status because of advantages such as reservations of seats in the State legislature and in government services, and various concessions, which it brings. In their anxiety to press their claim for being classified as a scheduled tribe they will go so far as to say that the Meenas of this area and the *Chowkidar* Meenas (the backward group with a criminal tradition) are one and the same people. But most Meenas will not agree with this view. They claim that they are a separate group—the *ujala* (clean, no criminal tradition) *Zamindar* (land-owner-cultivator) Meenas and are entitled to the social status given to other castes of cultivating owners.

An interesting facet of change in marriage customs is that they are more in the direction of high caste Indian traditional practices than in the direction of Western practices. Contact with Western culture and modern technology is the main motivating force for change in Indian society. It should be expected, therefore, that changes in customs, institutions, and ways of doing things would be in the direction of Western practice. This is happening over a wide area of economic activity and social practice in both urban and rural India, but in the case of marriage customs, work by women and their position in the family there is an opposite trend. The customs of the cultivating and scheduled castes are much closer to those of the West than those of the high castes. Yet they are losing ground to the customs of the high castes. The latter are not only not coming closer to Western customs but, as we have seen in case of dowry among the Brahmins, are to an extent becoming more pronounced. In this particular area of social behaviour, Sanskritsation[2] is getting the better of Westernization, even though contact with the west is the ultimate motivating force. The trend demonstrates the strength of high caste values and the esteem in which high caste social customs have been held by all sections of society, even though actual practice was not in accordance with these. Secondly, "it shows also that in this vital area of social behaviour (which constitutes the very essence of social existence) society must attain certain uniformity and get over marked inconsistencies within it before it is ready to adopt a new set of practices."

The other major trend—in consumption—is towards use of urban consumer goods and of modern social services in the fields of health, education, and so on. Here, we notice marked, and what would appear to us growing, disparities between Brahmins and Chammars on the one hand and Meenas on the other. The disparities appear to be due more to differences in occupations, especially in participation in non-agricultural occupations, than to any other single factor. They might be reduced in time with more widespread use of the new consumption goods and with longer experience with the new social services. But in view of the tendency of rural society to remain stratified and for the caste-occupation association to remain preserved, participation in non-agricultural employment will remain very different among different castes, so that differences in levels of living might increase instead of decreasing. (This has not been proved right as seen in Chapter 8 which captures the changes in the area in 2001, almost after forty years of the original study).

Accordingly, in the present stage of social evolution, while the forces of social advance and Sanskritization are tending to reduce traditional differences in consumption practices and social customs, the economic influences of urbanizations and non-agricultural employment are tending tc introduce new differences of rapidly growing range and magnitude.

The Role of Caste

All these changes in occupation and social practices have been accomplished with caste as the unit that is with members of caste functioning as the change making group. As a result, the role of caste in maintaining social norms has been reinforced and extended and the feeling of belonging to caste has been strengthened. Earlier this role had been mainly one of requiring maintenance of certain traditional practices and norms of behaviour, but now it includes adopting new ones, as a group. Caste emerges in the new role of the basic institution of social advance, and the individual sees rise in his social status as a part of the process of rise in status of the caste.

It is necessary to explain why these changes have been accomplished with caste as the unit and why individuals, even forward-looking, ambitious individuals, many of whom have served as leaders in the change process, have been content to see the rise in their individual status only as part of the process of rise in status of their caste. The initial motivation for the change among Chammars was provided by individuals who had got new ideas and aspirations as a result of urban contacts or education. Why did those individuals not break away from the practices of their caste and refuse to accept their disabilities as individuals? Why did they choose the much slower process of removing the disabilities and raising the social status of the entire caste? The most feasible explanation is that they felt that they would not be able to achieve their aspirations as individuals and that they could only advance as part of a group and that the only group through which they could advance was caste. Caste was and still is the basic social unit in village India.

These individuals felt that because all members of their caste suffered from the same disabilities they would take action if only they were suitably motivated; their task, they felt, was to provide this motivation. In this way, they argued, they would not only maintain their social relationship with their caste, but they would also achieve positions of leadership within the caste. On the other hand, if they try to do these things individually, they would have to break away from their caste, losing in the process their social relationships and encountering serious difficulties in such vital matters as marrying their sons and daughters, and still perhaps they would not be able to accomplish their objectives. It was obvious to them that in this process of casting off traditional obligations and disabilities they would encounter the opposition of the other castes, and would not be able to meet this opposition as individuals, however ambitious and determined they might be.

The successful accomplishment of this change, as well as the very significant experiences with political equality through the working of the *panchaya*t and *Panchaya*t *Samitis* has brought significant gains to the lower castes. One of these is that untouchablity is on the wane. This is clearly visible to any outside observer and is freely acknowledged by the villagers themselves. In a village like Manpur, where ten years ago, a Chammar would hesitate to go near a Rajput or Brahmin house, the fact that Chammar leaders are members of the village *panchaya*t and the executive committee of the cooperative society is accepted as a matter of course. The village has at least one well from which people of all castes, from Brahmins to Chammars, draw water freely. Restrictions on commensality are also waning—if not in the village, at least outside it. People of high and low castes do not yet sit and eat together in the traditional feasts, like those given on the occasions of marriage and death. Even castes with similar social status, such as *Malis* and *Gujjars* eat separately on such occasions. But on the new occasions for collective eating and drinking, such as taking tea in meetings of the *Panchayat Samiti* or the *zila parishads*, or eating in seminars and training camps, these restrictions are not observed and persons from different castes, from the highest to lowest, eat and drink together. Such violation of the traditional restrictions is being accepted.

It has also accepted that people of the scheduled castes can get goods and services freely in the town and in the railway station-district headquarter colony. The people of Manpur know that the Chammars of the hamlet go to the shopkeepers, restaurants, sweetmeat sellers, and barbers, in the shopping canter in the colony. But they accept this fact and neither protest against it nor withhold patronage from the shopkeepers. Within the village itself, high caste and Chammar students study together in the school and this is accepted: if milk distribution or even a mid-day lunch programme is started in the near future, there will most likely be no serious objection to it.

The attitude of the high castes to all these changes is healthy and could even be considered praiseworthy. It is in marked contrast to the widely prevalent stereotype of the high caste attitude towards untochability and treatment of the scheduled castes. The present attitude arises from partial acceptance of the view that untouchability and other disabilities suffered by the scheduled castes are wrong and must go. The younger men, many of whom are educated, have been influenced by the ideas of social equality and of the injustice of untouchability. These ideas were propagated by the Congress Party for a long time before Independence and have been advanced by all political parties since. They accept these changes and have a certain emotional identification with them. The older generation do not have any such identification; but they have reconciled themselves to the changes. They feel that the world has changed and it is no use protesting against the change. This 'change in the world' becomes dramatically clear to them when they see ex-*jagirdars* and other stalwarts of the old order hobnobbing with leaders of the scheduled castes at elections and urging better treatment and more concessions for these castes in their campaign speeches. Adoption of high caste practices by other castes is, they say, an important adjunct of the freedom in Independent India for every person to do what he likes. This is the reply which a direct question would most often evoke from them. This reply is also based on the perception, clear though not often expressed, that the nature of the new society is fundamentally different from that of the old; that the new society is essentially a commercial society in which ability to do a thing or to adopt a practice is governed mainly by the ability to afford it; that there are no other bars, and that the traditional restrictions on different castes, have no place in the new society.

There is of course apprehension about the more militant trends among the cultivating and the scheduled castes. The frank appeals to caste loyalty made during the 1960 *Panchayat* Elections were frequently cited by the high caste leaders as evidence of the growth of cateism—which, they felt, must be curbed. Some leaders went so far as to say that there could be no democracy in a caste-dominated situation.

The issues of growing caste consciousness and competition between castes are brought out most clearly by the reactions of cultivating castes to all these changes. The Meenas oppose change in occupation and social status of the Chammars toward whom they are definitely hostile. This opposition and hostility arose on socio-economic grounds. The Meena was the caste most directly affected by the economic and social consequence of Chammars' repudiating their customary obligations and trying to become cultivating owners. Loss of hides, as also of farm and general servants affected them most. Abandonment by Chammars of lands which they had cultivated earlier was a temporary advantage to the Meenas, but this was more than off-set by the growing Chammar competition, for allotment of new cultivable lands. The Chammars' aspirations for higher social status also affect them directly, because it means that the Chammars claim social equality with them. But a new dimension has been added to this hostility—their political rivalry. The feeling that Chammars are a major political force in the area adds to the resentment of the Meenas and brings the hostility into the open. The Chammars, for their part, are keenly aware that the Meenas are their principal opponents in economic and social advance as well as in local politics. The sentiments expressed in Chainpur and the Chammar hamlet of Manpur that "the Meena-dominated *Panchayat Samiti* will do nothing for us" is shared by Chammars in the whole area.

Caste and the Political Process

References have been made earlier to appeals to caste loyalty to win elections, especially elections to the *panchayats*, with slogans like "vote, and the daughter, for the Meena only"; which have become the symbols of these appeals; and to the tendency to place caste interests before all others in *panchayat* activities. The rivalry between castes reflects itself in the working of the *panchayat*, and the issues before the *panchayat* have begun to be viewed in terms of interests of particular castes. Many of the emerging village leaders are essentially "caste representatives". In fact, caste representatives are in a way the most significant persons among the new leaders, because the success of the *Panchayati Raj* institutions, and especially their acceptance as institutions of the entire rural community, will be influenced greatly by the personality and behaviour of these people.

But the studies also give insights into certain other significant developments. The high caste *Sarapanchas* of both Raipur and Manpur and a number of others have been elected with the support of the scheduled castes, in face of the opposition of the cultivating castes, and large numbers of their own castes. These leaders look to the interests of the scheduled castes and are anxious to ensure that they get their due in all matters. One result is that the influences which the scheduled castes should have in village affairs on account of their substantial numbers are already beginning to be felt. Another and perhaps even more important result is that the change in the nature of political power in rural society—from the authoritarian power of *Jagirdars* or the influence of a few selected people of the high and cultivating castes to the power of numbers—is being progressively grasped by all. In the *panchayat* of Raipur there is serious conflict. This conflict is only a reflection of conflicts in the village; to which the succession of social, economic and political changes that the village has experienced have contributed. While steps can certainly be taken to mitigate the problems, it cannot be avoided entirely.

One important role of emerging leaders is to serve as a link between village and administration, and the village and political leadership. This role is being played rather well. Leaders have completed the political chain between village level leadership of the *Sarpanch* on one hand and the State level leadership of the Minister and the M.L.As., on the other; they have greatly accelerated the process of transmitting the needs and problems of the villagers to the district headquarters and the State capital. Many of them show a remarkable understanding of "how things can be accomplished". The techniques of approaching people at various levels to press their claims are well understood and often very effectively applied. At the same time, they have brought State level politics squarely into the village. Both the aspirations of these people—many of them want to enter State level politics themselves, and the roles which they are being asked to play by the existing state and area level political figures, contribute to this development.

Outlook for the Future

The changes described in these studies have occurred in a society which is essentially pre-literate and tradition-bound. The great majority of adults who have experienced these changes are illiterate people brought up in the feudal-loyalist tradition. The microscopic minority with some education or greater contacts with the outside world, influenced by new social, political and economic ideas, have had a powerful influence as catalytic agents of change. Young, educated men or even young uneducated men have played an important part in the change processes. They have helped people understand the significance of the new change influences. They have urged them to accept change or as among the Chammars, motivated them to seek it.

But the situation of mass illiteracy and tradition-orientation is changing. A new generation is growing up. The new ideas, institutions and practices to which the present generation was exposed only in adulthood have been experienced by it from childhood. When people of the new generation become decision-makers, the change process will undoubtedly be more rapid. While it is hazardous to forecast its nature and direction—these will depend entirely upon how the new ideas have been grasped by this generation and what it makes of them—a few pointers can be given on basis of current trends.

The breakdown of the *Jajmani* system, which is quite far advanced already, will go further. The system will either disappear altogether, or if it does remain, it will be of marginal significance in the village economy. A few artisans (like carpenters, whose services are most essential for agriculture) may continue to have long term contractual arrangements with the cultivators; but, by and large, the village people will obtain the goods and services needed by them through payments in money.

The strong association of caste and occupation will remain, and the occupation of most villagers will continue to be influenced by their caste. There are two reasons for this. First, the majority of village people will continue to be agriculturalists, and since cultivation and land ownership will remain largely in the hands of traditional cultivating castes like the Meena, the *Mali* and the *Jat*, agriculture will continue to be associated with certain castes. Second, the influences which lead the high castes to seek white-collar and professional jobs, the scheduled castes to go towards unskilled labour jobs and artisans like the carpenters and the blacksmiths to seek modern counterparts of their traditional occupations will continue to operate, though with decreasing force.

The association of caste and occupation will be weakened as young men of all castes take up white-collar service and skilled work. It has been mentioned that educated young men of all castes aspire to become white-collar workers. The number of non-Brahmin young men in such service will increase progressively as education spreads among the other castes. The attraction of skilled work will be strongest for the scheduled castes. Indeed, the rapidly growing requirements for workers with modern skills will be met largely from these castes. Reference was made to the growing number of skilled workers, among the Chammar industrial labourers of Chainpur. This number will increase rapidly as the sons, nephews and younger brothers of men who made the change from agricultural labour to industrial employment grow up. These younger men, brought up in an industrial labour environment, will find it easier to move to higher paid skilled job than did the men of the earlier generation. At the other end of the social scale, the high castes will also move towards skilled labour jobs in somewhat larger numbers. That social considerations which have hampered this movement so far will weaken somewhat in future is indicated by the trend among the Rajputs, considerable number of whom has taken up such mechanical trades as driving and repairing motor vehicles. Since, the new trades obviously do not lower their social status, their example will be followed by young men of other high castes.

Combination of off-farm work with cultivation will become more widespread. The Meenas' disinclination to accept off-farm jobs altogether, may not disappear but an increasing number of young men from Meena families with small holdings will take up such work in an effort to increase the family income. The practice of young men doing non-agricultural work while the women and the older folks look after cultivation, which is already being followed by the Chammars hamlet of Manpur, may be followed by the Meenas also. Economic and social advantages of the practice—having two sources of income while staying in the village, maintaining the links with the family and the community and avoiding the disturbance and expense of setting up a separate establishment—are so marked that it is bound to spread. Moreover, it accords perfectly with the objective of social advance, because women remain on the farm and men go out for non-agricultural work.

Similarly, there will be a weakening of the tendency of the cultivators not to produce such high value farm products as milk, vegetables and fruit because of social consideration. There are signs of this change in this area but not in the villages included in these studies. Many educated young Rajput ex-*jagirdars* have laid out orchards for commercial production. A few have even started poultry keeping, a practice the majority of villagers consider fit only for the lowest castes and Moslems.[3] As in other changes, the lead of the high castes will be followed, by the other castes and attitudes will change.

The new generation will have a significantly different attitude towards technological change in agriculture. Response to improved techniques, including those introduced by community development programmes, has been rather slow in this area so far. The majority of the adults, who are illiterate and have a tradition-oriented outlook, think of change in techniques as a disturbance to their traditional ways of doing things rather than as an opportunity for better income or increased well-being. They may accept change; but they don't have the positive attitude of wanting or seeking it. The attitude of the younger generation will be different. They will want and seek changes, because they will be accustomed to seeking new things happening, to new techniques, materials, machines coming into use and bringing higher incomes or greater living comfort. Their attitudes toward manual labour will also be different. They will not be prepared to do back-breaking labour the way their fathers and countless generations before them have done. Nowhere, have educated people done such labour willingly, and it is most unlikely that the experience will be very different in village India. There will be a determined effort to eliminate the back-breaking labour and ridiculously low levels of productivity per person which obtain in agriculture. The change to capital intensive agriculture based on the use of machines may not come about. But there will be adoption of improvements like iron plough, the Persian wheel, the pump set for irrigation, and other small power driven machines like the small tractor or power tiller, which do not require large capital investment and which are already being successfully adopted by cultivators in some other parts of the country. Such change will be greatly facilitated by rural electrification[4]; further improvement in communication; establishment of facilities for distribution, service and repair of modern implements; and what is most important, availability of skilled youth in villages to operate and repair machines.

These and similar economic changes can be forecast with some confidence. But it is more difficult to foresee the nature of the social or socio-political changes. The social movement of recent years has been dominated by the striving of the scheduled castes and the cultivating castes for higher social status. Could this objective become less important after a time, as a result, perhaps, of effective reduction in social distance between different castes and the fact that difference—in social status based on birth are given less importance? Social disabilities, untouchability, and the ban on commensality—prominent features of the caste system in the past—have already become less important. The present generation has taken the initial step in weakening these restrictions. The next generation, used to freer mixing between castes on the basis of equality, will pay progressively less heed to them. Similarly, the process of the scheduled castes and the cultivating castes adopting the social customs and religious practices of the high castes will certainly go further, and since it is not likely to evoke any more resistance from the high castes than it has done so far, the difference between the customs and practices of different castes will be reduced further. Moreover, caste as a determinant of social status is far less important in contemporary urban society, in which wealth and profession of the individual are more important, than it is in the villages. And as economic activities are diversified and urban values percolate to the village, a similar position may prevail there.

The tendency of the cultivating castes and the scheduled castes to appeal to the bond of caste for political purpose could also weaken. These castes have at present a sense of new found power and political importance. Moreover, the motive of raising social status of the caste, which brings with it the feeling of inter-caste competition, is particularly strong among them. But if this motive is weakened, and longer experience with functioning of *panchayat*s and other institutions brings a clearer realization of the extent and the limitation of their powers, especially the fact that the institutions can be effective only to the extent that they command the allegiance of all castes, it is not unlikely that appeals to caste loyalty for political purposes will become less pronounced. That this could happen is brought out by the political behaviour of the high castes. Political contests among the high castes in this area have been based mainly on personal, group or factional considerations, and appeals to the caste loyalty are rarely made.

This should not lead one to the conclusion that caste will cease to be important. Untouchability, the ban on commensality and similar restrictions are but the outer trappings of caste. The influence of caste in local political institutions is a very recent addition to its many roles. The weakening or disappearance of these will not affect the essential structure of caste, which will remain a basic institution in village India.

There are several reasons for taking this view of which two are most important. First, with caste endogamy remaining inviolate, caste will remain the sole basis of kinship and the main determinant of the social and personal relations of the individual. In all these studies, in which changes in marriage customs have been analyzed, no reference has been made to caste endogamy. The main reason for the omission is that the rule of caste endogamy continues to be enforced as rigidly as ever. Indeed, the minor departure which occurred in the past, by way of a *Jagirdar* or a rich man taking a lower caste woman as concubine, has also disappeared. Secondly, as explained above, association of caste and occupation will continue for a large proportion of the rural population.

The picture which emerges from this analysis is of a society in which there is greater inter-mingling of agricultural and non-agricultural occupations, occupational structure is less rigid and there is greater readiness to accept technological change; but the association of caste and occupation remains for a large segment of rural population. But social distance between different castes and the disabilities of the lower castes have decreased. The motive to raise social status of the caste and the influence of caste on political institutions are possibly weaker. But caste remains the basic social institutions.

Need for a New Social Integration

Chapter 7 will trace the transition of the village from an integrated, though hierarchical society in which work, share in economic product and social status of each caste was fixed, to an increasingly competitive society in which each caste is striving for higher social status and greater political power. This pattern of history emphasizes the urgent need to evolve new patterns of association and social and economic interaction among rural people in order to achieve a new integration based on the principles of social and political equality, freedom of association and economic advance. Development of a suitable new social structure is the central problem of village India to which the coming generation will have to find a satisfactory solution.

The task of evolving the new social structure will not be easy. Building a valid basis of democratic functioning in a community in which caste remains a basic institution will be a unique experience. Its success will be influenced very greatly by economic factors—for example, the rate of expansion of opportunities in the non-agricultural sector, and whether economic inequalities between different groups in the rural community are allowed to grow. Accomplishment of the changes reviewed in these studies has been facilitated not a little by the fact that ideas of social and political equality began to spread and aspirations began to rise in a period in which economic conditions were relatively favourable. Rapid increase in opportunities for non-agricultural employment is especially important because the demand for such employment will increase with spread of education and the growing tendency among small cultivators to combine part-time non-agricultural work with cultivation. A slowing down of expansion of such opportunities could be a major factor in increasing inter-caste rivalries and retarding social change.

There is a need for conscious and determined emphasis on economic equality, especially ensuring effective availability of modern social services and new consumption goods to all sections of the village community. Marked inequalities in income and level of living will seriously impair efforts at social integration anywhere. Their influence is likely to be greater when the possibilities of economic inequality are increasing, and because of the tendency of different castes to avail themselves of new economic opportunities tends to follow caste lines. The differences in levels of living of the Brahmins, the Meenas and the Chammars, which are related to the occupational change among the three groups, are much greater than they were a generation earlier. And they will increase further if the Brahmins and the Chammars continue to advance towards non-agricultural employment much faster than the Meenas. The experience of these three groups represents a sample of much larger phenomenon. Modern industrial society has the potential of creating far greater differences in levels of living than any that the village had known.[5] The difference between the levels of living of the modern industrial magnate and his unskilled factory workers are far greater than any that existed in the village. The limited economic system of the village was egalitarian in comparison, simply because it could provide no more than bare subsistence for the majority of its people. Even the favoured few, like the *Jagirdar* and the rich money-lender-trader, had very limited choices in consumption.

As the new differences in levels of living will tend to follow caste lines, caste will not only influence social relations and economic activity of the individual but will also influence his level of living. The resultant economic disparities between castes could neutralize the social and political gains of recent years and give rise to new tensions. This possibility lends urgency to securing effective equality in basic areas of consumption and modern social services for all groups. Indeed it makes it the most important objective of social action in village India.

Footnotes

1. McKim Marriot (Ed): *Village India*, Chicago, 1955.

2. The term is used in the sense in which it has been used in: Srinivas, M.N. *Religion and society among the Coorgs of South India*. 1952. p. 30-31
3. Jai Singh is one of them and is very happy with the profits he is making in this enterprise.
4. A village near Sawai Madhopur town received electricity during 1963. This was immediately followed by installation of pumps on a dozen wells. The owners of these wells, who were already producing some vegetables for the urban market, began to concentrate on vegetable production.
5. This was perhaps one reason why the social system of the village could be sustained in spite of marked inequalities of social status and political power.

7

Social Change and the Village Community

The new integration (referred to in the last chapter) must be achieved primarily at the village level and with the village as the unit. The village has traditionally been the unit of settlement and of organization of social and economic relationships within rural society. And, it will remain so in future because the bulk of the rural population will continue to live in villages. It is, therefore, imperative that the village has a new social system through which the village people establish new patterns of social, political and economic interaction, which are satisfying to them and enable them to live as members of one community without conflict. The traditional social system of the village had, in spite of all its other defects and drawbacks this cardinal virtue; it enabled different castes and groups to live together without serious conflict. Otherwise, it could not have survived the political convulsions and periods of anarchy and unrest which India experienced from time to time.

That the Indian village is a distinct socio-economic unit whose inhabitants have a strong community feelings has been a dominant theme in writings on rural India during the last 100 years and more. Beginning with early British administrators[1], successive writers on rural India have emphasized this point. In recent years, sociologists studying villages have acknowledged the existence of the feeling of "belonging to the village" and have attempted to analyze the bonds that tie the villagers to his village and his caste, as contrasted with the nature of his contacts outside the village and the role of caste (which extends beyond the village). They have also dwelt at length on the question whether the feelings for caste contributes to the feeling for the village or serve as alternative, competitive focus of community feeling. Perhaps, the most interesting discussion onvc the subject are in the studies of Srinivas, McKim Marriott, and Oscar Lewis, reported in 'Village India'.[2]

In post-independence years, the idea that the people living in the village have a strong feelings of belonging together, has occupied an important place in thinking on the community development programme and on institutions such as the *panchayat* and the cooperative. It is a central idea in the community development programme, in which village and community are considered to be almost synonymous. Many activities of the programme, such as public works, the expense of which is shared by government and the village people, are based on the recognition of the villagers' loyalty to their village. Moreover, it is thought that by affording such opportunities for collective endeavor, the community development programme itself strengthens the feeling for the village and helps build a stronger, healthier community life. Many of the institutional activities included in the programme, such as organization of youth clubs, women's clubs and community centres, attempt to foster community feelings as a primary objective.

In the village *panchayats* similarly, the strong feelings of belonging, of being members of one community, has been recognized as a major source of institutional strength. That such wide authority and comprehensive role in the economic and social advance of the rural people could be envisaged for one institution is due, in the author's view, to implicit acceptance of the existence of this feeling. Moreover, the recent trend towards smaller *panchayats* in several States has been motivated by the idea that the *panchayat* will function better if the people of the *panchayat* area regard it as an institution of the community, and that this can happen only if its area is co-terminous with the existing unit of community life, the village. "One village, one *panchayat*"—this is the ideal. Bringing together two or more small villages into one *panchayat* is recognized only as compromise which has to be adopted because it is not feasible, for economic and administrative reasons, to have a *panchayat* for every small habitation.

In the case of cooperatives, there was for some time a controversy between the supporters of the comparatively large society, comprising a group of villages, and those who favoured the small society comprising a single village, or where necessary, a few small villages. The larger society was favoured on grounds of economic viability; the supporters of the small society was advocated so that members should know each other personally and that the successful working of the society should rest on their strong sense of community.[3]

Yet, it is recognized by all who have anything to do with rural life that the feeling of belonging to the village is weakening and changing in character. No modern writer could follow Metcalfe or Munro, and call the village communities little republics. The changes of the last 100 years and more—political, economics and social—have produced enormous changes in the feeling for the village. With Raipur as the example, an attempt is made here to analyze the character of change in the feeling for the village as well as the influence contributing to it. The changes are brought out by contrasting the present position with that obtaining about 60 years ago, i.e., just before the railway line came into the area. This event greatly increased the contact of the village with the outside world and accelerated the process of economic and social change. Its first effect was migration of Brahmins to cities to work as cooks and priests. This throw back to a historic date helps clearer perception of the basics on which the feeling for the village rested in the past and the change influences working on it.

Raipur Sixty Years Ago

Raipur is an old village; the villagers believe it was founded at the time of the historic battle at the Ranthambhore Fort early in the 14th century. The feeling of continuous living in the same village for generations and centuries, typical of most Indian villages and a powerful factor in contributing to the sense of belonging to it is particularly strong in Raipur, where there is the additional factor of pride in belonging to an historic village. This pride is shared by people of all castes, though the literate castes (Brahmin and Mahajan) feel it somewhat more strongly than others. Until 60 years ago the contacts of the village with the outside world were largely limited to some administrative and commercial relationships. Administration was concerned primarily with maintenance of law and order and of collection of land revenue. Jaipur State had appointed *patels* and posted *patwari* within the village for collection of land revenue. The *tehsil* and the *thana* (police station), the two important administrative offices of the State, were located in Sawai Madhopur town, six miles from the village. The villagers understood very well the duties of the *patels* and the *patwari* and the functions of these two administrative offices. They were also keenly aware that their village formed part of Jaipur State. There was a strong feeling of loyalty to the State and respect for the Ruler. But the administration had only limited functions: it did not enter into and affect the daily life of the villagers in innumerable ways as it does today.

The land of the village was the sole means of subsistence for the villagers. All castes depended upon it either directly as cultivators or indirectly as artisans, traders, priests etc., supplying goods or rendering services to the cultivators. Economic relations between different castes were regulated by the *Jajmani* system under which the goods and services to be supplied by each caste and the payments to be made to it (mainly in grain) were specified in detail. All villagers, cultivators and non-cultivators, shared in the produce of the land; the non-cultivators had as much stake and interest in the agriculture prosperity of the village as the cultivators. A year of good crops meant plenty, one of poor crops meant hardship for all. The village was not merely a place to live: it was a sole theater of economic activity and its land was the sole means of subsistence.

Commerce with the outside world was limited. The principal exports from the village were opium, some foodgrains and *ghee*. Imports were cloth, kerosene, salt and a few other consumer goods which had been introduced by this time. The village also served as a small commercial and service centre for surrounding small villages. Its artisans sold leather goods, ornaments and *lac* bangles; its merchants distributed consumer goods, lend money and bought agricultural produce, and its *Malis* sold vegetables. Marriages of most castes were concentrated within a radius of 30 miles. Exception were Brahmins and Mahajans in case of whom marriage with families living at longer distances were more common. Marriages were a major source of contact with other villages because it was common to visit one's relatives.

Travel was limited. Most travel was confined to visiting relatives in nearby villages or going to Sawai Madhopur town. The only exception was pilgrimage to holy places, which was the principal form of travel to longer distances.

The village was by no means isolated although that might have been the case earlier. But its contacts with the outside world were limited. What is more important, economic activity and day-to-day social life were concentrated in the village, and the outside world did not intrude into it and affect every aspect of life as it does today. As a result, the feeling of belonging to the village was all-pervading.

The feeling of belonging to one's caste was equally strong. Caste was the most important socio-economic institution in the life of the village people. It was the basis of all marriages, which were confined to caste. It determined occupation and social status; social and economic relations with people of other castes. Marriage and other social customs; consumption especially preference for or avoidance of certain foods; mode of dress and values and outlook towards life. The kind of life that an individual villager led from economic activity to outlook on life was determined mainly by his caste. Most villagers knew that their caste was found outside the village in neighbouring villages and beyond. But consciousness of the distribution of caste beyond the marriage zone was vague, and what is more important, not meaningful; because the fact did not appear to be of any great significance to an average villager.

To sum up, the average villager felt that he belonged to a particular village and to a particular caste. Both loyalties were strong and keenly felt. The feeling for the village rested on:

- Contiguous living in the village *abadi*;
- Concentration of economic activity and social relationship within the village, with the land of the village providing the sole means of substances and the *Jajmani* system binding the different occupational and social groups (castes) in the case of economic and social relationship which gave all of them a stake in the prosperity of the village; and
- Very limited contacts with the outside world.

The feeling for the caste was based on the vital roles it had in all aspects of the social and economic life of individual. But one loyalty contributed to the other: there were not many occasions when the villagers found the two loyalties competitive or conflicting. There were occasional conflicts between castes, no doubt; but the role of caste as a basis of the *Jajamani* system overrode these. Caste providing the social and economic stability and intra-group discipline essential for the functioning of the system. The socio-economic composition of the village upper-most in the mind of the villagers was of a unit composed of a number of castes, each of which performed an essential function and made possible it's functioning as a unit. This was expressed in the locally popular saying, "the village is an entity composed of *Saat Jaat*."[4]

Raipur Today

The position has changed radically during the past 60 years. The village is no longer the sole theater of economic activity; nor is its land the sole source of substances. Almost 40 per cent of the workers in Raipur (462 out of 1212) depend wholly or in large part upon income originating outside the village. The *Jajmani* system has all but broken down. *Jajmani* relations are now confined only to a few castes—the *Kumhars* (potters), the *Khatis* (carpenters), the *Lohars* (smiths) and the *Nais* (barbers). But even in these instances the traditional activities neither provide the main source of ir ome for the caste nor form main basis of supply of goods and services furnished by the caste to village. Thus, only four out of ten *Kumhar* families are engaged in their traditional occupation of making pots, and even these families supplement their earnings with other non-caste sources of income. On the other hand only a minority of the village families use *Jajmani* services. Non-cultivators and small part-time cultivators (e.g., *Rehgars* and Chammars—forty percent of all families in the village) do not participate in the *Jajmani* system at all. The main participants in the *Jajmani* system are the cultivating owners—Meenas and *Malis*—and a few cultivating households among the high castes. But even the families who participate in the system obtain only a few specified goods and services from the same artisans. Thus, only specified services like repairs to the plough are obtained from the *Khatis* under the *Jajmani* system, and all other goods, e.g., a *charpoy*, repairs to the house, are paid for in cash. Consequently, most of the transactions between the village artisans and other villagers are cash transactions, and the *Jajmani* system is of distinctly marginal significance in the economic life of the village.

Commerce with the outside world is extensive. A wide variety of manufactured goods is obtained from outside the village and earning money to pay for these, whether through sale of agricultural produce or through sale of one's labour, has become the most important objective of economic activity. Commercial contacts with the outside world are so active that a good deal of the buying and selling which would bc done in the village is done in Sawai Madhopur town instead. A major part of the agricultural produce of the village is sold in the town, not to traders within the village, because the producers feel they get better prices in the town. Similarly, many consumer goods available in the village shops are bought in the town because prices are lower, or there is greater variety. Even goods of the type produced by local artisans are purchased outside the village, and village artisans on their part sell their goods outside. The villagers buy country-type shoes, *charas* and other leather goods produced by the village *Rehgars* from Sawai Madhopur town, from *haats* (weekly markets) in other villages and form periodical fairs. The village *Rehgars* similarly sell their products in fairs, *haats* and Sawai Madhopur town. The *Rehgars* want a *haat* in the village so that they do not have to take their goods for sale outside. The village is part of a market area centering on the town of Sawai Madhopur, which in turn is linked with the markets of the State and the nation, and economic influences originating outside the village are constantly impinging on it. Most villagers see this quite clearly. The average cultivator understands that variations in prices of agricultural produce are the result mainly of factors originating outside the village or local area. During the two years preceding these studies, the price of *gur*, an important cash crop for these cultivators, had been low. They knew that this was not due to any local factor—production in the area had been low in 1960-61 and prices should have been high—but to over production in the country. The white-collar workers in government service and the skilled and unskilled workers in the cement factory and the railway station all realize that their employment depends upon decisions taken by people at the State capital, Jaipur, or in distant places like Delhi, Bombay, and Calcutta.

Changes in contiguous living have not been as marked, because most of the people of the village continue to live in the village *abadi.* But there is a growing tendency to live outside. Nearly half the Meena households now live in the hamlet which has grown to its present size during the last sixty years. In addition, two hamlets of Chammars' and *Rehgars*' have been established within the last twenty year; and a large proportion of families of these castes lived in them. The trend towards living outside the main *abadi* will grow. There is very little land available for expansion of housing within the *abadi,* and population increase and rise in the standard of living lead to a desire for bigger, more spacious houses and there will be pressure to move out of the *abadi.* This may result in the establishment of one or more new hamlets at some distance from the *abadi* or in a tendency among cultivators owning land irrigated by wells to live, homestead fashion near their wells.

Accordingly, all of the past reasons for the feeling of "belonging to the village" have been weakened and will weaken further as contacts with the outside world increase and economic activity outside the village becomes progressively more important. There is no influence in the development programme or development institutions which can counter this trend effectively. During eight years of operation of the community development programme, the only development activity in which the whole village participated as a unit was construction of middle school building. Participation was by no means equal: Brahmins and Mahajans made the largest contributions in money and were also the principal decision-makers, and participation of the scheduled castes was nominal. Still, this was the only activity in which all castes participated; there has been no other. All other works of the community development programme, e.g., construction of drinking water wells and paving streets, have been done on a caste or *mohalla* (quarter of the village) basis, and if there has been a village contribution it has been only from members of the caste or residents of the *mohalla* concerned. The development institutions associated with the community development programme—the *panchayt*, the cooperative society, the youth club, the women's club and the community centre—do require association on a village wide basis. But none of these institutions had been successful in countering the above trend and fostering village wide association. The *panchayat*, (Chapter 3) serves more as an area of struggle for power than as a medium for village-wide cooperative action. The cooperative society is not functioning well. If it had been more active, it would have been the means of village wide association for certain economic purposes. On the other hand, it could also, like the *panchayat*, be an arena for caste or group competition. The youth club is dominated by educated young men, mostly of the high castes, and has never been able to attract the youth of the cultivating or scheduled castes in large numbers. The women's club was also a high caste affair when it functioned. The community centre is inactive.

The three later institutions are intended to serve as media of informal association and recreation on a village wide, supra-caste basis. But because they do not function, this objective is not being achieved, and informal association and recreation remain confined largely within castes. Probably this was always the case; but the changes of the last two decades and those which are occurring now tend to confine them more and not less within caste. This needs some explanation. The main forms of informal association and recreation within the village at present are: meetings of men at *hatais* (place of informal group meetings) in the evening and in shops in the village *bazaar* during the day; meetings of women at the wells, and *keertans* (singing of devotional songs) by the young men in the temples at night. Feasts, fairs, and religious festivals are other important occasions when villagers get together. Meetings at *hatais* are generally within caste, confined to neighbors. Meetings in the village *bazaar* are supera-caste and are perhaps the most important means of day-to-day meetings between men of different castes. Meetings of women at wells have also tended to become more caste based because the number of wells has increased in recent years and each caste, including the scheduled caste, has now got its own well. Feasts at weddings and funerals are also caste affairs because most of the invitees are relatives of the host and belong to his caste. *Keertans* are an increasingly popular source of recreation for the villagers, especially the young men. But these are organized in temples, most of which are caste temples, and *keertan* parties are usually composed of members of the caste which patronizes and supports the temple. Most religious festivals are celebrated either in temples or in individual homes and do not afford opportunities for different castes to come together. There is only one festival in the year, the *Jaljhoolni Gyaras*, in which all the Hindus of the village come together. But when the scheduled caste claimed the right to participate in this festival and the high castes opposed it, the disagreement became a cause of tension and actual violence. Therefore, participation in this festival at present serves more to emphasize caste feelings than to foster the feelings of belonging to a supra-caste entity—the village. In the days of Jaipur State and the *Jagirdars,* there were rather more occasions for people of different castes to come together. The *Dussehra* and *Gangore*[5] festivals were celebrated by the State in the State capital and other large towns and by the *Jagirdars* in their village at their own expense, and all the people were expected to participate in these. Weddings and other ceremonies in the *Jagirdars'* homes were other occasions for people of different castes to come together, because they were all invited (or required) to attend. Integration of Jaipur State with Rajsthan and the disappearance of *Jagirdars* have spelt the disappearance of many opportunities for informal associations. The change is particularly marked in former *jagir* villages like Manpur, and it is often mentioned by the villagers.

The school is at present the only institution in which there is effective, daily association on a village-wide, supera-caste basis. Moreover, this association is on the basis of equality, without regard either for the traditional ideas of caste status or of the new force of caste competition. It is of great significance for the future, because it will have a fundamental influence on the attitudes and behaviour of the generation now going to school. But its present influence is rather limited, because the school going youth form only a small part of the population; as yet they have little influence on decision-making in the village.

The village is often thought of as a face-to-face society whose inhabitants see each other daily and do various activities together. This is undoubtedly true of small villages of agricuiturists like Bijaipur or the hamlet of Manpur. But as the above description brings out, this is not true of multi-caste village like Raipur.

Towards a New Society

The traditional feeling of belonging to the multi-caste village was dependent to a large extent on isolation or limited contacts with the outside world and the very restricted, essentially static economic and social life institutionalized in the *Jajmani* system. Moreover, the socio-economic system of the village was hierarchical in character and assigned a stated occupation, share in the economic product of the village, and most important, a particular social status, to each caste. It was inevitable, therefore, that with breakdown of isolation, increasing participation in the nation's economic and political life, and spread of ideas of social and political equality, this structure of socio-economic relations should suffer violent convulsions. The feeling of belonging to the village should weaken.

But this feeling was essentially secular and integrative in character. It symbolized the contribution of different castes in the functioning of a secular, supra-caste social unit. The feeling for the caste on the other hand is essentially sectarian and divisive. Therefore, decline of the feeling for the village and strengthening of the feeling for the caste, together with the change in the role of caste feeling from contributing to the feeling for the village to a competitor, are matters of concern. This is especially so because the village, as stated above, will remain a principal unit of community life. In rural India most activities of rural economic development and social advance will continue to be organized around it. Moreover, even though economic activity out side the village will become increasingly important in the life of the village people, they will continue to live in villages because of the very material advantages offered. Most of the people of Raipur who depend upon non-agricultural employment outside the village continue to live in the village, and even those who live outside for varying periods continue to maintain active links with the village.

That small units of settlement and community life have an important place even in modern industrially advanced societies is demonstrated by the recent movement towards living in suburbs and small towns in western countries. The entire community development movement in the west is based on the belief that life in the small community offers a unique opportunity for expression of deep seated human urges—the feeling of belonging to a significant group, the desire to know and to be known in it and to work with other members of the group in meaningful activities. Western writing on community development constantly emphasize that life in a small community is richer and happier because of the opportunities of informal association and collective effort for organizing recreation, social welfare and other activities that it offers.[6] In an ancient country like India the role of community development is much larger, because most economic development and social welfare programmes have to be organized around communities like the village.

But in order that the village may play the role envisaged for it, its social system must be organized on different principles. Unequal status of different castes and the *Jajmani* system must go, replaced by social relations based on the principles of social and political equality, freedom of association and an opportunity for every individual to accept new patterns of economic activities. This involves changes in attitudes, ways of doing things, institutions and leadership. Social strain and conflicts are inevitable in the process. But it is in the degree that this transformation takes place, that administration of local affairs and organization of social and economic activities within the village as the unit will become successful and satisfying to the people, and they will have a new sense of belonging together and a new loyalty to the village community.[7]

Footnotes

1. The following oft-quoted statement of Sir Charles Metcalf contained in his minutes of 1830 expresses this view most forcefully:

   "The village communities are little republics, having nearly everything that they want within themselves, and almost independent of any foreign relations. They seem to last where nothing else lasts. Dynasty after dynasty tumbles down; revolution succeeds to revolution. Hindu, Pathan, Moghal, Maharatta, Sikh, English, are masters in turn; but the village communities remain the same. In time of trouble they arm and fortify themselves. A hostile army passes through the country; the village community collects their cattle within their walls, and let the enemy pass unprovoked." As quoted in Dutt, R: *Economic History of India*, under early British rule, London, 1956. pp. 386-7.

   Metcalf had written about village communities in Northern India. Other British administrators of the time working in other parts of the country have expressed similar views. Thus, Munro in 1813 wrote about village communities in Madras as follows:

   "Every village with its twelve *Agagandaas*, as they are denominated, is a petty commonwealth, with its Mokuddum, Potsil, Rapod, Reddy or chief inhabitant at the head of it, and India is a great assemblage of such commonwealths. The inhabitants, during war, look chiefly to their own head-inhabitants; they give themselves no trouble about the breaking up and division of kingdoms while the village remains entire: they care not to what power it is transferred, on whomsoever it devolves, the internal management remains unaltered; the head-inhabitant is still the collector, magistrate, and head-farmer."—*ibid* page 141.

   And Elphinstone in 1819 wrote thus about village communities in the Deccan.

   "In whatever point of view we examine the Native Government in the Deccan, the first and most important feature is the division into villages or townships. These communities contain in miniature all the materials of a state within themselves, and are almost sufficient to protect their members, if all other governments are withdrawn. Though probably not compatible with a very good form of government, they are an excellent remedy for the imperfections of a bad one; they prevent the bad effects of its negligence and weakness, and even present some barrier against its tyranny and rapacity."—*ibid,* p. 346.

2. Marriott, McKim (Ed); *Village India,* University of Chicago Press, Chicago 1955. Chapter I, VI and VII.
3. The two points of views have been summarized in the Report of the *Committee on Cooperative Credit,* Government of India, Ministry of Community Development and Cooperation, May 1960, Chapter V and VI.
4. *Saat jaat*, lit. seven castes. The word 'saat' here means multiple.
5. *Dussehra or Vijaya Dashmi* is the festival which marks Rama's triumph over the demon king Ravana. Celebration of *Dussehra* was very popular with Hindu princes.
6. *Gangor* is a popular festival in Rajasthan. On this occasion, women worship Gauri (wife of Shiva) and pray for marital happiness and fertility. In the larger villages and towns celebrations of the festival culminates in a colourful procession of the images of Gouri and other Goddesses through the main streets. During the time of Jaipur State, this festival was celebrated by the State Government in all towns with much pomp and ceremony. The people of Sawai Madhopur still remember the grandeur of this festival.
7. See for instance, Morgan, Arthur E., *The Small Community,* New York, 1942; and other writings.

8

Self-Sustaining Development

A Study of Four Decades of Rural Development in Three Villages of Eastern Rajasthan

Differences in the progress of agriculture in different parts of the country have begun to attract attention. It is becoming increasingly clear that while in some areas agriculture has started to display considerable dynamism, its progress in other areas is still very slow. Identification of the physical, economic and social factors which are responsible for these differences is vital for understanding dynamics of agricultural change. A fruitful way of identifying these factors is through case studies of villages of specially rapid or slow progress. It is with this objective that the author undertook the studies of social and economic changes in three villages of eastern Rajasthan in 1961 where after efforts of one decade of development planning, agricultural farming methods were traditional, with low production and income levels for rural people and society traditional. However, in Punjab where author studied (1964) the effects of technical change in farming methods and use of improved varieties of seeds, chemical fertilizers and irrigation which were responsible for large increases in crops production, incomes and levels of living of the peasants, the improvement was accompanied with changes in health, education, transport and communication. The results of the Punjab study were published in several articles in *Economic and Political Weekly* during 1965 (The New Village) as were some articles on specific issues emerging from the study in the three villages of Rajasthan. The author had an opportunity of revisiting the Punjab village in 1976, 11 years after the publication of the findings of the first study and an article on 'The New Village 11 years after ...' was also published. The author's wife along with three researchers from Jawaharlal Nehru University revisited the three villages of Rajasthan in 2001, 40 years after the first study. The author had planned a similar resurvey of the Punjab village but could not undertake it due to his sudden demise in 2002.

This section gives detailed findings of the repeat study on economic and social change in village India in Rajasthan.

The Rajasthan Study

In 1961 a study was undertaken in three villages of Sawai Madhopur district of Rajasthan where author was posted as the District Collector. This is described in detail in the previous Seven chapters of this volume. The repeat study of the villages was done in 2001, four decades later in order to see the technological economic and social changes that had occurred in the villages during the intervening 40 years. This chapter gives the findings of the repeat study, written by the author in 2001.

Sawai Madhopur district, located about 130 km. from the State capital Jaipur, was one of the backward districts of Rajasthan. It borders Madhya Pradesh on the east, Bharatpur district to its north, Jaipur and Tonk to the west and Kotah to the south. Almost 2/3rd of the district as constituted in 1961, formed part of the former princely State of Jaipur until 1948. The remaining 1/3rd formed part of the former princely State of Karauli.

Until its abolition within 3-4 years of formation of Rajasthan in 1948, *Jagirdari* was the dominant system of land tenure. After its abolition, full and heritable rights in croplands were conferred on the actual cultivators of lands. Jaipur was a progressive State and had evolved a well-developed revenue administration during the 1940s. It also had a stable government for most of the 1950s and the 1960s and there has been political stability in the State during the last four decades also. The government launched an effective programme of rural development in the 1950s and the 1960s; it was the first state government in the country to establish *Panchayati*[1] *Raj* institutions.

The initial study revealed the effects of community development and other rural development programmes on people of the villages after a decade of their initiation; the repeat study shows effects of the programmes and technological, economic and social changes in the country during the intervening 40 years.

The initial study revealed that except the high castes—Rajput former *Jagirdars*, with relatively large land holdings, some *Mahajans* (trader-cum-money lenders) and Brahmins whose sons had become white-Collar workers, all others were poor. Wives of Meena cultivators would thank their stars if they could get enough cereals to eat through the year and avoid 'hunger' in the lean season, July-September, i.e. before the monsoon season crop of sorghum or millet was harvested in October. The scheduled castes—Chamaar, small cultivator-cum-agricultural or non-agricultural labourers and other scheduled castes were in a similar position.

Because of the poor level of nutrition of the women and the hard work that they did in the fields, maternal, infant and child mortality were high. Consequently, they could not bear to hear about family planning. Education of girls or even of boys was considered useless. In the 8-grade school located in village Manpur with a population of over 2500 there were 180 boys but only 5 girls.

There had been dramatic changes in all these respects during the intervening 40 years. By 2001, most of these people had enough cereals to eat; milk, vegetables and fruit in season formed an integral part of their diet. Production of wheat, the principal food-cum-cash crop had more than doubled. Production of mustard the principal cash crop had increased also. Increase in agricultural output in turn had been due to more intensive cultivation of croplands by tractors and irrigation by diesel oil operated pump sets. Irrigation has made it possible to grow high yielding varieties of wheat with chemical fertilizers and pesticides, as needed, and a large proportion of it is cultivated as a cash crop.

Even the Chammar and other scheduled castes small farmers-cum-labourers had enough cereals to eat and enough income from work in the neighbouring market town to buy milk, vegetables and fruit in season.

All the villagers had easy access to medical and preventive health care facilities from physicians in two large multi-facility hospitals, besides sub-dispensaries and *vaidyas* in two of the three villages. Maternal, child and infant mortality had been reduced greatly. Most of the boys and a large number of girls were being sent to schools. The farmers and the scheduled castes realize that educated boys could get white-collar jobs, and would know enough not to be cheated by merchants in the market and get minimum wages from unskilled work, fixed by the Government of Rajasthan.

They realized also that educated girls were better mothers and wives. They kept themselves, their houses and their children clean and were more willing to consult the physicians and *vaidyas* and take medicines for common diseases of the digestive and respiratory tracts. By 2001, most of the people of high castes and a large proportion of the farmers and the scheduled castes lived in brick and mortar homes. The high castes and many Meena farmers had piped water in their homes. They cared enough about having clean and adequate water to have spent several lakhs in construction of large overhead tanks outside the villages so that they could have piped water in their homes. Even those who depended upon wells, for drinking water, bathing or washing clothes took care to keep the wells clean.

A large number had black and white or colour T.V. receivers in their homes; almost all of them had radio receivers so that they were well aware of events in the district, the state and the country. For all these reasons, most of the villagers were not poor but had risen to lower middle or middle-income economic status.

Apparently, similar changes have occurred over a large area of Rajasthan as evidenced by major increases in output of wheat, mustard, ground nut and other cash crops. Use of chemical fertilizers and number of tractors has increased over 3 times between 1976 and 1992. Total, male and female literacy has increased steadily. The latter more than doubled between 1991 and 2001.

Thus the major change influences have been:

(i) Phenomenal increase in agricultural output due to adoption of improved agricultural practices which had lead to a major increase in income of farmers and change from subsistence to cash economy;
(ii) Major increase in health and productivity of farmers;
(iii) Increase in the proportion of household income from non-agricultural occupations; and
(iv) Major increase in education of males but particularly among females and awareness of rights and entitlements due to higher participation of people in local self-government.

The Study

The three villages—Manpur, Raipur and Bijaipur—studied are located in a rather backward district (Sawai Madhopur) of one of the most backward states (Rajasthan) in India. The villages were located along motorable roads between 3 and 8 kilometres from author's house and office in Maan Town where the district offices are located. Sawai Madhopur town is 6 kilometres east of it. He had strong interest in studying economic activities, social status and inter-caste relations of people of these villages and the effects of the community development and other rural development programmes on them. Before appointment to his post as collector, he had been Director for five years (1953-58) of the Programme Evaluation Organization of the Planning Commission, Government of India that had responsibility for concurrent and in-depth evaluation through sample surveys, of the impact of community development and other rural development programmes on the economic and social conditions of rural people in different states of the country.

Kamla Nath (his wife) participated in the study when she saw the abject poverty of women of two of these villages. The women worked on the family's farm; they did more farm work than the men. Both men and women of the small village, Bijaipur, which Kamla Nath had selected for intensive study, bathed in the pond located outside the village. They were too poor to afford use of soap or hair oil. Since, livestock also bathed in it, they were not much cleaner after the bath than they were before it. They were so poor that they thanked their stars, if they had enough cereals to eat and could avoid hunger in the lean season of June to September. There was no question of their consuming milk, vegetables or fruit themselves or giving milk to their growing children. Their only source of drinking water was a well, located in the village. As a result of their low level of personal hygiene and deficiency of protective foods in their diet, maternal, infant and child mortality was quite high. Consequently, they were very averse to accepting family planning.

Most of them were illiterate because men of the cultivating and the scheduled castes felt that education of girls was useless. The men were afraid that educated women would not work in the fields. Besides, they argued to themselves that since women were *Paraya Dhan* (the property of the husband) their parents should not spend on their education. Furthermore, girls as old as 9 or 10 years of age took care of their younger siblings, while their mothers worked in the fields. In the 8-grade school located in Maanpur (one of the two large villages), which was two kilometres from Bijaipur there were 180 boys but only five girls.

But, men of the high castes—Brahmin, Rajput and Mahajan—wanted that their women should be educated up to primary level. A large number of young men of these castes were working as *Patwaries*, village level workers, and secretaries of *Panchayats* or cooperative societies or schoolteachers in villages located not far from their homes. They could come home only during weekends or holidays but wanted that they should be in touch with their families. Some of them were clerks in offices of the Collector, the Superintendent of Police or other offices located in Maan Town. Furthermore, they wanted to marry their daughters to educated men of similar status as the parents and who were working in various white-collar jobs mentioned above.

The *Panchayat* of village Raipur in which people of the high caste were concentrated had, with contributions in money, materials or labour from the villagers and grants from the community development department constructed buildings for a primary (5-grade) school for girls and also for a 8-grade school for boys. It had obtained contributions also for improving the approach road to the village and other works described below. People of the high castes had contributed money, while the farmers and people of the scheduled castes had contributed labour or brought materials for these works.

As Collector, Dr. Nath could observe the rural people and their various problems in a way in which only a Collector can. They came to him for settlement of disputes about rights in land. They approached him with requests for assistance from the state government. Thus, they would request him to recommend to the state government remission of land revenue if there was a crop failure. He saw them also as electors to *Panchayati Raj* institutions, which had been established in the state during 1959, barely 18 months earlier. These institutions were established at the level of the village, the community development block and the district.

The village level institution, called the *Panchayat*, had responsibility for overseeing sustainable development of the natural resources (cultivable land, pastures and woodland, and cultivable or other wastelands if any) of the village; overseeing working of school teachers and other workers having responsibility for assisting the economic or social progress of the villages. It was established for every village that had a population of 5,000 or more. In case of small villages, five or more villages were grouped together to establish a *Panchayat* with a population of 5000. Alternatively, a fairly large village, its hamlets and one or more small villages in its vicinity were grouped to include a population of 5000.

The district was bifurcated in the late 1980s by constituting most of the area in its northern part plus a small area of the adjoining Jaipur district into a separate district, while Karauli earlier part of Sawai Madhopur district became a separate district. Both districts together had population of about 800,000 in 2001. The population of the five-community development blocks in the present Sawai Madhopur district averaged 160,000 in 1991. In village Raipur, in which people of the high castes were concentrated, the *Panchayat* includes the village and its 3 hamlets. In the other large village Maanpur, since the population of the village and its one hamlet was much below 5,000 in 1961, 5 neighbouring villages including Bijaipur were included in the area of the *Panchayat*. By 2001, the population within the jurisdiction of both *Panchayats* ranged between 7,000 and 8,000; but no change was made in their jurisdiction.

When the initial study was done, the villagers had already absorbed the effect of abolition, in the early 1950s, of *Jagirdari*, the system of land tenure that had existed in this area for centuries. Full and heritable rights in land had been conferred on the actual cultivators of croplands. The *Jagirdars*, whom the farmers used to pay land revenue and for serving whom men and women of various scheduled castes had clearly specified obligations, had now to content themselves with cultivation of the land left to them for self-cultivation. They cultivated the lands with the help of labourers that they employed or on basis of crop sharing with their former tenants. But there was no feeling of ranker among them. They had accepted the change as an integral part of the democratic process, which conferred equal rights on all.

The repeat study has revealed changes in economic and social status, skills, attitudes and aspirations of the people of these villages, during the four decades between the two studies, which could not even be imagined in 1961.

In 1961, most of the farmers and people of the scheduled castes were poor, illiterate and barely aware of events outside their immediate vicinity. By 2001, most of them had risen to lower middle income or middle-income status; their higher income was reflected in higher levels of consumption. They were healthier; as a result of more adequate and balanced food enough cereals and milk, vegetables and fruit in season and easy access to facilities for preventive health and medical care, better educated and well aware of events in the district, the state and the country. The farmers with land holdings as small as 10 hectares use tractors for cultivation of their croplands and diesel oil operated pump sets for irrigation. These machines, improved seed, chemical fertilizers and pesticides were available in the Maan Town market. There were facilities also for repair of the machines and sale of spare parts. But the farmers were skilled enough to correct small defects in the machines themselves. Otherwise, the use of the machines would be uneconomic. Their levels of skill and aspirations had been transformed. A large proportion of them lived in brick and mortar houses, had piped water and black and white or colour T.V. receivers in their homes. They sent their sons and daughters to schools; men and women of the high castes and the better-off farmers hoped that while one or two sons would remain in the village and look after the land, the others would become white collar workers. They wanted their daughters to be educated so that they could marry such workers; some of them could work as school teachers before they married. Holders of these jobs had relatively high income, security of service and those appointed as *Patwaries* or clerks in various offices had much "power"[4].

The Villages

Maanpur

Maanpur is a multi-caste village located 8 kilometres west of Maan Town, along the Sawai Madhopur—Tonk road. Bijaipur is also located along the road, but about 5 kilometres west of Maan Town. The high castes—Rajput, Mahajan (traders-cum-moneylenders) and Brahmin form about 1/3rd of the population of Maanpur. The rest are Meenas and various scheduled castes. The total population of Maanpur and its two hamlets of the Chammars and the Meenas was about 7000 in 2001, 2½ times the population in 1961. In 1961, the Meenas used to live to the west of the village, about 1 kilometre from the Sawai Madhopur, Jaipur road.

The increase in population is due mainly to natural increase, although there has been some influx of people from smaller villages both in the main village and the hamlets. The influx is due to facilities available in Maanpur for sale of produce, shopping and for education and primary health and medical care. The population of Bijaipur which is located about 3 kilometres from Maanpur and is included within the jurisdiction of Maanpur *Panchayat* is now more than 500; double the number in 1961. Except five households of Brahmins, all the others (107) are of Meenas. The five Brahmin households are offshoot from the one Brahmin household that existed in 1961 by all the five sons of the original settler having set up separate households.

Mr. Suraj Bhan Singh, our respondent for Maanpur is the younger brother of late Mr. Hari Singh who was *Sarpanch* in 1961. He is 81 but is quite fit. He was *sarpanch* for several years. At present a Mahajan friend of his holds the post. One son of Mr. Suraj Bhan Singh is teaching in the college located in Maan Town; a daughter is taking the bank officers' examination. Another daughter is married to an army officer. The families of Suraj Bhan Singh, late Hari Singh and another brother are living in separate houses, which are kept in very good repair. They have a jeep, a tractor and a diesel operated pump on their irrigation well. Their entire cropland is irrigated by the well, run by a pumpset. They sell cereals in excess of their needs and produce milk, vegetables and some fruit in season primarily for the needs of the families. One son of late Hari Singh has been settled in Jaipur for 35 years. Another son, a physician, is practicing in the village. His wife who is an Auxiliary Nurse Midwife (ANM) hails from south India. She assists women of the village and neighbouring villages in maternity cases and advises them on pre-natal and post-natal care of their children and themselves. She advises them also on family planning.

The above details of the families of Suraj Bhan Singh and late Hari Singh have been given in order to illustrate the changes in attitudes and aspirations of Rajputs of this village and this district during the intervening 40 years. In 1961, they would educate their sons so that they could become clerks or other white-collar workers or join the army. However, they would ensure that at least one son continued to stay in the village and looked after the family's cropland. Supervising cultivation of their cropland gave their families prestige and also provided a dependable source of income.

Although their women still wore the veil, in 2001, they did not expect their daughters to wear it. The aspiration for their daughters was that they should marry white-collar workers or farm owners or those working in the army. Both sons and daughters must be married among children of Rajputs of the neighbouring villages or those living in the adjoining *taluka* or Jaipur district or in Jaipur city itself. In 1961 educating their children to become professionals such as physicians or lawyers was far beyond their imagination. They could not even think of one of their children marrying a person from south India, ignoring all considerations of caste and economic status of the parental families.

The description of the occupation of children of Shri Sham Lal Sharma of Raipur, a Brahmin and of Mr. Fateh Singh, a Rajput given later show similar changes in attitudes, aspirations and practices of the Brahmins and the Rajputs in the area and that have been accepted by the older people.

A large number of houses in the village and a number of those in its two hamlets are made of brick and mortar, have electricity and black and white or colour T.V. receivers. There are 56 telephones in the village and a sub post-office. There is a small government dispensary staffed primarily by the ANM in Maanpur; a doctor visits it for a few hours in the week. The villagers can reach the multi-facility hospital, located in village Alanpur on the outskirts of Maan Town, in 30 minutes by bicycle or bus and sooner by their own motor bicycles or scooters. There are 16 doctors in the hospital besides nurses and paramedical personnel. This location was selected for the hospital because enough land for the hospital and residences of the staff was available there. The hospital is ten kilometres from Maanpur and seven kilometres from Bijaipur. This hospital and the one located just outside Raipur provide medical care to all the people of the district. In 1961, the only medical facility for people of Sawai Madhopur *tehsil* was the small hospital, with 2 doctors, two nurses and a dispenser located in Sawai Madhopur town, 15 kilometres away.

Education Facilities: The Situation in 2001

There are a degree college, a polytechnic and a higher secondary school in Maan Town. These are all located in Allanpur, a suburb of Maan Town, where there is enough land for them. The number of girl students is quite significant in all except the polytechnic although it is smaller than that of boys.

There is a secondary school (with ten classes) a middle school (with 8-classes) run by the Department of Education and a private middle school in Maanpur. There are 350 girls and 400 boys in three schools. The two hamlets of the Chammars and the Meenas have their own schools. The school in the Chammar hamlet, which was a primary school and was located in a temple in 1961 is a middle school now and has its own building. But it lacks a boundary wall and the people complain that the *Panchayat Samiti* does not give them its part of the money needed to build the wall because they are a scheduled caste and are poor. The Meena hamlet has a primary school: they have built eight rooms so that it can be converted into a middle school and run by the Department of Education.

There are a 10-grade school and a middle school for girls run by the Department of Education in village Raipur. This means an up-gradation of the middle school for boys and the primary school for girls of 1961. A large number of boys and a few girls go to the higher secondary school located in Alanpur. A number of boys and girls go also to the college. Besides, the two schools run by the Department of Education, there is an 8-grade school run by a private teacher. This school also has a large enrolment despite high fees in it because the 'quality' of education is considered to be better in it than in the schools run by the Department. The schools are a powerful medium of social change.

The teachers insist that the boys and girls come to them after a bath using soap and hair oil and in uniforms, which are washed at least once in two days and are well pressed. The habit of personal hygiene travels from the students to their parents. Salaries of teachers are quite high (Rs. 7,000-10,000) per month. The *Panchayat* supervises efficient running of the schools.

The 1961 attitude that girl's education is not needed has not completely gone among the cultivators or the scheduled castes. Nevertheless, girls are being sent to school by these castes. The Brahmins, Mahajans and Rajputs are very keen to educate their daughters. The principal reason for this is that they want to marry them to government servants and professionals who want well educated wives. The progress made in the life style of women is such that girls are driving cars and scooters in the Maan Town market and nobody bats an eyelid. Many women of Raipur are working as teachers and nurses in the hospital located within the game sanctuary and in the neighbouring villages including Bijaipur.

The habitation area of Maanpur and its two hamlets is much larger than it was in 1961. The hamlet of the Chamaars has more than 100 houses; in 1961 it had less than 50. About 50 *Meena* households who used to live to the west of the village are living now in a hamlet located along the Maan Town, Tonk road. Land for the hamlet was allotted to them in 1961. The location is convenient for supplementing their income from farming by unskilled labour in Maan Town market and on maintenance of the railway lines.

There is a primary school in the hamlet of the Meenas also. They have constructed an 8-room building for it so that it can be upgraded to a middle school by the Department of Education. Thus, in contrast to one 8-grade school in Maanpur and 1 primary school in the hamlet of the Chammars in 1961, there are 4 schools in Maanpur and its hamlets. The large enrolment in all the schools and the large expenditure by the people on construction and maintenance of the buildings show the value that people of all castes attach to education of their children.

Drinking Water Supply

The villagers of Maanpur have through contributions from all those who would have piped water in their homes (mainly Rajputs and Mahajans) contributed Rs. 4 lakhs for construction of an overhead tank located outside the village.

The State has constructed 3 tube wells and provided the operators to run the pumps, which lift the water to the tank. The residents of Bijaipur have also constructed the tank and the tube well and hire the operator to run them without any assistance from the state government. Spending such large amounts to construct overhead tanks, and having piped water in their houses demonstrates the importance that these people now attach to having adequate and safe water for drinking, washing and other uses. The Chammars and the Meenas of the two hamlets of Maanpur, however, use water of wells located in their hamlets. They too make every effort to ensure that the surrounding of their wells is kept clean. In 1961, all households in Maanpur and Bijaipur had to draw water manually from the wells. In Raipur, however, a few wells in the Brahmin locality had hand pumps installed on them.

Since Maanpur is located along the Maan Town, Tonk road there are eight teashops and four restaurants on its outskirts. The tax paid by the shops makes a sizeable contribution to the income of the *Panchayat*.

A large number of the houses in both Maanpur and Raipur have hand pumps. There is a well-kept storm water-drain in the centre as well as side drains for draining out the waste water from the houses along the paved main street of Maanpur so that the village is quite clean.

A number of employees of the railway (gang men), post office, and several clerks and others working in the district offices live in the village. Some of them belong to the village while others are outsiders who find the village a cheap place to live because rents are much lower in it than in Maan Town. Thus, the village has become a dormitory for workers in Maan Town.

Bijaipur

Informant Hira Lal Meena is a *Panchayat* Development officer in the office of the *Panchayat Samiti*. He was a primary school student in 1961. He became a Village Level Worker (VLW) by 1975, during our second visit to the village. He is a cultivator with a medium-sized land holding. He commutes to work on his motor bicycle. One of his nephews is a BDO. A son is a driver another two are lower division clerks (LDCs) and one is an Assistant Railway Station Master.

There are 108 households in the village as against 55 in 1961. Excepting one household of a Brahmin all the others were of Meenas in 1961 but by 2001, the number of Brahmin households has increased to five due to bifurcation of the one main household of 1961. Rest of the increase has been due to natural increase of the population resident in 1961; there has been some in-migration from very small villages located near it.

The main street of the village has been paved and has side drain which takes the waste water to a pond located at the end of the inhabited area of the village. As a result, the village is quite clean.

The Meenas of Bijaipur whose food consisted only of cereals and oil in 1961 now have milk and cooked vegetables as a regular part of their diet. They buy milk and vegetables from vendors who bring them from the Maan Town market, if they do not have their own. In 1961, the pond located outside the village was the principal place for bathing of men, women and livestock. It has dried up now. There are 2-3 community hand pumps in the village. The women walk to them to fetch water for drinking, bathing and washing clothes. Most of the houses have hand pumps within them connected from the overhead tank.

There are a number of *pucca* houses (made of brick and mortar). Agriculture production has more than doubled. Every household has a bicycle; 30-32 households (one third of the total) have motor bicycles. There are 26 tractors and a similar number of pumps for irrigation. The villagers have erected a temple of *Hanumanji* along the road to Tonk; it has cost Rupees seven lakhs. Its maintenance is self-financing because of large offerings by devotees from Maanpur, Bijaipur and a number of other villages in the vicinity. The villagers had a well-attended *puja* to inaugurate the temple in May 2000. It included a *Katha* (religious discourse) for a month. They had formed a construction committee to oversee construction of the temple.

There is an 8-grade (middle) school in the village: many girls besides boys attend the school. People prefer to send their young children both boys and girls to the private school in the village in which the teaching is better than in the government run schools. Many families send their children to attend secondary school in Alanpur (Maan Town) so that they can become white-collar workers. One boy of the village is a BDO Block Development Officer; 6-7 are LDCs (Lower Division Clerks).

A number of Employees of the railway (gang men), post office, and several clerks and others working in the district offices live in the village, because rents are lower in it than in Maan Town. Thus, the village has become a dormitory for workers in Maan Town.

The creamy upper layer of progressive and educated Meenas of Bijaipur, Brahmins and Mahajans of Raipur and Rajputs and Mahajans of Maanpur have entered white-collar service and professions. They have become affluent and have also acquired 'power' because of their professional skills and even more because of their nearness to officials.

Raipur

Raipur is a multi-caste village, located about eight km. from Maan Town and about 1½ km. from the road to the Ranthambhore Game sanctuary. A hamlet of the *Gujjars* located outside the village abuts on the road to the sanctuary. The village population of about 2800 in 1961 has increased to about 8000 in 2001. Almost all the increase has been due to natural increase of the population resident in Raipur; there has, however been some in-migration of Chammars from neighbouring small villages. The high castes—Brahmins, Mahajans and Kayasthas form about 1/3rd of the population; about 10 per cent are Moslems. They engage in cultivation—Meenas, *Malies and Gujjars* or the scheduled castes; leather workers and makers of leather goods—mainly Chammars and *Rehgars; Dhobies* (washermen) and others. The people of high castes, the Moslems and affluent Meenas and *Malies* live in the village itself; the remainder live in three hamlets of the Chammars, Meenas and *Gujjars*.

In 1961, a large number of Brahmin and *Mahajan* young men, after getting educated in the 8-grade middle school located just outside the village, were working as *Patwaries*, school teachers, VLW's (Village Level Workers), secretaries of *Panchayats* or cooperative societies or clerks in the offices of the Collector or the Superintendent of Police or others located in Maan Town. Most of them were posted in villages in the Sawai Madhopur *tehsil* from which they could visit their homes during Sundays or other holidays. They would keep in touch with their families through letters. They were therefore; keen that their wives should be educated up to the primary level.

The village had an 8-grade school for boys and a 5-grade primary school for girls. Buildings for them, located at the entrance of the village had been constructed through contributions (in money) primarily by the Brahmins and *Mahajans* but also by a few Meenas and others. By 2001, the 8-grade middle school had become a 10-grade school and the primary school for girls had become an 8-grade middle school. In addition, 2 private teachers had opened 8-grade middle schools. All the schools had large enrolment and their buildings were adequate to accommodate the large number of students. The number of girls in the higher secondary school is also quite significant although much smaller than that of boys. Most of the girls belong to the high castes for a reason which has been explained earlier. A large number of Brahmin and *Mahajan* men are working in white-collar jobs in various offices in Maan Town and in various services in the district.

A large number of boys and a number of girls were attending the higher secondary school in Allanpur. Some boys were attending the college also. A number of boys are studying in professional colleges in Jaipur and Kotah to become professionals such as lawyers, physicians, or engineers. Many of them were working as professionals or in offices in these or other cities. Their parents were proud of this fact.

After beginning of the community development programme in 1953, large grants had been received from the block development office for repair of the approach road to the village and for improvement of drinking water wells of the Chammars and the *Gujjars* and for construction of buildings for the offices of the *Panchayat*, the cooperative society, the residence of the VLW and a store for improved seeds, chemical fertilizers, pesticides and improved implements. The high castes had made contributions in cash, while the farmers and the scheduled castes contributed labour or locally available materials.

The main street of the village along which most of the Brahmins, *Mahajans* and the Moslems lived was paved with side-drains to drain the wastewater. However, the drains were not cleaned efficiently they overflowed often. As a result, the main street was and remains quite dirty. Water from drains enters into another shallow pond at the back of the Brahmin street. The pond is surrounded by several low caste houses including the house of a *Dhobin* (washer woman) who is the *sarpanch* of the village.

There are a number of *vaidyas* in the village. Besides a large multi-facility hospital with 40-beds, run by Tiger Watch, a foreign non-governmental organization, located about one kilometre from the village. A husband-wife team of doctors look after the hospital from day to day. This hospital specializes in operations for cataract and other eye diseases. A number of specialists from Jaipur and even from Delhi come to it for performing operations for cataract and other diseases. Thus, the villagers are very well served with facilities for preventive health and medical care.

In 2001, there were more than 50 telephones, many with STD facility and a sub-post office within the village. A large number of houses had electricity and black and white or colour T.V. receivers. The main street had 130 shops which sold a large variety of goods: (i) foodgrains and other provisions, cloth, clothes, shoes and other leather goods, general merchandise and medical drugs; (ii) black and white and colour T.V. receivers, spare parts for tractors and pump-sets, and cooking gas. The villagers needed to go to the Maan Town market only for buying tractors, pump sets and spare parts for them, which are not available in the village, or for getting greater variety or higher quality of goods than those available in the shops in the village. The Moslem quarter has a number of repair shops for bicycles, motorcycles and various machines. Besides a number of Moslem artisans work as repairmen for repair of motor vehicles, tractors, diesel operated pumps, TV receivers and other electrical appliances. They find opportunities also in the tourist hotels because they are the only ones who can cook meat. Some *Mahajans* or Brahmins of the village who had specialized in preparing festive meals at marriages of the high castes have opened shops of sweet meat in the Maan Town market and are doing very well. However, a few Brahmin widows who carry milk from the village to the market remain quite poor.

Fateh Singh, the game warden in 1961 has now retired. He runs the international NGO 'Tiger Watch' and has become an international personality. He accompanied President Clinton on his visit to the game sanctuary. The President arrived by helicopter and five helipads were specially built for his visit. Fateh Singh lives in a sprawling farm-house. He is a millionaire. One of his sons is a doctor working in the hospital built by the Tiger Foundation. He has got himself allotted about 125 hectares of land, some of which he plans to sell to the Oberois (owners of the hotel chain Oberoi) for building a hotel. Watching animals and birds in the sanctuary remain a passion with him. According to him, there are 25 tigers in the sanctuary but they are rarely seen. However, there are a large numbers of *sambhars* (heavy two horned deer), *cheetals* (the spotted golden deers) and *Neelgais*; their number has not been estimated by him. There are also a few elephants and a few crocodiles in the numerous ponds in the jungle.

The approach road to the village is full of potholes. The one kilometre approach road to Raipur from the main road to Ranthambhore is not in good condition despite constant repairs with funds provided by the *Panchayat Samiti* and the *Panchayat*. The village is dirty because of lack of drainage of waste water from the houses of the Brahmins and the *Mahajans*.

Farming Practices and Crop Production

Very few farmers cultivate their land by bullocks. There are tractors everywhere. Because of deeper ploughing of cropped area, some increase in the cultivated area, irrigation of most of the cropland by wells fitted with diesel operated pumps and use of improved dwarf, high-yielding seed varieties of seed, chemical fertilizers and pesticides for wheat, its production has gone up about three times. Production of sorghum, millets, gram (chickpeas) and oil seeds (mainly mustard) have increased also due to irrigation and use of tractors. Most of the cultivators grow the coarse grains and some wheat for food; oil seeds (mainly mustard) and much of the wheat is sold for meeting the cash needs of the families. As a result of increase in the irrigated area and use of tractors for culivation of cropland, production of cereals, wheat and chickpeas, in the winter and sorghum and millets in the summer, has increased. Total agricultural production is estimated to have increased about three times. The cultivated area has not increased much but yields per hectare have increased greatly due to use of improved methods of production and inputs, as described above. There is large production also of milk, fruit and vegetables. Sorghum and millets are produced for food; their stalks provide fodder for milch animals. A large number of buffaloes and fewer cows are kept to provide milk. There are only a few bollocks as compared to their number in 1961 because tractors now cultivate most of the land. Landless Chammars and other scheduled castes buy milk, fruit and vegetables in the Maan Town market or Raipur itself by paying for them with cash earned from wages for labour. Farmers produce much more milk and vegetables than they used to. Fruit such as papaya, banana and guava are produced in large quantities. In 1961, hardly any fruit was produced. Farmers in villages, such as Allanpur, that are near Maan Town, have sale of milk, fruit and vegetables to shops in the market as their main source of income. Other fruits imported from Jaipur, are bought only by the tourists, the district level officers living in Maan Town and professionals such as lawyers and physicians. All men of Maanpur and the two other villages drink numerous cups of tea in a day. In 1961, only the leaders of the villages drank tea when meeting officers visiting the villages.

The farmers of Raipur operate about 40 tractors. Most of the cultivators who have tractors also have diesel oil operated pumps on their irrigation wells, because supply of electricity by the State Electricity Board is so irregular. Farmers with small holdings who cannot afford to buy their own tractors can rent them from those who have them. The rate of renting is fixed at Rs. 300 per hour. Others lease out their own small plots for cultivation to farmers with large holdings or become sharecroppers on lands owned by Rajputs, Brahmins and *Mahajans*. This is true also of most of the Meena cultivators of Maanpur and Meena or Jat farmers of Raipur. The Gujjars cultivate land primarily to supplement their income from sale of milk and sale of sheep or goats that they graze in the forests.

Meenas, Chammars and other scheduled castes also do unskilled labour available in the Maan Town market, on the upkeep of the railway tracks, repair of the road to Jaipur or of the railway station itself. These require much unskilled and skilled labour because there is heavy traffic on the railway tracks and on the road and brisk activity in the market. The Maan Town railway station is much larger than it was in 1961 and is quite clean. There are several trains going between Delhi and Mumbai; in 1961, there were only two trains. There is also a direct fast train between Jaipur and Mumbai via Sawai Madhopur besides the two older trains between Sawai Madhopur and Jaipur. The road to Jaipur via Tonk is a tarmac coated, two-lane state highway. Traffic on it of jeeps, buses, trucks and other motor vehicles (passenger cars and motor bicycles or scooters) is heavy. The trucks bring goods needed by the people of the area and carry to Jaipur the surplus cereals, oilseeds and fruit that they produce. There is such large production of guavas that they are sent to Jaipur and even to Mumbai. However, the road is not well maintained and is full of potholes.

Maan Town and its Market

Maan town had no market in 1961 except a few shop out side the railway station. The security considerations during the visit of Queen Elizabeth II in 1961 necessitated the shifting of theses shops. The Collector ordered their rehabilitation in another locality in Maan Town now called the Maan Town Market. Maan Town initially a residential colony for the district officers surrounded by large uninhabited land is full of houses and shops and is crowded. The officers' colony including the houses of the Collector and the Superintendent of Police are part of this habitation area. The market has 700-800 shops in contrast with 40 shops allotted in 1961. The dealers sell everything: foodgrains and other provisions; milk, fruit, vegetables and medicines, cloth and clothes, shoes and other leather goods, utensils, spare parts for motor vehicles, tractors and irrigation pumps, T.V. receivers and other electrically operated kitchen gadgets. It has facilities also for repair of tractors, irrigation pumps and other farm implements and also of T.V. sets and other electrical gadgets. Since trucks are parked in the middle of the market, traffic within it moves very slowly.

There is a big petrol station in the Maan Town market. It sells petrol, diesel oil, kerosene and cooking gas. Many dealers sell gas also. There is a very large gas bottling plant on the way to the game sanctuary. It supplies gas to the whole district and is the main distribution centre for the entire state of Rajasthan.

There is a cloverleaf fly-over on the railway line at the junction station of Maan Town. The bridge has made communication between the districts headquarter and Sawai Madhopur town as well as villages like Raipur easy. In 1961, we always had to wait at the level railway crossing sometimes up to half an hour to go to Raipur. Next to the fly-over and near the railway line to Mumbai, there is a large, very modern cinema house in which are shown the latest Bollywood movies. In 1961, the 'cinema' was no more than a shed, which showed movies off and on.

The six kilometres road between Sawai Madhopur and Maan Town, which had few houses and farms in 1961, is now lined with brick and mortar houses and, orchards of vegetables and fruit. There are many milch animals in the farms along the road because of extensive pastures to the rear of the road. The population of Sawai Madhopur town has increased slowly but of Maan Town has increased about ten times. Instead of about 5000 in 1961 it was estimated at about 50,000 in 2001. The Maan Town metropolitan area stretches along the road to Bijaipur and Tonk. Bijaipur is however, just outside the metropolitan area.

Due to availability of all necessities of life and adequate facilities for education of their children and of access to primary and curative health care, most of the district and sub-division officers are now living in the officers' colony which has a much larger number of houses than in 1961.

The district medical and health officers who were earlier in Karauli and the executive engineer (buildings and roads) who was earlier in Tonk are now in Maan Town. The district forest officer and the district agricultural officer earlier in Tonk are also living in the officers' colony. The assistant executive engineer, rural electrification who lived earlier in Sawai Madhopur town is now an Executive Engineer and lives also in the colony. Due to the residence of the officers in Maan Town supervision of the game sanctuary and delivery of education and health services to the residents of the town and for villagers of the whole *tehsil* is much better. The road to Bijaipur via Tonk and those in the market and to the game sanctuary are full of potholes due to failure of the state government and *Nagar Palika* of Maan Town to sanction enough funds to maintain them in good conditions. The daily long power cuts are due to the failure of the Rajasthan State Electricity Board to maintain regular supply of electricity.

The offices of the Collector and the Superintendent of Police are two among many in Maan Town.

Maan Town is, however, a very crowded and polluted ghetto. The vacant land in front of the Collector's office and the house of the Collector and the Superintendent of Police has been walled and is used as a park/ for holding exhibitions. The officers' club constructed in 1961 is lying out of use and is now surrounded by small workshops and shops. There is a new circuit house in Allanpur with ten rooms, some of which are air-conditioned. The overcrowding in Maan Town has been caused by total violation of the development plan of the town by successive Collectors. They allowed the land in the area to be sold by the *Panchayat Samiti* or the *Nagar Palika* (municipal committee) for lakhs of rupees. As a result the beautiful view of vast stretches of vacant land in front and back of our (the collector's) house that we enjoyed so much when we slept on the terrace in the summer has completely disappeared.

The cement factory has been closed for many years because its operation was no longer profitable for the owners. No decision has been taken by the Government of Rajasthan to reopen it; it may never reopen. The unskilled and skilled workers who lived in the housing colony of the factory are still living there.

Due to the residence of the officers in Maan Town, supervision of the game sanctuary and delivery of education and health services to the residents of the town and for villagers of the whole *tehsil* has improved somewhat. The roads to Jaipur via Tonk and those in the market and to the game sanctuary, however, are full of potholes due to failure of the state government and *Nagar Palika* of Maan Town to sanction enough funds to maintain them in good conditions. In 1961, the officers' colony got its electricity from a power generation unit of the cement factory which kept its supply very regular. Now the Rajasthan State Electricity Board supplies the electricity and there are daily long power cuts.

There has been a major shift of population and business from Sawai Madhopur town to Maan Town. The Sawai Madhopur town market appeared like a sleepy street in the early evening hours of a working day in 2001; while the Maan Town market hums with activity till late at night. Besides a number of lawyers and merchants from Sawai Madhopur town have shifted their residence to Maan Town. Residence in Maan Town provides easy access to the district officers. The merchants find that there is far more business in Maan Town than in Sawai Madhopur.

The Game Sanctuary

The 2-lane tarmac coated road from the railway station to the game sanctuary is also full of pot holes because of heavy traffic of tourist jeeps during the cool season. There are several small hotels besides the deluxe hotel run by the Taj Group of Mumbai in the former Maharaja's shooting lodge for stay of tourists. The Oberois are planning to build a hotel and expect adequate occupancy during the tourist season.

Mr. Fateh Singh, the game warden in 1961 has now retired. He works now for Tiger Watch, and has become an international personality. He accompanied President Clinton on his visit to the game sanctuary. The President arrived by helicopter; 5 helipads were specially built for his visit. Mr. Fateh Singh lives in a sprawling farm house. One of his sons is a doctor working in the hospital built by Tiger Watch. Another son is in Mumbai training to be a male nurse. He has got himself allotted about 125 hectares of land, some of which he plans to sell to the Oberois for building the hotel. Watching animals and birds in the sanctuary remain a passion with him. He took Mrs. Nath and the researchers to the game sanctuary and remained with them for more than 4 hours. According to him, there are 25 tigers in the sanctuary but they are rarely seen. However, there is a large number of *Sambhars* (heavy two horned deer) cheetals (the spotted golden deer) and *Neelgais* (blue bulls). Their number has not been estimated by him. There are also a few elephants and several crocodiles in the numerous ponds in the jungle. There are innumerable birds of all colours. He explained that when a tiger is passing to drink water in a pond all the animals and birds become still so as not to attract his attention. The small 4-room facility located in the middle of the sanctuary, just below the Fort is not open to the tourists because their stay would disturb the animals and could encourage poaching.

Growth Poles in Rural India

Are Maanpur and Raipur Villages or Small Towns?

In 1961, both Raipur and Maanpur were villages with population between 2500 and 3000. Most of the people, including those of the high castes depended primarily on income from land. The high castes got their land cultivated by sharecroppers or by labourers hired by them. Even those whose sons were working as white-collar workers, had income from land as a secondary source of income. For Meenas, *Mallies* and Jats cultivation of their land provided the only source of income. The Chammars supplemented their income from their small plots of land, which they had been allotted by the state government by agricultural and/or non-agricultural labour and on maintenance of the railway tracks and the Jaipur-Tonk road. Some of them worked as share-croppers on farms of the high castes. Most people of the other scheduled castes also supplemented income from practice of their traditional craft and by agricultural labour.

In 1961, the world-view of most of the villagers was distinctly local. They sold any surplus grain that they had after meeting the food needs of the family to traders who bought it within the villages. For all except the high castes, Jaipur, which was 130 km. from their villages, was too far to be of any interest to them and Delhi, the national capital, might as well be in another country. Even the young men of high castes who worked as white-collar workers (VLWs, secretaries of cooperative societies or *Panchayats*, *Patwaries*, school teachers or clerks in various offices) had little interest in events outside the state. They were only vaguely aware of events in the country. Few of them read the newspapers or possessed radio receivers.

In 2001, however, both Raipur and Maanpur had populations of 7000-8000 and should be classified as small towns, by the Superintendent of Census of Rajasthan in 2001. They had also other attributes of a town—a sub-post office, more than 50 telephones; more than 100 black or colour television receivers and piped water in a large number of houses. Most of the houses of the high castes and of Meenas with even middle-sized land-holdings are of brick and mortar. The main street of Raipur had 130 shops, while that of Maanpur had 70 shops besides eight teashops and four restaurants. Both villages had a high 10-grade school and two 8-grade middle schools, sub-dispensaries, a resident physician and/or *vaidyas*.

Shops in Raipur and Maanpur markets sell everything—foodgrains and other provisions; cloth, clothes, shoes and other leather goods and furnishing and drugs. Dealers in them sell kerosene and diesel oils—the fuel for tractors, pump sets and other machines. Some of them sell spare-parts for these also. Dealers in Maan Town market located five km from Raipur and eight km. from Maanpur also sell various consumer goods. They sell also spare parts for the machines and have facilities for their repair of machines as well as building materials and inputs of improved agriculture—improved seeds, chemical fertilizers and pesticides. Some dealers in both the villages sell cooking gas. Farmers can sell their produce in Maan Town or in the villages themselves.

Most of the farmers produce mustard and groundnuts and some wheat for sale so that they can buy various consumer goods and consumer durables mentioned above. The farmers are part of the regional economy because they sell their crops in it and buy various consumer goods from it. The high castes whose sons are working as white-collar workers or professionals or whose daughters are married to them are part of the national economy. They are proud of the fact that their sons who are professionals are working in other states or their daughters are married to professionals living in Jaipur, Kotah or other cities.

The farmers take large short-term loans from cooperative societies for current cultivation and medium term loans from Land Mortgage Banks or from the branches of scheduled banks located in Maan Town or in the villages for buying tractors, pump sets or other machines, building materials for construction of houses and opening of shops. Farmers are keen to get the maximum prices for their crops and the non-agricultural labourers are keen to get the minimum wages fixed by the Government of Rajasthan. Replacement of dowry for bride price among all but the poorest farmers increases the need for cash further. Both Maanpur and Raipur would have attracted people from small villages in their vicinity to sell their produce or buy consumer goods or consumer durables, if they had not been so close to Maan Town. Thus both Maanpur and Raipur have all the characteristics of a small town.

Caste and Occupational Mobility

Caste played and continues to play a very important role in occupational change from the traditional village economy to a market economy. The economic motive although important is not strong enough to override caste considerations. By 1961, a large number of Brahmin young men had become *Patwaries*, VLWs, secretaries of *panchayat* and cooperative societies, teachers in primary school, *Vaidyas*, clerks in offices of the Rajasthan government and the cement factory. After getting educated up to the middle (8 grade) school, some of the Brahmin and *Mahajan* girls had also become teachers in primary schools. These jobs paid well and since the young men were posted within 30 km. of Raipur, they could visit their families on weekends and could keep in touch with them through letters. However, no Brahmin had taken to trading or become an artisan such as carpenter, mason, smith, driver of motor vehicles, etc. despite the high level of earnings in them. These occupations were literally closed to them.

The *Mahajans* of Raipur could become traders in the Maan Town market or like the Brahmins, white-collar workers after passing the necessary examinations. However, they preferred to remain traders-cum-money-lenders-cum-non-cultivating owners of their land within their own villages. Besides, relatively high earnings, prestige were a major consideration with staying in the village.

The Rajputs of Maanpur were satisfied with remaining non-cultivating owners of their lands that they could retain for self-cultivation. They employed Chammars, Meenas and *Mallies* as agricultural labourers or sharecroppers for managing cultivation of their lands. Their aspiration was that one or more sons should get educated and become white-collar workers. However, at least one son must remain to look after the land of the family. This gave prestige to the family and also provided sizeable income. They would marry their daughters to educated Rajput young men who were in the Army or were white-collar workers or were managing family farms.

The Meenas were satisfied with managing their farms better to increase agricultural production. Those with small holdings supplemented their income with unskilled work on repair of the railway tracks or the roads or work in the cement factory. They were interested primarily in producing field crops (sorghum, millet, wheat, chick-peas) and oil seeds but were not interested in producing vegetables, fruit or milk for sale. Producing fruit and vegetables for sale was the job of the *Malies* who in addition, produced wheat, sorghum and oilseeds. The *Gujjars* were helping to meet the demand for milk. Similarly, the large demand for meat was met by Hindu khatiks (butchers) and the Moslems.

The Chammars although interested in being recognized as a cultivating caste, the equal of the Meenas had, like the Meenas, become unskilled workers in the repair of railway tracks and roads. Some of them had become carpenters, masons, smiths, etc. who found well paid jobs in Maan Town market and building houses in Maan Town. The teachers in schools and doctors in hospitals could be Brahmins, Mahajans or Rajputs while nurses and mid-wives in hospitals could be mainly Chammars or Moslems; the women who performed these tasks by tradition. The great increase in demand for them in the two large hospitals had not induced women of any other caste to become nurses or midwives.

The high demand for meat had not led any Hindu caste except the *Gujjars* to increase the size of herds. The meat sold in the Maan Town market was all goat meat. Beef or meat of camels could not be sold because of the sensitivities of the people in this predominantly Hindu area. Cattle were reared in the woodlands to produce bullocks. *Gujjars* who grazed their herds on the stubble of the cultivated fields and in the forests sold meat of sheep and goats also. But this was done primarily to earn some cash and to keep size of their herds within the availability of the pasture. Thus, even in 2001, the economic motive had not become dominant; caste considerations remained important in the choice of new economic activities in the new market economy.

Change in Values

People of all castes including the Meenas, *Malies* and Chammars had accepted the fact that education of girls to the primary school level was a good thing. They feel that girls educated to primary schools may not work in the fields but had aspirations to marry their educated daughters to white-collar or school educated Meena boys who like the high caste educated men would like to have educated wives. Moreover, cultivation of land by tractors and use of other equipment such as mechanical shellers for sorghum and millets or dehuskers of wheat had reduced women's work in the fields. They could, therefore, devote their time to their work as mothers and homemakers. The men realized also that their educated wives would get prompt treatment for themselves and their children in case of communicable or other diseases of the children or themselves. Furthermore, clean homes and access to clean and more adequate drinking water supply from wells located in the villages or piped water from overhead tanks meant less disease among their men, children and themselves.

By 2001, most of the Meenas still said that they did not accept any bride price, but gave dowry on marriage of their girls. However, the truth of this statement could not be verified. Child marriages had been reduced greatly. The Brahmins, *Mahajans* and Rajputs married their daughters only when they were 16 or 18 years of age and the young men were 22-25 years old. By this time, both were mature and would not fall victim to communicable diseases. Even the Meena, Mali and other cultivators wanted that their daughters should be married when they were old enough to look after their homes and children. Although, widow's remarriage was allowed among the Meenas, *Malies*, Chammars and all other castes, except the high castes the widows did not have a high social status. Even the Moslems did not accord a high status to their widows. Widow remarriage allowed among all castes but was barred by the high castes. Widows had always been a burden among the high castes that wanted to keep their number to the minimum. The ban on remarriage of young widows must have relaxed among the high castes; in a recent announcement by one of the *panchayats* in Madhya Pradesh special efforts were being made to arrange marriages of young widows.

A few Moslem widows of Raipur had become tailors so that they could earn some money while sitting at home. A Delhi based NGO *Dastkar* had opened a centre near Raipur where Moslem women made quilted bed sheets for export to Europe and embroidered dresses for sale to the tourists but no Hindu woman took up this activity despite high earnings in it. In 1961, Brahmin widows carried milk from Raipur to the Maan Town market on their heads to earn a little money to support themselves. They were looked down upon by the rest of the community for being so poor. But these supposedly enlightened people were so stupid that they would not allow their widows to learn a remunerative trade like tailoring.

The Brahmin women just did not do this skilled work. The Brahmin cooks in 1961 use to cook for marriages in Raipur and some of them went to Mumbai and worked as cooks in *Marwari* homes. In 2001 they had stopped going there and had opened food and sweet-meat shops in the Maan Town market and were doing very well!

In 1961, almost all the district level officers were Brahmins, Rajputs, *Mahajans*; a few were *Kayasthas* oı Moslems. All the clerks in Collector's office belonged to these groups. Almost all the policemen were either Rajputs or *Jats*. The president of the Bar Association was a Brahmin lawyer who was also the chairman of the Sawai Madhopur Municipal Committee. These jobs preferences had changed by 2001 only to the extent that many Meenas have become clerks, village level workers, secretaries of *Panchayats* or cooperative societies or traders. Many Chammars have become clerks or junior officers.

Thus, most of the jobs in the new economy had been taken by those for whom the change to these jobs was permitted by tradition. The traditional job preferences or prohibitions had not changed between 1961 and 2001 despite the major economic and social changes that have been described in the foregoing sections.

Perception of Corruption

A perception widely shared by a large number of people relates to prevalence of corruption among officials and clerks in the offices of the Collector, the Superintendent of Police or other district level offices and even in the *Panchayat Samiti* and the *Zila Parishads*. This impression prevailed (and justifiably) in 1961 also. Furthermore, the people realize that the money to be paid for 'getting things done' is much higher in 2001 than it was in 1961.

A certain amount of monetary corruption was widespread in 1961. Its scale was limited however in those days. The clerks in the office and the junior officers talked about it. It was also known that the clerk in my office would take a bribe of Rs. 20 or more to handover to cultivator a decision in his favour. There was no stigma against it. However, there are also a few officers or clerks who were scrupulously honest and very competent. One of them was an old Brahmin who was a superb draftsman in Hindi. I could trust him to interpret the cases of the cultivators (I could not understand their language—*Haroti*—well and after a few attempts to write my judgements in Hindi, gave it up because he could write them better than I could). The SDO, Sawai Madhopur a Brahmin was also scrupulously honest. But two SDOs of Gangapur and Karauli were not.

There was much corruption at the state level also. One leader of the Jats from western Rajasthan had about 300 people eating at his official residence in Jaipur every night. He was a wealthy farmer but his main source of income was his position as Chairman of the Rajasthan Cooperative Federation which controlled distribution of improved seed, chemical fertilizers, pesticides and improved implements to the farmers through the cooperative societies.

We could not obtain any data on the scale of monetary corruption but it was known among the cultivators that in order to get any work done in the BDOs office one had to pay a bribe. The villagers recognised this as one routine official practice.

Role of Communication Facilities and Traders

Another major change relates to the role of communication facilities and of private traders in promoting rural development. In 1961, radio receivers were owned by a very few relatively affluent farmers or men of the high castes; there were no television receivers. Now about 1/5 of the households in Maanpur and a similar number in Raipur and some even in Bijaipur have television receivers in their homes; everyone can afford the radio receivers. The receivers provide information and entertainment. Furthermore, they motivate the people to educate their children, have clean drinking water supply, keep their homes and children clean, and have a balanced diet. These supplement and reinforce the advice and the facilities offered by the extension workers, teachers in primary and secondary schools and doctors and nurses in the hospitals.

In 1961, only the VLWs and agriculture extension officers provided information about improved agricultural practices and supply of inputs for crops. Veterinary assistants treated diseases of animals. Now, traders in the Maan Town market supplement the advice given by the VLWs and the extension officers on the choice and dosages of chemical fertilizers and pesticides for different food and cash crops. The traders who sell tractors pump sets provide fuel and facilities for repair of these. After observing the repairmen, most of the farmers have developed the skill to repair small defects in their machines themselves; otherwise the use of the machines would be too expensive.

In 1961, there were no telephones in these villages. The Collector, the Superintendent of Police and a few district or sub-divisional level officers, the MLA and a few professionals mainly lawyers and the two doctors in the Sawai Madhopur hospital were the only people who had telephones in their homes. Now there are more than 50 telephones with STD facility in both Maanpur and Raipur. In 1961, the only Post Offices were in Maan Town and Sawai Madhopur. Now there are sub post offices in both Maanpur and Raipur. The isolation of the villages has been broken not only by motorable roads, buses, and trucks and other motor vehicles but also by these means of communication.

Essentials for Leadership in PRIs

The essential qualifications in 1961, as well as in 2001, for leadership in the village and in local institutions are that: (i) the leader should belong to a family with a large land holding or an established position of affluence or prestige in the village; (ii) the leader should have good communication skills –convincingly vocal in pressurizing the district administration to attend to the villagers' needs, and (iii) he should have good relations with the villagers as well as the officers.

In 1961, late Hari Singh a Rajput with a large land holding in his family and who had been the principal functionary of the former *Jagirdar* of the village was the *Sarpanch* of Maanpur *Panchayat*. He had been *sarpanch* since the *Panchayat* was established in 1952. His position was unquestioned for two reasons. First he had the qualities that kept the leaders of various communities (Rajputs, Mahajans, Meenas, *Mallies* and the scheduled castes) satisfied and had also established good relations with officials. In 2001, the *Sarpanch* is a *Mahajan* successful businessman. But late Hari Singh's younger brother Mr. Suraj Bhan Singh an ex-*sarpanch* of the village is consulted by leaders of various castes in matters relating to the welfare of all the villages under the *Panchayat* because of his traditional position in the village. The leaders of the hamlets of the Chammars and the Meenas are also cultivators of more than average land holdings.. Late Hari Singh had and Suraj Bhan Singh has the qualities also of being convincingly vocal about the needs and problems of the village to the officials and at the same time convince the villagers that he can put forward the demands of all the villagers as well or better than any one else.

In Raipur, the two most respected leaders in 1961 were (i) middle aged Meena with a large land holding. He had been a member of the first *Panchayat* established in 1952. The second leader was a middle aged affluent *Mahajan*. The family owned a sizeable land holding and had besides money-lending as a principal economic activity. He too had been a member and for many years *Sarpanch* of the *Panchayat* established in 1952. The two leaders had mobilized funds, labour and materials contributions from the villagers for construction of the buildings of a middle school for boys and a primary school for girls, repair of the approach road to the village, pavement of streets in the habitation area of the village and construction of buildings for the *Panchayat* and the cooperative society cum-store for improved seed, fertilizers and other inputs. They had obtained grants or loans from the community development administration for construction of all these works and also for construction and repair of wells in the hamlets of the Chammars and *Gujjars*, located on the outskirts of the village.

Mr. Sham Lal Sharma, the *Sarpanch* of Raipur in 1961 was very critical of the regime of these leaders; he accused them of corruption a charge that they reciprocated. But he recognized that he could not mobilize the funds for the works mentioned above that the traditional leaders had done. The maximum that he could do was to maintain these works and at the same time ensure that the *Panchayat* had enough funds for maintaining clean drains in the habitation area of the high castes. The villagers did not allow him to raise taxes to undertake any new development works. Although he was a well-paid clerk in the cement factory, he came from a poor family. Thus he lacked one essential condition for leadership.

In 1961, two essential conditions for position of leadership at the block and district level were also that the leader should be well off enough not to appear to utilize his leadership to enrich himself from the grants or loans that were available for development works in the villages and he should be convincingly vocal about the demands and the difficulties of the villagers to the officials.

The *Pradhan* (chairman) of the Sawai Madhopur *Panchayat Samiti* in 1961 was middle aged Meena from the central part of the *tehsil* which was the stronghold of the Meenas. His family had a large landholding and the Meena community had chosen him for being a convincingly vocal representative of the Meena caste. Furthermore, he had such personal qualities that the decisions of the *Panchayat Samiti* were seldom overturned by the District Development Officer or the Collector.

In 1961, the MLA of the Sawai Madhopur (unreserved) constituency was a reasonably successful Moslem lawyer. His brother was also a successful lawyer in the Collector's office. Furthermore, he had the backing of the mostly Moslem forest contractors who mobilized men and money for his campaign in return for his ability to get permission to cut forest and other favours from the Collector and the state government. He was succeeded in the election of 1962 by a Rajput ex-*Jagirdar*, a traditional leader from a reasonably affluent family. Furthermore, the Rajput *Jagirdar* had the ability to approach the Meenas, *Malies* and the Chammars and to convince them that he would further their interests with the state government.

These conditions have remained unchanged in 2001, no matter who occupies the various positions in the *Panchayati Raj* institutions. The *Sarpanch* of Raipur in 2001 is a woman of washer men caste, the lowest in an extremely caste conscious village. She is completely ineffective. She is accused also of corruption because her husband drinks. She was elected because the seat had been reserved for a member of the scheduled caste and scheduled tribe (SC/ST) and also reserved for a woman. The SC/ST castes community men could not decide on any one candidate and had put up several women. The Dhobi woman won the election primarily as a proxy candidate for whom all high caste voters voted. However, the real leaders of the community remain a reasonably affluent Meena and two or more reasonably well off Mahajans and Brahmins.

Working of Panchayati Raj Institutions and Cooperative Societies in the Three Villages

In 1961, *Panchayati Raj* institutions had been established only two years earlier. The posts of *Sarpanchas* (Chairmen of the *Panchayat*) were occupied mainly by the high castes—a Brahmin in Raipur and a Rajput in Maanpur. The other members of the *Panchayat* of Maanpur agreed to whatever the *Sarpanch* (late) Mr. Hari Singh and his supporters decided. The co-opted women members also agreed with him. He had been the representative of the *Jagirdar* but had reconciled himself to his position as a non-cultivating owner of the land that had been left to him for self-cultivation. He had sharecroppers or wage labourers to cultivate his land.

He had utilized the grants available from the community development department to construct buildings of an 8-grade school and the offices of the *Panchayat* and the cooperative society. This large building served also as a store for improved seeds, chemical fertilizers, pesticides and improved implements. These were distributed to the farmers by a VLW—a residence had been constructed for him—at the rates fixed by the government. The *sarpanch* also ensured equitable distribution of sugar and kerosene oil, which was distributed through the Public Distribution System (PDS) in 1961.

Although a traditionalist, who would not allow the scheduled castes to worship in the temple of the high castes or draw water from their wells, the villagers respected him for his personal honesty and the development works that he had done for the village. Even the Chammars of the hamlet respected him because he had helped them obtain a grant from the government for improving their drinking water well and in opening of a primary school in their hamlet.

The *Sarpanch* of Raipur in 1961 was a young very vocal Brahmin. He was educated up to high school and worked as a clerk in the cement factory. He had been elected with the help of some young supporters against the opposition of the traditional leaders of the village—a relatively wealthy Mahajan and an affluent middle aged Meena. The latter's predecessors had been headmen of the village for more than two generations. The *Sarpanch* accused the traditional leaders of corruption; they returned the allegation. He tried to cultivate the officials, including the Collector by showing them the development works—buildings for a middle school for boys and a primary school for girls, offices of the *Panchayat* and the cooperative society; a building for residence of the VLW and a store for improved seed, chemical fertilizers, pesticides and improved implements.

But the traditional leaders of the village did not respect him, including several people of his own caste because he came from a poor family and was vocal in his criticism of the traditional leaders. He realized that he could not have mobilized the contributions for the various works that the traditional leaders had obtained. He could not even persuade the Brahmin and Mahajan families to maintain cleanliness in their streets by arranging effective drainage of the side drains. Thus, the drains in the main street which had as many as 130 shops in 2001 (selling everything from provisions to spare-parts for tractors and T.V. sets) often overflowed with waste water.

Hira Lal Meena our informant in Bijaipur is educated and is *Panchayat* development officer in the office of the BDO; he comes from a family which has a large landholding. He is well off; his children are in good jobs and he has been active in the construction committee for the big temple of *Hanumanji* for which more than Rs. 700, 000 were collected. He represents Bijaipur on the Maanpur *Panchayat* of which Bijaipur is a part.

The *Sarpanch* of the Maanpur *Panchayat* in 2001 was a *Mahajan.* He worked in close collaboration with the traditional leaders including Mr. S.B. Singh, younger brother of late Mr. Hari Singh who had also been *Sarpanch* of the village and the Mahajans. He maintained good relations also with the Meenas and the Chammars of the two hamlets and also with the Collector and other officials.

The *Sarpanch* of Raipur in 2001 is a Dhobi (washerwoman) woman. She comes from the lowest caste in a highly caste conscious village. She became *sarpanch* as mentioned earlier as a proxy candidate because member of the scheduled castes or the scheduled tribes and their leaders could not agree on any one candidate and put up several Meena women. The real leaders of the village, as mentioned earlier, remain unchanged by her election. She was getting no cooperation in her work from traditional village leaders—Brahmins, Mahajans and Meenas. They all feel she is incompetent and her husband is corrupt. They were openly talking about submitting a no-confidence motion against her leadership as soon as she has completed two years of her mandatory tenure. Even the women members of the *Panchayat*, who constituted 33 per cent of the total members and ward members who represented all castes, were supporting the traditional male village leaders in their efforts to replace the *Dhobin Sarpanch.*

Working of the *Panchayati Raj* institutions and the cooperative societies in both the large multi-caste villages Maanpur and Raipur can be considered satisfactory. The *Panchayats* of both villages had mobilized contributions in labour, materials and money to maintain various works mentioned earlier for the two villages. The contribution of people of the scheduled castes and the scheduled tribes had been in the form of materials and/or labour while that of the people of the high castes had been in money. The post of *Sarpanch* of *Panchayats* of both Maanpur and Raipur remained for almost 3 decades after 1961 with people of the high castes—Rajputs and Mahajans. Thereafter, people of the scheduled castes and the scheduled tribe have assumed it. The high castes have accepted this change in the caste of the leaders. The *Panchayat* of both villages have continued to be active in doing welfare work for the villages during 1961-2001. The *Panchayat* of Raipur, however, has not been able to make effective arrangements for drainage of wastewater from the main street, which remains quite dirty.

The *Panchayats* of both Maanpur and Raipur mobilized contributions in money, materials and labour amounting to about Rs. 4 lakhs each to construct overhead tanks from which piped water is supplied to a large number of houses in these villages. While the villagers have constructed the tanks the state government has provided funds for construction of tube wells, water of which is lifted to fill the tanks. It has provided also the operators to work the pumps. Heads of households who get the piped water supply pay a nominal amount for use of the water.

The leaders of Bijaipur have also concrete paved the main street; constructed side drains and ensured cleanliness in the village. Their principal source of drinking water is a tube well from which water is lifted to an overhead tank and supplied to about half of the houses. The remainders draw water from two wells located on the outskirts of the village. The village leaders ensure effective operation of the tube well and cleanliness around the wells. In Bijaipur, however, the overhead tank and the tube well have been constructed by the villagers themselves.

In all three villages, the schools operated by the government have well maintained buildings and the teachers recruited by the Department of Education do their duties efficiently. The *Panchayats* ensure this. This is not difficult because most of the teachers have their homes in neighbouring villages. Furthermore, the monthly pay (Rs. 7,000 to 10,000 per month) for a primary school teacher is quite attractive for a young man or a young woman who have obtained a teacher's certificate after passing their higher secondary school examination.

The willingness of the parents to pay high fees for "quality education" for their children has induced enterprising teachers to open 'private schools' in both Maanpur and Raipur. There are two 'private schools' in Raipur and one in Maanpur. Fees in them are much higher than in schools run by the Department of Education. But all the private schools have large numbers of students because 'quality' of education in them is much better than in schools run by the Department.

The working of the cooperative societies can also be considered satisfactory. The loans given by the cooperatives for current crop production range between Rs. 25-30 lakh in both the large villages. Recovery of loans is not a problem. On the contrary, the Maanpur society received a cash prize of Rs. 100,000 from the state government for timely recovery of the loans. The medium term loans given by the Land Mortgage Bank or by branches of nationalized banks for buying tractors, pump-sets and other machines for construction or improvements of homes are also repaid in time because the farmers realize that the flow of loans could not be maintained otherwise. Deposits with the branches of five national banks located in Maan Town market or in Raipur and Maanpur range between Rs. 2-4 crores.

The traditional leaders of the village who dominated the *Panchayats* and the cooperative societies in 1961 still maintain their leadership position. They did not have any formal positions in 2001 but they remained the decision-making elite. This is because the villagers have confidence in their commitment to work for all the villagers.

All the three villages have better access to facilities for education and preventive health and medical care than most of the other villages of the district because they are located near the district headquarters. For the same reason, they receive more funds for construction of various works and attention of officers of rural development departments than the other villages of the district. Their educated young men have privileged access to white-collar service in offices in the district headquarters.

There have been some important changes in attitudes and aspirations. Education of girls which was considered useless in 1961 was considered desirable in 2001. Dowry for marriages of girls has replaced bride money even among the not so affluent Meenas. Giving dowry, a traditional practice of the high castes, has become a status symbol for the middle income and affluent Meenas. The amounts of dowry are not small either, from Rs. 150, 000 to 300,000 for young men who have secure white-collar jobs—for VLWs and school teachers to clerks and junior officers in various offices in Maanpur. It was difficult to imagine in 1961 that changes of such magnitude would occur during the next four decades. Rural electrification was just starting in 1961; the cumbersome and inefficient *charas* system was used for irrigation of small areas of land. Installation of diesel-operated pumps on most of the irrigation wells has meant a large increase in the cultivated area that is irrigated—2/3rd of the total in Sawai Madhopur *tehsil.* High-yield varieties of wheat, use of which has resulted in large increases in output of wheat and income of farmers were not even heard of in 1961.

The Growth Poles in the village economy are:

1. ***Cultivation by Tractors and Irrigation by Diesel Operated Pumps.*** These have contributed to some increase in the cultivated area and much increase in the irrigated area. Production of cereals is 3-4 times higher than that in 1961. Besides since milk, vegetables and fruit in season have become an essential item of food of all except the very poor, they are produced much more than before. Surpluses of these are sold in the Maan Town market and make a significant contribution to the income of the producers. Due to adequate consumption of food and inclusion of protective foods in their diet, health of the people, men, women and children is much better. Due to much less farm work for women and men, the women devote their time to care of children

and keeping their houses clean. The men have time to work at the railway station; such labour makes a valuable addition to their income. The principal diseases are those of the digestive and respiratory tracks. Malaria the great killer that had been eradicated by the 1950s has made a comeback.

2. ***Labour:*** mainly unskilled but also skilled, find enough employment in up-keep of the railway station, the railway tracks and the state highway to Jaipur via Tonk. The carpenters, masons and smiths find enough work in construction and repair of shops and houses in Maan Town and its market and the hotels. The mechanics of motor vehicles, tractors and irrigation pumps have enough work in upkeep and repair of these. The electricians have enough work in repair of TV. receivers and electrical appliances used by housewives in Maan Town, in the officers' colony and in houses which have electricity in the villages.
3. ***The Market:*** There is so much work in it that it has replaced the factory as a source of employment. Besides it has contributed to the villages being part of a cash economy instead of a subsistence economy.
4. ***The Game Sanctuary:*** It provides jobs for labourers in maintenance of roads to it and employees of the various tourist agencies.
5. ***Much Greater Availability of Medical Facilities and Improvement in Supplies of Drinking Water***—has led to improvement in health of the people. Increase in education of boys and girls have also resulted in consciousness of a higher level of living. The TV. receivers tell them to live a better life having access to essentials of clean living, such as soap, hair oil, and medicines which cure diseases of men, women and children. They propagate also family planning. The village women report that they have accepted the 2-3 child norms. One son is a must, two sons are preferred. A large number of "operations" are reported to be performed every year. But the large number of children in all villages indicates that these statements have to be taken with a large pinch of salt.
6. ***The standard of living of the villagers*** is now comparable to that of Otalan[2] in 1963 or higher. Many houses have hand pumps besides the community hand pumps for bathing and drinking water. Ponds are used exclusively for bathing and drinking water of milch animals; buffaloes and cows. Both Maanpur and Raipur

and Bijaipur have paved streets and drains for drainage of waste water which is absorbed in the tanks outside the villages. Maanpur and its two hamlets and Bijaipur are located along a tarmac covered metalled road so that motorized transport is available through the day. Raipur is within a km. of an all weather motorable road. Because of this facility, villagers can go to and return from Jaipur, the capital for redressel of their grievances within a day.

Further, social development will mean absolute decline in practice of untouchability, greater education of women and children of school going ages and abolition of child marriages which is still widespread. It will mean even greater migration of sons of Brahmins, Rajputs and Mahajans to Jaipur, Kotah and other cities in Rajasthan and Delhi in search of white-collar jobs. At present there are educated men in Raipur and Bijaipur who are sitting idle due to lack of employment opportunities.

7. ***Bride price*** is stated to have disappeared among the better-to-do Meena cultivators. They pride themselves in giving dowry. The maximum dowry of Rs. 100,000–150,000 is commanded by even the lowest level white-collar worker who gets Rs. 10,000 to Rs. 15,000 as salary. They are the most desired grooms. However, there must be bride price among the poor cultivators because their women even now do much more work on the farm than the men. Their farm work as well as that of the men in well to do families is much less, however, than earlier because the small cultivators can hire tractors and pay also for irrigation water which are mainly the male tasks. They pay for these by working on the railway station, maintenance of railway tracks and on the road to Jaipur.

Due to much less farm work for women and men, the women devote their time to care of children and keeping their homes clean. The men have time to work at the railway station: such labour makes a valuable addition to their income.

Concluding Remarks

Although one cannot foresee new growth poles in the economy, there is little doubt that increases in income and consumption, improvement in education and health and attendant rise in aspirations of people of all castes will continue during the next two decades. Production of wheat and mustard in the cool season will continue to increase by more efficient use of chemical fertilizers, pesticides and irrigation water. More dependable supply of electricity by the Rajasthan State Electricity Board will greatly reduce the cost of irrigation because the price of electricity would be much lower than the cost of diesel oil. It will increase incomes of farmers and comfort in living and more households can have the comfort of electric lights and fans in their homes, besides substantial saving in expenditure on foreign exchange on import of kerosene or crude oil.

With rise in income and consumption, increase in education of children and improvement of health of women, children and men, there have been major changes in attitudes and aspirations of people of all castes during the last 4 decades 1961-2001. Women of all castes have accepted the need for family planning, mention of which was repugnant to them in 1961. Wives of Meena farmers with small land holdings realize that their land holding is small and can provide work for only one son; the others would have to work as share-croppers and supplement their income by unskilled labour in Maan Town market or repair of the railway track. Wives of Chammars and other scheduled castes realize similarly that even two sons could not find enough work as share-croppers on land or as non-agricultural labourers. With reduction in infant mortality, they are not afraid that most of their children would die in infancy and they would be left childless.

However, it is not certain that the realization has led to smaller families so far. Our respondents in the three villages and Mr. Fateh Singh our respondent for the game sanctuary, all have 3-5 children and are proud of the fact. Except Mr. Heera Lal Meena a leader of Bijaipur, whose sons are working in Maan Town, some sons of the others are living in Jaipur or in other states. Earlier after getting education up to high school, several high caste young men were working as secretary for cooperative society or *Panchayat*, a school teacher or a clerk in some office in Maan Town. Some Chammars had begun to get into such jobs but the Meenas were not interested. Now even Meenas are aspiring to get these jobs. Furthermore, the high castes are educating their sons to become college graduates or professionals who will get posts with much higher salaries; no matter that they would live at long distances from their homes. Sons of two of our three respondents, former *Sarpanch* of Maanpur and Raipur are professionals and are living in Jaipur, Kotah and other cities. One son of Mr Fateh Singh, a Rajput and our respondent for the Game Sanctuary is a doctor who works in the hospital maintained by an international Non-

Governmental Organization (NGOs) 'Tiger Watch' and located just outside Raipur. Another son is in Mumbai training to be male nurse. The parents do not mind this. On the contrary, they are happy at their sons' success as professionals. These are typical attitudes and aspirations of the urban middle class.

Since bride price has been replaced by dowry, the Meena farmers realize that they could not afford to provide a dowry for more than one daughter.

In 1961, most of the people of this area—all except the Meenas with relatively large land-holdings, Rajput, former *Jagirdars* or those who were their representatives and *Mahajans* or Brahmins whose sons had after education got white-collar jobs—were poor. By 2001, most of them had risen to lower middle-income status. Inequalities in social status of people of different castes have been greatly reduced. Assumption of posts of *Sarpanch* (chairmen) by men or even women belonging to the scheduled castes and the fact that some young men of these castes would get posts of clerks or junior officers in the offices of the district have been accepted by people of the high caste without protest.

Other changes in attitudes of great significance are:

(i) Realization of the value of education of girls;

(ii) Need for and practice of family planning by a significant percentage of couples in the reproductive age group.

(iii) Land reform of abolition of intermediary tenure holdings has not been effective or there is wide opposition to it from former landowners to its becoming effective. But the number of these areas is small. Over large parts of the country, the reform has been effective for four decades or more.

Assumption of Political Power by Cultivating Community

Assumption of Political Power by Cultivating caste been the norm in most of the states for almost 50 years, the high castes are fully reconciled to the fact. In two States—U.P. and Bihar—which are most populous, political power has been or is with leaders of other backward castes. There is resistance to it only in Bihar.

A perception, widely shared by large numbers of people relates to prevalence of corruption among officials and clerks in the offices of the Collector, the Superintendent of Police or other district level offices and even in the *Panchayat Samiti* and the *Zilla Parishad.* This impression prevailed (and justifiably) in 1961 also. Furthermore, the people realize that the money to be paid for 'getting things done' is much higher in 2001 than it was in 1961.

Role of Communication Facilities

Another major change relates to the role of communication facilities and of private traders in promoting rural development. In 1961, radio receivers were owned by a very few relatively affluent farmers or men in the high castes; there were no television receivers. Now about 20 per cent of the households in Maanpur and a similar number in Raipur have television receivers in their homes. The radio receivers can be afforded by everyone. The information to cultivators, about the need for education of children, having clean drinking water supply, keeping their homes and children clean, having a balanced diet and availing of medical facilities in case of sickness and family planning practices, can be conveyed to all men and women through radio and television receivers. These supplement and reinforce the advice and the facilities offered by the extension workers and teachers in primary and secondary schools, doctors and nurses in the hospitals.

In 1961, in Maanpur information about improved agricultural practices and supply of inputs for crops were provided only by the VLWs and agriculture extension officers. Veterinary assistants treated diseases of animals; the traders in the Maan Town market supplement the advice given by the VLWs and the extension officers on the choice and dosages of chemical fertilizers for different food crops—wheat and especially mustard which are the principal food and cash crops. The traders sell tractors and pump sets and provide fuel and facilities for repair of these. After observing the repairmen, a few farmers have developed the skill to repair small defects in their machines themselves.

In 1961, there were no telephones in these villages. The Collector, the Superintendent of Police and a few district or sub-divisional level officers, the MLA and a few professionals mainly lawyers and the doctors in the Sawai Madhopur hospital had telephones in their homes. Now there are more than 50 telephones with STD facilities in Maanpur as well as in Raipur. In 1961, the only post offices were in Maan Town and Sawai Madhopur. Now there are sub-post offices in both Maanpur and Raipur. The isolation of the villages has been broken not only by motorable roads, buses, trucks and other motor vehicles but also by these means of communication.

Is Development Self-Sustaining?

Meaning of Self-Sustainable Development

Self-Sustaining Development has two meanings in our view. First, it should not make undue demands on the natural resources of soil, water or vegetation. Second, it should mean that the improvements in health and productivity of people, education and awareness should be permanent and it should create aspirations to progress higher in the future.

The development described in the foregoing sections satisfies both criteria of self-sustaining development. The farmland is more productive in 2001 than it was in 1961. In 1961 most of the farmland was bare for more than 6 months in the year (after the monsoon season crops of sorghum or millets had been harvested) and was subject to wind or water erosion. Now, two-third of the farmland is irrigated and has two crops—grams (chick peas), wheat, mustard or pulses in the cold season and sorghum, millets or groundnut in the monsoon season. The crop rotation followed is such that the nutrients removed by one set of crops are replaced by another set. Thus, stalks of sorghum, millets and vines of mustard and groundnuts replace most of the nutrients removed by high-yield wheat. While some of the stalks of sorghum and millet and husks of wheat are fed to milch animals, the remainder is ploughed in to improve the physical structure of the soil. The vines of mustard and groundnut, which are ploughed in also improve the physical structure of the soil by taking nitrogen from the air. As a result the need for application of chemical fertilizers is reduced. The pastures are looked after better because production of milk is a major source of income for villages located between Sawai Madhopur and Maan Town. The Ranthambhore forest and game sanctuary are protected both by the forest guards and employees of Tiger Watch an international non-governmental organization (NGO), the sole object of which is to preserve the natural habitat of tigers and other wild beasts. Much of the cultivable land which had formed part of the *shikar* (hunting) preserves of former *Jagirdars* and was under trees has been cleared for cultivation and allotted to Chammars or other landless or appropriated by the *Jagirdars* for self-cultivation. There is no evidence yet of fall in the ground water table due to irrigation of most of the cropland.

Self-sustaining development also means that increase in income and consumption, improvement in health, increase in education of children and awareness of the people should lead to aspirations for further rise in these. This is also true in this area. In 1961 most of the people, all except the better off *Mahajans* and Meenas or Brahmins whose sons were working as village level white-collar workers, were poor. By 2001 most of them had risen to lower middle income or higher economic status. Even the farmers with small holdings and the scheduled castes agricultural or non-agricultural labourers have enough cereals to eat through the year; milk, vegetables, and fruit in season, which few could afford to eat earlier, are now an integral part of their diet. Their health is much better, because they have access to medical care facilities in the form of two very well equipped multi-facility hospitals, besides dispensaries and *vaidyas* in both the large villages. In addition, Maanpur has a resident physician and an auxiliary nurse midwife. They realize the value of adequate and safe drinking water supply for maintaining good health to have invested lakhs in construction of overhead tanks and tube wells to lift water to them in order to have piped water in the homes and constructed side drains along the main streets of all the three villages to drain the waste water. Two villages—Maanpur and Bijaipur are quite clean because drain water is discharged in ponds located to the rear of the villages.

Their homes and children are much cleaner because the need for manual work by women on the farms is much less than before, thanks to use of tractors for cultivation and mechanical shellers of sorghum and millet and de-huskers of wheat. A significant percentage of houses are made of brick and mortar which are much easier to clean than the mud and thatch hut in which most of the small cultivators and landless labourers lived in 1961 and that needed, in addition, annual repair. Maternal, infant and child mortality has been reduced so much that many couples in the reproductive age group are practicing family planning. In Maanpur most of the middle aged women with two or more children have opted for 'operations' against further pregnancies and the visiting doctor has conducted about 100 operations, during the last four months among couples.

The value of education of children has been realized so much that most of the boys and a large number of girls of school going ages are being sent to primary or secondary schools. People of the high castes and more affluent Meenas educate their daughters so that they can be wives of white-collar workers. Furthermore, even the poor farmers and landless labourers realize that educated wives keep their homes and children clean and know enough about preventive health care to avoid themselves or their children falling victims to communicable diseases.

Since a large number of high castes and affluent Meena households have black and white or colour T.V. receivers and even the poor have radio receivers, they are well aware of events in the area, district, and the state and even in the country. These receivers inform and entertain. They tell them the essentials of good living and create the desire to have the means to achieve it.

There has been a rise in aspirations of people of all castes. The high castes—Brahmins, Mahajans and Rajputs are educating their sons to go through degree or professional colleges in Jaipur or Kotah so that they can become professionals or officers in the state government who have much higher salaries than they had in 1961. They are educating their daughters so that they can be married to such officers. The parents are proud of the fact, that some of their sons are professionals living in Jaipur or other districts of Rajasthan or in other states. Even the Meenas who were not interested in white-collar jobs are now keen that their sons and daughters should be educated so that they can become white-collar workers.

There has been a major rise in level of skills of the farmers. In 1961, improved ploughs donated by CARE (Corporation for American Relief Everywhere) were lying unused in Maanpur because no one could repair some small defects in them. Now the cultivators who have tractors for cultivation and diesel operated pump sets for irrigation can remedy small defects in them themselves. Facilities for repairs to the machines are available with dealers in the market but the repairs would be too expensive, if the farmers could not repair the small defects in the machines themselves.

Will Development Described above in the Sawai Madhopur Villages be Self-Sustaining?

This question can be answered conclusively only during the next 2 decades when the technological, economic and social changes can be viewed over a longer-term perspective. However, from present indicators they would appear to be so, for the following reasons:

Most of the changes have been accomplished by the people themselves. The social service and infrastructure facilities provided and some of them maintained by the government have assisted the economic and social change process. However, using these facilities and ensuring that they are well maintained is entirely the initiatives of the people. In 1961, the cooperative of Maanpur could give short-term loans of a total of less than Rs. 100,000 for current crop production. Recovery was a problem. Now the short-term loans are taken by almost all cultivators and the amount runs into tens of lakhs and recovery is not a problem; the borrowers realize that prompt repayment of the loans is essential to availability of further loans.

Changes in skills and aspirations are even more important. In 1961, improved iron ploughs developed by CARE were lying unused in the *Panchayat* building of Maanpur because no one could remedy the small defects in them. The farmers have the skill now to correct small defects in the machines that they use themselves.

Development is self-sustaining because it is inconceivable that after having come this far, these people would allow them selves to be returned to their former poverty, illiteracy and ignorance.

It is true that these people located near the district headquarters have privileged access to education and medical facilities located in the district level; high schools, colleges and hospitals. They have privileged access to white-collar work for the same reason. Farmers located in distant villages would not have such access. However, the changes must be occurring over a large area in Rajasthan, as shown by a SIDA study which shows (a) Increase in agro-production; (b) Use of chemical fertilizers, and (c) Increase in number of tractors. Rajasthan which was deficit in foodgrains in the 1950s has large surplus.

PROGRESS OF RAJASTHAN

Data available on various indicators of economic and social development of progress of Rajasthan during the last two Decades 1981-2001 show that Rajsthan can be classified as prosperous and progressive state.

Rajasthan has since its formation in the early 1950s been classified as a BIMARU State (an acronyms for states which include Bihar, Madhya Pradesh, U.P., Orissa among others) in which slow economic progress and social change brings down the rate of increase in G.D.P. and other indicators of economic and social progress such as increase in literacy, decline in infant, child and maternal mortality, proportion of people below the poverty line. The following note indicates that on the basis of several indicators of economic and social development during the last two decades it should be classified now as a progressive state.

Growth of Population

The population of the State increased from 44.3 million in 1991 to 56.4 million in 2001. (Table 8.1) The rate of increase 2.5 per cent per annum was as high as in the previous decade. Apparently, the effects, if any, of

Table 8.1: Growth Rate of Population, 1981-1991 and 1991-2001 and Growth Rate of Per Capita Income 1980-81 to 1996-97

Sl. No.	India & States	Population in 1990-91	Population in 2000-01	Growth rate of population Per cent per annum		Female Literacy rate (%)	Per capita income at 1980-81 prices (Rupees)		
		(millions)	(millions)	1981-91	1991-2001	2001	1980-81	1996-97	Increase (%)
1	2	3	4	5	6	7	8	9	10
1	India	846.4	1027.5	2.01	1.93	54.16	1625	2814	70.5
2	Uttar Pradesh	132.0	166.0	2.28	2.30	43.0	1278	1628	27.4
3	Bihar	64.5	82.9	2.10	2.50	33.6	917	1010	10.1
4	West Bengal	68.0	80.2	2.14	1.64	60.2	1773	2641	49.0
5	Madhya Pradesh	48.6	96.8	2.41	2.18	50.3	1358	1877	38.0
6	Rajasthan	44.0	54.5	2.80	2.49	44.0	1228	2247	83.0
7	Punjab	20.3	24.3	1.89	1.80	63.5	2674	4171	56.0
8	Haryana	16.5	21.0	2.42	2.47	56.3	2330	3996	71.5
9	Orissa	31.7	36.7	1.83	1.48	50.1	1314	1595	21.4
10	Maharashtra	78.9	96.8	2.28	2.04	67.5	2425	4853	100.1
11	Gujarat	41.3	50.6	1.92	2.03	58.6	1940	3717	91.6
12	Kerala	29.1	31.8	1.34	0.90	87.9	1568	2274	45.0
13	Tamil Nadu	55.9	62.1	1.43	1.06	64.5	1448	2876	98.6
14	Andhra Pradesh	66.5	75.7	2.37	1.30	51.5	1380	2134	54.6
15	Karnataka	45.0	52.7	1.92	1.59	57.5	1380	2518	64.5
16	Goa	1.2	1.3	1.47	1.39	75.5	3145	6550	97.8

Nota: The 1991 populations of Uttar Pradesh, Bihar and Madhya Pradesh have been reduced to take into account the separation of Uttaranchal, Jharkhand and Chhattisgarh respectively from the three states.

Sources:

(a) Registrar General of India: Provisional Population Totals 1990/91 Paper No. 1 of 1991 and Provisional Population Totals, Paper 1 of 2001, New Delhi, India.

(b) For per capita income: *E.P.W.* Research Foundation: National Accounts Statistics of India 1950-51-1996-97, Mumbai, 1998 p. 84.

(c) For Data on agricultural output: SIDA (Swedish International Development Agency) Rajasthan: A Statistical Study, New Delhi, 1998.

family limitation by couples in the reproductive age groups have yet to be seen. The rapid growth reflects however, major improvement in health of the people due to eradication of malaria and control of diseases of the respiratory and digestive tracts as a result of intensive coverage with facilities for medical and preventive health care and improvement in water supply for villages and towns.

Increase in Per Capita Income

Despite the rapid increase in population, per capita income increased by 83 per cent between 1980-81 and 1996-97, the figures for the two years were Rs. 1220 and Rs. 2247 respectively (Table 8.1). The growth rate is much above the national average of 70.5 per cent. Among the 17 states with population above 20 million in 2001, the rates were higher than of Rajasthan only in Maharashtra, Gujarat and Tamil Nadu, the states which have high levels of industrial development and in which agricultural output has also increased rapidly. To be included among the states with rapidly increasing per capita income is a creditable achievement because it is explained below that the increase is almost entirely due to rapid increase in agricultural output, there being no other source of significant economic growth.

Agricultural Growth

There has been rapid increase in agricultural output in the following areas:

(i) Areas in north western Rajasthan which receive irrigation from a canal from the Sutlej River. The irrigated area has increased considerably after construction of the Bhakra Dam on the river in the 1950s. High-yield wheat and medium staple cotton are the principal crops.

(ii) The areas in eastern and south-eastern Rajasthan which extend from Alwar in the north, through Bharatpur, Jaipur, Kotah, Bhilwara and Udaipur in the south which receive irrigation from electric and diesel oil operated pumps. High-yield wheat and sorghum are the principal food crops. Output of mustard and ground nut the principal cash crops in these areas have increased also. Sale of these crops and also of wheat and medium staple cotton in north-western Rajasthan meets all the needs of the farmers for buying various consumer goods—cloth, clothes, shoes and other leather goods and building materials such as cement, corrugated iron sheets and steel rods for making brick and mortar houses. The Chammar landless labourers-cum-small farmers have income from cultivation of their small farms, plus non-agricultural labour in the market towns or as share-croppers for Rajput or *Mahajan Jagirdars*. They have become masons, carpenters and plumbers so that they can earn high wages in building brick and mortar houses and repairing defects in them. Other scheduled castes that practice their crafts have enough income from sale of goods that they produce to be above the poverty line.

(iii) Increase in agricultural output is due also to increase in use of chemical fertilizers by 450 per cent during *Kharif* and 300 per cent for *Rabi* cultivation. (SIDA, p. 36) Total consumption of (NPK) fertilizers increased by almost 3 times from 7.4 kg. per hectare in 1980-81 to 20.03 kg. Per hectare in 1993-94. (SIDA, p. 198-199)

(iv) Cultivation by tractors and performing other operations in the fields by power driven implements.

(v) Effective crop protection practices.

(vi) Intensive agricultural extension services and transfer of research results from the laboratory to the farms.

(vi) Extensive rural electrification and a state-wide network of roads connecting villages to market towns.

Thus Rajasthan, which was deficit in foodgrains in the 1950s, has a large surplus and besides has large export of oil seeds. The statistical data for the Sawai Madhopur district and the *tehsil* show that the average yield for wheat has increased by 2½ to 3 times per hectare; 3½ times for groundnut, 2 to 3 times for mustard. The most remunerative cash crop is mustard; it yields Rs. 800 per hectare. However, groundnut yields only Rs. 600 per hectare, whereas for wheat the return amounts to Rs. 1,375 per hectare.

Increase in Tourism

Jaipur, Ajmer, Jaisalmer, Udaipur and Mt. Abu are visited by a million or more tourists, for recreation or for worship. Hundreds of thousand of Moslems pilgrims worship at the *Dargah* (burial place) of Khawaja Moinudeen Chishti, a great Sufi saint of 15th century. Mt. Abu is visited similarly by hundred of thousands of Jain pilgrims from southern Rajasthan and northern Gujarat. Jaipur, Udaipur and Jaisalmer are the most visited cities by foreign and domestic tourists; Jaipur and Udaipur are visited by both groups for seeing their palaces and museums while Jaisalmer is visited mainly by foreign tourists to have a glimpse of its distinctive palaces and houses in a desert landscape.

Increase in Literacy

Increase in literacy has been noteworthy. The female literacy rate was as low as 20.4 per cent in 1990/91; the lowest among the then existing 15 major states with population above 20 million. It has more than doubled to 44.3 per cent in 2001 (Table 8.2).

Table 8.2: Progress in Literacy in BIMARU States, 1991-2001

(Percentage)

Sl. No	*State*	*Literacy rate in 1991*			*Literacy rate in 2001*		
		Total	*Male*	*Female*	*Total*	*Male*	*Female*
1.	Bihar	38.5	52.6	23.5	47.5	60.3	31.62
2.	U.P.	41.7	55.4	26.0	57.4	70.2	43.03
3.	Rajasthan	38.5	55.1	20.8	61.0	76.5	49.34
4.	M.P.	43.4	57.4	28.4	64.1	76.8	50.00

Source: Registrar General of India: Census of India, 2001. Paper No. 1 Provisional Population tables. New Delhi, 2001.

The literacy rate in 2001 was 76 per cent for males and 44.3 per cent for females higher than the rates in U.P., Bihar, Orissa, Assam and Jharkhand. The rates of 2001 put Rajasthan among states with medium literacy. This is a creditable achievement for a state which had a low level of literacy as late as 1990-91.

The increase is due to the following reasons:

> The men realise that if they were literate they would not be cheated by merchants who buy their crops or those who sell them various consumer goods. They appreciate also that wives with some education keep themselves, their children and homes clean and seek assistance in case of sickness. They should have adequate and safe supply of drinking water from tube wells or wells fitted with electric or diesel oil operated pumps. Besides with use of machines—tractors for cultivation, pump sets for irrigation, mechanical shellers of sorghum and millet and dehuskers of wheat

there is much less work in the fields. They have to look after milch buffaloes, ensure that they are cleaned after the buffaloes have been milked and tied in their yards at night.

Social Change

There have been noteworthy social changes during the last 50 years. *Jagirdari*, which was the dominant system of tenure for collection of land revenue and maintaining law and order in most of the areas of the state, was abolished in the early 1950s and full and heritable rights in land were conferred on the actual cultivators of croplands.

This reform which still rocks the peace and stability of States such as Bihar, was accomplished without protest from the *Jagirdars*. They contented themselves with management of the lands left to them for self-cultivation. They employed wage labourers or share croppers for cultivation. Now, most of them have purchased tractors for cultivation and installed diesel oil or electricity operated pumps for irrigation of the irrigable areas.

Primary health centres (mini-hospitals) at district headquarter towns with dispensaries, auxiliary nurses, midwives and *vaidyas* ensures that facilities for preventive health and medical care are within easy reach of residents of both large villages and towns.

Untouchability has been abolished by law and has disappeared in the urban areas and most of the rural areas. The Chammars, the largest group among the scheduled castes, have stopped performing their traditional tasks of flaying the hides and skins of dead animals and making leather goods. They have been allotted cultivable lands released by former *Jagirdars* and other by the state government and are making strenuous efforts to be recognized as a clean cultivating caste. They have also stopped performing their traditional tasks at the houses of the former *Jagirdars* or for the village. People of the other scheduled castes who carry out their traditional obligations are no longer considered untouchable.

The progress made by the Chammars is such that a few young men have after being educated to B.A. level, joined the Rajasthan or Indian Administrative Service. Others are working as white-collar workers in offices of the Collector, the Superintends of Police or other district offices after passing the higher secondary school examination. These young men are very assertive of their right to education in schools and colleges and for employment in offices of the state government. They cite the provision in the Constitution of India relating to reservation of seats for them in educational institutions and in government service. In the rural areas, many are clerks, school teachers or village level officials such as secretaries of *panchayats* and cooperative societies. Due to the provisions of reservation of seats for them in *Panchayati Raj* institutions, many of them have become *sarpanches* (chairman of *panchayats*), *pradhans* (chairman) or other influential members of *Panchayat Samitis*. Men of the high castes, who dominated these institutions for the first three decades after their formation, recognise this change inevitable in a democratic society.

Position of Women

There has been equally remarkable change in the position of women. Child marriage, which was widespread even in the 1960s, has been reduced greatly. There has been rapid progress in education of women. Large numbers of girls are being sent to primary (5-grade) and middle (8-grade) schools which are located in every large village. The men are not afraid (as they were until the 1960s) that educated women would not work in the fields. The need for their work in fields is much less because of extensive use of tractors for cultivation and of other machines (such as mechanical thrashers of sorghum and millets and dehuskers of wheat) and for various other tasks. Furthermore, the men realise that wives with some education keep themselves; their children and their homes clean and obtain medical assistance in case of sickness. The people of high castes are educating their daughters to high school or higher levels, so that they can marry white-collar workers including professionals and soldiers in the armed forces who have a steady high income and some power. Some of the high caste educated women have become professionals like teachers and bank clerks, etc. Their sons are being educated to higher secondary school or college level so that they can become white-collar workers and professionals such as physicians, engineers and architects.

The ability of Rajasthani society to make such far-reaching changes within five decades reflects a resilience which was quite unexpected even in the 1960s. It is the most important reason for the economic and social progress made by the state and the greatest hope for continuing progress in future.

Conditions Affecting Rapid Progress

The most important condition affecting rapid economic and social progress has been stable and development-oriented governments. After a few years of unstable governments after its formation in the late 1940s,

Rajasthan had a stable, development oriented government for about 20 years, from mid-1950s to the middle of the 1970s. It was succeeded by another government which stayed in power for more than a decade and continued the development process initiated in the 1950s. In recent years also there has been political stability. The present Chief Minister has been at the helm of affairs for almost a decade. His predecessor was at the helm of affairs for more than a decade. One result of this is that the officers of the IAS and the technical services can perform their duties without too much interference by ministers and MLAs. Corruption among ministers and influential MLAs is much less and their interference with work of the officers is also much less than in several other states.

Another condition affecting rapid progress is almost exclusive emphasis on development of agriculture and rural development. After not too successful efforts to promote industrial development, the government realised that the efforts could yield very limited results despite the large number of highly successful Rajasthani industrialists living in Kolkata and other cities. There are however, highly skilled craftsmen in Jaipur, Jodhpur and Udaipur who make jewellery, leather goods with exquisite designs, textiles and furnishings printed with distinctive Rajasthani designs. These are popular with domestic and foreign tourists.

The last condition affecting economic and social development is the determination of the people to acquire higher levels of income.

Role of Non-Governmental Organizations in Development of the Villages

We have experienced and read a lot about the role of non-governmental organizations in Rajasthan in economic and social development of villages. Some of the most outstanding models for self-sustainable village development have been developed and perfected by outstanding social workers some of who had given up lucrative government jobs to devote themselves to development in rural Rajasthan. In the three villages studied by us, however, there was no NGO working on an ongoing basis. The two NGOs—Tiger Foundation and *Dastakar* have been mentioned. Both have set-up offices outside Raipur. The Tiger foundation is devoted to providing medical and preventive health care facilities which as mentioned earlier has specific specialization and is mostly foreign-funded. *Dastkar* has no major thrust for social or economic development of the villages around it. It is located on the outskirt of Raipur, on the way to the game sanctuary and trains some potentially skilled Muslim men and women for getting their export orders for quilted bed sheets and colourful dresses made here and sell some of their products to the tourists. Mr. Fateh Singh, who is representative of the Tiger Watch, had encouraged *Dastakar* to open its office here. However, its impact on the social change and economic improvement of Raipur is minimal; none of its officers ever visit the village.

There are no other major social changes. Furthermore, there is no significant presence of economic development oriented NGOs in the district. Some small NGOs that exist are mainly catering to taking up government programmes and focus themselves on implementation of government programmes in areas for which funds are available. They are located in Maan Town/Sawai Madhopur town and shift their location of work from village to village depending upon the area for which funds have been earmarked and for the duration of the programme. Most of the social and economic changes that are described in this study are results of macro development change influences of the last forty years primarily introduced by the government, which have enabled the villages to achieve the current take-off stage of self-sustainable development. The development impetus as mentioned above has been unleashed by—education and health facilities, developments in agricultural infrastructure and shift from self-sufficient to market economy of the villages as well as awareness about the political rights and entitlements created by changes in the structure of local self government—role of *Panchayati Raj* Institutions.

Are Maanpur and Raipur Villages or Small Towns?

In 1961, both Raipur and Maanpur were villages with population between 2500 and 3000. Most of the people, including those of the high castes depended primarily on income from land. The high castes got their lands cultivated by sharecroppers or by labourers hired by them. Even those whose sons were working as white-collar workers, had income from land as a secondary source. For Meenas, Malies and Jats, cultivation of their land provided the only source of income. The Chammar and other scheduled castes supplemented their income from their small plots of land, which they had been allotted, by agricultural and/or non-agricultural labour and on maintenance of the railway tracks and the Jaipur-Tonk road. The world-view of most of the villagers was distinctly local. They sold any surplus grain that they had after meeting the needs of the family to traders who bought it within the villages. For all except the high castes, Jaipur that was 130 km. from their villages was too far to be of any interest to them and Delhi the national capital might as well be in another country.

Even the young men of high castes who worked as white-collar workers—V.L.Ws, secretaries of cooperative societies or *Panchayat*s, *Patwaries*, school teachers or clerks in various offices had little interest in events outside the state. They were only vaguely aware of events in the country. Few of them read the newspapers or possessed radio receivers.

In 2001, however, both Raipur and Maanpur had populations of 7000-8000 and should have been classified as small towns, by the Superintendent of Census of Rajasthan. They have also other attributes of a town—a sub-post office, more than 50 telephones, more than 100 black or colour television receivers and piped water in a large number of houses. Most of the houses of the high castes and of Meenas with even middle-sized holdings were of brick and mortar. The main street of Raipur had 130 shops, while that of Maanpur had 70 shops besides eight teashops and four restaurants. Both villages had one 10-grade high school and 2-8 grade middle schools, sub-dispensaries, a resident physician and/or *vaidyas*.

The shops in Raipur and Maanpur sell everything—foodgrains and other provisions and drugs, cloth, clothes, shoes and other leather goods and furnishings. Dealers in them sell kerosene and diesel oils the fuel for tractors, pump sets and other machines. Some of them sell spare-parts for them also. Dealers in Maan Town market, located 5 km. from Raipur and 8 km. from Maanpur also sell various consumer goods. They sell also spare parts for the machines and have facilities for repair of machines as well as building materials and inputs of improved agriculture—improved seeds, chemical fertilizers and pesticides. Some dealers in both the villages sell cooking gas. Farmers can sell their produce in Maantown or in the villages themselves.

Most of the farmers produce mustard and groundnuts and some wheat for sale so that they can buy various consumer goods and consumer durables mentioned above. The farmers are part of the regional economy because they sell their crops in it and buy various consumer goods from it. The high castes whose sons are working as white-collar workers or professionals or whose daughters are married to them are part of the national economy. The more affluent among them are proud of the fact that their sons who are professionals are working in other states or their daughters are married to professionals living in Jaipur, Kotah or other cities.

The farmers take large short-term loans from cooperative societies for current cultivation and medium term loans from Land Mortgage Banks or from the branches of scheduled banks located in Maan Town or within the villages for buying tractors, pump sets or other machines, building materials for construction of houses and opening of shops. Farmers are keen to get the maximum prices of their crops and the non-agricultural labourers are keen to get the minimum wages fixed by the Government of Rajasthan. Replacement of dowry for bride price among all but the poorest farmers increases the need for cash further. Both Maanpur and Raipur attract people from small villages in their vicinity to sell their produce or buy consumer goods or consumer durables. Thus both Maanpur and Raipur have all the characteristics of a small town.

What Next

Increase in the Number of Tourists

Make the 3 day Delhi-Agra-Jaipur circle a four-day circle by including a visit from Jaipur to the game sanctuary and back within a day. This would be possible if the road from Jaipur to the game sanctuary is improved so much that motor vehicles can easily go to the sanctuary and back in a day. The sanctuary has the unique feature of having tigers and other wild animals and of a great historical tradition.

Make the road to the Fort from its base negotiable by elephants as the road to the Amber Palace in Jaipur is at present. Restore the original majesty of the palace by repairs to it and repair the quality of the soldiers and other servants of the palace. The palace where Queen Padmini and her fellow wives of soldiers committed suicide should be very well maintained. Trained guides should explain in detail the story of the Pathan invader Allauddin Khilji, the Raja and Queen Padmini of Ranthambhore Fort. The sanctuary is unique in that it has wild animals, exotic birds and Ranthambhore Fort which has the legend of unfilled desire of a Pathan ruler of Delhi to catch a glimpse of a queen of legendary beauty. The road to it can be negotiated easily by jeeps and elephants.

Make Maanpur and Raipur model villages so that families coming from Jaipur by road and those coming from Delhi by train can see village life first hand.

The standard of living is now comparable to that in village Otalan of Punjab in 1961 with the following exception:

(i) Liberation of girls was much greater in Otalan even in 1963 than in the Rajasthan villages even now (2001)
(ii) A large number of young men of both—*Jats* and the scheduled castes went to the army from the Punjab village. Very few young men from this village go to the army.

(iii) Improvement of supply of electricity by Rajasthan State Electricity Board will greatly reduce cost of irrigation and contribute to increase in production.

(iv) The leaders of the hamlets of the Chammar and the Meenas were and continue to be cultivators of more than average land holdings.

The Future

There are indications of presence of a large field of natural gas in western Rajasthan, almost on the border with Pakistan. If such a field is discovered the scenario for agricultural and agro-industrial development will be totally transformed. With assured supply of power, the farmers who use diesel oil to operate pumps will use electric pumps. There would be large saving in foreign exchange now spent on import of diesel oil or kerosene used for lighting homes. The desert will bloom; the area was well wooded as late as the 16th century. The foliage in the area would be restored so that there is adequate pasturage for the large numbers of livestock (cattle, sheep and goats) that are kept by the herders.

The farmers in the small villages in this area who spend a day fetching two buckets of water for their needs, will be assured of clean drinking water from deep wells located near their villages. They will devote themselves to increase production of food in their farms. The periodic shortage of food, water and fodder that are experienced by this area that leads to migration of people and herds and deaths of thousands of live stocks due to scarcity of water and foliage will be a distant memory.

With completion of Indira Gandhi Canal there will be a large increase in the irrigated area and in agricultural output in the areas irrigated by it. The serious problems of large seepage of water due to wind erosion will be greatly reduced by plantation of trees all along the banks of the canal.

The development of industries in Karachi and rapid increase in irrigated area and agricultural output in west Punjab and Sindh with use of natural gas from the Sui field in Baluchistan illustrates the possibilities that would become reality with discovery of gas.

There is little doubt that increases in income and consumption, improvement in education and health and attendant rise in aspirations of people of all castes will continue during the next two decades. Production of wheat and mustard in the cool season will continue to increase by more efficient use of chemical fertilizers, pesticides and irrigation. More dependable supply of electricity by the Rajasthan State Electricity Board will greatly reduce the cost of irrigation and thus the cost of production, increase in income of farmers, increase in comfort of those who have electricity in their homes and saving in foreign exchange.

With rise in income and consumption, increase in education of children and improvement of health of women, children and men, there have been major changes in attitudes and aspirations of people of all castes during the last 4 decades 1961-2001. Women of all castes have accepted the need for family planning, mention of which was repugnant to them in 1961. Wives of Meena farmers with small land holdings realize that their land holding is small and can provide work for only one son; the others would have to work as share-croppers and supplement their income by unskilled labour in Maan Town market or repair of the railway track. Wives of Chammars and other scheduled castes realize similarly that even two sons could not find enough work as sharecroppers on land or as non-agricultural labourers. With reduction in infant mortality, they are not afraid that most of their children would die in infancy and they would be left childless. However, it is not certain that the realization has led to smaller families so far.

In 1961, only young men of the three high castes—Brahmin, Mahajan and Rajput- -aspired to and did become white-collar workers. Some Chammars had begun to get into such jobs; but the Meenas were not interested. Now even Meenas are aspiring to get these jobs. Furthermore, the high castes are educating their sons to become college graduates or professionals who will get posts with much higher salaries than those of workers in the district; no matter that they would live at long distances from their homes.

Mr. Fateh Singh himself is living now with a modern woman from Gujarat who is running a boutique from her house bringing the latest in ladies fashion to Sawai Madhopur elite and the foreign tourists. She had come to work with Dastkar Centre located just outside the sanctuary. The tourists love to spend an evening with Fateh Singh in his sprawling farmhouse with most elegant lay out for dinner by fireside and listening to stories of his life with the tigers in the sanctuary.

Most of the people of this area—all except some Rajputs, Mahajans or Brahmins or Meenas with large land holdings were poor in 1961. There had already been major changes in political, economic and social conditions during the previous 15 years (after Independence when the first study was done), which had been accepted by the people. The Rajputs and other *Jagirdars* had reconciled themselves to their changed status of non-cultivating managers of their land, which had been left to them for self-cultivation. The Meena cultivators were happy that they had got full and heritable rights to the land that they had been cultivating. The Chammars had ceased to flay the hides and skins of dead animals or do unpaid work in the houses of the *Jagirdars*, which they had been obliged to do earlier. Most of them had got allotted cultivable wasteland, which had become available following abolition of *Jagirdari*. They were trying desperately to be recognized as a clean caste, the equals of the Meenas. They and the Meenas had given up drinking and eating meat so that they could be recognized as a clean cultivating caste, the equivalent of the *Jats* or *Gujjars*.

Sanskritization in occupations and aspirations are very much visible among the Meenas and the Chammars. Since, the Chammars could not draw water from the wells of the high castes or worship in their temples, they had obtained grants from the community development department to improve the wells in their hamlets and had built their own temple. Practice of untouchability had been declared an offence and was disappearing in both rural and urban areas. By 1961 representatives of all castes elected to the *Panchayat* of both Maanpur and Raipur sat together to conduct the business of the statutory *Panchayats*. Furthermore, men of all castes drank tea from the same two shops located in Maan Town market. The *Sarpanches* of both Raipur and Maanpur were from the high castes in 1961. By 2001, although the *Sarpanch* of the Maanpur *Panchayat* was a *Mahajan*, that of Raipur was a woman of the dhobi (washer man) caste. People of the high caste or the cultivators did not respect her but there was no petition pending with the Collector requesting her removal. In Maanpur also, there had been periods when a Meena occupied the post.

There has been large investment by the state government in appointing agricultural extension and veterinary officers; opening schools, hospitals and dispensaries, providing loans through cooperative societies and branches of nationalized banks located in both Maanpur and Raipur and the Land Mortgage Bank for current cultivation, for improvement of cropland or buying tractors, pump sets and other machines and building houses. At the same time, as their income has increased, the people have themselves made large investments in buying tractors, pump sets, and other machines and improved seed, fertilizers and pesticides. Large investment has been made by the state also in rural electrification and in construction of tube-wells for lifting water to overhead tanks, which supply drinking water to large numbers of homes in all these villages. The villagers have constructed the overhead tanks, which cost about Rs. 4 lakh each in Raipur and Maanpur and somewhat less in Bijaipur. This expenditure shows the value that they now attach to having adequate and safe drinking water.

These changes in lifestyle, attitudes, and political structures and in the desire of the government and political parties to empower people and realization that development of rural areas is an essential component for self-sustainable development exist. We have no doubt that the direction of development in the villages recorded above will proceed at much greater speed than witnessed during the last 40 years because massive development inputs of the past half a century have already started bringing out the desired results and with additional support and investment the area will experience exponential growth.

The above is a micro study of technological change in agriculture, rise in income and consumption of people of all castes, rise in social status of the scheduled castes and women and changes in inter-caste relations that have occurred over large areas of eastern Rajasthan, adjoining areas of western Madhya Pradesh and over large areas in several other states.

Sawai Madhopur: A Long Term Projection

The agricultural district of Sawai Madhopur has made enormous progress in the last 40 years. A similar progress was noticed in the Punjab village between 1963 and 1975. This book has chronicled the success of the community and the area. What do the next twenty years hold?

To answer this question, it becomes important to review the development process in other parts of India, as well as the development of farming communities in other parts of the world. After examining the developments of these regions, we will outline potential scenarios for Sawai Madhopur.

In India, the Punjabi farming communities have moved farthest along the development cycle. Agricultural development in Punjab is characterized by the following:

- Increasing agricultural productivity and rural wealth. This has led to increased capital outlays for larger farm machinery. As the farming activity has become more mechanized, labour requirements have declined.
- Movement of agricultural labour into the service sector. As labour needs declined, farm families have seen their sons become truck drivers, and other service workers. Many have immigrated to other parts of the world where they work in service occupations like taxi drivers, shop attendants, etc.
- The investment in larger farm machinery has often not paid off in high enough returns. Larger farm machinery, like combines,

requires large farms and the Punjabi farms are not large enough to take full advantage of the capabilities of the machinery. Many farmers have not been able to pay off their machinery loans and have lost their farms.

The farmers of Sawai Madhopur are likely to follow the same pattern as the Punjabi farmers. There is a tendency to over-invest, once the returns of initial investment become apparent. Eventually too many people make too many investments in the same thing and there is a winnowing out of the marginal producers. The remaining producers consolidate the farms into larger tracts and can make use of the efficiencies of large scale mechanization. If the experience of Punjab is repeated in Sawai Madhopur, there will be fewer farm families, larger farms and greater mechanization. The farmers, who succeed, will be more prosperous.

But it Need not be this Way

As mentioned in the Introduction the author had mused based on his review of the way farming has been organized in the United States, France and Japan and his projection of shapes of things to come in the villages studied by him that it need not be this way because the different structures supply us an alternative way to look at the future.

American farming is characterized by mega farms and a high level of automation. The food industry in the United States is homogenous and national. Farm produce, whether it is wheat, fowl or dairy are collected at central points, processed and distributed nationally. The chicken breast purchased in Maine are exactly the same as the chicken breasts purchased in Honolulu, and they are both packaged in a factory in Arkansas; same with cheese, milk, bread, etc. Scale brings efficiencies to the production of food and also allows national standards of cleanliness to be enforced. The food is cheap and good. But the food is the same everywhere and is neither as tasty nor as healthy as small batch food processing would allow it to be. As a result, there is now the emergence of local bakeries and food processors who service a local, more affluent clientele and fine dining restaurants. Locally grown tomatoes and herbs and lettuce are finding a preferred position in many restaurants; local (sometimes neighbourhood) bakeries are finding unexpected success because they can vary their offerings and experiment with different ingredients.

French farming has always maintained its local traditions. The local markets with fruits, vegetables and other farm products (jams, jellies, mustards, herbs, etc.) complement the local bakery and the local meat shop. Farm employment remains relatively high and vibrantly innovative. Recently, high priced French jams have been finding success in specialty food stores in the United States. While the food is more varied and innovative, healthier and tastier, the cost of the food is significantly higher. The French consumer is more than willing to pay the higher prices...after all he is French!

The farm sector in Japan has an interesting twist. Japanese farmers form a strong political block and have been able to have many protectionist laws passed. Japan is dotted with small inefficient rice farms and the farmers are protected by competition from other countries ("Japanese rice is just better than Chinese rice"). Due to the regulation of the market, the Japanese food market is neither as vibrant as the French market, nor as efficient and inexpensive as the American market. It is a politically driven market.

We would recommend that the farmers of Sawai Madhopur or Punjab do not ask the politician for help in safeguarding their farms.

It is clear that the Indian food market is beginning to be dominated by large scale national and international food processors. The American model of food production and distribution will eventually be the way the Indian market is organized. We do not have the cultural snobbery or affinity to local produce that the French have; our industrialists have also shown an unseemly adeptness to manipulate the political system to their own uses, so the Japanese model is unlikely here.

However, India is a much more varied society than America and there will be a better possibility of regional producers of particular products to flourish. In the case of Sawai Madhopur, the area has been found to be exceptionally suitable for the growing of guavas. Additionally, there is a local sweet called *rabri* for which the area is famous. Proper branding of these products would lead to the movement of farming from commodity products to higher margin products. A guava canning factory, a Tiger brand of guava juice with extra protein, Sawai Madhopur *rabri* are all possibilities.

There will continue to be a viable farming community in Sawai Madhopur—many people will continue to produce commodity items for sale to large food processors, and there will be some local products which may find regional or national fame.

It is clear, however, that many farmers will not be able to survive. The children of the farmers will move to cities, many will enter service industries like trucking and retailing. In order for the children to continue to progress and become wealthier, it is crucial that they are educated and trained. Higher education results in greater individual productivity, which means increasing wealth.

There is one unique thing about Sawai Madhopur which separates it from many other villages in India. It is the location of one of three forest reserves for the endangered Bengal tiger. The Bengal tiger is a magnificent species and has caught the fancy of conservation groups around the world; it is one of three "glamour endangered species", the other two being whales and the bald eagle.

It would be to the benefit of Sawai Madhopur to establish itself as a centre for tiger research. This will bring in good service jobs to the area, as well as increase the level of education for the local population. As tiger research increases and the number of tigers increase, there will be a larger number of tourists visiting the Ranthambore Forest Reserve which will lead to more jobs in the tourist industry.

If the local or state government establishes a plan to purchase the farms of bankrupt farmers to expand the Ranthambore Forest Reserve, the economic development of the area will be assured. We will then have come full circle—from 1961 when the Chammars wanted to cut the forest so that they could have cultivable land, to 2010, when farms will be given back to the forest and to the tiger, so that people from around the world can visit and see it. Sawai Madhopur has a rare resource in the tiger and the forest; the development of the area and the wealth of its people will be most benefited by the conservation of the forest and its expansion. Who could have imagined that in 1961.

Footnotes

1. The word *panchayat* is being used for various types of institutions—statutory village *panchayats*, traditional institutions of castes (caste *panchayats*) or villages; sometimes even for *ad hoc* meetings of caste or villagers, called on a particular occasion e.g. to decide a particular dispute. In this book, unless the context indicates otherwise, the word has been used only to mean statutory *panchayats*.
2. Otalan is the village in Punjab, which the author studied in 1963 and revisited it in 1975. (See chapters 10-12 in this Volume).

Annexure 8.1
RAJASTHAN: A STATE STUDY

Swedish International Development Agency (SIDA)

This is a compilation of statistics about Rajasthan and its various districts with detailed explanatory notes on the tables. The coverage is exhaustive because all sectors of the economy from per capita income and incidence of poverty to agriculture and animal husbandry are covered. The social sectors include total population; its growth rate during 1981-91, literacy rates among males and females and health status of the population. There are a large number of small black and white maps, showing boundaries of various districts besides a large number of tables. All the tables have explanatory notes on them. About half of the tables give aggregates about Rajasthan while others give district-wise details on the subject of the tables. The explanatory notes explain that the Rajasthan government has made successful efforts in several areas such as:

(i) Increasing production of milk in northern Rajasthan and organizing milk producers' cooperatives on the pattern of Amul dairy in Gujarat in order to supply milk to Delhi, Jaipur and other towns;

(ii) Increasing production of meat by improving breeds of sheep. The owners of both the bovine and ovine animals are given instructions on preventive diseases of cows and sheep and given regular injections to all the stock in case of outbreak of a disease, and

(iii) Promoting tourism by successful advertising and increasing facilities for stay of foreign and Indian tourists to places of pleasure and religious tourism—Jaipur, Udaipur and Jaisalmer (pleasure tourism) and Ajmer, Ranakpur and Mt. Abu (religious tourism).

The emphasis in various Five Year Plans has changed from projects aimed at increasing agricultural output to industrial development, improvement of infrastructures especially by building roads and poverty alleviation programmes. Emphasis on increase in agricultural output continues.

Among the cities in Rajasthan, none except small percentages of the populations in Jaipur, Jodhpur and Udaipur have access to piped water supply with the result that easily preventable diseases such as malaria, diarrhoea, dysentery and tuberculosis are common. This, despite a large network of primary health centres at the community development block level, hospitals at district headquarters and a large number of private practitioners in the cities. The most disease prone areas have been indicated.

The literacy rate is very low. In 1991, only 20 per cent of the females and 55 per cent of the males were literate. There is great difference in the literacy rate between urban and rural areas. In urban areas 65 per cent of the population was literate in 1991, in rural areas it was only 39 per cent. However, even these dismal figures indicate a great improvement over the situation in 1951 when only 9 per cent of the population was literate. Despite this progress, the figure for the state is much lower than the all India average of about 40 per cent. However, life expectancy at birth is close to the all India average, so is child mortality. The family planning programme has not been too successful. Average number of births per woman is 4.6 compared to 3.6 for all India.

Rajasthan remains a backward State despite efforts of the government and NGO's to increase agricultural production, literacy, percentage of children going to school and improve health and productivity of the population. This is due primarily to environmental constraints. Two examples illustrate this. Almost half of the area of the State is desert or semi-desert and is visited by severe drought in one or two years out of every three. In the drought years, all efforts of the government are directed towards providing food and water to people in the drought-affected areas and fodder for their livestock. Despite large expenditure by the government and large financial assistance from the central government, thousands of people and tens of thousands of animals die. More than ten per cent of the area in the south is hilly and is inhabited by tribal who are very backward. Economic development in this area is difficult and efforts aimed at it have not yielded quick results. Two reasons for this are: bureaucratic delays and misappropriation of funds by officials and the politicians in-charge of expenditure of the programme. The latter is indicated by a recent incident when the tribal attacked those who were in-charge of distributing funds for their development in Rajsamund (*The Economist*, London, January 13-19, 2001 pp. 29-39).

Beginning with a project to reduce incidence of guinea worm in Udaipur division to improvement of water supply in villages of the division in the mid 1980s, SIDA has undertaken a number of projects to promote economic and social development in Rajasthan. This book is a part of the effort.

Special Acknowledgements

We are grateful to Dr. Giri and the three researchers who accompanied him along with Kamla Nath and conducted the resurvey. We are grateful to the Collector of Sawai Madhopur, Mr. P.K. Goel, who arranged for stay of Mrs. Nath and 3 researchers led by Dr. D.K. Giri in the circuit house in Maan Town. Our thanks go next to Mr. Bijai Singh, who has retired after long years of work as a messenger in the collector's office including two years with Dr. Nath. He arranged our travel to the villages, to the game sanctuary and the Ranthambhore Fort by jeep. We are grateful to Mr. Fateh Singh of Tiger Watch, who was the game warden in the game sanctuary in 1961. He spent hours with us in the sanctuary, providing valuable information about the number of tigers and other wild animals and birds in the sanctuary.

Our thanks go next to Messrs. Sham Lal Sharma and Suraj Bhan Singh the ex-*sarpanches* of Raipur and Maanpur respectively. Both were the *Sarpanches* (Presidents) of the *Panchayats* of their villages for several years. Mr. Sharma, who was *Sarpanch* of Raipur in 1961, was a most enthusiastic informant of Dr. Nath about his village. He literally forced him to study the village by showing him the various development works that the *Panchayat* was doing under his leadership. This time both the ex-*sarpanches* spent hours with us explaining the changes in the economy of the villages and in inter-caste relations during the last 40 years. Furthermore, they sent detailed replies to our questions, information in great detail on topics which had been left uncovered during our discussions. Mr. Heera Lal Meena, the leader of village Bijaipur, who is now a clerk in the office of the BDO made a similar contribution for his village.

Dr. Nath could not participate in the fieldwork for reasons of health, but has provided detailed notes interpreting the results of the field study on the basis of the information provided by the research team and relating them to conditions in 1961. This draft is the result of our joint effort. We are of course fully responsible for any errors in it.

SECTION B
Economic Development and Social Change in the Punjab

9

Farming Communities in the Irrigated Areas of Western Punjab (Pakistan)*

Economic Development and Social Change in the Punjab

Introduction

During the last few years attention has begun to be directed towards differential progress in agriculture in different parts of the country. It is becoming increasingly clear that while in some areas agriculture has begun to display considerable dynamism, its progress in other areas is still very slow. Identification of the factors—physical, economic and social—which contribute to these differences in progress is important for understanding the dynamics of agricultural progress. Case studies of villages of especially rapid or slow progress is a fruitful method of identifying these factors because the sharp contrasts between the two situations bring out these factors prominently. Moreover, the case study method by describing change in different aspects of the economy and social life of the selected village makes it possible to bring out the inter-relationship between these. The author had studied his own village—Jhawaria—in west Punjab, now in Pakistan during his several visits to the village from Lahore (where he lived and was a student in school and college) in the 1940s, to spend his summer holidays and to attend marriages and births in the extended family. He wrote about the socio-economic composition of the village and land use and work patterns in the village as part of his application for a Witbeck scholarship in 1946. The essay was later published in *American Geographer*. We include the essay as part of his studies in technological change in agriculture in the Punjab. The study captures the effects of canal and well irrigation on the income and standard of living of the farmers.

---

* Written in 1946 and published in *American Geographer*;........exact data of publication not available.

Later in the 1960s he studied three villages in Sawai Madhopur district of Eastern Rajasthan during his stay there as Collector in 1961-62. Sawai Madhopur is one of the backward district in one of the then most backward states of the country. The villages selected were, however, less undeveloped than the many in the district because of nearness to the town and a cement factory. The author's interest in making a comparative study of more progressive rural areas in one of the fast developing State—Punjab—led him to select Jitpur a village in central Punjab for the 1960s study (Chapter 6).

This study of a village in Central Punjab, an area which has experienced rapid technological change in agriculture and economic progress had been undertaken with these objects in view. It describes the various changes in agriculture experienced by the village, the inter-action between these, the shape of the agricultural enterprise and of the village after the improve practices advocated by extension workers have been largely adopted and, finally, the problems which agricultural progress and relative prosperity created. Although the study is focused on change in agriculture, progress in other directions—health, education, transport and communications and levels of living—has also been described. A major conclusion emerging from the study is that change in agriculture is part of a larger process of social and economic change, as a result of which the complexion of the village and the character of village life are changing rapidly and a 'New Village' is emerging; hence the main heading. It is hoped that this study will be followed by case studies of slow progress in agriculture in north India and studies of both slow and rapid progress in other parts of the country so that the dynamics of agricultural progress are more adequately understood*.

This study is based on a three weeks' stay in 1963 in village Jitpur of Ludhiana district of Central Punjab. This is a comparatively large, multi-caste, village with a population of about 1850. A village of this size was selected in order to observe the effects of change in agriculture and of economic progress on cultivators as well as non-cultivators and especially to see how far the latter had contributed to these changes and had benefited from them.

* The author had studied three villages in 1961 in one of the most backward areas in a then one of the backward states, Rajasthan. Analysis of data of the study on several socio-economic aspects of the Rajasthan villages have been included in Chapter 1-8 in this volume.

A major part of the study consisted of discussions with individuals and groups of cultivators about agricultural techniques and seeing the improved practices and devices at work. Several group discussions in which anybody from the village could participate were held. In addition individual interviews were held with the *Sarpanch* of the village *Panchayat*, the Chairman and the Secretary of the service co-operative, the Manager of the seed and fertilizer depot, the Village Level Worker (VLW), the *Patwari*, a few progressive farmers (on their farms), some Harijan leaders, one of the two fabricators of agricultural implements, and one young man who does electrical installation work in the village.

Data on demographic characteristics land-holdings and economic activity were collected for all households in the village through a household census. More detailed data on agricultural operations of medium-sized cultivators (those having holdings between 8-14 acres) and on employment and earnings of the *Harijans* were collected on a sample basis. Ten families of medium-sized cultivators and ten of *Harijans* were included in the sample. The object of the survey of the cultivators was to obtain a closer acquaintance with their farm operations and to obtain an approximate idea of their levels of production and income. It was also useful in seeing how far improvements like use of chemical fertilizers, for which data on consumption for the block and the village were given by the block staff, were being followed by these cultivators. The sample survey of the *Harijans* was intended to obtain a more precise idea of their level of income.

Besides work in this village, several other villages in the Block were visited in order to see other noteworthy developments. One of these villages had a successful co-operative milk producers' society supplying milk to the Government Dairy at the State capital. Another had a number of progressive farmers settled in a garden colony, which is one of several such colonies established in the Punjab in the post-Partition years. Detailed discussions about agricultural progress and extension activities were held with the Block Development Officer and other members of the Block extension staff, and later with the Pilot Project Officer of the 'Package Programme', and a few specialists at the Punjab Agricultural University, Ludhiana. I am indebted to all these people, and especially to the BDO and his staff who had to spend considerable time with me, for their assistance in this study. The 'New Village', was resurveyed in 1976 after the Green Revolution and findings of the resurvey are given in chapter 11.

THE CULTURE OF FARMING COMMUNITIES IN THE IRRIGATED AREAS OF WESTERN PUNJAB (1946)

Introduction

India is a country of small farmers and small villages. About 75 per cent of the people are farmers and village is the typical form of rural settlement in most parts of the country. An Indian village is a collection of huts or small houses, all made of wood, straw, leaves, mud, brick or any other material which might be locally available. The fields of the farmers radiate out from the village. Most of these fields are very small. The average holding varies from 3 to 10 acres of cultivated land in different parts of the country; and this holding is seldom in one contiguous block. It is composed of several scattered tiny plots[1]. As in most old agricultural countries farming in India, is not a commercial enterprise, but a way of living. Perhaps the most important characteristic of this way of living was the organization of production with the village as a self-sufficing unit. Family and social relationships, customs, traditions, religion and even the outlook on life have been deeply influenced by the agricultural way of life and the economic organization which accompanied it.

Division of labour was fairly well developed in the Indian village. Each village (or group of villages) had its own weavers, carpenters, smiths, shoemakers, bakers, butchers, barbers, oil pressmen and other craftsmen. All these artisans[2] worked for the farmers and were paid at the time of the harvest. This payment was supplemented by gifts at festivals, marriages and other ceremonies. The artisans made their huts on the landowners' land, and were often allotted plots of land to cultivate for fodder for their animals (usually pair of oxen or a milch-buffalo). They furnished the extra-help needed at seedtime, harvest and other busy periods. The artisans did not enjoy the same status as the landowners. But they were not serfs. If they were dissatisfied they could move out.

This may be called a barter-economy, but there was a very strong element of benevolent paternalism in it. Every community had to take care that its artisans were satisfied and well off. If they were not, that would lower the community in the estimation of neighbouring communities. Prestige was the regulator of conduct.

Besides these artisans, there was one (or more) shopkeeper in the village. He handled the commerce as well as the credit (lent money hence often called money-lender). He was often, a very important person, because he was better educated and informed, and his advice was frequently sought in important matters. Local disputes were resolved by the village council of elders. There was the general belief that when five elders sat down for a decision God came among them to guide them, and an unjust decision was therefore, not possible. In general, age was a fairly strong claim to respect and prestige.

The system rested on faith in God, and on mutual confidence. Esteem, "Face" (*Ijjat*), and traditional loyalties were more important than pecuniary gain. It is not implied that there were no frictions and frustrations. There was at times, exploitation, by the elders, by the money-lenders, by the priests. But on the whole, the system worked fairly well. It helped preserve the economic and social independence of the people through the political disorders which were frequent.

The system was a natural response to the times when communication and transportation was extremely difficult; and travel was slow and hazardous. Trade had to be kept at a minimum; and was generally limited to salt, spices and a few other necessaties which could not be produced locally. The only other contacts with the outside world were through pilgrimage and through payment of land revenue (in kind) to the ruler. The latter in turn, gave protection or lack of it, depending upon his way of ruling, and his power. British rule has revolutionized this more or less stable socio-economic structure. With the introduction of centralized administration, and compulsory payment of land revenue in cash, construction of railways and roads, making trade and travel quick, cheap and safe, and with the introduction of machine made goods, with which the products of the local artisans cannot compete, the old system has broken down. Money and not custom has become more and more, the regulator of economic relationships.

The old status systems, based on caste (occupation), ownership of land, age and sex are rapidly losing their significance. The high value put on family and community loyalty, on custom and tradition, is giving place to the emphasis on making money.

The transformation is by no means complete. The traditional structure still exists, but its foundations are crumbling, and unless there is a swing of public sentiment or policy in the other direction, its collapse is only a matter of time.

I feel that any description of the culture of the present day India cannot but emphasize the rapid change which that culture is undergoing. The agricultural communities of the irrigated plains of Western Punjab offer an excellent illustration of this process. In the Western Punjab plains, agricultural settlements along the rivers date back to ancient times. But they were confined to the vicinity of the rivers, and the remaining area was sparsely settled. The construction of canals, (between 1890 and 1933) made agricultural settlement possible over most of this area. It was settled by a definite land policy adopted by the British Government. Most of the land was "Crown Land" (Equivalent of American "Public Domain"). It was disposed of by sale, but care was taken that big landlords or businessmen did not get large blocks of it. Settlement on family-size-farms (about 25 acres) was encouraged by direct gifts to veterans of First World War and other settlers and by instalment-payment-plans. The prices charged were lower than the value of land was estimated to be. The native population was supplemented by immigration of veterans and settlers from the densely populated districts of Eastern Punjab. These settlements are called "Canal Colonies".

The settlement meant quite a change for the settlers. The natives had to change from their grazing, dry farming or well-irrigation methods to canal-irrigation-agriculture. The immigrants had not only to change their techniques, but also to adapt themselves to a new area. They all had to fit themselves into the pattern already laid for them. The fields, roads, villages, towns, were built according to plan. Water rights, rates, land-revenue etc. had been determined before the settlers arrived. They had the benefit of a fairly active Agriculture Department to help them choose crops suited to the area, and adopt modern methods of farming and marketing. They were settled in villages, and along with them settled the artisans, shopkeepers and priests. But the idea was not to develop self-sufficing communities but to develop a type of agriculture which would be half way between purely commercial agriculture (as prevails in parts of U.S.A., for example) and the old Indian self-sufficient economy. Although village was still to remain a producing unit, money was to be an integral part of the economy. Land revenue, water rates, new seeds, implements and manufactured goods had to be paid for. Crops therefore, must be sold in the market.

In this area, therefore, we find two distinct types of settlement—the new canal colony settlements and the old settlements along the rivers. The former are characterized by their bigger, rectilinear fields; straight irrigation ditches and roads; villages and towns with broad straight streets, wide squares, and a general air of orderliness and neatness. The latter can be distinguished by smaller, haphazardly divided fields; winding roads; large number of wells; old towns and villages with narrow, crooked streets and a less orderly, if more picturesque appearance. Both are experiencing the socio-economic changes described above, only the former are farther along the road towards modernization than the latter.

Location of the Area

The observations made in this paper apply (with minor variations) to the area bounded by the rivers Jhelum and Satluj, and a line drawn North-South just east of the city of Lahore. These boundaries are arbitrary, like any other. But they are satisfactory for our purpose. They define fairly well the area where canal colony settlement has been best developed during the last half a century.

To the north and west of the Jhelum there is virtually no canal irrigation yet.[3] To the South of the Satluj, canal colonies have been developed since 1933. But the greater proximity of the area to the Indian desert (*Thar*) and different culture of the people induced me to keep the Satluj as the boundary. The least satisfactory boundary is perhaps, the eastern. Here, there is no sharp line, but a somewhat narrow transitional zone. To the east of this zone, the country takes quite a different aspect. It is more humid (less arid), agriculture with the help of well-irrigation, was fairly well developed over most of the cultivable land, before the canals were constructed. Among the people, Hindus and Sikhs constitute the majority. The Mohammedans are in a minority. Nearly all this area now forms part of the Dominion of India, while the West Punjab area, is all a part of the Dominion of Pakistan.

Within the West Punjab canal colonies, Lyallpur District shows the highest development of canal colony culture.

Ecological Factors

Topography and Soils

Topographically, the area is very much like the rest of the Indo-Gangetic plain—a level to undulating plain formed by the alluvium brought by the rivers[4] from the Himalayas. In this area, however, a greater proportion of the alluvium is "young alluvium" (as contrasted with "old alluvium") than is the case in most of the Ganges Plain. The young alluvium is much less leeched, and therefore, more fertile than the old alluvium. Along the rivers, soils are continually renewed by floods.

Small remnants of an old mountain chain rise from the plains as low hills. They occupy only a small area and have no economic significance.

Climate

The climate is warm continental, sub-humid to arid. Summers are hot. June is thc hottest month with mean temperatures over 90°F over most of the area. (Lahore 93°F). At most stations the mean maximum temperatures for the three hot season months May, June and July exceed 100°F. Winters are cool. January is the coolest month with mean temperatures round 55°F (Lahore 54.7°F. Multan 56.5°F).

The average annual rainfall varies from over 30" (Sialkot 31.0") in the northeast to less than 10" (Multan 7.2") in the Southwest. Over most of the area it ranges between 12-18". As in most areas of low rainfall, variability from year to year is very high (30-40"). About 2/3 of the rain comes in the three months of the summer monsoon—July, August, September. Most of the remainder comes in light showers, with the cyclonic storms which enter the area from the northwest and west in winter and early spring. There are three well recognized seasons—the Hot Season—April to June; the Rainy Season—July to October and the Cool Season—November to March. Frosts are rare and two crops a year are the rule.

Natural Vegetation

The natural vegetation is largely bunch grass and thorny scrub, intersperse with acacia. Along the rivers are stands of open forest of broadleaf trees.

Land Use

In the old 'river settlements', irrigation was practiced by wells or overflow canals. The over-flow canals brought water to the fields only when the water level in the rivers was high (rainy season, generally). In the low water season, the fields were irrigated by shallow wells, worked by oxen (Persian wheels). The limits of this type of agriculture were formed by the distance to which the water of the river could be carried by the overflow canals, and the distance up to which the water tube was high enough to make well irrigation practicable. It varied in different parts of the area, from less than a mile to more than 10 miles depending upon the amount of rainfall and level of the river relative to that of the plain. It fluctuated from year to year with the level of water in the rivers at the high-water season which in turn depended on the rainfall in the mountains.

The new irrigation canals have been constructed by controlling the waters of the rivers by dams at suitable points. Somewhat over 5 million acres have been brought under cultivation, by this means, in this area. This extension of the limits of agriculture is probably the most remarkable expansion of this kind in India in recent times[5]. The physical conditions were peculiarly favourable to this development. The major streams are snow fed and have sufficient water throughout the year to make perennial irrigation possible. Gradients in the alluvial plains are low and water can be easily carried by gravity canals.

Crops

Crops, in India, are officially divided into two groups:

(a) Cool season (Rabi) crops.
(b) Warm season (Kharif) crops.

I have found this division useful, and have maintained it in this discussion.

(a) Cool Season Crops

Wheat is the principal crop in this group. It is the principal grain crop, and the staple grain in the area. It is one of the two major cash crops (cotton is the other); and it is an important source of fodder. Some wheat is cut green for fodder. Wheat straw is perhaps as important in the diet of the farmers' animals as the grain is in his own.

Wheat is sown in October and November. Shortly, after the last monsoon rains, and just as the cool season is beginning. It continues to grow rather slowly till January, with the rapid rise in temperatures in February and March, it matures quickly and is ready for harvesting about the first week of April.

Barley and Gram are the two other grain crops in this season. The latter is principally a grain for livestock. Both can tolerate poorer, sandier soils, and a shortage of water better than can wheat.

Among the fodder crops grown in this season, the most important are Lucerne, alfalfa and other hay crops, and turnips. Turnips have been grown in the Punjab for quite a long time, but Lucerne, Alfalfa and other hays have been only recently introduced. They have however, expanded very rapidly, because they give high yields (six cuttings of Lucerne are not uncommon) and because they provide green forage between March and June when no other green is available, and when the farmer's stock of wheat-straw is low. (New straw is not ready before May, and the previous years' supply is almost exhausted).

Warm Season Crops

Among these cotton is the most important. The variety grown is mostly "Punjab-American" (locally called "*Narma*"). This is a variety evolved by crossbreeding native Punjab cotton with the American upland variety. It has been very successful on irrigated farms. It yields a longer finer fibre (7/8" to 1") which is highly prized because most of the other Indian cottons are coarse and of short staple (5/8" to ¾").

Cotton is sown late in May or early in June, a few weeks before the beginning of the monsoon rains. Picking begins in late November and lasts till the end of January. Cotton is almost entirely a cash crop.

Rice is also grown at this season, but acreage is small, and is mainly confined to the more humid north-eastern parts of the area.

Maize, Sorghum (*Juar*) and Millet (*Bajra*) are the three principal fodder crops of this season. All the maize, and nearly all the sorghum is cut green for feeding. Millet, however, is important also as a grain crop. It is the poor man's grain. Maize is more important in the more humid eastern section. Sorghum and millets become more important as we go westwards.

Wheat, cotton and fodder crops are thus, the principal crops of the area. There is more emphasis on fodder crops in this area than in most parts of India. The animals (oxen, buffaloes and cows) are about the best and strongest that can be found anywhere in the country. They come from good breeds that were developed mostly along the rivers, (the Sahiwal breeds developed along the Ravi are most famous) and the farmers take pride in their livestock. The above order, bullocks, buffaloes, cows, reflects their relative importance (in descending order). Oxen are most important. Ploughing and most of the other work around the farm is done with their help. The male buffalo is also used for this purpose. But he cannot stand the summer heat as well, and farmers feel that he is less intelligent, more stubborn and more difficult to manage. The female buffalo, however, is much more important as a milk producer than the cow. Her average milk yield is 50-100 per cent greater than that of the average cow. Her milk has a high fat content (about 6%). Most farmers (farmers' wives rather) supplement their cash earnings by selling Ghee (butter heated to eliminate whey and moisture).

The Agriculture Department has done some of its best work in this area. Most of the crops are grown from seed originally developed at the experiment stations. Cotton and hays have been mentioned above. The same is true of wheat. The experiment Station varieties have almost replaced the old hard, small brown varieties. The former give higher yields, and because they look better (the grain is bigger and whiter) they fetch better prices.

Work Rhythms

I have found it most convenient to start with April. Harvesting of wheat begins about the first week of April, and the operations connected with it (cutting, thrashing, winnowing) continue till the latter part of May. This is the busiest time of the year and is full of considerable anxiety. Thunderstorms are quite common at this time. The farmer wants to get the grain in his grain-house and the straw in his storage pit as soon as possible. The wheat would not spoil if left standing for sometime, after it is mature. But once cutting is started, all the operations must be completed as rapidly as possible. If a thunderstorm comes when the thrashed wheat is lying on the ground (waiting to be winnowed) it may blow away most of the straw and the farmer may also lose a portion of the grain (by soaking in the ground). The village artisan works with farmers in the fields. Neighbourly help is quite common too. It is customary to invite neighbours and friends to do the cutting. The men work in the field all day (often the Mirasi or professional entertainer is in attendance with his drum or a string instrument). At dinner everybody is fed by the hostess with Ghee and Shakkar (purified butter and sugar, a combination which is considered quite a delicacy when eaten with chapattis or unleavened wheat bread).

Of course, the operations are done by the traditional hand methods. Wheat is cut by the scythe, thrashed by making the oxen trample over it, and winnowed with a basket. The work is slow and hard but is quite picturesque.

Planting of cotton begins about the latter half of May and lasts through early June. If the farmer is not growing cotton, he may plant fodder crops at this time. These latter take only two months to be ready for cutting. They can, therefore, be planted at any time between May and August. Millet is planted somewhat later than the others. At this time also farmers begin to prepare the land for the cool season crops.

Monsoon rains begin about the first week of July. Before that time, the farmer must make sure that every thing is in good order and able to stand the rain—that his house is in good repair, and will keep him dry (most of the houses are of mud, and require constant care); that his grain-house and storage pit will keep the grain and straw from getting wet.

By the end of July, the most pressing tasks are over. Wheat has been harvested, cotton and fodder has been planted, cotton given one or two weeding, and the land to the cool season crops given a few ploughings. If the rains are good, the need for irrigation is also not so urgent. There is generally sufficient new grass around the farm for the animals. The farmer can afford to relax. August is therefore a month of comparative leisure. Marriages, *Kabbaddi* (a local game) and wrestling bouts, *Kawwallis* (somewhat resembling a musical meeting) take place at this time.

The height of the monsoon is over by the middle of September. More attention has to be given to irrigation, and to the preparation of land for cool season crops. Planting of these crops begins in the first half of October and continues through November. Millet for grain is also harvested at this time. (Rice somewhat earlier in late September and early October). Wheat planting time is again a busy time, but not as busy as the wheat harvesting period. After the farmer has done the planting he is ready to take his turn at malaria, if he has not done so early. Malaria is very common from September through November, and in certain years few escape it.

Cotton picking begins about the middle of November. This is the time for the artisans' wives to work in the fields. There is not much rush however, because this is dry season, and unless there is an unusually heavy storm (in late December or January) there is little danger of cotton being spoiled. Irrigation of fall-sown crops continues in this period. Water in the rivers is low, and the need greatest (the winter showers have not arrived yet). Thefts of water and disputes over its use are most common at this time.

The farmer looks at the winter showers as a gift from God. The amount of rainfall is small (about 5" at most stations) but it comes in light showers and is considered very beneficial for the crops. Of course it provides welcome relief to the oxen in the "river settlements" and to men in the canal irrigation areas.

February and March are months of comparative leisure. Winter fodder crops are harvested for livestock and land is prepared for summer crops. Of course irrigation continues. This is the time when the farmers sell their cotton, settle their disputes (go to courts) get their implements and their bodies ready. As some farmers say, "they build their reserve for the strenuous days ahead".

Institutions

Land Tenure Systems

Both peasant proprietorship and sharecropper system are common. In the latter the cultivator supplies labour, stock, seed, and implements. The landowner supplies the land and water rights, pays land revenue and water rates. The produce is shared half and half (with variations). There are a few large farms which are run by managers. Land revenue is the oldest tax in India, and even today, the most important. In the Punjab, it is collected in two instalments, after the harvesting of the two major crops. The village headman is responsible for payment from the whole village, but assessment is on individual basis. The District Magistrate (the head of the District Government) is also the District Revenue officer, a clear indication of the importance of the tax. In every village there are one or more *Patwaris* (assessors and record keepers) whose job is to record the crops planted in each field, and yields (good, bad or fair) for purposes of future assessment. The *Patwari* is a very important officer. But his position becomes precarious, when two powerful factions claim the same piece of land, or there is some dispute over water rights.

Religion

Religion is the most powerful institution. Most of the farmers are Mohammedans. A considerable proportion of the immigrants from Eastern Punjab are Sikhs, who have settled mostly in separate communities. All the districts have a Mohammedans' majority. The Hindus are mostly traders, and most of them live in the towns and larger villages.

The *Quoran* orders five prayers a day. I do not believe that the majority of the farmers get to perform all five every day, but they all consider it a very worthy ideal and try to pray as often as they can. On my evening walks, I would often see a farmer stop by an irrigation ditch, take off his shoes, wash his hands and feet and start praying with his face towards the setting sun. They are also quite particular about observing *Ramazan*. In this month the devotees cannot eat or drink or smoke when the sun is in the sky. Because the Mohammedans follow the lunar year, their festivals circulate through the year. I am not a Mohammedan, and cannot hope to understand their feelings, but it seems to me that observance of Ramazan must be extremely difficult when it falls in summer. Going without food or drink for 14 or 15 hours, in the middle of the Punjab summers with temperatures rising to about 110°F (or more), almost every day, is no mean performance, especially when it has to be done for 30 days consecutively.

The high percentage of *Ramazan* fasts that are observed is an eloquent tribute to the religious devotion of the people.

Religious festivals are the times of greatest festivity. Many of the most popular fairs are held at the shrine of some religious saints. These fair are a unique sight. Crowds of villagers, townsmen and entertainers, mostly booths and stores, sweet meat shops, cheap novelty stores, joy rides, gambling houses, quacks selling their cure-alls with eloquent speeches—there is a peculiar air of excitement around them. It is not unusual to find villagers walking 10-20 miles to see a fair. The Agriculture Department and other welfare agencies have made good use of these fairs. New implements, seeds and farming methods are demonstrated. Livestock shows are held. Methods of controlling and preventing common diseases, or co-operative living, and modern hygienic practices are taught by exhibitions and lectures.

Drinking, eating pork and music are forbidden by *Quoran*. Of the three the second is considered the worst. Even bringing pork in a village where Muslims are in a majority is to invite trouble. The taboo against drinking has not altogether eliminated the use of liquor. Mohammedans drink, but drinking is not common and there are few habitual drinkers. Marriages and other festive occasions (not religious festivals though!) are the times when most people drink, if they ever do. Sikhs drink much more than either Mohammedans or Hindus. They are not allowed to smoke and hence compensate by drinking.

Music and Dancing

The injunction against music and dancing has hampered the development of folk music and dancing. These have become the special faculty of *mirasis*—a caste of professional entertainers. The *mirasi's* services are generally required at marriages and other festivities and at harvest time. Most *mirasis* work in the fields or have some other occupation besides their main job. Religious music figures prominently among the Hindus and Sikhs. Almost every temple of any size has some musical instruments and religious courses are quite frequent. Folk dances are common at Sikh festivals. The standard of performance is not high. The Punjabis (Muslim, Sikh or Hindu) do not look upon dancing as an accomplishment which a cultured young gentleman or lady must acquire. It is looked upon as a business of entertainers—to be enjoyed once in a while but not to be practiced.

Of the folk songs that have grown out of this area the most famous is the story of Heer Ranjah—the tragic love of Heer, the daughter of a wealthy land-lord for Ranjah, a poor cow-herd. A few verses of this famous story are an essential part of the extra-curricular education which the village boy gets as he grows up. A shrine commemorates the site of the tragedy and a fair is held there every year in honour of the heroic lovers.

Education

Most of the people are illiterate. The mosque and the temple are the old schools. But their use is limited, especially that of the mosque because the Mohammedans scripture (*Quorran*) is in Arabic and every one cannot hope to read it. (The Sikh scriptures are in Punjabi and easy to follow).

The schools established by the District Boards are fairly well patronized—when we consider that children have often to walk two or three miles to get to a school. The turnover in schools is very high, and few pupils go beyond the fourth grade. There is a general feeling among the farmers that education does not help the boys do farm work better. There is considerable justification for this feeling. Most of the boys who go to high school or college do not wish to return to their farms. They go to town and get a job, and are lost as far as farm-work is concerned. Also education is mostly academic, and very little has been done to relate it to the farmer's problems. Of late some efforts have been made to teach farmers' boys better methods of farming, but much more remains to be done.

Community Life

The community clubhouse is the headman's *Dera*—a raised platform with a roof, but generally no walls. Here the farmers come to discuss the village politics, and their common problems. On the Mohammedans' *Dera* a fire for the smoking pipe is always burning, and sharing the smoking pipe is considered a sign of fraternity. The newspaper is the modern addition to the *Dera*. The number of newspaper fans increased considerably during the war.

The other places of communal gatherings are the Mosque and the Temple. Religious sermons and often-formal political speeches are made here. The priests have a strong hold upon the people, especially the Mohammedans priests. Party spirit is quite well developed, especially among the older river settlements. From the names of the villages and the names of their inhabitants it appears that each village was originally settled by one or two families (or tribes). These old family or tribal affiliations are quite strong, and play an important part in local politics.

Party fights are common. They often lead to stick-fights (sometimes murders) and costly and often ruinous litigation. Land rights, water rights and women are the most common causes of these disputes.

The most powerful man in the village is the headman (*Lambardar*). His authority is recognized in official circles. He is responsible for payment of land revenue and maintenance of law and order in the village. In larger villages there are several headmen. Every villager has to be in good graces of the headman. They are big landlords or have strong backing to begin with, and the official recognition which they get further increases their power. The village and area officials (the *Patwari*, Police Constables and Sub-Inspectors) seldom, go against the headmen. They are mighty little despots in their limited areas.

Changing Institutions

As we have said earlier, the self-sufficiency of the village has broken down, and the breakdown is more complete in the canal colonies than in the older "river settlements". Motorbuses, trucks, railroads, and highways have made trade and travel, quick and cheap. The villagers can go to town very easily and can afford to do their shopping there. The articles in the stores in town are more attractive and there is an infinitely larger variety. The village weaver can probably make only coarse cotton cloth, and the dyer may be able to dye only a few colours. The farmer's wife would have to spin the cotton herself, exchange the yarn for cloth with the weaver, wait till the cloth is made, and then take it to the dyer for dying. It may take a month before the thing is ready. In stead, she can go to town and buy a fine print for no more and frequently less than what it costs to get the cloth made locally; and she does not have to do the spinning or wait for a month.

The village potter can make only earthen pots. He cannot make the shiny glass and porcelain ware. But there must be a few of these in farmer's house, because the neighbours next door have them, and they look so pretty and modern. After all, every housewife wants to keep with the times.

The village *Mirasi* presents the same old songs and the same old jokes every time. Movies are much more fun and they are always different.

The radio has interesting programmes, including "farm programmes" and latest news. "When we listen to the radio we don't require the *mirasi*, and we get the latest market reports so the village shop keeper cannot take advantage of us"

The above examples have been given to throw light on some of the motives which are bringing about the rapid change towards commercialization.

Canals, improved seeds, implements, and new medicines have demonstrated that there is a lot to be learned from the new education "which is coming from the town", that the traditional lore is not sufficient. The younger generation feels that the elders do not fully appreciate the significance of the new ideas. They (the younger people) do not have implicit faith in the wisdom of their elders any longer. The joint family system, based on obedience to elders, is thus deprived of its very foundation.

Conclusion

Not all the results of this growing individualism have been good. Under the old system the villagers took care of their affairs themselves. They did not depend on outsiders, and therefore could not be exploited by outsiders. Communal good (as the elders saw it) was all important, and anybody who wanted to live in the community had to conform to the pattern i.e. to keep communal good foremost. The necessity of living together, and the high value placed on "prestige" kept selfishness within reasonable limits.

Now the villagers depend upon outsiders. Exploitation is rife because the outsiders generally have the advantage of education, official position or social status. The *Patwaris*, policemen, court attendants and lawyers, Irrigation Overseers, and all the other petty members of the official hierarchy with which the villagers come in contact take advantage of them. There is nothing to restrain them.

Within the village itself, the headman, the big landlord and the money lender help themselves as best as they can, at the expense of the other members of the community. Prestige, traditional loyalties, and regard do not operate as checks any more. The material losses which the average villager suffers, under these circumstances are often noted by writers and welfare workers. But the emotional losses—the humiliations, and frustrations—these are not sufficiently emphasized. Yet these are just as important.

All workers connected with rural welfare have noted the decline in-group co-operation with distress. They have recognized the necessity for group-cooperation and it is being emphasized from the very (official) quarters which brought about its decline. Perhaps the greatest task of the social worker will be to bring home to the villagers that individualism and a money economy are not incompatible with group co-operation. For the present, the villagers have lost their old equilibrium, what the new equilibrium will be, on what values it will be based, only time can tell. Yet the growing recognition of the problem is an encouraging sign.

Footnotes

1. The serious problems of wastes of labour and of social friction which this 'sub-division and fragmentation of holdings' raises has been engaging the attention of government and economists for some time, and some efforts have been made to consolidate the holdings. Much more needs to be done, however.
2. This is not the best word, but it is generally used, and I retained it, for want of a better one.
3. With the completion of the Bhakra Dam on the Indus, irrigation will be extended to parts of the area west of the Jhelum.
4. Satluj, Beas, Ravi, Chenab and Jhelum are the five rivers which give the Punjab its name. Punjab = Five + rivers; the land of five rivers. They are all perennial streams, tributary to the Indus.
5. The province of Punjab claimed to have the largest and finest system of canal irrigation in the world!

10

Technological Change and Agricultural Growth in a Village in East Punjab

The New Village*

The Area and the Period

Ludhiana is one of the more progressive agricultural districts of Punjab. Since 1960, it has been selected for the Intensive Agricultural Development (Package) Programme of the Ministry of Food and Agriculture. Accordingly, the intensity of agricultural extension effort in it is greater and the resources being made available for agricultural development are much larger than in an average district of the State. However, this more intensive effort began only in 1961; the district had not received any special attention earlier. The changes described in this study are the results mainly of developments which had taken place before the inception of Package Programme and, as the discussion brings out, are related to the social and economic changes which have occurred all over Central Punjab in the post-Partition years and to development activities undertaken in all parts of the State. But it is well to keep in view the fact that the very selection of Ludhiana as the Package Programme district indicates a relatively high standard of agricultural development and a potential for attaining rapid increases in agricultural production as a result of the Programme.

Secondly, Ludhiana and a number of smaller towns of Central Punjab have seen rapid growth of small-scale industry in recent years. The centre of this development is the town of Ludhiana itself, in which there has been a phenomenal growth of machine tool and light engineering industries. Lately, this development has overflowed to the larger villages, especially those, which have certain advantages like location along the

---

* Published in Economic Weekly, 1965.

Delhi-Amritsar (Grand Trunk) Road. This growth of small-scale industries has important effects on the rural economy and agricultural techniques, which are discussed below. Moreover, the agricultural changes described in this study and growths of small-scale industry in towns are both part of a larger process of socio-economic change. However, for the purposes of this study, I took care not to select an industrial village. Such villages are still few in number and selection of one of these would have interfered with analysis of agricultural change, which is the main theme of this study. The influence of industrial growth described in this study is the regional effect, which has been felt by all villages in this area.

The selected village is well served with road transport, has electricity and has attained a high level of agricultural productivity. But, it is not exceptional in any of these respects in this area. The majority of the villages in this CD block are within two miles of an all-weather motorable road and the motor transport facilities available to them are almost as good as those available to this village. Electric supply has been extended to 88 out of 107 villages of the block. As regards agricultural productivity, the average yields of crops reported for this village are comparable to yields reported for the block. Similarly, in the level of use of fertilizer, which is a good index of acceptance of agricultural improvements, the village is not exceptional. The average figure of 34.0 kg of chemical fertilizers used per acre under crops reported for this village has been attained and exceeded by a number of other villages in this block and by several blocks in this district.

The Village and the People

Jitpur is a medium-sized multi-caste village, having 299 households and a population of about 1,850. It is located at a distance of two miles from *tehsil* and block headquarters town, Samrala, which itself has a population of only about 6,000 and is not much more than a large village. Jitpur is situated on an all-weather motorable road, which links it with this town on one side, and with a market town (population about 25,000) on the other. There is a regular bus service with 12 buses plying each way on this road. In addition, four three-wheeler Tempos are plying continuously. As a result, a motor transport vehicle is available on this road every ten minutes through the day. The village is not suburban in character; Ludhiana, the nearest large city (population over 5 lakhs) is about 25 miles from it. But these details about frequency of road transport have been given in order to indicate how quickly and easily the villager can move out of the village. This fact was brought home to me during the first visit to the village. When I reached the village, I was told that a prominent village leader, whom I had expected to meet, had left for the State capital that very morning. I was disappointed at the prospect of not being able to see him. But before I left the village four hours later, the man had returned. The entire trip to the State capital, located about 40 miles away, including his making certain enquiries about his work in the capital had taken just six hours. The rapidity of travel by road, in which this village or the villages of this block are by no means exceptional and is a very powerful factor in the travel of new ideas to the village and in lessening of the distance—in time, in ways of thinking and in levels of living—between the people of the villages and those of the towns, which in turn is an important factor in technological progress in the villages.

Another first impression may be recorded also, in order to give a perspective of the technological level to which the village has access now. The village has two shops of fabricators of agricultural implements. These are owned by two extended families of *Ramgarhiya Lohars* (smiths), residents of the village. One of these shops is on the approved list of fabricators of agricultural implements for the State Department of Agriculture. It manufactures *rahats* (iron Persian wheels), iron ploughs, buckets, steel trunks and similar articles of sheet steel, besides doing repair work. This shop with its electric motors, a power press, lathes and other power-driven machines is comparable in equipment and technical skill of its workmen to any small manufacturing unit in the neighbouring *tehsil* town or even in Ludhiana. Several young men from *Lohar* (smith) families of Jitpur are working in Ludhiana as skilled workers in small engineering units and the men working in the village have stayed behind, not because they are inferior in skill or capacity to work to those who have gone out, but only because they feel that they can make as much or more money by running the family shops in the village. These men understand machines—electric motors, tractors, trucks, flour mills, almost any machine that is likely to be used in the village—and their presence in the village is a major factor in technological progress. It means that if an electric motor or other power driven agricultural implement like a chaff cutter or sugarcane press goes out of order, it will be repaired quickly and efficiently, and if the repair cannot be done locally or a part need to be replaced, the cultivator will be suitably advised to get this done from the block headquarter town or Ludhiana. He need not be afraid of being left helpless in case of a breakdown or of long expensive delays or heavy repair costs. It means further that the cultivator or his young son has a high standard of technical competence to look up to. The fact that this standard already exists in the village gives an impetus to him and to his young son to handle machines and to correct small defects himself. During subsequent discussions in the village, many cultivators explained that they seldom have any problem with their electric motors; that they could correct small defects themselves and went to the *tehsil* town only in case of a major trouble like a burnt armature. One elderly cultivator went so far as to say that the longer they worked their motors the fewer breakdowns these had.

This level of competence in handling machines is in striking contrast to that found in an average village in many parts of the country, where the village smith or carpenter confines himself to making and repairing the traditional agricultural implements and is either incapable of, or does not care to handle, even such non-power-driven improved implements as iron ploughs or sugarcane crushers.[1]

The People

The distribution of households by caste is given in Table 10.1.

The *Bazigars* are not permanent residents of the village. They live in semi-permanent huts in one corner of the village and are dependent mainly

Table 10.1: Distribution of Households by Caste

	Caste	*No of Households*	*Population*
1.	Jat	105	780
2.	Ramgarhiya Mistri (smith, mason, carpenter)	37	205
3.	Mahajan* (Brahmin, Khatri, and Arora)	46	289
4.	Harijan (Ramdasia, Balmiki, Julaha)	87	517
5.	Other artisans: Darzi (tailor); Kumhar (potter); Nai (barber); Jhur (water-carrier); Teli (oil-presser); Gujjar (grazier)	15	92
6.	Bazigar	9	48
	Total	299	1,831

* The term Mahajan is used by the villagers for all these three castes of traders-cum-white-collar workers. It has been retained here for the sake of convenience even though I realize that quite different castes like Brahmin and Khatri are included in the group. The number of households by individual caste is as follows: Brahmin, 27; Khatri, 17; Arora 2.

upon casual agricultural or non-agricultural labour. They also rear buffaloes or cattle for sale of milk or animals. They are a semi-nomadic people who stay at the outskirts of large villages and small towns for months at a time. In recent years they have been trying to settle down as cultivators or cultivators-cum-labourers and are being assisted in this process by the state Government with allotment of land for cultivation and with financial assistance.

There are sharp differences in land-ownership and occupation among the different castes as will be seen from Table 10.2. The Jats are the principal land owner-cultivators: they own and cultivate practically all the land of the village. Among the other casts, Mahajans, *Mistris* (mason, carpenters and smiths) and 'other artisans' are essentially non-cultivators. The Harijans have agricultural labour as an important source of income; but they have no rights in land. Of the 104 land-owning families in the village, 96 are of Jats, and of the 82 families of cultivators, 76 are of Jats. These cultivate 96 per cent of the land of the village. The concentration of land-ownership and cultivation in the hands of a single caste could hardly be greater.

Table 10.2: Land Ownership and Cultivation

(in acres)

		Land Ownership		*Cultivation*	
		Families	*Area Owned*	*Families*	*Area Owned*
1.	Jats	96	1,033.0	76	1,065.0
2.	Mistris	3	11.5	2	9.5
3.	Mahajans	4	28.5	4	28.5
4.	Harijans	1	6.0*	0	0
	Total	104	1,079.0	82	1,103.0

* Just allotted in a neighbouring village; cultivation not begun.

Further, as the data of the Appendix 10.I bring out, the participation of Jats in non-agricultural occupations is relatively small. A number of Jats have gone out of the village in the Army and elsewhere but among those living in the village; more than 90 per cent are engaged in cultivation.

Mistris, Mahajans and the 'other artisans' depend upon occupations other than cultivation. In the case of *Mistris*, the principal occupations are those of mason, carpenter and smith, the latter including skilled work in machine shops in the village and outside. Out of 56 *Mistries* workers living in the village, as many as 43 are classified as engaged in skilled work. Fourteen of these are masons, 12 are carpenters, and 11 are smiths.

The principal occupations of Mahajans are petty shop-keeping and white-collar services. Four families take up cultivation of their small holdings. Agricultural and non-agricultural labour is also reported by a few persons, obviously those who are uneducated or are too poor to do anything else. A number of persons among the Mahajans are not doing any work. These are old people, who depend upon their pensions and/or remittances from sons in service outside the village.

The 'other artisans' follow their traditional occupations, supplementing earnings from these by labour, agricultural and non-agricultural. Their numbers are sufficiently small (1-3 households each) to enable them to make a meagre living in this way.

The Harijans are the big landless group. A few families have their traditional occupations—scavenging for six families of *Balmikis*, weaving for six families of *Julahas* (weavers)—as important sources of income. But the great majority (75 families), who are called *Ramdasias* or *Ravidasias*[2]; depend almost exclusively upon agricultural and/or non-agricultural labour. These people gave up their traditional *Chamaars'* work, i.e. flaying of carcasses of dead cattle and making of leather goods, about 40 years ago. But even when they practiced it, it contributed only a small proportion to their incomes, and their main reliance was on labour. Out of 110 Harijan workers living in the village, as many as 91 were reported to be engaged in agricultural and/or non-agricultural labour. Fifteen among these were *sanjhees* (attached agricultural labourers) working for cultivators for an annual payment, given in most cases as a share of produce; 13 are non-agricultural labourers, while the remainders take up casual agricultural or non-agricultural work as one or the other becomes available.

Since the *sanjhees* get a share of the produce, it may be thought that they are share-croppers and not labourers. The impression is strengthened by the fact that some *sanjhees* besides contributing labour pay proportionate share of the land revenue and cost of seed, fertilizer, etc. The annual contract (usually verbal) between the cultivator and the *sanjhee* specifies the items to be contributed by the latter and the crops of which he is to receive a share. (Usually the *sanjhee* gets a share of the grain and cash crops; but is not given any share in fodders or by-products like chaff, cotton sticks, etc.) But the cultivators were emphatic in maintaining that the *sanjhees* were agricultural labourers, that they had no part in decision making in cultivation and that giving them a share of the produce was only another method of paying for their labour. The Harijans themselves did not contest these claims nor did they make any reference to their having had rights in land at anytime in the past.

The remarkable adherence of castes to their traditional occupations and roles in the village may be noted. Ownership and cultivation of land is concentrated in the hands of the Jats. The only other participants in cultivation are Harijans; but their role is confined entirely to furnishing labour. The Mahajans and the *Mistris*, the two other major castes of the village, have confined themselves to their traditional roles of traders-cum-white-collar workers and skilled artisans respectively. This adherence of traditional occupations and roles is in striking contrast to the technological and economic progress, which the village has made in recent years. It shows that economic progress need not involve basic changes from the traditional roles and patterns of economic activity of the different castes. On other hand, as the following discussion will bring out, this very adherence, voluntary or forced, has provided a major incentive to economic and social progress. The fact that castes like the Mahajans and the *Mistris* did not have an opportunity for participation in land-ownership and cultivation within the village, meant that as population increased and aspirations rose with spread of education and increasing contacts with the outside world, these castes sought an escape from the limitation of local economic opportunity in emigration. Each caste chose the occupation(s), for which it was best suited because of its traditional occupation and role in the village. Among the Jat cultivators also, young men from families with small holdings sought an escape from declining incomes at home in emigration. As a result, the area acquired an active tradition of emigration, which has been a major influence in economic and social progress. The alternate response of traditionally non-cultivating castes participating in land-ownership and cultivation with varying degrees of combination between cultivation and the traditional occupation of the caste, which is found in villages in many parts of the country, was not made here[3]. Both the social situation and the laws were responsible for this. The land-owning cultivating Jats were too powerful and too deeply attached to the land to allow non-cultivators to acquire rights in it. Secondly, acquisition of land by non-cultivators was prohibited under the well-known Punjab Land Alienation Act of 1901.

Emigrantion

The figures given in the Appendix 10.I include data on those emigrants from the village who are unmarried and those who are married but keep their families in the village. These persons have been included for two reasons. Firstly, since emigration is an important factor in technological and social change in the village, some data on numbers who have gone out of the village are of interest for this study. Secondly, people of these two categories, even though living outside the village are part of the social and to an extent the economic situation of the village. The men with families living in the village send remittances and themselves visit the village as frequently as possible. Most of those from cultivating families continue their interest in land. The unmarried ones have equally strong links and interests. Their parents, uncles and other relations in the village are the only family they have. They look to them for assistance in getting married and in setting up their own homes in future. These two categories of emigrants are best thought of as constituents of village families, who are living outside it. Many of them will come back; others will remain 'men of the village', until they establish themselves sufficiently to take their wives and children with them.

The emigrants included in the Appendix total 89. Most of them are Jats, Mahajans and *Mistris*; the number of Harijans and other artisans is very small. Emigration from this village (and this area generally) has been mainly from castes, which are socially and economically the most advanced, and the least from groups like the Harijans which were poor and depressed. The largest number of emigrants (42) is in the Army. More than half of these (23) are Jats; the remainder being Mahajans (10) and Harijans (7). The other occupations of the emigrants are skilled work (22), and white-collar services and professions (32). The Mahajans are either in white-collar services and professions or in military service. The *Mistris* are mostly skilled workers though a few are in white-collar services and professions also. They are conspicuous by their absence from the Army. The eleven Jats, listed under skilled work, are mostly drivers of buses and trucks. They are about the only people in the village who take up this form of skilled work: the *Mistris* avoid it. This was explained by the villagers with the remark that the Jats alone have the physical strength and stamina required for this exhausting work.

The area has a long tradition of military service. The Jats and, to a lesser extent, the Brahmins, were the first to join such service. The first recruits to the British Indian Army went in the last quarter of the 19th Century and there are many men in the village today, who have served in the first or the Second World War. On the other hand the recruitment of Harijans to the Army is a very recent phenomenon. Six of the 7 young men reported as being in military service, joined the service only after the declaration of the Emergency.

Migration to take up white-collar services and professions and skilled work also began several decades ago. The Mahajans were prominent in the former and the *Mistris* in the latter. Masons of this village have been going out for work on public works and private house construction for several decades. Before, the partition, they used to go for work on the canals in West Punjab, and to towns like Lahore, Lyallpur and Rawalpindi. This tradition continues and several of them are now working in Delhi and towns of the Punjab.

This tradition of emigration has had very important economic and social consequences some of which are related to the main theme of this study. Emigration with its inflow of money, and new ideas especially from persons who came back to live in the village, brought rise in economic level of the families of the emigrants and rising aspirations and widening mental horizons for the whole village. The village people saw that there was opportunity outside, and that it was possible to avail of it instead of enduring a low and declining income at home. In case of cultivators, emigration meant also that the process of sub-division and fragmentation of holdings was less rapid than it would have been otherwise. The relatively comfortable size of holdings, which we note below (Table 10.3) as a major reason for successful technological change, is the result partly of emigration.

Two aspects of emigration, which deserve special mention, are going to canal colonies of West Punjab and to foreign countries. The canal colonies were a major avenue of emigration for cultivators of this area in the early years of this century, and the area is now full of cultivators who have come back to their ancestral villages after the partition of the Punjab in 1947. This return migration has, as explained later, has been a significant factor in agricultural progress. But this particular village did not participate in migration to canal colonies. The explanation given for this was interesting. It was explained that the then *Zaildar*[4] of the village when asked by Government whether he or any person from his village would like to take land in the canal colonies, had refused the offer. His grandson, a prominent leader of the village, was mildly proud of this attitude of his ancestor, though many others were of the view that this had retarded the progress of the village.

Emigration to foreign countries from villages of this area has been mainly to Malaya, Thailand and East Africa. From this particular village, several Brahmin families have settled in East Africa. But the latest phase of such emigration is migration of young men to the UK for taking up jobs as un-skilled or semi-skilled workers. Large numbers of young men from Ludhiana and other districts of Central Punjab have been going to the UK during the last few years and during the course of this study I had occasion to experience the ferment which news of employment in UK on "good wages" was causing in the area. Employment vouchers, wage rates, cost of living and living conditions in UK and the possibility of saving money and sending it home, were the talk of the small block headquarter town. Information on these points obtained from all possible sources—letters and remittances from the young men who had gone to the UK, news picked up at Ludhiana, Delhi and other towns—was pooled and discussed at length by the young men from the villages who gathered at restaurants and other shops in the town. The consensus of opinion was that wages were "good"; but cost of living was high, and one could save money only by living in overcrowded tenements and enduring physical hardship. Since, the average young man of this area is quite prepared for these there was considerable enthusiasm for going abroad, especially among young men with some education who did not want to engage in farming or other ancestral occupations.[5]

Technological Change in Agriculture

Pattern of Land Holdings

It has been noted in Table 10.2 that the eighty-two farmer families of the village cultivate a total of 1103 acres. This gives a crude average of 13.45 acres per cultivating family. The distribution of families by sizes of cultivated holdings is given in Table 10.3:

Table 10.3: Distribution of Families by Sizes of Cultivated Holdings

Below 5 acres	3
5 to 10 acres	22
10 to 15 acres	30
15 to 20 acres	18
20 to 30 acres	4
30 acres and above	5

The largest number of families (70 out of 82) cultivate between 5 and 20 acres. Families cultivating less than 5 acres are very small in number and have only a part-time interest in cultivation Families cultivating above 20 acres are also very few. Several of them are undivided joint families.

On further classification by one-acre divisions, it is found that the largest number of families (21) cultivated between 10 and 11 acres, and that the median cultivated holding is 10.5 acres. The villagers consider those cultivating between 8 and 14 acres as medium sized cultivators. Such cultivators number 38, somewhat less than half of the total. Data on farm operations of the 10 sample cultivators of this group are presented in Table 10.4.

It will be seen that the net disposable income of these cultivating families ranged from about Rs. 1,200 to over Rs. 5,500 per year; the variation being dependent upon the number of workers in the family, the area cultivated, whether irrigation was being done by bullocks or by electric motor and the level of fertilizer use. This income remained with the family after meeting all its needs of food, providing for fodder for livestock including milch animals, and paying all the cultivation expenses (e.g. for seed, manures and fertilizers, labour, etc). The value of the food-grains and other produce (*gur, khandsari* sugar and cotton) retained by the families for domestic use varied from Rs. 1,275 to Rs. 2,360. Each family was keeping besides bullocks, two or more milk-yielding buffaloes and since the milk yields are fairly high (8 kg per buffalo per day or higher) the milk was sufficient for meeting all the milk and *ghee* requirements of the family. Further, all families grew some vegetables and had kept a few poultry birds also. Accordingly, the food needs of the families were met almost fully, and at a fairly satisfactory level of nutrition; and the disposable income was available for expenditure on clothing, repair or extension of the house, education, travel and miscellaneous expenses.

The calculation is not very refined, but it is adequate for the purpose of obtaining an approximate idea of the economic level of the middle cultivator. It is clear from it that this cultivator is considerably above the subsistence level; that he has a small surplus for education, travel and other needs after meeting his elementary needs for food, clothing, housing, etc. Data on the character of housing, facility of electricity and water supply in the house, and possession of durable goods and other general observations in the village also point to a similar conclusion. The main significance of this conclusion is that since the cultivator is not constantly pre-occupied with meeting his barest minimum needs, he can afford to bring a business approach to his cultivation, to take some risks and to make experiments with new practices. The extension staff emphasized that this latter had been one major result of the economic changes of the last fifteen years. As the VLW stated it, "Earlier the sole aim of the cultivator was to feed his family and that of the Harijan who worked for him. Now however, several of them aim at making more money and are looking for changes in practices which would enable them to do so".

Table 10.4: Farm Operations of Ten Sample Medium Cultivators

Sl. No.	*Area cultivated (acres)*		*Motive power for irrigation*	*Persons in the household*	*Workers in the household*	*Value in rupees of*		*Cash expenditure on*			*Net disposable income*		*Livestock*	
	Total	*Irrigated*				*Home consumption of products*	*Sale of produce*	*Labour*	*Electric power*	*Fertilizers*	*Total*	*Per family worker*	*Work animals bullocks*	*Milch animals buffaloes*
1	2	3	4	5	6	7	8	9	10	11	12	13	14	15
1	9	9	Bullocks	8	3	1700	3960	100	–	181	3679	1226	3 +1 camel	3
2	13	13	–do–	5	1	1495*	750†	100	–	92	1158	1158	2	2
3	8	8	–do–	8	1	1280	1410	160	–	64	1186	1186	2 +1 camel	2
4	11	11	–do–	10	3	1275	2650	100	–	197	2353	784	2 +1 camel	2
5	14	14	–do–	12	4	1906	2950	100	–	122	2728	682	4 +1 camel	3
6	13	13	Elec. Motor	17	5	1905	3225	–	522	140	2563	513	4	2
7	14	14	–do–	10	3	2360	6925	100	850	437	5538	1846	3	4
8	8	8	Bullocks	6	2	1266	1270	60	–	42	1168	584	2 +1 cow	1
9	14	14	Elec. Motor	10	2£	1591	3500	100	400	158	2842	1411	4	4
10	13	13	Bullocks	8	2	1515	2404	100	–	72	2232	1116	4 +1 cow	2

* Has other dependants also. † Plus Rs. 600, income from carting.

£ In addition one *sanjhee* kept and paid 1/9 share of production.

Land Use and Cropping Pattern

Data on distribution of the cropped area among principal crops in 1951-52, 1956-57 and 1961-62, as obtained from the records of the Revenue Department, are given in Table 10.5.

Table 10.5: Distribution of the Cropped Area among Principal Crops

(*in acres*)

	1951-52	*1956-57*	*1961-62*
Total geographical area	1,238	1,239	1,239
Net area sown:	1,132	1,118	1,118
Irrigated	786	771	951
Unirrigated	346	346	167
Gross cropped area:	1,637	1,663	1,639
Irrigated	1,256	1,271	1,440
Unirrigated	381	372	199
Area sown more than once	505	545	521
Percentage of net area sown	44.6	48.7	46.6
Area under crops			
Kharif: Maize	121	188	240
Cotton	–	198	143
Sugarcane	191	99	178
Summer fodders:	295	231	195
Charl	249	155	127
Other	46	76	68
Wheat	474	357	436
Other Rabi grains and mixtures	319	276	237
Winter fodders (mainly berseem)	92	154	164
Vegetables	4	4	7
Other crops	16	6	11

These figures do not show any noteworthy change either in the net area sown or in the gross cropped area during this period. But there is an increase of about 200 acres in the irrigated area. In 1961-62, 85.6 per cent of the cropped area of the village received irrigation. Irrigation was almost entirely from wells. Out of 951 acres irrigated in 1961-62, 940 acres were irrigated by wells. The increase in irrigation during this period has been due to increase in number of wells (from 30 to 51) and electrification of a large number (36) of these. The area under canal irrigation is very small, only 11 acres. A distributary of a canal passes through the village; but very few cultivators take water from it. The main reason given for not taking water from the canal is that there is sufficient water in the wells, and cost of lifting it is not too high. The fear of water logging, a major problem in some of the canal-irrigated areas of Central Punjab, also discourages use of canal water.

The figures of Table 10.5 show significant changes in the cropping pattern, with increases in areas under more remunerative and higher-yielding crops like cotton, maize and the winter fodder *berseem*, and decreases in those under low-yielding crops like gram, *rabi* grain mixtures (wheat-gram, gram-barley) and the summer fodder *chari*. The area under maize has doubled during this period; cotton, which was not grown in 1951-52, has become an important crop and acreage under *berseem* has also increased. All these crops yield much more than the crops they have replaced. Maize and cotton are higher yielding or are more remunerative than gram or wheat-gram or barley-gram mixtures. *Berseem* similarly yields much more than *Chari*. It gives 5, 6 or more cuttings in one season, compared to one cutting of *Chari*. The value of fodder from an acre under *berseem* is estimated about three times that from an acre under *Chari*.

This change in the cropping pattern has become possible because of increased availability of irrigation, and especially because the cultivator has a much larger quantity of water entirely under his control. He can follow an intensive cropping pattern and ensure adequate attention to each of the crops grown by him. During discussions in the village, the cultivators repeatedly referred to the latter fact.

Consolidation and Electrification

All cultivators were agreed that the present phase of rapid improvement in agriculture started after consolidation of holdings, which was completed in the village during 1951-52. The advantages of consolidation of holdings for more efficient and intensive cultivation are so well known that it is not necessary to explain these here. However, the case of the *Sarpanch* may be mentioned to illustrate the point. He said, "Before consolidation my family had share in lands falling under 13 wells; but after consolidation all our lands came under one well, though we constructed another well later." Consolidation of holdings was followed by a spurt of development activity, the most important feature of which was extension of well irrigation. The village had 30 wells in 1951-52. By 1961-62 the number had increased to 45. In addition, there were 6 *kutcha*-bore tube-wells in the latter year, bringing the total number of irrigation units to 51. The village received electricity in 1954; it was among the first villages in the block to receive it. Electrification was followed by a wave of installation of electric motors on the wells. Eleven motors were installed, within one month, in 1955 when a large *Taccavi* loan was sanctioned for this purpose by the State Government. At the time of this study, 29 out of 45 wells had electric motors and one had a diesel engine. In addition, the 6 *kutcha*-bore tube-wells mentioned above were also fitted with electric motors. This *kutcha*-bore is an interesting innovation because it enables a cultivator to start irrigating his land without constructing a *pucca* well. A tube is inserted in the ground by digging a *kutcha* hole, a pumping set and electric motor are installed on it and irrigation is started immediately but the *pucca* well is constructed after two, three or more years when the cultivator can spare the capital. It was also reported that some farmers in neighbouring villages had two or three such bores in different parts of their farms and used portable motors which they took from one hole to the other. This latest innovation, which saves time and investment, is an indication of the facility which the cultivators have acquired in the technique of irrigation with the help of electric motors.

Installation of electric motors was helped by liberal grants of *Taccavi* loans by the State Government. Loans for 8 electric motors totalling Rs. 13,000 were sanctioned during 1955, when the first set of motors was installed and till the time of this study, loans totalling Rs. 26,300 had been sanctioned for 15 electric motors. Thus, *taccavi* loans have financed electrification of half the village wells.

Electrification makes possible lifting of water at a markedly lower cost, besides allowing a saving of time in irrigation. The estimate given in Table 10.6 of the comparative cost of irrigation of one acre of wheat by electric pumping and by lifting water with the help of bullocks was given by one cultivator and is generally accepted. Irrigation with an electric pumping set besides being much cheaper is also much more intensive and adequate. It was explained that with an electric pumping set four watering for the wheat crop were adequate; but with bullocks six to seven watering were required.

The effect of electrification of wells has not been so much increase in area under irrigation, as more adequate and intensive watering of the irrigated land. The saving of labour of man and beast, which electrification has brought about, has been utilized by cultivators mainly in the form of more adequate and intensive irrigation of their crops, which along with increased use of fertilizers and other improved practices, has resulted in increased yields. Improvement in the quality of livestock has been another striking benefit. This has resulted both from reduced strain on bullocks—lifting water for irrigation is considered extremely strenuous for the bullocks—and better feeding, which has become possible as a result of

Table 10.6: Comparative Cost of Irrigation with an Electric Pumping Set and Bullocks

Rauni irrigation (first irrigation after preparing the land) of one acre of wheat			
With Electric Pumping Set	(Rs)	With Bullocks	(Rs)
Consumption of electricity for 6 hours (approx)	2.00	Wages of 2 men for 2½ days @ Rs. 2.50 per man per day	12.50
Wages of 1 man for three quarters of a day @ Rs. 2.50 per day	1.87	Expenses of two bullocks for 2½ days @ Rs. 5 per day	12.50
Total	3.87	Total	25.00
Or say,	4.00		

larger area under green fodders. Explaining this point, one cultivator said, "Now we have green fodder the year round, with the result that we feed our animals better and also make a saving on the grains which we used to feed them earlier".

More Intensive Manuring

This is possibly the second most important aspect of technological change in agriculture. It consists both in better use of farm-yard manure and greatly increased use of chemical fertilizers. The latter, which began only during the early 50s, has shown a rapid increase especially during the last five years (Table 10.7).

This village is not exceptional in the progress of fertilizer use or in the average quantity of fertilizer used per acre. The total fertilizer consumption in the block itself had increased from 295 tonnes in 1956-57 to 2,141 tonnes in 1961-62 and is expected to reach 4,000 tonnes in 1963-64. The average figure per cultivated acre in the village was 34 kg per acre as compared with 25.3 kg for the block. The highest average of almost 100 kg per cultivated acre was reported from the garden colony village mentioned later.

Use of chemical fertilizers has become an integral part of the agricultural pattern of the village. The VLW mentioned that practically every cultivator in the village was using chemical fertilizers and that a large number was following the dosages recommended by him. One reason for the popularity of chemical fertilizers is that the average cultivator realizes that the increasingly intensive cropping pattern, which he is now adopting, cannot be sustained without their use. He understands that he

Table 10.7: Use of Chemical Fertilizers

	1958-59	*1959-60*	*1960-61*	*1961-62*	*1962-63**
Nitrogenous: Ammonium Sulphate CAN (Calcium ammonium nitrate)	20.00	23.00	24.00	31.00	36.05
Phosphate: Super phosphate	2.00	3.05	2.00	7.04	10.01
Total	22.00	26.05	26.00	38.04	46.06

* Sale of fertilizer between April and November 1963 was about 75 tonnes and it was estimated by the VLW and the BDO that the total for 1963-64 would be between 90 to 100 tonnes because top dressing of rabi crops had yet to be done.

just does not have adequate farm-yard manure for all his crops and must use chemical fertilizers in addition. There is good awareness also of the relative cost and returns from fertilizer use. In one of the discussions, a cultivator mentioned that in case of the wheat crop, the cost of the chemical fertilizer was recovered from the additional chaff, which they got as a result of the higher yield, and the additional grain was their profit. There was general agreement with this view. Another indication of the cultivators' understanding of chemical fertilizers may be had from the speed with which the new fertilizer CAN (Calcium Ammonium Nitrate) had spread. In the early years of the CD block, the extension staff popularized the use of ammonium sulphate but during the last three years, when there has been a shortage of ammonium sulphate and CAN from the Nangal Fertilizer Factory has been freely available, they have been propagating use of the latter.

The BDO explained that while ammonium sulphate was still demanded by cultivators for certain crops—it was considered particularly well for groundnut—the majority of the cultivators had already switched over to the use of CAN. They had understood that their crops needed nitrogen, and that CAN supplied it just as efficiently as did ammonium sulphate. They might not know the English word 'nitrogen'; but they had grasped the basic idea that ammonium sulphate, CAN and other manures (like farm-yard manure) supplied the same essential element to the soil.

Use of super phosphate for the wheat and groundnut crops is also increasing rapidly. The latest introduction is potash. Its use is being propagated by the extension staff for the wheat crop from this year (1963-64) only, and eight tons of potash had been distributed in the block area. As the results are considered to be promising, the block staffs feel that the quantity could be increased to about 100 tons next year. The main advantage of potash is that it gives a polished appearance to the grain, which fetches a higher price in the market. The yield is also reported to be somewhat higher with its use.

Better Use of Farm-Yard Manure

This is linked with consolidation of holdings on the one hand, and use of chemical fertilizers on the other. Consolidation gave a fillip to use of farm-yard manure, because as a result of it, all cultivators and most non-cultivators who had livestock were allotted sites for compost pits on the outskirts of the village. This allotment removed the difficulty of land for pits, which many cultivators and non-cultivators like *Harijans* who kept cattle faced. All these pits are well utilized. In addition many cultivators have pits in their holdings also. Experience with use of chemical fertilizers has aided use of farm-yard manure because it has made the cultivators conscious of the value of their own farm-yard manure. So long as the cultivators did not buy fertilizers they were not acutely conscious of the monetary value of the farm-yard manure which they produced themselves or which they obtained from *Harijans* and others in the village. But, when they began to buy fertilizers they began to be aware of the value of farm-yard manure also, because they began to compare what a cartload of farm-yard manure could do for their crops in comparison with what a bag of chemical fertilizers did. Moreover, as a larger number of *Harijans* and other non-cultivators began to have manure from their newly allotted pits, buying and selling of manure (for cash or in exchange for fodder) became more common. In 1963, the price of one cartload of manure, during the *kharif* sowing season (May-June) when most of the farm-yard manure is applied to the fields, was more than Rs. 6 per cart, and many cultivators were commenting that this was an all time high.

However, even though there is greater awareness of the value of farm-yard manure, and its use has increased, the practice of burning cow-dung has not stopped. The compost Inspector of the block explained that the cultivators realized that the practice caused a serious loss to agriculture and that the more progressive and prosperous ones would be quite willing to stop it if an alternate fuel was available easily and cheaply, and the problem of heating milk for making *ghee* could be solved. As regards the latter, he explained that cow-dung cakes were essential for heating milk for *ghee* making, because of the slow heat and the particular flavour which they imparted to the *ghee* and which was especially fancied by the village people. This preference may result in some cow-dung continuing to be burnt for heating milk, even after the households switch over to other fuels. But the main problem is obviously that of providing an alternate fuel.

The Problem of Fuel

The present fuel consumption pattern of the village is somewhat as follows:

The cultivators and the *Harijans* depend upon home produced fuel—cow dung and agricultural wastes like cotton sticks. Most Mahajan and Mistri families, who do not keep milch animals, buy fuel. They buy cow-dung cakes, agricultural wastes, fire-wood, charcoal or kerosene depending upon availability and price of different fuels, and the income and level of living of the family.

Cow-dung cakes are sold mostly by the *Harijans* and "other artisans". Fire-wood and charcoal are sold in three fuel shops located in the village. As many as ten families have kerosene stoves, which they use for a part of their cooking.

The chief requisite for reducing consumption of cow-dung as a fuel is making available alternate fuels at a cheap price. The families, which are already buying fuel, will buy any fuel which is cheap and easily available. They will gladly use soft coke or fire-wood or even electricity if it is cheap. The cultivators and *Harijans* will have greater resistance to buying fuel. But even they will buy fuel, if it is cheap and conveniently available. The value of cow-dung for agriculture is realized by the cultivators and it is not considered free. But it is used, because it is there and is cheap. The *gobar* gas plant and more efficient *chulhas*, especially those which can use agricultural wastes like cotton stocks also have good possibilities of being adopted.

Use of Improved Implements

The third notable aspect of technological change is use of improved implements. Use of improved iron ploughs, chaff-cutters and iron sugar cane presses, which began to be used in the Punjab villages 30-40 years ago have become universal, and newer improvements like furrow-turning and soil-stirring ploughs, bullock carts with pneumatic tyres, chaff cutters and sugarcane crushers driven by electric motors have also been introduced in considerable numbers. The number of implements, including improved implements, at the time of the study is given in Table 10.8.

Table 10.8: Number of Implements

Ploughs	
Desi (unimproved)	82
Iron (improved)	142
Iron, furrow turning	44
Cotton drills	6
Maize sellers	3
Tractors	–
Chaff cutters	
Manual	70
Bullock-driven	30
Motor-driven	8
Sugarcane crushers	
Bullock-driven	58
Motor-driven	4
Bullock carts with	
Wooden wheels	34
Pneumatic tires	38

It will be seen from the above Table 10.8 that the stage of acceptance of small improvements, e.g. iron ploughs or chaff-cutters, is long past. Even the bullock cart with pneumatic tyres, which involves considerable investment, is in general use. The cultivator is now at a stage when he is prepared to adopt any improved implement which is distinctly superior to the one he is using already and which he can afford to buy or hire. Secondly, he is prepared to accept any innovation or modification in existing practice, which results in a clear saving of time, labour or money. This last is very well illustrated by the recent change in the practices regarding threshing of wheat and selling of maize.

Wheat has been threshed in Indian villages from time immemorial by bullocks going over piles of harvested wheat placed on the ground. This process involves back-breaking labour by men and bullocks for two or three weeks in April and May. Winnowing is done by throwing the wheat and chaff against the breeze. Both these processes have been replaced in the West by the combined harvesters. These machines are beyond the reach of the Indian cultivator; but during the last few years a number of small mechanical threshers costing between Rs. 2,000 and 3,000 have appeared in the markets of the Punjab. Some of these have begun to be used by cultivators in this area also and it was reported that some cultivators of this village had got their wheat threshed by one such machine the previous year. However, more significant than use of this machine is the new practice of using the chaff-cutter (which most cultivators possess) for threshing wheat. In this new process, whole stocks of wheat are fed through the chaff-cutter which cuts the chaff into smaller pieces and separates the ears of grain. The mixture is then gone over lightly by bullocks for a few hours and the grain is separated. Another method is to put the ears of grain through the maize-Sheller described below. It was reported that nearly 40 per cent of the wheat crop of the village had been threshed in this way during the previous year.

The advantages of the new process are obvious. It results in considerable saving of time and labour during April and May, which are among the busiest months of the year. This is the time when cotton and early summer fodders have to be sown and weeding of sugarcane has to be attended to. The cultivator does not have to do back breaking labour in the hot sun as he had to do in the past, and can devote himself to more fruitful work. The practice has two other advantages also. It reduces risk of loss of grain and chaff from dust-storms and thunder-storms, which are quite common at this time of the year, and yields better, cleaner grain and chaff because these do not get mixed with the dust. Secondly, it does not involve use of any special, expensive equipment, but depends upon use of tools, which the cultivator possesses already. But the most significant point about it, from the point of view of this study, is that it has become popular mainly through the initiative of the cultivators themselves. An extension worker might have evolved the practice and extension staff might have had some part in popularizing it. But it was obviously not evolved at a research station and was not propagated by the extension staff as an important recommended practice.

The mechanical maize-Sheller is a simple device, which consists of nothing more than an old Mobil oil barrel, fitted with wooden pedals, mounted on a horizontal wooden shaft. It operates with mechanical or bullock power. There are three such machines in the village, one of which is owned by an agricultural implement fabricator and the other two are owned by the two flour mill owners. These people undertake shelling of maize for cultivators at a charge of one *seer* per *maund* (1 kg per 40 kg) of grain shelled. It was reported that about half of the maize crop of the village was being handled by these machines and that five machines would be adequate to handle the entire crop. Here, again is an instance of a simple machine evolved through local ingenuity giving substantial benefits—saving of time, labour and a much better product.

One result of these technological advances is that the extension workers and the engineers working on improved implements have acquired a new hope and confidence. I had occasion to visit the agricultural implements workshop attached to the Agricultural University and to see the work being done on evolving improved implements like improved ploughs, a combined seed-cum-fertilizer drill and an improved hoe. Many of the improved ploughs and other implements devised at the workshop are improvements on the implements used by the cultivators earlier and have proved to be very popular. From discussions with these people it was clear that they had acquired the confidence that any implement which was distinctly superior to the one used by the cultivator and met all his requirements would be accepted. This confidence is a very important fact.

At this workshop experiments were also being made with small tractors. The main objective of these experiments is to evolve a tractor which meets all the needs of a medium cultivator with a holding of 10 to 15 acres and which sells at a price which this cultivator can afford to pay. The engineers and some of the other specialists at the University were very confident about the success of these experiments. They felt that among the models available abroad there are some which could meet all these conditions and could with suitable modifications is successfully placed in the Punjab market.

Use of Improved Seed

The Punjab cultivator has long been familiar with the use of improved seed of some crops. Improved varieties of wheat like C-591 and of sugarcane like CO-312 were accepted several decades ago and have been in general use since. The most important change in this area during the last ten years has been introduction of longer staple 'American' varieties of cotton. The practice of growing American cotton was brought to the area by refugee cultivators returning from the canal colonies. It spread very quickly in the early 50s when it nearly replaced the shorter staple *desi* varieties. However, it received a set-back later, because the price differential in favour of the American variety was reduced and it was found that the American variety was more susceptible to disease. As a result both American and *desi* varieties are now grown in the area. In this village, most of the cotton grown is of the American variety but as the figures in Table 10.5 show, the area under cotton has declined after 1956-57, partly because of damage from disease.

In case of wheat also the older C-591 variety has been largely replaced by a new variety, C-273, which is more resistant to disease, has bolder grain and consequently fetches a better price. The experience with the spread of this new variety is interesting because it brings out the speed with which a new, distinctly superior variety can replace an older one. This variety was introduced by the Department of Agriculture about seven years ago and it is claimed by the extension staff that it almost replaced the C-591 variety in this block within a period of about four years. When one considers that one season must elapse before the first demonstrations on cultivators' fields can give results, this time span of four years is quite small and shows a high degree of receptivity of cultivators to improvements like improved seed with which they have long been familiar.

Another noteworthy development is that some of the more progressive cultivators are themselves looking for new varieties. One such cultivator had obtained from a cultivator in another block, seed of a new variety of wheat, which was supposed to give very high yields with intensive application of chemical fertilizers. This new variety has not yet been released by the Department of Agriculture because experiments on it are still in progress. But this cultivator had obtained it himself and during my interview with him, gave quite a sophisticated analysis of the economics of high yields with heavy doses of fertilizer. Another cultivator was experimenting with a new *kharif* fodder evolved by crossing *bajra* with Napier grass which gives very high yields and is also very nutritious.

Use of Chemical Pesticides

Use of pesticides is the latest among the improvements advocated by the extension staff, and is not as widespread as use of improved seed or of chemical fertilizers. This is due partly to the fact that the chemicals and equipment like power sprayers needed for spraying the crops are expensive and partly to the fact that chemical pesticides are ineffective in case of some important plant diseases of the area. Thus, there is as yet no chemical cure for the Gurdaspur borer which attacks sugarcane and causes heavy damage to the crop in some years. But, wherever, the cultivators can use pesticides cheaply and effectively they are doing so. This is illustrated by the use of pesticides against storage pests. The practice of using BHC on grain kept in storage has been advocated by the extension staff during the last three years and the VLW claimed that it has already been adopted by the majority of cultivators in this village. Some of them mix BHC with the grain in the storage bin while others spray it by hand on the bags.

Livestock Husbandry

The standard of livestock husbandry in the Punjab has always been comparatively high. Some of the best breeds in the country like the Haryana bullocks and Murray buffaloes come from the Haryana (south-east Punjab) area, which is not far from this district. Moreover, recent technological changes in agriculture and rise in agricultural productivity have also contributed to improvement in the quality of livestock. Mention has been made above of improvement in feeding, resulting from larger areas under green-fodders, and of less strain on the working animals as a result of introduction of electric motors for lifting water. The bullocks and buffaloes are now seen in the village would rank among the best in the country.

The villagers are also keenly aware of the value of good breeding. Two pure-bred bulls, a Haryana cow bull and a Murray buffalo bull, are maintained by the *panchayat* through the traditional practice of being allowed to roam freely in the fields. Castration is universally done and early, in order to avoid indiscriminate breeding. However, artificial insemination has not become popular, even though this facility, which is available at the veterinary hospital in the block head-quarter town, can be availed of without difficulty. Certain other attitudes, e.g. towards treatment of disease and taking up commercial production of livestock products, also indicate that considerable progress has yet to be made before scientific attitude towards livestock husbandry and a commercial outlook towards production and sale of livestock products become widely established.

Treatment of Disease of Animals and Birds and Attitudes towards Sale of Milk and Eggs

The block headquarters town has a well-equipped veterinary hospital. Similar hospitals are located in other towns at distances of 5-10 miles. Besides, there are sub-centres in the larger villages. With this network of hospitals and sub-centres, facilities for treatment of sick animals and of breeding with animals of pure breeds are within easy reach of most villages. The veterinary doctor in-charge of the hospital explained that the hospital and sub-centres were quite popular with the villagers; that large number of animals were brought to these daily; that he and his assistants were called frequently in case of serious sickness of animals and that programmes of control of epidemic diseases like HS and foot-and-mouth disease were effectively organized from time to time.

While all this would be correct, another experience, which I had, gives a revealing insight into the present attitudes towards treatment of livestock diseases. During my first visit to the village, I was told that the village was going through an outbreak of foot-and-mouth disease, and that a special ceremony, a *jag* (from Sanskrit *yajna* or sacrifice) would be organized the next day to bring it under control. It was explained that a special messenger had been sent to a neighbouring town to obtain a charm (*taweez)* from a well-known practitioner of charms and that the ceremony would consist in collecting in the morning all the cattle of the village at its various gates, passing them through the gates, and sprinkling on them, while they passed, water in which the charm and leaves and fruit of the *neem* tree had been dipped. They added that a large quantity of rice would be cooked at one place and distributed to all the households in the village, and that no fire would burn, i.e. no cooking would be done in any individual house, and that no person would be either allowed to come into the village from outside or to leave it, on that day.

The *jag* was duly held the next day; but I was not able to witness it because of the ban on entry of outsiders. The *Sarpanch*, an educated wide-awake man with extensive urban contacts, was a leading figure in organizing the *jag*, and the other village leaders, most of whom are equally educated and wide-awake, took a prominent part in it. Even the young VLW, an excellent extension worker who was otherwise quite progressive in his outlook, appeared to share the villagers' belief in the *jag.* When I mentioned celebration of the *jag* to the veterinary doctor, he admitted that celebration of such *jags* at the time of outbreaks of foot-and-mouth disease was common in the area. He mentioned also that villagers frequently resorted to treatments of this kind when their animals were sick, and that these treatments were often done simultaneously with the veterinary treatment obtained from hospitals.

Dairying and Poultry Farming

The attitudes towards commercial dairying and poultry production also show that the traditional prejudices against these are being overcome only slowly. There is widespread prejudice against sale of milk by cultivators in Punjab and adjoining state of northern India. This prejudice has been weakening in recent years when, with the growth of urban demand for milk, sale of milk has become very profitable. In this area, the city of Ludhiana and other towns obtain most of their milk supply from villages, through vendors who collect milk in the villages and bring it to the towns on bicycles. The block headquarter town obtains its milk supply in this way. In addition, there is a large and growing demand for milk from the government dairy at the State capital. The dairy obtains its milk supply from milk producers' co-operative societies, several of which are located in villages of this block.

This village sends milk to the block headquarter town, the quantity being estimated at between 120 and 150 kg daily. Besides, there is considerable sale of milk within the village itself. Most Mahajans and *Mistris* and many *Harijans* do not keep milch animals and buy milk, the quantity varying with the size and income of the family. Many Jats also buy milk when their animals are dry. But commercial milk production is much less than it could be, and the prejudice against production of milk for sale among cultivators is partly responsible for this. It is significant that sale of milk was reported by only 5 people and three of these were non-Jat—one Brahmin and *two Harijans*. Some village leaders mentioned that the number of milk sellers was in fact higher and that many cultivators, who were actually selling milk had not reported the sale, because of the stigma attached to it.

A milk producers' co-operative society for supplying milk to the government dairy at the State capital had been formed in the village two years earlier. It had worked for some time, and had then failed. Its failure was attributed by the village leaders to dishonesty and inefficiency of the staff attached to the milk collection centre located in the village. But later, when I discussed this subject again with them after having seen the successful operation of such a centre in a neighbouring village, they agreed that the main reason for the failure of the scheme was lack of interest in commercial dairying among the cultivators.

The same attitude prevails towards production of eggs for sale. The cultivators have no prejudice against consumption of eggs or other poultry products or against keeping some birds for meeting their domestic requirements of these. In fact, the practice of keeping birds for meeting domestic requirements has increased greatly in recent years, as the cultivators have become more prosperous. The VLW estimated that as many as 75 families (mostly of Jat cultivators) were keeping poultry. But only one person had started commercial production in a small way, by keeping a flock of about 50 birds.

However, both successful dairying and commercial poultry farming were seen elsewhere in the block. Dairying was seen in the adjoining village, which had a co-operative milk producers' society supplying milk to the Government dairy at the State capital. The society has 20 members from the village, and in addition collects milk from non-members in other villages. The supplies range between 400 and 600 kg of milk daily. The members of the society were very satisfied with its working and explained that they received good income from sale of milk. Many of them had steadily increased milk production during the one year working of the society. It was an experience also to see delicate instruments like the Babcock butter-fat tester being operated by an old illiterate member. The Chairman of the society, a young man, educated and very progressive dairy farmer, was extremely enthusiastic about its working. He mentioned that the members of his society had recently bought 60 quality buffaloes from an adjoining district to increase their production of milk. His own herd of about 15 buffaloes was among the best in the block and two of his buffaloes had received prizes for high milk production. He explained that the average milk yield of a buffalo among the members of the society was 8 kg per day (some of the buffaloes in his own herd yielded 16 to 18 kg per day, at the peak of the lactation period), that one buffalo could yield a net profit of Rs. 75 to 100 per month to its owner and that several members of the society with only 2 or 3 buffaloes were having incomes of Rs. 150 to 200 per month.

Commercial production of poultry was also seen in this village and elsewhere in the block. This is one of the blocks selected for intensive development of poultry in the State. As part of the poultry development programme a poultry extension centre and a marketing society were established at the block headquarters about a year ago. These provide all the assistance and facilities—one-day old chicks to start a new flock, balanced feed, medical assistance, especially inoculation against disease like *Ranikhet*, incubators for hatching of eggs and agreements for marketing of eggs and birds—which a farmer needs to start and run a poultry farm. The block has about a dozen poultry farms with flocks of 100 to 500 birds each, and the number is increasing.

The poultry farmer in this village was an educated young man, the son of a government officer, who had turned to poultry keeping about a year earlier when he was unable to get a suitable white collar job. He explained that he had obtained one-day old chicks from the government poultry farm at Ludhiana and got technical assistance from the extension staff at the poultry extension centre. He was a member of the poultry marketing society, bought his feed and marketed his eggs through it. During the previous winter he had made good money by selling eggs for hatching to the IADP people at Ludhiana. He mentioned that he could get a net income of Re 1 per bird and that he was making more money by keeping poultry than he would have made in any white-collar job. He had started with about 300 birds in his own residential house, but was so satisfied with one year's working of his enterprise that at the time of my visit he was building a new, scientifically designed poultry house outside the village, with plans to increase his flock to 1,000 birds.

Later, I had occasion to see several other poultry farms, including one located at the block headquarter town, which was being managed by the wife of a white-collar worker. This woman was keeping about 400 birds in the yard of her home. She had started keeping poultry about three years earlier, and her initial success had so encouraged her that she had bought her own incubator and had set herself up as a supplier of chicks to new poultry farmers.

Poultry farming is making rapid progress in the block and in the district. The number of poultry farms has increased during the last three years and will increase even more rapidly now, since it has caught the attention of the people. The main attraction is the high price of eggs in the markets of Delhi and the Punjab towns. The staff of the poultry extension centre and several of the poultry farmers themselves explained that the new, scientific method of keeping poultry, which had eliminated the risk of heavy mortality from disease, had made poultry farming quite profitable. Indeed, it has transformed poultry keeping—a neglected branch of animal husbandry to which only the poor scheduled castes or Muslims paid any attention earlier—into a profitable enterprise.

But it is interesting to note that this new development of poultry is mainly in the hands of educated people. Some of them are cultivators; but others like the wife of the white-collar worker mentioned above are non-cultivators. The enterprise requires a certain amount of capital and what is more, strict adherence to certain recommended practices, e.g. inoculation of birds at stated periods, balanced feeding, culling etc., which the average farmer still finds too tedious; but which the educated person can adopt easily.

The speed with which commercial poultry farming is spreading leads the author to think that commercial dairying can also make similar progress, if there are comparable advances in technique and similar facilities for marketing, etc. are made available. The main requirements for development of dairying are improving the milk yields of animals and more efficient organization of milk collection. As regards the former, one specialist at the Agricultural University was of the view that through systematic breeding and improvements in feeding practices, the milk yields of buffaloes in this area could be increased by 50 to 75 per cent within a few years.

The Problem of Excessive Numbers

In any discussion on animal husbandry in India, the problem of numbers assumes prominence, because the number of cattle is much in excess of the requirements of agriculture and their low quality is considered to be due mainly to this fact. The prevailing practice in many parts of the country is that animals, especially cows and young stock, are turned loose on village pastures and other common lands and fallows, and subsist on whatever grazing is available in these. The situation in this respect is strikingly different in this village today. The number of cattle is not too large and the practice of grazing on common lands and fallows, never widespread, has almost disappeared. The number of livestock at the time of this survey as reported is given in Table 10.9.

Thus there were only 131 pairs of bullocks for over 1,100 acres of intensively cultivated, well-irrigated land, which has a high intensity of double cropping. This number is not excessive, but appears to be barely sufficient for meeting the requirements of agriculture. The only other animals kept in appreciable numbers are milch buffaloes, which are the primary source of milk supply. On the other hand, the number of cows and young stock, which form such a large proportion of cattle in several other parts of the country, is comparatively small. One reason for this is that the cultivators do not attempt to be self-sufficient in their requirements of bullocks by breeding cows and raising young stock. They do not find this practice economical. The prevailing practice is to buy either mature bullocks or young calves of between 1 and 4 years of age, and to bring them up until they are old enough for work. Buying of young calves is preferred to buying of mature bullocks, because these are cheaper. These bullocks and calves are brought mainly in the *mandis* of the Haryana area which are not far from here. Most cultivators do not rear buffaloes either. These are reared by *Harijans* or other castes like *Bazigars*, for whom it is an important source of income. Even buffaloes, which have gone dry are often given by cultivators to *Harijans* to keep through their dry periods and are taken back, when they are in milk.

Table 10.9: Number of Livestock

Bullocks	262
Cows	89
Young stock	123
She-buffaloes	261
Young stock of buffaloes	197
Goats	109

It is clear from this that the cultivator has a very practical attitude towards livestock husbandry. He keeps only those animals, which are most useful to him, and keeps feeding of unproductive animals or even of productive animals through their unproductive periods at a minimum. But the animals, which he does keep, he feeds well. Unlike farmers in many parts of the country, he does not have the attitude of keeping large numbers of animals (and allowing them to starve) just because it does not cost him anything to do so.

This attitude is related to the fact that the practice of allowing the cattle to graze in pastures, etc, has been stopped and there is now almost exclusive reliance on stall-feeding. Growing of fodder crops and stall-feeding of cattle have been prominent features of the farm enterprise in Punjab for a long time; but in villages of this area, these have received further emphasis after consolidation of holdings and electrification of wells. First, with consolidation even the small areas of pastures, which had been available earlier, were eliminated. Secondly, with the growing intensity of cropping, hardly any areas of fallow lands are available for grazing of animals. Thirdly, as explained earlier, with increase in irrigation and in agricultural productivity, cultivators now grow much larger quantities of green-fodder.

Therefore, if the present phase of mechanization, i.e. electrification of wells, is followed by the further step of introduction of small tractors, the presence of a large number of surplus cattle will not prove an intractable problem. The introduction of tractors will be accompanied by progressive reduction in the number of cattle through the simple process of cultivators selling their existing bullocks and not buying new ones. Buffaloes will continue to be kept however for their milk and their numbers may even increase, if commercial dairyfarming makes progress. The need for farmyard manure will then be met increasingly from the buffaloes. These developments will be similar to those in USA and Western Europe, where the farm-work animal, the horse, has disappeared after introduction of tractors, and there has been a sharp increase in the number of cows of specialized dairy breeds.

On the Eve of a Technological Revolution

The picture which emerges from the above description is that of an agricultural community in which there has been notable advance in methods of utilization of resources. A process of rapid adoption of improved agricultural practices is now well under way. This process began with consolidation of holdings, which was followed by a rapid increase in the number of irrigation wells and electrification of most of these. These developments made possible a more intensive cropping pattern, more adequate irrigation and care of all the crops grown, and increasing attention to adoption of recommended improvements, notably use of chemical fertilizers. Much progress still remains to be made in intensifying agriculture and extending adoption of improved practices to all the farmers. The use of chemical fertilizers for instance, could be increased ten-fold, before the level considered adequate by the agricultural scientists are reached. But a stage has now been reached when adoption of improved practices has become part of the agricultural enterprise of the average farmer; when proved improvements like improved seeds of several crops, and nitrogenous fertilizers are adopted by the majority of the farmers and a new seed variety or a new fertilizer takes only a few years (3 to 5) to get widely accepted. There are farmers in these villages that are not only ready to adopt recommended improvements; but are themselves looking for these in an effort to increase their production and incomes. Their number is small; but their presence has an influence which is far greater than their numbers. Further, beginnings of highly specialized types of commercial farming or livestock enterprises, like commercial poultry production, have already been made.

The area is now ready for larger changes, which would bring about major changes in farming techniques and make farming significantly more specialized and commercial. Expansion of poultry farming and of commercial dairying; much larger and more scientific use of commercial fertilizers and pesticides; large-scale introduction of the small tractors and mechanization of a variety of agricultural operations will be some of these changes. The successful experience with technological change has put the farmers in a mood in which a large number will be ready to adopt the larger and more fundamental changes. The economic level of the upper half of the farmers (those with holdings above 10 acres) makes it possible for them to be receptive to these changes, and there are no problems like that of a large number of unproductive cattle, which would present insuperable obstacles in the adoption of these.

Impact of Change

The Mahajans

The non-cultivator castes in the village are the Mahajans, the Artisans and the Harijans. The Mahajans need not detain us long. It has been explained earlier that for several decades they have sought their economic destiny outside the village, through joining services and professions after getting education. The economic changes of recent years have not altered this trend significantly.

The majority of the Mahajan families of Jitpur are dependent to a greater or lesser extent upon income originating outside the village. Some depend upon pensions; others receive remittances from sons, nephews, etc., working outside the village. Among the 83 workers listed in the Appendix 10.I as many as 30 are 'emigrants' with active links with village families. Even among the remaining 53 workers, who live in the village, as many as 13 are in service jobs outside the village. Within the village, the principal occupation of the Mahajans is petty shop-keeping. A few have recently taken to mechanical trades like repair of bicycles and flour-milling. But the scope for such petty commerce is rather limited. The village is not a commercial centre and is not likely to become one in the future, because it is located so close to the block headquarter town. The aspiration of the Mahajans has for several decades been to seek employment outside the village after education, and must remain so.

The Artisans

As mentioned earlier, the village has two main groups of artisans: the *Ramgarhia Mistris*—smiths, masons, carpenters—having 37 households, and 'other artisans'—potters, oil pressers, etc.—represented by 15 households. The impact of the changes on these two groups has been markedly different. Most of the *Mistri* families have done well; but the majority of the families of 'other artisans' have benefited little and continue to be among the poorest people in the village.

The families of smiths are among the most progressive and prosperous in the village. The two families of agricultural implements fabricators are doing a flourishing business in fabrication of agricultural implements and in repair work. Two other families have gone into business—owning brick-kilns and trucks and taking up small government contracts. They are among the most prosperous people in the village. A large number of young men from families of smiths have got remunerative employment outside the village, in the machine shops in the block headquarters town and in Ludhiana. The masons are also doing well. As explained earlier, they are very good craftsmen, and as a result of increase in house-building activity, they have managed to get remunerative employment in the village, in the block headquarter town and in neighbouring villages. The wages of a mason range between Rs. 4-5 per day plus food, so that an average worker can make about Rs. 150 per month. The carpenters have not displayed the same enterprise as the smiths or the masons have. They remain closely connected with agriculture and have repairs of ploughs and other agricultural implements as their major source of income. But even they have benefited from increase in demand for wood-work, resulting from increased construction activity.

In contrast, the 'other artisans' have benefited very little. The potters and the oil pressers continue their traditional occupations and follow the traditional techniques. But since these do not give them full-time employment, they supplement their earnings from these with agricultural and non-agricultural labour. The potters also haul earth for house construction. The traditional craft of the weavers (6 Harijan families) has been steadily declining as mill-made fabrics have replaced the cloth woven by them, and the recent economic changes have only hastened the decline. The only cloth now produced by them is coarse, heavy *khadi* and *khes* (bed-spreads). Weaving of these two types of cloth survives only because these fulfil some of the more specific needs of rural life. The *khes* for instance is useful not only as a bed-spread, but serves also as a cheap and durable cotton shawl, which can be used as much for protection against rain and cold as for bringing straw or green fodder from the fields.

In case of all these crafts, there is neither any marked increase in demand for the products nor any technological improvement. Nor does continuation of the current change of processes hold any prospects of revival in the foreseeable future. The economic redemption of the artisans practicing these crafts lies in change of occupation—taking up white-collar service after education or entering other skilled occupations after learning new skills.

The Harijans

As explained above, the Harijans of Jitpur are primarily a labouring group. The 75 families of *Ramdasias* depend mainly upon labour, agricultural and/or non-agricultural. The six families of *Julahas* (weavers) and six of *Balmikis* (scavengers) have their traditional occupations as supplementary sources of income. The labourers can be divided into two groups:

(i) *Sanjhees* or attached agricultural labourers with cultivators; and

(ii) Casual unattached labourers who take up labour, agricultural or non-agricultural, according as it becomes available.

Among the latter, 18 men work with trucks, loading and unloading bricks. They could also be regarded as attached labourers, more or less, because they do this work for about ten months in the year and take up other work only during the rainy season when this work is not available.

The other economic activities of the Harijans are service (8 workers) and shop-keeping (3 workers). Service is mainly of the unskilled work type, though two young men are skilled workers and one is a white-collar worker. Eleven Harijan young men of the village are included among the emigrants in the Appendix. Seven of these are in military service and the other four are in other services. The families of shop-keepers and service-men living in the village, and of the young men who have gone out for service are the most progressive and prosperous Harijan families in the village. And, with spread of education and rise in aspirations there is a growing tendency among the young people to look up to these occupations as the means to a higher income and better life.

Wages and Employment

The wages of casual agricultural labourers are Rs. 2 per day plus food or, less frequently, Rs. 2.50 per day without food. Wages for certain agricultural operations like harvesting of wheat or maize, and making of *gur,* which are paid in kind, are considerably higher. But such work is available only for a few days in the appropriate seasons. The Harijan casual labourers figuring in the sample survey reported having done such work for 15 to 25 days in the year.

The wages of casual non-agricultural labourers are Rs. 2 per day without food, though workers who load and unload bricks from trucks make much more, up to Rs. 4 per day. These workers have also greater security of employment, because this work is available for about ten months in the year.

From the data of the sample household and from discussions with Harijans in the village, it appears that a casual agricultural and non-agricultural labourer can get employment for about 25 days in a month in most months of the year, and that the only slack period when he is unemployed for any length of time is the rainy season (July-August). Assuming a total work year of 250 to 300 days, taking into account the fact that when he does agricultural work he gets food in addition to money wages, and that in specified agricultural operations like harvesting of wheat or making *gur*, he makes much more than Rs. 2 per day, the average annual earnings of a casual agricultural-cum-non-agricultural labourer come to about Rs. 600 per year. There was general agreement among the villagers on this point.

The women do not take up wage labour, agricultural or non-agricultural. The only work for which they get wages (in kind) is picking cotton. The women of the sample household had obtained 15 to 25 kg of cotton in the previous years, and all of it was retained for household consumption. The main contribution of the women to the income of the household is made through the livestock enterprise. This income comes through increment in the value of the animals kept, less frequently from the sale of milk, and is reported to range between Rs. 200 and Rs. 300 per year. Including this income, an average Harijan household with one male earner working as casual agricultural or non-agricultural labourer makes between Rs. 800 to 1,000 per year. The *sanjhees* and those working with trucks are better off. The latter get higher wages. The *sanjhees* have assurance of obtaining all their needs of food and other agricultural produce fairly comfortably, and have also greater financial security, because they can depend upon financial assistance from their employers in times of need.

Most *sanjhees* are given a share of the produce, the proportion varying with the size of holding, especially depending on whether one or more pairs of bullocks are kept, on the productivity of the farm and the need of the owner for labour. In a holding with one pair of bullocks, the share varies from one-fourth to one-sixth of the produce, and in one with two pairs of bullocks, it varies between one-eighth and one-eleventh. If more than two pairs of bullocks are kept, the proportion is correspondingly smaller. Until about 20 years ago, the *sanjhee's* share in the produce was decided as follows: if a cultivator had a pair of bullocks and two workers of his own family, the *sanjhee* got one-fifth of the produce, bullocks and men being counted equally for this purpose. Now-a-days however, this principal is not always adhered to, mainly because the cultivators feel that productivity of land has increased with intensive irrigation, use of chemical fertilizers and other improved practices, and the *sanjhee*, who does not contribute to the cost of these, is not entitled to the same share which he was getting earlier. Therefore, progressive cultivators with high level of productivity generally give the *sanjhee* a smaller share of the produce. Some of them prefer to pay their *sanjhee* in cash. In such cases the payment to the *sanjhee* varies between Rs. 500 and Rs. 600 per year plus food. On the other hand, a *sanjhee* working with a farmer who has not enough workers of his own, or whose cultivation is not efficient, may get a larger share. There was one case in the sample in which the *sanjhee* was getting one-fourth of the gross produce from a cultivator having one pair of bullocks. But as the man was not an efficient cultivator, and production on his farm was low, the *sanjhee* was no better off than the other *sanjhees* included in the sample.

The *sanjhee* gets a share only in foodgrains and other products like *gur* and cotton, but not in fodder crops, agricultural wastes or by-products like cotton sticks. Most *Harijans* do keep some milch animals for sale or for meeting the milk needs of their families, and do need fodder. They obtain it in two ways—in exchange for farmyard manure, which they have from their animals, and by their women cutting grass growing along field boundaries or as weeds in the fields with standing crops. The cultivators do not object to Harijan women, especially of the families of *sanjhees* and others with whom they have relations, cutting grass in their fields; and the facility of obtaining grass from the employer's fields is one attraction for a *sanjhee* and even for a causal agricultural labourer.

During the interviews with them, the cultivators complained that because of greatly increased availability of agricultural and non-agricultural employment in recent years, they were experiencing difficulty in obtaining labour for agriculture, especially in the months of April-May and September-October, when agricultural work was the heaviest. They also complained that the labourers preferred non-agricultural work to agricultural work in spite of higher wages in the latter because agricultural work was harder and involved longer hours of work. The *Harijans* agreed that more employment was now available, but explained that there were still some periods in the year like the rainy season, when they had to remain unemployed for some time. They also admitted that they preferred non-agricultural to agricultural work, and for the reasons given by the cultivators. Their main complaint was that increase in agricultural productions in recent years had not benefited them very much. They stated that the wages for casual labour had not risen in proportion to the rise in prices and that in case of *sanjhees* rise in agricultural productivity had been neutralized by reduction in share of the produce.

We now come to the question: how far have the economic changes of recent years benefited the *Harijans* and what attitudes do they have to these? The answer may be given somewhat as follows:

- The casual agricultural-cum-non-agricultural labourers are still essentially at the subsistence level.

- The *sanjhees* and the workers with trucks are better off. The *sanjhees* have participated differently in the increase in agricultural productivity, though their participation would have been larger if their share had not been reduced. The workers with trucks have a new remunerative source of employment.
- The best-off families among Harijans are those in which one or more members are engaged in occupations like shop-keeping or service.

The *Harijans* are keenly aware of the fact that economic progress in the village has so far failed to lift most of them above the subsistence level and has only increased the economic disparity between themselves and the cultivating-owners. This creates dissatisfaction among them, especially among the young men.

The largest gains to the *Harijans* have come through changes in social attitudes and improvement of social services. Untouchability, never as rigorous in this area as in other parts of the country (partly because of the influence of Sikh religion) has almost disappeared. Improvement in health services, construction of works like pavements of streets and *pucca* wells in the Harijan quarter, and loans for housing have also benefited them. But the main benefit has come through education. It has been explained earlier that the most prosperous and progressive Harijan families in the village are those of shopkeepers and men in service, or families from which boys have gone out for service. All these people have been able to enter these more remunerative occupations because of education. It appears that spread of education will be the main instrument for economic and social progress of the Harijans and such progress will come mainly through the social process—education, wider outlook, higher aspirations, striving for and getting better paid jobs, mainly outside the village. The recent extension of compulsory primary education, which has brought a large proportion of the *Harijan* boys into the schools, is a major step in this direction.

Other Aspects of Change

Education

The tradition of modern type school education is quite well established in this area, especially among groups like Mahajans and *Ramgarhia Mistris* from which large numbers have been going out in services, professions and skilled work. Among the Jats too, education has been widespread because of the tradition of emigration and military service. But in recent years education has been spreading rapidly among all groups including the Harijans. The village has two primary schools now, one for boys and the other for girls, which have 285 students. In addition 83 boys and girls go to the three high schools in the block headquarters town and three boys attend the college located in the *mandi* town. Thus, the total number of students in the village is 371. Their distribution by sex, caste and type of school attended is given in Table 10.10.

Compulsory primary education was introduced in the village three years ago. It has been effectively enforced in case of boys and with the exception of a stray case here and there, every boy of school going age now goes to school. In case of girls, however, enforcement is not equally strict and there are many girls especially among the Harijans, who do not attend school. The figures in Table 10.10 bring out clearly the effect of enforcement of compulsory education on school going. The sharp increase in the number of Harijan boys in the first three classes is particularly noteworthy. The number of Harijan girls going to school has also shown a marked increase though it is still small. Among the Jats also the number of girls going to school is much less than the number of boys but the effect of introduction of compulsory primary education is clearly seen in the increase in number of girls in the first three classes as compared with that in the higher classes. Among the *Ramgarhia Mistris* and Mahajans on the other hand, the number of girls going to school including high school is comparable to or higher than that of boys. In both these groups, education of girls has become an accepted social practice.

Table 10.10: Distribution of School Students by Sex, Caste and Type of School Attended

Caste	Number of Children Going to School										
	Primary School						High School			Total	
	Ist 3 Classes			Class IV & V							
	M	F	T	M	F	T	M	F	T	M	F
Jats	46	31	77	22	9	31	23	9	32	91	49
Mistris	16	16	32	8	3	11	6	10	16	30	29
Mahajans	13	19	32	4	9	13	15	12	27	32	40
Harijans	44	14	58	6	5	11	6	-	6	56	19
Other artisans	5	3	8	2	1	3	1	-	1	8	4
Bazigars	3	2	5	4	-	4	1	-	1	8	2
Total village	127	65	212	46	27	73	52	31	83	225	143

The number of boys and girls in classes 1 to 9 is estimated to be about 66 per cent of those in the age-group 6-15. The percentage of boys and girls of the age-group 6-11 going to school would be higher still because the numbers in primary classes are much higher than those in the post-primary classes. But the village is still far from universal literacy. The percentage of literates among adults (above 15 year) was found, in this survey, to be only 23.8. The position of universal literacy will be reached only after a generation when the boys and girls who are now going to school become adults. But a situation has already been reached, in which because of the large number of boys and girls in schools, presence in the village of a number of educated men, and of growing awareness and knowledge of things even among the illiterates, ignorance has ceased to be a relevant fact in village life. This is a most significant fact for the education and cultural progress of village India; because it means that the point at which ignorance ceases to be important can be reached considerably before universal literacy has been attained. Literacy and education are important as ends in themselves. But they are equally important as means of banishing ignorance and superstitions, and changing the mental outlook from a basically tradition-oriented one to a change oriented one. Experience here shows that the water-shed between ignorance on one side and knowledge on the other can be crossed and a change oriented outlook produced even before the entire population becomes literate.

Health

By far the most significant recent development in the field of health in this area, as in most others in India, has been eradication of malaria. This has meant elimination of the greatest killer that debilitates men. Moreover, since other diseases like cholera and dysentery, which are prevalent in most other parts of India, have always been less important in the Punjab, eradication of malaria has meant elimination of epidemic disease as a major problem in village life. Campaigns for eradication of small-pox and trachoma are now being carried out as part of country-wide campaigns, and it is expected that these two diseases will also be eliminated in a few years' time.

The author had occasion to discuss the availability of medical facilities and attitudes towards treatment of disease with the village leaders and with the lady doctor in charge of the hospital at the block headquarter town. The hospital, which has 24 beds, has one doctor, besides nurses and other auxiliary staff. Similar hospitals are located at distances of 5 to 15 miles along all the roads going out from the town. In addition, there are sub-centres located in the larger villages, which provide maternity aid and guidance in child-care. Three such sub-centres are located in this block, and this village is included in the area of one of these.

The doctor explained that as part of the work of the sub-centres, house-to-house surveys of all pregnant women were conducted from time to time, that the women were persuaded to come to the sub-centres for ante-natal consultation and were given advice and necessary medicines. Cases in which any complication was likely at the time of delivery were detected at this stage, and deliveries of such women were attended to either by the nurse-midwife in their homes, or if necessary, at the hospital. At the time of this survey, about a dozen women from this village were visiting the sub-centre for ante-natal or family planning consultation. All the three *dais* of the village had received the training prescribed by the Health Department and were associated with the programme of the sub-centre. The maternity and child guidance service now available to this village is comparable to that available to any protected section of the population of the middle or lower income group, e.g. participants in the Employees State Insurance Scheme, and is very much better than that available to any ordinary urban group.

Attitude Towards Treatment of Disease

Treatment of disease, especially serious disease or injury by modern medicine has become accepted. All cases of serious sickness or of injury are taken normally to the hospital at the block headquarter and more serious ones are taken to the hospital at the district headquarter town. But, for treatment of common diseases, there is considerable resort to private practitioners, a *vaidya* in the village and two *vaidyas* and two medical practitioners in the block headquarter town. The reason for the popularity of the private practitioners is either because the hospital cannot provide all the medical facilities that a villager may need or desire e.g. supply of medicines—or because he feels that he will get better medical attention with a private practitioner. But since even the *vaidyas* have begun to use sulpha-drugs and anti-biotic, use of modern medicines is extensive, and the knowledge that a penicillin injection is an effective cure for many a disease has become part of the culture of the village.

Family Planning

A beginning has been made with this programme also. Facilities for consultation and free contraceptives are provided to the women at the sub-centres, and to both men and women at the hospital. The hospital provides facilities for vasectomy also and six of these were reported to have been done during the two years preceding this survey. The doctor, the BDO, the VLW, some workers of the Family Planning Programme and the village leaders with whom the author had occasion to discuss the subject, summed up the present practice and attitudes towards family planning as follows:

The number of people using family planning practices is still quite small. The Mahajans and the *Mistris* use these practices more than people of the other castes.

But knowledge of family planning practices is spreading rapidly, and the number of people who have begun to be aware of the need for these practices is growing. The cultivators in this area have always been acutely conscious of the limitation of land in supporting an increasing population—the tradition of migration among the Jats is one indicator of this awareness—and the threat to size of holding, and level of income posed by a large number of births is being increasingly realized by them.

Many, cultivators, especially the young ones, are only watching the experience of those who have begun following family planning practices and especially those who have undergone vasectomies, before adopting these themselves. Use of family planning methods will spread very rapidly in the next few years, as the experience of the small number that is practicing these now becomes widely known.

Sanitation

There has been enormous improvement in sanitation and water supply in the village during the last 15 years. Most of the village streets have been paved and provided with *pucca* side drains with financial assistance from the Community Development Block. Several wells have been made sanitary by provision of well-designed platforms, parapet walls and *pullies*. But the biggest improvement in water supply has come through installation of hand-pumps in a large number of houses. Sanitary water supply now remains a problem only for the Harijans and 'other artisans', who continue to draw water from the wells.

The main sanitation problems of the village now relate to use of latrines and provision of drainage. The drainage problem has been aggravated in recent years, with installation of hand-pumps in the houses and construction of drains because much larger quantities of waste-water now flow into the village pond. No way for draining the pond has been found yet. The *Sarpanch* mentioned that he had sent a proposal to the State Government for draining the pond through a long drainage channel into a *nullah*, and was expecting that a survey of the scheme would be taken up by the State Drainage Department in the near future. However, from the discussions with him and other people in the village it was clear that there was not enough concern about this problem among the village people and progress on it would not be rapid. Similarly, no progress has been made in use of latrines and none can be made unless flush-type latrines, which an average farmer can afford to install in his own house, are introduced. Dry latrines are impractical for the simple reason that no body would be prepared to clean them. The sweepers of the village already confine themselves to sweeping of only cow dung and other litter and in the prevailing social climate, it will be impossible to get them to clean latrines.

Levels of Living

Some limited data on character of housing and possession of certain durable consumer goods were collected as part of the household survey. The main object was to get some indication of the advance towards modernization and of improvement in levels of living. The items were selected with this end in view. Another consideration was to select those items which would show significant differences in economic status within the village. Thus possession of a radio set was considered far more significant than possession of several other modern type consumer goods like a torch, a hurricane lantern or even a wristwatch. These latter have become common place in the villages, but the number of radios is still small enough to indicate significant differences in level of living. Similarly, possession of a sewing machine, a kerosene stove or an electric iron indicates not only a certain economic level but even more a definite urban orientation in the household. The items selected for the survey were: type of house—*kutcha, pucca*, or semi-*pucca*; whether having electricity and hand pump or not; possession of bicycle, sewing machine, radio, kerosene stove and other electric appliances like a fan and electric iron. The data are presented caste-wise in Table 10.11.

Table 10.11: Levels of Living

	Village	*Jat*	*Ramgarhia*	*Mahajan*	*Harijan*	*Other Artisans*	*Bazigar*
Total number of households	299	105	37	46	87	15	9
No. of households living in houses							
Kutcha	163	41	18	21	62	12	9
Semi-pucca	58	18	7	14	12	2	—
Pucca	83	46	12	11	13	1	—
With electricity	108	45	24	31	3	5	—
With hand-pump	168	83	25	35	17	7	1
No. of households possessing							
Bicycles	130	55	33	28	7	6	1
Sewing machine	83	30	23	23	2	5	—
No. of households possessing other appliances	Radio 20; Electric Iron 16: Kerosene stove: 10						

It will be seen that about 45 per cent of the households are living in *pucca* or semi-*pucca* houses; about 35 per cent are in houses fitted with electricity; but as many as 55 per cent are in houses having hand-pumps. Over 45 per cent of the households have bicycles and over a quarter have sewing machines. But the number of radios, kerosene stoves and electric irons is rather small.

It may be noted also that living in *pucca* or semi-*pucca* houses with facility of electricity or hand-pump and possession of these durable consumer goods is confined mainly to the three upper groups, the Jats, the *Ramgarhia Mistris* and the Mahajans. The Mahajans are visibly lower than the other two groups. This may appear surprising at first; but is readily understood when we consider the fact that a large number of Mahajans are either old people or widows living on pensions or remittances from sons and other relatives.

On the other hand the Harijans, the other artisans and the *Bazigars* have these benefits of modernization to a very limited extent. As compared with nearly 40 per cent of Jat families living in electrified houses, only three Harijan families (4 per cent of the total) are living in such houses. Harijans come out very poorly even in possession of the bicycle which has come to be accepted as a necessity over large parts of rural India. This contrast in level of living between the three upper groups and the Harijans reinforces the observations about the failure of the Harijans to rise above the subsistence level and the growing disparity between them and the Jats made earlier. It focuses attention on what is perhaps the biggest problem of the village for the future, namely, taking the fruits of higher productivity and income to this large section of the population.

Factors behind Technological Change

The Man

The Jat generally, and the Sikh Jat particularly, is known to be a good cultivator, combining hard work with intelligent use of resources. This fact has been repeatedly stressed by administrators, agricultural officers and others who have had occasion to work with Jat cultivators. (See for instance Darling, 1925).In the canal colonies of West Punjab, Sikh Jats proved to be particularly adept at intelligent use of irrigation waters, and some of the highest standards of farm husbandry, yields per acre and agricultural incomes to be found anywhere in the country were reached on their farms. The refugee cultivators from the canal colonies are among the most progressive cultivators in this area, and their presence has made a major contribution to Jitpur's agricultural progress, as explained below. Already the standard of farm husbandry in this area was fairly good in pre-Independence years. Cultivation was intensive and crop yields were moderately high. The average yield of sugarcane in 1951-52, just before the opening of the CD block, was 40 to 45 kg (of *gur*) per acre, as compared with 55 kg per acre today. The standard of livestock husbandry was also high, as evidenced by the fairly high yields of milch animals.

Agricultural extension work was well organized in pre-Partition Punjab, its Department of Agriculture being among the best in the country. Several important improved practices such as use of C-591 wheat, and CO-312 sugarcane, growing of *berseem* as green-fodder and use of improved implements like iron ploughs, iron Persian wheels, chaff-cutters and improved sugarcane presses, had become universally accepted in this area by the time of Independence. The people of Jitpur mentioned in particular the work of a Deputy Director of Agriculture who had in the 1930's taught them the improved method of making *khandsari* sugar, which they are following to this day.

But, rapid advance in techniques and agricultural productivity, with which we are concerned in this study, has occurred only after Independence, and the explanation for it must be sought in the factors operating in this period. A number of factors have been operating simultaneously, and we shall content ourselves with listing the most important among them.

Influence of Refugee Cultivators

After the partition of the Punjab in 1947, large numbers of cultivators from the canal colonies came to East Punjab to their ancestral villages from where they had emigrated 30 or 40 years earlier, or to other villages in which they had been allotted lands. The canal colonists, as stated earlier, had attained high standards of farm husbandry and agricultural incomes in West Punjab and were used to improved methods of farming advocated by the Department of Agriculture. When they came to East Punjab and were given holdings, which were much smaller than those they had left behind, their first endeavour was to re-attain the standard of agricultural income which they had enjoyed earlier. They started building up their new holdings through methods which had given good results in the canal colonies—use of improved seed, use of iron ploughs and other implements, thorough preparation of land and last, but most important, intensive irrigation. From these practices they soon went on to new practices, which were necessary for obtaining higher per acre yields from their smaller holdings. Thus, they were in the forefront of the movement for irrigation by pumping sets, because they realized that irrigation was the key to intensive farming and that the only way to increase water supplies in this area was through the use of mechanical power for lifting water from wells.

Besides generally stimulating the movement towards more progressive, intensive agriculture the refugee cultivators were responsible for popularizing several specific improvements. The rapid spread of American cotton in East Punjab in the early 1950s was due mainly to their influence. They started growing American cotton, which they used to grow in the canal colonies, and the local cultivators followed their example. The large price difference between American and *desi* cotton in the early 1950s aided this movement and growing of American cotton became universal in several districts of the Punjab within a few years.[6] The rapid increase in popularity of the fodder crop, *berseem*, was also because they preferred *berseem* to other fodder crops. Some of the prosperous refugee cultivators, who had owned citrus orchards in the canal colonies, started planting orchards. The Punjab government encouraged the practice by establishing planned garden colonies, in which besides specialized advice, liberal *Taccavi* loans and other facilities were also given to the planters.

Of course, the refugee cultivators were not successful in everything they introduced. Citrus orchards were not successful, because the climate and soils of the Central Punjab districts are different from those of the West Punjab canal colonies. The author saw an instance of failure of citrus plantation in the garden colony, located in this block, at a distance of about ten miles from Jitpur. The colonists had all planted citrus orchards in the early 1950s; but they had to give up later when they found that the trees did not survive after two or three years, partly because of the presence of a "hard pan" in the sub-soil. The American cotton was also not without its defects. It was more susceptible to diseases like jessids and boll-worm. As a result, after the first wave of spread of American cotton, the *desi* variety staged a comeback. Many agricultural officers now feel that the area is more suitable for *desi* than American cotton.

But the idea of intensive agriculture, use of improved methods and following the advice of extension workers received a definite stimulus from the example of the refugee cultivators. The leadership provided by a refugee cultivator in the village with the co-operative milk producers' society has been described earlier. The garden colony people, though unsuccessful at planting orchards, have nevertheless attained a high standard of cultivation. They are acknowledged to be the best cultivators in the block and are frequently held up by the extension workers as models for other cultivators. In all our discussions, with the extension staff at the block and the district level, and even with specialists at the Ludhiana Agricultural University, the role of refugee cultivators in providing a stimulus to the movement towards improved agriculture was emphasized.

Ex-Servicemen and Educated Cultivators

The other groups whose presence has had a significant influence on technological and economic progress in the area are ex-servicemen and educated cultivators. The major contribution of the ex-servicemen has been in spreading the idea of better living—better and cleaner homes, cleaner villages, use of modern medicine, modern-type consumer goods, etc. The block staff and the village leaders said that ex-servicemen were particularly enthusiastic about building *pucca* or semi-*pucca* houses and installing electricity and hand-pumps in houses. They also took active interest in village sanitation programmes. The spread of the tea-drinking habit after Second World War was also attributed to them. Several ex-servicemen were also active in popular institutions like the co-operatives and the *Panchayats* and rose to positions of leadership in them. The extension staff thought that they were good at working the co-operatives because they understood the 'co-operative principle' and were more honest; but they were not particularly successful in the *panchayats*. Several ex-servicemen, when elected to *panchayats*, proved unpopular and lost in the subsequent elections. The explanation given for this was that 'they were too strict in the observance of principles'.

But the role of ex-servicemen in the improvement of agriculture was some-what limited. They undoubtedly influenced technological change, because they were familiar with modern technology and were anxious to adopt labour-saving devices. They were among the first to install electric motors on wells, and to adopt innovations like power or bullock-driven chaff-cutters, sugarcane crushers, in this and the neighbouring villages. But their influence in adoption of other improvements has not been much, because the average cultivator feels that they are not willing to do hard labour and are not particularly good cultivators. This impression is based on the fact that many ex-servicemen were not really interested in agriculture. They drifted to non-agricultural jobs after a period of stay on the farms, and those who did stay back were not happy at doing hard manual labour.

As for educated people, few persons with education above the middle-standard stay in agriculture. They are after non-agricultural employment, and leave cultivation as soon as they get suitable jobs. But to the extent that they do stay in agriculture, they are an influence for progress. Some of them like the garden colonists and the chairman of the milk producers' society, are good cultivators. Moreover, like the ex-servicemen, they are anxious to adopt new techniques, especially new implements and other labour-saving devices; and for the same reasons. They have also shown a noteworthy aptitude for taking up new, remunerative types of farm production. The new commercial poultry production is entirely in the hands of educated men. They do not have the prejudice against keeping poultry, which the average cultivator still has. They also have the added advantage of understanding and following the rigorous routine which commercial poultry production requires.

The Environment of Progress

But the most significant influence of the post-Independence years has been the environment of progress. A number of factors, ranging from steady and high prices of agricultural produce and interest shown by government in improvement of agriculture, to the growing inter-action between the town and the village, have gone into the making of this environment. Since, prices of agricultural produce have remained high, and the government has been making propaganda and giving various incentives and facilities for increasing production, the cultivators feel that the increasing agricultural production is profitable and is likely to remain so for a long time. The various steps taken by the government to increase production have also had their direct effects. It has been explained that in this village, consolidation, digging of new wells and electrification laid the basis of a more progressive agriculture. The work of the extension organization has also been a constant influence for progress. Currently, the propaganda for use of chemical fertilizers, backed by readily available *Taccavi* loans, is a major factor in rapid increase in the use of chemical fertilizers.

Increasingly, these influences have operated in a peasantry, which was rising above the subsistence level, was becoming less subject to tradition, and was, therefore, more responsive and better able to benefit from them. The size of holdings in the area is such that with the improved methods of resource use—possible after consolidation and electrification of wells—the average cultivator could raise himself substantially above the subsistence level. As this happened, he acquired not only a desire for a higher standard of living, but also a confidence in his ability to attain it. Eradication of malaria removed a major impediment to economic efficiency—a cause of chronic lassitude and lack of ambition. Spread of education meant penetration of new ideas, decline in influence of tradition and growth of new aspirations, especially among the young who form a steadily more influential section of the population. Even though large numbers of educated young men have gone out after receiving education, the ones who have stayed behind have been on the look-out for improvements which lighten the burden of work or increase incomes. And as they succeed in their efforts, their influence increases.

Finally, rapid growth of transport and communications has effectively linked the villages with the towns, and made the village people an integral part of contemporary culture and aspirations. Reference was made in the beginning to the ease and rapidity with which the people of Jitpur can travel to the neighbouring town and other places. The material advantages of this which have a direct influence on agricultural improvement are, facility and low expense of taking produce to the market, buying implements, equipment and consumer goods at lower prices and getting repairs and replacement of parts done quickly and cheaply. But the non-material advantages are of equal, if not greater, importance. The average resident of Jitpur today is a full participant in the news, ideas and social currents of contemporary society. Any news or new idea can reach him just as quickly as it reaches a person in the neighbouring town. To an extent he is better informed than the latter, because the channels of informal communication and discussion are much better preserved in the village. Moreover, with his present income and the network of social services available to him, he has a standard of living, which is comparable if not superior in many respects, to that of the resident of the town. All this means that the villager and the town-dweller are part of the same culture and share its values and aspirations. This constant interaction between town and village and the establishment of cultural continuum extending from the large city to the village is a most important influence for economic progress. The distinction between the town and the village—in food, dress, housing conditions, modes of economic activity, patterns of social relation and values—which is still pronounced in many parts of India, has almost disappeared in the Punjab.

Simultaneous development of small-scale industry in the towns and technological change in agriculture in the villages is only another aspect of this cultural continuity. The two developments are related in many ways, starting from a common dependence on cheap electricity and mechanical aptitude and skills of the Punjab artisans. Within the village, the relationship between them is expressed in two ways: facility in adoption of new agricultural implements by cultivators because of existence of facilities for repair and manufacture of these in the neighbouring towns; and opportunities for young men of the village for employment in small-scale industry in the towns. An investigation of the relations between the two developments is a fascinating subject for further research.

One result of establishment of this cultural continuum is seen in the mental make-up of the extension workers. The extension agency has here, as in other States, its problems of administrative co-ordination, supplies, credit, etc. But what impresses one here is the lack of distance—social, economic and psychological—between the agricultural extension workers and the cultivators. The Village Level Workers (VLW) and even the block and district level Extension Officers speak the language of the cultivators. They have an understanding of their problems and an emotional identification with their interests, which is not found among extension workers in many parts of the country. One reason for this is that most of them come from cultivators' families. But an even more important reason is the fact that levels of living, awareness and income of the average cultivator are comparable to those of the average extension worker. As a result, the extension worker considers the cultivators to be his social and economic equals: he does not think that by joining government service he has become superior to them. Moreover, more extension workers realize that they will have to settle down and work on farms after retiring from service. And since cultivation is profitable, they look forward to it. It may be of interest to mention that many highly paid government officers, especially of the Department of Agriculture, have settled down after retirement, on 15-20 acre farms, and are quite happy with the income and living conditions, which these farms provide. This aspiration to return to agriculture, even more than the farm background, is responsible for ready and sympathetic appreciation of the problems of the cultivators. When both the cultivator and the extension worker feel that they have not merely a common past but also a common future, mental reservations disappear and a community of interest is established, which is rarely established otherwise.

The Role of Emigration

It has been explained earlier that the area has a tradition of emigration.

The effect of the recent economic and social changes has been to accelerate the rate at which aspirations for non-agricultural employment and emigration grow. It is true that two reasons for emigration of educated young men from the village in the past-low productivity in agriculture and unattractiveness of village life—no longer operate. A 10-acre holding now offers a similar or higher income than clerical or skilled jobs in town. Secondly, life in the village after coming of electricity, hand pumps, roads and bus transport is not unattractive. But these changes cannot check growth of off-farm employment and emigration, because continued advances in agriculture and levels of living are themselves dependent upon a continuing exodus of workers from the village.

Let us analyze this separately for each of the principal castes. Among the Jat cultivating owners, continued agricultural progress and prosperity are dependent upon the size of holding not falling much below the present level. This means that a certain proportion of young men must continuously go out. The Mahajans already have a limited economic role in the village. They depend mainly upon income originating from outside and their position cannot change significantly unless some manufacturing industry or urban-oriented commercial activity, in which a large number can get employment, is established in the village. As for the *Mistris*, technological change has undoubtedly opened opportunities for work within and near the village. But as explained above, even they have found employment outside the village more attractive. Increasing number of *Mistri* young men is either going out of the village or are working outside while living in the village. Emigration and work outside the village have been the least among the Harijans and 'other artisans', who are the poorest and most backward people in the village.

The much repeated argument that emigration of its educated and most intelligent people robs the village of its best talent and slows down economic and social progress has no relevance in this situation. As stated earlier the major role of emigration has been to provide opportunities for gainful employment to people who had only a limited role in the economic system of the village and to bring into the village money, new ideas, new techniques and higher aspirations. This contribution of emigration has been far more significant than any loss caused to the village by migration of its educated young men.

Gains of Progress and the Weaker Sections

It has been explained above that the gains of recent economic progress have not been shared equally by all sections of the village community and that the Harijans and other artisans in particular have not benefited, adequately from such progress. These groups have made some economic gains undoubtedly, but they are much smaller than those made by the Jat cultivators and the *Mistris*. The difference in levels of living of different castes and groups in the village is much larger today than it was a generation ago, simply because conveniences like electricity and hand-pumps in the homes or durable consumer goods like bicycles and sewing machines which the Jats and the *Mistris* have in considerable numbers and which the Harijans do not have, were not available earlier. Moreover, from the (limited) data on earnings of Harijans given earlier, it would appear that increase in agricultural productivity has not been accompanied by a proportionate increase in earnings of agricultural labourers. The result is that the difference between owners of land and their labourers has increased.

But the *Harijans* cannot obtain a significantly higher income within the economic framework of the village. (Revitalization of their traditional crafts offers no solution to their economic problem, because the economic changes of recent years have accelerated the decline of these crafts.) They can achieve it only through greater participation in the economy of the area, the State and the country. In other words they must do what the Mahajans and the *Mistris* (and to a lesser extent the Jats) have done before them. They must take up white-collar and skilled-labour jobs in increasing numbers. The process has begun already—recent increase in the number of Harijan young men going into the armed forces is an indicator—and will gather momentum as education spreads among the Harijans. Already, the more advanced and prosperous families among Harijans are those in which skilled work or white-collar service, or other non-agricultural pursuits, is an important source of contribution. As the number of such families increases, the economic and social levels of the group will rise.

Conclusion

This chapter based on a study of technological change in agriculture and in certain other aspects of change, e.g. in levels of living, education, health and attitudes of people, have been analyzed with a view to seeing the relation between them and change in agriculture. Perhaps, the most significant conclusion emerging from the study is that change in agricultural techniques is part of a larger change process, which affects many aspects of the life of the villagers, and also the entire region. Change in agriculture is but one aspect of the process of economic growth in Central Punjab. Further, it is necessary to mention that what we have described here is the *beginning* of a process of technological change. It should gather momentum in future and produce larger and more important changes—intensive use of chemical fertilizers and pesticides, use of small tractors, increasing emphasis on specialized farming (poultry keeping, dairying, horticulture), and change in attitudes towards the role of agriculture. These changes can be seen already among the more progressive farmers like the dairy farmers and the garden colonists.

This study throws up many questions relating to the analysis of change, e.g. the role of innovators, channels of communication within the village, reasons for acceptance or rejection of specific practices, and the contribution of Sikh religion, better nutrition or health to the enterprise and vigour of the villagers. These and other questions are being investigated by a number of investigators working in different parts of India which will give us a better understanding of the process described in this study.

Footnotes

1. I know of villages in another States where cultivators who grow sugarcane and make *gur* do not own the cane presses, but hire these from smiths in towns, who look after the repairs also because the local smiths cannot repair these presses.
2. The correct word appears to be Ravidasias, i.e. followers of Ravidas, the celebrated *Chammar* Saint; but the word Ramdasias is more commonly used.
3. See the occupational change among *Berwa Chammars* in Sawai Madhopur district of Eastern Rajasthan described in Chapter 2.
4. Headman of a group of villages. The post was abolished after Independence.
5. No young man from Jitpur had gone for such work to the UK till the time of this study. But two young men explained to me that they were thinking of going and had sent the necessary applications for employment vouchers, passports, etc.
6. The Programme Evaluation Organization (PEO) of the Planning Commission made a study of the spread of American cotton in certain Community Development Blocks of PEPSU in 1954. It was found in this study that 70 to 90 per cent of the cultivators were growing American cotton and that the example of the refugee cultivators who had brought American cotton with them was a major factor in it s spread ("Cotton Extension in PEPSU" 1955. PEO Planning Commission).

Appendix 10.I

Selected Economic Data for Households – Caste-wise, Jitpur 1963

		Jats	Ramgarhia Mistris	Mahajans	Harijans	Other artisans	Bazigars	Total
Number of households		105	37	46	87	15	9	299
Population	Male	472	110	154	281	57	25	1099
	Female	308	95	135	236	32	23	832
	Total	780	205	289	517	92	48	1931
Population above 15 years	Male	271	74	94	134	37	12	622
	Female	170	56	77	108	19	9	439
	Total	441	130	171	242	56	21	1061
Number of literate persons above 15 years	Male	68	37	71	30	8	1	215
	Female	8	17	13	–	–	–	38
	Total	76	54	84	30	8	1	253
Number of children going to school	Male	91	30	32	56	8	8	225
	Female	49	29	40	19	4	2	143
	Total	140	59	72	75	12	10	368
Land Ownership and Cultivation								
Number of land–owning households		96	3	4	1	–	–	104
Area owned (acres)		1033	11.5	28.5	6	–	–	1080
Number of cultivating households		76	2	4	–	–	–	82
Area cultivated (acres)		1065	9.5	28.5	–	–	–	1103

Appendix (Contd.)

Economic Activity							
Number of workers							
(i) including migrants	245	70	83	120	29	13	
(ii) excluding migrants, i.e. in village	213	56	53	110	26	13	
Number of workers in village in:							
Cultivation	194	–	9	–	–	–	203
Agricultural labour	1	–	1		4	1	127
Non–agricultural labour	4	4	4	91	5	12	64
Skilled work	1	43	7	5	8	–	25
Service	1	1	13	8	2	–	
Others (inc. shop keeping, contract work, traditional village crafts, etc.)	5	7	14	5	5	4	40
Emigrants in:							
Military service	24	–	10	7	1	–	42
Skilled work (inc. drivers of motor vehicles)	11	9	2	–	–	–	22
White-collar services and professions	6	4	18	2	2	–	32
Others	–	1	–	2	–	–	3
No. of households living in houses							
Total	105	37	46	87	15	9	299
Kutcha	41	18	21	62	12	9	163
Semi-pucca	18	7	14	12	2	–	53
Pucca	46	12	11	13	1	–	83
With electricity	45	24	31	3	5	–	108
With hand-pumps	83	25	35	17	7	1	168
No, of households owning							
Bicycles	55	33	28	7	6	1	130
Sewing machines	30	23	23	2	5	–	83

11

Women in the New Village*

Kamla Nath

The rapid technological change in agriculture and economic progress sweeping through some of the villages in Central Punjab are also affecting the women of the area. In this chapter an attempt has been made to describe the pattern of work, practices relating to home-making, treatment of diseases, maternity and child care and attitudes towards education of girls among women of Jat cultivator households of a small village about three miles from Jitpur.

The agricultural economy and techniques in this village are very similar to those described for Jitpur. It received electricity at about the same time: the bulk of the cropped area is irrigated, and majority of the irrigation wells are fitted with electric motors. The cropping pattern and use of improved practices (chemical fertilizers, improved seeds, and improved implements) are also similar to Jitpur. I selected this village in preference to Jitpur because it is a small village of Jat cultivators, and it was much easier for me to know the women. Besides, the extremely co-operative attitude of women of the family of the *Sarpanch* (father) and President of the dairy cooperative (son) enabled me to know the women of the village. The educated young wife of the President is much respected in the village for her family background—she comes from a well-known Jat family of the district—education and competence in managing the home. She introduced me to the village women, helped explain the object of my work, and was always available for any assistance that I might need. I found discussions with her and the older women of the family an interesting supplement to the data collected through the sample survey. The *dai* of the village, a *Chammar* woman, assisted me as a companion

---

* Kamla Nath, the wife of the author studied the impact of technological change in agriculture on women in the New Village. However, she selected a neighbouring village located at a distance of couple of miles from Jitpur for her study. Her findings were also published in Economic and Political Weekly in 1965.

and interpreter, and also gave useful information on local customs and practices. I am grateful to these women for their assistance.

The village had a total of 104 households and population of 626 (1961). There are 76 households of *Jats*, but only 36 of them are cultivators. In the remaining households, the small holding is given out for cultivation on *batai* (crop sharing) and work outside the village, army pensions or remittances from sons or nephews working outside are the principal sources of income. This study was confined to the *Jat* cultivators. A sample survey of 18 households (50% of the total) was undertaken, with a view primarily to meeting and knowing a sufficiently large number of women. Emigration and dependence upon outside income is rather more in this village than in Jitpur. The *Jats* of the village have been prominent in the military service. Several even received awards for valour in First and Second World War. A *pucca* well situated at the entrance to the village was built by the District board in 1937 in recognition of the services rendered by men of the village during the First World War.

The 18 households have 123 persons; an average of 6.8 persons per household. The comparatively large size of households is due to the strength of the institution of joint family. As many as 10 households consist of joint families—7 are two unit families, while the remaining 3 are three unit families. The number of males is much larger than of females (68 males and 55 females). The excess of males creates a serious problem of finding wives for men. The problem is discussed at the end.

Pattern of Work

The women's pattern of work is described first, because of its influence on home-making, child care, personal hygiene and even attitude towards education of girls. Most women of the sample households reported that they did not do any work in the fields. One of them to emphasize her point said, "We do not go out to even pick *sag* (green leaves of mustard, turnips etc used as a vegetable). Only two women said that they went to the fields to pick cotton or to supervise the work of hired labourers, during peak period of agricultural work.[1]

Women in the villages of this area probably never worked in the fields in the way in which women of some other cultivating groups in North India do. But the trend towards women not doing any work in the fields is more recent. The change has occurred only during the last 15-20 years and is related to agricultural prosperity, increase in education and urban influences. The older women in several households said that earlier they used to go to the fields to pick cotton, bring fuel and vegetables for the home and fodder for the livestock. One woman regretting the change said, "The young women do not do hard work now, they do not work in the fields and they do not have to grind corn on the *chakki* (hand mill) or to fetch water from the wells, as we had to do. This is why they cannot deliver their babies easily". Domestic work for the women has also become much lighter. Since hand pumps have been installed in most homes the women do not need to bring water from the village wells. Grinding corn on the *chakki* is no longer necessary, because there is a flour mill in the village. This work, which was generally entrusted to the young daughter-in-law, was often the cause of quarrels in the joint family. Its elimination has been welcomed particularly by the younger women.

The main work of the women now, besides looking after the home, is care of the livestock. This takes a lot of their time, because the animals are kept within the houses at night and also for part of the day. Indeed they go out to the fields mainly for exercise. The women feed and look after the animals, and milk the buffaloes and cows. But they will not clean the cattle shed; cleaning the cattle shed and carrying refuse to the compost pit are the jobs of the sweeper women. The women do not mind looking after the animals—indeed they are proud of it, because presence of such animals in the house has always been considered a sign of prosperity in Punjab villages. Even the educated wife of the President of the Dairy Cooperative Society spent lot of time attending to her milch animals and disposing of the milk.

Poultry farming is now becoming popular in this area. In this village, one young man is keeping about 400 birds in a part of his house. His mother and wife do all the work—feeding the birds, collecting the eggs, cleaning the bird house periodically. Two other men have also started keeping a few birds each. One of them is thinking of setting up a big modern poultry farm. But the attitude of women towards this work is not favourable. In some of my group interviews, women jeered at the mother of the young poultry farmer and showed pity for the young wife. "Chicken are dirty", they said, "and looking after them is the job of the sweeper women. Besides, what is the use of keeping poultry, when we can get the same income from one buffalo as from a hundred chickens"! These attitudes may change, if poultry farming continues to be as profitable as it has been during the last few years, and the movement towards establishing poultry farms continues among educated farmers.

Elimination of farm work and lighter domestic chores have given these women a lot of free time, which they are now devoting to cooking, better care of home, the children and themselves and to practicing of traditional crafts such as *durry* making, and learning new ones such as knitting and sewing.

These women devote much more time to cooking than do women who work in the fields. Two full meals (sometimes three) are cooked daily[2] and the food is substantial and adequate.[3] They are also becoming increasingly conscious of personal hygiene and their own appearance. They bathe much more frequently than they did in the past. A daily bath is now the rule in the summer; but in the winter they bathe only once in two or three days. Presence of hand pumps in the houses encourages frequent bathing. A number of women use cheap face cream or talcum powder. The wife of the President of the dairy cooperative was using cream, face powder and lipstick of well-known brands. All the younger women said that they used toilet soap and applied oil to the hair. But some of the older women continue the old practice of applying *ghee* to the hair. None of the women, young or old had ever used mud for washing their hair, which the Meena women of Sawai Madhopur use. The children too were clean and well clothed.

Most women possess quite a few changes of clothes. Every time the family goes to the town, new clothes and sometimes new shoes are bought for one or the other member. Silk or rayon clothes are bought for festive occasions, woollens are bought for winter. All men, women and children were wearing some woollen garment at the time of this study which was conducted during December. Some men possess western style woollen suits and the women have woollen *salwar-kamiz* suits. These are worn on special occasions—visiting the town to see a 'high officer', or visiting a prosperous relative. A large proportion of the cash income of the families is spent on clothing. It is interesting to note that with somewhat higher incomes, the trend among the Meenas of Sawai Madhopur is to spend more on silver ornaments; but in this group the emphasis is *now* on clothing. That they have gone through the stage of spending more on ornaments was clear from the remarks of the 90-year old mother of the *Sarpanch*. She said, "I have seen three *Zamanas* (periods) in my life. First there was the 'silver age' when all of us wore silver ornaments. Then there was the 'gold age'; now it is the 'cloth age'. "The women do have gold and silver ornaments but they were not wearing any ornaments at all. This is a significant trend, for it shows that in course of time possession of ornaments may not retain the same value it enjoys today with villagers in most parts of India.

Washing clothes is almost a daily routine. Frequent washing of clothes is necessary because of the preference for lighter shades of colours in clothes, in contrast to the dark colours worn in Rajasthan. Ordinary washing soap, surf and even Lux flakes are used.

Houses and Household Goods

Most of the houses (16 out of 18 among the sample households) are *pucca*. All houses have hand pumps, nearly two-third are fitted with electricity. Electricity is used mainly for lighting; only 5 households possess radios and 3 have electric fans. However, 13 households possess bicycles, 11 own sewing machines and 9 have kerosene stoves or electric heaters. In the house of the President of the Dairy Co-operative Society; the drawing room was furnished with a cane sofa set (without cushions), chairs, a dressing table, a bedstead and curtains. There was some modern furniture in his father's house also. But the family is clearly an exception. The other households cannot set apart a room in their small crowded homes as a drawing room. The only modern furniture in their homes was a few chairs. However, old style bedsteads (called *palangs*) of good workmanship were seen in a number of homes.

There is a definite trend towards modernizing the home and buying new durable consumer goods. Several women showed me their radios, sewing machines and other possessions with obvious pride. In most cases the articles had been brought by the daughter-in-law married to the educated son employed in the town in her dowry.

But most of the houses are congested and are not very clean. This is due partly to the large size of families and partly to the practice of keeping animals within the homes. Moreover, installation of hand pumps has made the houses damp—a portion of the courtyard always remains wet. It has also made the lanes outside the houses wet and dirty, and given the village pond a permanent existence. Most of the women did not show any concern about the unsanitary conditions of the street or the congestion and damp within the houses. This lack of concern may be due partly to the feeling that nothing can be done about these things. Tightly clustered houses, narrow dirty lanes, lack of drainage and presence of stagnant water at various places are common features of villages (and most towns) in North India, and are accepted. But some of the younger men and women are thinking of getting away from it all, by building their new houses outside in the fields.

The need for additional space felt by these families has been met in the recent past by construction of one or more rooms on the first floor.

These rooms are well lighted and are of relatively modern design. They are generally used either by the young educated daughter-in-law (if she is staying with the family) or are reserved for guests, such as the son-in-law.[4] But addition of rooms on the first floor has cut off sunlight from the ground floor rooms and has made the principal living quarter darker and more dingy.

Women in the two households having *kucha* houses said that they had not made their houses *pucca* because they were thinking of building new houses outside the village. But the movement towards living outside the village has not yet started. So far, only the *Sarpanch*, a *refugee* from the West Punjab canal colonies, has built a house on the outskirts of the village. His house with its enormous courtyard (*aahata)*, cattle sheds, and feeding stalls, well separated from the living rooms, is patterned after houses in the canal colonies. It presented a pleasant contrast to the other houses. But no other family has followed his example so far.

Health

Modern facilities for treatment of diseases, maternity and child-care are within easy reach of the village and are being used by the people. There is good hospital at the block headquarters' town. Samrala. Besides, there are three sub-centres, each under the charge of a trained nurse-midwife, which provide assistance for maternity and family planning. The village is in the area of the sub-centre located in the next village, a mile away. The village *dai* is undergoing training at the sub-centre. She assists the nurse mid-wife in conducting delivery cases and will be authorized to handle these cases on her own, after she has completed the one-year training course. According to an order of the Punjab Health Department, no untrained *dai* can handle delivery cases on her own. I did not have the opportunity to investigate how strictly this order was actually being followed.

All the women reported that for all ailments, major or minor; they consulted a doctor, the qualified private medical practitioner at Samrala. He lives in the next village and can make the rounds of the village on his way to and from the town. They said that they went to the Government Hospital only when this doctor was not available. Cases of serious sickness or serious injury were taken to one of the hospitals at Ludhiana. The city has a number of good hospitals including one attached to Medical College. In half of the sample households, the women reported that they kept medicines such as Anacin, Tincture Iodine, *Amritdhara*, and brandy at home, and used them for minor ailments. Women in the other households also knew about these medicines, but they were not keeping them. Resort to the doctor is so common that one woman said, "We go to the doctor, even when a thorn pricks us".

All pregnant women are expected to be registered with the sub-centre and visit it regularly for getting ante-natal advice. The nurse mid-wife is also expected to conduct house-to house surveys periodically, in order to make sure that all pregnant women are contacted. But she is confronted with an interesting problem arising from the practice (in this area as in many others in India) of women going to their parent's homes for child-birth. She said that a number of women for whom she had been maintaining ante-natal records went away for their deliveries to their parents' homes while she had to conduct deliveries of many women for whom she had no records!

The sub-centres also provide advice and assistance on family planning. Of the 32 women in the sample households, three, all below age 35 were using family planning devices. Two more showed interest, but were not using any device. One woman, who complained about having a large number of children, was hesitant about using any family planning devices. Most women knew about family planning practices and were not unwilling to talk about them; some expressed a desire for birth control pill. The lady doctor at Samrala hospital mentioned that some men of the village had vasectomies done. But no such case was mentioned among the sample households.

Education

All the girls of primary school age 6-11 years are going to the village school. Half a dozen of the older girls go to higher secondary school at Samrala. I used to meet these girls going to school or returning from the school, on their bicycles, on my way to or from the village. They all rode gent's bicycles: the families perhaps could not afford to buy separate ladies' bicycles. This phenomenon—young girls going out on bicycles—would have been unthinkable a generation earlier, when a girl was not allowed to go out of the village unescorted. Girls from some of the more prosperous and progressive families are receiving education in colleges (or other training institutions) in towns. They stay in hostels. Two daughters of the President of the dairy co-operative are studying outside the village—one is in a college in Ludhiana while the other is in a higher secondary school at Samrala. The daughter in another household is receiving the Physical Training Instructor's training at Patiala. In another household, the daughter is receiving basic teacher's training. Among girls (not of the sample households) one is studying for the Bachelor of Teaching (BT) diploma. A sister of this girl had recently flown to Canada to get married to a man (of the caste) settled in Canada. The village women were referring to this as an example of the 'forwardness' of the family. There was no hint of disapproval or of embarrassment that such a thing should have happened in their village.

Education of girls has become a thing of value with the group. All families are sending their girls to school, and the more progressive ones are sending them to institutions of training, which will equip them for careers. Some young women from the village have already taken up jobs. The Deputy Inspector of Schools at Samrala is the daughter-in-law in one of the sample households. Both the teachers in the village school are women from the village. The preference for 'career training' to getting a university degree is significant. Some of the women said that they would like to see their daughters equipped for a career in time of need.

But education of girls is a recent phenomenon. This is brought out very well by data on the number of educated females of different age groups presented in the Table 11.1. It will be seen that all the 14 women above age 35 are illiterate; among those below 35 more than half are educated, but all the girls of school-going age are attending school. It may be noted that all the daughters-in-law living outside the village are educated. These women married to educated men—their husbands are all in white-collar or military service—had to be educated to get married to educated men. This shows a pattern of selectivity in emigration, and also provides a clue to the motivation for education of girls. Girls are being educated because educated men, who are in service and who are the prized grooms, want educated wives. The changed work pattern of the women—their being at home all the time and having adequate time

Table 11.1: Number of Educated Women of Different Age Group in 18 Households

	Total	*Educated*	*Illiterate*
No. of Women			
Above age 35	14	–	14
Below age 35	22	12	10
Daughters-in-law of the households living outside the village	10	10	–
No. of girls of Age (6-14 years) Total going to school Not going School	18	18	–

for household work and child-care—also helps education of girls. Older girls are not needed to look after younger brothers and sisters or to help the mothers with household tasks.

But this trend towards education of girls, with a view to marrying them to educated young men in service, is creating an interesting situation within the group. On the one hand, the problem of finding suitable grooms for educated girls and giving an adequate dowry—problems characteristic of the urban middle class—are appearing. The recent journey of a girl to Canada shows how far families are prepared to go to meet these problems. At the same time, it is becoming increasingly difficult for illiterate or barely literate, young men who remain in the village and work on the farm to get married. This difficulty caused by the absolute shortage of women referred to earlier has always been there, but it is accentuated by the tendency to educate the girls and to marry them to educated young men in service. The gravity of the problem will be appreciated from the fact that among the 43 males, above age 18 in the sample households as many as 15 are unmarried. Reference was made to the problem by the women in three sample households, that of a small farmer with a holding of only 6 acres, four unmarried young sons were living with their aged father and mother. They had no hope of getting married because their holding is so small. In another household, only one of the three sons was married. Their father said, 'The *Jats* will not give their daughters to us because our holding is small, and we are not prepared to buy women from outside. He is a lucky father, who can marry all his sons!" The difficulty of finding wives is met to some extent by buying women from outside the State. These women, usually from poor families of low castes, are bought from U.P., West Bengal or the South. There were no such women among the sample households: but there were three in the village. I could meet all three women and listen to their interesting life histories. I met some of them in the neighbouring villages of the sub-centre also. The men of the village are well-known in the area for bringing women from outside, and there were about a dozen such women in that village.

Footnotes

1. The Meena women of Sawai Madhopur district of Rajasthan among whom I had conducted a similar study earlier (the findings of the Rajasthan study are given in chapter 5), do all agricultural work except ploughing. In fact, from an analysis of the farm work in this area, I came to the conclusion that they do more work than their men.

2. The Meena women of Sawai Madhopur would finish most of their cooking for the day in the morning, before leaving for the fields, and would cook only *chappaties* in the evening.
3. I did not collect any data on food consumption. But use of plenty of milk and *ghee* and vegetables especially green leaf '*saag*' was so evident.
4. The women used the Punjabi word for guest (*Paraohina*) also for son-in-law. Obviously, sons-in-law are the most frequent or the most honoured guests.

12

The New Village
12 Years After*

Introduction

Jitpur[1], the subject of this study, is relatively a large village, which had population of 2114 according to the Population Census of 1971. It is situated about 175 miles west of India's capital, New Delhi, in the Ludhiana District of the Punjab State. The State bordering Pakistan is the richest in the Indian Union, with an average per capita income during 1970-72 of Rs. 1053, almost 60 per cent above the national average. The bases of its prosperity are a progressive agriculture—the State has been in the forefront of India's Green Revolution of the late 1960s—and diversified small-and-medium-scale industries. Ludhiana, the district headquarters, located about 30 miles from Jitpur, is a city with a population of nearly 500,000. It is the principal industrial centre of the state and is also the seat of the Agricultural University, an important centre of agricultural education and research in northern India. Jitpur is located on an all-weather motorable road at a distance of one and a half miles from the market town of Samrala (population 7,500). A second market town, Khanna, with a population of about 25,000 is nine miles from Jitpur at the other end of the road. The principal castes of the village are Jat, Harijan[2], *Mistri* and Mahajan. The Jats are the most numerous followed by the Harijans. The caste-wise distribution of the village households in 1975 was as follows:

The Jats, besides being the largest caste, are also the most powerful. They own and cultivate nearly all the land, and the village has always

* This part of the study was published as: *The New Village—Twelve Years After'* in *Indian Urbanization and Planning—Vehicles of Modernization;* eds. Noble, Allen G and Dutt Ashok K. Tata McGraw-Hill Publishers, 1977.

Caste	*Number of Households*
Jat	182
Harijan	101
Mistri	13
Mahajan	25
Others	23
Total	344

been regarded as a Jat village. The traditional occupation of the Harijans is stated to have been leather-work, but their principal source of livelihood was until recently agricultural labour. Many Harijan heads of households worked as attached labourers to farmers under the crop-sharing *sanghee* (lit. share-holder) system. Although bearing all the risks of cultivation and providing bullock power in addition to their own, they had no rights on the land. With growth of opportunities for non-agricultural work in or near the village during the last twenty-five years, however, they have taken increasingly to this work, principally as casual, day labourers. A few enterprising young men have become skilled workers, shopkeepers, or white-collar workers. The *Mistries* (lit. artisans), the traditional carpenters, smiths and masons, have with growth of small industries in the region, sought employment in them in increasing numbers. Some, who have become successful entrepreneurs, are the richest people in the village. The Mahajan is the composite name for the Brahmins, the *Khatris* and the *Aroras*, The Brahmins were the traditional priests while the other two were merchant money-lenders. All the three castes have had white-collar service and commerce as their principal occupations for a long time. The 'other castes' group includes castes with traditional occupations of barber, tailor, potter, oil-presser water-carrier-cum-cook, etc. All the castes except the Mahajans, who are Hindus, follow the Sikh religion.

The village is well served with social and economic service facilities. It has two primary schools (both co-educational); a maternity, child-welfare-and family planning centre; a primary cooperative society whose principal functions are provision of agricultural credit and distribution of chemical fertilizers and other agricultural inputs; a bank and a training centre for rural artisans. Frequent minibus service on the road is the principal means of transport. There are ten shops (general stores) and a machine shop, which repairs and fabricates agricultural implements. Furthermore, because of proximity to two market towns, the village has easy access to the various service facilities located in them. Agricultural extension and related rural development services form part of the Community Development Block

Organization[3]. Jitpur is included in the Samrala Community Development Block, which has a total of 153 villages and a rural population of approximately 120,000.

Method

The village was first studied in 1963 when a series of five articles describing changes in agricultural technology and various other aspects of economic and social change were published in the *Economic Weekly*. Later in the year, the articles were reprinted as a monograph entitled '*The New Village*' (Nath, V., 1965). The present study is based on a two-week revisit undertaken in December 1975; its primary objective is to describe the changes in the village and the region during the period since the first study; particularly as result of the Green Revolution. It may be mentioned that the 1963 study had, after describing the rapid economic and social changes experienced by the village and the region during the preceding twelve years, forecast "larger and more rapid changes" in the future.

The focus of the present study and its method are somewhat different from those of the original study. Thus greater attention has been given than in the first study to analyzing the regional aspects of the change and to assessing the prospects for the future. The study within the village concentrates on those aspects, which appeared most significant either for understanding the change process of the preceding 12 years or as indicators of future trends. Accordingly, listing of all households in the village with collection of detailed data on demographic characteristics and economic activities of the members and housing conditions; a survey of holdings of all farmers and a sample survey of production and income of the medium sized farmers, which had been done in the 1963 study, have not been repeated. The principal method of enquiry has been interviews with knowledgeable respondents in the village, with officials of the Community Development Block and local leaders in Samrala, and with district-or-state level officials in Ludhiana. We hope that what the study may have lost in depth is more than compensated by the gains in terms of broader and more future-oriented perspective.

It should be repeated that this is not a study of an average Indian village but of a village in one of the richest and most progressive region of the country. But, while economic and social changes are relatively slow in most regions of India, this regions is by no means unique in the speed or the scope of changes: similar or somewhat less rapid changes have been experienced in the post-Independence period in a number of other regions or micro-regions of the country. The principal value of this and other studies of progressive rural communities is that—(a) they demonstrate the possibility of rapid economic and social changes within the matrix of peasant agriculture and the social structure of rural India which is dominated by the institution of caste; (b) describe the nature of the changes, outlining the areas of rapid and slow advance; and finally (c) draw attention to the factors which induce or retard the change process.

The Village and the Region in 1963

The principal points made in the study were the following:

(i) The village was, like the central Punjab region[4] of which it formed a part, in the midst of the process of rapid economic and social change. The process began with the land reform of consolidation of land holdings[5] which was undertaken at the initiative of the state government in the early 1950s. It was aided by the well developed physical and economic infrastructures of the region, but its vigour, speed and broad range were due primarily to the people of the region. They had shown a remarkable readiness and capacity to use the various infrastructure facilities effectively; to adopt the changes in agricultural production techniques, health practices, consumption, living patterns, etc., recommended by the various extension and service agencies quickly, and finally, to innovate and adapt the recommended practices, as also commercially viable tools and equipments, more closely to their particular needs and financial resources.

The principal component of the infrastructure were approach roads linking most of the villages of the region with trunk highways; bus, minibus and truck services providing motorized transport to almost all villages; the extensive rural electrification network; primary schools in almost all villages, secondary schools in the larger villages and the market towns and collages in the latter; medical, maternity and family planning services provided both by the centre and run by the government as well as by private practitioners; agricultural and animal husbandry extension services supported by services for distribution of inputs, needed for modernization of agriculture (improved seeds, chemical fertilizers, improved implements etc.) and for provision of agricultural credit at low rates of interest and finally, markets regulated by committees dominated by the farmers themselves.

The people had demonstrated their readiness to contribute to the creation and operation of the services, their capacity to use them effectively and their innovative ability in various ways. They had readily contributed land needed for building the approach roads, often destroying their standing crops so that these could be built earlier. The bus service run by the state government was extremely popular while the minibus and truck service, provided by the local operators, extended the range of motorized transport service to all villages. Similarly, the land reform of consolidation of holdings, which involved pooling of all the village lands and their redistribution and which could proceed only slowly in some parts of the state, had been undertaken speedily in the region with Land Holders' Committees, which had been established in every village, playing an active role in the decision-making process. Furthermore, it had been followed rapidly by the farmers undertaking reclamation of the uncultivated lands allotted to them and expansion of irrigation by sinking new wells and tube-wells, and installing electric pumps on wells.[6] The change-over from lifting water with the aid of bullocks to electric pumps greatly reduced the cost of irrigation.[7] In addition it made possible extension of the areas irrigated by a well; increase in the intensity of cropping, besides extension of areas under highly remunerative crops, such as sugarcane, which, however require intensive irrigation. Adoption of improved agricultural practices, notably use of improved seed, chemical fertilizers and improved implements, and generally more efficient farm management were also aided by consolidation of holdings, expansion of irrigation and improvement in its efficiency. The total effect was a rapid change process, resulting in significant increase in total agricultural output, through more intensive and efficient use of the resources of land and water, and the labour and capital committed to agriculture. The farmers had also shown a capacity to operate successfully new power-driven implements, notably the electric pumps and mechanical grain threshers, which was quite exceptional for Indian farmers, while the small machine-shops located in the villages or the market towns could service and repair the machines quickly, efficiently and at low cost. The artisans of the region not only provided these services to the farmers but also displayed considerable innovative ability; the mechanical corn-shellers and wheat threshers, which had rapidly become popular, were noteworthy products of this ability. The latest development in the agricultural change process had been growth of poultry keeping, dairying and market gardening in response to the growing urban demand for their products. These were being taken up both by progressive farmers and by other small entrepreneurs; their growth was significant both because of their potential for making major additions to the farmers' incomes and also because it involved giving up strong traditional prejudices against them. The Jats did not keep poultry, which was considered dirty; only the Harijans (and before their migration to Pakistan in 1947 the Muslim residents of the region) kept poultry. Market gardening had been the traditional activity of specialized casts like the Sikh *Sainies* and the Muslim *Arains*. As regards dairying, while the farmers kept milch animals, there was a very strong prejudice against selling milk by farmers; it was considered a mark of extreme want or degradation.[8]

(ii) The change in agriculture and animal husbandry which had been the most noticeable and perhaps also the most significant from the economic stand point, had been accompanied by noteworthy advances in literacy, education and use of modern medical and public health services; major changes in the patterns of employment, consumption and levels of living as well as social changes affecting the attitudes and values of the people, inter-group relations and institutions. Attending primary school had become the norm for all children of the relevant age-group (6-11 years) of the upper castes and for most children of the Harijans. Besides large number of boys and girls were attending secondary schools and colleges. Opportunities for non-agricultural employment had expanded rapidly with the growth of construction following increase in agricultural incomes and in economic activity generally. As a result there was accelerated migration from the villages (see below); wage rates had increased, shortages of labour had begun to be experienced, especially in the peak period of agricultural activity during April and May in which several labour-intensive operations, notably harvesting of wheat and planting of cotton and sugar cane were in progress and the traditional *sanjhee* system of crop sharing between the farmer-land-owner and their attached Harijan agricultural labourers had begun to decline. Among the changes in consumption and level of living the most noticeable to the outside observer were those resulting from the following:

(a) Improvement in housing and environmental sanitation with construction of new *pucca* (brick and mortar) houses in place of the traditional *kucha* or mud houses; electrification of the houses and installation of hand-pumps in them for water supply—earlier the women had to go some distance from their homes to fetch water from communal wells—and pavement of village streets with bricks and construction of drains along their sides for efficient flow of waste water;

(b) The rapid increase in the use of durable consumer goods such as bicycles, sewing machines, radio receivers and small kerosene stoves for cooking; and

(c) Cessation of farm work by women of all but the poor Harjan households.

In Jitpur about 50 per cent of the households were living by 1963 in houses that were entirely or partly *pucca*, more than 50 per cent had hand-pumps in their homes while 36 per cent lived in electrified houses. All the streets of the village except a few in Harijan quarters had been paved and provided with drains. Electrification had made the homes brighter while installation of the hand-pumps had eliminated the drudgery of carrying water from the wells for the women. Cessation of farm work by the women and the education of the girls and the young women had been major factors contributing to improvement in home-making, child care and personal hygiene. Freed from farm work, the women had more time for their homes and the children and the educated ones among them acquainted the others with new ideas, practices and consumption goods.

Finally, with the spread of education and of the ideas of freedom and equality, especially during the periodic elections to the state and central legislatures and to village *panchayats*; increasing participation of Harijans in non-agricultural work outside the villages; increasing emigration from the villages and frequent travel of villagers to towns following improvements in transport and communications, there had been a significant decline in untouchability. It had in any case been weak in the region because of the influence of the Sikh religion, which advocated equality of all men before God and prohibited the practice of untouchability.

(iii) Conditions in the region were exceptionally favourable for rapid economic and social change. The region had a strong tradition of peasant proprietorship, and land holdings were on an average larger and the proportion of landless agricultural labourers smaller than in most parts of India.[9] The Jats, who constitute the majority of the farmers in the region, were well known for their hard work and love for farming. The *Mistries* were similarly known for their industry, mechanical aptitude and innovative capacity; they were recognized to be the best carpenters, masons and machine workers in India. The Sikh religion, with its doctrines of monotheism and equality of all men, had acted as a major liberating influence. However, the Ludhiana district, the micro region of Jitpur, was until the beginning of the above mentioned change process in the early 1950s, a relatively poor area because large part of it either had sandy soil or formed part of the poorly drained floodplain of the river Satluj. But the town of Ludhiana had long been the Centre of the hosiery industry, which provided the nucleus for rapid growth of small, light engineering industries after cheap hydro-electric power became available and industrial development began to be encouraged by the state and central Governments through a variety of promotional measures. Secondly, the micro-region had abundant ground-water, exploitation of which became feasible after the cost of lifting water was reduced with electrification of wells, and construction of electric-or-diesel-powered tube-wells made possible lifting of water from much greater depths than had been possible with the aid of bullocks. The consequent rapid expansion of irrigation was the most important factor contributing to increase of agricultural output in the district.

(iv) The willingness and capacity for rapid economic and social change; the mechanical aptitude and the innovative capability owed not a little to the century-old tradition of emigration among the people of the region. Emigration had begun with large numbers of people joining the British Indian army during the 50s and 60s of the last century, and had continued: the region had remained a major source of recruitment for the British Indian (and after Independence of the Indian) army. Besides, it had sent out large numbers of white collar workers, operators of trucks and taxis, and repairmen for machinery and equipment to cities and towns all over India. Furthermore, large numbers had gone down to settle as farmers in the canal colonies of Western Punjab, which were settled in the first two decades of the century, and in foreign countries notably Malaysia and East Africa. Remittances from the young men working in the towns but maintaining close ties with their 'families' in the villages, and from the emigrants had been an important source of income in the region, while the new ideas and practices introduced by returning migrants had been a major change influence. The ex-soldiers returning after Second World War and the refugees, returning from the canal colonies after the creation of Pakistan, had been the leaders in the above-mentioned change process. Both groups had useful skills as well as strong motivation for change. Large number of ex-soldiers had worked in the armed forces as electricians, auto mechanics, drivers etc.; all had got used to living in neat quarters, to preventive health practices, such as use of quinine and mosquito nets, and to modern consumer goods such as bicycles and radios. They were not considered to be particularly good farmers by the villagers because of their unwillingness to work hard, but they were recognized as leaders in adoption of environmental sanitation practices, acceptance of education and modern medicine and in running development-oriented institutions such as the cooperative societies, the *panchayats*, and the market committees. The *refugees* had been used to following improved agricultural and animal husbandry practices advocated by the extension services in the canal colonies and had also, because of relatively large irrigated land holdings, enjoyed much higher income levels than the farmers of the region.[10] On return to their ancestral villages and faced with the need to work much smaller holdings, they had a strong motivation to intensify land use and increase agricultural output and incomes. In this process, they not only continued practices such as use of improved seeds and implements, growing of fodder crops and stall-feeding of cattle which they had been following in the colonies but also readily took up new ones, such as use of chemical fertilizers and pesticides. They were also the leaders in construction of tube-wells and installation of electric pumps on wells and in taking up remunerative agricultural or animal husbandry enterprises such as growing of vegetables and fruit, dairy farming and poultry keeping which had been shunned by the local farmers because of traditional prejudices. The *refugees* were generally the most progressive cultivators in the villages in which they had settled while the 'garden colonies', established by the most progressive and affluent among them, had the highest level of husbandry and income to be seen in the region.

(v) At the same time, the process had itself further stimulated migration and added new dimensions to it, notably (a) spread of migration to the Harijans who had been relatively unaffected by it earlier; (b) much larger intra-regional movement from the villages to the towns because of the above-mentioned growth of small-scale industries in the latter; and (c) emigration to Britain for work in factories there.

(vi) The cumulative effect of all these changes was so large that a "new village", which was different from the traditional Indian village in every significant economic and social respect, appeared to be emerging. Hence, the title of the study. In the `new village', not only were the levels of agricultural technology and income much higher than in the old, but in contrast to the inward-orientation, conservative tradition-bound attitudes and values and a rigid social structure, dominated by the institution of caste of the latter, it had multiple and expanding relations with the regional and national economies, and attitudes, values and inter-group economic and social relations, that were increasingly responsive to the demands of the changes in technology, employment opportunities, consumption patterns and levels of living.

(vii) But the changes in agriculture and animal husbandry were considered to be only, "the beginning of a process which should gather momentum in future and produce larger and more important changes—intensive use of chemical fertilizers and pesticides, use of small tractors, increasing emphasis on specialized farming (poultry keeping, dairying and horticulture) and changes in attitudes towards the role of agriculture. These changes can be seen already among the more progressive farmers like the dairy farmers and the 'garden colonists'." (Nath, V. *op. cit.*, p. 47)

The Green Revolution

The impetus for the "larger and more important changes" came with introduction in 1965-66 of the high-yielding, dwarf varieties of wheat. The region was exceptionally well equipped to benefit from the high yield potential of the new varieties. Wheat was its most important crop; it already had most of the pre-requisites for obtaining the high-yields and could create the others by further, more rapid progress along lines which were already well established. Thus it had assured adequate and controlled water supplies, provided by well developed irrigation facilities. Use of non-power-driven improved implements, such as improved ploughs, harrows and seed drills, was widespread and power-driven implements, such as tractors and grain threshers, were beginning to be used in increasing numbers particularly by farmers with relatively large land holdings (above 20 acres). Similarly, increasing appreciation of the benefits of using chemical fertilizers had been added to the well established tradition of intensive manuring of the wheat crop. Finally, the farmers had become change-oriented after experience with rapid economic and social change for over 15 year during which their productivity, income and level of living had risen rapidly, and the best among them were themselves looking for new improvements in techniques and other ways to increase their income. The high yield potential of the new varieties provided a powerful incentive for further rapid progress while provision of liberal agricultural credit by the State and Central Governments at subsidized, low rates of interest (10-12 ½ per cent per annum)[11] provided the funds needed for adopting the new capital-intensive techniques. Short and medium-term loans, needed for financing current agricultural operations, such as purchase of seeds and chemical fertilizers, payment for labour, or for quick-yielding investments such as purchase of livestock, were given by village-level, primary cooperative societies, while long-term loans, with repayment periods of 7-10 years, needed for investment in land reclamation, development of irrigation facilities and purchase of tractors etc, were given by institutions such as the newly-created Land Mortgage Bank (LMB). By 1969-70, four years after the introduction of the new varieties, almost 70 per cent of the total area under wheat in Punjab had been sown with them, while the figure for Ludhiana district was 86 per cent. Production of wheat increased very rapidly, as a result both of increase in yields, and diversion of land from other crops to wheat; the diversion was made because with the high yield given by the new varieties, production of wheat became much more remunerative than that of alternative crops. In Ludhiana district; production of wheat increased by 142.8 per cent between 1964-65 and 1971-72; more than half of the increase was contributed by increase in area, which went up by 63.6 per cent, while the remainder was due to increase in yield per acre which went up by 48.4 per cent.

In order to provide a background to the agricultural changes in village Jitpur, described in the next section, and to relate them to the regional change process, data on a number of indicators of agricultural progress are given for Ludhiana district in Table 12.1. Although progress under the Green Revolution was concentrated during the five years, 1966-67 to 1971-72, the figures are given for 1961-62 and 1972-73 in order to facilitate the comparison with Jitpur.

It will be seen from Table 12.1 that the gross cropped area in the district increased by more than one-third during the eleven-year period. The increase was achieved mainly by increase in the intensity of cropping from 1.25 to 1.61; the physical area under crops went up by only 7 per cent. Expansion of irrigation was even more rapid than the expansion of cropping; the gross irrigated area more than doubled and by 1972-73, 86 per cent of the Gross Cropped Area was irrigated. Changes in the cropping pattern were equally rapid. The areas under wheat, corn and groundnut more than doubled while those under all other crops decreased, the reductions in the areas under the fodder crops and pulses (beans) being the most pronounced. Thus wheat, corn and groundnut were not only the principal beneficiaries of expansion of the cropped area but gained also at the expense of other crops, particularly fodders and pulses.

The changes were related to the introduction of high-yielding varieties of wheat and associated programmes, particularly expansion of irrigation, and reflected also changes in the relative profitability of the different crops or crop combinations following the introduction of the new varieties.

Table 12.1: Selected Indicators of Agricultural Progress in Ludhiana District, 1961-62–1972-73

Indicator	*1961-62*	*1972-73*	*1972-73* (with 1961-62=100)
Land use and the Cropping Pattern (Areas in 000 acres)			
Gross cropped area	933.7	1284.4	137.6
Gross irrigated area	521.2	1104.1	211.8
Percentage of gross cropped area			
Irrigated	55.8	86.0	154.6
Areas under			
–Wheat	285.3	624.9	219.0
–Corn	98.3	231.2	235.2
–Sugarcane	25.7	17.8	69.2
–Cotton	74.1	59.3	80.0
–Groundnut	71.1	145.2	204.2
–Pulses	126.7	19.3	14.4
–Fodder Crops	232.2	127.0	54.7
Consumption of Chemical Fertilizers			
Total (000 tonnes)	13.4	251.0	1873.1
Per acre of Gross Cropped Area (kg)	14.4	195.5	1360.1
Loans advanced by Cooperative Credit Societies			
Short-term (Million Rupees)	12.5	120.2	963.6
Medium-term (Million Rupees)	3.4	2.5	72.4
Total (Million Rupees)	15.9	122.7	772.4
Total per acre of gross cropped area (Rupees)	17.0	95.5	561.8

Source: *Twelve-Years' Assessment of Intensive Agricultural District Programme.* Ludhiana, 1960-61–1972-73. IADP. Ludhiana, Punjab 1975.

In order to give some indication of the latter, data on changes in average yields, prices and gross returns for five important crops of the district[12] wheat, corn, sugarcane cotton and groundnut, are given in Table 12.2. The data relate to the period, 1960-61-1962-63 to 1970-73; three-year averages have been used at both ends of the time period in order to minimize the influence of year-to-year fluctuations in yields or prices, both of which were quite considerable.

Prices of all the five crops more than doubled during the period. As regards yields, while that of wheat and that of groundnut decreased slightly, those of the remaining three crops increased by 30-40 per cent. As a

Table 12.2: Increase in Yields, Prices and Gross Returns from Selected Crops between 1960-61 - 1962-63 to 1970-71 - 72-73 in Ludhiana District

Crops	*Yield*	*Price*	*Gross Returns (3-year Averages of 1971-72 to 1972-73 and 1960-61 to 1962-63)*
Wheat	1.99	2.04	4.06
Maize	1.29	2.08	2.68
Sugarcane	1.39	2.00	2.78
Cotton (American)	1.29	2.18	2.82
Groundnut	0.97	2.15	2.09

Source: Twelve-Years' Assessment of IADP.

result, the gross return from wheat increased four-fold, that from groundnut more than doubled while those from the other three crops increased nearly three-fold. The rapid increase in the area under wheat was due clearly to its becoming the most profitable crop. But the reasons for increases in the areas under corn and groundnut were somewhat different as were those for reductions in the areas under sugarcane, cotton or other crops. The principal reason for the increase in the acreage under corn was that being a shorter duration crop than cotton it fits into the new crop rotation cycle much better. Growing two crops a year on the same field has become much more feasible, than it had been earlier, because the high-yielding varieties of wheat have a shorter growing season than the older varieties, and the water needs of both crops can be met adequately by the improved irrigation facilities. Accordingly, corn followed by wheat has become the most popular crop rotation. On the other hand, sugarcane, which occupies the land for about ten mouths in the year, makes double cropping impossible. The other disadvantage of sugarcane, and to a lesser extent of cotton, is high requirement of labour: its importance has increased during the period because of increase in the cost of labour and emergence of a shortage of labour at the peak periods of agricultural activity.

The area under groundnut has expanded rapidly despite it giving relatively the lowest increase in gross return because it is the most suitable crop for the areas with sandy soils of low productivity.

The relationship between the changes in relative profitability of different crops and in the areas under them would be seen more clearly if data on costs of production and net returns were available also. But the large changes in the cropping pattern in a time-span of little more than a decade give a clear indication of the responsiveness of farmers to changes in the relative profitability of alternative crops, arising from technological and price changes, and their readiness to transfer their resources of land, labour and capital from production of crops giving lower returns to those giving higher returns. This responsiveness confirms the findings of many studies of peasant agriculture which show a remarkable ability on the part of the peasants to make relatively rapid changes in resource allocation in response to changing economic conditions[13].

The Village and the Region in 1975

By the time of the revisit to Jitpur in December 1975, the rapid changes associated with the Green Revolution, and described above, had already been completed; the new cropping pattern production practices were well established, and there had been time also for reflection of the effects of the higher incomes in changes in consumption particularly through improvement of housing and possession of durable consumer goods. The changes in land use and the cropping pattern are indicated in Table 12.3 while data on selected other indicators of economic change area given in Table 12.4. In Table 12.3 figures are given for 1951-52 also in order to make possible comparison with the land use and the cropping pattern prevailing in the village before the beginning of the rapid agricultural and economic change process described in Chapter 10.

Changes in Land use and the Cropping Pattern

Of the total geographical area of 1239 acres, 1121 acres or more than 90 per cent was cultivated in 1973-74. The latter figure had remained virtually unchanged since 1951-52 indicating that the limit of expansion of cultivation had been reached by that time (perhaps much earlier). The intensity of cropping also remained almost unchanged during the period, 1951-52 to 1961-62, at 1.45-1.47. More than three-fourths of the cropped area was already irrigated by 1951-52, the further expansion of irrigation brought the proportion up to 88 per cent by 1961-62. But the most notable changes were in the cropping pattern.

The acreage under corn nearly doubled, that under the fodder crops grown in the winter (mainly *barseem* clover) increased nearly 80 per cent and cotton which was not grown earlier became an important crop. The increases in the area under corn and cotton were achieved mainly at the expense of the fodder and other crops grown in the summer, while that under the winter fodders resulted from reduction of the area under "other grains and mixtures". This group includes gram or chick-pea and barley, sown either by themselves or in combination with each other or with wheat.

Table 12.3: Changes in Land Use and the Cropping Pattern 1951-52 to 1973-74-Village Jitpur

	1951-52	*1961-62*	*1973-74*	*% change during*	
				1951/52 to 1961/62	*1961/62 to 1973/74*
	(1)	(2)	(3)	(4)	(5)
1. Total geographical area	1239	1239	1239	--	--
2. Net area sown	1132	1118	1121	-1.2	+ 0.3
3. Gross cropped area	1637	1639	2034	0.0	+ 24.1
4. Intensity of cropping (Line 3/line 2)	1.45	1.47	1.81		
5. Gross Irrigated area	1256	1440	2034	+14.5	+ 41.3
6. Percentage of gross cropped area irrigated	76.7	87.9	100.0		
Crops					
(a) kharif (Summer)					
7. Corn (Maize)	121	240	604	+98.3	+151.7
8. Cotton	--	143	92	–	–35.7
9. Sugarcane	191	178	95	–6.8	–46.6
10. Fodder crops	295	195	202	–33.9	+3.6
11. Other	125	28	50	–77.6	+78.6
12. Total	732	784	1043	+7.1	+26.6
(b) Rabi (Cool Season)					
13. Wheat	474	436	845	–8.0	+93.8
14. Other grains and mixtures	319	237	37	–24.7	–84.4
15. Fodder crops	92	164	94	+78.3	–42.3
16. Other	20	20	15	–	–25.0
Total	905	855	991	–5.5	+15.9
18. Grand Total (Line 12 + Line 17)	1637	1639	2034	0.0	+24.1

Changes in land use and cropping pattern between 1961-62 and 1973-74 were much greater. The gross cropped area increased by 24 per cent, from 1639 to 2034 acres, as a result of increase in the intensity of cropping; The intensity of cropping reached the figure of 1.81 by 1973-74 indicating that 81 per cent of the cropland was double-cropped during that year. Corn and wheat were the principal crops benefiting from the increase in double-cropping. The acreage under corn increased from 240 to 604 acres and that under wheat from 436 to 845. But land had to be diverted also from other crops to achieve theses increases in corn and

Table 12.4: Selected Other Indicators of Economic Change, between 1963 and 1975—Village Jitpur

Indicator	1963	1975
1. Population	About 1850	2 114*
2. No. of households	299	344
3. Irrigation units (No):		
Wells	45	55
Tube-wells	–	16
Additional bores	6	14
Total	51	85
No. of units with motive power provided by:		
Electricity	36	69
Diesel oil	–	16
Bullocks	15	–
4. Use of chemical fertilizers:		
Total (tonnes)	46.1	152.3
Per acre of gross sown area (kg)	28.1	74.9
5. Tractors (No.)	–	14
6. Trucks (No.)	3	16
7. Institutional agricultural credit:		
Loans advanced by the primary cooperative society:		
Short-term (000 rupees)	n.a.	273.6
Medium-term (000 rupees)	n.a.	30.0
Total (000 Rupees)	n.a.	303.6
Short-term loans per acres of gross sown area (rupees)	n.a	134.5
Long-term loans advanced by:		
The Land Mortgage Bank (000 rupees)	–	208.6+
The Central Bank of India (000 rupees)	–	50.0
8. Daily wage or earning level of male workers:		
Casual agricultural labour:	Rs. 2 + food or Rs. 2.50	Rs. 6 + food or Rs. 8**
Loading and unloading bricks on trucks	Rs. 4	Up to Rs. 10-15
9. Housing		
Percentage of households living in:		
Pucca or Semi-Pucca houses	47	70
Houses with electricity	36	81
10. Durable consumer goods (Nos.)		
Bicycles	130	n.s.
Sewing machines	83	n.s.
Radio receivers	20	n.s.
Cars/jeeps	–	5
Motor cycles/scooters	–	13
Refrigerators	–	4

* 1971 Census

\+ cumulative total for 9 years, 1967-75.

** Rs. 4 plus food for in-migrants from U.P.

n.s.: too numerous to be used as significant indicators of change.

wheat acreage; areas under all the other crops, except the fodders and 'other' crops grown in the summer went down. The area under sugarcane was reduced by almost half and that under 'other grains and mixtures' grown in the cool season from 237 to 37 acres.

The other notable change was expansion of irrigation: the gross irrigated area increased by nearly 600 acres, or by more than 40 per cent during this period and by 1973-74 all the cropped area was reported to be irrigated. The number of irrigation sources, which had increased from 36 in 1951-52 to 51 by 1961-62, increased further to 85 by 1973-74 (Table 12.4). Sixteen of the new irrigation sources were tube-wells, which, as mentioned earlier, tap deeper layers of sub-soil water. They also have much larger irrigation capacity; the average capacity of a tube-well is 3-4 times that of an average well. Most of the tube-wells were powered by diesel engines. Expansion of irrigation met the water supply requirements of the increased intensity of cropping and also made possible extension of irrigation to about 12 per cent of the cropped area that had remained unirrigated by 1961-62 Improvement of efficiency of irrigation, i.e., providing adequate water supply to all the crops, and reduction of the cost of irrigation were secured by further substitution of bullocks by electric-or-diesel-oil-operated pumps for lifting the water; substitution had been completed by 1973-74.

Use of Chemical Fertilizers

As may be expected, use of chemical fertilizers, the other essential ingredient of the new agricultural technology, also increased very rapidly during the period. The figures given in Table 12.4 show increase between 1962-63 and 1974-75 from 46.1 tonnes to 152.3 tonnes in the total quantity of fertilizers used, and from 28.1 kg to 74.9 kg per acre of gross cropped area. They do not, give an adequate indication of the trends in fertilizer use during this period because they are partial and are also not comparable. First, they relate only to sales by the village primary cooperative society, which gives short-term (repayable within one year) loans for the purchases. In 1962-63, when supplies were scarce the society was almost the only source of supply of fertilizers; but by 1974-75, additional large quantities were being bought by the farmers from private dealers located in the market towns, against cash payments or under mutually agreed credit arrangements. Second, the figures are for quantities of fertilizers, and not for plant nutrients, so that different fertilizers with different concentrations of nutrients—ammonium sulphate has 16 per cent of nitrogen while urea has 45 per cent—are lumped together in them. In 1962-63, only three of chemical fertilizers-ammonium sulphate, calcium-ammonium nitrate and super phosphate were being used. But by 1973-74, the number had increased to six; these included both high concentration fertilizers, such as urea, and balanced fertilizers, such as di-ammonium phosphate and NPK, which contained two or three nutrients. Thus the change in fertilizers use during this period included, besides a major increase in the quantity, increasing application of highly concentrated and/or balanced fertilizers, and increasing willingness of farmers to buy fertilizers on their own.

Mechanization

Substitution of electric or diesel-driven pumps for bullocks for lifting water for irrigation is one important constituent of mechanization of agriculture. The other is represented by increasing use of tractors, combines, grain threshers, corn shellers and other implements driven by mechanical power. In 1963, while two-thirds of the wells in the village were already being worked by electric pumps, the use of the other power-driven implements was limited. There was not a single tractor or grain-thresher although farmers had begun to use their chaff-cutters, eight of which were run by electricity, for partial threshing of the wheat, and there were only three corn shellers. By 1975, however, use of other power-driven implements was widespread. There were 14 tractors and as many as 55 grain threshers (Table 12.4) and three large farmers had hired combine-harvesters from the state Cooperative Marketing Federation (MARKFED) for harvesting their wheat crop during April-May 1975. The charges for hiring, reported to be Rs. 150 per acres, were high but the combines were preferred because they saved the farmers the trouble of hiring and supervising the labour needed for the operation. The tractors were all owned by relatively large farmers who cultivated 20 acres or more, but the other farmers could hire them when they were not being used by the owners. Hiring of tractors from owners within the village or others in the neighbouring village of the market town of Samrala was common, the rate being Rs. 12-15 per acre of ploughing.

Increase in Agricultural Output

Precise estimation of the increase in agricultural output during the period is not possible in the absence of data for the village on the yields of crops. However, an approximate estimate has been made by using the district data on yields and prices of the principal crops of the village and is shown in Table 12.5. It will be seen that the gross value of agricultural output in 1973-74 was four times that in 1961-62. Somewhat over half of the increase was due to increase in prices—the prices of corn, wheat and sugarcane doubled while those of cotton and gram increased by 118 and 155 per cent respectively—and the remainder represented real increase in output, resulting from expansion of cropped area, substitution of less profitable crops by more profitable ones and increase in crop yields.

It should be emphasized, however, that the increase in net incomes of the farmers would be considerably less than four times, because of the increases in expenditure on inputs, particularly chemical fertilizers, electricity, diesel oil and labour. The increases must be quite large because, as mentioned above, fertilizer use has increased by more than four times. Furthermore, apart from the quantitative increases in the inputs, their unit costs have increased. Thus wage rates have gone up about three times. An estimate of the net increase in income can be made only if figures on cost of cultivation of all the important crops are available for both the years. However, even after making allowance for all the cost increases, there can be no question that the increase in output represents a substantial gain in real incomes for the farmers.

The Role/Institutional Finance

Institutional finance, i.e. short, medium and long-term loans, bearing relatively low interest rates and provided by specialized credit institutions or directly by the State Government, has been the principal sources of

Table 12.5: Estimated Value of Output of Principal Crops in 1961-62 and 1973-74—Village Jitpur

(*Value Figures in Rupees*)

Crop	*1961-62*			*1973-74*		
	Area (Acres) (Y)	*Gross Value (per acre) (p)*	*Total (y × p)**	*Area (Acres)*	*Gross Value (per acre)*	*Total (y × p)**
Corn	240	197.2	47,328	604	506.9	306,161
Wheat	436	264.3	115,235	845	1075.7	908,994
Cotton	143	115.8	16,552	92	298.5	27,466
Sugarcane	178	815.0	145,070	95	2016.1	191,530
Other rabi grains and mixtures	237	161.6+	38,302+	37	460.2+	17,029+
Total		1234	362,578		1673	1,451,180

*represents product of average yield per acre (y) and price (p).

+ For *gram* or chick pea which is the principal grain among them.

financing the investment needs of agricultural development. The primary co-operative credit society located in the village has been the principal source of short-term and medium-term loans while long-term loans, repayable in 7-10 years and needed for financing investment in irrigation or farm machinery such as tractors, have been provided since its establishment at Samrala in 1967 mainly by the Land Mortgage Bank. Until the middle 1960s the State Government used to provide medium and long-term-loans directly: the loans were the principal source of institutional finance for construction of wells and electrification during the 1950s. But they were discontinued with the growth of lending by the specialized credit institutions. The commercial banking system could emerge as a major source of institutional finance in the future: fostering the banking habit among the rural people and meeting the investment needs of development of agricultural and rural industry were among the most important objectives of nationalization of the 14 largest commercial banks by the Indian Government in 1969. In pursuit of these objectives there has been rapid increase in the number of branches of the banks in the small towns and the large villages since nationalization: there were four such branches in Samrala in 1975 and one, opened in 1970, in the village itself.

The cooperative society had advanced short-term loans totalling Rs. 273,600 during 1974-75 (Table 12.4). Most of them were given in kind, in the form of chemical fertilizers or other inputs distributed by the society. The loans, which bore an interest rate of 12 ½ per cent per annum had been taken by nearly 400 of the 542 members of the society.

The Land Mortgage Bank (LMB) had advanced a total of Rs. 208,600 to 32 farmers of the village during the nine years of its existence. The loans, ranging from 2,000 to 24,000 rupees each, had been given to finance construction of tube-wells, purchase of tractors, purchase of land or redemption of land from mortgage, etc. Twenty-three loans totalling Rs. 119,500 had been given for development of irrigation, of which 21, totalling Rs. 108,000, had been given for construction of tube-wells. The 16 tube-wells in operation in the village in 1975 had all been constructed with the aid of these loans, which ranged between Rs. 4,000 to 6,000 each. Five tube-wells for which loans had been given during 1974 and 1975 were not operational by the time of this study. The bank had also financed purchase of five tractors to the extent or Rs. 100,600; the individual loans had ranged between Rs. 12,000 and 30,000. The branch of the Central Bank of India, located in the village, had advanced only two loans totalling Rs. 50,000 for purchase of tractors; but at the time of the study it was financing purchase of milch buffaloes by the members of the newly-formed Milk Producers' Cooperative Society. Medium-term loans totalling Rs. 30,000 had been advanced to 15 of the 52 members of the society and the applications of the others were being processed. The loans were being given under a special programme of the Central government aimed at assisting the small and marginal farmers.

Comparison with Changes in the District

Comparison of the figures of Tables 12.3 and 12.4 with the corresponding figures for the district given in Table 12.1 shows that in case of most of the important indicators of agricultural change—gross cropped area, gross irrigated area, acreage under wheat and consumption of chemical fertilizers—the rates increase were lower in the village than in the district. In case of gross cropped area and gross irrigated area the lower rates were due to the village having already achieved significantly higher intensity of cropping and proportion of irrigated cropped area than the district by 1961-62, so that the scope for further progress was less. The difference is not large; in case of increase in acreage under wheat, while in case of consumption of chemical fertilizers the village and district figures area not comparable because while the former relate only to the quantities distributed by the cooperative society, the latter include also sales by the private dealers.

Other Aspects of Change

Employment, Wages and the Social Position of the Harijans

Perhaps the most serious criticism of the Green Revolution (or rather of the capital-and-technology-intensive strategy of increasing agricultural output that underlies it) is that it has increased disparities in rural incomes agricultural output that underlies it) is that it has increased disparities in rural incomes and aggravated the problems of labour surplus in agriculture, which was already very serious in many less developed countries, including India, and has thus increased rural social tensions and unrest. It is explained that the large farmers have benefited most from the new technology because they could afford to make the large investment needed for expansion of irrigation and purchase of machinery, chemical fertilizers and other input, and also obtained large increments in output and incomes from the higher productivity of the land; that small farmers have benefited little because of their limited capacity for investment and the small size of their operations, while the landless agricultural labourers are worse off than before because mechanization of agriculture has reduced the demand for labour. It is alleged also that over large regions of India in which the majority of the small farmers are tenants, introduction of the new technology has given the land-owners both the incentive and the opportunity to dispossess them by reclaiming the land for 'personal cultivation'.[14] Further since the landless labourers, the tenants and other small farmers belong mainly to the socially depressed scheduled castes and scheduled tribes while the large or medium-size farmers belong to the socially privileged and powerful high castes, the increases in economic disparities adds to the tensions generated by the social cleavages.[15]

A case study of a single village is not a suitable medium for systematic investigation of such issues for various reasons including the fact that the selected village may not be representative of the region. Thus the size—distribution of cultivated holdings in it may differ significantly from that in the region. The situation relating to the supply or demand for labour may also be different from that in the region because of differences relating to the proportion of landless labourers in the population, the patterns of land use and cropping or the opportunities for off-farm employment. Accordingly, the following observations on changes relating to employment, wages and the social position of the Harijans in village Jitpur during the period 1963-75 are not intended in any way to indicate trends in the district or the state. Their primary objective is to describe how the agricultural changes described above have affected this important section of the village community, which comprises more than one-fourth of its total population. In the process, they draw attention also to some aspects of the change in the labour situation resulting from the Green Revolution which need to be given greater attention in studies of the Revolution.

The principal changes in the labour situation in the village and in the social position of the Harijans since 1963 have been the following:

(i) Virtual disappearance of the slack in the demand for labour during the monsoon months of July and August, which had existed in 1963, despite growth of employment opportunities during the 1950s and the early 1960s and emergence in its place of seasonal labour shortage which is being met by import of in-migrant labour from the neighbouring State of Uttar Pradesh. The change is reported to have taken place towards the end of the 1960s. The labour shortage is pronounced during the peak period of agricultural activity in April and May when harvesting of wheat is in progress along with various operations connected with planting of the summer crops. About 50-75 in-migrant workers come to work in the village for 1-2 months during this period. The monsoon months of July and August instead being a slack period has, with emergence of corn as the second most important crop of the village, become another period of heavy demand for labour which is needed for the weeding of corn. Some farmers face difficulty in obtaining sufficient labour at this time but it is not serious enough to require import of in-migrant labour.

(ii) Progressive replacement of the traditional *sanjhee* system of crop-sharing between the farmer-owner and his attached agricultural labourer and of the traditional practice of paying for particular agricultural operations such as harvesting of wheat and picking of cotton in kind, by employing workers on daily-wage basis and paying the wages in cash, which had been noted in the 1963 study, has gone even further. The *sanjhee* system, which was still adopted in 1963 study by farmers whose need for agricultural work could not be met by their own family labour has practically disappeared. Employment of agricultural workers on a daily basis is the norm. Secondly, while payments are still made in kind for some operations, notably harvesting of wheat, the dominant mode of payment of wages is in cash. The prevailing rates for the males are Rs. 6 per day plus food (mid-day meal and tea in the late morning and the afternoon) or Rs. 8 without food for local workers, and Rs. 4 plus food for the in-migrants from U.P. The wage differential between the local and the in-migrants workers is justified by the farmers on the ground that the in-migrants do not work as hard or as well as the local workers. They have less stamina than the local workers on account of poor health and small physique and they lack knowledge of local agricultural conditions. They are also considered to be less dependable.

These changes are closely related to the agricultural changes described above, as also to the growth of demand for off-farm labour, notably in construction and transport activities, which is in turn related to a large extent to the agricultural changes. The seasonal slack in demand for labour has disappeared because with more than 80 per cent of the cropland growing two crops in the year, agriculture has become a year-round operation in which there is no slack season, only periods of more or less intensive activity. As regards the total demand for agricultural labour, the increases resulting from expansion of cropped area and the various requirements of obtaining high yields per acre have to be set off against reductions brought about by replacement of bullocks by electric or diesel irrigation pumps and increasing use of tractors, grain threshers, etc. A precise estimate of the net effect on demand can be made only through a detailed study of labour inputs in agriculture.[16] Such a study is needed also for determining the relative contributions of increase in demand for agriculture and growth of off-farm employment in changing the labour situation from one of seasonal labour surplus to that of seasonal shortage.

The agricultural changes of the last 25 years have contributed to the decline of the *sanjhee* system and of the traditional practices of making payments for labour in kind because in a period of rapidly rising yields and prices of crops, the farmers have been increasingly unwilling to share the gains with their labourers particularly since the resource of labour (or of the bullock power, contributed by the *sanjhee)* is not critical to achieving the gains and the labourers cannot contribute the resources of capital and technology that are critical. But as a result of the decline the economic relationship between the farmers and the labourers is no longer governed by tradition, but by the market forces of demand and supply for labour. As a result, the labourers have become a more purely proletarian group with a much less direct stake in the productivity of the land or the profitability of the farm enterprise than they were when they shared the crops with the farmers.

The growth of off-farm employment is a major factor affecting the labour situation in the village. It adds to the demand for labour and keeps wage rates high. The principal sources of such employment are construction works in or near the village; loading and unloading of bricks with trucks which transport them form brick kilns to the constructions sites; hauling produce in the produce market (*mandi)* in Samrala town and various white-collar or unskilled jobs or commercial activity in or near the village. The following admittedly approximate estimates of employment provided by these sources are based on interviews with several knowledgeable respondents in the village; estimates given by different respondents were checked and rechecked in the course of the interviews:

Sources of Employment	*Number of Workers**
Construction work (housing, roads, etc.) 15 Masons 2 Carpenters	50-60 unskilled workers
Loading and Unloading of bricks	40-60
Carrying produce in the market	15-20
White-collar and skilled jobs	20-25
Other* (shop-keeping, repairs of Motors and other skilled work)	15-20
Total	160-200**

* The range of number indicates variations in employment in the course of the year.

** The total number of workers is less than this figure because many workers take up two or more types of work during the year. Furthermore, many workers combine non-agricultural work with agricultural labour.

Since only 637 persons were listed as workers in Jitpur at the time of the Census of Population 1971 it is clear that about one-fourth of the labour force of the village is engaged in non-agricultural work. For most of them it is a year-round activity and the principal source of livelihood.

Agricultural changes have contributed to the growth of off-farm employment because increase in activity levels in most of the source of such employment is related, directly or indirectly, to them. The increase in construction activity, which is responsible for the increase in employment in construction works as well as in loading and unloading of bricks with trucks, is the result mainly of increases in agricultural investment or in house construction resulting from increase in income. The principal forms of the activity have been construction of wells, tube-wells, storage facilities and other farm buildings; construction of new houses, shops and community buildings and making additions to or improvements in existing houses. About 100 new *pucca* houses were estimated to have been built during the 12 years since the 1963 study, while the scale of improvements and renovations is indicated by the fact that the proportion of households living in *pucca* or partially *pucca* dwellings had gone up from 47 to 70 per cent and of electrified houses from 36 to 81 (Table 12.4). Construction of new houses and improvements or additions to existing houses has also been the most important indicator of improvement in the level of living and the most important avenue for investment of the higher incomes. That the Harijans and other labouring groups in the village have also benefited from the improvement is indicated by the high proportions of households of these groups that now live in *pucca,* partially *pucca* or electrified houses.

Construction works in the vicinity of the village include besides houses and farm-or-business-related structures in the neighbouring villages, public works such as roads. The second reason for the construction and related haulage of bricks becoming important sources of employment in Jitpur is that its residents own 7 brick kilns and 16 trucks; the more affluent and enterprising; Jat and *Mistri* families have found these to be a lucrative business enterprises. In 1963, Jitpur residents owned only three brick kilns and three trucks and only 18 Harijans were in employment on haulage of bricks

Wages or earnings in off-farm employment are generally higher than in agricultural work. The workers hauling bricks generally make 10-15 rupees a day, more in periods of brisk activity; the earnings of those hauling produce in the market are similar, while skilled workers such as masons, earn Rs. 15 to 20 a day. These relatively high wages or earnings combined with the large volume of off-farm employment keep up the wage level of the agricultural labourers also. Their current wage level of Rs. 6 per day plus food or Rs. 8 with out food represents a three-fold increase since 1963, when the prevailing rates were Rs. 2 plus food or Rs. 2.50 without food. The increase has been somewhat higher than the increase in crop prices but less than that in the gross value of agricultural output. It has been explained above that average crop prices in 1970-71 to 1972-73 were twice as high as those during 1960-61 to 1962-63, and that the gross value of agricultural output has gone up by four times during the period, although the increase in net returns to the farmers had been less because of increase in expenditure on inputs. But crop prices have gone up further since 1970-71 to 1972-73 with corresponding increases in the value of agricultural output. Thus the current (Dec. 1975) price of Rs. 110 per quintal of wheat represents a 31.3 per cent increase over the average price of Rs. 83.80 during 1970-71 to 1972-73.

The increase in the total volume of employment, especially disappearance of the period of enforced idleness during the slack season in agricultural activity, and increase in various forms of non-agricultural employment, in several of which wages or earnings are so much higher than in agricultural work, have been major gains for the Harijans (and others such as barbers, oil-pressers, etc) who depend mainly on labour. It has contributed more to improvement in the economic condition of these groups than the rise in the wages of agricultural labourers.

Another development which has contributed to improvement in both the economic and social position of these groups has been increase in their employment in white-collar or skilled jobs. Ten Harijans of the village are employed as white-collar workers; and five are working as masons; in 1963 there was only one Harijans white-collar worker and no Harijan mason or other skilled worker. The upward occupational mobility of the Harijans, as also its principal cause—grant of scholarships by Government for education of Harijan children and reservation of posts for them in the Government service—are accepted by the Jats and other high castes and are also considered justified and necessary by the more enlightened members of these castes. The acceptance has gone to the extent that a Harijan youth of the village was working as the successful secretary of the primary co-operative society. The job carries a good salary and is, besides, a position of some power because of the role of the society in disbursement of low interest short-term loans and in distribution of chemical fertilizers.

Improvement in the Levels of Living

The following brief remarks are limited to a few, more obvious changes which were observed during this study: an adequate discussion would have to be based on a detailed survey of the level of living. Reference has already been made to improvements in housing resulting from construction of new houses and improvements in existing ones. This constitutes, in our view, the most important change in the level of living. Most of the new houses, built outside the circular road round the village, which was demarcated at the time of the consolidation of holdings and was built soon after, are spacious and well built. Some of them, belonging to the more affluent households, are built in the architectural styles, which are popular in the Punjab towns. Another notable change relates to possession of durable consumer goods. In 1963, possession of goods such as bicycles, sewing machines and radios was considered by the villagers to be significant indicators of modernization of consumption and of improvement in the level of living. But not so in 1975! The goods had become common, because their price was low in relation to the income level of the villagers. The price of a bicycle represented 40-60 days' wages of an agricultural labourer and that of a radio the wages for only 15-20 days. The new goods regarded as significant indicators of rise in level of living were automobiles, motor cycles, scooters and refrigerators. But their number was small and would remain so for a long time

(Table 12.4) because of the high cost of buying and keeping them. With the possible exception of refrigerators, we regard theses goods more as indicators of economic status, which distinguish the affluent from the rest of the community, than as indicators of improvement in level of living. Their appearance in the village is an indicator primarily of increase in disparities in income and the level of living.

An interesting change, which indicated the villagers' readiness to adopt urban middle class norms, was the opening in 1969 of an English-medium, 'model' primary school. It had been opened by a woman teacher belonging to the village who had returned home after teaching for some years at an English-medium high school, located at Dehra Dun in Western Uttar Pradesh. In contrast to the Government primary school in which instruction was free, the new school charged a high fee of Rs. 20 per month per child. But it was popular and as many as 110 children including 10 Harijan children were attending it because the level of instruction in it was considered to be higher than that in the Government School.[17] The Government primary school had 250 children. Thus with a total of 360 children in the two schools, almost every child, boy or girl, of the age-group, 6-11 years, appeared to be attending school. The change since 1963 related primarily to increase in school going by the children of the Harijans, because at that time a proportion of their children were not attending school. The headmaster of the Government school mentioned that the primary school would be raised to the middle level (grade VI to VIII) from the 1976-77 school year; the villagers had built at their own expense a handsome new three-room wing to the school building to provide accommodation for the new classes.

The Prospect

The process of rapid change in agricultural technology (and associated increase in agricultural output) which has been the main theme of this study had been completed by 1971-72 and the next three year was a period of stagnation or retrogression. This is indicated by data on several indicators of agricultural change for both Ludhiana district and the village. Thus output of cereals in the district declined from its peak of 1009,000 tonnes in 1971-72 to 969,000 tonnes in 1972-73 and 964,000 tonnes in 1974-75. Consumption of chemical fertilizers had peaked at 251,000 tonnes in 1972-73 and was only 160,000 in 1974-75. The yield of wheat had declined form 33.1 quintals per acre in 1971-72 to 29.7 quintals by 1974-75. In case of the village, data on gross cropped area, gross irrigated area, and distribution of chemical fertilizers and short-term credit by the primary cooperative society showed similar stagnation or small decline after 1971-72 or 1972-73. This development was attributed to a combination of unfavourable factors; low rainfall in 1972-73 and again in 1974-75; shortages of chemical fertilizers and diesel oil and sharp increases in their prices after the quintupling of the prices of crude oil by the OPEC countries in 1973-74; and finally, shortage of electricity because of fall in generation as result of the low rainfall (most of the electricity in the state is supplied by a hydroelectric plant). In 1975-76, a favourable monsoon had resulted in a bumper summer crop and the cool season crop was also expected to be very good. But the farmers had found themselves caught in a squeeze between rising prices of inputs and falling prices of crops. The prices of chemical fertilizers and diesel oil had continued to rise and the electricity rates were raised by the State Electricity Board during the summer of 1975. The rates had been earlier held unchanged for several years despite rising generation costs, because of the state governments' policy of encouraging the use of electricity by farmers. On the other hand, the price of corn had, with the end of the scarcity of food grains, come down from a peak of about Rs. 130 per quintal in 1974-75 to Rs. 65-70 by December 1975. In the case of wheat, the price at which the Central Government made purchases for meeting the needs of the public distribution system, had remained unchanged at the 1974-75 level of Rs. 110 per quintal, but the premium above it which the farmers got for sales in the free market, had disappeared and the official purchase price had become the support price for the crop.

Do theses developments foreshadow a period of stagnation or retrogression for the region or do they constitute only a temporary setback in a vigorous growth process? A definite answer is not possible at this stage because we are so close in time to the period of growth and the period of stagnation. Instead we list below some of the factors, which are relevant to analysis of this issue and also indicate some developments which have a bearing on the possible directions of future advance.

(i) The rapid progress achieved by the region has been due primarily to two factors—well developed physical and economic infrastructures and the initiative and dynamism of the people. Both have been added to and strengthened very considerably during nearly 25 year of rapid economic growth. The Green Revolution years, in particular, have witnessed significant expansion of irrigation facilities, major additions to the stock of agricultural capital and expansion or strengthening of the institutional structures of agricultural research and extension, supply of inputs, and agricultural credit. The capacity of the people for making rapid progress has been enhanced because of increase in literacy, improvements in health, nutrition and level of living and, most notably, by the experience of rapid progress during the Green Revolution years. The experience has shown them the possibility of rapid economic advance within their own socio-economic matrix besides greatly increasing their technological and income levels.

(ii) The stagnation or retrogression during 1972-73 to 1974-75 had been due either to natural causes or to national level factors, relating to supplies of inputs or prices of inputs or outputs. As for the national level factors, while the exceptionally favourable situation of the Green Revolution years could not continue indefinitely—a period of adjustment was inevitable—it would be unrealistic to assume that in a situation of rapidly rising demand for food and bare self-sufficiency or marginal scarcity in supply, they could long remain unfavourable to growth in the few regions in which rapid growth of food output had been achieved and the potential for further rapid growth demonstrated. According to projections made by the National Commission on Agriculture the demand for foodgrains (cereals and pulses) is expected to increase by 46-64 per cent between 1975 and A.D. 2000 (National Commission on Agriculture, 1973). The rate of increase may turn out to be higher because the estimates of the commission on the growth rates of population and per capita income on which the projections are based appear to us to be on the low side. On the other hand despite the Green Revolution in the wheat-growing region of North Western India, the rate of increase of food output during the 1960s (1960-61 to 1971-72) was only marginally higher, at 2.7 per cent per annum, than the rate of 2.5 per cent achieved during the first 12 years of planned development (1952-53 to 1964-65). This was because food output in most of the other regions, which grow rice or other grains continued to be very low. Thus while wheat output increased at an average rate of 8.8 per cent per annum during 1960-61 to 1971-72 the rate for rice was about 2.5 per cent and that for jowar, India's third ranking cereal in acreage and production, was negative (Saran, 1975).

(iii) Further growth of agricultural output in this region may be expected to come from two principal sources: (a) continuing increase in crop output through more careful adoption of recommendations of the extension services, relating particularly to application of chemical fertilizers, and irrigation; progressive improvements in the recommendations as a result of research, and improvements in management by farmers who are increasingly conscious of increasing the efficiency of resource use; and (b) growth of dairying, poultry-keeping market gardening and other highly remunerative forms of production resulting in progressive transformation of the region's agriculture from a field-crop producing to a mixed, crop-and-livestock enterprise.

(iv) The effect of the price squeeze was reflected in the widespread feeling in the region that agriculture was no longer as 'remunerative' as it had been in the late 1960s and the early 1970s. The feeling was expressed by respondents in Jitpur, by officials and local leaders in Samrala and Ludhiana and by two state-level leaders, the Vice-Chancellor of the Agricultural University and an ex-Minister of Agriculture. Although some of them were pessimistic about the future, most were not, and thought that steady progress could continue if appropriate changes were made in the pattern of production. The best prospects for growth were seen in development of dairying and poultry keeping. The popular slogan that "The Green Revolution must be followed by a White Revolution" was repeated by several officials and leaders. The State government was encouraging expansion of dairying, poultry-keeping, market-gardening, etc. through a variety of promotional measures. It had drawn up a long-term plan for development of dairying, which was built round establishment of a chain of central dairies, and a dense network of milk collection centres to supply them with milk. Four such dairies located in the principal cities of the state and supplying the cities with fluid milk and products such as butter and ghee (butter oil) were already functioning; besides two large, privately owned, milk processing plants which produced powdered milk, baby food, etc. Three additional dairies were under construction and the plan projected establishment of a dairy or processing plant in each of the 12 districts of the State. The plan envisaged also a major increase in the efficiency of

> milk production by progressive replacement of the existing milch animals with high-yielding animals developed by cross-breeding local cows with high-yielding European stock of the Holstein, Jersey and Brown Swiss breeds; and (b) development of the Punjab as a major dairy State supplying milk and milk products to cities all over Northern India. The latter objective was based on appreciation of the fact that the level of animal husbandry and the milk yield per animal were already much higher in the state than in the other states of Northern India.

Among the promotional measures being undertaken to increase milk production, the most important was encouraging formation of "milk producers" co-operatives, consisting primarily of marginal farmers of landless agricultural labourers and giving the members liberal medium-term loans for purchase of milch animals or other needs. Besides increasing milk output the measure was expected to provide a source of supplementary income to theses poorer sections of the agricultural community. It may be recalled that such a co-operative had been established in village Jitpur in 1975 and loans totalling Rs. 30,000 had already been given to 15 of its 52 members, and that a milk collection centre for the central dairy located at the state capital Chandigarh was proposed to be opened in the village early in 1976.

Poultry farming, which had been growing rapidly in the State in the late 1950s and early 1960s but had gone through a period of stagnation and consolidation thereafter was a well organized promotional service, consisting of extension officers posted at the Community Development block and multi-village levels; facilities for disease control and treatment of birds, hatching of eggs and supply of chicks to the poultry farmers; provision of credit and supply of inputs particularly balanced feed to them, and marketing of their products. But, as in the case of the dairy development programme, the emphasis in this case also was on encouraging poultry keeping by small farmers of landless labourers in order to provide them with a source of supplementary income. The Samrala Community Development Block was one of the "intensive development areas" in the State and had a number of relatively large poultry units with 1,000 laying birds or more, besides small units with 100-500 birds, Jitpur had five poultry units in 1975 with the number of birds ranging between 300 and 800. All were owned by small farmers and had been started during the previous two years,

It will be noticed from the above description of the dairy and poultry development programme that the primary economic objective of razing income in the agricultural sector of the State's economy and increasing the long-term growth potential of the sector and the welfare objective of raising the income of the poorer section of the agricultural community were mixed in them. While a clear choice between the two objectives may not be necessary immediately, the choice on establishment of priorities between them was essential in order to improve efficiency of performance.

To conclude, the prospect is of:: (a) continuation of the process of vigorous agricultural and economic growth in the region and the village to which the Green Revolution has given a 'big push'; but (b) progressive change in the character of the region's agriculture from concentration of production of field crops to mixed crop-and-livestock economy similar to that of many countries of Western Europe. Most studies of the Green Revolution emphasize technological change in agriculture and the resulting changes in output, income and employment. This case study brings out, however, that even the purely economic changes associated with the Green Revolution have been broader in scope and more complex in character. Thus it shows that non-agricultural employment, resulting mainly from the increase in construction activity, has increased to such an extent that it is now the principal source of livelihood for about one fourth of the labour force of the village. Second, with the virtual disappearance of the *sanjhee* system and further decline in the practice of making payments of agricultural labour in kind, the traditional, institutionalized patterns of inter-group and inter-personal economic relationships have been replaced almost completely by relationships determined by the market forces of demand and supply for labour. Together, these two changes have altered profoundly the relationship between the land of the village and its people. Not only do the labouring groups not share directly in the current crop, but for a substantial proportion of them the land is no longer the source of livelihood. Indeed for the non-agricultural workers working outside the village, the village is not much more than a dormitory. They live in it because of family and community ties and the very considerable advantage of free or cheap housing. But their economic interests are primarily in the wider, micro-regional economy.

The village economy itself is more closely integrated with the larger regional and national economies than ever before and is more dependent upon policies, and programmes originating in the changing needs of the latter. These policies and programmes have been the dominant agents in the change process of the past 25 years. The people of the region and the village have readily accepted the programmes and have through their own initiative and innovative ability added to their beneficial effects. But that does not alter the change-agent rolc of the policies and programmers. And as the reference to economic stagnation during 1972-73 to 1974-75 indicates, even temporary changes in national-level factors, such as supplies of inputs or prices of inputs and outputs have a profound effect on the village economy. We believe that the 'self-sufficiency' of the Indian village was always over-stated. But with the economic changes, such as those reviewed here, the village is now as much a part of the wider regional and national economies as any urban community.

Footnotes

1. The name is fictitious.
2. *Harijan*: (lit. children of God). The term was first used by Mahatma Gandhi, the great leader of India's Independence, for the socially depressed, untouchable Hindu castes, such as leather-workers and sweepers, in his campaign for abolition of untouchability and improvement of the social and economic status of these castes. After the Independence of India, the castes are designated as "scheduled castes", but the term 'Harijans' continues to be used in many regions including this one.
3. The Community Development Block organization was developed as part of the community development programme, the broad ranging rural development programme which the Indian Government started in 1952. The rural areas of India are covered by nearly 5,500 blocks with population varying between 50,000 and 150,000. Every block has a team of specialists in agricultural extension and related rural development services.
4. The pre-1966 State of Punjab was divided into three parts in that year. The central region in which Sikhs are in a majority, was constituted into the new state of Punjab; the eastern region was constituted into the new state of Haryana, while the small Himalayan portion was merged with the existing state of Himachal Pradesh.
5. Consolidation of holdings is the reform through which the small, scattered plots of land owned by the land-owning families of a village are pooled and each family is then allotted in their place one to three much larger plots. It makes possible more efficient and more intensive cultivation.
6. Wells tap shallow layers of groundwater, located in this region at depths of 15 to 50 feet while tube-wells tap the layers at depths of 50 to 150 feet. The motive power for lifting the water in wells had been provided traditionally by bullocks which have however been replaced increasingly by electric to diesel powered pumps: tube-wells are generally powered by the latter.

7. The comparative cost figures for irrigating a field preparatory to sowing of wheat in it were estimated in 1963 as follows:

	Rs. per acre
(i) Using electric pump set	3.87
(ii) Using a pair of bullocks	25.00

8. A popular Punjabi proverb equates selling milk by a farmer with selling his son.
9. According to the Census of Population, agricultural labourers constituted 17.3 per cent of the agricultural labour force and 9.7 per cent of all workers in Punjab in 1961; the corresponding figures of India were 23.7 per cent and 16.7 per cent respectively (Registrar General and Census Commissioner, India: *Census of India.* Series 1. India Paper 1 of 1971. Supplement: *Provisional Population Totals* (New Delhi: 1971) pp. 62-63.
10. The canal colonies of Punjab had among the highest level of agriculture and animal husbandry and of rural incomes in pre-Independent India. The extension service had made a major contribution to this achievement. They were efficient and the farmers, new to a region with an unfamiliar, harsh environment, were more receptive to their advice than farmers in most regions of India.
11. Rate of interest for loans taken from village money-lenders vary between 25 and 100 per cent per annum.
12. Pulses or beans of several kinds have an important place in cropping system in most regions of India. They are the principal source of protein in diet of the Indian farmers. Secondly being legumes, they increase the fertility of the soil.
13. An interesting historical analysis of price responsiveness of Sierra Leonean peasants (in West Africa) whose principal commercial crops are palm kernels, cocoa and coffee and of substitution between the first two are contained in: Saylor, R.G., *The Economic System of Sierra Leone.* (Durham, N.C.: Duke University Press, 1967) pp. 58-73.

14 & 15. See for instance:

Ladejinsky, Wolf. "*Ironies of India's Green Revolution*". *Foreign Affairs,* Vol. 48, No 4 (July 1970) p. 764.

—— "*Green Revolution in Bihar, the Kosi Area; A field Trip*" refers specifically to ejection of tenants as a result of the Green Revolution in a field trip report on Bihar *Economic and Political Weekly,* Bombay, Vol, IV No. 39 (September 27, 1969) pp. A-147-162.

Frankel, F., "Agricultural Modernization and Social Change." *Mainstream* (November 29, 1969)

16. One such study, which contains a detailed analysis of the supply and demand for labour in agriculture of Punjab-Haryana, in 1968-69 and projections up to 1983-94 is Billings, Martin H., and Arjun Sigh, "Mechanization and rural Employment," *Economic and Political Weekly*, Bombay, Vol. V., No. 26 (June 27, 1970) pp. A-61-69. The study indicated that the marginal shortage of labour in the peak demand months for September and October

already experienced during 1968-69 would become progressively worse unless the conventional technology was replaced by increasing use of machinery particularly pump-sets, tractors and threshers.

17. Sending children to English Medium 'model' or public schools (following the British practice the term 'public' is used for expensive private schools) has become very popular among the urban middle and upper income groups in the Punjab. The older and best known among the 'public' schools were originally established in the pre-Independence period for the children of British officers or the Indian Princes and many parents make considerable financial sacrifice to send their children to them in order to give them a better start in life.

References

Billings, Martin H., and Arjun Sigh, "Mechanization and rural Employment" *Economic and Political Weekly*, Bombay, Vol. V., No. 26 (June 27, 1970) pp. A-61-69

Frankel, F., "Agricultural Modernization and Social Change." *Mainstream* (November 29, 1969)

Ladejinsky, Wolf. "Ironies of India's Green Revolution". *Foreign Affairs,* Vol. 48, No 4 (July 1970) p. 764.

—— "*Green Revolution in Bihar, the Kosi Area; A field Trip*" refers specifically to ejection of tenants as a result of the Green Revolution in a field trip report on Bihar, *Economic and Political Weekly,* Bombay, Vol. IV No. 39 (September 27, 1969) pp. A-147-162

Nath, V., "The New Village" *The Economic Weekly* Bombay 1965 p. 58.

National Commission on Agriculture, *Projections of Demand for Selected Agricultural Commodities in India, A.D. 1975-2000.* (Mimeo.) New Delhi 1973.

Saran, Ram, "*Growth in Indian Agriculture: An Analysis*", Presidential Address to the, *Second Annual Conference of the North India Economic Association* (Mimeo.) New Delhi 1975 pp. 3-6.

13

Capturing Change in Rural India

Final Analysis

It has been mentioned in the village studies that the process, speed and direction of development in the villages studied by the author has been such that the development appears to be self-sustaining; if so, is it exceptional or an all India phenomena. In other words has India been experiencing self-sustaining economic and social development during the half century after Independence and if so, would the speed and direction of this development continue in the next two decades at an accelerating rate?

The macro development indicators show that this is not an isolated phenomenon. Before we give explanation for this statement, it is important to know what we mean by self-sustainable development.

What is Self-Sustainable Development?

Stated simply, a country is supposed to be experiencing self-sustaining development if there is improvement in economic and social condition of all the people without deterioration to the physical environment.

(i) **Improvement in Economic Condition of All the People:** Increase in per capita income and in consumption of all the people means increase in consumption of food, cloth, shoes and other items of consumption and in conditions of homes, environment and in social infrastructure.

(ii) It also means **absolute decline in the number of poor**. The poor are designated as those not obtaining enough calories to maintain themselves in good health, that they also do not have access to clean drinking water and easy access to facilities for treatment in case of sickness. It means also that there are no facilities for education of their children. Most of the poor in rural areas are those who do not have enough remunerative work in agriculture or in allied agricultural activities—animal husbandry forestry or fishing or in industrial and service sector units.

(iii) **Improvement in social conditions of people** means abolition of untouchability and discrimination against scheduled castes and scheduled tribes.

The question is difficult to answer for the two decades. However, the quantum and speed of development of the past four decades and current growth rates, captured below, indicate that the development will continue but at what speed and in which direction will depend upon numerous internal and external factors.

Capturing Economic Development: Soon after India became independent it experienced an acute shortage of food for its population of over 350 million. The areas which produced large surpluses of wheat and medium staple cotton in west Punjab and Sindh had gone over to Pakistan. Similarly, the areas which produced the best quality jute and rice are now Bangladesh. Fish had also gone over to the then East Pakistan (now Bangladesh). Therefore, the first priority of the Government of India was to meet these shortages and avoid an impending famine.

The Government launched a country-wide programme of development of its villages in which more than 75 per cent of its population lived. By the end of the 1950s, all the problems, inherited by the Government of India on Independence had been largely solved. The rains which had failed in the early 1950s were adequate during the mid 1950s. The farmers helped by the agricultural extension effort of the previous five years, produced enough wheat and rice to feed the entire population. Similarly, production of rice and jute increased in West Bengal, although some quantities had to be imported from East Pakistan (Bangladesh) to feed the jute mills. Since export of jute and jute products was one of the biggest items in India, it was essential that these should be maintained.

The programme of integrated rural development resulted in improving greatly supplies of drinking water for 75-80 per cent of the villages because loans and subsidies were given to the beneficiary population to dig new wells and clean up old wells and tanks and step wells, water of which is used in many areas to get water for drinking. Approach roads were built to serve a large proportion of the population living in villages; roads were metalled so that they could be motorable. All villages with a population of 500 were assisted to have a 1-6 grade school; secondary 6-11 grade schools were opened in all the larger villages. All the programmes were executed with participation of villagers and the government. Thus in construction of wells and approach roads while the beneficiary villagers provided labour and locally available materials, the Government provided subsidies to meet the remaining costs. Roads to large villages were made motorable by the public works department. Similarly, while the villagers built and maintained the buildings for the schools and health Centres, the government provided the teachers for the schools and equipments for medical and preventive health care. The government opened a primary health care centre (mini hospital with 6 beds, 1-2 doctors, 2 or more nurses and other paramedical staff) for every group of villages which had a population of 60-100 thousand; it opened dispensaries and paid for *vaidyas* in the large villages. The staff of these institutions was required also to propagate the need for maintaining sanitation within the villages and how to avoid falling prey to communicable diseases of the respiratory and digestive tracks.

The programmes had the desired effect. Helped by two favourable monsoons, production of foodgrains (cereals and pulses) increased enough to make the country self sufficient in cereals. The deficiency in medium staple cotton was overcome by increasing production in the Coimbatore area of Tamil Nadu and somewhat later, by late 1950s and the 1960s, increasing its production in Haryana where large areas were irrigated by a canal from Satluj River after construction of the Bhakra-Nangal irrigation-cum-power project which brought a large area under irrigation in Punjab, Haryana and three districts of north western Rajasthan and also provided hydro-electric power in these areas. Supply of electricity also encouraged modernization of existing industries and development of agro-processing and other industries in Punjab and Haryana. Production of jute increased and its quality improved in West Bengal, so that the need for import of raw jute for the jute mills was reduced. This was essential for maintaining India's export of jute products which earns large foreign exchange earnings. Production of rice increased in West Bengal and other States.

Later when food shortage developed for two years in the 1960s, it was alleviated by import of wheat and other grains from the USA under its PL-480 programme. But just when the US President, refused to give further aid for several reasons, improved very high yielding varieties of seed of wheat and rice began to be available from Mexico (wheat) and the International Rice Research Institute in the Philippines. These were adapted by Indian scientists to suit conditions in the main producing areas of wheat in Punjab, Haryana, North West Rajasthan and Western UP. Output of wheat increased dramatically so that by the end of the 1960s India became self-sufficient in cereals. The increasing demand for rice was met by Indian scientists adapting the improved high-yield varieties to the large variations in environmental conditions under which rice is grown in India. India has been self sufficient in cereals since the late 1960s; it produced 200 million tonnes or more, at the end of the 1990s, more than 3 times the output in the late 1950s. Currently, the country has so much surpluse that it does not have space to store the excess grain.

The increase has been more than adequate for the need of the population, which grew around 2.5 per cent annually. Increase in output of cotton and man-made fibres for manufacture of cloth has been such that consumption of cloth by the average Indian is about 80 per cent higher in 1996-97 than in 1973-74. Consumption of sugar has also approximately doubled and that of cooking oil has increased by three times.

Income and Standard of Living

The standard of living is higher. The sales of refrigerators, air-conditioners, washing machines, gas-operated cookers, motor bicycles, mopeds and even cars has been growing rapidly every year; the latter despite bad roads. Consumption of electricity increased five times. This has meant total rural electrification in large number of states and more use of electricity at home and on farms for irrigation. Thus the average Indian is better fed, better clothed and perhaps better housed than his father or grand-father was in the 1950s. This development has been entirely due to the efforts of the Indian people because the share of foreign aid as investment in stimulating economic growth is negligible. The development is self-sustaining also because it is doubtful if we are ruining the natural resources. On the contrary, the area under forest cover, and the area under cultivation and irrigation is higher than earlier. Yields of major crops, wheat and rice have increased, so has production of sugar and other foods except oil seeds. These increases are due to higher yields on the same area of cropland. The increase in consumption of soap, hair oil, toothpaste, furniture and radio and T.V. receivers and use of medicines and health services in rural areas show that people wish to live better be cleaner and healthier than they were 20 years ago.

Improvement in health with attendant decline in infant and maternal mortality is such that the average life span is 67 years for males and 69 years for females. He or she is also much healthier. With expansion in education and health services, phenomenal increase in circulation of newspapers and the immense reach of the radio and television among people of all classes and income groups, the population is better fed, better clothed, physically better looked after and better informed and entertained.

Industrial Development

Beginning with the early 1960s and lasting up to the early 1970s the Government implemented, with financial and technical assistance from the Soviet Union, Germany, Britain and Canada, and with some technical assistance from Switzerland and the USA, large programme of industrial development. Under it were constructed five integrated steel mills with a capacity of one million tones each; a factory each for manufacturing heavy machine tools, light machine tools, and locomotives and associated equipment for the railways. Two factories for making coaches for the railways; two mills for manufacturing turbines and other heavy electrical equipment. After discovery of crude oil, off-shore Mumbai and off-shore and on-shore Gujarat, large investments were made by a Public Sector Undertaking—ONGC—for exploration and development of the oil fields and by the Indian Oil Company for refining the crude-oil (in partnership with various private sector companies) and in setting up a network of distributors for its petroleum products all over the country. This investment has however been self-financing and in fact the Indian Oil Company and the other two oil companies contribute a significant amount to the Government budget every year. Among the other industrial projects mentioned above, Hindustan Machine Tools has been profit making from the beginning and BHEL has been self financing after a few years. The largest unit that is a drag on Government's finances is SAIL (Steel Authority of India). Now since the government is getting out of owning industrial units; it can devote full attention to development of physical infrastructures—roads, electricity, and supply of drinking water to rural areas and cities—and to education and health care programmes. Very large investment is required in these sectors every year because of the deficiencies, particularly in the rural areas of some states like UP, Bihar, Orissa, Rajasthan and Madhya Pradesh. Very large investment will be required also for financing construction of roads both link (inter-state) highways which connect principal cities and the state highways which connect small towns and large villages. In the context of increasing urbanization very large investment is required for providing dependable supplies of drinking water to residents of metropolitan cities, because of large deficiencies in them.

Both investments will be self-financing because they will meet urgent needs of the population which will increase level of comfort and productivity of the population. In rural areas a literate farmer or agricultural labourer, who is also well served with medical and preventive health care, can manage his economic activities better and the woman is a better manager of the household. Literacy is the foundation on which various skills required in the industrial and service sectors are built.

Population Growth and Economic Development

The economic trends of the last three decades, especially of the 1991-2001 indicate that such development is being achieved and will continue in the next 15 to 20 years. The rate of population growth has declined after four decades of increase. The decline is due to voluntary decision of couples in the reproductive age group to limit the number of their children after observing that the survival rate of babies is higher. The Census Commissioner has estimated that the number of babies born to a woman in her reproductive age (total fertility rate) has gone down from 4.6 in 1991 to 3.1 in 2001 and would go down further to 2.5 in 2011-2016. The first results of the Census of Population of 2001 and the data on growth rate of GDP during the decade, 1991-2001 (published by the CSO) indicate that the process may have just begun.

Both the Census Commissioner and UNDP projected that the decline in growth trend would continue and during 2001-2015, the rate of growth of population would average 1.3 per cent per annum. Projecting this trend over the next 15 years, the Census Commissioner has estimated that the need to migrate to cities in search of work will decline.

The country is self-sufficient in food and fibre and has the infrastructure to reduce the deficit of oilseeds or to pay for the import. Industrial output has been increasing for meeting both domestic and export demands. The increase is spread over a large range of commodities—processed food, cotton silk and woollen textiles, shoes and other leather goods, furnishings for homes and offices and consumer durables—motor vehicles (cars, buses and trucks, two-and-three wheeler cycles), refrigerators, air conditioners washing machines and kitchen appliances operated by electricity, furniture for homes and offices. In service sectors while the share of personal services has not increased, there is rapid increase in trade and transport and information technology. As a result, exports have increased. Indian industrialists and entrepreneurs have a massive presence not only within Indian but are spreading themselves out acquiring industrial units—Tatas, Bharati airtel, Ambanis, Mittals to name a few.

Development at States Level

From all indicators available so far it appears that in a number of states such development has started and it will continue in the next 15-20 years.

In a number of areas production of food and of fibre crops has increased, there is no evidence of deterioration of the natural environment. These areas are not only self-sufficient in food and processed raw materials—cotton or other textiles and cooking oil but also export these to deficit areas. In other areas deficits in food has been eliminated as a result of extension of the irrigated area and reduction of soil erosion or soil degradation.

It is of interest to note that most of the areas in which agricultural output is high and agro-processing industries are well developed and others in which such development is recommended are either in the northern plains or are in the east and west coast plains—The only exceptions are in the south in which the whole of Tamil Nadu and adjoining areas of south western Karnataka are well developed. The areas in Rajasthan and western Madhya Pradesh in which such development is recommended are along the valleys of the rivers such as Banas and Chambal that flow into the plains from the Aravali Hills. It is also of interest to note that all have good railway facilities. The railway lines in the peninsula, define the axes of development in this large region.

The Dichotomy between Plains and the Hills

It should be mentioned also that there could develop as a consequence of the expected development a dichotomy in peninsular India between the residents of the plains and the tribal living in the adjoining hills as a consequence of which there are two Indias: one of the plains, rich and prosperous, and the other of tribal which are poor and backward. The residents of the plains would be much better educated and skilled and also much better off than the tribal. The tribal poor will not work in India's metropolitan cities but remain poised in their own hilly and forested areas.

However, since this dichotomy cannot be sustained for long · leading to violent clashes between the two groups, strategies mu evolved through which tribal youth can be brought in the main-stre They must be trained in industrial skills, so that they can work as skil. workers in the numerous industrial units that are located in their region. They must also be literate and educated so that they can do the white collar and professional jobs within their own areas. With skills and education they will also be able to fight for their rights effectively as well as their exploitation by the people of the plains. They will lead modernization of agriculture to increase output of food grains and other crops which are grown by their people. At present their protests are limited to Naxalite types attacks over the plains' dwellers settled in their midst.

Other Pockets of Development

It should be mentioned also that some of the areas which produce most of the cereals, medium staple cotton and sugar in the country were less than 50 years ago classified as drought prone and required food for work programmes to avert starvation. Western Maharashtra, Western Haryana and Western Rajasthan, and Saurashtra are examples. They were made productive by efficient use of the groundwater in some areas, such as Maharashtra and by surface water as in West Haryana and North-West Rajasthan. In Eastern Rajasthan and Western Madhya Pradesh it is productive use of the underground and surface water that would make the areas more productive. It is the inter-manage of a natural resource—underground and surface-wells or tube-wells—and improved technology which has led to increase in production and income. Tractors for reclamation of the lands and pump sets that greatly increase the cultivated and irrigated areas and increase agricultural output and development of agro-industries—wheat, and rice flour mills and preserving potatoes in cold storages and packing mangoes in season (May-July-August, for consumption in the cities). As a result of these developments there is much more work for rural population.

In Rajasthan

The study of three villages in Eastern Rajasthan shows that increase in agricultural production due to use of tractors and irrigation by diesel oil operated pumps has induced the process of increase in the income and level of living of the farmers. The wages and income of the scheduled castes of agricultural-cum-non-agricultural labourers is also higher. People are healthier—thanks to increased and more nutritious food with adequate content of foodgrains (cereals and pulses); milk, vegetables, sugar and oil supply. Facilities for curative and medical care are within easy reach. Children including girls are getting educated. They are becoming teachers, VLWs, secretaries of cooperative societies and *panchayats* and clerks in various offices. The high caste young men are becoming clerks and professionals. The aspirations of all have increased so that they will want to have a higher level of income and living in future.

There is no undue draft on the environment; on the contrary the farmlands are more productive being less subject to wind and water erosion. Macro-level statistics from Rajasthan indicate that development in this area is not isolated but is happening over large parts of South East and Eastern Rajasthan as well as North West Rajasthan.

Other areas where similar development has taken place are Punjab, Haryana, West UP, West Bengal, Coastal AP, Tamil Nadu, South East Karnataka, Kerala, Western Coastal Gujarat, Himachal Pradesh and Uttaranchal.

Areas which need self-sustaining agricultural development are:

- Eastern and Central U.P. and Bihar—North and South.
- Hill states of North East and part of Assam which needs to be cleaned of sand and silt.

Measures to start agricultural and agro-industrial development in these areas are as follow:

Central and East UP and Bihar

Complete effective land reform, especially in Bihar.

Check flood damage of Gomti, Gandok and Kosi Rivers—Forestation and other soil erosion measures in the hills.

Give loans and subsidies to farmers to clean the sand and silt by manual methods and to buy improved seeds of grain (wheat, rice, gram, peas, and other pulses, and oilseeds—mustard).

Give loans to former *Zamindars* to buy tractors for cultivation of their croplands and electric or diesel oil pump sets for the irrigable land which have been left to them for self-cultivation. Similar, loans and subsidies to farmers with relatively large holdings will enable them to produce food crops and small quantities of vegetables and fruit.

The former *Zamindars* and farmers with large holdings will grow potatoes and high quality mangoes (which Bihar, especially North Bihar produces in large quantities and which are sent to Kolkata and other cities). They will build cold storages in cooperation with traders, to preserve their produce, give loans and subsidies to similar producers to increase production of high quality mangoes in Lucknow to Varanasi in UP.

Provide facilities for preventive and curative health facilities to all. Make existing Public Health Officers (PHO) and hospitals more efficient by effective supervision of the staff. The village leaders should be charged with responsibility for ensuring full attendance of staff of the Public Health Oficers. Besides provisions should be made for increased facilities for primary and secondary level schools.

Immediately, the environment of villages will improve through investment in improved housing and provision of clean drinking water and drainage facilities in their homes. The specific measures in different areas should be different. But this is common to all. In some of the areas there is water logging especially in coastal areas of Andhra Pradesh and parts of Tamil Nadu. In these areas the villagers have to have effective drains to have enough dry land in and around their villagers so that their water supply is clean.

Community Development programme had improved the living environment of the villages in all the areas of high productivity and also in the plains of East UP and North Bihar. They have provided drains and drinking water supplies, which is most important for improving the health of the people. Pavement of streets and construction of side drains are needed to take out waste water. Drinking water supplies were improved by cleaning wells, increasing number of wells, and installation of taps for drawing water from tube wells and tanks.

In south Bihar there are thousands of wells, which are worked by bullocks. A large percentage could be fitted with diesel oil or electric operated pumps. This would increase agricultural output in their command areas.

West Bengal

The present Government of West Bengal has increased production of rice dramatically and of jute by effective land reforms, control of floods of rivers and reclamation of the land which used to be flooded by giving loans and subsidies for all these purposes to former *Zamindars* and farmers.

Peninsular India

Increasing agricultural production and agro-industrial development in Jharkhand.

Jharkhand was created as a new state by separation from Bihar in 2000. The first year was spent in setting up of the new state including the infrastructure and additional buildings in Ranchi, the capital. The area has large deposits of coal, iron ore, mica, manganese and other minerals. Excepting mica, the three other minerals are used in its steel mills in Jamshedpur and Bokaro, thermal and hydro electric power stations, mills processing steel to make rails and rolling stock for the railways, and its two aluminium mills. However, agricultural output is not enough to meet the needs of the population mainly of tribal. Their dry fields of rice or coarse grains are often wasted away during the monsoon rains and they have to be fixed annually and given loans and subsidies to clear the fields of rubbish and to plant the crops again. The first step in this area is to build check dams above the fields so that the area which is flooded and destroyed during the monsoon is greatly reduced.

The tribal youth—young men and women who are not going to work in the mines or mining companies or power stations should be given loans and subsidies to be educated so that they can become white collar and skilled workers. The white-collar workers will work in the secretariat at Ranchi, in district headquarters and offices of the companies which are running the steel plants and other industrial units. They will replace the workers from other states who are working in the plants, various industrial or power producing units.

There is great dissatisfaction in some areas that they have neither been given enough cultivable land in lieu of the lands that were taken away from them to build steel, power, cement and other mills, nor given adequate or timely compensation for this land. This grievance will have to be removed by the new Jharkhand government in consultation with the central Government and pay these people with loans and subsidies.

Similar measures should be taken in East and South East Madhya Pradesh, inland Orissa and in Chhatisgarh, These are hilly and forested and have large population of tribal. The problems of South East Madhya Pradesh and Inland Orissa which are also hilly and forested are similar with the difference that communications are much less developed than in Jharkhand.

Eradication of Poverty

Eradication or alleviation of poverty: This has been an important objective of Indian planning and development since the beginning of the First Five Year Plan. However, the estimates of 36 per cent of the population or lower estimate of people below the poverty line in the mid-1990s indicate that progress made in this direction has not been satisfactory.

During the 1990s while GDP has been increasing at 5-9 per cent per annum and per capita income has been increasing at 3-5 per cent per annum, the proportion of people below poverty line is estimated to have declined as seen from following data. The decline of 50 per cent between 1993-94 and 2001-2002 is most significant.

Proportion of People Below Poverty Line

1973-74	*1987-88*	*1993-94*	*1996-97*	*2001-02*
54.9	38.9	36.0	29.3	18.0

Source: Table 242 (p. 212) *Statistical Outline* 2002.

The principal groups which are poor are small farmers and agricultural labourers in the 65 per cent of the cropped area which is rain-fed and are located in the plains of former *Zamindari* areas of UP, Bihar, West Bengal and Orissa or in hilly and forested areas or drought prone areas of a number of States in Peninsular India and in Tamil Nadu and Andhra Pradesh, in which rainfall in the monsoon or post-monsoon seasons is fluctuating and undependable.

The measures to increase productivity in these areas may differ in detail, but can be divided into two main categories:

1. Increasing the irrigated area by a combination of measures for preserving moisture through a programme of creating small tanks by checking soil erosion. The tanks small and large would provide irrigation water to crops (rice or coarse cereals). They should be repaired and renovated annually by food-for-work programmes financed by the state governments.
   These programmes should receive financial assistance from the central government.
2. Food-for-work programmes in these and other drought prone areas should be accompanied by education to the recipients, particularly, lactating and pregnant mothers in principle of

nutrition and environment preservation. The number receiving such assistance should be progressively reduced as more and more farmers can adopt practices which preserve productivity of their farms.

Two examples will illustrate the point. In sub-Himalayan areas of UP, Bihar and West Bengal where large areas of potentially fertile land are rendered unproductive by deposits of coarse sand and boulders after every monsoon flood.

However, the present West Bengal government has reduced the areas through two measures.

(i) Construction of check dams and large reservoirs to protect land below them from being flooded. The dams and reservoirs are being repaired annually by the state government and by farmers themselves. Land released as a result of these measures is allotted to marginal farmers and landless labourers together with distribution at highly subsidized prices of improved seed and chemical fertilizers. They are also given medium term loans to buy bullocks and other farm equipment. The results have been a major increase in agricultural production and rapid increase in number of farmers who ensure that their small but economic holdings retain their productivity.
The Government of UP and Bihar could undertake similar programmes with assistance from the Central Government.

(ii) The drought prone areas of Maharashtra and Karnataka have been progressively reduced by a combination of measures to check soil erosion and construction of check dams. Some formerly drought prone valleys in inland Maharashtra now produce fruit and vegetables and high yield sugarcane. Some of the drought prone areas along the coast now produce mangoes which command a very high price.

Some of the former drought prone areas in Gujarat are major producers of milk for sale to the cities and for manufacture of dairy products.

A large proportion of milk for Delhi as well as for cities in Rajasthan is obtained from areas which are drought hit but in the summer have numerous reservoirs, large and small, in which large herds of milch animals are stall fed on fodder crops during the cool season.

Punjab Sikhs who migrated to the UP—Terai—in the 1950s and the 1960s have reclaimed large areas of formerly flooded croplands to produce large crops of wheat and rice. Such areas could be increased by assistance from the state governments.

Influence of the Large Farmers

When the Governments of India and of several states implemented, successfully in the early 1950s, the land reform of abolition of *Jagirdari* and *Zamindari* the former *Zamindars* appeared to have accepted this change peacefully and accepted their new position of cultivators of land which they were allowed to retain for self-cultivation. They got them cultivated with labour provided by their former tenants belonging to the scheduled castes or other backward castes. Forty years later, in many areas of the country, such as Eastern UP, Bihar and parts of Madhya Pradesh and Orissa, the land reform does not appear to have changed social stratification as much as one would expect. It is true that millions of former tenants or share-croppers belonging to the scheduled castes or other backward castes have become peasant proprietors, but during the time the former *Zamindars* have managed to remain the power group in all States of UP, Bihar, MP, Orissa and Rajasthan. They hog the loans and grants given by the government for agricultural and rural development in collusion with officials responsible for implementation of these programmes. With the same collusion, they appropriate a considerable proportion of the funds provided for food-for-work and other programmes to provide gainful employment to the rural poor. In some areas, parts of Bihar and Telengana region of Andhra Pradesh, their resistance to any change is so great that there is literally a class war on between the former *Zamindars* and their former tenants. Burning the villages of the latter and killing them by attacks at night, just like ku kus Klan in the southern USA after the civil war, are common. The scheduled castes retaliate by murdering, particularly in the garb of Naxalites, oppressive landlords.

After the Government of India had implemented the abolition of *Jagirdari* and *Zamindari* in the early 1950s, it should have implemented further reform of fixing a ceiling on land holdings, so that cultivable land in excess of the ceilings held by large farmers (mostly former *Zamindars*) were taken away from them and distributed among the landless members of the scheduled castes and marginal farmers of these and other backward castes. However, the opposition to the reform is so strong that the legislation has never been implemented, so that inequalities in land holdings among farmers remain a dominant feature of rural India in large parts of the country.

The influence of these farmers is so strong that the government cannot formulate support prices for cereals, sugarcane, cotton or oilseeds which are dictated by the market. It has to fix higher prices so that the large farmers who have most of the marketable surplus are assured high incomes.

Thus despite all attempts to reduce their power; the large farmers remain an important pressure group in most of the States. One reason for this is that most of the legislators in the states and members of Parliament are large farmers.

Land Use Patterns

A number of large villages become small towns if productivity of agriculture in their hinterlands increases rapidly. Is this the only settlement possible or is there any alternative?

The question can be answered definitely only in 2021 on the basis of trends during the next two decades. However, this seems to be the best feasible scenario at present from all available evidence.

An indication of this is provided by a report made to the National Council of Applied Economic Research in the mid-1960s, by an American Expert, E.A.K.J. Johnson, which proposed that India should build 5000 new towns in strategic locations and provide them with all facilities needed for a market town. He proposed that the towns should be built on green field locations, because the existing large villages are already overpopulated and polluted and would become more so. Fortunately no action was taken on the recommendation, because any action would have been a waste of precious funds which could be put to better uses.

A small town is at the centre of small villages, residents of which mainly farmers and labourers come to it to buy provisions, cloth, clothes, drugs or other necessities, building materials and other needs. It serves however, primarily the needs of its own.

Growth of relatively large villages to mini-market towns is a natural process. The factors that contribute to this process, such as surplus from high productivity agriculture, remittances from residence of workers in industrial units or service sector jobs located in a neighbouring large town or metropolitan city and others are primarily local and partly regional. They become urban in some cases, particularly villages located in the peri-urban area of metropolitan cities. We have observed that the towns have grown in areas in which productively of agriculture has increased or the ones located in the peri-urban areas of metropolitan cities. It is conspicuous by its absence in areas such as large parts of UP, Bihar, much of West Bengal, Orissa and Assam, where such processes have not operated for different reasons.

Changes in Rajasthan

Rajasthan despite its adverse geoclimatic conditions has a surplus in food-grains. The present per capita production per annum in Rajasthan is 205 kg. as against a national consumption of 160 kg. Per adult per annum." (See Rajasthan: A State Profile; p. 36-37) Thus Rajasthan that was deficit in food grains in the 1950s has large surplus and besides has large export of oil seeds.

There has been large investment by the state government in appointing agricultural extension and veterinary officers; opening schools, hospitals and dispensaries; providing loans through cooperative societies and branches of nationalized banks (located in both Maanpur and Raipur) and the Land Mortgage Bank for current cultivation, for improvement of cropland or buying tractors, pump sets and other machines and building houses. At the same time, as their income has increased, the people have themselves made large investments in buying tractors, pump sets, and other machines and improved seed, fertilizers and pesticides. Large investment has been made by the state also in rural electrification and in construction of tube-wells for lifting water to overhead tanks, which supply drinking water to large numbers of homes in all the villages (studied). The villagers have constructed the overhead tanks, which cost about Rs. 4 million in Raipur and Maanpur and somewhat less in Bijaipur. This expenditure shows the value that they attach to having adequate and safe drinking water.

Social Development

As seen in the villages of Rajasthan since the Chammars could not draw water from the wells of the high castes or worship in their temples, they had obtained grants from the Community Development Department to improve the wells in their hamlets and had built their own temples. Practice of untouchability had been declared an offence and was disappearing in both rural and urban areas. By 1961, representatives of all castes elected to the *panchayat* of both Maanpur and Raipur sat together to conduct the business of the statutory *panchayat*s. Furthermore, men of all castes drank tea from the same two shops located in Maan Town market. The *Sarpancha*s of both Raipur and Maanpur were from the high castes in 1961. By 2001, although the *sarpanch* of the Maanpur *panchayt* was a Mahajan, that of Raipur was a woman of the dhobi (washer man) caste. People of the high caste or the cultivators did not respect her but there was no petition pending with the Collector, requesting her removal. In Maanpur also, there had been periods when a Meena occupied the post.

Further, social development will mean absolute decline in practice of untouchability, greater education of women and children of school going ages and abolition of child marriages that is still widespread. It will mean even greater migration of sons of Brahmins, Rajputs and Mahajans to Jaipur, Kotah and other cities in Rajasthan and Delhi in search of white-collar jobs. At present there are educated men in Raipur who are sitting idle due to lack of employment opportunities.

"As mentioned earlier hunger has been eliminated due to increased availability not only of grains but even protective foods." There has been increase in education and improvement in health and productivity of the people. The principal diseases are those of the digestive and respiratory tracks. Malaria the great killer had been eradicated by the 1950s but has made a slow comeback.

There is enough work both for skilled and unskilled non-agricultural workers in and around Sawi Madhopur district headquarter Maan Town market and the railway station.

Increase in education of boys and girls have also resulted in consciousness of a higher level of living and having smaller families. The standard of living of most of the villagers can be considered to be that of lower middle income while others with white collar jobs can be considered to be in middle-income category. Bride price is stated to have disappeared among the better-to-do Meena cultivators and dowry has appeared. However, there must be bride price among the poor cultivators due to the fact that women do much more work on the farm than the men. Their farm work is much less, however, than earlier because the small cultivators can hire tractors and pay also for irrigation water. Improvement of supply of electricity by RSEB (Rajasthan State Electricity Board) will greatly reduce cost of irrigation and contribute to increase in production.

The standard of living is now comparable to that in village Otalan of Punjab in 1961 with the following exception:

- Liberation of girls was much greater in Otalan even then, than in the Sawai Madhopur villages now.

- A large number of young men of both—Jat and the scheduled castes went to the army. Very few young men from this village go to the army.

The developments in this area explained in the foregoing sections satisfy both criteria of self sustaining development in our view. The farmlands are more productive in 2001 than they were in 1961. In 1961, most of the farm land was bare for more than six months in the year i.e. after the monsoon season when crops of sorghum or millets had been harvested and was subject to wind or storm erosion. Now, almost all the farmland is irrigated and grows crops—gram (chick peas), wheat, mustard or pulses in the cold season and sorghum, millets or groundnut in the monsoon season. The crop rotation followed is such that the nutrients removed by one set of crops are replaced by another set. Thus, most of the nutrients removed by high yield wheat are replaced by stubs of sorghum, millets and vines of mustard and ground nuts. While some of the stubs of sorghum and millet and husks of wheat are fed to milch animals, the remainder are ploughed in, which improve the physical structure of the soil. The remains of groundnut and mustard mix in addition, nitrogen from the air. The pastures are looked after better because production of milk is a major source of income for villages located between Sawai Madhopur and Maan Town. The Ranthambhore forest and game sanctuary are protected both by the forest guards and employees of Tiger Watch an international non-governmental organisation, the sole object of which is to preserve the natural habitat of tigers and other wild beasts. Much of the cultivable land which had formed part of the *shikar* (hunting) preserve of former *Jagirdars* and was under trees has been cleared for cultivation and allotted to Chammars or other landless or appropriated by the *Jagirdars* for self-cultivation. There is no evidence yet of fall in the ground water table due to irrigation of most of the cropland.

Increase in income and consumption, improvement in health, increase in education of children and rise in aspirations for further rise in these.

In 1961, most of the people, all except the better off Mahajans and Meenas or Brahmins whose sons were working as village level white collar workers, were poor. By 2001, most of them had risen to lower middle income or higher economic status. Even the farmers with small holdings and the scheduled castes agricultural or non-agricultural labourers have enough cereals to eat through the year and also have protective foods—milk, vegetables, and fruit in season—which few could afford to eat earlier are now an integral part of their diet. Their health is much better, because they have access to medical care facilities in the form of two very well equipped multi-facility hospitals, besides dispensaries and *vaidyas* in both the large villages. In addition, Maanpur has a resident physician and an auxiliary nurse midwife. They realise enough the value of adequate and safe drinking water supply for maintaining good health, and constructed side drains along the main streets of all the three villages to drain the waste water for cleanliness. Two villages—Maanpur and Jeenapur are quite clean because drain water is discharged in ponds located to the rear of the villages.

Their homes and children are much cleaner because the need for manual work on the farms is much less than before, thanks to use of tractors for cultivation and mechanical shellers for sorghum and millet and de-huskers of wheat. A large percentage of houses are made of brick and mortar which are much easier to clean than the mud and thatch huts in which most of the small cultivators and landless labourers lived in 1961. Maternal, infant and child mortality has been reduced so much that many couples in the reproductive age group are practicing family planning.

There is a multi facility hospital near the base of the sanctuary. It was built and is being maintained by the Tiger Foundation, an NGO. It specializes in treatment of cataract. About 1000 operations are performed in it every year. Patients come from Sawai Madhopur, Maan Town and villages and towns of the whole district. Eye specialists come to the hospital also from Delhi for cataract operations. One of the specialists goes twice a month from Jaipur to perform operations. One husband and wife team manages the hospital on a daily basis with large number of nurses and other paramedical and administrative staff.

The value of education of children has been realised so much that most of the boys and a large number of girls of school going ages are being sent to primary or secondary schools. People of the high castes and more affluent Meenas educate their daughters so that they can be wives of white-collar workers. Furthermore, even the poor farmers and landless labourers realize that educated wives keep their homes and children clean and know enough to avoid themselves or their children falling victims to communicable diseases.

Since a large number of high castes and affluent Meenas household have black and white or colour T.V. receivers and even the poor have radio receivers, they are well aware of events in the area, district, and the state and even in the country. These receivers inform and entertain. They tell them the essentials of good living and create the desire to have the means to achieve it.

There has been a rise in aspirations of people of all castes. The high castes Brshmins, Mahajans and Rajputs are educating their sons to go through degree or professional colleges in Jaipur or Kotah so that they can become professionals or officers in the state government who have much higher salaries than they had in 1961. They are educating their daughters so that they can be married to such officers. The parents are proud of the fact that some of their sons are professionals living in Jaipur or other districts of Rajasthan or in other states. Even the Meenas who were not interested in white collar jobs are now keen that their sons and daughters should be educated so that they can become white collar workers.

Development is self-sustaining because it is inconceivable that after having come this far, they would allow themselves to return to their former poverty, illiteracy and ignorance.

It is true that these people located near the district headquarters have privileged access to education and medical facilities located at the district level; high schools, colleges and hospitals. They have privileged access to white-collar work for the same reason. Farmers located in distant villages would not have such access. However, the changes must be occurring over a long area in Rajasthan, as seen from the statistics on increase in agro-production, use of chemical fertilizers and increase in number of tractors.

Changes in skills and aspirations are even more important. There has been a major rise in level of skills of the farmers. In 1961, improved iron ploughs developed by CARE were lying unused in the *panchayat* building of Maanpur because no one could remedy the small defects in them. Now most of the farmers have the skill to run tractors and diesel oil operated pump sets. Facilities for repair of major defects in them are available with the dealers in Maan Town market. However, the farmers have the skill to correct small defects in these machines themselves; otherwise their operation would be too expensive.

Would this progress continue? Most likely, yes, the growth rate is due to the efforts of the private sector without intervention of the government except to remove some of the hurdles in the path of fastest growing industries. And the World Bank and other agencies are of the opinion that it would mean faster development if these hurdles were removed faster.

The progress is primarily due to the efforts of the rural and urban people. This despite the fact that India has had a week government with coalition of 25 political parties which make it difficult to take major policy decisions. The growth would be faster if the hurdles were removed.

The farmers of Sawai Madhopur are likely to follow the same pattern as the Punjabi farmers. There is a tendency to over-invest, once the returns of initial investment become apparent. Eventually too many people make too many investments in the same thing and there is a winnowing out of the marginal producers. The remaining producers consolidate the farms into larger tracts and can make use of the efficiencies of large scale mechanization. If the experience of Punjab is repeated in Sawai Madhopur, there will be fewer farm families, larger farms and greater mechanization. The farmers who succeed, will be more prosperous.

But it Need not be This Way

It is instructive at this point to review the way farming has been organized in the United States, France and Japan. The different structures supply us an alternative way to look at the future.

American farming is characterized by mega farms and a high level of automation. The food industry in the United States is homogenous and national. Farm produce, whether it is wheat, fowl or dairy are collected at central points, processed and distributed nationally. The chicken breast purchased in Maine are exactly the same as the chicken breasts purchased in Honolulu, and they are both packaged in a factory in Arkansas; same with cheese, milk and bread etc. Scale brings efficiencies to the production of food and also allows national standards of cleanliness to be enforced. The food is cheap and good. But the food is the same everywhere and is neither as tasty nor as healthy as small batch food processing would allow it to be. As a result, there is now the emergence of local bakeries and food processors who service a local, more affluent clientele and fine dining restaurants. Locally grown tomatoes and herbs and lettuce are finding a preferred position in many restaurants; local (sometimes neighbourhood) bakeries are finding unexpected success because they can vary their offerings and experiment with different ingredients.

French farming has always maintained its local traditions. The local markets with fruits, vegetables and other farm products (jams, jellies, mustards, herbs etc.) complement the local bakery and the local boulangerie (meat shop). Farm employment remains relatively high and vibrantly innovative. Recently, high priced French jams have been finding success in specialty food stores in the United States. While the food is more varied and innovative, healthier and tastier, the cost of the food is significantly higher. The French consumer is more than willing to pay the higher prices; after all he is French!

The farm sector in Japan has an interesting twist. Japanese farmers form a strong political block and have been able to have many protectionist laws passed. Japan is dotted with small inefficient rice farms and the farmers are protected by competition from other countries ("Japanese rice is just better than Chinese rice"). Due to the regulation of the market, the Japanese food market is neither as vibrant as the French market, nor as efficient and inexpensive as the American market. It is a politically driven market.

We would recommend that the farmers of Sawai Madhopur or Punjab do not ask the politician for help in safeguarding their farms.

It is clear that the Indian food market is beginning to be dominated by large scale national and international food processors. The American model of food production and distribution will eventually be the way the Indian market is organized. We do not have the cultural snobbery or affinity to local produce that the French have; our industrialists have also shown an unseemly adeptness to manipulate the political system to their own uses, so the Japanese model is unlikely here.

However, India is a much more varied society than America and there will be a better possibility of regional producers of particular products to flourish. In the case of Sawai Madhopur, the area has been found to be exceptionally suitable for growing of guavas. Additionally, there is a local sweet called *rabri* for which the area is famous. Proper branding of these products would lead to the movement of farming from commodity products to higher margin products. A guava canning factory, a Tiger brand of guava juice with extra protein, Sawai Madhopur *rabri* are all possibilities.

There will continue to be a viable farming community in Sawai Madhopur—many people will continue to produce commodity items for sale to large food processors, and there will be some local products which may find regional or national fame.

It is clear, however, that many farmers will not be able to survive. The children of the farmers will move to cities, many will enter service industries like trucking and retailing. In order for the children to continue to progress and become wealthier, it is crucial that they are educated and trained. Higher education results in greater individual productivity, which means increasing wealth.

Bibliography

SECTION A

Village Studies and the Caste System

A number of village studies conducted by sociologists and cultural anthropologists in villages in different parts of India have appeared in recent years. They describe the working of the social system of the villages: several of them refer also to social, economic and political changes being experienced by the villages. A selected list is given below. Dube's work, *India's Changing Villages*, and the studies of Mrs. Epstein, Carstairs and Mayer, are of particular interest for this work. The first two deal specifically with social change; the others are of interest because they are studies of villages of former princely States located in the same socio-cultural area. Carstairs studied a village in the former Udaipur State of Rajasthan; Mayer's work is based on village of Devas, a small princely State in Central India (now Madhya Pradesh).

Besides these recent works, some earlier works on caste are also of interest. Ibbotson's Punjab Castes (Lahore, 1916) is a basic document on the castes of Northern India. Hutton, J.H. in his report on the Census of India 1931 and in *Caste in India* (Oxford, 1951) gives detailed accounts of caste, its character, origin and functions, and especially interesting accounts of the changes experienced by the lower castes during the 1920s (and earlier).

Bailey, F.G., *Caste and the Economic Frontier*. Oxford University Press, Bombay, 1958

Carstairs, G.M. *The Twice Born.* The Hogarth Press, London, 1957.

Dube, S.C. *Indian Village*, Rutledge and Kegan Paul, London, 1955.

Dube, S.C. *India's Changing Villages: Human Factors in Community Development.* Routledge and Kegan Paul, London, 1958

Epstein, T. Scarlett, *Economic Development and Social Change in South India.* Oxford University Press, Bombay, 1962

Lewis, Oscar. *Village Life in Nothern India*. University of Chicago Press, Chicago, 1955.

Mayer, Adrian C. *Caste and Kinship in Central India*, Rutledge and Kegan Paul, London, 1960.
Srinivas, M.N. (Ed) *Indian Villages*. Asia Publishers, Bombay, 1955.

2. Panchayats and Panchayati Raj Institutions

Legislation

The Rajasthan Panchayat act 1953 as amended up to 1960. Government Central Press, Jaipur, 1960
The Rajasthan Panchayat Samitis and Zila Parishads Act 1959. Government Central Press, Jaipur, 1959.

Concepts, History, Working etc.

Committee on Plan Projects, Government of India. Report of the Team for the Study of Community Projects and National Extension Service. Volume I. New Delhi, 1957.
Dey, S.K., *Panchayati Raj; A Synthesis;* Asia Publishing House, Bombay, 1961.
Evaluation Crganization, Government of Rajasthan, *Report on Panchayat Elections in Rajasthan. Jaipur, 1961.*
Indian Journal of Public Administration, *Special Panchayati Raj Number*, Volume III, No. 4, 1962. Indian Institute of Public Administration, New Delhi.
Jayraman, K. A., *Study of Panchayats in Madras*. Indian Society of Agricultural Economics, Bombay, 1947.
Maheshwari, B., *Studies of Panchayati Raj*. New Delhi Metropolitan Book Company Pvt. Ltd. 1963
Malavaya, H.D., *Village Panchayats in India*. All India Congress Committee, New Delhi, 1956.
Programme Evaluation Organization Planning Commission, Government of India. *A study of Panchayats*, New Delhi, 1958.

Community Development

Dey, S.K., *Community Development* (2 Volumes). Kitab Mahal, Alahabad, 1960.
Mukerji, B., *Community Development in India*. Orient Longmans, Bombay, 1961.
Mayer, Albert., *Pilot Project, India; the Story of Rural Development at Etawah, Uttar Pradesh*. University of California Press, Berkeley, 1958.
Krishnamachari, V.T., *Community Development in India*. Publications Division, Government of India, New Delhi, 1958.
Programme Evaluation Organization Planning Commission, New Delhi, *Evaluation Reports on the Working of Community Projects and N.E.S. Block*. Seven annual Reports from 1954 to 1960.

Taylor, Carl. C., *Critical Analysis of India's Community Development Programmes. Community Projects Administration,* Government of India, New Delhi, 1956.

United Nations, Commissioner for Technical Assistance. Report of a Community Development Evaluation Mission in India. Ministry of Community Development and Cooperation, Government of India, New Delhi, 1959.

Planning and Development

Lewis, John P., *Quite Crisis in India.* Brookings Institution, Washington D.C., 1962

Melenbaum, W., *Prospects for Indian Development.* George Allen and Unwin, London, 1962.

Planning Commission, Government of India, New Delhi. First Five Year Plan; Second Five Year Plan; Third Five Year Plan.

Planning Commission, Government of India, *The New India; Progress through Democracy.* Macmillan, New York, 1958.

Singh, Tarlok, *Poverty and Social Change. A study in the Economic Reorganization of Indian Rural Society.* Longmans, Green and Company, London, 1945.

Progress of Scheduled Castes and Scheduled Tribes

Reports of the Commissioner for Scheduled Castes and Scheduled Tribes, Government of India, New Delhi. Annual, 1952 onwards

Other Subjects

Dutt, R.C., *Economic History of India,* Rutledge & Kegan Paul, London 1956.

Gadgil, D.R., *Industrial Evolution of India in recent times.* Oxford University Press, Bombay 1924.

Khera, S.S., *District Administration in India,* Asia Publishers Bombay 1964.

Park Richard L. and Tinker Irene (Ed)., *Leadership and Political Institutions in India,* Princeton, the University Press, 1959.

Index